Some chemistry texts are factual...but not very readable.
Some are attractive...but not very thorough.
If you're searching for a book that has
*both* depth and clarity...

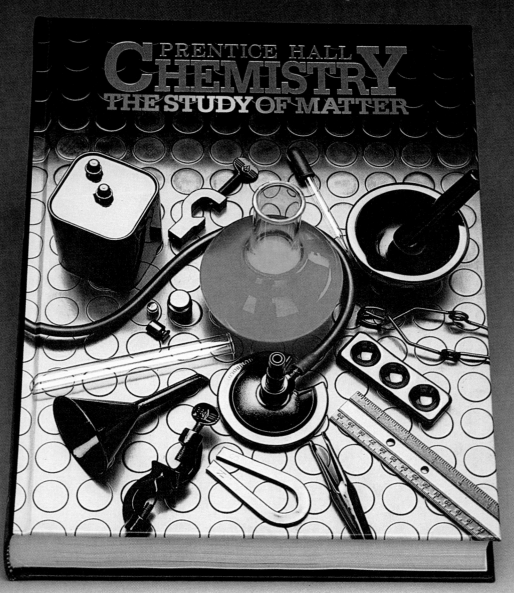

# THE CHEMISTRY IS RIGHT!

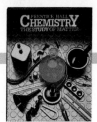

# If you value content, concept mastery, and proble

*Chemistry: The Study of Matter* covers thoroughly all the topics you expect to find in an introductory course. Content was never sacrificed when new features were added.

Our carefully developed narrative communicates the energy of the subject with utmost clarity and precision. With this new edition, readability continues to be an asset.

All new diagrams, drawings, and photographs **simplify** the most challenging concepts... make them vivid and tangible.

More sample problems **than ever before demystify concepts... and prepare students for independent problem solving.**

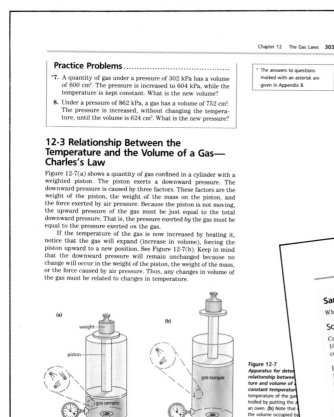

Chapter 12   The Gas Laws   **303**

### Practice Problems ........................................

*7. A quantity of gas under a pressure of 302 kPa has a volume of 600 cm³. The pressure is increased to 604 kPa, while the temperature is kept constant. What is the new volume?

8. Under a pressure of 862 kPa, a gas has a volume of 752 cm³. The pressure is increased, without changing the temperature, until the volume is 624 cm³. What is the new pressure?

> * The answers to questions marked with an asterisk are given in Appendix B.

### 12-3 Relationship Between the Temperature and the Volume of a Gas— Charles's Law

Figure 12-7(a) shows a quantity of gas confined in a cylinder with a weighted piston. The piston exerts a downward pressure. The downward pressure is caused by three factors. These factors are the weight of the piston, the weight of the mass on the piston, and the force exerted by air pressure. Because the piston is not moving, the upward pressure of the gas must be just equal to the total downward pressure. That is, the pressure exerted *by* the gas must be equal to the pressure exerted *on* the gas.

If the temperature of the gas is now increased by heating it, notice that the gas will expand (increase in volume), forcing the piston upward to a new position. See Figure 12-7(b). Keep in mind that the downward pressure will remain unchanged because no change will occur in the weight of the piston, the weight of the mass, or the force caused by air pressure. Thus, any changes in volume of the gas must be related to changes in temperature.

**Figure 12-7**
*Apparatus for dete... relationship betwee... ture and volume of ... constant temperatur... temperature of the gas... trolled by putting the a... an oven. (b) Note that ... the volume occupied by ... (a), the volume here is ... cause the temperature is ... pressure was kept consta...*

**Frequent** Section Reviews **check recall of content** from the previous one or two sections through review questions and practice problems.

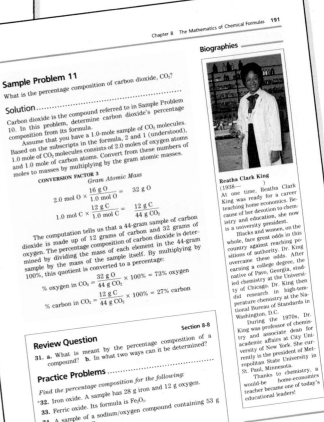

Chapter 8   The Mathematics of Chemical Formulas   **191**

Biographies

### Sample Problem 11

What is the percentage composition of carbon dioxide, $CO_2$?

### Solution ........................................

Carbon dioxide is the compound referred to in Sample Problem 10. In this problem, determine carbon dioxide's percentage composition from its formula.

Assume that you have a 1.0-mole sample of $CO_2$ molecules. Based on the subscripts in the formula, 2 and 1 (understood), 1.0 mole of $CO_2$ molecules consists of 2.0 moles of oxygen atoms and 1.0 mole of carbon atoms. Convert from these numbers of moles to masses by multiplying by the gram atomic masses.

CONVERSION FACTOR 3
*Gram Atomic Mass*

$$2.0 \text{ mol O} \times \frac{16 \text{ g O}}{1.0 \text{ mol O}} = 32 \text{ g O}$$

$$1.0 \text{ mol C} \times \frac{12 \text{ g C}}{1.0 \text{ mol C}} = \frac{12 \text{ g C}}{44 \text{ g } CO_2}$$

The computation tells us that a 44-gram sample of carbon dioxide is made up of 12 grams of carbon and 32 grams of oxygen. The percentage composition of carbon dioxide is determined by dividing the mass of each element in the 44-gram sample by the mass of the sample itself. By multiplying by 100%, this quotient is converted to a percentage:

$$\% \text{ oxygen in } CO_2 = \frac{32 \text{ g O}}{44 \text{ g } CO_2} \times 100\% = 73\% \text{ oxygen}$$

$$\% \text{ carbon in } CO_2 = \frac{12 \text{ g C}}{44 \text{ g } CO_2} \times 100\% = 27\% \text{ carbon}$$

Section 8-8

### Review Question

31. **a.** What is meant by the percentage composition of a compound?   **b.** In what two ways can it be determined?

### Practice Problems ........................................

*Find the percentage composition for the following:*

*32. Iron oxide. A sample has 28 g iron and 12 g oxygen.

33. Ferric oxide. Its formula is $Fe_2O_3$.

34. A sample of a sodium/oxygen compound containing 53 g Na and 37 g O.

35. Sodium peroxide. Its formula is $Na_2O_2$.

**Reatha Clark King**
(1938—     )
At one time, Reatha Clark King was ready for a career teaching home economics. Because of her devotion to chemistry and education, she now is a university president.

Blacks and women, on the whole, face great odds in this country against reaching positions of authority. Dr. King overcame these odds. After earning a college degree, the native of Pavo, Georgia, studied chemistry at the University of Chicago. Dr. King then did research in high-temperature chemistry at the National Bureau of Standards in Washington, D.C.

During the 1970s, Dr. King was professor of chemistry and associate dean for academic affairs at City University of New York. She currently is the president of Metropolitan State University in St. Paul, Minnesota.

Thanks to chemistry, a would-be home-economics teacher became one of today's educational leaders!

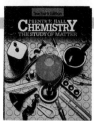

Teacher's Edition
**CHEMISTRY**
THE STUDY OF MATTER

## Extensive Chapter Reviews check comprehension of content, thinking skills, and concept understanding:

- *Summary:* reviews key ideas.
- *Chemical Terms:* lists new vocabulary.
- *Content Review:* checks recall once again.
- *Content Mastery:* goes beyond memory to check understanding.
- *Concept Mastery:* asks students to apply skills to reveal the depth of their understanding of key concepts.
- *Cumulative Review:* a review of important content and concepts from prior chapters.
- *Critical Thinking:* trains students to develop higher-order thinking skills.
- *Challenge Problems:* Poses the ultimate challenge for students as they integrate thinking skills, concepts, and problem solving.

---

104   Chapter 5   Energy

# Chapter Review

5

## Chapter Summary

- Energy is the ability to do work.   *5-1*
- Potential, kinetic, chemical, electrical, electro-magnetic, and magnetic energy, sound, and heat all are forms of energy.   *5-2*
- Energy can b...

## Content Review

1. What is the mathematical relationship among the quantities of work, force, and distance?   *5-1*

30. Some objects become electrically charged when rubbed together. If a balloon becomes neg-atively charged when rubbed with wool flannel, what is the charge on the flannel?

31. Explain the energy conversions that occur in the pile driver illustrated here.

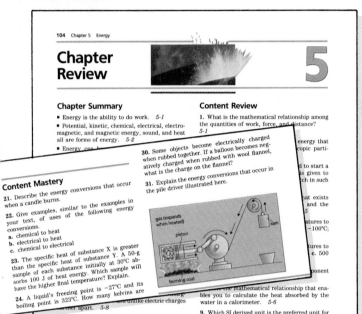

gas (expands when heated)

piston

ram

burning coal

## Content Mastery

21. Describe the energy conversions that occur when a candle burns.

22. Give examples, similar to the examples in your text, of uses of the following energy conversions.
a. chemical to heat
b. electrical to heat
c. chemical to electrical

23. The specific heat of substance X is greater than the specific heat of substance Y. A 50-g sample of each substance initially at 30°C ab-sorbs 100 J of heat energy. Which sample will have the higher final temperature? Explain.

24. A liquid's freezing point is −27°C and its boiling point is 323°C. How many kelvins are ... ...her apart.   *5-8*

...like electric charges

...mathematical relationship that ena-bles you to calculate the heat absorbed by the water in a calorimeter.   *5-6*

9. Which SI derived unit is the preferred unit for measuring heat energy?   *5-6*

10. How much heat energy (in joules) is required to raise the temperature of 200 g of water from 20°C to 50°C?   *5-6*

11. Make the following conversions.
a. 8000 J to kJ;
b. $3.5 \times 10^4$ J to kJ;
c. 2.1 kJ to J;
d. $4.7 \times 10^{-1}$ kJ to J.   *5-6*

12. If 700 g of water at 90°C loses 27 kJ of heat energy, what is its final temperature?   *5-6*

## Chemical Terms

| | | | |
|---|---|---|---|
| enery | 5-1 | absolute zero | 5-5 |
| work | 5-1 | Kelvin scale | 5-5 |
| kinetic energy | 5-2 | calorie | 5-6 |
| joule | 5-2 | calorimetry | 5-6 |
| law of conservation | | calorimeter | 5-6 |
| of energy | 5-3 | specific heat | 5-6 |
| exothermic | 5-4 | electrostatic force | 5-8 |
| endothermic | 5-4 | electric current | 5-8 |
| activation energy | 5-4 | electrical | |
| Celsius scale | 5-5 | conductors | 5-8 |

...energy that ...opic parti-

...d to start a ...s given to ...ch in such

...at exists ...and the ...5

...atures to ...−100°C;

...tures to ...e. 500

...ponent

---

Chapter 14   The Periodic Table   **385**

20. Which of the following pairs belong to the same family?
a. H, He;   c. C, Pb;
b. Li, Be;   d. Ga, Ge.

21. Given the following three bonds: N:H, N:F, and N:Cl. In which bond are the shared electrons a. most attracted to nitrogen?   b. least attract-ed to nitrogen?

22. How does the general trend of metallic char-acter compare with electronegativity as you move a. horizontally across the periodic table? b. vertically down the periodic table?

23. a. What are the lightest alkali metal and the lightest halogen? b. What are the heaviest noble gas and heaviest alkaline earth metal?

24. What is the name of the energy required in the following reaction?

$$M(g) + energy \rightarrow M^+(g) + e^-$$

25. Which of the following three elements has the highest ionization energy: Sn, As, or S?

26. What is the primary difference between Men-deleev's periodic table and Moseley's periodic table?

27. a. Which alkali metal belongs to the sixth period? b. Which halogen belongs to the fourth period?

28. What element is in the fifth period and 11th column?

### Physical Properties of Elements on Xeno

| Element | Color | Hardness | Melting pt. (°C) |
|---|---|---|---|
| A | turquoise | soft | 1050 |
| B | silvery, black | hard | −300 |
| C | yellow | soft | 1000 |
| D | gray | hard | 400 |
| E | pink | soft | 1200 |
| F | silvery, black | hard | −100 |
| G | silvery, black | hard | −200 |
| H | black | hard | 300 |
| I | aqua | soft | 900 |
| J | brown | soft | 1000 |

30. In the second stage, you collect data on the chemical properties of the elements. Using the data listed below, modify your original periodic table. Justify your new arrangement.

### Chemical Properties of Elements on Xeno

| Element | Reacts with water | Reacts with acid | Reacts with oxygen | No reaction |
|---|---|---|---|---|
| A | | | X | |
| B | X | X | X | |
| C | | | | X |
| D | | X | X | |
| E | | | | X |
| F | X | X | X | |
| G | X | X | X | |
| H | X | X | X | |
| I | | | X | |
| J | | X | X | |

## Concept Mastery

*Imagine that you are a sci...*
*world...*

...mine the relative ...s on Xeno. Using ...ur periodic table.

...ents on Xeno

| | Relative atomic mass |
|---|---|
| | 15 |
| | 9 |
| | 14 |
| | 2 |
| | 6 |

---

## More problems in the Teacher's Resource Book!
- Stoichiometry Problems
- Additional Practice Problems

---

### CHAPTER 10

## Practice Problems

1. Given the balanced chemical equation

$$Br_2 + 2NaI \rightarrow 2NaBr + I_2$$

how many moles of sodium bromide (NaBr) could be produced from 0.172 mole of bromine ($Br_2$)?

2. How many moles of oxygen ($O_2$) would be needed to produce 79.60 moles of sulfur trioxide ($SO_3$) according to the following balanced chem-...

10. Calculate the volume of chlorine gas ($Cl_2$) that will be required at STP for complete reaction of $7.15 \times 10^{25}$ atoms of iron (Fe) accord-ing to this balanced chemical equation:

$$2Fe(s) + 3Cl_2(g) \rightarrow 2FeCl_3(s)$$

11. Calculate the mass of mercury metal (Hg) that is required to produce 29.8 g of mercu-ry(I) oxide ($Hg_2O$) according to the following bal-anced chemical equation.

$$4Hg(l) + O_2(g) \rightarrow 2Hg_2O(s)$$

... = 16.0 g/mol)

---

STOICHIOMETRY PROBLEMS

## Empirical Formulas of Hydrates

Sometimes water is an integral part of a compound known as a *hydrate*. In finding the empirical formula of a hydrate, the number of moles of water of hydration per formula unit must be found.

### Sample Problem

A 5.00-gram sample of hydrated copper sulfate was heated until all of the water was driven off. After heating, the remaining 3.19-gram sample contained 1.27 grams of copper, 0.64 gram of sulfur, and 1.28 grams of oxygen. Find the empirical formula of the hydrate.

### Solution

**Step 1**   Find the number of moles of each ele-ment and moles of water present. The solution of this hydrate problem is similar to the solutions of the problems studied earlier with one additional consideration. The ... ...sult of the loss of water ...You find

5.00 g mass before heating
− 3.19 g mass after heating
  1.81 g mass of water in the hydrate

$$\frac{gram\ atomic}{mass\ or\ gram} \quad (inverted) \quad moles$$
$$molecular\ mass$$

mass

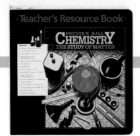

# When you want a text that's both relevant and challenging...*the chemistry is right!*

Special features put chemistry into a real-world context.
Students learn quickly that chemistry isn't just memorizing.

## APPLICATIONS IN CHEMISTRY
### Self-cooling Cans

A change in phase of carbon dioxide is the key to the biggest breakthrough in soda-can technology since the pop top popped up in 1962. The self-cooling can is able to cool its contents to 0.6°C to 1.7°C, or just above freezing, from beginning temperatures of up to 43°C. The cooling takes less than a minute and a half. Soon, the refrigerator may be the least likely place to find a soda.

The self-cooling can looks like any other can, except it has a cone-shaped container about 5 cm long just inside the top of the can. Within the cone is a capsule containing liquid $CO_2$ under high pressure. When the tab is pulled to open the can, a release valve connected to the tab opens the capsule. As the liquid $CO_2$ escapes from the capsule and enters the cone, it changes to a gas. The gas rushes through the cone and escapes through the top of the can. The

nal, through the bulb, and back into the battery at the positive terminal.

"Applications" reveal everyday uses of chemistry and remind students of the practicality of what they're learning. And there are more "Applications" suggestions in the Teacher's Edition.

## BREAKTHROUGHS IN CHEMISTRY
### Superconductors

Superconductors are materials that can carry electricity with virtually no loss of energy. At present, as much as 20% of the electricity sent through high-tension power lines is lost in the form of heat. The heat is generated as the current encounters resistance in the copper wire. If the electricity were sent through a superconducting material, practically no energy would be lost. The utilities and consumers would save billions of dollars.

Besides allowing for cheap energy, superconductors could result in: trains that travel hundreds of miles per hour on a cushion of electrically generated magnetism; widespread use of electric cars; and tiny but powerful computers. Eventually they could lead to the large-scale building of nuclear generators that operate not on nuclear fission, but on nuclear fusion (see Chapter 26).

To understand superconductors, you first must understand how electricity works. Electricity is the movement of electrons through a material. Resistance is a measure of the energy lost in the form of heat from electron collisions. Materials with extremely high resistance, such as rubber and glass, are called insulators. In these materials, electrons are tightly bound to atoms and cannot be jostled loose to sustain a flow of electricity. Conductors are materials with lower resistance, usually metals. In conductors, some electrons are loosely bound and can form a current when a voltage is applied. But

**Insulator**
negative charge    positive charge
Electrons

**Conductor**

"Breakthroughs" recognize recent advances and achievements in the field of chemistry.

---

### Critical Thinking

**53.** Place the following substances in order of increasing basicity. (Use Figure 20-6 to help you.)
**a.** 0.1 $M$ sodium hydroxide
**b.** 0.1 $M$ hydrochloric acid
**c.** lemon juice
**d.** 0.1 $M$ acetic acid
**e.** tomato juice
**f.** milk

**54.** Why do people take antacid tablets to settle their upset stomachs?

**55.** Compare and contrast a buffer solution with an unbuffered solution.

**56.** If a given solution turns methyl violet indicator blue and bromophenol blue indicator yellow, what color do you predict it will turn methyl yellow indicator? What is the approximate pH of the solution?

methyl violet indicator    bromphenol blue indicator    methyl yellow indicator

**57.** Whic...

**d.** methyl yellow
**e.** litmus

**58.** Which of the following would not make good buffer solutions? Explain.
**a.** a solution of 1.0$M$ $HC_2H_3O_2$ and 1.0 $M$ $NaC_2H_3O_2$.
**b.** a solution of 1.0 $M$ HCl and 1.0 $M$ NaCl.
**c.** a solution of 1.0 $M$ $NH_3$ and 1.0 $M$ NaOH.

### Challenge Problems

**59.** The following reaction takes place in a solution of NaHS: $HS^- + H_2O \rightleftharpoons H_2S + OH^-$. The $K_h$ for this reaction is $9.1 \times 10^{-8}$. **a.** Write the hydrolysis constant expression for this reaction. **b.** What is the $[OH^-]$ of a 0.10 $M$ solution of NaHS? **c.** What is the $[H^+]$? **d.** What is the pH?

**60.** Assuming no change in volume, **a.** what is the change in pH if 0.10 mol of acid is added to 1.00 $dm^3$ of neutral water? **b.** what is the change in pH if 0.10 mol of acid is added to 1.00 $dm^3$ of a buffer solution? The $K_a$ for the weak acid used in the buffer solution is $1.0 \times 10^{-7}$, and the amounts of undissociated weak acid and its salt are equal (1.00 mol of each). **c.** How does the pH change in **b** compare with the pH change in **a**?

**61.** Collect samples of various cleaning solutions, cosmetic solutions, cough syrups, and beverages that are available in your home. Based on their functions, predict whether these solutions are acidic, basic, or neutral. Then devise a way to verify your predictions.

---

Critical thinking skills—essential to scientific inquiry—are integrated throughout the program:
- in the student book chapter reviews
- in the Teacher's Edition—a special section on the hierarchy of critical and creative thinking skills ...plus chapter suggestions
- in the Teacher's Resource Book—special activities

"Can You Explain This" shows chemistry demonstrations with unexpected results. Challenges students to apply their chemistry concepts and thinking skills.

**32.** What volume of a 0.300 $N$ solution of HCl will completely neutralize 36.0 cm³ of a 0.225 $N$ solution of NaOH?

## CAN YOU EXPLAIN THIS?
### Electrolytic Titration

**(a)** The beaker contains a solution of barium hydroxide, $Ba(OH)_2$, dissolved in water. The buret contains sulfuric acid diluted with water. **(b)** When the sulfuric acid is added to the beaker from the buret, a white precipitate forms.

As more of the acid is run into the beaker, the light gets dimmer and finally goes out. As still more of the acid is run into the beaker, the bulb begins to light up again, finally reaching its original brightness.

1. What kind of substance is barium hydroxide if the light bulb lights when the electrodes are dipped into its aqueous solution? (Write an equation showing what happens when solid $Ba(OH)_2$ is added to water.)
2. As more and more acid is added to the beaker, why does the bulb at first get dimmer, then go out, and finally light up again to its original brightness?

**Circuit Drawing**
plugged into wall outlet

(a)    (b)

---

Date _____  Class _____

Name _____

### CRITICAL AND CREATIVE THINKING

## Comparing and Contrasting

The act of comparing and contrasting can be a powerful thinking tool because it can help you discover things that you might not otherwise notice, and it can lead to sound decision-making. When you compare, you determine the similarities or common characteristics as well as the differences among objects, ideas, or events. When you contrast, you compare their differences. When very similar things are compared and contrasted, previously unseen patterns may be revealed.

Let's look at a real life example: You are eating a hamburger for lunch and your friend is eating a cheeseburger. You compare the hamburger and the cheeseburger by noting that each contains a round patty of beef, a pickle, and a wholewheat

bun. You also observe that each patty has been seasoned and cooked in the same way. The cheeseburger, however, contains a slice of American cheese, while the hamburger does not. Also, it takes longer to prepare than the hamburger, costs twenty-five cents more, and tastes different. To contrast the cheeseburger and the hamburger, therefore, you note that the cheeseburger takes 12 minutes to prepare while the hamburger takes 10 minutes, and, the cheeseburger costs $2.25 while the hamburger costs $2.00. In addition, you find that you prefer the taste of your friend's cheeseburger to the somewhat more bland taste of your hamburger. In fact, it may just be this difference in the taste of the two burgers that helps you decide which to choose next time.

### Think Critically

In the laboratory, you will be given two groups of substances to compare and contrast. One of these groups is labelled as ionically bonded compounds and the other as covalently bonded compounds.

First, observe the appearance of several examples of each group. Use a binocular microscope or a hand lens if they are available. Record your observations.

1. In what ways are ionic and covalent solids alike in appearance? Are there any differences between
2. Consider all of the examples presented to you. Are there any differences between groups at room temperature?  volatility of the groups. Record your judgment of the

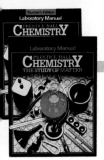

# If you seek lab support that's both reinforcing and enriching...*the chemistry is right!*

## Hands-on applications make chemistry spring to life!

PRENTICE HALL

## STUDENT LABORATORY MANUAL

**52 labs**–all tested and reviewed, with safety suggestions–enable students to reinforce skills and concepts they've learned. Extensive *Safety Notes* and *symbols* keep students "on their toes." And there are even more safety suggestions in the Teacher's Edition.

---

Name _____ Date _____ Class _____

### Types of Chemical Reactions Lab **14**

Text reference: **Chapter 9, pp. 215–217**

#### Pre-Lab Discussion

There are many kinds of chemical reactions and several ways to classify them. One useful method classifies reactions into four major types. These are: (1) direct combination, or synthesis; (2) decomposition, or analysis; (3) single replacement; and (4) exchange of ions, or double replacement. Not all reactions can be put into one of these categories. Many, however, can.

In a synthesis reaction, two or more substances (elements or compounds) combine to form a more complex substance. Equations for synthesis reactions have the general form $A + B \rightarrow AB$. For example, the formation of water from hydrogen and oxygen is written $2H_2 + O_2 \rightarrow 2H_2O$.

A decomposition reaction is the opposite of a synthesis reaction. In decomposition, a compound breaks down into two or more simpler substances (elements or compounds). Equations for decomposition reactions have the form $AB \rightarrow A + B$. The breakdown of water into its elements is an example of such a reaction: $2H_2O \rightarrow 2H_2 + O_2$.

In a single replacement reaction, one substance in a compound is replaced by another, more active, substance (an element). Equations for single replacement reactions have two general forms. In reactions in which one metal replaces another metal, the general equation is $X + YB \rightarrow XB + Y$. In those in which one nonmetal replaces another nonmetal, the general form is $X + AY \rightarrow AX + Y$. The following equations illustrate these types of reactions:

Zinc metal replaces copper(II) ion:

$$Zn(s) + CuSO_4(aq) \rightarrow ZnSO_4(aq) + Cu(s)$$

Chlorine (a nonmetal) replaces bromide ions:

$$Cl_2(g) + 2KBr(aq) \rightarrow 2KCl(aq) + Br_2(l)$$

In a double replacement reaction, the metal ions of two different ionic compounds can be thought of as "replacing one another." Equations for this type of reaction have the general form $AB + CD \rightarrow AD + CB$. Most replacement reactions, both single and double, take place in aqueous solutions containing free ions. In a double replacement reaction, one of the products is a precipitate, an insoluble gas, or water. An example is the reaction between silver nitrate and sodium chloride in which the precipitate silver chloride is formed:

$$AgNO_3(aq) + NaCl(aq) \rightarrow AgCl(s) + NaNO_3(aq)$$

All of the types of reactions discussed here may be represented by balanced molecular equations. Reactions involving ion exchanges may be represented by ionic equations also. In this investigation you will be concerned only with molecular formulas and equations. In a balanced equa-

69

## TEACHER'S LABORATORY MANUAL

*All* labs are annotated with answers and sample data. "A Shorter Lab Period" feature for longer labs presents helpful strategies for completing the lab in a shorter time span. Most labs can be completed in 45 minutes.

---

## TEACHER'S RESOURCE BOOK

**Open-ended Labs** challenge students' creativity. Not only must they solve problems; they must determine *how* to solve them.

---

Name _____ Date _____ Class _____

OPEN-ENDED LABORATORY EXPERIMENT          Text Reference: **Section 5-6**

### Relative Temperature in a Bunsen Burner Flame

#### Pre-Lab Discussion

A Bunsen burner makes use of the combustion of a carbon-hydrogen fuel to provide heat for laboratory purposes. Such a burner, when properly adjusted, will produce a relatively nonluminous (nonbright) cone-shaped flame. Careful inspection of this flame reveals that it is made up of two visible parts: an outer transparent, dim blue cone; and an inner, less 'transparent, and brighter greenish-blue cone.

**Material and Equipment**

Water
Bunsen burner
Ring clamp
Wire gauze
Beaker, 150-mL
Graduated cylinder
Thermometer
Clock
Beaker tongs
Safety goggles

[figure: Two types of laboratory gas burners — labeled "gas valve", "air adjustment", "gas adjustment", "outer, transparent, dim blue cone", "inner, less transparent, brighter greenish-blue cone"]

**Two types of laboratory gas burners.**

The flame as a whole is obviously a good source of heat. However, the parts of the flame —both the outer and inner cones, and specific regions within them—may differ in temperature.

**Safety**

Follow good lab safety practices. Observe caution in dealing with the Bunsen burner and heated objects.

**Procedure**

1. Read the entire remainder of this lab before carrying out the next step of this procedure.
2. Prepare a written plan of action that describes the way you plan to proceed with the work. *Get your teacher's approval of your plan before you begin any lab work.*

**Preliminary Question**

As part of your plan of action, answer the follow-

---

Students should understand that the law of conservation of matter requires balanced equations for all chemical reactions. Make sure they know that subscripts cannot be altered to bring about balance in an equation. Only coefficients can be used for this purpose. And mention the use of vertical arrows to indicate the formation of a precipitate (down-pointing) or an insoluble gas (up-pointing).

**LAB TIME: 50–60 minutes**

**A Shorter Lab Period**
Time: 40 minutes
If your laboratory period is shorter than 50–60 minutes, do either of the following. (1) Demonstrate the two reactions involving possible safety problems—the burning of Mg ribbon and the reaction of sodium sulfite with hydrochloric acid. These fall at the beginning and at the end of the procedures respectively, so they can be done easily as demonstrations. (2) Have students work in teams of two or more, with procedures split among team subgroups. The subgroups should work simultaneously, pausing only to observe results obtained by each subgroup.

**Safety**
Review safety procedures for working with open flames, heating chemicals in test tubes, handling acids, and wafting gases toward the nose. Stress the need to wear safety goggles when working with 6 *M* HCl. Caution students to avoid inhaling HCl fumes. Emphasize the hazards of the burning magnesium.
Call attention to the caution alert symbols. Advise students on the proper disposal of all materials.

tion, the number of atoms of any given element must be the same on both sides of the equation. Multiplying the coefficient and the subscript of an element must yield the same result on both sides of the balanced equation.

In this investigation you will observe examples of the four types of reactions described above. You will be expected to balance the equations representing the observed reactions.

**Purpose**

Observe some chemical reactions and identify reactants and products of those reactions. Classify the reactions and write balanced equations.

**Equipment**

burner                          wood splints
crucible tongs                  sandpaper, fine
microspatula                    evaporating dish
test tubes, 15×180-mm (7)       safety goggles
test tube holder                lab apron or coat
test tube rack

**Materials**

zinc, mossy (Zn)                1 *M* copper(II) sulfate (CuSO₄)
copper wire, 10 cm (Cu)         0.1 *M* zinc acetate (Zn(C₂H₃O₂)₂)
magnesium ribbon, 5 cm (Mg)     0.1 *M* sodium phosphate (Na₃PO₄)
copper(II) carbonate (CuCO₃)    1 *M* sodium sulfite (Na₂SO₃)
6 *M* hydrochloric acid (HCl)

**Safety**

In this investigation you will be working with open flames, heating chemicals, handling acids, and producing gaseous products. You should review the safety procedures for these activities given on pages ix–x.

Burning magnesium produces a very bright, hot flame. Make sure you hold the burning metal at arm's length and do not look directly at it.

Remember never to smell a chemical directly. Review the accepted method of wafting gases toward your nose as illustrated on page xi.

Pay special attention to the safety symbols beside certain steps in the procedure. Refer to page xi to review the special precautions associated with each symbol.

Wear safety goggles and protective clothing at all times when working in the lab.

**Procedure**

**PART A  SYNTHESIS**

1. Use fine sandpaper to clean a piece of copper wire until the wire is shiny. Note the appearance of the wire.

2. Using crucible tongs, hold the wire in the hottest part of a burner flame for 1–2 minutes. Examine the wire and note any change in its appearance caused by heating.

3. Place an evaporating dish near the base of the burner. Examine a piece of magnesium ribbon. Using crucible tongs,

70

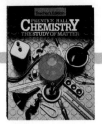

# When you need practical teaching suppo[rt]

So you can concentrate on what you do best – TEACH – our Teacher's Edition gives you professional support by doing the things you've always wanted to do …but never had the time.

## The Gas Laws

### Chapter Planning Guide

| Text Section | | Labs (Lab Manual) and Demonstrations (TE) | Supplementary Materials (Teacher's Resource Book) |
|---|---|---|---|
| 12-1 | Development of the Kinetic Theory of Gases, p. 297 | Demo 12-1: The Exploding and Shrinking Marshmallows, p. TG-185 | Transparency Master: Boyle's Law—Table of Data, p. 12-5 |
| 12-2 | Relationship Between the Pressure and the Volume of a Gas—Boyle's Law, pp. 298-303 | Lab 19: Boyle's Law | Review Activity: Boyle's Law, p. 12-15 Concept Mastery: Pressure and Volume Changes, p. CM-22 |
| 12-3 | Relationship Between the Temperature and the Volume of a Gas—Charles's Law, pp. 303-309 | Demo 12-2: Ballooning, p. TG-186 Lab 20: Charles's Law (demonstration) | Transparency Masters: —Charles's Law—Data Table 1, p. 12-6 —Plotting the Temperature of a Gas against Its Volume at Constant Pressure, p. 12-7 —Plotting the Temperature of a Gas against Its Volume at Constant Pressure (answer), p. 12-8 —Charles's Law: A Graphical Representation, p. 12-9 —Charles's Law Data: The Constant $V/T$ Ratio, p. 12-10 Review Activity: Charles's Law, p. 12-16 Open-Ended Demonstration: Differences in the Behavior of Rubber and Mylar Balloons, p. 12-13 |
| 12-4 | Relationship Between the Temperature and the Pressure of a Gas, pp. 310-311 | Demo 12-3: Water Balloon in the Bottle, p. TG-186 Demo 12-4: The Handboiler, p. TG-187 | Concept Mastery: Temperature Changes, p. CM-23 |
| 12-5 | The Combined Gas Law, pp. 311-313 | Lab 21: The Molar Volume of a Gas | Critical and Creative Thinking: Conditional Arguments, p. CCT-55 |
| Application | Self-cooling Cans, p. 313 | | |
| 12-6 | The Densities of Gases, pp. 314-315 | Lab 22: Determining the Molecular Mass of a Gas | Stoichiometry Problems: Density of Gases, p. SP-34 Stoichiometry Problems: Determining Molecular Mass from Density, p. SP-35 |

TG-180

## TEACHER'S EDITION

**Planning guides** for every chapter
- color-coded section headings for Core, Optional, and Advanced material
- suggestions for integrating all labs and demonstrations
- references to black-line masters from the Teacher's Resource Book

**Section-by-section teaching suggestions** with motivating demonstrations in every chapter

Chapter 4   Matter   TG-85

### Chapter Overview

In Chapter 4, we define matter and explain why mass, not weight, is used as a measure of the quantity of matter. We classify matter into elements, compounds, and mixtures. The differences between extensive and intensive properties are discussed, and students solve density problems. The three phases of matter—gas, liquid, and solid—are characterized. The difference between physical properties and chemical properties is explained, and physical changes are differentiated from chemical changes. We describe the evidence that led Lavoisier to state the law of conservation of mass. The chapter closes with a description of the two states—free and combined—in which elements occur in nature, and symbols for some elements are given.

### Chapter Objectives

After students have completed this chapter, they will be able to:
1. Explain why mass is used as a measure of the quantity of matter. *4-1*
2. Describe the characteristics of elements, compounds, and mixtures. *4-2, 4-3,* and *4-10*
3. Solve density problems by applying an understanding of the concept of density. *4-4* and *4-5*
4. Distinguish between physical and chemical properties and physical and chemical change. *4-6* to *4-8*
5. Demonstrate an understanding of the law of conservation of mass by applying it to a chemical reaction. *4-9* to *4-11*

### Teaching Suggestions

4-1 Mass, pp. 63-64,

4-2 Varieties of Matter—Elements and Compounds, pp. 64-65, and

4-3 Varieties of Matter—Mixtures, pp. 66-69

#### Planning Guide
Labs (Lab Manual) and Demonst[...]

■ Display a lab balance and a spring scale and ask students what quantity each piece of equipment is used to measure. Although both balances and scales are commonly used to measure weight—in, for example, food stores—point out that only a balance can truly measure mass. For your students studying space-age topics who probably know that weight is defined in terms of gravitational force, you may want to recall (or use here for the first time) the discussion in Section 2-1 of the newton, the SI unit of weight. Masses are usually measured in grams.

■ Tell students that chemists could not make much progress toward understanding the nature of matter until they had classified samples as elements, compounds, and mixtures. To help students distinguish among these categories in terms of their physical and chemical properties, use Demonstrations 4-1, 4-2, and 4-3. To help students understand the distinctions at the molecular level, use the Transparency Master "Elements, Compounds, and Mixtures" before Section 4-3.

You may want to look ahead to the classification of elements as metals, nonmetals, semimetals, and noble gases. This classification is introduced in Section 7-7 and discussed further in later chapters. You might also look ahead to Section 4-11 and have students locate in the periodic table in text Figure 7-7 the elements named in text Figure 4-21. Have them name several examples of metals, nonmetals, semimetals, and noble gases.

■ **Application.** You may want to give students the following information about some familiar substances. The "chlorine" used to purify swimming pools is not the element chlorine at all, but rather a compound containing chlorine, usually sodium hypochlorite. This chlorine is the same substance that is used to wash clothes. The fluoride in toothpastes is a compound of fluorine, usually stannous fluoride or sodium monofluorophosphate (MFP). However, the iodine in tincture of iodine is actually the element iodine, dissolved in alcohol.

■ **Concept Mastery.** You may wish to use Concept Mastery question 44 (chapter-end [...]) students' under[...]

**Worked-out solutions** to all problems at your fingertips – not in another ancillary

**Annotated answers** right next to all questions and problems

228   Chapter 9   Chemical Equations

## Chapter Review

### Content Review

1. Write the word equation for the reaction of zinc with copper(II) chloride to form copper and zinc chloride. *9-1* zinc + copper(II) chloride → copper + zinc chloride

2. What is the law of conservation of mass? *9-2* Total mass before reaction = total mass after reaction.

3. Interpret the following equations. *9-2*
   a. $2Na + 2H_2O \rightarrow 2NaOH + H_2$
   b. $CaCO_3 + 2HCl \rightarrow CO_2 + CaCl_2 + H_2O$

4. Tell which of the following are balanced equations. Assume that all formulas are correctly written. *9-3*

c. tin + oxygen → tin(IV) oxide
d. zinc nitrate + hydrogen sulfide → zinc sulfid[e] + nitric acid

11. Write balanced formula equations for th[e] reactions in question 10. *9-8*

12. Complete and balance the following equa[-] tions: *9-9*
   a. $N_2 + ? \rightarrow NH_3$   $N_2 + 3H_2 \rightarrow 2NH_3$
   b. $SO_2 + ? \rightarrow SO_3$   $2SO_2 + O_2 \rightarrow 2SO_3$
   c. $? + O_2 \rightarrow H_2O$   $2H_2 + O_2 \rightarrow 2H_2O$
   d. $Fe + ? \rightarrow Fe_2O_3$   $4Fe + 3O_2 \rightarrow 2Fe_2O_3$

13. What is a catalyst? *9-10* a substance that increases the rate of a reaction

14. Complete and balance the following equa[-] tions: *9-10*
   a. $KClO_3 \rightarrow KCl + ?$   $2KClO_3 \rightarrow 2KCl + 3O_2$
   b. $CuO \rightarrow ? + ?$   $2CuO \rightarrow 2Cu + O_2$
   c. $NO \rightarrow ? + ?$   $2NO \rightarrow N_2 + O_2$

TG-118   Chapter 6   Structure of the Atom

= (mass of $^{12}C$) (abundance) + (mass of $^{13}C$) (abundance)

= (12.000000) (0.9889) + (13.003354) (0.0111)

= 11.8668000 u + 0.1443372 u

= 12.0111372 u = 12.01 u

c. Both express the same value, but the periodic table states more significant figures.

41. $E = hf$. First calculate frequency from $c = \lambda f$:

$f = \frac{c}{\lambda} = \frac{3.00 \times 10^8 \text{ m/s}}{4.86 \times 10^{-7} \text{ m}}$

$= 0.617283395 \times 10^{8-(-7)}$ /s

$= 0.617 \times 10^{15}$ /Hz = $6.17 \times 10^{14}$ Hz

$E = hf = (6.6 \times 10^{-34} \text{ J/Hz})(6.17 \times 10^{14} \text{ Hz})$

$= 40.74 \times 10^{-34+14} = 41 \times 10^{-20} = 4.1 \times 10^{-19}$ J

42. An electron absorbs light when it moves into an excited state.

43. The symbol for any element is $^A_Z P$ where [ ] = symbol for the element (in periodic table), $A$ = mass number (number of nucleons), $Z$ = atomic number (number of protons), and charge = number of protons minus number of electrons. Therefore for [ ] [ ]
   a. The element is $^7_3Li$, because $Z = 3$.
   b. The atomic number, $Z$ (the subscript), is 3.
   c. Its mass number, $A$ (the superscript), is 7.
   d. It has 7 nucleons because $A = 7$.
   [...]trons $= A - Z = 7 - 3 = 4$.

47. Wavelength is inversely proportional to frequency, $\lambda = c/f$. Since frequency is directly proportional to energy ($E = hf$), wavelength is inversely proportional to energy.
   a. Gamma rays have a higher frequency than visible light, so visible light has a longer wavelength.
   b. Ultraviolet light has a shorter wavelength than infrared light, so ultraviolet light has more energy.

48. Using the law of definite proportions, we know:
   $\frac{95.110 \text{ g chlorine}}{200.00 \text{ g KCl}} = \frac{\text{unknown g chlorine}}{153.20 \text{ g KCl}}$
   Therefore the amount of chlorine is
   $\frac{95.110 \text{ g chlorine}}{200.00 \text{ g KCl}} \times 153.20 \text{ g KCl} =$   72.85426 g Cl
   $\approx 72.854 \text{ g Cl} = 7.2854 \times 10^1 \text{ g Cl} = 72.854 \text{ g Cl}$

Page 143, Concept Mastery

49. **Concept:** *Atomic structure versus molecular arrangement.*
   **Solution:** The different properties of graphite and diamonds are due to the arrangements of the carbon atoms. The structures of the atoms themselves are indistinguishable.

50. **Concept:** *Electrons in atoms have fixed energy.*
   [...]*tion:* Planets in the solar system travel in [...] the sun. Electrons

# ithin your reach...*the chemistry is right!*

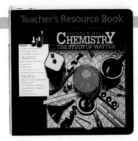

## More extra help than any other program!

## TEACHER'S RESOURCE BOOK
Full-color, 38″ x 55″ poster of the *Periodic Table of the Elements*

And, sections on:
- Laboratory Safety
- Skills Development
- Stoichiometry Problems
- Critical and Creative Thinking
- Societal Issues
- College Board Review
- Reference Tables
- Additional Practice Problems
- Overhead Transparency Masters
- Open-ended Labs and Demonstrations
- Review Activities
- Additional Resources

Plus...Chapter Tests and *Alternate Chapter Tests*

**50 FULL-COLOR CRITICAL-THINKING SKILLS TRANSPARENCIES**—with a Teacher's Guide—assist you in teaching the most difficult concepts.

## COMPUTER SOFTWARE
Computer Test Bank contains over 2,300 questions in a state-of-the-art test generating program.

Prentice Hall Courseware Programs
- Periodic Table
- Chemical Bonding
- Dynamic Equilibrium
- Boyle and Charles' Laws
- Gas Laws and the Mole

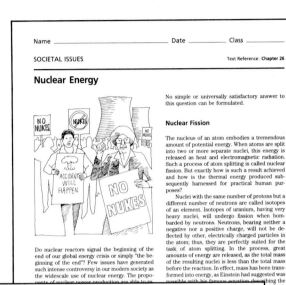

Name _____ Date _____ Class _____

SOCIETAL ISSUES                            Text Reference: **Chapter 26**

### Nuclear Energy

Do nuclear reactors signal the beginning of the end of our global energy crisis or simply "the beginning of the end"? Few issues have generated such intense controversy in our modern society as the widescale use of nuclear energy. The proponents of nuclear power production are able to re...

No simple or universally satisfactory answer to this question can be formulated.

#### Nuclear Fission

The nucleus of an atom embodies a tremendous amount of potential energy. When atoms are split into two or more separate nuclei, this energy is released as heat and electromagnetic radiation. Such a process of atom splitting is called nuclear fission. But exactly how is such a result achieved and how is the thermal energy produced subsequently harnessed for practical human purposes?

Nuclei with the same number of protons but a different number of neutrons are called isotopes of an element. Isotopes of uranium, having very heavy nuclei, will undergo fission when bombarded by neutrons. Neutrons, bearing neither a negative nor a positive charge, will not be deflected by other, electrically charged particles in the atom; thus, they are perfectly suited for the task of atom splitting. In the process, great amounts of energy are released, as the total mass of the resulting nuclei is less than the total mass before the reaction. In effect, mass has been transformed into energy, as Einstein had suggested was possible with his famous equation describing the...

OPEN-ENDED LABORATORY DEMONSTRATION          Text Reference: **Section 10-5**

### Limiting Quantities

#### The Demonstration

1. Make the following preparations in advance of class. Into each of three 125-mL conical (Erlenmeyer) flasks put 100 mL of 1.0 *M* HCl. Into the neck of the first flask, put a coil of magnesium ribbon whose mass is 0.60 g. Arrange the coil of metal so that friction holds it wedged into the neck of the flask, away from the acid below. In a similar way, put into the second flask a coil of magnesium ribbon whose mass is 1.20 g. Into the third flask, put a coil whose mass is 2.40 g. Seal the mouth of each flask by stretching the end of a balloon over it. While doing so, keep the balloon from inflating, so that it hangs limply along the outside of the flask. Attach to each flask a sign that tells the students the mass of the magnesium ribbon in that flask.

2. Tell the class that the flasks hold identical amounts and concentrations of hydrochloric acid, and that each sign shows the mass of magnesium ribbon.

3. Pick up the first balloon-sealed flask (with 0.60 g Mg) and carefully poke the balloon to push the coil of magnesium into the acid. Allow the students to observe the balloon being inflated by the hydrogen generated by the reaction. Allow some students to come to the front...note the warmth of the flask.

4. Repeat the...

Name _____
TEST A

**17 Kinetics and Thermodynamics** (continued)

____ 18. The kinetic energies of the molecules of...
   a. are all the same.
   b. vary over a wide range.
   c. change only when the temperature ch...
   d. are independent of the temperature of the reactan...

____ 19. Increasing the temperature of the reactan...
   rate of many reactions to
   a. increase slightly.
   b. decrease slightly.

____ 20. Most chemical reactions occur as a result...
   a. two particles.
   b. three particles.

#### B. Problems
Solve the following problems in the spaces provided. S...

**21.** How much heat is given off when 24.0 g of methan...
reaction is:

$$CH_4(g) + 2O_2(g) \rightarrow CO_2(g) + ...$$

**22.** The $\Delta H$ for the complete burning of a mole of octa...
of heat released when 1.0 kg of octane is burned? The...

$$C_8H_{18}(l) + 12\frac{1}{2} O_2(g) \rightarrow 9H...$$

Name _____
TEST B

**17 Kinetics and Thermodynamics** (continued)

____ 19. Substances that speed up chemical reactions but are not permanently changed themselves are called
   a. mechanisms.        b. catalysts.        c. inhibitors.        d. activators.

____ 20. The study of rates of chemical reactions is called
   a. thermodynamics.        b. kinematics.        c. dynamics.        d. kinetics.

#### B. Problems
Solve the following problems in the spaces provided. **Show all your work.**

**21.** How much heat is given off when 40.0 g of methane is burned in air? The equation for the reaction is:

$$CH_4(g) + 2O_2(g) \rightarrow CO_2(g) + 2H_2O(l) + 890 \text{ kJ}$$

**22.** The $\Delta H$ for the complete burning of a mole of octane, $C_8H_{18}$, is $-5450$ kJ. What is the amount of heat released when 2.5 g of octane is burned? The equation for the reaction is:

$$C_8H_{18}(l) + 12\frac{1}{2} O_2(g) \rightarrow 9H_2O(l) + 8CO_2(g)$$

PRENTICE HALL

# Compare! See if *this* chemistry is right...*for you!*

# CHEMISTRY: The Study of Matter THIRD EDITION

### Authors: Henry Dorin • Dorothy Gabel • Peter Demmin

Teacher's Resource Book   Computer Test Bank
Student Book   Teacher's Edition   Laboratory Manual
Teacher's Edition Laboratory Manual   Chemistry Courseware   Transparencies

For more information, please write to:

**PRENTICE HALL**
School Division of Simon & Schuster
4343 Equity Drive  P.O. Box 2649
Columbus, Ohio 43216-2649

Or, call TOLL FREE: 1-800-848-9500

Printed in USA.
© 1988 by Prentice Hall
Englewood Cliffs, NJ
All rights reserved.

# PRENTICE HALL
# CHEMISTRY
## THE STUDY OF MATTER

### Teacher's Guide

# PRENTICE HALL
# CHEMISTRY
# THE STUDY OF MATTER

## Third Edition

## Teacher's Guide

**Henry Dorin**

formerly

Assistant Professor
Chemistry Department, New York University
Chairperson, Physical Science Department
Boys High School, New York City

**Peter E. Demmin**

Chairperson, Science Department
Amherst Central Senior High School
Amherst, New York

**Dorothy L. Gabel**

Chairperson, Science Education
Indiana University
Bloomington, Indiana

**Prentice Hall, Inc.**
Needham, Massachusetts
Englewood Cliffs, New Jersey

# Credits

**Staff Credits**

| | |
|---|---|
| Editorial Development | Robert J. Hope, Edward M. Steele, Diana G. Kessler, Lois B. Arnold, Joel R. Gendler |
| Design Coordination | Jonathan B. Pollard |
| Production Editor | George Carl Cordes |
| Book Manufacturing | Bill Wood |
| Art Direction | L. Christopher Valente |
| Marketing | Paul P. Scopa, Michael Buckley |

**Outside Credits**

| | |
|---|---|
| Critical and Creative Thinking Consultant | Robert J. Swartz Coordinator of Critical and Creative Thinking Program University of Massachusetts, Boston |
| Computer Software Consultant | Donald P. Kelley South Burlington, Vermont |
| Editorial Services | Mary C. Hicks, Mary Jo Diem, Camillo Cimis, Sylvia Gelb, Julie Schofield, Carol Botteron |
| Writing Services | Jan A. Harris, Lawrence Kershnar, Barbara Stine, James J. Banks, Audrey Friedman, Charles E. Gittins, Judith A. Kelley, John Swanson, Mary Zoll |
| Book Design | John and Coni Martucci, Martucci Studio |
| Design Consultant | Constance Tree, Martucci Studio |
| Illustrations | Martucci Studio: Jerry Malone |
| Production Services | Mary N. Babcock, Lois McDonald, Lesli A. Palladino, Martucci Studio, The Book Department, Inc. |

**Cover Design**

| | |
|---|---|
| Design/Photography | John Martucci and L. Christopher Valente |
| Art Direction | Jonathan B. Pollard |

**Photo Credits**

TG-10: Martucci Studios. TG-65: S. Grohe Studio. TG-74: (c) L. Jones, 1987. TG-81: H. Wagner/(Phototake). TG-91: (c) D. Muench, 1988. TG-101: F. Siteman/(Taurus Photo). TG-116: Dan McCoy/(Rainbow). TG-125: Chemical Design/Science Photo Library/(Photo Researchers, Inc.). TG-137: Martucci Studios. TG-152: Ken O'Donoghue. TG-162: Martucci Studios. TG-176: K. Heacox/(Woodfin, Camp. Assoc.). TG-189: F. Myers/Click/Chicago. TG-199: Craig Aurness/(West Light). TG-210: D. Karlson/(The Picture Cube). TG-227: Scott Camazine/(Photo Researchers, Inc.). TG-259: B. Hrynwych/(Southern Light). TG-270: B. Ross/(West Light). TG-282: R. Arnold. TG-292: Martucci Studios. TG-303: D. Budnik/ (Woodfin, Camp. Assoc.). TG-318: G. Stein Studio. TG-328: M. Furman. TG-345: Martucci Studios. TG-354: Martucci Studios. TG-365: D. Lehman/(After-Image).

**1990 Printing**
A Simon & Schuster Company
© Copyright 1989, by Prentice-Hall, Inc.

Previous editions were published by **Cebco · Allyn and Bacon, Inc.** © 1982 and **Allyn and Bacon, Inc.** © 1987.

ISBN 0-13-129883-6

Printed in the United States of America
4 5 6 7 8 9     96 95 94 93 92 91 90

# Contents
# of the Teacher's Guide

# Philosophy of the Course

## Introduction

All high school chemistry courses have many goals, but there are three goals that are basic to a superior chemistry course:

1. that students learn the facts, formulas, and principles that compose the standard high school curriculum,
2. that students understand the basic concepts underlying the facts, formulas, and principles, and
3. that students develop critical-thinking and problem-solving skills, not only to use in chemistry but, by extension, to use in everyday life.

Most chemistry courses accomplish the first goal, but unless a conscious effort is made, courses can be grossly deficient in effecting the other two goals. *Prentice Hall Chemistry: The Study of Matter* is a program designed to help teachers achieve all three basic goals. By programmatically infusing concept mastery, critical thinking, problem solving, and laboratory experimentation strands, this program both underpins and expands upon the facts, formulas, and principles of chemistry.

## Concept Mastery

Whatever goals you and your students may have for the high school chemistry course, they will not be met unless students are given the opportunity to do more than simply absorb facts and formulas. Students must be encouraged to develop a full understanding of chemical concepts. That is, they must be guided to actively construct their own mental models of the basic concepts. Passive acceptance of the teacher's own mental model will not suffice.

Too often, students depart from their high school chemistry course confused and without the intellectual satisfaction that occurs when they truly understand the underlying concepts. As a result, they not only may be reluctant to enroll in another chemistry course but may even develop a negative attitude toward science as a whole. This limits their career choices and discourages them from intellectually debating societal issues involving science. And lack of concept understanding may even help explain the bewildering study finding that shows that taking a high school chemistry course does not lead to higher levels of achievement in a college chemistry course.

Unless the understanding of chemical concepts is the primary goal of a high school chemistry course, the experience will be a sterile one for students. Further, the long-term effect will be detrimental to the individual's prospects for success in future scientific study. Therefore, concept mastery is stressed throughout this program.

**Rationale.** A true understanding of basic concepts is essential both as a foundation for the acquisition of new concepts and for the successful application of knowledge in novel situations. Possessing knowledge without concept understanding is analogous to perceiving the three-dimensional world as a flat, two-dimensional surface. Under such circumstances, it is inevitable that misconceptions about the nature of the world arise.

For example, chemistry teachers usually assume that students have mastered fundamental concepts such as volume. Actually, many students never acquire this concept; instead, they memorize a formula such as "length times width times height" and then unthinkingly apply it to figures of any shape, including pyramids and cylinders. When asked to find the volume of the following figure, many college sophomores multiplied $6 \times 3 \times 3$, to come up with 36. They did not even attach units to the number, because the units had no meaning for them.

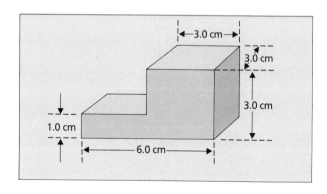

Many chemistry teachers also make the assumption that students are familiar with the particle nature of matter. For example, many teachers assume that students realize that when water evaporates, molecules of water escape into the atmosphere, or that when water boils, the large bubbles inside the water are gaseous water molecules. Yet there is evidence that many 17-year-olds think that the water has been broken down into hydrogen and oxygen.

**Teaching Strategies.** Chemistry students frequently fail to understand the concepts that are presented in class because they tend to memorize facts and the descriptions of processes without thinking through the meaning of the processes or relating them to the physical phenomena they represent. For example, it might appear that a student who can balance an equation understands the chemical concepts that the equation represents. Yet in one study, 50% of the students who balanced equations correctly were unable to distinguish the meaning of the coefficients in terms of molecules and atoms. For example, when given the formula for hydrogen preceded by the coefficient ($2H_2$), they did not distinguish between

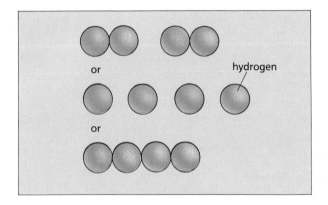

*Prentice Hall Chemistry: The Study of Matter* has many features that will enable you to teach chemistry so as to develop concept mastery in your students. The following suggestions should facilitate concept understanding:

1. *Focus on few concepts, but in greater depth.* In this program, you will find that a large portion of the presentation has been devoted to fundamental concepts. Material is arranged so that more advanced concepts are set apart, so that they can be omitted for certain classes or students.

2. *Use a variety of teaching strategies.* Different students may learn from different strategies. Some will learn using computer software. Others will learn from a laboratory approach or from demonstrations. The use of overhead transparencies is frequently helpful. The Teaching Suggestions in the Teacher's Edition of the text, as well as the Suggestions given in the Teacher's Resource Book, will provide a number of strategies for teaching the same content using a variety of strategies.

3. *Present concepts from several different viewpoints.* The same concept needs to be addressed in many different ways. For example, consider the concept of volume. Although it means the space occupied by a material object, it can be considered from the standpoint of the units used to measure it, the formu-

las that can be used to calculate it, the displacement of water, the laboratory measurement, etc. Students need to encounter as many meanings as possible, because each different approach will broaden his or her conception of the meaning of volume.

When dealing with matter, students will need to see that all matter can be thought of as having mass, volume, and being composed of particles. Frequently, students do not attach the same meaning to matter that chemists do. For example, when you, the chemistry teacher, think of water, you probably think of a clear, liquid substance, made of molecules containing two hydrogen atoms and one oxygen atom, and having the formula $H_2O$. On the other hand, students may only be thinking of the liquid water.

For a conceptual understanding of chemistry, it is necessary for students to attach the microscopic (molecular) and the symbolic (formula) meanings to the word "water" as well as the macroscopic properties (clear, liquid). To help students do this, pictures in the text frequently show the particles of which the substances are composed. Because students may gloss over these, you will find a special section in the *Teacher's Resource Book* that contains Concept Mastery worksheets that should be assigned at various points in the course to reinforce the particle nature of matter. Asking students to explain on the microscopic level what appears on the macroscopic level will deepen their conceptual understanding. They must be required to think about the phenomena rather than to simply memorize facts and formulas.

4. *Elicit students' misconceptions and directly address them in class.* Sometimes students have developed misconceptions from observing nature and interpreting it in the same way that early scientists did. For example, a student in an air-conditioned room may notice that the metal parts of a chair feel colder than the cloth-covered seat. The student may erroneously conclude that the metal has a lower temperature than the cloth. Other times, students may have misconceptions because they have learned something in an incomplete way in a previous course, through reading, etc. No matter how students have arrived at such misconceptions, the misconceptions are very difficult to erase. At the end of every chapter in the text, you will find a section of questions titled "Concept Mastery." These questions should be quite helpful in identifying students' misconceptions. You may wish to use some of these questions before you teach each chapter. If a misconception persists, use an alternative strategy to dispel it.

5. *Encourage students to discuss concepts with one another.* Students frequently understand each other's thinking better than adults do. Having one student explain a concept to another helps both the

student who is doing the explaining and the student who is listening. Students will feel more comfortable revealing their misconceptions to a classmate than to a teacher.

6. *Include concept mastery questions on tests.* Students will learn to please you by limiting their study of chemistry to the types of tests that you give. Include some test questions on the particle nature of matter. (The chapter tests in the *Teacher's Resource Book* contain some concept mastery questions.) Ask students to explain their answers. Give partial credit on problems when they supply the correct steps.

# Critical and Creative Thinking

Another major goal of a high school chemistry course must be the development of critical and creative thinking skills. Critical thinking, the use of reason to make a decision or form an opinion, is a skill essential to successful learning in any subject area. Evaluative and analytical skills are required for the acquisition of productive knowledge, that is, true concept understanding. The active construction of mental models of concepts often involves such activities as classifying a list of items, considering the relationships among constituent parts, and detecting similarities and differences so as to reveal a pattern—all analytical skills of critical thinking. Inferential skills, induction and deduction, make it possible to apply concepts to concrete situations so as to explain perceived phenomena.

**Rationale.** Creative thinking comes into prominence when challenging problems are posed. Faced with a non-routine or "ill-defined" problem, the student should be willing and able to propose novel ideas and have the flexibility to change direction when a particular approach proves futile. By practicing a combination of critical and creative thinking, students will become adept problem solvers.

Fostering scientific literacy is an equally important reason for teaching critical and creative thinking. When their education has been completed, all students, whether or not they have chosen to pursue careers in chemistry, will be faced with the need to make decisions about societal issues that pertain to science. Mastery of the basic concepts of chemistry in conjunction with the ability to analyze, evaluate, and reason is what scientific literacy demands.

**Teaching Strategies.** Throughout this program, opportunities for developing critical and creative thinking skills have been provided. A separate, clearly identified group of questions at the end of each chapter of the textbook is devoted to critical thinking. In the *Teacher's Resource Book*, there is a special group of

Critical and Creative Thinking worksheets, each of which concentrates on a single subskill. Another group of worksheets in the *Teacher's Resource Book—Societal Issues*—calls upon students to apply their scientific understanding and critical thinking skills in the examination of vital issues facing society. Both the Open-Ended Demonstrations and Open-Ended Laboratories are worksheets that demand the exercise of critical and creative thinking skills.

To optimize the effectiveness of the critical and creative thinking exercises provided throughout the program, classroom activities stressing metacognition should be provided. Metacognition, or the conscious reflection on the mental steps involved in a thinking skill, helps students gain a deeper understanding of the important elements of good thinking. A powerful method for fostering metacognition is encouraging students to "think out loud."

Because many students might be reluctant to reveal their thinking processes, it is important to provide a classroom atmosphere of acceptance and approval. Some suggestions for creating an environment conducive to thinking are listed below.

1. *Create a supportive environment.*
   - Encourage an open, receptive atmosphere in the classroom.
   - Stress that the focus is on the process of thinking, not on "getting the right answer."
      Do not label answers as "right" or "wrong."
      Do not single out responses for special praise, which tends to suggest a "right" answer and thus inhibit the flow of more unconventional responses.
      Listen carefully as students verbalize their thinking, in order to identify flaws in their thinking.
      Use a series of How, Why, and What-if questions to redirect the thinking of a student who has proposed flawed reasoning.
      Encourage students to offer somewhat unconventional responses.
   - Be deliberate in your use of "wait time."
      Allow for a pause of possibly long duration prior to the initiation of student responses.
      Impose no time limit on student responses so as to encourage further thought and develop confidence.
      Pause again after the students' initial outpouring of ideas has ceased in order to open up new vistas for contemplation. (For example, a student who is comparing and contrasting might ex-

haust comparisons by size and shape. A willingness to wait for further response may well allow the student to open up to the possibility of comparison by color, texture, function, and so on.)

2. *Concentrate on metacognition.*

■ Make use of classroom configurations that encourage metacognitive thinking, such as:

*Demonstration:* Demonstrate in front of the class with a volunteer. The student volunteer thinks out loud to solve a problem; you record the thinking steps on an overhead projector or the chalkboard.

*Pair/Share:* Students pair off; one solves aloud, the other records the thinking processes and then shares them with the class.

*Fishbowl:* A small group of up to eight students solves aloud; the rest of the class records and reports the thinking processes of the group.

*Class Discussion:* Summarize with the class what comprises the essential elements of a particular skill.

# Problem Solving

Successful problem solving involves several factors, including a systematic approach, specialized techniques, concept understanding, and critical and creative thinking. Depending on where a particular problem falls in the spectrum from well-defined to ill-defined, students will have more or less success depending on the extent of their concept understanding and the strength of their critical and creative thinking skills. In all cases, though, the application of a systematic method of approach like the five-step Read/Collect Information/Plan/Solve/Check method presented in Chapter 3 of the textbook can be helpful. By organizing students' thinking, these simple steps can serve as a frame upon which students can build. Also presented in Chapter 3 are two specialized techniques—dimensional analysis and the use of scientific notation—that prove useful in solving many of the problems encountered in a high school chemistry course.

However, neither such special techniques nor a systematic approach is more than an elementary starting point along the path to successful problem solving.

**Rationale.** Within the past 10 years, several studies have been conducted on how students go about solving chemistry problems in high school and in introductory college chemistry courses. The conclusion of almost every study is that a major reason students cannot solve problems is that they do not understand the underlying concepts. For example, in one study stu-

dents were asked to solve molarity problems aloud. A greater percentage of students could get a correct answer to a problem that asked for the molarity of a solution given the mass of a solid and volume of the solution than could describe how to make 1 liter of a 2 *M* solution of the same substance in the laboratory. An explanation for this inconsistency was that in solving the molarity problem, students simply had plugged values into a memorized formula. There was no memorized procedure for making up the molar solution.

Additional information about why chemistry students are poor problem solvers has been obtained by comparing students' success in solving simple but analogous problems. Students were given information about the mass and volume of the ingredients needed to make up lemonade of normal concentration. They were then asked how to make up larger quantities or more concentrated solutions. Analogous chemistry problems based on solutions of sodium hydroxide also were used. Results indicated that as long as the problems were simple, students could solve the lemonade problems. However, when the lemonade problems involved adding or evaporating off water, the percentage of students solving correctly was virtually the same as for the dilution and concentration problems involving sodium hydroxide (this percentage was very low). In other words, it is not because students do not understand moles that they cannot solve these more complex problems. It is because they do not understand the fundamental concept of solution. When students took the lemonade test again after having completed their study of molarity, the percentage of students solving the lemonade dilution and concentration problems correctly was unchanged. This offers more evidence that students' study of chemistry does not increase their understanding of the world unless they understand basic concepts.

In teaching students to solve problems, you will want to do everything in your power to encourage them to think about the method of solution rather than to mechanically apply a formula to produce an answer. Reliance on memorization should be discouraged because it can stifle the creativity that leads to the generation of ideas. Flexibility, another aspect of creative thinking, is also beneficial because it prevents the solver from persisting in the pursuit of an unproductive strategy. But critical rather than creative thinking usually is the primary mental activity involved in problem solving. Analytical skills come into play when sifting through the data: relating parts to the whole, examining similarities and differences, classifying according to various criteria, ranking or ordering items for a particular characteristic, and so on. Distinguishing among reasons, assumptions, and causes often can help students clarify a problem situation.

**Teaching Strategies.** Several features of *Prentice Hall Chemistry: The Study of Matter* will aid you in helping your students become better problem solvers. The following suggestions incorporate some of the features that you will find in the text, in the Teacher's Guide, and in the *Teacher's Resource Book*.

1. *Listen to your students solve problems aloud.* You might even wish to have them taped for later study so you can pinpoint their difficulties. In this way, you will determine their misconceptions or lack of qualitative understanding of the underlying concepts.

2. *Teach concepts thoroughly before teaching problem solving.* The text is well suited to help you do this. Students should understand that any quantity of a substance that appears in a problem is matter that has mass and volume and is composed of particles. The worksheets in the special Concept Mastery Section of the *Teacher's Resource Book* should reinforce this. In solving problems, if students are always asked to compare the given quantity of each substance with the standard quantity, the mole, they may see the relationships that exist between these quantities. An example of solving problems with this under consideration is shown on page CM-15 of the *Teacher's Resource Book*.

3. *Teach students to be systematic in their problem solving.* The dimensional-analysis method helps some students because it organizes the given information.

# The Laboratory

The laboratory plays an important role in the teaching of science. All the information contained in the chemistry text has its roots in the chemistry laboratory. Many chemists have spent a lifetime collecting and interpreting data to formulate the theories that are the backbone of chemistry today. Although high school students cannot be expected to make new scientific discoveries, there are many other goals in including laboratory work in an introductory chemistry course. Several of these are described as follows:

1. *Chemistry becomes more interesting, so motivation to learn increases.* Some chemistry teachers believe that this is the primary goal of laboratory work. There always will be some students who enroll in a chemistry course in order to see "the explosions and color changes." Chemistry experiments also can provide the release that some students need in the course of the school day. It is hoped, however, that the chemistry lab will arouse students' curiosity about natural phenomena.

2. *Understanding of chemical concepts is facilitated.* Laboratory activities provide students with direct contact with substances and the changes these substances undergo under different sets of circumstances. These concrete experiences provide another context for construction of mental models of concepts that are presented in a more abstract manner in the text.

Care must be taken that students have the necessary experiences they need to form acceptable concepts. All too frequently, in the interest of saving time, teachers demonstrate parts of experiments that should be left to students. For example, in an experiment calling for solutions of various molarities, students should make up the solutions to extend their concept of molarity.

Teachers also may think that computer simulations can substitute for laboratory work. Although computer simulations teach some concepts well, some early research results indicate that students are not always able to relate what they see on the computer screen to the phenomena of the real world.

3. *The lack of absolute certainty in scientific results is underscored.* Post-laboratory discussions of the data and conclusions that are reached by students are essential if students are to come to the realization that there is a degree of uncertainty in all measurements and conclusions that can be drawn from experiments.

4. *Critical thinking skills are exercised.* First-hand observation, a significant critical thinking skill, is at the heart of all laboratory work. Even those students who approach lab experiments as if they were cookbook recipes cannot escape the necessity of making careful observations. Many experiments also require the analysis of data through the techniques of comparing and contrasting, ordering, and classifying. With skillful questioning during the pre- and post-laboratory discussions, students can be guided to refine their analytical and reasoning skills. Before performing an experiment, students should be asked to explain why the given procedure will fulfill the stated goal of the activity. When the experiment has been completed, students should be asked to use inferential skills to draw conclusions from the data.

5. *Psychomotor and organizational skills are exercised.* When students prepare for an experiment, they must set up the equipment, organize their work space, and decide how they will collect the data. Although giving students a ready-made data table helps to some extent, students must at least determine how the available lab time will be spent. Actually handling the equipment makes students more adept at using screws, clamps, and other mechanical devices.

# Design of the Text

## Organization

The text for *Prentice Hall Chemistry: The Study of Matter* is divided into 26 chapters. Each chapter is broken down into from five to 23 sections. In a textbook, chapters that run on without convenient stopping points pose a psychological barrier for students. There is a limit to the amount of new information that any person can absorb at one time, and students frequently need to go back over part of a reading assignment before continuing with it. This is especially true of difficult sections that must be understood before the material that follows can be read meaningfully.

## Objectives

Listed at the beginning of each chapter are general objectives for that chapter. These objectives are intended to provide an outline or framework for instruction. Use them as a means to an important end: effective teaching by you, the teacher, and efficient learning by each student.

An objective is a specified educational goal, described in terms of the observable behavior of a student who has attained that goal. Objectives are useful for the secondary school teacher for several reasons:

*Communication.* Clearly conceived and written objectives allow the teacher to communicate ideas precisely to others, including to students, parents, and other teaching professionals. It is especially helpful for students to know the types and levels of performance they are expected to achieve at the end of a section, chapter, or course.

*Planning.* Objectives facilitate the planning of instruction and the selection of teaching materials and aids. Expressing objectives in terms of ideal behavior delineates the changes you wish to bring about in students and helps to disclose the best way to accomplish them.

*Initial Diagnosis.* Objectives enable the teacher more effectively to diagnose students' skills and preparedness. By examining students' current behavior, you can determine which topics to emphasize, bypass, or move on to. In addition, objectives allow you to monitor students' progress.

*Testing/Evaluation.* Objectives allow the teacher systematically to evaluate learning by students. Expressing behavioral goals helps you to determine the relevant materials and methods with which to measure learning.

*Results.* Consequently, objectives enable the teacher to supply "evidence" that learning has indeed occurred. Students' achievements of the goals you have set for them are your "proof" that your teaching methods have been successful.

## Types of Sections

The chapter objectives are followed by the chapter text, which is made up of the following types of sections:

*Core:* The content of the core sections is within the grasp of all high school chemistry students in the academic track.

*Advanced:* The advanced sections are suitable for students with above average ability.

*Optional:* At the teacher's discretion, the optional sections may or may not be given as part of the reading assignment.

## Types of Optional Sections

There are several types of optional sections:

*Breakthroughs:* A series of essays describing recent, exciting developments in chemistry.

*Applications:* A series of essays illustrating the ways in which chemical concepts are used in a practical way.

*Biographies:* Brief biographies of people, from the past and the present, whose work in chemistry has been outstanding.

*Careers:* A series of essays describing some careers that require training in chemistry.

*Can You Explain This?:* A series of demonstrations and photographs illustrating chemical phenomena that can be explained by an application of chemical principles.

# Using the "Can You Explain This?" Demonstrations

Demonstrations are an integral part of the teaching of chemistry, and most teachers routinely perform a number of standard demonstrations that illustrate particular points. The demonstrations in the "Can You Explain This?" series challenge students to account for the observed results by applying chemical principles or concepts.

Although the demonstrations are described in the text, we strongly recommend that teachers do the demonstrations in class where possible. Live demonstrations are more interesting and can generate additional questions and answers.

These demonstrations are a reminder that scientists attempt to explain observed phenomena in terms of theory. The answers students give to the questions should be judged on the basis of how much sense they make, not on whether they are "correct." Challenge your students either to prove or disprove a proposed explanation, allowing them to set up and carry out procedures to make their point, where this is safe and practicable.

As teachers, we too often allow ourselves to be cast in the role of the all-knowing sage. When students ask us for an explanation of something they observed in a lab experiment or classroom demonstration, we might feel embarrassed if we cannot explain the phenomenon, and we might employ various devices to cover up our ignorance. It is better to admit our ignorance but then to challenge the students to suggest a thought experiment or lab procedure that might reveal the answer.

# Section-End Questions

To help you in assigning homework, Review Questions and Practice Problems have been interspersed throughout the chapters instead of appearing only at the ends of the chapters. A block of these questions typically appears after two or three sections of the chapter but might appear after a single section if that section is longer or has more difficult material in it. If a reading assignment goes beyond a block of these questions, students should answer the questions before continuing the reading. The Review Questions and Practice Problems are an integral part of the reading assignment. Students should answer all Review Questions and do all Practice Problems for the sections they are assigned to read.

Some of the Review Questions and Practice Problems are marked with an asterisk. The answers to these questions and problems are given in the back of

the book in Appendix B. These answers provide students with immediate feedback on their progress. Obtaining a correct answer indicates to a student that he or she is ready to go on with the assignment. Obtaining an incorrect answer indicates that the student should go back over the pertinent section and restudy it. A student getting an incorrect answer on the first try often will succeed in getting a correct answer on the second attempt. By making these answers available to the students, we hope to have eliminated some of the instances where students, through a misunderstanding of their reading, conscientiously do all of the assigned questions but get incorrect answers for all of them.

# Chapter-End Questions

At the end of each chapter, there is a wealth of chapter-end questions of varying levels of difficulty. These questions are grouped under the following headings:

*Content Review:* a review of the basic content of the chapter by section. At the end of each question, the section of the chapter to which the question pertains is indicated, making it easy for students having difficulty with a question to find the related text.

*Content Mastery.* a review of the basic content of the chapter but with section references given only to the teacher in the Annotated Teacher's Edition.

*Concept Mastery:* a review of the important concepts in the chapter.

*Cumulative Review:* a review of important content and concepts from prior chapters.

*Critical Thinking:* a review that emphasizes the use of critical thinking skills. A numbered listing of the critical thinking skills that are used in this course appears in this Teacher's Guide on page TG-41. Each of the critical thinking questions that appears at the end of a chapter is referenced by number to the critical thinking skill used to answer the question.

*Challenge Problems:* a review consisting of difficult problems suitable for extremely able students.

The questions in all six of the categories are within the capabilities of *above average* students, although most teachers will find that time limitations make it necessary to assign only some of these questions. All of the questions in the *first four* categories and *some* of the questions in the last two categories can be handled by average students. Choose those questions that you feel are most appropriate given the time available. All of the questions in the first *two* categories and *some* of the questions in the next three categories could be assigned to below average students. Once again, time constraints will prohibit most teachers from assigning all of these questions.

# Courses of Instruction for Different Ability Levels

Over the past 40 years, there has been a trend toward heavier chemistry books as ever greater amounts of material have gone into them. These heavier books also are more ponderous with respect to chemical concepts as the descriptive chemistry in the older texts has been replaced by theoretical chemistry. Even in the "good old days," when chemistry books were much thinner, most chemistry teachers did not attempt to "cover" an entire book.

Given these circumstances, you might wonder, "How much of this book should I attempt to teach?" We doubt whether any teacher, even one with the most gifted students, could teach the entire book and use all the other components of the program in a typical 180-day school year.

Students taking introductory chemistry in high school fall into three groups:

- above average college preparatory students (honors)
- average college preparatory students
- non-college-bound students

In the third category are two types of students: (1) those who would like to study chemistry in high school even though they have no plans to attend college, and (2) those who aspire to go to college but are not likely to be enrolled because they lack the ability for college-level work. These are the students who, often responding to parental pressure, become enrolled in a college preparatory course against the advice of their guidance counselors.

The table that follows categorizes each section of the text in terms of its suitability for the three ability levels just listed. When a section is designated as suitable for a particular ability level, it means that the material in the section readily can be understood (with conscientious study) by students having that particular ability level. "Suitable" does not mean that every section so marked should be taught. This book contains considerably more material than can be learned in a 180-day school year by a typical high school chemistry class. In the last half of the book, many of the topics can be omitted without depriving the students of a good understanding of the fundamentals of introductory high school chemistry. Especially in that part of the book, you will want to exercise some choice concerning which topics to teach and which to omit. This choice will allow you to vary your emphasis and will provide you with flexibility in teaching students of varying ability.

We especially advise inexperienced teachers not to "race through" the earlier chapters. Students will need a good understanding of the first 15 chapters of the text in order to be able to understand the rest of the book. If you go through the earlier chapters at too fast a pace, you (and your students) will have some insurmountable difficulties while wrestling with the later chapters. Of the last 11 chapters in the text, most chemistry teachers would consider Chapters 16 (Solutions), 19 (Acids, Bases, and Salts), 20 (Acid-Base Reactions), 21 (Oxidation and Reduction), and 22 (Electrochemistry) the chapters deserving the most careful attention.

It is important for you, the teacher, to find the teaching pace that will maximize learning. This pace will vary from class to class, depending on the abilities of your students. Rather than attempting to "cover" the book, your goal should be, given the time constraints, to teach as much of the most important material as possible at a depth of understanding that is appropriate for high school chemistry. To accomplish this goal, you might have to cover fewer topics so that more learning can occur.

# Categorization of Text Sections by Ability Level

| | Above Average College Prep. | Average College Prep. | Non-College Track |
|---|:---:|:---:|:---:|
| **Introduction to Chemistry** | | | |
| 1-1    Introduction | ✔ | ✔ | ✔ |
| 1-2    The Scientific Method | ✔ | ✔ | ✔ |
| 1-3    Controlled Experiments | ✔ | ✔ | ✔ |
| 1-4    Making a Graph | ✔ | ✔ | ✔ |
| 1-5    Safety—A Primary Concern | ✔ | ✔ | ✔ |
| **Measurement** | | | |
| 2-1    Chemical Quantities | ✔ | ✔ | ✔ |
| 2-2    The International System of Units | ✔ | ✔ | ✔ |
| 2-3    Advantages of Using SI | ✔ | ✔ | ✔ |
| 2-4    SI Prefixes | ✔ | ✔ | ✔ |
| 2-5    SI Derived Units | ✔ | ✔ | ✔ |
| 2-6    Non-SI Units Found in Chemistry Writing | ✔ | ✔ | ✔ |
| ▨ 2-7    The Newton, an SI Derived Unit | ✔ | | |
| 2-8    The Meter, Kilogram, and Cubic Meter | ✔ | ✔ | ✔ |
| 2-9    Uncertainty in Measurement | ✔ | ✔ | |
| 2-10    Accuracy versus Precision | ✔ | ✔ | |
| 2-11    Significant Figures | ✔ | ✔ | |
| ▨ 2-12    The Use of Plus-or-minus Notation | ✔ | | |
| 2-13    Calculating with Measurements | ✔ | ✔ | |
| 2-14    Percent Error | ✔ | ✔ | |
| **Problem Solving** | | | |
| 3-1    Introduction | ✔ | ✔ | ✔ |
| 3-2    Dimensional Analysis | ✔ | ✔ | ✔ |
| 3-3    Scientific Notation | ✔ | ✔ | ✔ |
| 3-4    Using Scientific Notation for Expressing the Correct Number of Significant Figures | ✔ | ✔ | |
| 3-5    A General Procedure for Solving Problems | ✔ | ✔ | ✔ |

▨ Advanced Topic

# Categorization of Text Sections (continued)

| | Above Average College Prep. | Average College Prep. | Non-College Track |
|---|:---:|:---:|:---:|
| **Matter** | | | |
| 4-1 Mass | ✔ | ✔ | ✔ |
| 4-2 Varieties of Matter—Elements and Compounds | ✔ | ✔ | ✔ |
| 4-3 Varieties of Matter—Mixtures | ✔ | ✔ | ✔ |
| 4-4 Properties | ✔ | ✔ | ✔ |
| 4-5 Density | ✔ | ✔ | ✔ |
| 4-6 Changes of Phase | ✔ | ✔ | ✔ |
| 4-7 Physical and Chemical Properties | ✔ | ✔ | ✔ |
| 4-8 Physical and Chemical Change | ✔ | ✔ | ✔ |
| 4-9 Conservation of Mass | ✔ | ✔ | ✔ |
| 4-10 Relative Abundance | ✔ | ✔ | ✔ |
| 4-11 Symbols of the Elements | ✔ | ✔ | ✔ |
| **Energy** | | | |
| 5-1 The Concept of Energy | ✔ | ✔ | ✔ |
| 5-2 Forms of Energy | ✔ | ✔ | ✔ |
| 5-3 Conversion of Energy and Its Conservation | ✔ | ✔ | ✔ |
| 5-4 Energy and Chemical Reactions | ✔ | ✔ | ✔ |
| 5-5 Heat Energy and Temperature | ✔ | ✔ | ✔ |
| 5-6 Heat and Its Measurement | ✔ | ✔ | ✔ |
| 5-7 The Kinetic Theory of Heat and Temperature | ✔ | ✔ | ✔ |
| 5-8 Interactions Between Electric Charges | ✔ | ✔ | ✔ |
| **Structure of the Atom** | | | |
| 6-1 Atoms Today | ✔ | ✔ | ✔ |
| 6-2 Historical Background | ✔ | ✔ | ✔ |
| 6-3 The Law of Multiple Proportions | ✔ | ✔ | |
| 6-4 Dalton's Atomic Theory | ✔ | ✔ | ✔ |
| 6-5 Updating the Atomic Theory | ✔ | ✔ | ✔ |
| 6-6 Electrons, Protons, and Neutrons | ✔ | ✔ | ✔ |
| ■ 6-7 Charge and Mass of the Electron | ✔ | ✔ | |

## Categorization of Text Sections (continued)

| | Above Average College Prep. | Average College Prep. | Non-College Track |
|---|:---:|:---:|:---:|
| 6-8    The Rutherford Model of the Atom | ✔ | ✔ | ✔ |
| 6-9    Shortcomings of Rutherford's Model | ✔ | ✔ | ✔ |
| 6-10   The Bohr Model | ✔ | ✔ | ✔ |
| 6-11   The Charge-cloud Model | ✔ | ✔ | ✔ |
| 6-12   Scientific Models | ✔ | ✔ | ✔ |
| 6-13   The Nature of Light | ✔ | ✔ | |
| 6-14   The Emission and Absorption of Radiation | ✔ | ✔ | ✔ |
| ■ 6-15   Light as Energy | ✔ | ✔ | |
| 6-16   The Major Nucleons | ✔ | ✔ | ✔ |
| ■ 6-17   Quarks | ✔ | | |
| 6-18   The Concept of Atomic Weight | ✔ | ✔ | ✔ |
| 6-19   Mass Number | ✔ | ✔ | ✔ |
| 6-20   Modern Standard of Atomic Mass | ✔ | ✔ | ✔ |
| ■ 6-21   Determining Atomic Masses from Weighted Averages | ✔ | | |

## Chemical Formulas

| | Above Average College Prep. | Average College Prep. | Non-College Track |
|---|:---:|:---:|:---:|
| 7-1    Using Symbols to Write Formulas | ✔ | ✔ | ✔ |
| 7-2    Kinds of Formulas | ✔ | ✔ | ✔ |
| 7-3    Types of Compounds | ✔ | ✔ | ✔ |
| 7-4    Ionic Substances | ✔ | ✔ | ✔ |
| 7-5    Predicting Formulas of Ionic Compounds | ✔ | ✔ | ✔ |
| 7-6    Naming Ionic Compounds | ✔ | ✔ | ✔ |
| 7-7    Formulas of Molecular Compounds | ✔ | ✔ | ✔ |
| 7-8    Naming Molecular Compounds | ✔ | ✔ | ✔ |
| 7-9    Naming Acids | ✔ | ✔ | ✔ |

## The Mathematics of Chemical Formulas

| | Above Average College Prep. | Average College Prep. | Non-College Track |
|---|:---:|:---:|:---:|
| 8-1    Stoichiometry | ✔ | ✔ | ✔ |
| 8-2    Formula Mass | ✔ | ✔ | ✔ |
| 8-3    Gram Atomic Mass and Gram Formula Mass | ✔ | ✔ | ✔ |
| 8-4    The Mole | ✔ | ✔ | ✔ |
| 8-5    Moles and Atoms | ✔ | ✔ | ✔ |
| 8-6    Moles and Formula Units | ✔ | ✔ | ✔ |
| 8-7    Mole Relationships | ✔ | ✔ | ✔ |

■ Advanced Topic

# Categorization of Text Sections (continued)

| | | Above Average College Prep. | Average College Prep. | Non-College Track |
|---|---|:---:|:---:|:---:|
| 8-8 | Percentage Composition | ✔ | ✔ | ✔ |
| 8-9 | Determining the Formula of a Compound | ✔ | ✔ | |
| ■ 8-10 | Another Way to Determine Empirical Formulas | ✔ | | |

## Chemical Equations

| | | | | |
|---|---|:---:|:---:|:---:|
| 9-1 | Word Equations | ✔ | ✔ | ✔ |
| 9-2 | Interpreting Formula Equations | ✔ | ✔ | ✔ |
| 9-3 | Determining Whether an Equation is Balanced | ✔ | ✔ | ✔ |
| 9-4 | Balancing Chemical Equations | ✔ | ✔ | ✔ |
| 9-5 | Showing Energy Changes in Equations | ✔ | ✔ | ✔ |
| 9-6 | Showing Phases in Chemical Equations | ✔ | ✔ | ✔ |
| 9-7 | Ions in Water Solution | ✔ | ✔ | |
| 9-8 | Classifying Chemical Reactions | ✔ | ✔ | ✔ |
| 9-9 | Direct Combination or Synthesis Reactions | ✔ | ✔ | ✔ |
| 9-10 | Decomposition or Analysis Reactions | ✔ | ✔ | ✔ |
| 9-11 | Single Replacement Reactions | ✔ | ✔ | ✔ |
| 9-12 | Double Replacement Reactions | ✔ | ✔ | ✔ |
| ■ 9-13 | Writing Ionic Equations | ✔ | | |

## The Mathematics of Chemical Equations

| | | | | |
|---|---|:---:|:---:|:---:|
| 10-1 | The Importance of Mathematics in Chemistry | ✔ | ✔ | ✔ |
| 10-2 | Coefficients and Relative Volumes of Gases | ✔ | ✔ | ✔ |
| 10-3 | Mass-Mass Relationships | ✔ | ✔ | ✔ |
| 10-4 | Mixed Mass-Volume-Particle Relationships | ✔ | ✔ | |
| ■ 10-5 | Limiting Reactant Problems | ✔ | | |

## Phases of Matter

| | | | | |
|---|---|:---:|:---:|:---:|
| 11-1 | The Study of Phases | ✔ | ✔ | ✔ |
| 11-2 | The Meaning of Pressure | ✔ | ✔ | ✔ |
| 11-3 | Atmospheric Pressure | ✔ | ✔ | ✔ |
| 11-4 | Measuring Gas Pressure | ✔ | ✔ | ✔ |
| 11-5 | Boiling and Melting | ✔ | ✔ | ✔ |

# Categorization of Text Sections (continued)

| | Above Average College Prep. | Average College Prep. | Non-College Track |
|---|:---:|:---:|:---:|
| 11-6    Theory of Physical Phase | ✔ | ✔ | ✔ |
| 11-7    Temperature and Phase Change | ✔ | ✔ | ✔ |
| 11-8    The Kinetic Theory of Gases | ✔ | ✔ | ✔ |
| 11-9    Vapor-Liquid Equilibrium | ✔ | ✔ | ✔ |
| 11-10   Vapor Pressure and Boiling | ✔ | ✔ | ✔ |
| 11-11   Liquefaction of Gases | ✔ | ✔ | ✔ |
| 11-12   Heat of Vaporization | ✔ | ✔ | ✔ |
| 11-13   Distillation | ✔ | ✔ | ✔ |
| 11-14   Solids and the Kinetic Theory | ✔ | ✔ | ✔ |
| 11-15   Melting and the Heat of Fusion | ✔ | ✔ | ✔ |
| 11-16   Sublimation | ✔ | ✔ | ✔ |
| 11-17   Crystals | ✔ | ✔ | ✔ |
| 11-18   Water of Hydration in Crystals | ✔ | ✔ | ✔ |
| 11-19   Hygroscopic and Deliquescent Substances | ✔ | ✔ | ✔ |
| 11-20   Densities of the Solid and Liquid Phases | ✔ | ✔ | ✔ |

## The Gas Laws

| | Above Average College Prep. | Average College Prep. | Non-College Track |
|---|:---:|:---:|:---:|
| 12-1    Development of the Kinetic Theory of Gases | ✔ | ✔ | ✔ |
| 12-2    Relationship Between the Pressure and the Volume of a Gas—Boyle's Law | ✔ | ✔ | ✔ |
| 12-3    Relationship Between the Temperature and the Volume of a Gas—Charles's Law | ✔ | ✔ | ✔ |
| ▩ 12-4   Relationship Between the Temperature and the Pressure of a Gas | ✔ | ✔ | |
| 12-5    The Combined Gas Law | ✔ | ✔ | ✔ |
| 12-6    The Densities of Gases | ✔ | ✔ | |
| ▩ 12-7   Volume as a Measure of the Quantity of a Gas | ✔ | ✔ | |
| ▩ 12-8   Mass-Volume Problems at Non-standard Conditions | ✔ | | |
| 12-9    Dalton's Law of Partial Pressures | ✔ | ✔ | ✔ |
| 12-10   Graham's Law of Diffusion | ✔ | ✔ | |
| 12-11   The Kinetic Theory and the Gas Laws | ✔ | ✔ | |
| 12-12   Deviations from Ideal Behavior | ✔ | ✔ | |
| ▩ 12-13   The Ideal Gas Law | ✔ | ✔ | |

▩ Advanced Topic

# Categorization of Text Sections (continued)

| | | Above Average College Prep. | Average College Prep. | Non-College Track |
|---|---|:---:|:---:|:---:|
| **Electron Configurations** | | | | |
| 13-1 | Wave Mechanics | ✔ | ✔ | ✔ |
| 13-2 | Probability and Energy Levels | ✔ | ✔ | ✔ |
| 13-3 | Energy Levels of the Wave-Mechanical Model of the Atom | ✔ | ✔ | ✔ |
| 13-4 | Orbitals | ✔ | ✔ | ✔ |
| 13-5 | The Shapes of Orbitals | ✔ | ✔ | ✔ |
| 13-6 | Electron Spin | ✔ | ✔ | ✔ |
| ▨ 13-7 | Quantum Numbers | ✔ | | |
| 13-8 | Notation for Electron Configurations | ✔ | ✔ | ✔ |
| 13-9 | Electron Configurations for the First 11 Elements | ✔ | ✔ | ✔ |
| 13-10 | Electron Configurations for Elements of Higher Atomic Numbers | ✔ | ✔ | ✔ |
| 13-11 | Significance of Electron Configurations | ✔ | ✔ | ✔ |
| 13-12 | Electron Configurations for Atoms in the Excited State | ✔ | | |
| **The Periodic Table** | | | | |
| 14-1 | Origin of the Periodic Table | ✔ | ✔ | ✔ |
| 14-2 | Reading the Periodic Table | ✔ | ✔ | ✔ |
| 14-3 | Periods of Elements | ✔ | ✔ | ✔ |
| 14-4 | Groups of Elements | ✔ | ✔ | ✔ |
| 14-5 | Periodicity in Properties | ✔ | ✔ | ✔ |
| 14-6 | Ionization Energy and Periodicity | ✔ | ✔ | ✔ |
| 14-7 | Electronegativity and Periodicity | ✔ | ✔ | ✔ |
| ▨ 14-8 | Position of Electrons | ✔ | | |
| 14-9 | Atomic Radius and Periodicity | ✔ | ✔ | |
| 14-10 | Ionic Radius | ✔ | ✔ | |
| ▨ 14-11 | Isoelectronic Species | ✔ | | |
| 14-12 | Metals, Nonmetals, and Semimetals in the Periodic Table | ✔ | ✔ | ✔ |

# Categorization of Text Sections (continued)

| Chemical Bonding | Above Average College Prep. | Average College Prep. | Non-College Track |
|---|:---:|:---:|:---:|
| 15-1    The Attachment Between Atoms | ✔ | ✔ | ✔ |
| 15-2    Ionic Bonding | ✔ | ✔ | ✔ |
| 15-3    Covalent Bonding | ✔ | ✔ | ✔ |
| 15-4    Hybridization | ✔ | ✔ | |
| ■ 15-5    Dot Diagrams for Molecules and Polyatomic Ions | ✔ | ✔ | |
| 15-6    The Shapes of Molecules—the VSEPR Model | ✔ | ✔ | |
| ■ 15-7    Exceptions to the Rule of Eight | ✔ | | |
| 15-8    Polar Bonds and Polar Molecules | ✔ | ✔ | ✔ |
| 15-9    Hydrogen Bonding | ✔ | ✔ | ✔ |
| 15-10    Metallic Bonding | ✔ | ✔ | ✔ |
| 15-11    Molecular Substances | ✔ | ✔ | ✔ |
| 15-12    Network Solids | ✔ | ✔ | ✔ |
| 15-13    Ionic Crystals | ✔ | ✔ | ✔ |
| 15-14    Bond Energy—The Strength of a Chemical Bond | ✔ | ✔ | |

| Solutions | Above Average College Prep. | Average College Prep. | Non-College Track |
|---|:---:|:---:|:---:|
| 16-1    Mixtures | ✔ | ✔ | ✔ |
| 16-2    Solutions | ✔ | ✔ | ✔ |
| 16-3    Types of Solutions | ✔ | ✔ | ✔ |
| 16-4    Antifreeze | ✔ | ✔ | ✔ |
| 16-5    Degree of Solubility | ✔ | ✔ | ✔ |
| 16-6    Factors Affecting the Rate of Solution | ✔ | ✔ | ✔ |
| 16-7    Solubility and the Nature of A Solvent and a Solute | ✔ | ✔ | ✔ |
| 16-8    Energy Changes During Solution Formation | ✔ | ✔ | ✔ |
| 16-9    Solubility Curves and Solubility Tables | ✔ | ✔ | ✔ |
| 16-10    Saturated, Unsaturated, and Supersaturated Solutions | ✔ | ✔ | ✔ |
| 16-11    Dilute and Concentrated Solutions | ✔ | ✔ | ✔ |
| 16-12    Expressing Concentration—Molarity | ✔ | ✔ | ✔ |
| 16-13    Expressing Concentration—Molality | ✔ | ✔ | |
| ■ 16-14    Freezing Point Depression | ✔ | | |
| ■ 16-15    Boiling Point Elevation | ✔ | | |

■ Advanced Topic

# Categorization of Text Sections (continued)

| | Above Average College Prep. | Average College Prep. | Non-College Track |
|---|:---:|:---:|:---:|
| **Chemical Kinetics and Thermodynamics** | | | |
| 17-1 Two Major Topics in Chemistry | ✔ | ✔ | ✔ |
| 17-2 Rate of Reaction and the Collision Theory | ✔ | ✔ | ✔ |
| 17-3 Reaction Mechanisms | ✔ | ✔ | |
| 17-4 The Nature of the Reactants and Reaction Rate | ✔ | ✔ | |
| 17-5 Temperature and Reaction Rate | ✔ | ✔ | |
| 17-6 Concentration of Reactants and Reaction Rate | ✔ | ✔ | |
| 17-7 Pressure and Reaction Rate | ✔ | ✔ | |
| 17-8 Catalysts and Reaction Rate | ✔ | ✔ | ✔ |
| 17-9 Activation Energy and the Activated Complex | ✔ | | |
| ■ 17-10 Reaction Mechanisms and Rates of Reaction | ✔ | | |
| 17-11 Potential Energy Diagrams | ✔ | ✔ | |
| ■ 17-12 Activation Energy: Temperature and Concentration | ✔ | | |
| ■ 17-13 Activation Energy and Catalysts | ✔ | | |
| 17-14 Heat Content, or Enthalpy | ✔ | ✔ | |
| 17-15 Heat of Formation | ✔ | ✔ | |
| 17-16 Stability of Compounds | ✔ | ✔ | |
| 17-17 Hess's Law of Constant Heat Summation | ✔ | | |
| ■ 17-18 The Direction of Chemical Change | ✔ | | |
| ■ 17-19 Entropy | ✔ | | |
| ■ 17-20 The Effect of Changes in Entropy on the Direction of Spontaneous Change | ✔ | | |
| ■ 17-21 The Gibbs Free Energy Equation | ✔ | | |
| ■ 17-22 Application of the Gibbs Equation to a Physical Change | ✔ | | |
| ■ 17-23 Free Energy of Formation | ✔ | | |
| **Chemical Equilibrium** | | | |
| 18-1 Reversible Reactions | ✔ | ✔ | ✔ |
| 18-2 Characteristics of an Equilibrium | ✔ | ✔ | ✔ |
| 18-3 The Mass-Action Expression | ✔ | ✔ | |
| 18-4 The Equilibrium Constant | ✔ | ✔ | |
| ■ 18-5 Applications of $K_{eq}$ | ✔ | | |

# Categorization of Text Sections (continued)

| | | Above Average College Prep. | Average College Prep. | Non-College Track |
|---|---|:---:|:---:|:---:|
| 18-6 | Effects of Stresses on Systems at Equilibrium: Le Chatelier's Principle | ✔ | ✔ | |
| 18-7 | The Role of the Equilibrium Constant | ✔ | ✔ | |
| 18-8 | Le Chatelier's Principle: Changing Temperature or Pressure, Adding a Catalyst | ✔ | ✔ | |
| ■ 18-9 | Solubility Equilibrium | ✔ | | |
| ■ 18-10 | The Common-Ion Effect | ✔ | ✔ | |

## Acids, Bases, and Salts

| | | Above Average College Prep. | Average College Prep. | Non-College Track |
|---|---|:---:|:---:|:---:|
| 19-1 | The Theory of Ionization | ✔ | ✔ | ✔ |
| 19-2 | The Dissociation of Ionic Electrolytes | ✔ | ✔ | ✔ |
| 19-3 | Ionization of Covalently Bonded Electrolytes | ✔ | ✔ | ✔ |
| 19-4 | Acids (Arrhenius's Definition) | ✔ | ✔ | ✔ |
| 19-5 | Ionization Constants for Acids | ✔ | ✔ | |
| 19-6 | Properties of Acids | ✔ | ✔ | ✔ |
| 19-7 | Arrhenius Bases and Their Properties | ✔ | ✔ | ✔ |
| 19-8 | Salts | ✔ | ✔ | ✔ |
| 19-9 | Brønsted-Lowry Acids and Bases | ✔ | ✔ | |
| 19-10 | Conjugate Acid-Base Pairs | ✔ | ✔ | |
| 19-11 | Comparing Strengths of Acids and Bases | ✔ | ✔ | |
| 19-12 | Amphoteric Substances | ✔ | ✔ | |

## Acid-Base Reactions

| | | Above Average College Prep. | Average College Prep. | Non-College Track |
|---|---|:---:|:---:|:---:|
| 20-1 | The Self-ionization of Water | ✔ | ✔ | |
| 20-2 | The pH of a Solution | ✔ | ✔ | ✔ |
| ■ 20-3 | Calculating pH Values | ✔ | ✔ | |
| ■ 20-4 | Buffer Solutions | ✔ | | |
| 20-5 | Acid-Base Indicators | ✔ | ✔ | ✔ |
| 20-6 | Acid-Base Neutralization | ✔ | ✔ | ✔ |
| 20-7 | Acid-Base Titration | ✔ | ✔ | ✔ |
| 20-8 | Hydrolysis of Salts | ✔ | ✔ | |
| 20-9 | Choice of Indicators | ✔ | ✔ | |
| ■ 20-10 | Gram Equivalent Masses | ✔ | | |
| ■ 20-11 | Normality | ✔ | | |

■ Advanced Topic

# Categorization of Text Sections (continued)

| | Above Average College Prep. | Average College Prep. | Non-College Track |
|---|---|---|---|
| **Oxidation and Reduction** | | | |
| 21-1   The Use of the Terms Oxidation and Reduction | ✔ | ✔ | ✔ |
| 21-2   Oxidation Numbers | ✔ | ✔ | ✔ |
| 21-3   Identifying Oxidation-Reduction Reactions | ✔ | ✔ | ✔ |
| ■ 21-4   Balancing Redox Equations with Oxidation Numbers | ✔ | ✔ | |
| ■ 21-5   Balancing Redox Equations—The Half-reaction Method | ✔ | | |
| **Electrochemistry** | | | |
| 22-1   Two Branches of Electrochemistry | ✔ | ✔ | ✔ |
| 22-2   Half-reactions and Half-reaction Equations | ✔ | ✔ | ✔ |
| 22-3   The Electric Current | ✔ | ✔ | ✔ |
| 22-4   Current Through an Electrolyte—Electrolysis | ✔ | ✔ | ✔ |
| 22-5   Electrolysis of Molten Sodium Chloride | ✔ | ✔ | |
| 22-6   Electrolysis of Water | ✔ | ✔ | ✔ |
| 22-7   Electrolysis of Concentrated Sodium Chloride Solution (Brine) | ✔ | ✔ | |
| 22-8   Electroplating | ✔ | ✔ | ✔ |
| 22-9   The Electrochemical Cell | ✔ | ✔ | ✔ |
| 22-10   The Porous Cup and Salt Bridge | ✔ | ✔ | ✔ |
| 22-11   The Voltage of an Electrochemical Cell | ✔ | ✔ | |
| 22-12   The Standard Hydrogen Half-cell | ✔ | ✔ | |
| 22-13   Standard Electrode Potentials | ✔ | ✔ | |
| 22-14   Voltages of Galvanic Cells Not Containing the Standard Hydrogen Half-cell | ✔ | ✔ | |
| 22-15   The Chemical Activities of Metals | ✔ | ✔ | |
| 22-16   Some Practical Applications of Electrochemical Cells | ✔ | ✔ | ✔ |
| 22-17   The Corrosion of Metals—An Electrochemical Process | ✔ | ✔ | ✔ |
| **The Chemistry of Selected Elements** | | | |
| 23-1   Descriptive Chemistry | ✔ | ✔ | ✔ |
| 23-2   The Alkali Metals | ✔ | ✔ | ✔ |
| 23-3   The Alkaline Earth Metals | ✔ | ✔ | ✔ |

# Categorization of Text Sections (continued)

| | Above Average College Prep. | Average College Prep. | Non-College Track |
|---|:---:|:---:|:---:|
| 23-4  The Transition Metals | ✔ | ✔ | ✔ |
| 23-5  Aluminum | ✔ | ✔ | ✔ |
| ■ 23-6  Iron and Steel | ✔ | ✔ | |
| ■ 23-7  The Recovery of Copper | ✔ | ✔ | |
| 23-8  Oxygen | ✔ | ✔ | ✔ |
| 23-9  Hydrogen | ✔ | ✔ | ✔ |
| 23-10  Sulfur | ✔ | ✔ | ✔ |
| 23-11  Nitrogen | ✔ | ✔ | ✔ |
| 23-12  The Halogens | ✔ | ✔ | ✔ |
| 23-13  The Noble Gases | ✔ | ✔ | ✔ |

## Organic Chemistry

| | Above Average College Prep. | Average College Prep. | Non-College Track |
|---|:---:|:---:|:---:|
| 24-1  The Nature of Organic Compounds | ✔ | ✔ | ✔ |
| 24-2  General Properties of Organic Compounds | ✔ | ✔ | ✔ |
| 24-3  Bonding in Organic Compounds | ✔ | ✔ | |
| 24-4  Structural Formulas and Isomers | ✔ | ✔ | ✔ |
| 24-5  Hydrocarbons | ✔ | ✔ | ✔ |
| 24-6  Saturated Hydrocarbons—The Alkanes | ✔ | ✔ | ✔ |
| 24-7  IUPAC Naming System | ✔ | ✔ | ✔ |
| 24-8  Unsaturated Hydrocarbons—Alkenes, Alkynes, and Alkadienes | ✔ | ✔ | ✔ |
| ■ 24-9  Aromatic Hydrocarbons—The Benzene Series | ✔ | ✔ | |
| ■ 24-10  Reactions of the Hydrocarbons | ✔ | | |
| ■ 24-11  Petroleum | ✔ | | |
| 24-12  Alcohols | ✔ | ✔ | ✔ |
| 24-13  Aldehydes | ✔ | ✔ | ✔ |
| 24-14  Ketones | ✔ | ✔ | ✔ |
| ■ 24-15  Ethers | ✔ | ✔ | |
| 24-16  Carboxylic Acids | ✔ | ✔ | ✔ |

■ Advanced Topic

# Categorization of Text Sections (continued)

| | | Above Average College Prep. | Average College Prep. | Non-College Track |
|---|---|:---:|:---:|:---:|
| ■ 24-17 | Esters and Esterification | ✔ | ✔ | |
| 24-18 | Soaps and Detergents | ✔ | ✔ | ✔ |

## Biochemistry

| | | | | |
|---|---|:---:|:---:|:---:|
| 25-1 | The Compounds of Life | ✔ | ✔ | ✔ |
| 25-2 | Carbohydrates | ✔ | ✔ | ✔ |
| 25-3 | Lipids | ✔ | ✔ | ✔ |
| 25-4 | Proteins | ✔ | ✔ | ✔ |
| 25-5 | Biochemical Reactions and Enzymes | ✔ | ✔ | |
| ■ 25-6 | Nucleic Acids | ✔ | | |
| ■ 25-7 | The Role of Energy in Biochemistry | ✔ | | |

## Nuclear Chemistry

| | | | | |
|---|---|:---:|:---:|:---:|
| 26-1 | Changes in the Nucleus | ✔ | ✔ | ✔ |
| 26-2 | Types of Radiation | ✔ | ✔ | ✔ |
| 26-3 | Half-Life | ✔ | ✔ | ✔ |
| 26-4 | Natural Radioactivity | ✔ | ✔ | ✔ |
| 26-5 | The Uranium-238 Decay Series | ✔ | ✔ | |
| 26-6 | Artificial Radioactivity (Induced Radioactivity) | ✔ | ✔ | |
| 26-7 | Biological Effects of Radiation | ✔ | ✔ | ✔ |
| 26-8 | Beneficial Uses of Radioisotopes | ✔ | ✔ | ✔ |
| ■ 26-9 | Radioactive Dating | ✔ | | |
| ■ 26-10 | Particle Accelerators | ✔ | | |
| 26-11 | Nuclear Energy: The Mass-Energy Relationship | ✔ | ✔ | |
| 26-12 | Nuclear Fission | ✔ | ✔ | ✔ |
| 26-13 | Fission Reactors | ✔ | ✔ | |
| 26-14 | Fusion Reactions | ✔ | ✔ | ✔ |

# How to Use
# the Program Components

The components of the Prentice Hall chemistry program are:

Student text: *Prentice Hall Chemistry: The Study of Matter*
Teacher's edition: *Prentice Hall Chemistry: The Study of Matter, TE*
Lab manual: *Laboratory Manual, Prentice Hall Chemistry: The Study of Matter*
Teacher's edition: *Laboratory Manual, Prentice Hall Chemistry: The Study of Matter, TE*
Resource book: *Teacher's Resource Book*
Computer software: *Boyle's and Charles' Law*
*Gas Laws and the Mole*
*Periodic Table*
*Chemical Bonding*
*Dynamic Equilibrium*
Computer Test Bank
Critical Thinking Skills Transparencies

## Using the Program with Students of Different Abilities

In some schools, college preparatory science students are grouped homogeneously. In other schools (especially in smaller schools), students representing the complete spectrum of ability levels may be enrolled in the very same class. Whereas some of the slower students never make it to college, some of the faster ones are capable of college-level work while still in high school. As we prepared this chemistry program, we (the authors and editors) put considerable effort into designing the program so that it could be effectively used with students having a wide range of abilities.

## Student Text

The student text is the centerpiece of the Prentice Hall chemistry program. It presents all of the essential facts and concepts that constitute a comprehensive high school chemistry course. It is designed to help students learn the subject matter and to apply it to new situations through analysis, synthesis, and evaluation.

**Core, advanced, and optional sections.** The text contains a number of elements that can be adapted to different teaching and learning styles. Each chapter is broken into a number of sections, each of which falls into one of three categories: core, advanced, and optional. The advanced sections will challenge your fastest students. All of the core sections are within the grasp of your average students, although you will want to exercise some choice concerning which core topics to teach because time limitations will prevent you from teaching them all. Some teachers might elect to teach all of the chapter on nuclear chemistry but only part of the chapter on kinetics and thermodynamics. Other teachers will have a different emphasis. All teachers, however, will want their students to understand thoroughly the chapters in the first half of the book because many of the later chapters cannot be understood without this foundation.

Not all of the core sections are equally important for a fundamental knowledge of introductory chemistry. Therefore, not all of them need be taught to below average students. See the section of this Teacher's Guide titled "Courses of Instruction for Different Ability Levels" for guidance concerning which core sections can be used with below average students. We suggest that, with a class of slower students, you teach fewer of the core sections but spend more time on each section you assign.

**Interspersed and chapter-end questions.** The interspersed questions (the questions that appear typically after every two or three sections of the chapter) and the chapter-end questions are an important tool for teaching the chapter content. The interspersed questions should be answered by all students after they finish reading the sections to which the questions pertain. The chapter-end questions should be assigned selectively. With the exception of the Cumulative Review questions, these questions are grouped according to their degree of difficulty. Accompanying Figure 1 gives the headings for each group of chapter-end questions and the ability level for which each group of questions is suited.

**Figure 1**
*Suitability of chapter-end categories of questions for students of varying abilities.*

| Suitability of Chapter-end Question Categories | | | |
|---|---|---|---|
| **End-of-chapter question heading** | **Ability level** | | |
| | **Below average** | **Average** | **Above average** |
| Content Review | suitable | suitable | suitable |
| Content Mastery | suitable | suitable | |
| Concept Mastery | some questions | suitable | |
| Cumulative Review | some questions | suitable | |
| Critical Thinking | some questions | some questions | |
| Challenge Problems | | some questions | |

In addition to core sections and advanced topics, the text contains the following special features (optional sections):

Applications in Chemistry
Breakthroughs in Chemistry
Biographies
Careers
Can You Explain This?

For a description of each feature, consult the section of this Teacher's Guide titled "Design of the Text." You can either give these features as part of a reading assignment or make them optional. Either way, most students will read them because of the features' high level of interest and their brevity.

**End of text.** The text ends with a glossary, table of contents, and some appendices. One appendix gives some problems with non-SI units commonly found in the chemical literature. Another appendix gives the answers to selected interspersed questions. The remaining appendices are reference tables.

## Teacher's Edition of the Text

The Teacher's Edition of the text contains all the material in the pupil's edition along with additional information of special interest to the teacher. This information appears in two places: in the margins of the text itself as teacher's annotations, and in the Teacher's Guide, which is the section of the Teacher's Edition at the front of the book.

**Teacher's Guide.** The Teacher's Guide provides two types of information: general program information and specific information pertaining to each chapter. The general program information appears in several sections in the Teacher's Guide. The specific information pertaining to each chapter appears in the chapter-by-chapter section—the last section of the Guide.

We suggest that you look at the table of contents for the Teacher's Guide at this time to review its contents. By perusing the table of contents and by skimming the pages in the Guide, you will get a good understanding of the Guide's organization and general contents.

**Chapter-by-chapter section of the Teacher's Guide.** The chapter-by-chapter section of this Teacher's Guide is by far the largest section. There is one subsection for each chapter in the book. Each chapter-by-chapter subsection is in turn divided into the following parts:

- *Planning Guide:* a table that lists all the lab experiments, demonstrations, and materials in the *Teacher's Resource Book* that relate to the chapter.

- *Chapter Overview:* a brief description of the content of the chapter.

- *Teaching Suggestions:* a description of effective ways to teach the chapter. In addition, this section contains a description of some ways in which the chemistry of the chapter is applied in the everyday world, a discussion of important concepts presented in the chapter, and a discussion of a critical thinking skill that has special relevance for the chapter.

- *Demonstrations:* a listing of typically three or four demonstrations that help to motivate students and to focus their attention on important concepts.

- *Answers to Questions:* complete answers to all the questions and problems in the text.

**Teacher's marginal annotations.** For many of the questions and problems in the text (both those interspersed within the chapter and those in the chapter end), a *short* answer appears in the margin of the text or below the question or problem. *Complete* answers are given in the chapter-by-chapter section of the Teacher's Guide. Whereas a marginal annotation adjacent to a problem may simply give the final result of a calculation, the complete answer in the Teacher's Guide shows how that result was arrived at. The complete answers also include the answers to essay questions that require more space than is available in a margin.

## Lab Manual

Chemistry is a laboratory science, and the Prentice Hall chemistry program includes both a student lab manual and an annotated teacher's edition of the lab manual. The lab manual complements the topics covered in the text. By doing laboratory work, students become actively involved in the process of investigation and develop an appreciation for the scientific method of inquiry. The laboratory activities give students many opportunities to exercise a variety of skills, including firsthand observation and other higher-level thinking skills.

The student lab manual begins with a safety section and a descriptive section to help students become familiar with the techniques and equipment they will use in the laboratory. The lab manual also contains one or more labs for each chapter in the text. Each lab contains a text reference that indicates the text material with which the lab correlates. By providing more labs than any class has time to do in one school year, the program allows you to select the labs that are most appropriate for your class.

You can use labs to teach in two ways. If you assign a lab before the corresponding material is covered in class, students can "discover" important chemical concepts before they are introduced in the text. If you assign a lab after the corresponding material is covered in class, laboratory activities will reinforce or clarify concepts learned in class.

The annotated teacher's edition (TE) of the lab manual is an expanded version of the student lab manual. In the TE, all of the information, teaching suggestions, sample data and calculations, art, and answers to questions, are located on the corresponding student pages. Labs that require more than 40 minutes to complete contain a section with suggestions for modifying the lab procedure to permit students to complete the experiment within a 40-minute period. We strongly recommend that you, the teacher, test all

lab procedures before assigning them to your students in order to pinpoint any possible problem areas.

## Teacher's Resource Book

The *Teacher's Resource Book* (TRB) for *Prentice Hall Chemistry: The Study of Matter* was especially created for this edition of the text. It contains a wealth of material that will permit greater flexibility in the way you conduct the course. The TRB contains both support and background material for the teacher and blackline masters for student activities. The activities are of a varied nature so as to serve the needs of students having a wide range of abilities, including above- and below-average students. The materials will make your teaching more effective and your classroom a more exciting learning environment. The TRB is divided into 15 sections, and each section contains teacher's notes that contain specific suggestions for using the materials in each section. Each section also contains an answer key. The following are brief descriptions of each of the TRB sections.

**Laboratory Safety Information.** This section starts with an article for the teacher that discusses safe conduct in the laboratory and the proper storage and disposal of chemicals. Blackline masters containing instruction on lab safety and first aid are provided. The information contained therein prepares students to sign a Laboratory Safety Agreement and to take a Safety Quiz, both of which are also provided in blackline form.

**Stoichiometry Problems.** These blackline masters supply insights into important concepts in the mathematics of problem solving in chemistry. Each lesson describes clearly the underlying concepts upon which the practice problems are based. This emphasis on understanding the concepts helps eliminate the mindless memorization of the steps in sample problems to which students resort when their comprehension of concepts is poor. The clarity of the writing will enable students to understand the material with a minimum of assistance from the teacher.

**Concept Mastery.** These blackline masters are designed to help students understand the three levels on which chemists visualize matter: macroscopic, microscopic, and symbolic. Students must understand how matter reacts at each of these levels in order to truly understand the underlying concepts upon which chemical principles are based.

**Critical and Creative Thinking.** These blackline masters introduce students to critical and creative thinking skills as they are applied to appropriate examples in chemistry. Eighteen of these concentrate on a single thinking skill applied to a natural chemistry context. In addition, there is a special problem-solving worksheet in which a number of the skills are used together in an organized way so that students can see how the skills are integrated to solve a problem effectively. This problem-solving worksheet involves the kind of broad and multifaceted problem that is typical of applied chemistry.

**Skills Development.** These blackline masters provide instruction and practice in applying research, reading, thinking, and mathematics skills to the study of chemistry.

**Societal Issues.** These blackline masters contain essays that present several sides of a chemistry-related social issue. The critical-thinking questions that follow each essay focus attention on the importance to society of a citizenry capable of understanding the technical aspects of a problem.

**Chapter Tests and Alternate Chapter Tests.** These blackline masters provide two tests for each chapter. The content of the two tests is similar, but the A and B forms provide greater flexibility in the program. For example, if you teach two chemistry classes, you may wish to give one test to your first class and the other test to your second class.

**Chapter-by-chapter activities.** The TRB contains specific support materials and student activities for each of the text chapters. These include:

*Transparency Masters.* These masters for making overhead transparencies contain illustrations, graphs, and tables to enhance classroom lectures and discussions.

*Open-ended Laboratory Demonstrations.* These teacher demonstrations challenge students to answer the questions:

- What did you observe?
- How would you explain your observations?
- What would you do to test the validity of your explanation?

*Open-ended Laboratory Experiments.* These blackline masters contain experiments that are less structured than those found in traditional laboratory manuals for chemistry. Students are presented with a problem and are challenged to find a solution using a procedure that they have had a part in devising themselves. These experiments allow students to use critical- and creative-thinking skills, as well as problem-solving skills.

*Computer Laboratory Experiments.* These activities make use of a variety of some of the best available software for chemistry instruction.

*Review Activities.* These blackline-master worksheets help reteach technical vocabulary and concepts covered in the text chapters.

*Practice Problems.* These blackline masters provide additional practice in solving problems similar to the Practice Problems contained in the text chapters.

*Non-SI Supplementary Problems.* These blackline masters provide additional problem-solving practice using non-SI units.

**College-Board Review.** These blackline masters contain questions similar in format and content to those on the college-board test. They can be used to help interested students prepare for that test.

**Additional Resources.** This section includes a list of books, articles, audiovisual aids, and computer software for each of the chapters in the text. These references provide you with background information and teaching aids to help teach and review the chapter.

# Computer Software

Prentice-Hall Science Courseware for chemistry takes advantage of the unique capabilities of the computer while offering learning experiences that cannot be provided by more traditional text or lab materials. These programs allow students to manipulate variables, observe effects, interpret data, and solve problems as a scientist would. They also can provide interactive supportive tutorials as an option for those students who need more in-depth conceptual information.

Each software title includes a program Evaluation with automatic Reteach and a Record-Keeping System that can hold 100 students' scores. Each title also provides a complete Teacher's Guide that includes reproducible activities, discussion questions, and library investigations, along with suggestions on how to use the program.

# Computer Test Bank

The *Teacher's Resource Book* for *Prentice Hall Chemistry: The Study of Matter* contains chapter tests in blackline-master form. In addition to these tests, a computer test bank of more than 2300 chemistry questions has been prepared for the course. The questions, which are new questions not found among those on the blackline masters, are recorded on nine 5¼″ floppy disks. Accompanying the disks is a printed copy of all the questions.

**Using the Computer Test Bank.** To construct a test, you make a note of the questions in the printed copy of the test bank that you want to include in the test and you type the number of each of these questions into the computer. With a few keystrokes, the printer will then print out the desired number of copies of the test. Alternatively, you can print a single copy and reproduce the desired number of copies on a photocopying machine. The program also prints answer sheets and an answer key.

The test bank can be used not only for constructing chapter tests, it can just as easily create quizzes, unit tests, semester tests, and final exams.

With a few simple keystrokes, you can print a scrambled version of any test—that is, a test that contains exactly the same questions but that lists the questions in a different order.

Ample unused storage space has been reserved on each disk for adding questions of your own.

In the printed copy of the test bank, questions are grouped by chapter and correlated with chapter sections and chapter objectives. This correlation allows you to easily refer students to the appropriate text material for review of questions answered incorrectly.

**Types of questions.** The questions for each chapter fall into five categories, the first four of which are objective questions:

1. Vocabulary (matching questions)
2. Knowing Facts (multiple choice and true/false)
3. Understanding Concepts (multiple choice)
4. Solving Problems (multiple choice)
5. Essay (essay questions requiring one or two paragraphs of exposition)

**Hardware.** The disks may be run on an Apple IIe, Apple IIc, and Apple IIgs. Programs also can be run on IBMs. The questions can be printed on a variety of commonly used printers, including the Apple Imagewriter, Apple DMP, Epson, Okidata, Panasonic and IBM. Still other printers may be used after a simple "customizing" procedure.

## Critical Thinking Skills Transparencies

The *Critical Thinking Skills Transparencies* consist of 50 four-color acetates of selected figures in the student text. An accompanying manual provides teacher's notes on how to use each transparency to help you explain the concepts in the text and to help your students develop their critical thinking skills. The accompanying manual also contains a student worksheet for each transparency. These worksheets are provided in blackline master form so you can easily duplicate them for your students.

# Developing Skills in the Chemistry Classroom

Recent studies have revealed that many students do not possess the basic skills students must have if they are to be successful learners. *Prentice Hall Chemistry: The Study of Matter* and the ancillary materials to be used with it (the lab manual, *Teacher's Resource Book*, and computer software) provide students with a large variety of activities that teach thinking skills, study skills, reading skills, and laboratory skills.

## Thinking Skills

Higher-level thinking skills are essential to the development of scientific literacy, the stated goal of science education. For many students, chemistry might be their last science course before entering college. It is important for students to develop higher-level thinking skills *before* they reach college.

Taxonomies of cognitive processes define a variety of thinking skills. The categories used in this book, listed from the simplest to the most complex, are as follows:
1. *Recall of Fact:* recalling from memory specific information.
2. *Comprehension:* understanding operations and concepts.
3. *Critical Thinking:* rational processing of facts, opinions, and arguments.
4. *Creative Thinking:* envisioning original explanations, relationships, or solutions.
5. *Problem Solving:* using critical and creative thinking to resolve an issue identified as a problem.

Figure 2 summarizes the taxonomy of thinking skills applied throughout the *Prentice Hall Chemistry: The Study of Matter* program. The information in Figure 2 is elaborated on in Figure 4 (page TG-42), which describes the various kinds of thinking skills, provides examples of each, and identifies where each skill has been incorporated into the program.

## Thinking Skills: The Text

In the text, the questions at the end of each chapter and the feature titled "Can You Explain This?" give particular emphasis to thinking skills. Chapter-end questions and problems lead students through a cognitive hierarchy. The categories of questions that appear at the end of each chapter are listed under the following headings:

*Content Review* and *Content Mastery:* questions that test the recall and comprehension of important factual information.

*Concept Mastery:* questions that test the comprehension of concepts.

*Cumulative Review:* questions that pertain to prior chapters. They require recall of factual information and comprehension of concepts.

*Critical Thinking:* questions that challenge students to use their higher-level thinking skills, such as analyzing, classifying, inferring, and evaluating.

*Challenge Problems:* problems that require students to use higher-level thinking skills (including critical and creative thinking skills).

**Text feature.** "Can You Explain This?" is a feature that challenges students to explain observed phenomena by applying chemical principles they have learned in the course.

## Thinking Skills: Lab Manual and Teacher's Resource Book

Just as the text provides exercises that develop and apply a variety of thinking skills, the other major components of the program—the *Teacher's Resource Book* (TRB) and lab manual—contain instructional and assessment materials designed to develop a variety of thinking skills.

Figure 3 lists the thinking skills students must use to do each kind of activity in the *Teacher's Resource Book*.

Because the Prentice Hall chemistry program contains a large variety of materials, you will find it easy to involve your students in the study of chemistry at a level of difficulty that is appropriate for each class.

## Study Skills

The Educational Equity Project of the College Entrance Examination Board has declared, "Successful study skills are necessary for . . . achieving the desired outcomes in the basic academic subjects. Students are unlikely to be efficient in any part of their work without study skills." This observation has been reinforced by the National Commission on Excellence

**Figure 2**

*Thinking skills in science.* Figure 4 gives an elaboration of this schema.

I. Recall of Fact
II. Comprehension
III. Critical Thinking
    A. Collecting Evidence and Judging Reliability
        1. Firsthand Observations
        2. Secondhand Sources
    B. Analysis, Grouping, and Classification
        1. Analyzing Parts-Whole Relationships
        2. Comparing and Contrasting
        3. Ordering Information
        4. Classifying
        5. Identifying Reasons
        6. Identifying Assumptions
    C. Inference (Reasoning)
        1. Induction
            a. Generalization
            b. Causal Explanation
            c. Reasoning by Analogy
            d. Predicting Consequences
        2. Deduction
            a. Categorical Arguments
            b. Conditional Arguments
    D. Making Value Judgments
        1. Judgments of Usefulness
            a. Judging Things and Ideas
            b. Ranking Things and Ideas
        2. Ethical Judgments
    E. Making Decisions
IV. Creative Thinking
V. Problem Solving
    A. Well-defined Problems
    B. Ill-defined Problems

**Figure 3**

*Major thinking skills required for various components of the* Teacher's Resource Book

| TRB section | Type of activity | Major thinking skills required |
|---|---|---|
| Stoichiometry Problems | exposition with problems | problem solving |
| Societal Issues | essay with questions | critical thinking |
| Critical and Creative Thinking | essay with questions | critical and creative thinking |
| Concept Mastery | questions | comprehension |
| Tests | | all |
| Chapter-by-chapter | Review Activity worksheets | recall of fact and comprehension |
| | Practice Problems | problem solving |
| | Non-SI Practice Problems | problem solving |
| | Open-ended Demonstrations | critical thinking |
| | Open-ended Laboratories | critical and creative thinking |
| | computer laboratories | all |
| College Board Review | questions | all |

Table title: **Thinking Skills Required for *Teacher's Resource Book*** in Education report, *A Nation at Risk*. That report asserts that "effective study and work skills . . . are essential if school and independent time is to be used efficiently."

Study skills are those basic abilities that enable every student to learn effectively and efficiently in all content areas. Just as other mental and physical skills can be taught, so too can teachers instruct their students in the critical area of *how* to learn.

Students of all ability levels need programs that develop fundamental study skills. This program provides activities to teach and promote four classes of study skills.

1. *Work and study habits:* establishing an effective routine.
2. *Reference skills:* finding information and using a library.
3. *Organizational skills:* organizing, analyzing, and interrelating information.
4. *Specialized skills for attaining specific goals, such as better test scores, or accomplishing specific tasks associated with content areas.*

Many educators believe that instruction in study skills is most effective when combined with instruction in the content areas. The high school chemistry class, with its broad scope and laboratory work, makes special demands on the learner. The development of strong study skills will enable students to meet the challenge of this and future science courses.

Teachers can vary the amount of basic instruction in study habits according to the needs of particular classes or individuals. In the "Skills Development" section of the *Teacher's Resource Book*, there are essays and activities on a variety of study skills, including reading science materials, using science reference materials. writing library research papers, graphing, displaying experimental data, and distinguishing observation from interpretation.

# Reading Skills

Many educators believe that instruction in reading comprehension should be combined with instruction in content areas. To learn chemistry, students must be able to obtain information from written sources. Teaching reading skills in the chemistry classroom, especially as those skills pertain to the reading of science materials, will facilitate learning. Reading skills are developed in the "Study Skills" section of the *Teacher's Resource Book*.

# Laboratory Skills

Three major types of laboratory skills are addressed in the Prentice Hall chemistry program: safety skills, technical skills, and analytical skills. Safety and technical skills are practiced during laboratory investigations. Analytical laboratory skills are used in planning an investigation and interpreting its results. The development of these skills, along with their observational skills, will enable students to understand better how to solve scientific problems.

**Safety skills.** Safety information for the teacher is provided in this Teacher's Guide as well as in the Laboratory Safety Information section of the *Teacher's Resource Book*. Safety guidelines addressed to the student appear in the text, the lab manual, and the *Teacher's Resource Book*. At the beginning of the course, before beginning any laboratory work, students should read these guidelines, pass the Safety Quiz in the *Teacher's Resource Book*, and, to formalize their commitment to safe laboratory procedures, sign the safety agreement provided in the *Teacher's Resource Book*.

**Technical laboratory skills.** The section on laboratory equipment and skills at the front of the lab manual introduces the skills that students need to use while working in the chemistry laboratory. These skills include how to use a laboratory burner and a balance, how to handle chemical reagents, how to measure liquids in volumetric glassware, how to filter a mixture of substances in the solid and aqueous phases, and how to break, bend, and polish glass tubing.

**Analytical laboratory skills.** In the lab manual, the "Conclusions and Questions" section at the end of each lab encourages students to apply analytical skills to the laboratory situation. Some of the questions in that section emphasize those critical thinking skills essential to observing and assessing the results of a laboratory experiment.

In Chapter 1 of the textbook, the scientific method and the importance of controlling the variables in an experiment are discussed. The proper technique for graphing laboratory data is discussed in both Chapter 1 of the text and in the *Teacher's Resource Book* (Skills Development Section). Creative thinking skills, used to plan an experimental procedure, are encouraged by the open-ended laboratory experiments in the *Teacher's Resource Book*.

# Thinking Skills in Science

| Skill | Subskill | Description |
|---|---|---|
| **I. Recall of Fact** | | Remembering items of information learned or experienced. |
| **II. Comprehension** | | Understanding received ideas well enough to express them in one's own words.     Neither *analysis* (see III.B.) nor *inference* (see III.C.) is required. |
| **III. Critical Thinking** | | The use of rational thought to make a decision or form an opinion. (The skills and subskills are discussed below.) |
| | **A. Collecting Evidence and Judging Reliability** | Collecting evidence is obtaining information on a subject. Judging reliability is forming an opinion about its accuracy and objectivity. |
| | **1. Firsthand Observations** | Using one or more of the senses, either unaided or aided by instruments, to obtain information.     Reliability varies with the experience, attentiveness, etc., of the observer, as well as with the quality of the instruments used. |
| | **2. Secondhand Sources** | Any reports, such as those in newspapers and magazines, that are not firsthand observations. |
| | **B. Analysis, Grouping, and Classification** | Analysis is the breaking down or separating of a whole into its parts in order to examine them. Grouping and classification involve the assignment of the parts to various groups or classes according to some system. |

**Figure 4** *Thinking skills in science.*

| Example of use | Development, application in the program |
|---|---|
| Q. What is the chemical formula of water?<br>A. The chemical formula of water is $H_2O$. | ■ Chapter-End Questions: Content Review, Content Mastery, and Cumulative Review<br>■ *Teacher's Resource Book:* Review Activities |
| Q. In any sample of the substance whose formula is $MgCl_2$, how many chloride ions will there be relative to the number of magnesium ions?<br>A. There will be twice as many chloride ions. | ■ Chapter-End Questions: Content Mastery, Concept Mastery, Cumulative Review<br>■ *Teacher's Resource Book:* Concept Mastery Section, Review Activities |
| (See below for examples of the use of each subskill.) | ■ Chapter-End Questions: Critical Thinking<br>■ Text Feature: Can You Explain This?<br>■ *Teacher's Resource Book:* Societal Issues, Critical and Creative Thinking, Open-Ended Laboratory Experiments, Open-Ended Demonstrations |
|  |  |
| Q. A technician reports the concentration of a toxic substance in synthetic building materials as 12 parts per million. Should this finding be accepted as accurate?<br>A. Yes, if the technician is skilled in measuring with the instrument used, is impartial, and the results can be corroborated by the measurements of others. | (Firsthand observation skills are developed and applied in the laboratory activities.) |
| Q. Conflicting reports on whether a company has contaminated drinking-water wells appear in the following publications: a neighborhood newspaper, a city newspaper, the company's magazine, and a government agency's report. Which report would you take as being the most reliable? Why?<br>A. Probably the report, depending on the expertise and lack of bias of its authors and the thoroughness of the study. The company's magazine might be the least credible, depending on similar factors. |  |

# Thinking Skills in Science (continued)

| Skill | Subskill | Description |
|---|---|---|
| | 1. Analyzing Parts-Whole Relationships | Consideration of the parts in relation to the whole or in relation to one another. |
| | 2. Comparing and Contrasting | Comparing is examining things in order to identify similarities and differences. Contrasting is examining in order to emphasize differences.<br>    When the things compared are similar, patterns may be detected. |
| | 3. Ordering Information | Establishing a sequence according to size, weight, time, or some other characteristic. |
| | 4. Classifying | Arranging into groups according to some system or organizing principle. |
| | 5. Identifying Reasons | Identifying ideas people use to justify thoughts, actions, or statements.<br>    A *reason* is distinct from a *cause*, which is what makes something happen. |
| | 6. Identifying Assumptions | Recognizing ideas that are accepted as true without proof or examination. |
| | C. Inference (Reasoning) | Drawing a conclusion by the use of logic—induction or deduction. |
| | 1. Induction | Drawing a conclusion from empirical data.<br>    *Induction produces only probable—not certain—conclusions.* |
| | a. Generalization | Drawing a conclusion about *all* cases, based on information or experience of only some cases (called a *sample*). |

| Example of use | Development, application in the program |
|---|---|
| Q. Explain the relationship between atoms and molecules.<br>A. Atoms are the building blocks of molecules. | ■ Chapter-End Questions: Critical Thinking<br>■ Text Feature: Can You Explain This?<br>■ *Teacher's Resource Book:* Societal Issues, Critical and Creative Thinking, Open-Ended Laboratory Experiments, Open-Ended Demonstrations |
| Q. Compare and contrast a mixture and a compound.<br>A. Mixtures and compounds are similar in that they are both *combinations*. They are different in that when two or more elements combine physically, they form a mixture; when they combine chemically, they form a compound. | |
| Q. Order any three elements by atomic mass. Explain.<br>A. Aluminum, silicon, and phosphorus (listed from the smallest atomic mass to the largest). | |
| Q. Classify the following as either compounds or mixtures: salt, orange juice, water, toothpaste.<br>A. Salt and water are compounds. Orange juice and toothpaste are mixtures. | |
| Q. Natural gas has no odor or color. Why does the gas company add a gas to it that has an odor?<br>A. So leaks can be detected. | |
| Q. Before Rutherford's time, people thought the atom was the smallest particle of matter. What assumptions were those people making?<br>A. Most people assumed that the atom was indivisible (one of the assumptions of Dalton's atomic theory). | |
| | |
| | |
| Q. Several nails left in a beaker of water rusted overnight. Will all other nails left in water rust overnight?<br>A. Yes, if the nails are made of the same material and there is dissolved oxygen in the water. | |

# Thinking Skills in Science (continued)

| Skill | Subskill | Description |
|---|---|---|
| | **b. Causal Explanation** | Drawing a conclusion about a probable cause (that is, about why something happened), based on evidence. |
| | **c. Reasoning by Analogy** | Extending a conclusion about one class to another class judged to be similar. |
| | **d. Predicting Conse-quences** | Drawing a conclusion, based on evidence, about the probable effects of a given cause whose effects have not yet occurred. |
| | **2. Deduction** | Drawing a conclusion that *necessarily follows* from one or more statements (called *premises*). <br> *Through deduction you can achieve certainty if the premises are certain.* |
| | **a. Categorical Arguments** | Applying deductive methods to determine whether or not something belongs to a particular class or category. |
| | **b. Conditional Arguments** | Applying deductive methods to draw conclusions from *conditional*, or "if-then," statements and given information. |
| | **D. Making Value Judgments** | Assessing whether something is desirable or undesirable. |
| | **1. Judgments of Usefulness** | Assessing how well, or badly, some thing, action, idea, etc., serves a particular purpose or functions in a particular situation. |
| | **a. Judging Things and Ideas** | Applying judgments of usefulness to individual things and ideas. |
| | **b. Ranking Things and Ideas** | Comparing and ordering according to how well a particular function or purpose is served. |

| Example of use | Development, application in the program |
|---|---|
| Q. What caused the candle in the sealed jar to go out?<br>A. The candle probably went out because combustion requires oxygen, and the burning candle used up all the oxygen. | ■ Chapter-End Questions: Critical Thinking<br>■ Text Feature: Can You Explain This?<br>■ *Teacher's Resource Book:* Societal Issues, Critical and Creative Thinking, Open-Ended Laboratory Experiments, Open-Ended Demonstrations |
| Q. Sodium forms a chloride salt. Does cesium?<br>A. Yes, probably. Because cesium is in the same group of the periodic table, many of its properties are similar to those of sodium. | |
| Q. Will chlorine bleach remove this food stain from the cotton shirt?<br>A. Yes, probably, because chlorine bleach has in the past removed most food stains from cotton. | |
| | |
| Q. Is rubidium a chemically active element?<br>A. Rubidium is an alkali metal. All alkali metals are chemically active. Therefore, rubidium must be chemically active. | |
| Q. Will this rubber stopper sink in water?<br>A. If it is denser than water, the stopper will sink. It is more dense. Therefore, it will sink. | |
| | |
| Q. Is it useful to fluoridate a rural town's drinking water supply?<br>A. It depends on how effective fluoridation is in preventing tooth decay, whether there are any unwanted side effects, and the cost. | |
| Q. Rank the following containers in order of suitability for keeping a liquid hot: a beaker, a Styrofoam cup, a vacuum jug.<br>A. The jug is best suited (because of the vacuum), the cup is next best (because of air cells in Styrofoam). The beaker is least suited. | |

# Thinking Skills in Science (continued)

| Skill | Subskill | Description |
|---|---|---|
| | **2. Ethical Judgments** | Assessing how well something accords with ideals such as justice, respect for human life, and truth. |
| **IV. Creative Thinking** | | Generating Ideas, or combining ideas in new ways (*synthesis*)—characterized by originality and imagination.<br>　　Creative thinking is *divergent* (''to go in different directions'') thinking, rather than convergent, because it generates several possible ideas or hypotheses. It may involve the generation of many ideas of a single type (*fluency*) and/or of different types (*flexibility*). |
| **V. Problem Solving** | | Systematic thinking that involves gathering information and using reasoning (including critical and creative thinking skills). This thinking is directed towards reaching the goal of a well-supported conclusion or course of action that resolves an issue identified as a problem. When problem solving is used to choose a course of action, it is known as *decision making*. |
| | **A. Well-defined Problems** | Problems are more well-defined as more information on the goals, strategy, or pertinent facts are given to the solver. |
| | **B. Ill-defined Problems** | Problems are more ill-defined when little information is provided. The solver must determine the problem objectives, invent a strategy, and develop the needed information. |

| Example of use | Development, application in the program |
|---|---|
| Q. Should a chemist develop new compounds for chemical warfare?<br>A. (Answer depends on values such as political beliefs, concern for the environment, and regard for human, animal, and plant life.) | |
| Q. How can we solve the energy crisis?<br>A. (flexibility) 1. Do not waste any of the energy we already have. 2. Use all sources of energy available. 3. Develop new sources of energy. (fluency) 1. Conserve, ration, regulate, recycle. 2. Fossil fuels, wood, hydroelectric, nuclear, solar. 3. Tidal, biological, photosynthetic, electrochemical. | ■ Chapter-end Questions: Critical Thinking Challenge Problems<br>■ *Teacher's Resource Book:* Open-Ended Laboratory Experiments, Critical and Creative Thinking worksheets |
| | ■ Chapter-end Questions: All sections, especially Challenge Problems<br>■ *Teacher's Resource Book:* Stoichiometry Problems, Practice Problems |
| Q. Convert 60 degrees Celsius to degrees Fahrenheit.<br>A. Calculate the answer from the known formula:<br>$°F = \frac{9}{5}°C + 32$<br>$°F = \frac{9}{5}(60°C) + 32$<br>$°F = 140$ | |
| Q. Given a particular tomato, how could the percentage of water in the tomato be determined?<br>A. Objective: To determine the mass of the water. Possible strategy:<br>■ Measure and record the mass of the tomato.<br>■ Remove the water by squeezing and drying.<br>■ Measure and record the mass of the dried tomato.<br>■ Calculate the percentage of water from the recorded measurements. | |

# Using Computers in the Classroom

The "Additional Resources" section of the *Teacher's Resource Book* (TRB) contains a list of applicable computer software for each chapter in the text. Each list includes books, magazine articles, and audiovisual aids, as well as computer software. The "Additional Resources" section of the TRB also includes a list of sources for the referenced computer software.

If you wish to rent or purchase computer software, the following information might be helpful.

**Selection Criteria.** A large number and variety of computer software programs is available to teachers of high school chemistry. However, the quality of these programs varies widely. Program quality can be judged on the basis of the following characteristics:

*Content:* The content should be appropriate for the study of high school chemistry. Programs should be *accurate* and free of spelling errors and gender and race bias. Directions should be clear and easy to follow.

*Control:* For many software programs, it is desirable for the user to be able to control the pace and the sequence. Good programs often provide the user with helpful feedback.

*Graphics:* Program graphics should be used effectively. The screen should be clear, uncluttered, and easy to read.

*Approach:* The program should be interesting. It should provide the user with a learning experience not easily duplicated by other media, such as films, filmstrips, and overhead transparencies. Many of the better programs enable students to play an active role in the learning process by interacting with and responding to the program. Good programs offer a novel approach to the subject that heightens the interest of the student. Programs of this kind make computer-assisted learning a unique learning experience.

**Types of Programs.** Computer programs include tutorials, simulations, drill-and-practice (some of which are presented in a game format), lab interfaces, and what might be termed "classroom tools."

In *Periodic Table* (available from Prentice Hall, 4343 Equity Drive, P.O. Box 2649, Columbus, OH 43216), students gain an understanding of the chemical behavior, composition, and periodic properties of the elements. Interacting with the program, students review such terms as atomic mass, number, shell, and more. Then, by arranging a list of elements according to their atomic numbers, students actually create the periodic table.

The programs in the category "classroom tools" are not in and of themselves instructive, but the teacher can make them so. For example, *Molecular Animator*, (available from COMPress, P.O. Box 102, Wentworth, NH 03282) constructs a three-dimensional image of a molecule from information entered into the computer by the student or the teacher. The image can then be rotated, reduced, or enlarged so as to give the viewer a better understanding of the structure of the molecule.

Be aware that some programs fit into more than one category. A program that is primarily tutorial (a program teaching or reviewing content or concepts) also might include some drill-and-practice or involve simulation.

Programs that use simulations are recommended for use in demonstrations or lab exercises. Programs of this kind often make use of probeware. For example, *Experiments in Chemistry* (available from HRM Software, 175 Tompkins Avenue, Pleasantville, NY 10570) records and plots temperature, pH, and conductance data inputted through probes and an interfacing device, most of which come with the program (the pH probe must be obtained separately).

# Laboratory Safety Information

This section on laboratory safety and chemical storage and disposal is included as a resource for the teacher. Rather than providing definitive rules and regulations, the information is intended to be a basis for establishing good, safe laboratory practice. Prentice Hall makes no claim as to the completeness of this material. Not all precautions necessitated by the storage, use, and disposal of chemicals are covered here. Additional steps and safeguards might be required.

## Laboratory Safety

The safety and well-being of the participants in a science laboratory are the responsibility of all those involved in that lab, but especially the teacher. Teachers should promote a "safety first" philosophy to avoid health hazards and accidents while maintaining a stimulating learning environment. This can be accomplished both through personal example and the careful planning and implementation of safety strategies. Here are listed some recommendations that should be helpful in the pursuit of a safe laboratory.

1. Set up a laboratory safety committee made up of both teachers and administrators. Arrange to meet regularly to set safety policy for the school, discuss any safety problems that might arise, and organize periodic inspections of laboratories.
2. Develop detailed plans concerning what to do in case of emergency; review the procedures periodically throughout the school year.
3. Inform students of these emergency plans, and carry out unannounced drills.
4. Keep up-to-date in first aid and CPR (cardiopulmonary resuscitation) training.
5. Post emergency phone numbers (ambulance, fire, police, hospital, poison control center) next to the laboratory telephone.
6. Perform laboratory investigations before assigning them to the students. (However, we recommend that you not work in the laboratory alone.) Take note of any potential hazards; devise plans for dealing with any possible mishaps or emergencies.
7. Read the Material Safety Data Sheet (MSDS) furnished by chemical manufacturing companies for each chemical used, noting any possible hazards, as well as directions for proper handling. These sheets are now required by law to be provided with every chemical purchased. Upon request, companies will provide you with MSDSs for chemicals you bought before the law went into effect.

8. Emphasize safety considerations in pre-laboratory discussions. Posters dealing with safety issues might be hung in both the classroom and the laboratory as reminders.
9. The laboratory room should have two exits.
10. Make sure laboratory aisles and exits are kept clear from obstruction.
11. Insist on serious, proper conduct in the lab:
    - No horseplay
    - No smoking, eating, or drinking
    - No unauthorized experiments
    - No working alone.
    - Long hair, dangling jewelry, and loose clothing should be restrained, and the wearing of open shoes is prohibited.
12. Encourage students to keep the lab bench neat and clear of extraneous matter (e.g., books and jackets) in order to avoid accidents.
13. Make sure that exercises using toxic or flammable materials are performed in the fume hood.
14. Keep the hood clear of unnecessary chemicals and equipment.
15. Have your hood checked periodically to ensure that it is operating safely and efficiently.
16. Store chemicals in the storeroom rather than the lab itself.
17. Demonstrate the proper handling of glass materials, such as tubing, pipets, and cylinders.
18. Only wastepaper should be discarded in wastepaper receptacles; keep a separate container for broken glass.
19. Emphasize that suction bulbs are to be used with pipets—students are never to use their mouths to create suction.
20. Consider the use of dispensing devices for liquids: They help to prevent (a) spills, (b) skin contact with chemicals, and (c) waste.
21. Require the use of safety shields during experiments in which there is a chance of explosion or implosion.
22. Use hot plates in place of open flames whenever possible. Never use open flames when flammables are present in the room.
23. Do not leave running equipment unattended.

## Laboratory Safety Equipment

Important laboratory safety equipment includes fire extinguishers, a safety shower, fire blankets, spill kits, an eye wash, and a first-aid kit. Teachers and students should be familiar with the functioning of this equipment and aware of its location in the room. Special consideration should be given to handicapped students as regards the use of these devices.

1. Safety equipment should be easily accessible and kept up to date.
2. Smoke alarms and fire detectors are recommended, especially if there is no water sprinkler system.
3. Fire extinguishers (multipurpose, ABC) should be kept in good working order.
4. The eye wash should be plumbed in (not portable) and be able to provide a continuous stream of water at body temperature for 15 minutes. Proper use consists of holding the eyelids back and rolling the eyeballs to effect a thorough flushing of both eyes for at least 15 minutes.
5. Spill kits can be purchased from supply companies or be home-made (sand, cat litter); the latter, however, do not absorb gases as do professionally prepared kits.
6. Lab aprons or coats should be worn to cover and protect clothing.
7. Insist that all individuals entering the laboratory wear safety goggles; when these are not individually owned but school property, sanitizers may be purchased from supply companies to clean goggles after each use. (Goggles must be worn over contact lenses; contacts, particularly soft lenses, may provide an additional hazard in the event of a chemical splash into the eye.)

## Chemical Storage

Proper storage of chemicals is an essential part of an overall laboratory safety program. With a well-thought-out and implemented storage system, safety hazards and accidents can be avoided to a large extent. Following are recommendations for safe chemical storage for a high school chemistry program.

1. Rather than storing chemicals in the lab itself, a separate room designated solely for storage of chemicals is recommended; access to this room should be restricted.
2. There should be two means of exit from the storeroom; a window will suffice as one exit if the room is on a low enough floor of the building.
3. The storeroom should be well ventilated.
4. A circuit breaker for the storeroom should be easily accessible in case of emergency.
5. A telephone should be close by. Have emergency numbers (ambulance, fire, police, hospital, poison control center) posted next to the phone.
6. Safety equipment, such as first aid kit, spill kit, fire extinguisher (multipurpose, ABC), eye wash, and shower, should be readily available to the storeroom.
7. Use wood shelving, rather than metal, for chemical storage, and make sure that the shelves are stable, with no chance of collapse.
8. Shelving structures should be arranged so that there are no blind alleys; exiting should be easily accomplished.
9. Shelves should have a no-roll lip on their edges.
10. Do not overload shelves.
11. Avoid using the floor or shelves above eye level for storage.
12. Place large containers on lower shelves, in trays to catch leaks.
13. Fireproof cabinets are recommended for the storage of flammable and toxic materials. If cabinets are not available, these chemicals should be stored in safety cans.
14. Use only explosion-proof refrigerators for chemical storage.
15. Coated bottles are available from chemical supply houses and are useful in preventing accidents.
16. Many chemical companies provide detailed information on the hazards, storage, and safety of their chemicals on the reagent labels. Examine these labels carefully for pertinent information. More information may be obtained from the MSDSs (Material Safety Data Sheets) provided with the chemicals.
17. Arrange chemicals on shelves in compatible chemical families; alphabetical arrangement is not recommended. See the table on page TG-53 for some examples of incompatible chemicals. Several chemical supply companies have devised systems of compatible chemical families, complete with color-coded reagent labels that make it easy to arrange chemicals on the shelves in compatible groups.
18. In general, store oxidizing agents away from organic chemicals.
19. Keep only the minimum amount of chemicals necessary on hand; remember this goal while making orders.
20. Write the date received, and expected shelf life on incoming chemicals.
21. Perform an inventory of the storeroom periodically and dispose of any chemicals that are old or unlikely to be used.

## Chemical Disposal

The disposal of wastes comes under a variety of federal and state regulations. The Resource Conservation and Recovery Act of 1976 (RCRA), as administered by the U.S. Environmental Protection Agency

# Table of Incompatible Chemicals

The selected chemicals on the left should be stored as far away as possible from those on the right.

| | |
|---|---|
| acetic acid | chromic acid, ethylene glycol, hydroxyl compounds, nitric acid, perchloric acid, permanganates, peroxides |
| acetone | concentrated nitric and sulfuric acid solutions |
| alkali and alkaline earth metals (Ca, Li, Na, K, and powdered Al and Mg) | carbon dioxide, carbon tetrachloride (and other chlorinated hydrocarbons), halogens, water |
| ammonia | calcium hypochlorite, halogens, hydrofluoric acid, mercury |
| carbon (activated) | calcium hypochlorite, oxidizing agents |
| carbon tetrachloride | sodium |
| copper | acetylene, hydrogen peroxide |
| flammable liquids | ammonium nitrate, chromic acid, halogens, hydrogen peroxide, nitric acid, sodium peroxide |
| hydrogen peroxide | acetone, alcohols, aniline, chromium, combustible materials, copper, iron, organic materials, most metals or their salts |
| iodine | acetylene, ammonia, hydrogen |
| nitrates | sulfuric acid |
| nitric acid | acetic acid, chromic acid, copper, flammable liquids or gases, heavy metals, hydrocyanic acid, hydrogen sulfide |
| nitrites | acids |
| oxygen | flammable liquids/solids/gases, grease, hydrogen, oils |
| phosphorus (white) | air, alkalis, oxygen, reducing agents |
| silver | acetylene, ammonium compounds, oxalic acid, tartaric acid |
| sulfides | acids |
| sulfuric acid | chlorates, perchlorates, and permanganates of light metals |

(EPA), addresses the disposal of hazardous solid wastes. Some individual states have made regulations for waste disposal even more stringent than those required by this act, however. Be sure to check with your local environmental agencies to obtain more complete and current information on this issue.

At this time, according to RCRA, a hazardous waste is defined to be an ignitable, corrosive, reactive, toxic, and/or acutely hazardous substance (gas, liquid, or solid) of no value, i.e., of no further use.

When a substance cannot conceivably be reused or recycled but must be disposed of, several options are open to institutions. Disposal contractors can be hired to pack up, label, and deliver hazardous and other wastes to EPA-sanctioned disposal sites, and then certify that these measures have been taken. This is generally a very expensive option. In some cases, the institution itself may pack the wastes in Department-of-Transportation-approved steel drums, containing absorbent material, which then can be hauled away by a contractor. Another alternative is for individuals to attempt to dispose of substances themselves using chemical procedures published by certain supply houses. This last method is *not* recommended by the American Chemical Society. Although some reactions might transform a hazardous material into a less hazardous or non-hazardous one, some are potentially dangerous. In addition, the procedures often do not comply sufficiently with RCRA directives.

A useful resource for the teacher concerning chemical disposal is *Prudent Practices for Disposal of Chemicals from Laboratories*, published by the National Academy of Sciences (1983).

Following are recommendations for chemical disposal for the high school chemistry laboratory.

1. Before each lab, instruct your students concerning where and how they are to dispose of chemicals that are used or produced during the lab.

2. Keep each excess or used chemical in a separate container; do not mix them. Keeping excess chemicals separate allows for their potential recycling or reuse and also obviates the need for expensive separation by a contractor (often required by RCRA) if the wastes must be disposed of professionally.

3. Use minimal amounts of reagents in experiments in order to limit the quantity of waste chemicals.

4. Keep drainage lines for laboratory sinks separate from sanitary lines.

5. Only nonflammable, neutral, nontoxic, and water-soluble chemicals should be flushed down the drain.

6. Provide special disposal containers for water-insoluble liquids that are denser than water, since they can clog the drain. If the liquids are volatile, the container should be kept in the hood. The liquids may be disposed of by evaporating them in the hood. (Caution: Do not allow volatile liquids to sit in an uncovered container in the hood while the hood motor is off, even if the hood door is closed.)

7. Consult reagent MSDSs (Material Safety Data Sheets) for handling and disposal instructions.

8. Contact other local high schools, colleges, and universities to find out how they deal with their waste disposal. Perhaps your school could join others in sharing the cost of hiring a disposal contractor.

9. Keep a permanent record of waste material that is removed from your institution, including the identity of the chemicals, their amount, the date they were labeled "waste," the date of disposal, the disposal contractor, and the disposal site. You are liable for these materials even after they have been removed from your school. For this reason, it is necessary to hire only a reputable contractor who will dump your wastes at an EPA-approved site.

# Selected Bibliography

Bretherick, L. *Hazards in the Chemical Laboratory*, 4th ed. Royal Society of Chemistry, 1986.

Committee on Chemical Safety. *Safety in Academic Chemistry Laboratories*, 4th ed. American Chemical Society, 1985.

Committee on Hazardous Substances in the Laboratory, Assembly of Mathematical and Physical Sciences, National Research Council. *Prudent Practices for Handling Chemicals in Laboratories*. National Academy Press, 1981.

Committee on Hazardous Substances in the Laboratory, Commission on Physical Sciences, Mathematics, and Resources, National Research Council. *Prudent Practices for Disposal of Chemicals from Laboratories*. National Academy Press, 1983.

Flinn Scientific, Inc. *Chemical Catalog/Reference Manual* (current edition).

Gerlovich, J., ed. *School Science Safety: Secondary*. Flinn Scientific. 1985.

Lefévre, M. J. *First Aid Manual for Chemical Accidents*. Dowden, Hutchinson & Ross, 1980.

National Fire Protection Association. *Fire Protection for Laboratories Using Chemicals*. 1986.

National Fire Protection Association. *Manual of Hazardous Chemical Reactions*, 1986.

National Fire Protection Association. *Fire Protection Guide on Hazardous Materials* (current edition).

National Institute for Occupational Safety and Health. *Safety in the School Science Laboratory*. 1980.

National Institute for Occupational Safety and Health. *Manual of Safety and Health Hazards in the School Science Laboratory*. U.S. Dept. of Health and Human Services. 1980.

Patnoe, R. L. "Chemistry Laboratory Safety Check." *Science Teacher*, October 1976.

Pipitone, D. A., ed. *Safe Storage of Laboratory Chemicals*. Wiley-Interscience, 1984.

Pipitone, D.A., and D. D. Hedberg. "Safe Chemical Storage: A Pound of Prevention Is Worth a Ton of Trouble." *Journal of Chemical Education*, 1982, Vol. 59.

"Safety in the Chemical Laboratory," Vols. 1-4 of *Journal of Chemical Education*, American Chemical Society, Division of Chemical Education, 1964-1980.

Young, J. A. "Safety Tips. Academic Laboratory Waste Disposal: Yes, You Can Get Rid of That Stuff Legally." *Journal of Chemical Education*, June 1983.

For information about RCRA and the Superfund, call toll-free 1-800-424-9346; for information about the Toxic Substances Control Act, call toll-free 1-800-424-9065.

# How to Address İndividual Needs in the Chemistry Classroom

Meeting the needs of individual students is an important aspect of effective teaching. To meet these needs, teachers must be able to provide a variety of learning activities and materials at varying levels of difficulty. The Prentice Hall chemistry program provides this kind of flexibility. The text and its ancillaries contain a variety of instructional, motivational, and evaluative activities.

## Using the Program Components

**The text.** Each chapter of the text is comprised of three kinds of sections: core, advanced, and optional. The content of the core sections is within the grasp of all average and above average students in the academic chemistry track. The advanced sections, which can be omitted without loss of continuity, have been designed for students with above average ability. Many of the core sections can be understood by below average students if the students are allowed to proceed at a pace that is appropriate for their levels of ability. The optional sections, assigned at the discretion of the teacher, are described in the article in this Teacher's Guide titled "Design of the Text." These optional sections can be used to motivate and enrich students who easily master facts and concepts. The section of this Teacher's Guide titled "Courses of Instruction for Different Ability Levels" gives guidance concerning which sections are appropriate for various levels of students.

Many of the core sections in the first 15 chapters of the book must be well understood by all of your students in order for them to understand the content in the remaining 11 chapters. In assigning material in the last 11 chapters, you will want to decide which chapters and sections to assign because the book contains more material than can be mastered in 1 year even by most classes of above average students. This will allow you some flexibility in assigning work according to your personal preferences and the composition of your classes.

The questions that appear at the ends of each chapter have been categorized according to their level of difficulty in order to aid in the individualization of instruction and evaluation. Those under the headings "Content Review" and "Content Mastery" emphasize the recall and comprehension of basic factual information. The "Concept Mastery" questions test the comprehension of important chemical concepts. The questions under "Critical Thinking" and "Challenge Problems" exercise higher level thinking skills.

**Lab manual.** The lab manual, which contains 52 experiments, also has been designed to facilitate individualization of instruction. At least one lab is provided for each text chapter, and more than one lab is provided for most chapters. Each lab is correlated to a specific text section or sections. This allows you to choose labs that emphasize the principles that are most important for your students. With above average students, you might wish to assign labs before the corresponding material is covered in class. This allows students to develop their critical thinking and problem solving skills as they "discover" important chemical concepts. With average and below-average students, you probably will want to assign labs after the corresponding material is covered in class in order to reinforce or clarify the concepts covered.

***Teacher's Resource Book*** The activities in the *Teacher's Resource Book* (TRB) are varied in nature and ideally suited to individualizing the Prentice Hall chemistry program. These TRB activities cover the full range of teaching goals, from remediation to enrichment and evaluation. The materials in some sections of the TRB enhance the development of learning skills, critical and creative thinking, laboratory and safety skills, problem solving, concept mastery, and College Board Review preparation. Other activities in the TRB are related to the content of specific chapters. These activities are organized on a chapter-by-chapter basis and include overhead transparency masters, review worksheets, practice problem worksheets, open-ended laboratory experiments, open-ended demonstrations, and computer laboratories.

Many of the activities in the TRB are suitable for students of all ability levels. Other activities are intended for students of particular ability levels. For example, the skills development and review activities stress the acquisition of basic facts, concepts, and learning skills, whereas the critical and creative thinking worksheets, the open-ended laboratories and demonstrations, and the college board review questions promote higher level learning.

**Computer software.** These programs provide you with yet another way to meet the individual needs of your students. The programs allow above average students to manipulate variables, observe facts, interpret data, and solve problems as a scientist would. The programs also can provide interactive tutorials for your students who need additional help to understand the concepts covered in class.

The computer software titles available from Prentice Hall are:

*Boyle's and Charles' Law*
*Gas Laws and the Mole*
*Periodic Table*
*Chemical Bonding*
*Dynamic Equilibrium*

**Critical Thinking Transparencies:** These four-color reproductions of selected figures in the text provide above average students with another way to develop their critical thinking skills. The accompanying teacher's notes allow you to take students beyond the information provided in the text.

## Accommodating Special Needs

In the past, students with physical, mental, or emotional disabilities often were segregated from their nondisabled schoolmates. Some attended special schools. Far too many grew up with less than adequate schooling.

Federal Law PL 94-142 completely changes this situation. Today, every student with a disability or disabilities must be integrated into the school community. The disabling condition or conditions must be identified, analyzed, and evaluated, and a suitable educational plan must be devised for the student. Such plans may call for partial integration into the school community, with some instruction taking place in special education classes, or total integration, with selected special services, such as speech therapy.

In all cases, a fundamental goal is the integration of the disabled student into the mainstream of the school community, and ultimately into the mainstream of society. The mainstreaming plans should reflect agreement among student, parents, and school authorities with respect to what are the most suitable learning activities.

It is the responsibility of the science teacher, indeed, of all teachers, to become familiar with the educational plan of each disabled student in a class. Then, whatever is needed to facilitate learning by the disabled student must be developed and put in place.

**Nature of disabilities.** It might be useful to review the different types of disabilities that can turn up in the classroom. Poor sight, blindness, mechanical impairments involving the arms, legs, and spine, and other health problems are known as *physical impairments*.

*Emotional disturbance* is any condition involving the emotions, such as a tendency to unprovoked outbursts of anger, that interferes with normal functioning in social and educational settings.

Conditions that interfere with a student's ability to use language are called *communicative disabilities*. These include deafness, hearing loss, speech problems, and certain specific learning disabilities—dysfunction in one or more of the psychological processes involved in either using or understanding language.

Disorders such as dyslexia, developmental aphasia, perceptual problems, and minimal brain damage are called *specific learning disabilities*.

Finally, intellectual functioning slower than the range of function considered normal is referred to as *mild mental retardation*.

**Reaching disabled students.** Students with disabilities, like other students, continuously interact with their environment while learning about it and developing skills. However, a considerable body of research has established that certain disabled students can be hindered in their growth when classroom instruction is based primarily on reading, listening and writing. Meaningful instruction of these students must meet their special needs. These needs depend on the nature of their disabilities and their experiential backgrounds. Generally, what is required are appropriate experiences focused on student participation before, during, and after presentation of concepts.

Participatory experiences provide the background necessary for disabled students to structure, interpret, and assimilate the concepts. The experiences affect the time for processing ideas, the form of sensory input, the quality of interpretive discussion, and other elements involved in a successful science lesson. For example, visually impaired students benefit greatly by being allowed to manipulate lesson objects and materials before and during the time of instruction. This provides a background of physical characteristics that the teacher can use to great advantage. Students with no visual disability can readily obtain the same background by viewing the objects as the lesson begins. It follows that carefully constructed experiential activities, allowing participation to the extent permitted by a student's disability, are essential to meaningful learning.

A teaching strategy consistent with the definition of the disabled student given earlier is as follows. First, students should be permitted to solve simple open-ended problems by means of manipulative activities. Handling materials and equipment used for classroom demonstrations and carrying out any other activities specially designed, with teacher assistance as needed, will meet this need. For some students, laboratory activities will be suitable. Second, students should read, or have the text paraphrased for them, as needed, and then interact directly with the teacher. As the concepts being taught are discussed, reference should be made to the concrete activities previously carried out to help students assimilate and integrate the desired content. Third, students should be given simple convergent problems that call for the use of concepts covered. A useful technique, when feasible, is to modify chapter-end questions so that they can be performed rather than responded to in writing. For example, suppose that a question calls for the definitions of atoms and molecules. Allowing the disabled student to manipulate spheres that represent atoms can both demonstrate understanding and further reinforce learning. Finally, if needed, remedial learning activities can be devised and administered.

Teachers desiring more information and ideas will find the following title useful: *Sourcebook: Science Education and the Physically Handicapped*, edited by H. Hofman and K. Ricker, National Science Teachers Association, 1979.

## Gifted Students

Far too often, the gifted student is neglected on the grounds that bright students need little attention or guidance to achieve at a satisfactory level. Then, when such students fail to achieve up to their potential, teachers complain that their lack of performance is incomprehensible. It is probably true that bright students need as much attention as disabled students if they are to avoid becoming casualties of the system.

Left to his or her own resources and required to master only the content and skills presented to the average learner, the gifted student often tunes out and experiences anger and frustration. Such students very quickly master whatever is taught and thus are bored by the lack of mental stimulation inherent in plodding through learning activities that fail to challenge them. Some of these gifted students rebel and become behavior problems.

The Prentice Hall chemistry program provides a large number of learning activities to meet the needs of most, if not all, gifted students. Most chapters in the text contain advanced topics. All contain critical thinking questions and challenge problems. The *Teacher's Resource Book* contains many activities (open-ended laboratory experiments, open-ended demonstrations, computer labs, and college board review questions) suitable for students with above average ability.

# Introduction to Chemistry

## Chapter Planning Guide

| Text Section | Labs (Lab Manual) and Demonstrations (TE) | Supplementary Materials (Teacher's Resource Book) |
|---|---|---|
| **1-1** Introduction, pp. 1-2 | Demo 1-1: Mystery Sign, p. TG-62<br>Demo 1-2: Patriotic Colors, p. TG-62<br>Demo 1-3: The Alchemist's Dream, p. TG-63 | |
| **1-2** The Scientific Method, pp. 2-4 | Lab 1: Qualitative Observations of a Chemical Reaction<br>Lab 2: Quantitative Observations of a Chemical Reaction<br>Demo 1-4: The Drinking Bird, p. TG-63 | Transparency Master: Two Explanations for What Happens When an Object Burns, p. 1-2<br>Review Activity: The Scientific Method, p. 1-5<br>Skills Development: Observation versus Interpretation, p. SD-23<br>Critical and Creative Thinking: Creative Thinking, p. CCT-71<br>Laboratory Safety Information:<br>—Safety in the Chemistry Laboratory, p. LSI-7<br>—First Aid in the Chemistry Laboratory, p. LSI-9<br>—Laboratory Safety Agreement, p. LSI-10<br>—Safety Quiz, p. LSI-11 |
| **1-3** Controlled Experiments, pp. 4-6 | | Open-Ended Experiment: Viscosity of Motor Oils, p. 1-3<br>Societal Issues: The Vitamin C Controversy, p. SI-11 |
| **1-4** Making a Graph, pp. 7-9 | | Skills Development: Graphing, p. SD-21<br>Skills Development: Producing and Displaying Experimental Data, p. SD-24 |
| **Application** Bioluminescence, pp. 6-7 | | |

| Text Section | Labs (Lab Manual) and Demonstrations (TE) | Supplementary Materials (Teacher's Resource Book) |
|---|---|---|
| **1-5** Safety—a Primary Concern, pp. 9-10 | | Skills Development: <br>—Reading Science Books and Articles, p. SD-3 <br>—Using Science Reference Materials, p. SD-5 <br>—Writing a Library Research Paper, p. SD-7 <br>—Preparing for and Taking Tests, p. SD-8 <br>—Writing Lab Reports, p. SD-27 |
| **Career** Chemist in Occupational Safety, p. 9 | | |
| | | Test—Form A, p. AT-3 <br>Alternate Test—Form B, p. BT-3 |

■ Core   ■ Advanced   ■ Optional

## Chapter Overview

In Chapter 1 we introduce chemistry as a science and address its relevance to contemporary concerns. The nature of science, both pure and applied, is discussed, and the issue of the beneficial and harmful effects of technology is raised. We explain six steps of the scientific method with special emphasis on the controlled experiment and the technique of graphing results. The chapter closes with a discussion on the importance of learning safe procedures for using hazardous chemicals at home, in school, and in the work place.

## Chapter Objectives

After students have completed this chapter, they will be able to:
1. Distinguish between pure science and applied science or technology.                              *1-1*
2. Explain the scientific method.                              *1-2*
3. Set up a simple controlled experiment.                              *1-3*
4. Prepare a correctly made graph of laboratory data.                              *1-4*
5. Understand the rules of safe conduct in the chemistry classroom and lab.                              *1-5*

## Teaching Suggestions

### 1-1 Introduction, pp. 1-2

| Planning Guide | |
|---|---|
| Labs (Lab Manual) and Demonstrations (TE) | Supplementary Materials (Teacher's Resource Book) |
| Demo 1-1: Mystery Sign, p. TG-62 <br>Demo 1-2: Patriotic Colors, p. TG-62 <br>Demo 1-3: The Alchemist's Dream, p. TG-63 | |

■ After the teaching suggestions for this chapter, there are a group of demonstrations that complement this chapter:

Demonstration 1-1, Mystery Sign
Demonstration 1-2, Patriotic Colors
Demonstration 1-3, The Alchemist's Dream
Demonstration 1-4, The Drinking Bird

At the beginning of the first class, you can do one or more of these demonstrations to spark interest in the course. These demonstrations also help teach the content of the chapter. The overview to each demonstration summarizes the action and purpose.

When you do demonstrations, set a good example by wearing safety goggles and protective clothing.

Follow the rules of safety that you will require of your students when they begin their laboratory work.

■ As you begin class discussion on the relevance of chemistry to the lives of students, point out that chemical discoveries have led to the production of drugs, dyes, plastics, fertilizers, antibiotics, and special alloys. Such products have helped people to live longer and more comfortably. However, the harmful effects of chemical products are so widely publicized that the word "chemical" may have a negative connotation to your students.

You may have students bring up examples of the harmful effects of chemicals they have heard of or read about, or you may mention examples such as the effects of DDT and other pesticides, cigarette tars, oxides of sulfur and nitrogen, and morphine and its derivatives. Fluorocarbons are eroding the ozone layer. Acid rain is damaging rivers, lakes, and forests. Pesticides and other chemicals are tainting ground water, and the threat of nuclear war is ever present.

On the positive side, nations have begun to deal politically with the nuclear threat and with acid rain. Point out to students the influence of individuals in effecting change—for example, Rachel Carson's book *Silent Spring*, which helped to bring about a ban on DDT and to save the bald eagle and other birds from extinction.

## 1-2 The Scientific Method, pp. 2-4

| Planning Guide | |
| --- | --- |
| **Labs (Lab Manual) and Demonstrations (TE)** | **Supplementary Materials (Teacher's Resource Book)** |
| Lab 1: Qualitative Observations of a Chemical Reaction<br>Lab 2: Quantitative Observations of a Chemical Reaction<br>Demo 1-4: The Drinking Bird, p. TG-63 | Transparency Master: Two Explanations for What Happens When an Object Burns, p. 1-2<br>Review Activity: The Scientific Method, p. 1-5<br>Skills Development: Observations versus Interpretation, p. SD-23<br>Critical and Creative Thinking: Creative Thinking, p. CCT-71<br>Laboratory Safety Information<br>—Safety in the Chemistry Laboratory, p. LSI-7<br>—First Aid in the Chemistry Laboratory, p. LSI-9<br>—Laboratory Safety Agreement, p. LSI-10<br>—Safety Quiz, p. LSI-11 |

■ In connection with your discussion of step 2 of the scientific method ("Collecting observations"), you may have the students do Laboratory 1, "Qualitative Observations of a Chemical Reaction," in which they observe changes in shape, color, etc., that occur when a candle is burned. Then have them do Laboratory 2, "Quantitative Observations of a Chemical Reaction," in which they observe the change in the mass of a candle after it is burned and the change in the temperature of water after it is heated.

Before students do any labs, be sure to discuss the information in "Safety in the Chemistry Laboratory," which appears in the lab manual and also in the TRB. As part of your own preparation, read "Laboratory Safety Information" in this Teacher's Edition, pp. TG-51-TG-54, and "Safety Information for the Teacher," found in the Laboratory Safety Information section of the TRB. (See also the teaching suggestions for Section 1-5 below.)

To launch a discussion of step 4 ("Formulating hypotheses") of the scientific method you may use Demonstration 1-4, "The Drinking Bird." Students hypothesize about a glass bird that repeatedly bends over to "drink" water. In addition to (or instead of) the demonstration, you may use the Skills Activity "Observation versus Interpretation," in which students observe and interpret what happens when they prepare a solution and then boil away some of the solvent.

In everyday usage, the terms *hypothesis*, *theory*, and *scientific law* are often used loosely. Stress the importance of using these terms correctly in all contexts, whether "scientific" or not. The nonscientist may refer to a certain idea as "just a theory," with the implication that some theories become facts. This is, of course, not the role of a theory.

Use the Transparency Master "Two Explanations for What Happens When an Object Burns" to point out that theories change and why they change. Ask students to state some observations that might have lent support to the phlogiston theory and some that might have led to its abandonment.

■ **Concept Mastery.** Students often have the erroneous idea that when someone uses the scientific method, he or she follows a set number of predetermined steps in a certain order. They may believe that all scientists work in the exact manner implied by the stepwise presentation of the scientific method. Emphasize that this is not the case. You may wish to use Concept Mastery Question 23 (chapter-end question) to help clarify the point. Tell students that some theoretical scientists approach the solving of a problem from a mathematical point of view, while others make scientific discoveries by chance.

■ **Critical Thinking.** Throughout the course there will be many opportunities for students to use the skill of creative thinking. The Critical and Creative Thinking worksheet "Creative Thinking" directs students to generate new ideas in the context of a laboratory experiment. Students then evaluate their ideas, using critical thinking skills that will be covered in greater depth later in the course. This worksheet is a good introduction to Critical and Creative Thinking because it uses many of these skills together.

## 1-3 Controlled Experiments, pp. 4-6, and

## 1-4 Making a Graph, pp. 7-9

| Planning Guide | |
|---|---|
| **Labs (Lab Manual) and Demonstrations (TE)** | **Supplementary Materials (Teacher's Resource Book)** |
| | Open-Ended Experiment: Viscosity of Motor Oils, p. 1-3 |
| | Societal Issues: The Vitamin C Controversy, p. SI-11 |
| | Skills Development: Graphing, p. SD-21 |
| | Skills Development: Producing and Displaying Experimental Data, p. SD-24 |

■ Controlled experimentation has led to the discovery of many scientific laws. Measurement is usually an important factor in producing results. After students have done Laboratory 1 and Laboratory 2, have them compare the two laboratory experiments and point out that although conclusions reached in a qualitative procedure may be correct, a quantitative procedure can produce information that is more accurate and/or useful.

Students may use the Open-Ended Laboratory Experiment "Viscosity in Motor Oils" for practice in a laboratory procedure that—if well designed—should include both the use of controls and the graphic representation of data collected in the laboratory.

Suggest everyday situations for controlled experimentation. Is my watch running correctly? Is the "silk" in my shirt real silk or a synthetic fiber? Should my homework be done before or after dinner? Students may pose their own problems and describe how they might go about solving them with the aid of controls.

■ The Societal Issue, "The Vitamin C Controversy," is appropriate for use with the study of controlled experimentation.

■ **Concept Mastery.** Students often perform experiments in an introductory chemistry course in a routine manner as if they were baking a cake or putting together a model airplane. You need to help your

students to analyze each experiment they perform for the kind of variables involved. You may wish to use Concept Mastery question 22 (chapter-end question) to improve student understanding of variables. Discuss how to identify the manipulated (independent) variable, the responding (dependent) variable, and the controlled variables in experiments. Some students will confuse the manipulated variable with a controlled variable because they reason that when the variable is manipulated in a systematic fashion, such as 0.1 g, 0.2 g, etc., it is controlled.

You can also point out that although in most experiments only one variable is manipulated at a given time, one variable sometimes interacts with another in such a way that the two variables must be systematically changed at the same time to determine the maximum effect. This idea of making systematic changes and keeping a record of those changes is what you will want students to understand about the control of variables.

■ **Application.** Your students will be interested to know that controlled scientific experimentation is conducted not only by scientists but also by the business community and the government. For example, extensive testing by automobile companies and consumer agencies has produced data showing that the wearing of safety belts significantly reduces injuries from accidents. Similarly, data continue to show that the severity of accidents and the consumption of gasoline are significantly reduced by lowering the speed limit on highways from 65 mph to 55 mph.

## 1-5 Safety— A Primary Concern, pp. 9-10

| Planning Guide | |
|---|---|
| **Labs (Lab Manual) and Demonstrations (TE)** | **Supplementary Materials (Teacher's Resource Book)** |
| | Skills Development: —Reading Science Books and Articles, p. SD-3 —Using Science Reference Materials, p. SD-5 —Writing a Library Research Paper, p. SD-7 —Preparing for and Taking Tests, p. SD-8 —Writing Lab Reports, p. SD-27 |

■ Before you or your students do any laboratory work, a thorough discussion of the information in "Safety in the Chemistry Laboratory" and "First Aid in the Chemistry Laboratory" is in order. Add information from your own experience to that given in the TRB materials, and have students make their own additional suggestions for safe procedures. Each student should also hand in a duly signed "Laboratory Safety Agreement" and score 100% on the "Safety Quiz" before being allowed in the laboratory.

■ You may close the chapter by assigning one or more of the following Skills Activities: "Reading Science Books and Articles," "Using Science Reference Materials," "Writing a Library Research Paper," "Preparing for and Taking Tests," and "Writing Laboratory Reports." Any of these activities may be postponed to a time when students have an immediate need for the skills in question.

# Demonstrations

## 1-1 Mystery Sign

**Overview:** In this demonstration, you spray window cleaning solution containing $NH_3$ on a large piece of paper, and a message in pink appears and then disappears. This demonstration is a good one to carry out on the first day of class, to show that chemistry deals with changes in matter.

**Materials:** solution of phenolphthalein indicator; cotton swab, small sponge brush, or paint brush; large piece of paper (somewhat absorbent); spray bottle of window cleaning solution containing $NH_3$.

**Advance Preparation:** 1. **Phenolphthalein:** Prepare the phenolphthalein solution by mixing 0.1 g indicator in 50 mL ethyl alcohol. 2. Add a few cubic centimeters of concentrated ammonia solution to the window cleaning solution containing $NH_3$ to increase basicity.

**Procedure:** 1. Use a small paint brush, sponge brush, or cotton swab to paint a message, using phenolphthalein indicator solution, on a large piece of paper. If the paper is not very porous, the window cleaning solution containing $NH_3$ will run down the paper and can cause a mess. Have paper towels handy. Keep the message short and simple (for example, "Chemistry is fun!" or "Chem is try"). Allow the paper to dry thoroughly and tape it to the chalkboard in front of the classroom. 2. Spray window cleaning solution containing $NH_3$ on the message so as to cover the entire message as quickly as possible. 3. Repeat step 2 several times.

**Results:** The basic window cleaning solution containing $NH_3$ will turn the indicator pink. The color will fade quickly because the ammonia will evaporate and the carbon dioxide in the air will produce an acidic solution that will neutralize any ammonia that may remain on the paper.

## 1-2 Patriotic Colors

**Overview:** In this demonstration, you add a colorless solution to three other colorless solutions to produce red, white, and blue solutions. The reactions that occur when you mix these solutions illustrate that chemistry deals with changes in materials.

**Materials:** ammonia water; 0.05% phenolphthalein solution; 0.5 $M$ magnesium nitrate or magnesium chloride; copper(II) sulfate solution that is almost colorless; three 125-mL Erlenmeyer flasks; 50-mL beaker

**Advance Preparation:** 1. Prepare ammonia water by mixing one part concentrated ammonia with three parts water. 2. Prepare the phenolphthalein solution by mixing 0.05 g of indicator in 50 mL of ethyl alcohol. 3. Prepare a 0.5 $M$ magnesium solution by mixing 7.4 g of magnesium nitrate in 100 mL of water or by mixing 4.8 g of magnesium chloride in 100 mL of water. 4. Prepare a near colorless dilute solution of copper(II) sulfate by mixing a few crystals in water.

**Procedure:** 1. Place the three Erlenmeyer flasks onto a piece of white paper. 2. Place about 100 mL of distilled water and 5–10 drops of the phenolphthalein solution into the first flask; 100 mL of magnesium solution into the next; and 100 mL of the very dilute copper(II) sulfate solution into the last flask. 3. Have the students note that all of the flasks seem to look like water (clear, colorless liquids). 4. Pour some ammonia water into the 50-mL beaker and add a few milliliters of this solution to each flask.

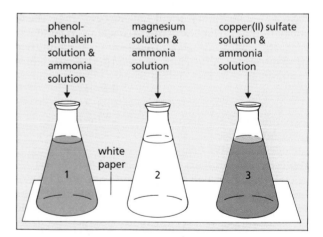

**Figure 1-1**

**Results:** The first flask should turn a clear, dark rose color because phenolphthalein turns pink or purple in a basic solution. The second flask should form a white precipitate of magnesium hydroxide. The last flask should turn a deep blue because copper forms a blue complex with ammonia.

**Disposal Tips:** Carefully pour the contents of the flasks down the drain and flush with large amounts of water.

## 1-3 The Alchemist's Dream

**Overview:** In this demonstration, you can appear to be successful in achieving what the alchemists of the Middle Ages tried, but failed, to do. You first heat a penny in a sodium hydroxide solution containing zinc dust, and the penny appears to turn into silver. After you heat the "silver penny," it changes into "gold."

**Materials:** 6 $M$ NaOH; 0.50 g of zinc dust; evaporating dish; hot plate; tongs or tweezers; beaker of water; burner or candle; penny

**Advance Preparation:** Use the following procedure to prepare the 6 $M$ NaOH. Dissolve 24 g of NaOH in 70 mL of distilled water in a 250-mL beaker. Place this beaker into a cold water bath to absorb the heat given off and to speed up the dissolving. Stir until all of the solid has dissolved. Dilute with water to get 100 mL of solution.

**Safety:** Be careful when handling 6 $M$ NaOH; it is very corrosive and can cause burns. Also be cautious with the zinc dust because metallic dusts can be toxic if they are inhaled. Heat the NaOH solution containing the zinc dust and penny gently to prevent spattering that can occur as the zinc dust coats the penny.

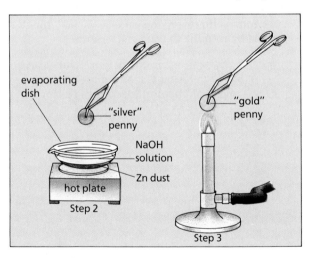

**Figure 1-2**

**Procedure:** 1. Carefully add the zinc dust to the evaporating dish and add about 15 mL of the sodium hydroxide solution. Set the dish onto a hot plate and heat on medium heat. Do not allow the solution to boil. 2. Add a penny to the solution and allow the reaction to continue for about two minutes or until the penny has changed to a silver color. Remove the penny with tongs or tweezers and dip it in water. 3. Using tongs or tweezers, hold the "silver" penny in the top of a flame and heat it until it changes color. Place the penny in water and dry it with a paper towel. The penny should look like gold.

**Results:** In step 2, the penny is coated with zinc atoms. When the coated penny is heated in step 3, the zinc coating mixes with the copper atoms in the penny to form a brass alloy, which looks like gold.

**Disposal Tips:** When the evaporating dish is cool, decant the solution into a large beaker of tap water, and pour the water down the drain. Use a wet paper towel to wipe any remaining zinc particles from the dish.

## 1-4 The Drinking Bird

**Overview:** In this demonstration, you put the beak of a glass "drinking bird" into a glass of water, and the bird repeatedly bends over to "drink" water from the glass and continues to bend even after the glass is removed. You ask students to hypothesize about this phenomenon, to make predictions as to the effects of various changes in conditions, to carry out procedures, and to draw conclusions. In other words, you are teaching students to use the scientific method.

**Materials:** glass drinking bird (Fisher Scientific: S41712, approximately $3.00; or from novelty stores); plastic cups (tall enough to allow the beak of the bird to touch the fluid in the cup when the bird bends over); water at room temperature; ethyl alcohol; hot water; ice-cold water; acetone or nail-polish remover.

**Advance Preparation:** Shortly before class, heat roughly 300 mL of water to just below boiling, and cool another 300 mL of water by adding a large amount of ice.

**Procedure:** 1. Fill a plastic cup completely with water at room temperature. Position the bird so that when it bends over to "drink," its beak will touch the water. The teacher should start the bird drinking. Ask students to explain the result. 2. Remove the cup of water. Ask students to try to explain what happens. Accept all answers without making judgments. 3. Tell students that more information may be needed to explain these phenomena. Replace the cup of water with a cup of ethyl alcohol. Repeat step 1. Ask students to list some differences between the water and the alcohol that might account for what they observe. Accept all answers. Place a drop of the alcohol onto a student's arm and have him or her note the resulting sensation. 4. At this point, take the bird around the room and show how the bird is constructed. Draw a picture of it on the board. Hold the bulb of the bird in your hand and have students observe what happens. 5. Ask students to predict what will happen to the bending rate when each of the following is carried out: fanning the bird; using a cup of hot water instead of water at room temperature; using a cup of ice-cold water; and using acetone or nail-polish remover. Now try each of these to see how close their predictions come to the actual behavior. 6. Tell students they have just used the scientific method to solve the mystery of the drinking bird and to make and test predictions.

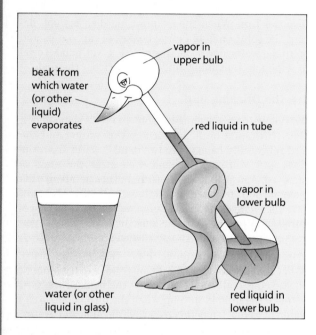

**Figure 1-3**

**Results:** In step 1, the bird will continue to bend over repeatedly to drink. After the beak touches water or any other sufficiently volatile liquid, the evaporation of the liquid from the beak results in cooling. This produces condensation of vaporized Freon or methylene chloride within a glass bulb inside the bird's head and a resulting decrease in vapor pressure. This, in turn, causes liquid Freon or methylene chloride (dyed red) to be pushed up a tube from a second bulb, which is located below it and which contains the liquid and some trapped vapor. The resulting gravitational imbalance causes the bird to bend over. At that point, however, the bottom end of the tube is no longer below the surface of the red liquid, which allows vapor from the lower bulb to rise up through the tube and liquid to run back down into the lower bulb. The bird then straightens up. The process repeats itself, even after the glass of water is removed (step 2) as long as there is still liquid evaporating from the beak. In step 3, the bending rate increases because ethyl alcohol is more volatile than water, as is indicated by the sensation of coolness produced by the evaporation of alcohol from

the student's arm. In step 4, the heat of your hand will cause red liquid to move up the tube from the bulb. In step 5, fanning the bird, using hot water, and using acetone or nail-polish remover all increase the bending rate because they all increase evaporation rate of liquid from the beak. Using cold water decreases the evaporation and bending rates.

## Answers to Questions

### Page 6

1. The second attempt was not a controlled experiment because two quantities were changed at the same time and there was no way of knowing the effect of each change individually. In a controlled experiment, one would vary the quantities of one ingredient and note the effect on the taste and texture. When this was found to be satisfactory, the experimenter would vary the amounts of the second ingredient to be mixed with the desirable amount of the first ingredient.

### Page 9

2. The graph shows that the volume of a gas increases with an increase of temperature. There is a certain regularity in this change because, for practically every 5°C rise in temperature, the volume increases by 1.7 cm³. However, the volume is not directly proportional to the Celsius temperature.

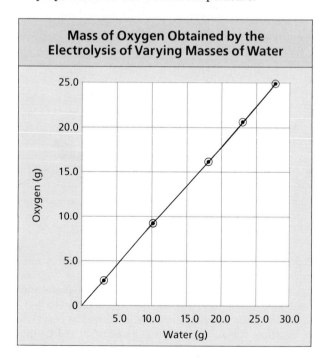

**Figure 1-4**

**3.** Student graph should resemble Figure 1-4 and show a direct proportion between quantity of water used and quantity of oxygen produced.

## Chapter Review

Page 11, Content Review

**1.** The principle of cause and effect states that everything that happens (an effect) is the result of something that happened earlier (the cause).

**2.** Pure scientists attempt to understand the world. They seek truth for its own sake. Applied scientists look for practical uses for discoveries.

**3.** An experiment is a carefully planned procedure that allows the scientist to make observations about the world in order to solve a problem.

**4.** When the current theory does not explain a new observation, the theory is modified. Sometimes, however, the old theory has to be discarded and a new theory proposed.

**5.** A controlled experiment is one in which certain factors are fixed, or controlled, by the scientist. The scientist varies these factors one at a time to determine how each factor affects the results. Controls are necessary to isolate the effect of one factor from the combined effect of all factors.

**6.** Some of the variables in the process of baking bread are the nature and amount of each ingredient, the time and temperature for rising and baking, and the size of the pan.

**7.** In a controlled experiment, the measurements collected are called data.

**8.** The independent variable is placed on the horizontal axis ($x$-axis); the dependent variable is placed on the vertical axis ($y$-axis).

**9.** A graph makes it easier to see patterns in the data, if there are any.

**10. a.** Figure 1-5 shows that the total distance traveled increases with time. The rate of increase decreases with time (the slope drops off).

**b.** If the bicycle rider keeps going, the curve will continue to increase at a slower and slower rate as the rider gets tired. If the rider has a burst of energy or a strong tail wind, it is possible for the slope to increase. If the rider quits for the day, the curve will level off.

**c.** At 10:30 am, the bicycle rider has traveled about 29 km, assuming a constant speed between 10:00 am and 11:00 am. This value is not

certain, however. If the rider stopped between 10:00 am and 10:30 am and traveled 10 km between 10:30 am and 11:00 am, then the distance at 10:30 am would be 23 km.

**d.** The bicycle rider covered 12 km the first hour and 5 km the last hour. Perhaps the rider was getting tired. The slower rate of travel is shown by the curve's leveling off.

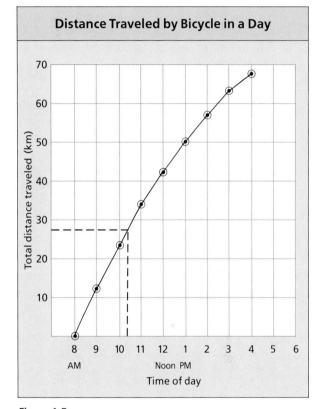

**Figure 1-5**

**11.** The benefit of penicillin is its ability to kill certain bacteria that cause infection. The risk is a possible allergic reaction.

**12.** We use products that carry a certain risk because we think the benefits are worth the risks.

**13.** Safety is a major concern of the chemical industry, which has spent time, money, and resources to establish and maintain a good record.

**14.** Some occupations in industrial safety are industrial hygienist, toxicologist, public health official, doctor, and nurse.

Page 12, Content Mastery

**15. a.** In the experiment, the temperature of the tank is increased and the pressure is recorded. The temperature is the independent variable, and the pressure is the dependent variable.

**b.** The temperature goes on the horizontal axis because it is the independent variable.

16. Advances in technology are often used to solve problems, but sometimes they create new problems. For example, technology has produced chemicals to control insects. Unfortunately, some of these chemicals also pollute the environment.

17. **a.** The scientific method can be broken down into six steps: 1. stating a problem, 2. collecting observations, 3. searching for scientific laws, 4. forming hypotheses, 5. forming theories, and 6. modifying theories.

**b.** Searching for scientific laws involves stating a relationship without explanation.

**c.** Forming theories involves unifying many pieces of diverse information into a grand design.

18. Make a mental or written list of possible causes, such as an empty gas tank, a dead battery, a clogged fuel line, or a short circuit. Check one possibility at a time, starting with the simplest one. For example, check the gas gauge. Continue gathering information until you find the cause. Fix the problem.

19. **a.** Chemical drain cleaners are easy to use and usually effective, but they can burn the skin or eyes.

**b.** Gasoline is a cheap fuel, but it is flammable.

**c.** Insulation helps to conserve energy but can damage the lungs of the workers who install it.

**d.** Automobiles are a comfortable, convenient means of transportation, but they can be involved in accidents and cause air pollution.

20. **a.** Figure 1-6 shows the water temperature increases from a low on February 1 to a high on August 1, then decreases again until the last value recorded. This pattern agrees with the change in air temperature with the seasons in Massachusetts.

**b.** The graph gives a water temperature on July 15 of 17.5°C. This value is only an estimate and not a certain fact because data are recorded only for the first day of each month. Temperatures for other days have to be estimated from the graph. The actual temperature might have been different due to an unusual weather pattern or storm.

**c.** Although the actual data recorded for the first day of each month would be different, the temperature graph should show the same general pattern (cold in the winter, warm in the summer).

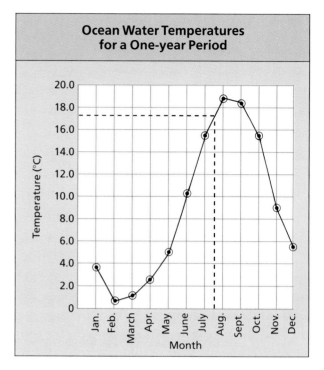

**Figure 1-6**

Page 12, Concept Mastery

21. **Concept:** *In a controlled experiment, all variables important to the outcome are controlled. More than 1 variable can be manipulated at a time.*

**Solution:** The variables of interest are the amount of water and the amount of hormone. All other factors (such as species of plant, age and size of plant, type of soil, and amount of sunlight) must be held constant. The amount of water and of hormone can be varied independently or together, but it must be done in a systematic way.

22. **Concept:** *A controlled variable is a factor that would affect the results if it were not held constant. A variable that varies in a regular or consistent manner is not a controlled variable. Controlled variables do not vary.*

**Solution:** The controlled variables are the volume and nature of the oil, the size of the strip of fabric, the size of the test tube, the volume of water, the brand of detergent, the number of times the test tube is shaken, and the method of evaluating the results.

Many students will think the mass of

detergent and the nature of the fabric are controlled variables because they vary regularly throughout the experiment—but they are not. A controlled variable is controlled, meaning it does not vary. A variable is controlled if it has the same value for each data point collected in the whole experiment.

**23.** ***Concept:*** *Sometimes a scientist uses the scientific method without using all six steps or without using them in the order presented in the text.*

    *Solution:*    The scientist is still using the scientific method even though some of the steps are missing.

### Page 13, Critical Thinking

**24.** There are many branches of science. Chemistry is only one of them.

**25.** Collecting observations is a good way of proving or disproving a hypothesis. If the observations are explained by the hypothesis, then they agree with or support the hypothesis and make it more believable. If the observations are not explained or if they are contradicted by the hypothesis, then the hypothesis is proven incomplete or incorrect.

**26.** A theory is the statement of a general pattern that unifies many individual facts, observations, or hypotheses.

**27.** Proponents of the phlogiston theory assumed that burning substances released phlogiston. As the concentration of phlogiston increased in the air, the substance could no longer burn.

**28.** Even though a theory can never be proved beyond all doubt, it is useful to state theories because they organize many facts into a recognizable pattern. A theory does not have to be completely discarded when new facts are discovered. Usually a theory can be modified to account for new facts. It is usually easier to modify an existing theory than to start all over again with a new theory.

**29.** The independent variable is the item you have control over, or what order you mass the marbles in. For example, you can choose to mass the blue marble first, then the green one, then the white one. The dependent variable is the measurement you record, the results of your experiment (in this case, the masses of the different marbles).

**30.** This is a judgment question, and students' answers will certainly vary. Some students may say that no risk, even a small one, is acceptable.

### Page 13, Challenge Problems

**31.** Answers will vary. For example, if brushing your teeth was an activity, then you might say that chemists developed the formula for the most effective toothpaste; they made the plastic that the toothpaste tube, the toothbrush handle, and the bristles are made of; they made the inks for writing the label on the tube; perhaps they even treated and purified the water that comes out of your faucet.

**32.** This problem asks students to conceptualize and conduct a simple experiment and to record their data. For example, they might mass five marbles, count the number of pages in five books, or read the temperature outside on five different days. Depending on their experiments, their graphs may or may not reveal a pattern.

**33.** Temperature is the only variable in this experiment. You need several samples of milk and a refrigerator. Decide how you will measure the rate of spoiling and what instruments you might need. If you have only one refrigerator, you can investigate the effect of only one temperature at a time. If you have several refrigerators, each set at a different temperature, you can study several temperatures simultaneously. Record how long it takes for a sample of milk to spoil at each temperature.

**34.** First, you need to decide what makes a house paint competitive. Some possible factors are its price, the range of available colors, its ability to cover various surfaces, and its durability. Then, measure the paint's performance on these factors and compare it with the performance of the other paints on the market.

# Measurement

## Chapter Planning Guide

| Text Section | | Labs (Lab Manual) and Demonstrations (TE) | Supplementary Materials (Teacher's Resource Book) |
|---|---|---|---|
| 2-1 | Chemical Quantities, p. 15 | Lab 3: Measuring Mass<br>Demo 2-1: Unaided Senses versus Measuring Devices, p. TG-72 | Transparency Master: SI Base Units of Measurement, p. 2-1 |
| 2-2 | The International System of Units, p. 16 | | |
| 2-3 | Advantages of Using SI, p. 17 | | |
| 2-4 | SI Prefixes, pp. 17-19 | Demo 2-2: A New Measurement System, p. TG-72<br>Demo 2-3: The Metric System in Everyday Life, p. TG-72 | Transparency Master: SI Derived Units, p. 2-2 |
| 2-5 | SI Derived Units, pp. 19-21 | | |
| 2-6 | Non-SI Units Found in Chemistry Writing, pp. 21-22 | | |
| 2-7 | The Newton, an SI Derived Unit, pp. 22-24 | | |
| 2-8 | The Meter, Kilogram, and Cubic Meter, pp. 24-26 | Demo 2-4: Precision versus Accuracy, p. TG-73 | Review Activity: The International System of Units, p. 2-3<br>Critical and Creative Thinking: First-hand Observations, p. CCT-3 |
| 2-9 | Uncertainty in Measurement, pp. 26-28 | | |
| 2-10 | Accuracy versus Precision, pp. 29-30 | | |
| 2-11 | Significant Figures, pp. 30-31 | | |
| Breakthrough | Space Spheres, pp. 28-29 | | |
| 2-12 | Use of Plus-or-minus Notation, p. 32 | | |

| Text Section | | Labs (Lab Manual) and Demonstrations (TE) | Supplementary Materials (Teacher's Resource Book) |
|---|---|---|---|
| **2-13** | Calculating with Measurements, pp. 33-36 | | Skills Development: Significant Figures, p. SD-19<br>Review Activity: Precision, Accuracy, and Significant Figures, p. 2-4<br>Skills Development: Fractions, Decimals, Percentages, p. SD-9<br>Practice Problems, p. 2-6<br>Societal Issue: Radon, p. SI-14 |
| **2-14** | Percent Error, pp. 36-37 | | |
| **Career** | Environmental Chemist, p. 34 | | |
| | | | Test—Form A, p. AT-6<br>Alternate Test—Form B, p. BT-6 |

■ Core    ■ Advanced    ■ Optional

## Chapter Overview

In Chapter 2 we emphasize the reliance of science on measurement and the need for universally accepted units of measurement. We describe the International System of Units (SI) and provide practice in using SI base units, prefixes, and derived units. The meter, the kilogram, the cubic meter, and the newton receive special attention. Uncertainty in measurement, and accuracy versus precision are explained. Students develop skills in the use of significant figures and plus-or-minus notation in expressing measurements and calculated results. The chapter closes with a discussion of percent error.

## Chapter Objectives

After students have completed this chapter, they will be able to:
1. Express measurements in the International System of Units (SI). *2-1* to *2-4,* and *2-8*
2. Be able to combine SI base units to form SI derived units. *2-5* to *2-7*
3. Determine the amount of uncertainty in a measured quantity. *2-9* and *2-12*
4. Apply correctly the terms *accuracy* and *precision.* *2-10*

5. Report measurements and the results of calculating with measurements. *2-11* and *2-13*
6. Calculate the percent error of an experimental result. *2-14*

## Teaching Suggestions

### 2-1 Chemical Quantities, p. 15,

### 2-2 The International System of Units, p. 16, and

### 2-3 Advantages of Using SI, p. 17

| Planning Guide | |
|---|---|
| Labs (Lab Manual) and Demonstrations (TE) | Supplementary Materials (Teacher's Resource Book) |
| Lab 3: Measuring Mass<br>Demo 2-1: Unaided Senses versus Measuring Devices, p. TG-72 | Transparency Master: SI Base Units of Measurement, p. 2-1 |

■ As a motivating starter, use Demonstration 2-1, "Unaided Senses versus Measuring Devices." This demonstration will help students to appreciate the need for measuring tools and to engage their interest before any reading or discussion of text material. You may also have students do Laboratory 3, "Measuring

Mass," before presenting the SI system so that they already have practical knowledge of one commonly used SI unit, the gram. In this lab, students acquire skill in performing three basic types of measurement: measuring mass directly, "measuring out" a substance, and determining mass by difference.

■ The nature of chemistry as a quantitative science, touched upon briefly in Chapter 1, is developed in Chapter 2. Tell students that the phlogiston theory was accepted for a long time because it was not tested quantitatively, and that its overthrow resulted from Lavoisier's measurement of the masses of reactants and products in his experiments. After his explanation of the nature of burning, the emphasis on measurement contributed greatly to progress in chemical knowledge.

■ The SI system—or the metric system (see Section 2-6), which uses most of the same units as the SI system—is used in nearly all countries except the United States. In December 1975, President Ford signed a bill calling for voluntary conversion to metric measures. Since then, deadlines have been established but have not been met. Students will be aware that metric measurements have been introduced for many grocery items, for some gasoline pumps, and on some road signs. Many industries also have converted to metric measures, but the cost of retooling has been a main factor in the failure of others to convert.

## 2-4 SI Prefixes, pp. 17-19,

## 2-5 SI Derived Units, pp. 19-21, and

## 2-6 Non-SI Units Found in Chemistry Writing, pp. 21-22

| Planning Guide | |
|---|---|
| **Labs (Lab Manual) and Demonstrations (TE)** | **Supplementary Materials (Teacher's Resource Book)** |
| Demo 2-2: A New Measurement System, p. TG-72 Demo 2-3: The Metric System in Everyday Life, p. TG-72 | Transparency Master: SI Derived Units, p. 2-2 |

■ Of the 16 SI prefixes given in text Figure 2-5, students need to learn the meanings of no more than the six that are in common usage: *mega-*, *kilo-*, *deci-*, *centi-*, *milli-*, and *micro-*. Use Demonstration 2-2, "A New Measurement System," to give students practice in applying their knowledge of SI prefixes.

■ The SI system is a modification of the older metric system, and some common metric units have been replaced by newer SI units. Among the units given in text Figure 2-9, students may be most familiar with

the liter and milliliter, now often being used, for example, on soft drink containers and kitchen measuring cups. Point out that this book uses the cubic decimeter and cubic centimeter, which are the SI equivalents of the liter and the milliliter, respectively. Use Demonstration 2-3, "The Metric System in Everyday Life" to help familiarize students with the use of grams, kilograms, centimeters, and cubic centimeters.

■ **Application:** You may want to point out that understanding SI units is necessary in other contexts besides that of the science laboratory. With the popularity of imported cars has come the need to recognize the pascal as the unit of air pressure. Complex audio systems with graphic equalizers allow us to control various frequency bands, expressed in hertz and kilohertz. (For example, 125 Hz adjusts the middle frequency sounds of vocals.) The distances of many track events and marathon races at the Olympics are designated in meters and kilometers.

## 2-7 The Newton, an SI Derived Unit, pp. 22-24

■ If you elect to teach this topic, you may want to tell students that the derived units for force, pressure, and work are obtained from the following formulas:

$$\text{Force (newtons)} = \text{mass} \times \text{acceleration} = \text{kg} \times \text{m/s}^2$$
$$= \text{m·kg/s}^2$$
$$\text{Pressure (pascals)} = \text{force per unit area} = \frac{\text{m·kg/s}^2}{\text{m}^2}$$
$$= \text{kg/m·s}^2$$
$$\text{Work (joules)} = \text{force} \times \text{distance} = \text{m·kg/s}^2 \times \text{m}$$
$$= \text{m}^2\text{·kg/s}^2$$

## 2-8 The Meter, Kilogram, and Cubic Meter, pp. 24-26,

## 2-9 Uncertainty in Measurement, pp. 26-28,

## 2-10 Accuracy versus Precision, pp. 29-30, and

## 2-11 Significant Figures, pp. 30-31

| Planning Guide | |
|---|---|
| **Labs (Lab Manual) and Demonstrations (TE)** | **Supplementary Materials (Teacher's Resource Book)** |
| Demo 2-4: Precision versus Accuracy, p. TG-73 | Review Activity: The International System of Units, p. 2-3 Critical and Creative Thinking: Firsthand Observations, p. CCT-3 |

■ To help students to literally get a "feel" for the actual sizes of SI (and metric) volumes and masses, have them handle dm³ cubes (which students themselves may construct). Then have them select the appropriate technique from those learned in Laboratory 3 and use it to determine the mass of 1 cm³ of water.

You may wish to use the following demonstration to determine your students' understanding of mass, volume, and surface area. Ask students which of two identical pieces of paper will, when dropped from equal heights, hit the floor first. Crumple one piece of paper and repeat the question. Then drop the two pieces. Ask whether the mass and volume have changed, and how you could prove they have not. Next, you might want to stack several dm³ cubes in various ways. Ask students to compare the volume, mass, and surface area after you change the position of the cubes. The demonstration should help show that mass and volume are constant but that surface area is not.

Use Demonstration 2-4, "Precision versus Accuracy," to reinforce the text explanation of these concepts. Emphasize that accuracy in measurement depends not only on the care and skill of the experimenter, but also on the limitations of the measuring instrument. An instrument may be suitable for one type of measurement but not for another. Ask students what instrument they would use to measure the thickness of a wooden board. Would the same instrument be appropriate for measuring the thickness of a piece of sheet copper? See text Figure 2-20.

With proper care and good technique, students should be able to make measurements that are fairly accurate. Point out that in spite of care and technique, the result may be poor because of faulty measuring instruments.

■ You may want to have students examine measuring devices with the scales marked in different gradations, such as graduated cylinders ranging in capacity from 1000 cm³ to 10 cm³ and a 50-cm³ buret. Ask students to read these, or make enlarged sketches on the chalkboard of the scales on each and ask students to make readings at predetermined points. Include measurements that fall on the heavy and fine lines and be sure that students use the proper number of zeros.

■ To give students practice with significant figures, have each student measure a given length with a metric ruler and then take the reading of a Celsius thermometer. In each case they should estimate the final figure of the reading. Then have the students indicate the number of significant figures in the measurements. Have them compare their results and note the variation in the final figures.

■ **Concept Mastery.** Many students enrolled in an introductory chemistry course do not have a good conceptual grasp of length, mass, and volume. Some will confuse mass and volume. They may define volume as the length × width × height of an object without realizing that this formula applies only to rectangular solids and even without being able to point out the three dimensions of an object. To help students overcome such deficits, you can use Concept Mastery questions 56, 57, 60, and 61 in the Chapter

Review, which are based on questions researchers have found to be difficult for some students. You may wish to set up these items as demonstrations and/or experiments. Use Concept Mastery questions 58 and 59 in the Chapter Review to check students' ability to distinguish volume from surface area, which they can do if they understand the concept of volume.

■ **Critical Thinking.** The Critical and Creative Thinking worksheet "Firsthand Observations" can be used to sharpen students' understanding of precision and accuracy. Students are asked to evaluate the experimental observations of several people based on human factors such as bias or inexperience. The worksheet will help them to see how the observer must be taken into account when determining the accuracy or precision of observations.

## 2-12 Use of Plus-or-minus Notation, pp. 32

■ If you elect to assign this topic, explain how the use of plus-or-minus notation pinpoints the uncertainty in a measurement more precisely than does the use of significant figures alone. Have students examine several examples of measured lengths and state the implied ranges. They can get help from Figure 2-22. Compare the uncertainties of values that state implied ranges with values that use the plus-or-minus notation.

## 2-13 Calculating with Measurements, pp. 33-36, and

## 2-14 Percent Error, pp. 36-37

| Planning Guide | |
|---|---|
| Labs (Lab Manual) and Demonstrations (TE) | Supplementary Materials (Teacher's Resource Book) |
| | Skills Development: Significant Figures, p. SD-19 |
| | Review Activity: Precision, Accuracy, and Significant Figures, p. 2-4 |
| | Skills Development: Fractions, Decimals, Percentages, p. SD-9 |
| | Practice Problems, p. 2-6 |
| | Societal Issues: Radon, p. SI-14 |

■ Tell students that the rules for determining the correct number of significant figures in the results of multiplication, division, addition, and subtraction are a basic tool that they will use repeatedly throughout the course. Thus, it is important that they study the rules carefully and that they understand the rationale behind each one.

■ To help students appreciate the nature of percent

error, ask them to measure the densities of objects made of pure zinc, aluminum, or copper. If available objects have regular shapes, students can measure the linear dimensions of the objects and calculate their volumes. Then have students determine the masses of the objects by using the procedure learned in Lab 3 (see teaching suggestions for Sections 2-1 through 2-3) and use the calculated volumes and measured masses to compute the densities of the objects. Alternatively, they may use the relevant parts of the procedure in Lab 5, "Density Determination," anticipating the textbook discussion of the topic in Chapter 4. From the data obtained, have the students calculate the percent errors. Let the class decide which errors are acceptable and which are not.

■ You may use the Societal Issue "Radon" at this time. This worksheet pertains to a practical application of measurement.

## Demonstrations

### 2-1 Unaided Senses versus Measuring Devices

**Overview:** In this demonstration, you ask students to use their sense of sight to determine which of two containers can hold more fluid and to use their sense of touch to determine which of two metal objects feels heavier. Students are usually incorrect in these selections and thus are made to see the need for using measurement devices.

**Materials:** either 100-mL graduated cylinder and 250-mL Florence flask or 250-mL graduated cylinder and 500-mL Florence flask; 4-cm-high iron cylinder; aluminum cylinder about twice the mass of the iron cylinder; 500-mL beaker full of colored water; balance.

**Advance Preparation: Colored water:** Prepare colored water by adding a few drops of food coloring to approximately 1 L of water.

**Procedure:** 1. Show the graduated cylinder and flask to the class and ask students to decide which will hold more water. Pour colored water from the beaker into the graduated cylinder and into the flask. 2. Pass the iron and aluminum cylinders around the room and have each student hold the cylinders in his/her hands and decide which cylinder seems heavier. Using a two-pan balance or electronic balance, determine and compare the two masses. Ask students why the iron feels "heavier," and discuss the density of the metals. 3. Discuss how the senses failed to help students in making the correct selections. Point out the need for an objective system of measurement and proper measuring instruments.

**Results:** The flask holds about twice the amount of liquid as the graduated cylinder. The aluminum cylinder is about twice as massive as the iron cylinder, but seems "lighter" because its density is lower.

### 2-2 A New Measurement System

**Overview:** In this demonstration, students learn how to develop a new system for measuring length by using a rod and applying a knowledge of prefixes.

**Materials:** a rod of metal or wood more than 0.5 m but less than 1 m long.

**Advance Preparation:** none

**Procedure:** 1. Show the rod of metal or wood to the class and tell the students you want them to develop their own system of measurement by using the rod as the basic unit of length. Give the rod some special unit name of your own or their choosing. 2. Try to measure the length of your desk by using the rod, and record the measurement on the board. 3. Ask students how they could use the new basic unit to measure the length of a given object that is shorter than the rod. Suggest developing a smaller unit that is 1/10 the size of the basic unit and ask them what the unit should be called. Use masking tape to mark off the rod into tenths. Have one of the students use this rod to make the measurement of the smaller object. 4. Ask one of the students to try to use this rod to measure the diameter of a thin pencil or toothpick. Ask students to suggest what might help make this job easier. They should suggest further subdividing each deciunit into ten equal lengths—into centiunits. 5. Ask students how they could use or modify the basic unit to measure the length of the school and the distance to a neighboring town, and develop units that include the appropriate prefixes. Discuss the problems involved in developing a measurement system, and emphasize the importance of standards. Significant figures and uncertainty in measurement can even be introduced as you try to measure various items. 6. End your discussion by stating that the students do not have to go to all the trouble of inventing a measurement system because one that can do all the things mentioned already exists: the metric system.

**Results:** The prefixes *deci-*, *centi-*, *deca-*, and *kilo-* should be added to the name of the basic unit in steps 3, 4, and 5. The actual magnitude of the quantities measured will depend on the length of the rod.

### 2-3 The Metric System in Everyday Life

**Overview:** In this demonstration, you display various household products. You ask students to estimate and measure mass, length, and volume, and to determine percent error. Students should gain a better perspective on how the metric system affects their lives, as well as a better sense of the size of metric units.

**Materials:** any container or other object that has a mass of 2.2 pounds, or 1 kg; triple-beam pan balance that can be used for kilogram masses; balance (electronic works best for quick comparisons); nickel coin; candy bar in wrapper that states mass in grams and in ounces; meter stick whose opposite side is calibrated in inches; 3″×5″ index card for each student; short plastic metric ruler or photocopy of one for each student; 1000-mL graduated cylinder or volumetric flask; 10-mL graduated cylinder for each group of three or four students; small test tube for each group.

**Advance Preparation:** none

**Procedure:** 1. Show the 1-kg object to the class, and find its mass on a triple-beam balance. Pass the object around so students can get a sense of the magnitude of 1 kg of mass. 2. Ask students for objects that they think have a mass of about 1 g. Determine the masses of all the objects until you find one whose mass is close to 1 g. Tell students to think of this object when trying to remember how small 1 g actually is. 3. Ask students to predict the mass of a nickel coin. Find the mass. 4. Show the candy-bar wrapper, with its statement of the net mass of the candy. Have a student volunteer determine the mass of the bar and wrapper and the mass of the wrapper alone. Ask whether the printed and measured net masses agree. 5. Show the meter stick to the class and discuss the division of the stick into decimeters, centimeters, and millimeters. Have the class find something that is the size of each of these units so that in the future they can more easily remember how small or how large each unit is. 6. Hand out an index card to each student, along with a metric ruler. Have the students visually estimate the width of the card, in centimeters, and then have them actually measure the width. Discuss significant figures. Have students volunteer their measurements, and record the results on the board. Discuss why their measurements are not all in perfect agreement. Give students the correct value of width for an index card, and have each student determine his/her percent error. 7. Show students 1000 cm³ (1000 mL) of volume by using a 1000-mL graduated cylinder or volumetric flask. 8. On the board, draw a cube, 1 cm on a side, and tell students its volume is 1 cm³, or 1 mL. Show them the 10-mL graduated cylinder and tell them that 10 of the drawn cubes would fill the cylinder. 9. Give each of the students a small test tube and tell them to try to place 5 mL of water into the tube by estimation. Have them pour the water into a 10-mL graduated cylinder and find out how close their estimation was. 10. Have student volunteers determine the volume of a measuring cup, a tablespoon, and a teaspoon. Ask students whether they think recipes printed in the future will express volume in cubic centimeters instead of in cups, tablespoons, and teaspoons.

**Results:** In step 2, students will be likely to volunteer objects whose masses are significantly greater or less than 1 g. The nickel coin in step 3 has a mass of about 5 g. In step 5, the width of a hand, for example, is about 1 dm; a little fingernail or pen might be 1 cm wide; and the tip of a pencil is about 1 mm wide. In step 6, the width of an index card (3 inches) is 7.62 cm. In step 10, 1 cup equals roughly 237 mL, 1 tablespoon equals roughly 15 mL, and 1 teaspoon equals roughly 5 mL.

## 2-4 Precision Versus Accuracy

**Overview:** In this demonstration, students use darts on a dart board to help them visualize the difference between precision and accuracy.

**Materials:** dart board and darts (or a transparency of a dart board to be used on the overhead projector, and cork stoppers to serve as darts).

**Advance Preparation:** If you do not use an actual dart board, draw a picture of one on a transparency.

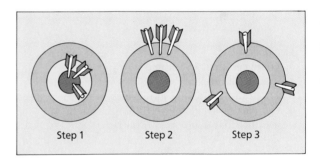

Step 1    Step 2    Step 3

**Figure 2-1**

**Procedure:** 1. Place three darts in the bull's-eye and ask students to describe the accuracy and precision of these "hits." 2. Place three darts near each other in the outer ring. Ask the question on accuracy and precision again. 3. Place three darts in various places in the outer rings. Ask the question again.

**Results:** In step 1, accuracy and precision are high. In step 2, precision is high and accuracy is low. In step 3, accuracy and precision are low.

## Answers to Questions

**Page 17**

1. All measurements are comparisons between the quantity being measured and a standard quantity. It is only in this way that measurements can be objective.
2. Calculating using SI metric units is easier than

calculating using English units because quantities that are not whole numbers are expressed as decimals rather than as fractions.

3. meter, m; kilogram, kg; kelvin, K; second, s

### Page 19

4. *kilo-*, 1000; *centi-*, 0.01; *milli-*, 0.001
5. cm, kg, mm, s, K
6. The kilogram is the only SI base unit that contains an SI prefix.
7. **a.** hectosecond, hs; **b.** millimeter, mm; **c.** kilogram, kg; **d.** microgram, $\mu$g
8. **a.** mass; **b.** length; **c.** temperature; **d.** time
9. **a.** 1000; **b.** 1/1000; **c.** 1/100; **d.** 1/1 000 000

### Page 21

10. *Base units:* **b.** kg, kilogram; **d.** s, second; **e.** K, kelvin; **g.** m, meter. *Derived units:* **a.** m$^2$, square meter; **c.** m/s, meter per second; **f.** m$^3$, cubic meter
11. The unit is the pascal, i.e., kilograms per meter per square second, or kg/m·s$^2$.

### Page 24

12. The newton (force) = kg·m/s$^2$; area = m$^2$
    Pressure = force/area = kg·m/s$^2$ ÷ m$^2$ = kg/m·s$^2$

### Page 26

13. cubic centimeter; volume
14. mass; kilogram
15. kilogram, gram, and milligram
16. (10 cm)$^3$ = 1000 cm$^3$ = 1000 mL = 1 L; yes; because 1 mL = 1/1000 L
17. False. Cubic meters are derived by calculation and can be used to measure any volume.

### Page 28

18. 5.9°C

### Page 30

19. Precision describes the closeness to one another of measurements of the same quantity.
20. Accuracy describes how close a measurement is to the true value.
21. Using a defective measuring device can result in measurements that are precise but not accurate.

### Page 31

22. All the digits in a measurement that have values known with certainty, plus one digit that is estimated.
23. There are three significant figures and one uncertain figure.

### Page 32

24. **a.** 13.2 ± 0.05 m; **b.** 20.15 ± 0.005 cm

### Page 35

25. **d.** 432 m$^2$

26. **b.** 0.21 cm$^2$
27. **a.** 67
28. **a.** 0.7863 g/cm$^3$

### Page 36

29. 346.9 g
30. 22.04 m
31. 15.236 s
32. 3.50 cm

### Page 37

33. It would mean that the true value is greater than the observed value.
34. % error = $\dfrac{(2490 \text{ cm}^3 - 2500 \text{ cm}^3)}{2500 \text{ cm}^3} \times 100\% = -0.40\%$
35. [(1.43 − 1.42) g/1.42 g] × 100% = 0.7%

## Chapter Review

### Page 38, Content Review

1. A quantity is a term for something that can be measured, such as length.
2. Five quantities that one might use in the kitchen are volume, mass, time, temperature, and length.
3. A measurement of quantity consists of a number followed by a unit of measure, e.g., 16 tons.
4. Three units of measurement associated with an automobile are miles/hour, miles/gallon, and horsepower.
5. The quantities being measured in question 4, above, are speed, fuel consumption, and power, respectively.
6. meter, m; kilogram, kg; second, s; kelvin, K; mole, mol; ampere, A; candela, cd
7. The five SI base units commonly used by chemists are the meter, the kilogram, the second, the mole, and the kelvin.
8. **a.** A; **b.** m; **c.** s; **d.** K; **e.** kg
9. Two advantages of the SI system as compared with the English system are (1) decimals are used rather than fractions and (2) converting from one SI unit to another is simpler.
10. **a.** centimeter; **b.** meter; **c.** gram; **d.** kilogram; **e.** second; **f.** millimeter; **g.** centisecond
11. **a.** cg; **b.** km; **c.** s
12. **a.** 100 cm × 1 meter/100 cm = 1 m
    **b.** 1000 cm × 1 m/100 cm = 10 m
    **c.** 1000 m × 1 km/1000 m = 1 km

**d.** 10 km × 1000 m/1 km = 10 000 m

**e.** 100 mm × 1 cm/10 mm = 10 cm

**13. a.** centigram, cg; **b.** microsecond; $\mu$s; **c.** kilometer, km; **d.** nanometer, nm

**14. a.** 2.3 megabucks × 1000 megabucks/1 dollar = 2 300 000 dollars

**b.** 0.19 km × 1000 m/l km × 100 cm/1 m = 19 000 cm

**c.** 2.1 GW × 1000 MW/1 GW = 2100 MW

**d.** 37 mg × 1 g/1000 mg × 1  kg/1000 g = 0.000 037 kg

**e.** 68 $\mu$g × 1000 ng/1$\mu$g = 68 000 ng

**15.** SI derived units are combinations of SI base units.

**16. a.** 7.0 m²; **b.** 2.0 g/s; **c.** 4.5 kg/cm²; **d.** 25 kg·m/s²; **e.** 4.0 g/K

**17. a.** The newton is the SI unit of force. **b.** The newton is a kilogram·meter/second².

**18. a.** gram; **b.** millimeter; **c.** meter; **d.** cubic meter; **e.** kilogram; **f.** cubic centimeter

**19. a.** 4.0 m × 2.0 m × 0.25 m = 2.0 m³

**b.** 2.0 m³ × (100 cm/1 m)³ = 2.0 × 10⁶ cm³

**c.** 2.0 × 10⁶ cm³ × (1 mL/1 cm³) = 2.0 × 10⁶ mL

**d.** 2.0 × 10⁶ mL × (1 L/1000 mL) = 2.0 × 10³ L

**20.** One uncertain digit is reported.

**21.** One cause of uncertainty is the measuring instrument. The other cause is the person doing the measuring.

**22.** The measurements are precise because they are so close to each other. They are not accurate because they differ significantly from the true length of the bar, which is exactly one meter.

**23.** Assuming the bull's-eye to be the area aimed for, the placement of the arrows shows a lower accuracy (nearness to desired result) than precision (reproducibility).

**24. a.** 38.6°C has three significant figures. **b.** One. The 6 is the only uncertain digit.

**25. a.** 2; **b.** 3; **c.** 3; **d.** 4; **e.** 3; **f.** 3

**26.** A measurement would be reported as 18.0 cm instead of 18 cm to show that the measurement has three significant figures, not two, and that the zero is the uncertain figure, not the eight.

**27. a.** ±0.5 kg; **b.** ±0.005 g; **c.** ±50 km

**28.** 10.0 cm³ has three significant figures, and 9.6781 g has five. The quotient should be rounded to the smaller number of significant figures, three. The rounded answer is 0.968 g/cm³.

**29. a.** 14 cm²; **b.** 12.0 m²; **c.** 38 g/cm

**30. a.** 202.4 g; **b.** 185 m; **c.** 2.7 s; **d.** 42.0 kg

**31.** (11.00 s − 10.67 s) × 100% / 10.67 s = 3.1%

**32.** (19.81 g − 20.00 g) × 100% / 20.00 g = −0.95%

**33.** (3612 s − 3600 s) × 100% / 3600 s = 0.33%

## Page 40, Content Mastery

**34.** This problem involves multiplication, or moving the decimal. The quantity 9.73 has three significant figures, while the relationship 1 g = 100 cg involves defined quantities with infinite numbers of significant figures, so the three significant figures in 9.73 are what limits the number of significant figures in your answer.

**35. a.** (12 km)(1000 m/1 km) × (4.5 mm)(1 m/1000 mm) = 54 m²

**b.** (8.6 g)(1 kg/1000 g) / (2.0 cm³)(1 m/100 cm)³ = 4300 kg/m³

**c.** (90 km)(1000 m/1 km)/(1 hr)(60 min/1 hr) (60 s/1 min) = 25 m/s

**36. a.** The absolute error is |458 K − 453 K| or |453 K − 458 K| = 5 K

**b.** The percent error is |458 K − 453 K| × 100% / 458 K = 1%

**37. a.** Since 1 kg = 1000 g, move the decimal three places to the right: 56.8 kg = 56 800 g. **b.** Since 1 g = 1000 mg, move the decimal three more places to the right: 56 800 g = 56 800 000 mg

**38. a.** The chewing gum found stuck to the bottom of the balance will make every object appear heavier. Therefore, precision will not be affected, but accuracy will be affected. **b.** A balance placed in a very drafty area will randomly make objects heavier or lighter. Therefore, both precision and accuracy will be affected.

**39. a.** kg; **b.** ms; **c.** cm

**40. c, d, f, h,** and **i** can be scientifically measured. Thickness is a quantity of length that can be measured—i.e., Thickness = l. Area is a quantity of length times length that can be measured—i.e., Area = (l)(l). Volume is a quantity of length times length times length that can be measured —i.e., Volume = (l)(l)(l). Speed is a quantity of length divided by time that can be measured—i.e., Speed = l/t. Density is a quantity of mass divided by length cubed that can be measured— i.e., Density = m/l³. All other terms are subjective and/or qualitative terms.

**41. a.** Volume = (length)³ = m³.

**b.** Concentration = amount/volume = mol/m³.

**c.** Acceleration = distance/time² = m/s².

**d.** Density = mass/(length)³ = kg/m³.

**e.** Speed = distance/time = m/s.

**f.** Temperature = K.

**42. a.** Absolute error = 100.0°C − 98.6°C = 1.4°C

**b.** Percent error = 1.4°C × 100%/100.0°C = 1.4%

**c.** Because all three measurements are the same, precision is very good. Because the measured value is off by more than its calibration, the accuracy is marginal at best. That is to say, the thermometer has markings that imply measurements are valid to the nearest 0.2°C when, in fact, accuracy is off by more than 1°C.

**43.** Since 1 mg = 0.001 g or 1 g = 1000 mg, move the decimal three places to the right: 1 carat = 0.2 g = 200 mg.

**44.** Because 1 ns = 0.000 000 001 s and 1 s = 1 000 000 000 ns, move the decimal nine places to the left: 30 ns = 0.000 000 030 s.

**45. a.** $(3.0 \text{ yd}^3)(3 \text{ ft/yd})^3 = 81 \text{ ft}^3$

**b.** $(2.0000 \text{ yd}^3)(3 \text{ ft/yd})^3(12 \text{ in/ft})^3 = 93312 \text{ in}^3$

**c.** (28 lb/gal)(16 oz/lb)(1 gal/8 pt) = 56 oz/pt

**d.** (55.0 mi/hr)(5280 ft/mi)(12 in/ft)
        (1 hr/60 min)(1 min/60 s) = 968 in/s
Times will vary (approximately 10–15 minutes).

**46. a.** (3.0 metric tons)(1000 kg/ton)(1000 g/kg) = 3 000 000 g

**b.** $(2.0000 \text{ m}^3)(100 \text{ cm/m})^3 = 2 000 000 \text{ cm}^3$

**c.** $(28 \text{ kg/m}^3)(1000 \text{ g/kg})(1 \text{ m/100 cm})^3 = 0.028 \text{ g/cm}^3$

**d.** (55.0 km/s)(1000 m/km)(100 cm/m) = 5 500 000 cm/s
Times will vary (approximately 5–10 minutes).

**47.** If students are proficient in using scientific notation, they should complete question 46 in less time than question 45.

**48.** A decisecond, ds, is ¹⁄₁₀ of the base unit of time.

**49.** 10.00 cm has four significant figures and one uncertain figure.

**50.** 7.328 g/2.1 cm³ = 3.489 523 81 g/cm³; rounding to two significant figures gives 3.5 g/cm³.

**51.** The addition yields an answer of 152.8152 kg; rounding to one decimal place gives 152.8 kg.

**52.** The answer should have no decimal places because 12 dollars has no decimal places. The answer will have two significant figures.

**53. a.** 2 × (168.2 ± 0.1 cm) + 2 × (14.4 ± 0.1 cm) = 365.2 ± 0.4 cm

**b.** To one decimal place, the perimeter is 365.2 cm.

**c.** (168.2 cm) × (14.4 cm) × (0.6 cm) = 1453.248 cm³; rounding to one significant figure gives 1000 cm³.

**54.** Answers will vary. **c.** Usually the item that has the most uncertainty is the item that limits the number of significant figures in the total.

**55.** 504.7 K − 505.12 K = −0.42 K; rounding to one decimal place gives −0.4 K.
(−0.4 K) × 100%/(505.12 K) = −0.79 189 103%; rounding to one significant figure gives −0.1%.

### Page 41, Concept Mastery

**56. Concept:** *When volume is measured by the displacement of water, the mass of the object displacing the water is immaterial.*

*Solution:* The water levels in the two cylinders will be the same. It is the volume of the solid that is added that causes the additional volume in the graduated cylinder. Because both the lead ball and the wood ball have the same diameter, they have the same volume. The mass of the object is not important.

**57. Concept:** *Volume cannot be computed by simply multiplying the length × width × height. The "hole" in the object must be subtracted out, or the object must be divided into parts that are added together.*

*Solution:* First, divide the object into two rectangular boxes. One is 4 cm by 3 cm by 2 cm. Multiplying length by width by height yields a volume of 24 cm³. The second box is 2 cm by 1 cm by 2 cm. Multiplying length by width by height yields a volume of 4 cm³. The volume of the object is the sum of these two volumes: 24 cm³ + 4 cm³ = 28 cm³.

**58. Concept:** *The shape of an object does not affect its volume.*

*Solution:* The volumes of the two configurations are equal. The volume of a given amount of matter is independent of its arrangement or shape. Twelve 1-cm³ cubes will always have a volume of 12 cm³.

**59. Concept:** *The surface area of an object is affected by its shape.*

*Solution:* The surface area of a side of a 1-cm³ cube is 1 cm². The surface area of the first arrangement is (6 cm²)(4 sides) + (4 cm²)(2 sides) = 32 cm². The surface area of the second arrangement is (12 cm²)(2 sides) + (2 cm²)(2 sides) + (6 cm²)(2 sides) = 40 cm². They are not the same. The surface area of a given volume is dependent on arrangement or shape.

60. ***Concept:*** *When a solid is added to water, it displaces the water, and volume rises. Sand does not absorb water.*

    *Solution:* When 10 cm³ of sand is added to 50 cm³ of water, some of the water will be replacing the spaces between sand particles that had been filled by air. The new volume, therefore, will be more than 50 cm³ but less than 60 cm³.

61. ***Concept:*** *When a small amount of water is added to a solid, the water displaces the air in the spaces between the molecules of the solid.*

    *Solution:* All of the 5 cm³ of water will fill up spaces between sand particles previously filled by air. The volume will remain at 80 cm³.

## Page 42, Cumulative Review

62. **a.** The temperature of the water is the independent variable because the amount of sugar that will dissolve in the water samples is dependent on the samples' temperature. **b.** The amount of sugar that dissolves should be graphed on the vertical axis because the amount of sugar dissolving is the dependent variable.

63. Variables that might affect the length of time a log burns in a fireplace include the size of the log, the type of wood, the dryness of the wood, and the design of the fireplace.

64. The explanation in the magazine article is not a scientific law. Scientific laws describe natural events but do not explain them.

65. If a super-cooled gas did not behave according to the kinetic theory of gases, the theory would probably be modified to fit the new observations.

66. Answers will vary. Examples: **a.** A pure scientist might learn the effect of humidity on the rate of rusting. **b.** An applied scientist might develop a new way to protect iron from rusting.

67. Answers will vary. However, in all cases the samples of cloth should be washed the same number of times in the same way, and the procedure for testing flammability should be the same for all samples.

## Page 42, Critical Thinking

68. The order from the smallest to the greatest is **b, a, d, e, c.**

69. Possible problems include errors in conversions, slowed down research, and increased difficulty in calculations depending on the type of unit used, for example, fractions.

70. A micrometer caliper is a more accurate instrument than the metric ruler and is the instrument of choice for measuring very small thicknesses.

71. Both precision and accuracy deal with measurement; precision is the ability to reproduce a measurement, while accuracy deals with how close the measurement is to the actual value.

72. Possible causes include the possibility that all students may have been using a defective instrument; they may have all been taught an inaccurate way to measure or to use the instrument; chemical X may be of unknown origin; chemical X may have been contaminated.

73. **a.** penicillin; **b.** pennies; **c.** time for the job

## Page 43, Challenge Problems

74. One caplet = 500 mg aspirin

    One regular aspirin tablet
    = 5 grains aspirin
    = 5 grains × (0.0647989 g/grain)×(1000 mg/g)
    = 324 mg
    The caplet contains more aspirin than a regular aspirin tablet.

75. $E = kg \times m^2/s^2 = (mass)(m/s)^2 = (mass)c^2 = mc^2$. Einstein first proposed this equation.

76. Answers will vary. Examples: can of soda, 354 cm³; quart of milk, 0.946 L; 10-ounce package of frozen vegetables, 284 g; 5-pound bag of potatoes, 2.27 kg; 4.6-ounce tube of toothpaste, 130 g.

77. Only one weight, either having a mass of 1 kg or 40 kg, is needed if you adjust the fulcrum of the balance; otherwise, a minimum of five weights— 1 kg, 3 kg, 5 kg, 10 kg, and 20 kg—is necessary. Other answers are also possible.

78. **a.** The mass could be as great as 3.215 g or as little as 2.832 g, a difference of about 0.4 g, so one decimal place should be reported. **b.** The total of the values is 15.186 g, giving an average of 3.0372 g, which rounds to 3.0 g. Therefore, the data can be expressed as 3.0 ± 0.2 g.

# Problem Solving

## Chapter Planning Guide

| Text Section | Labs (Lab Manual) and Demonstrations (TE) | Supplementary Materials (Teacher's Resource Book) |
|---|---|---|
| **3-1** Introduction, p. 45 | Demo 3-1: Dimensional-Analysis Cards, p. TG-80 | Skills Development: Algebraic Equations, p. SD-12 Non-SI Supplementary Problems, p. 3-4 |
| **3-2** Dimensional Analysis, pp. 45-50 | | |
| **3-3** Scientific Notation, pp. 50-53 | Lab 4: Uncertainty in Measurement | Transparency Master: Examples of Scientific Notation, p. 3-1 Review Activity: Scientific Notation, p. 3-2 Skills Development: Exponents and Scientific Notation, p. SD-15 Lab Skills Test, p. SD-29 |
| **3-4** Using Scientific Notation for Expressing the Correct Number of Significant Figures, pp. 54-55 | | |
| **3-5** A General Procedure for Solving Problems, pp. 55-58 | | Practice Problems, p. 3-3 Critical and Creative Thinking: Problem Solving, p. CCT-75 |
| **Career** Research Chemist, p. 57 | | |
| | | Test—Form A, p. AT-10 Alternate Test—Form B, p. BT-10 |

☐ Core  ☐ Advanced  ☐ Optional

## Chapter Overview

In Chapter 3, we stress the importance in chemistry of developing skills in problem solving. We explain the use of dimensional analysis in converting units of measurement, and students practice using this method. Then scientific notation is presented. We explain the rules for calculating with numbers in scientific notation and describe how it is used to express the correct number of significant figures. The chapter closes with a general problem-solving procedure.

## Chapter Objectives

After students have completed this chapter they will be able to:

1. Convert from one SI unit to another using dimensional analysis. *3-1 to 3-3*
2. Express large and small numbers in scientific notation. *3-3 and 3-4*
3. Be familiar with a general procedure for solving problems. *3-5*

# Teaching Suggestions

## 3-1 Introduction, p. 45, and

## 3-2 Dimensional Analysis, pp. 45-50

| Planning Guide | |
| --- | --- |
| **Labs (Lab Manual)<br>and Demonstrations (TE)** | **Supplementary Materials<br>(Teacher's Resource Book)** |
| Demo 3-1:<br>Dimensional-Analysis<br>Cards, p. TG-80 | Skills Development:<br>Algebraic Equations,<br>p. SD-12<br>Non-SI Supplementary<br>Problems, p. 3-4 |

■ To get started, you might have students imagine being a shopkeeper who is asked by a visitor from France what an item that is priced in dollars costs in francs. Then suppose the next customer is from Britain and wants to know the price of the item in pounds. With the assumption that the current exchange rates, as reported in the daily newspaper, are available, ask students how they would approach this type of problem. To make the problem a bit more complex, ask how, given only the exchange rates between dollars and the other two currencies, the price in pounds could be converted into the price in francs. You may then introduce the concepts of conversion factors, factor labels, and dimensional analysis by having students do Demonstration 3-1, "Dimensional-Analysis Cards."

■ Be sure students understand how using the appropriate conversion factor will lead to the correct unit in the answer. They should see that the right factor causes the other unit in the fraction to be "cancelled," or divided out, while the incorrect factor does not. For Sample Problem 5 in the text, as for the conversion of pounds into francs in the previous discussion, have students note that two equalities are involved.

■ **Application.** You may want to discuss with students the widespread use of dimensional analysis in everyday life. The calculation of gross weekly pay is a simple case: hours × rate per hour. Grocery bills contain many "number of items × cost per item" calculations. The cost to carpet or to paint a room is computed by dimensional analysis. The cost of pencils to a school district is determined in a manner such as "number of students × number of pencils per student × cost per pencil."

■ **Concept Mastery.** Emphasize that although the factor-label method of solving problems can be helpful, students must be careful not to substitute this method for reasoning. You can use Concept Mastery question 31 (chapter-end question) to help students realize that the factor-label method has its limitations.

## 3-3 Scientific Notation, pp. 50-53, and

## 3-4 Using Scientific Notation for Expressing the Correct Number of Significant Figures, pp. 54-55

| Planning Guide | |
| --- | --- |
| **Labs (Lab Manual)<br>and Demonstrations (TE)** | **Supplementary Materials<br>(Teacher's Resource Book)** |
| Lab 4: Uncertainty in<br>Measurement | Transparency Master:<br>Examples of Scientific<br>Notation, p. 3-1<br>Review Activity: Scientific<br>Notation, p. 3-1<br>Skills Development:<br>Exponents and Scientific<br>Notation, p. SD-15 |

■ Remind students that although in many texts groups of three digits in very large and very small numbers are separated by commas, spaces are used in the SI system, as described in Section 2-2. However, we often express these numbers in scientific notation, i.e., as the product of two factors that includes the correct number of significant figures. Be sure students understand how to rewrite numbers of any size in scientific notation and can apply the rules for computation with such numbers.

Have students review the topic of significant figures (Section 2-11) and then ask them to indicate the number of significant figures in measurements written in scientific notation. Emphasize that the answers to problems using scientific notation must show the correct number of significant figures according to the rules in Section 2-13. Be sure students can also apply correctly the rules in text Figure 3-6.

■ Laboratory 4, "Uncertainty in Measurement," is appropriate for students to do at this time. The lab reinforces and integrates a number of concepts studied in Chapters 2 and 3—calibration, accuracy, precision, significant figures, and uncertainty—and the use of these concepts in problem-solving calculations. In the lab, students make measurements of mass, length, temperature, and volume, using calibrated instruments. They report data using the correct number of significant figures and scientific notation and indicate the uncertainty of that data.

■ **Concept Mastery.** You can use Concept Mastery question 30 in the Chapter Review to help students reinforce their understanding of the limitations of measuring instruments. Instead of simply telling students to read the graduated cylinder to one decimal place, discuss how this limitation was determined. The scale is marked in milliliters, so the number of milliliters can be read directly off the scale and the tenths of a milliliter must be estimated. In addition, the question points out how writing a number in scientific notation accounts for the number of significant zeros in the measurement.

## 3-5 A General Procedure for Solving Problems, pp. 55-58

| Planning Guide | |
|---|---|
| **Labs (Lab Manual) and Demonstrations (TE)** | **Supplementary Materials (Teacher's Resource Book)** |
| | Practice Problems, p. 3-2 Critical and Creative Thinking: Problem Solving, p. CCT-75 |

■ Discuss with students the advantages of understanding the meaning and logic of a problem as opposed to the all-too-common approach of memorizing the procedure in a sample problem. Ask students to apply the five steps of the general problem-solving procedure to common personal problems they face, such as the choice of a college or a career, or smaller problems they deal with in their everyday lives.

■ **Critical Thinking.** While students have had experience solving well-defined problems, they are often at a loss when it comes to tackling a problem they have not seen before. The Critical and Creative Thinking worksheet "Problem Solving" provides a framework for approaching such open-ended problems. By working through the thought process of problem solving, students will acquire a skill that has practical applications for both chemistry and "real life" problems.

# Demonstration

## 3-1 Dimensional-Analysis Cards

**Overview:** By playing a domino-like game, students learn a technique that can be used to set up factor-label problems. By converting money values from one currency into another, they learn to convert measurements expressed in one unit into other units.

**Materials:** demonstration-size dominoes made from poster board; demonstration-size cards showing money equalities above and below a middle line, such as the line on the dominoes (the back sides of these cards should show the inverse equalities); demonstration-size cards showing metric mass equalities (conversion factors), with the back sides showing the inverse relationships.

**Advance Preparation:** Use poster board, scissors, and a marking pen to prepare the domino cards shown in Figure 3-1, along with any others you may wish to prepare to make the choice process more challenging.

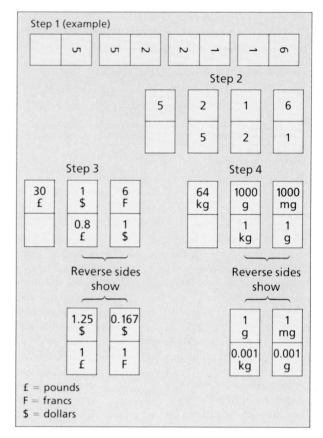

**Figure 3-1**

**Procedure:** 1. Place a domino card that has only one number on it on top of the chalkboard horizontally, and tell your students you want to "play" dominoes until the last number showing is a 6. (See step 1 in Figure 3-1.) Review the rules for domino play, if necessary. Explain that the left end of each domino that is laid down must contain a number that matches the number on the right end of the preceding domino. Ask them to select the domino that should be placed next to the one on the board, and continue to do this until all of the proper cards are used to end up with a 6 at the end. 2. Now place each of the cards in a vertical position so that, for example, the first domino shows a given number on its top half (above its center line) and the next card shows that number on the bottom. (See step 2 in Figure 3-1.) 3. Tell your students you are going to use a variation of the preceding technique to solve a type of problem. Ask them to determine how many French francs are equal to 30 British pounds, using cards that show approximate equalities between francs and U.S. dollars (6 francs/1 dollar) and between U.S. dollars and British pounds (1 dollar/0.8 pound). On the chalkboard, place a card that shows 30 pounds on top of the center line and nothing below the line, and ask a student volunteer to place the other cards (pounds shown below dollars, and dollars shown below francs, respectively) in the proper manner. Have the class determine the answer after the correct setup has been established so as to yield francs as the answer. (See step 3.) 4. Display the cards that contain metric–metric mass conversion factors. On the chalkboard, place a card that says "64 kg" and ask students to determine how many milligrams that quantity equals. Tell students to set up the conversion-factor cards in the proper manner and then determine the answer. (See step 4.)

**Results:** See the accompanying figure. The correct setup in step 3 yields

$$30 \text{ pounds} \times \frac{1 \text{ dollar}}{0.8 \text{ pound}} \times \frac{6 \text{ francs}}{1 \text{ dollar}} = 250 \text{ francs}$$

The correct setup in step 4 yields

$$64 \text{ kg} \times \frac{1000 \text{ g}}{1 \text{ kg}} \times \frac{1000 \text{ mg}}{1 \text{ g}}$$
$$= 64\,000\,000 \text{ mg} = 6.4 \times 10^7 \text{ mg}$$

## Answers to Questions

**Page 50**

**1. a.** 1 meter = 1000 millimeters; **b.** 1 meter/1000 millimeters and 1000 millimeters/1 meter;
   **c.** ? mm = 5.43 m × 1000 mm/1 m; **d.** 5430 mm

**2. a.** 1 kg = 1000 g and 1 g = 1000 mg; therefore, 1 kg = 1 000 000 mg; **b.** 1 kg/1 000 000 mg and 100 000 mg/1 kg; **c.** ? kg = 0.642 mg × 1 kg/1 000 000 mg; **d.** 0.000 000 642 kg

**3. a.** 1 km = 1000 m; 1 m = 100 cm; **b.** 1 km/1000 m and 1000 m/1 km; 1 m/100 cm and 100 cm/1 m; **c.** ? km = 86 000 cm × 1 m/100 cm × 1 km/1000 m; **d.** 0.860 km

**Page 53**

**4. a.** $4.0 \times 10^1$;   **b.** $4.00 \times 10^2$;   **c.** $4 \times 10^{-1}$;
   **d.** $4.04 \times 10^2$;   **e.** $4.004 \times 10^3$;   **f.** $4.400 \times 10^3$;
   **g.** $4 \times 10^{-3}$;   **h.** $4.04 \times 10^{-2}$

**5. a.** 610; **b.** 6010; **c.** 0.060;   **d.** 66; **e.** 0.000601;
   **f.** 60 100

**6. a.** $4.20 \times 10^2$;   **b.** $4.8000 \times 10^4$;   **c.** $3 \times 10^{-2}$;
   **d.** $7.8 \times 10^{-4}$

**7. a.**   2400;   **b.**   623 000;   **c.**   0.301;   **d.**   0.0082;
   **e.** 0.0000543;   **f.** 0.00036

**8. a.** $1.2 \times 10^{10}$;   **b.** $1.8 \times 10^3$;   **c.** $8.0 \times 10^{-2}$;
   **d.** $3.0 \times 10^2$;   **e.** $4.0 \times 10^{-3}$;   **f.** $5.0 \times 10^5$;
   **g.** $5.0 \times 10^4$

**Page 55**

**9. a.** 2; **b.** 3; **c.** 2; **d.** 3
**10. a.** 4; **b.** 3; *c.* 1

**Page 58**

**11.** $1.84 \text{ g/cm}^3 = ? \text{ g/24.2 cm}^3$
   Mass of acid = $24.2 \text{ cm}^3 \times 1.84 \text{ g/cm}^3 = 44.5 \text{ g}$

## Chapter Review  ③

**1.** Problem solving is an important skill that you can learn through practice. The method you use to solve problems in chemistry also works for problems you face in your everyday life.

**2.** Dimensional analysis is an approach to solving problems in which a given number and its unit are converted to the answer through the use of conversion factors.

**3.** Use dimensional analysis to convert cm to mm. 846 cm = ? mm
$$846 \text{ cm} \times \frac{10 \text{ mm}}{1 \text{ cm}} = 8460 \text{ mm}$$

**4.** 35 g = ? kg
$$35 \text{ g} \times \frac{1 \text{ kg}}{1000 \text{ g}} = 0.035 \text{ kg}$$

**5.** In this solution, the given number (1.8 kg) is multiplied by 2 conversion factors to get the answer.
$$1.8 \text{ kg} \times \frac{1000 \text{ g}}{1 \text{ kg}} \times \frac{1000 \text{ mg}}{1 \text{ g}} = 1\,800\,000 \text{ mg}$$

**6.** $5420 \text{ cm} = \dfrac{1 \text{ m}}{100 \text{ cm}} = 54.2 \text{ m}$

**7. a.** 1 g = 1000 mg
$$\frac{1 \text{ g}}{1000 \text{ mg}} \text{ and } \frac{1000 \text{ mg}}{1 \text{ g}}$$

   **b.** 0.725 g = ? mg
$$0.725 \text{ g} \times \frac{1000 \text{ mg}}{1 \text{ g}} = 725 \text{ mg}$$

   **c.** 163 mg = ? g
$$163 \text{ mg} \times \frac{1 \text{ g}}{1000 \text{ mg}} = 0.163 \text{ g}$$

**8.** Assuming that a trailing zero is not significant,
   **a.** $6 \times 10^2$;   **b.** $7.77 \times 10^3$;   **c.** $1.25 \times 10^{-1}$;
   **d.** $2.5 \times 10^5$;   **e.** $2.5 \times 10^{-5}$

**9. a.** 0.0025;   **b.** 0.000 006 25;   **c.** 505;   **d.** 20;
   **e.** 0.000010;   **f.** 81 000

**10. a.** $1.0 \times 10^{-6}$;   **b.** $1.0 \times 10^8$;   **c.** $6.0 \times 10^2$;
   **d.** $2.0 \times 10^2$;   **e.** $3.0 \times 10^5$;   **f.** $4.1 \times 10^1$

**11.** $302 \times 30.0 = 9060 = 9.06 \times 10^3$

**12.** $\dfrac{9.03 \times 10^{-2}}{3.00 \times 10^{-3}} = \dfrac{9.03}{3.00} \times 10^{-2--3} = 3.01 \times 10^1$

**13. a.** You cannot tell how many significant figures are in 150 from the number. It has either 2 or 3 significant figures, depending on whether the trail-

ing zero is significant or is just a place holder.
**b.** You can be sure about $1.50 \times 10^2$. It has 3 significant figures.

14. **a.** 4; Zeroes in the middle of a number are significant.
 **b.** 3; Every non-zero digit is significant.
 **c.** 4; The trailing zero is significant because it is to the right of the decimal point.
 **d.** 1; Leading zeroes are never significant.
 **e.** 2; The last zero is significant; the first 3 are not.
 **f.** 3; Since the trailing zero to the right of the decimal point is significant, the zero in the middle of the number must also be significant.

15. 1) Read the problem carefully and make a list of knowns and unknowns. 2) Look up any information you need. 3) Work out a plan for solving the problem. 4) Following your plan, do the arithmetic and get an answer. 5) Check your work.

16. $\text{density} = \dfrac{\text{mass}}{\text{volume}} = \dfrac{27.50 \text{ g}}{2.62 \text{ cm}^3} = 10.5 \text{ g/cm}^3$

17. $\text{mass} = \text{density} \times \text{volume}$
 $= 1.11 \text{ g/cm}^3 \times 45.8 \text{ cm}^3 = 50.8 \text{ g}$

### Page 60, Content Mastery

18. Because the number of significant figures is ambiguous, 200 is either $2 \times 10^2$ or $2.0 \times 10^2$ or $2.00 \times 10^2$.

19. **a.** $7.5 \times 10^1$;  **b.** $7.05 \times 10^2$;  **c.** $7.5 \times 10^3$;
 **d.** $7.5 \times 10^{-3}$

20. **a.** $920 \text{ cm} = ? \text{ m}$

 $920 \text{ cm} \times \dfrac{1 \text{ m}}{100 \text{ cm}} = 9.20 \text{ m}$

 **b.** $32500 \text{ g} = ? \text{ kg}$

 $32500 \text{ g} \times \dfrac{1 \text{ kg}}{1000 \text{ g}} = 32.5 \text{ kg}$

 **c.** $74.6 \text{ cm} = ? \text{ mm}$

 $74.6 \text{ cm} \times \dfrac{10 \text{ mm}}{1 \text{ cm}} = 746 \text{ mm}$

21. $\text{density} = \dfrac{\text{mass}}{\text{volume}} \qquad \text{volume} = \dfrac{\text{mass}}{\text{density}}$

 $\text{volume} = \dfrac{20.0 \text{ g}}{1.26 \text{ g/cm}^3} = 15.9 \text{ cm}^3 = 1.59 \times 10^1 \text{ cm}^3$

22. **a.** $32000$;  **b.** $0.00030$;  **c.** $0.302$;  **d.** $320$

23. $111 \text{ g} \times \dfrac{1 \text{ kg}}{1000 \text{ g}} = 0.111 \text{ kg}$

24. $935 \text{ mm} \times \dfrac{1 \text{ m}}{1000 \text{ mm}} = 0.935 \text{ m}$

25. **a.** $(5.0 \times 10^3)(3.0 \times 10^{-2}) = 15.0 \times 10^{3+-2} =$
 $15.0 \times 10^1 = 1.5 \times 10^2$
 **b.** $(4.4 \times 10^{-2})(2.2 \times 10^{-7}) = 9.7 \times 10^{-2+ -7} =$
 $9.7 \times 10^{-9}$

**c.** $\dfrac{1.8 \times 10^5}{6.0 \times 10^2} = 0.30 \times 10^{5-2} = 3.0 \times 10^2$

**d.** $\dfrac{3.6 \times 10^{-2}}{1.8 \times 10^{-2}} = 2.0 \times 10^{-2--2} = 2.0$

26. **a.** 4; All zeroes in the middle of a number are significant.
 **b.** 1; Leading zeroes are never significant.
 **c.** 1
 **d.** 3; The trailing zeroes are significant because they are to the right of the decimal point. The leading zeroes are not significant.

27. $\text{density} = \dfrac{\text{mass}}{\text{volume}} = \dfrac{64.8 \text{ g}}{54.0 \text{ cm}^3} = 1.20 \text{ g/cm}^3$

28. **a.** 1;  **b.** 2;  **c.** 3;  **d.** 5

29. $255 \text{ km} \times \dfrac{1 \text{ hr}}{85 \text{ km}} = 3.0 \text{ hrs}$

### Page 60, Concept Mastery

30. ***Concept:*** *The number of significant figures in a measurement depends on the markings on the instrument.*
 *Solution:* No, $15.00 \text{ cm}^3$ is not correct because it has too many significant figures. The correct volume is $15.0 \text{ cm}^3$. The 15 is read directly off the scale, and the 0 is estimated.

31. ***Concept:*** *Dimensional analysis is not always useful. You should solve problems from a basic understanding of the concepts, not by mechanically applying a particular method.*
 *Solution:* Dimensional analysis does not help with this problem because the unit in the numerator is the same as the unit in the denominator for both conversion factors. Dimensional analysis does not tell you whether the correct conversion factor is $\dfrac{93.3 \text{ kPa}}{99.9 \text{ kPa}}$ or $\dfrac{99.9 \text{ kPa}}{93.3 \text{ kPa}}$ because the units cancel out in both cases.

### Page 61, Cumulative Review

32. **d.** Since one of the dimensions (3.78 cm) has only 3 significant figures, the answer must have only 3 significant figures: $470 \text{ cm}^3$.

33. **b.** $25.0 \text{ m} \times \dfrac{100 \text{ cm}}{1 \text{ m}} = 2500 \text{ cm}$

34. Absolute error is the difference between the measured and the true value. Percent error is absolute error divided by the true value, times 100%.
 **a.** $81.0°C - 79.5°C = 1.5°C$ absolute error

**b.** $\dfrac{1.5°C}{79.5°C} \times 100\% = 1.9\%$ error

35. A controlled experiment is one in which a variable is held constant.

36. Pure science is the pursuit of truth for its own sake. Applied science is the search for a solution to a problem, an attempt to put knowledge to some practical use.

37. **a.** centimeter, cm; **b.** milligram, mg; **c.** kilogram, kg; **d.** nanosecond, ns

## Page 61, Critical Thinking

38. Using scientific notation makes handling large or small numbers more convenient. It also completely eliminates the ambiguity about the number of significant figures.

39. Yes, you can multiply a quantity by 1 without changing the value of the quantity. Because each conversion factor is a form of 1, you can multiply a quantity by as many conversion factors as you want to. Keep going until you get the number into the desired units.

40. The sixth-grade student assumed that each piece of information stated in the problem had to be used in solving the problem. This assumption is incorrect. The solution to this sample problem is the same regardless of the identity of the acid. Often, you have more information than you need to solve a problem. Part of the skill in problem solving is determining which information you do need and how to get it.

41. Solving chemistry problems can help you to improve your problem-solving skills. Solving problems requires you to list the known information, identify the answer you are trying to find, gather needed information, set up the problem, do any required calculations, and check your answer. You can apply each of these steps to solving problems in everyday life as well as solving problems in chemistry.

42. A number by itself is an incomplete answer to a numerical chemistry problem. A complete answer includes both the number and its unit.

## Page 61, Challenge Problems

43. **a.** Answers will vary. Students may choose to do Sample Problem 9 as a proportionality, for example. **b.** Advantages and disadvantages will depend on which problem students chose to do and what steps they followed to reach a solution.

44. $1.7 \times 10^{30}$

# Matter

## Chapter Planning Guide

| Text Section | Labs (Lab Manual) and Demonstrations (TE) | Supplementary Materials (Teacher's Resource Book) |
|---|---|---|
| **4-1** Mass, pp. 63-64<br><br>**4-2** Varieties of Matter—Elements and Compounds, pp. 64-66<br><br>**4-3** Varieties of Matter—Mixtures, pp. 66-69 | Demo 4-1: Elements, Compounds, and Mixtures, p. TG-87<br>Demo 4-2: Classification of and Separation of Matter, p. TG-88<br>Demo 4-3: Solutions versus Pure Substances, p. TG-89 | Transparency Master: Elements, Compounds, and Mixtures, p. 4-2 |
| **4-4** Properties, pp. 69-70<br><br>**4-5** Density, pp. 70-74 | Lab 5: Density Determination<br>Demo 4-4: Sink or Swim, p. TG-89<br>Demo 4-5: Density of Iron, p. TG-89 | Transparency Master: Densities of Some Common Substances at 20°C, p. 4-3<br>Open-Ended Experiment: The Density of Sand, p. 4-5<br>Practice Problems, p. 4-9<br>Non-SI Supplementary Problems, p. 4-10 |
| **Can You Explain This?** Layers of Liquids, p. 75 | | |
| **4-6** Changes of Phase, pp. 74-75<br><br>**4-7** Physical and Chemical Properties, pp. 75-76<br><br>**4-8** Physical and Chemical Change, pp. 76-77<br><br>**4-9** Conservation of Mass, pp. 77-78 | Lab 6: Physical and Chemical Change<br>Demo 4-6: Properties of Matter, p. TG-90<br>Demo 4-7: Changes in Matter, p. TG-90 | Review Activity. Classification of Matter, p. 4-7<br>Review Activity: Properties, p. 4-8<br>Critical and Creative Thinking: Classifying, p. CCT-23 |
| **4-10** Relative Abundance, pp. 78-79<br><br>**4-11** Symbols of the Elements, pp. 79-80 | | Transparency Master: Distribution of Elements in the Earth's Crust, p. 4-4 |
| **Biography** George Washington Carver, p. 78 | | |
| | | Test—Form A, p. AT-13<br>Alternate Test—Form B, p. BT-13 |

☐ Core  ■ Advanced  ☐ Optional

# Chapter Overview

In Chapter 4, we define matter and explain why mass, not weight, is used as a measure of the quantity of matter. We classify matter into elements, compounds, and mixtures. The differences between extensive and intensive properties are discussed, and students solve density problems. The three phases of matter—gas, liquid, and solid—are characterized. The difference between physical properties and chemical properties is explained, and physical changes are differentiated from chemical changes. We describe the evidence that led Lavoisier to state the law of conservation of mass. The chapter closes with a description of the two states—free and combined—in which elements occur in nature, and symbols for some elements are given.

# Chapter Objectives

After students have completed this chapter, they will be able to:

1. Explain why mass is used as a measure of the quantity of matter.                               *4-1*
2. Describe the characteristics of elements, compounds, and mixtures.         *4-2, 4-3,* and *4-10*
3. Solve density problems by applying an understanding of the concept of density.      *4-4* and *4-5*
4. Distinguish between physical and chemical properties and physical and chemical change.   *4-6* to *4-8*
5. Demonstrate an understanding of the law of conservation of mass by applying it to a chemical reaction.                           *4-9* to *4-11*

# Teaching Suggestions

### 4-1 Mass, pp. 63-64,

### 4-2 Varieties of Matter—Elements and Compounds, pp. 64-65, and

### 4-3 Varieties of Matter—Mixtures, pp. 66-69

| Planning Guide | |
| --- | --- |
| **Labs (Lab Manual) and Demonstrations (TE)** | **Supplementary Materials (Teacher's Resource Book)** |
| Demo 4-1: Elements, Compounds, and Mixtures, p. TG-87 Demo 4-2: Classification and Separation of Matter, p. TG-88 Demo 4-3: Solutions versus Pure Substances, p. TG-89 | Transparency Master: Elements, Compounds, and Mixtures, p. 4-2 |

■ Display a lab balance and a spring scale and ask students what quantity each piece of equipment is used to measure. Although both balances and scales are commonly used to measure weight—in, for example, food stores—point out that only a balance can truly measure mass. For your students studying space-age topics who probably know that weight is defined in terms of gravitational force, you may want to recall (or use here for the first time) the discussion in Section 2-1 of the newton, the SI unit of weight. Masses are usually measured in grams.

■ Tell students that chemists could not make much progress toward understanding the nature of matter until they had classified samples as elements, compounds, and mixtures. To help students distinguish among these categories in terms of their physical and chemical properties, use Demonstrations 4-1, 4-2, and 4-3. To help students understand the distinctions at the molecular level, use the Transparency Master "Elements, Compounds, and Mixtures" before Section 4-3.

You may want to look ahead to the classification of elements as metals, nonmetals, semimetals, and noble gases. This classification is introduced in Section 7-7 and discussed further in later chapters. You might also look ahead to Section 4-11 and have students locate in the periodic table in text Figure 7-7 the elements named in text Figure 4-21. Have them name several examples of metals, nonmetals, semimetals, and noble gases.

■ **Application.** You may want to give students the following information about some familiar substances. The "chlorine" used to purify swimming pools is not the element chlorine at all, but rather a compound containing chlorine, usually sodium hypochlorite. This chlorine is the same substance that is used to wash clothes. The fluoride in toothpastes is a compound of fluorine, usually stannous fluoride or sodium mono-fluorophosphate (MFP). However, the iodine in tincture of iodine is actually the element iodine, dissolved in alcohol.

■ **Concept Mastery.** You may wish to use Concept Mastery question 44 (chapter-end question) to check students' understanding of the term "substance." Students frequently use the word loosely to refer to any type of matter. For example, they may think of butter or margarine as a substance when, in the chemist's sense, each is a mixture of substances. That both materials get soft when heated (before they melt) indicates that they are composed of a variety of substances, each with its own melting point. Ask students to name materials that melt at only one temperature and are, therefore, substances. They might be able to name only one, ice.

## 4-4 Properties, pp. 69-70, and

## 4-5 Density, pp. 70-74

| Planning Guide | |
| --- | --- |
| **Labs (Lab Manual) and Demonstrations (TE)** | **Supplementary Materials (Teacher's Resource Book)** |
| Lab 5: Density Determination<br>Demo 4-4: Sink or Swim, p. TG-89<br>Demo 4-5; Density of Iron, p. TG-89 | Transparency Master: Densities of Some Common Substances at 20°C, p. 4-2<br>Open-Ended Experiment: The Density of Sand, p. 4-5<br>Practice Problems, p. 4-9<br>Non-SI Supplementary Problems, p. 4-10 |

■ Ask students why intensive properties can be used to identify substances but extensive properties cannot. Density is an example of an intensive property. Use the graph in Figure 4-15 to discuss the relationship between the mass and volume of a substance. Help students realize that the slope of the line on such a graph is equal to the density of the substance for which mass and volume have been plotted. You may wish to discuss this same concept using Demonstration 4-5, "Density of Iron." You can also use Demonstration 4-4, "Sink or Swim," and the Can You Explain This? feature, Layers of Liquids, to help students understand the concept of density.

To illustrate that density, as an intensive property, is used to identify substances, have students do Laboratory 5, "Density Determination." In the lab, students are asked to calculate densities for various substances and use density to identify an unknown.

■ If you have average or above average students, you may wish to have them do a less structured lab such as the Open-Ended Laboratory Experiment "Density of Sand." In this lab, students are asked to prepare and execute a plan for determining the density of a sample of sand with air around the sand granules and then the density of the sand alone.

■ Explain that density values for different substances vary widely. Ask students why the densities of gases are so small compared with the densities of liquids and solids. Also ask students why the densities of gases are significantly affected by temperature and pressure changes, whereas the densities of liquids and solids are only slightly affected.

■ **Application.** If you live in a cold climate, your students know about the use of antifreeze to prevent freezing of the water in automobile radiators. The antifreeze, mixed with water, forms a solution with a freezing point lower than that of the water alone. You may want to point out that the hydrometer used to check the level of antifreeze actually measures the density (or specific gravity, which is numerically equal to the density expressed in grams per cubic centimeter) of the solution. The density can be correlated with the amount the freezing point has been lowered.

## 4-6 Changes of Phase, pp. 74-75,

## 4-7 Physical and Chemical Properties, pp. 75-76,

## 4-8 Physical and Chemical Change, pp. 76-77, and

## 4-9 Conservation of Mass, pp. 77-78

| Planning Guide | |
| --- | --- |
| **Labs (Lab Manual) and Demonstrations (TE)** | **Supplementary Materials (Teacher's Resource Book)** |
| Lab 6: Physical and Chemical Change<br>Demo 4-6: Properties of Matter, p. TG-90<br>Demo 4-7: Changes in Matter, p. TG-90 | Review Activity: Classification of Matter, p. 4-7<br>Review Activity: Properties, p. 4-8<br>Critical and Creative Thinking: Classifying, p. CCT-23 |

■ The term "phase" was used originally to indicate a homogeneous substance with uniform composition and properties. Most texts today use the term to mean "physical state of a substance." You may wish to anticipate the text discussion of an unusual property of water, namely, that its liquid phase has a greater density than its solid phase (see Section 11-20).

■ Emphasize that many physical properties and all chemical properties are defined in terms of changes that substances undergo. Use Demonstration 4-6 "Properties of Matter" to help students observe various properties and classify them as physical or chemical and as intensive or extensive.

■ Use Demonstration 4-7 "Changes in Matter" to show students examples of physical and chemical changes that they can classify. Then have students do Laboratory 6, "Physical and Chemical Change." In this lab, they will carry out procedures that lead to further observations of changes in matter. Point out that energy changes take place in both types of changes in matter. Ask students what evidence of energy change could be observed in the demonstration and/or the lab.

Tell students that energy changes occur in both physical and chemical changes. Ask why energy in steam is greater than that in an equal mass of boiling water, and why oceans have a moderating effect on the temperature of the air in nearby areas.

■ Tell the students that the experiment shown in text Figure 4-19 is similar to that done in 1789 by Lavoisier, who stated that he had found no change in mass from the beginning to the end of a chemical reaction. Actually, some mass, too small to be measured by ordinary instruments, is lost or gained in chemical reactions because of the energy change. However, the combined total of mass and energy in any chemical reaction, or in the universe as a whole, is fixed and unchangeable. This modification of Lavoisier's law of conservation of mass is called the law of conservation of mass-energy.

■ **Application.** You may want to tell students that because of the range of the properties of carbon in its various forms, this element is unusually versatile. As graphite, carbon is dark gray, slippery, and soft, properties that make it useful in pencils and as a lubricant. As diamond, carbon is highly reflective and the hardest substance known, properties that make it useful for jewelry and for industrial tools. As activated charcoal, carbon removes impurities from water. When we burn coal and charcoal for fuel, we make use of a chemical property of the carbon that is the major component of these fuels.

■ **Concept Mastery.** Although students will memorize that mass is conserved in a chemical reaction, they may think mass is gained when a precipitate is formed and that mass is lost when a gas is formed. To help students correct such errors, you may wish to discuss Concept Mastery questions 45 and 46 (chapter-end questions). As an alternative, you may carry out the directions in the question as a class demonstration. Students also tend to think that because mass is conserved, volume is conserved. Use Concept Mastery question 47 (chapter-end question) to focus students' attention on this confusion. You may easily turn the question into a demonstration in which students predict what will happen in the experiment.

■ **Critical Thinking.** In the Critical and Creative Thinking worksheet "Classifying," students are asked to classify materials based on their properties. The open-ended approach used here develops the skill of finding relationships between different classes of materials. The worksheet will also help students to appreciate the utility of grouping materials according to chemical and physical properties.

## 4-10 Relative Abundance, pp. 78-79, and

## 4-11 Symbols of the Elements, pp. 79-80

| Planning Guide | |
|---|---|
| Labs (Lab Manual) and Demonstrations (TE) | Supplementary Materials (Teacher's Resource Book) |
| | Transparency Master: Distribution of Elements in the Earth's Crust, p. 4-4 |

■ To help students visualize the relative abundance of the elements, use the Transparency Master "Distribution of Elements in the Earth's Crust." Tell students that some elements, such as nitrogen, the noble gases, and the noble metals, occur free because of their relative inactivity. Others occur free because they are produced by some natural process, such as oxygen from photosynthesis and sulfur from volcanic activity.

■ Use symbols when referring to specific elements so that the students will become familiar with them. The text mentions one example of a symbol derived from its Latin name (*ferrum*). Have students use Figure 4-21 to find symbols derived from other Latin names (*cuprum, plumbum, hydrargyrum,* etc.) and then locate those symbols in the periodic table.

By way of contrast to the names of those elements known since antiquity, have students look in the periodic table for the symbols of the most recently identified elements, those with atomic numbers of 104 and above. The symbols for these elements are exceptions to the rule in that they have three letters, not just one or two. Pending the settlement of disputes over their so-called trivial names, the International Union of Pure and Applied Chemistry (IUPAC) has approved the use of systematic names and symbols. These names are derived directly from the atomic number of the element using the following numerical roots: 0 = nil, 1 = un, 2 = bi, 3 = tri, 4 = quad, 5 = pent, 6 = hex, 7 = sept, 8 = oct, and 9 = enn. The roots are combined in order of the digits that make up the atomic number and terminated by the suffix "ium." The final "n" of "enn" and the final "i" of "bi" and "tri" are dropped when needed to avoid a double "n" or double "i." Examples of these names and their symbols are: 104 Unnilquadium, Unq; 109 Unnilennium, Une. Some students may enjoy using the rules to figure out the names of elements with atomic numbers 105 through 108. You may also wish to mention that elements with atomic numbers 93 through 109, known as the transuranium elements, are all synthetic, as explained in Chapter 26. The synthesis of element number 110 was claimed by Soviet scientists in 1986, although the claim was still unconfirmed as of January 1988.

## Demonstrations

### 4-1 Elements, Compounds, and Mixtures

**Overview:** In this demonstration, you use an overhead projector and large and small paper clips in various combinations to illustrate the concept of elements, compounds, and mixtures. Students should be able to classify the paper clip examples and should be able to observe that mixtures can be separated without destroying the "substances" making them up.

**Materials:** box of large paper clips; box of small paper clips, overhead projector transparency printed with the headings "Elements," "Compounds," and "Mixtures."

**Advance Preparation:** Mark the headings on the transparency.

**Procedure:** 1. Place the transparency onto the overhead projector. Tell students you are going to use paper clips to represent two different elements. Place a few small paper clips under the heading "Elements." Mention that each paper clip looks exactly like all of the others and has properties identical to those of the others. Place a few large paper clips under the same heading but farther down the column and make a similar statement about this "element." 2. Make a "compound" out of one large and two small paper clips and place it under the heading "Compounds." Make a few more "molecules" of the same kind and place them together under the "Compounds" heading. Tell students that a formula in which $L$ stands for large and $S$ stands for small can represent this combination, and ask students to state what the formula should be. Also, point out that all of the molecules look alike and have identical properties. 3. Move all of the paper clips and combinations over to the "Mixtures" heading and tell the students that the resulting set is a mixture of substances. Using your hand, begin to separate the three substances from each other, and tell students you are doing so by physical means. Ask students what aspects of substances remain the same after such a physical process. 4. Make up some other examples of paper-clip "elements," "compounds," and "mixtures," and have students attempt to classify each.

**Results:** In step 2, the formula is $LS_2$. In a physical process (step 3), each substance keeps its identifying properties, is not changed in composition, and looks just as it did before the mixing occurred.

## 4-2 Classification and Separation of Matter

**Overview:** In this demonstration, students observe various types of matter in closed containers and try to classify each as solid, liquid, or gas, and as element, compound, solution, or heterogeneous mixture. Students also try to determine how many different substances are in each container and to propose how to separate the substances from each other by physical means. Students gain practice not only in classifying matter but also in suggesting how to separate and purify the components of mixtures of matter.

**Materials:** jars or stoppered flasks containing various combinations of elements, compounds, solutions, and heterogeneous mixtures (suggestions: (a) iron filings,

sand, and sugar; (b) salt water; (c) alcohol and water; (d) copper(II) sulfate solution and corn oil; (e) rocks and sand; (f) powdered sulfur; (g) air; (h) lead shot); magnet; separatory funnel (A separatory funnel may be hard to find. As an alternative, you can use measuring cups used to separate meat juices to make gravy.); filtering apparatus; hot plate; evaporating dish and watch glass; tweezers; distillation apparatus; magnifying glass.

**Advance Preparation:** Prepare the samples and set up the filtering and distillation apparatus.

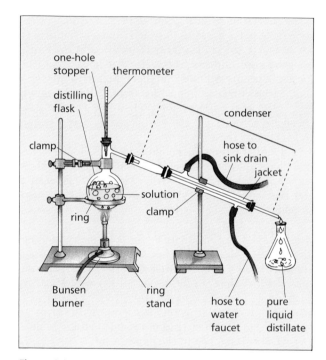

**Figure 4-1**

**Procedure:** 1. Display all of the jars and ask students to classify the matter in two ways: by phase, and by whether the matter is made up of an element, a compound, a solution, or a heterogeneous mixture. Allow the students to work in groups and to observe each jar. 2. Discuss and demonstrate various techniques used to separate matter, such as distillation (see the accompanying figure), filtration, decanting, use of a magnet, use of a separatory funnel, and use of tweezers. Tell the students to attempt to estimate how many different kinds of substances are in each jar and to state how they might test out their hypotheses.

**Results:** Suggested samples (a), (e), (f), and (h) are solid. Samples (b), (c), and (d) are liquid. Sample (g) is gaseous. Samples (f) and (h) each are made up of a single element. None of the samples is made up of a single compound. Samples (b), (c), and (g) are made up of solutions. Samples (a), (d), and (e) are made up of heterogeneous mixtures. Samples (f) and (h) each contain one substance. Samples (b) and (c) each contain two substances. Sample (a) contains three substances. Samples (d), (e), and (g) contain many substances. Suggestions for testing hypotheses in step 2 will vary.

## 4-3 Solutions versus Pure Substances

**Overview:** In this demonstration, students learn how to distinguish solutions and pure substances.

**Materials:** 5 watch glasses; solution (roughly 0.5 $M$) of salt water; solution (roughly 0.5 $M$) of iron(III) chloride ($FeCl_3$) in water; distilled water; ethyl alcohol; solution of distilled water and ethyl alcohol in equal proportions by volume; hot plate.

**Advance Preparation:** 1. **Salt water:** Prepare 0.5 $M$ salt water by dissolving 29.2 g NaCl in enough water to make 1.00 L of solution. 2. **$FeCl_3$:** Prepare 0.5 $M$ $FeCl_3$ by dissolving 162.3 g $FeCl_3$ in enough water to make 1.00 L of solution.

**Procedure:** 1. Show the class five watch glasses, each containing one of the liquids listed above. Ask students to observe each liquid carefully and to describe each. 2. Ask students how they can determine whether a given liquid is a solution or a pure substance. Demonstrate that one method is to place a watch glass containing the liquid onto the hot plate, heat it carefully on low setting and in a fume hood, and look for a residue. In the case of the solution of alcohol and water, students will not be able to use this method in order to tell that two different liquids are present. Ask the students to suggest a better method to use when two liquids are involved. 3. Set up a distillation apparatus, if possible, and distill the solution of ethyl alcohol and water. Have students look up the normal boiling point of each pure substance in the *Handbook of Chemistry and Physics*, or tell them the boiling points if no reference is handy.

**Results:** In step 1, all of the samples are homogeneous, two (ethyl alcohol and water–alcohol) have an odor, and one ($FeCl_3$) has a color. The normal boiling points of pure ethyl alcohol and of pure water are 78.4°C and 100.0°C, respectively.

## 4-4 Sink or Swim

**Overview:** In this demonstration, objects are placed into liquids and are observed either to sink or to float, depending on their densities. This demonstration helps to show that an object sinks if its density is greater than the density of the liquid into which it has been placed.

**Materials:** beaker ⅔ full of water; beaker ⅔ full of ethyl alcohol; 2 quarters; 2 pieces of ice; large bucket full of water; 2 cans of the same brand of soft drink, one "regular" and one "diet."

**Advance Preparation:** Obtain the appropriate soft drinks and arrange to have ice on hand.

**Procedure:** 1. Without telling the class which liquids are in them, place the two beakers onto white paper and ask students to observe and to explain what occurs when you drop a quarter into each beaker. 2. Add a piece of ice to each beaker, and ask students to hypothesize as to the reason for the result. Students will have assumed that both beakers contain the same liquid and now need to account for why something different occurs in the two beakers. Tell them what is in each. 3. Show the two cans of soft drink, and ask what will happen when each is placed into the large bucket of water. Some may predict that both will sink. Carefully add both cans to the water, and ask students to hypothesize as to the result. Reinforce the idea that an object will float if its density is less than that of the liquid in which it is placed. Relate this to occurrences such as oil spills at sea (if you wish, pour some oil into a test tube containing water to show that oil is less dense than water).

**Results:** In step 1, the quarters will sink in both liquids, since the quarters are more dense than the liquids. In step 2, the ice will float in the liquid water, whose density is greater than that of the ice. The ice will sink in the ethyl alcohol, whose density is less than the ice's density. In step 3, the "regular" soft drink has sugar in it and is of higher density than the "diet" drink; the can of "regular" drink sinks in the water, which is less dense than the can of "regular" drink, but the can of "diet" drink floats in the water.

## 4-5 Density of Iron

**Overview:** The mass and volume of three different-sized samples of a metal are determined and graphed. The density is calculated and used to identify the metal. The students learn that although the masses and volumes of different samples of the same metal may be different, the density is the same for all of the samples.

**Materials:** three different-sized samples of iron (or some other metal); balance; graduated cylinder.

**Advance Preparation:** none

**Procedure:** 1. Show the samples of metal to the class and tell the students you want to identify the metal by finding its density. 2. Find the mass of each sample of iron and record it on the board. 3. Discuss the water-displacement method for finding volume. Select an appropriate graduated cylinder and fill it half full of water and record the volume. Tilt the cylinder and carefully add the first sample of metal. Read and record the new volume and calculate the volume of the metal alone. 4. Repeat the procedure for the other two samples. 5. Have students observe and describe the relationship between changing mass and changing volume. Construct a graph on the board and plot the values. 6. Discuss the concept of density, and calculate the density (mass/volume) of each sample and record it with the other data. 7. Show how to find the slope of the graphed line, and ask students to comment on its value. 8. Have students determine the identity of the metal by comparing the calculated density to the values in a chart of densities.

**Results:** In step 5, as mass increases, so does volume. In step 6, the densities of all of the samples are equal: 7.87 g/mL. In step 7, the slope is equal to the calculated density.

## 4-6 Properties of Matter

**Overview:** In this demonstration, students make observations of the properties of a substance and then classify the properties as physical or chemical and as intensive or extensive.

**Materials:** cubes of sugar; watch glass; hot plate; balance; tweezers or spatula.

**Advance Preparation:** none

**Procedure:** 1. Have students observe a cube of sugar that has been placed onto a watch glass. Ask them to describe the properties of the sugar. 2. Ask students to suggest other procedures that might allow them to determine more properties. Carry out as many of the reasonable procedures as is possible. 3. Write each observed property on the board. Ask students to classify each as a physical property or a chemical property after reviewing the difference between physical and chemical properties. 4. Ask students to classify the properties as intensive or extensive, and point out that intensive properties are generally used in identifying substances.

**Results:** The sugar is white, crystalline, solid, and odorless. In step 2, answers may include: attempting to dissolve it in water or other solvents; finding its mass; trying to melt it; finding its density; and adding an acid or base to it. Physical properties include color, crystalline form, odor, phase, solubility, density, and melting point. Tendency to react with an acid or base is a chemical property. Mass is an extensive property; the other physical properties listed are intensive.

## 4-7 Changes in Matter

**Overview:** In this demonstration, examples of physical and chemical changes are illustrated. Accompanying energy changes are also noted. Students classify a change in matter by observing a reaction and determining whether a new substance has been formed.

**Materials:** mortar and pestle; test tubes in a rack; sugar cube and loose sugar; aluminum foil; hot plate; 50-mL beaker; concentrated sulfuric acid; vinegar; baking soda; ice; 0.01 $M$ solution of lead(II) nitrate ($Pb(NO_3)_2$); 0.10 $M$ solution of potassium iodide (KI); dry ice; seltzer tablet; beaker tongs; crucible tongs; small plastic bag.

**Advance Preparation:** 1. **$Pb(NO_3)_2$:** Prepare 0.10 $M$ $Pb(NO_3)_2$ by dissolving 3.31 g $Pb(NO_3)_2$ in enough water to make 100 mL of solution. 2. **KI:** Prepare 0.10 $M$ KI by dissolving 1.66 g KI in enough water to make 100 mL of solution.

**Safety:** Carry out the reaction between the sulfuric acid and sugar in a fume hood. Take special care in working with the acid, which is very corrosive. The black carbon column that is produced will have some acid on it, so use crucible tongs in handling it.

**Procedure:** 1. Place the sugar cube into a mortar and crush the cube to powder. Note that it took energy to crush the cube. 2. Place some of the power into a test tube of water and stir. Have a student do the touch test. Feel the bottom of the tube and determine whether it feels cooler or warmer than it did before the sugar was added. 3. Place sugar onto some foil and place the foil onto a hot plate set on "low." 4. Begin to heat the sugar on "high" and have students note what happens. They should also compare the amount of energy needed to decompose the sugar with the amount necessary to dissolve it. 5. Fill a 50-mL beaker one-third full of sugar, and add an equal amount of concentrated sulfuric acid. 6. Ask the students to classify each of the changes that have occurred in steps 1 through 5 as either physical or chemical. 7. Demonstrate the following changes, and ask students to classify each. Add some vinegar to baking soda. Place an ice cube onto a watch glass and allow the cube to melt. Add a colorless solution of lead(II) nitrate to an equal quantity of colorless potassium iodide. Add a seltzer tablet to water. Place a piece of dry ice onto a watch glass.

**Results:** In step 2, the bottom of the tube will probably feel slightly cooler. In step 3, the sugar will slowly melt. In step 4, the large amount of energy will cause the sugar to turn black, as it decomposes to form carbon. In step 5, the sugar will turn from white to brown to black. As the sulfuric acid removes the hydrogen and oxygen from the sugar, a porous column of carbon will form and rise. The changes in steps 1, 2, and 3 are physical. Those in steps 4 and 5 are chemical. The addition of vinegar to baking soda will cause carbon dioxide gas to be released (chemical change). The melting of the ice cube is a physical change. The mixing of the $Pb(NO_3)_2$ and KI solutions will produce a yellow precipitate of $PbI_2$ (chemical change). The seltzer tablet will release carbon dioxide gas in water (chemical change). The dry ice will sublime to gaseous carbon dioxide (physical change).

**Disposal Tips:** Use beaker tongs to move the beaker containing the carbon column and excess sulfuric acid from the fume hood to the sink. Carefully rinse the contents of the beaker with a great deal of water to dilute the remaining sulfuric acid and to wash the acid down the drain. Use crucible tongs to pick up the rinsed carbon column, and place it into a plastic bag.

## Answers to Questions

**Page 66**

1. Mass is not affected by changes in temperature, location, pressure, etc.
2. A sample of an element or compound has the same properties as any other sample of the same element or compound.
3. Compounds can be broken down into two or more substances by chemical change; elements cannot be broken down by chemical change.
4. No. The properties of a compound differ from those of the elements of which it is composed.
5. $? \text{ g H}_2 = 150 \text{ g H}_2\text{0} \times \dfrac{11.2 \text{ g H}_2}{100 \text{ g H}_2\text{0}} = 16.8 \text{ g H}_2$

**Page 68**

6. Elements and compounds may be in mixtures.
7. The compound has a definite composition, is homogeneous, has properties different from the substances of which it is composed, and can be broken down into its components only by chemical change. The mixture has a variable composition, may or may not be homogeneous, has the properties of its components, and can be separated into its elements by physical change.
8. The composition of the compound is definite while that of the mixture is variable.
9. **a.** Add sugar to salt but do not stir.
   **b.** Add sugar to salt and stir the mixture thoroughly.

**Page 70**

10. Intensive properties, such as melting point and boiling point.
11. Extensive properties vary with the quantity of the substance on hand.

**Page 74**

12. The units and temperature are not given.
13. Units, temperature, and pressure are not given.
14. density of Pb/density of Al =
    $11.35 \text{ g/cm}^3/2.70 \text{ g/cm}^3 = 4.20$
    The lead sample has 4.2 times the mass of the aluminum sample.

15. 7.87 g
16. $57.9 \text{ g}/3.00 \text{ cm}^3 = 19.3 \text{ g/cm}^3$
17. volume = mass/density = $31.5 \text{ g}/10.5 \text{ g/cm}^3 =$
    $3.00 \text{ cm}^3$
18. mass = density × volume = $7.9 \text{ g/cm}^3 \times 10 \text{ cm}^3 =$
    $79 \text{ g}$
19. The mass represented by the red line in text Figure 4-15 is 14.0 g − 2.0 g = 12.0 g. The volume represented by the blue line is $1.2 \text{ cm}^3 - 0.2 \text{ cm}^3 = 1.0 \text{ cm}^3$. Dividing the mass by the volume gives the slope of the line:

    $$\text{Slope} = \frac{14.0 \text{ g} - 2.0 \text{ g}}{1.2 \text{ cm}^3 - 0.2 \text{ cm}^3} = \frac{12.0 \text{ g}}{1.0 \text{ cm}^3} = 12.0 \text{ g/cm}^3$$

    *Significance of the slope:* On a graph showing the mass of a substance on the vertical axis plotted against its volume on the horizontal axis, the slope shows the density of the substance.
20. The curve indicates a direct proportion between the variables. Because masses occupy space, an "object" with no mass (zero mass) would occupy zero volume.

**Page 75, Layers of Liquids**

1. The liquids remain in layers because each liquid will not dissolve in the liquids with which it makes contact. For example, water will not dissolve in the mineral oil above it or in the corn syrup below it.
2. The density of each solid is intermediate between the densities of the liquids above and below it. For example, paraffin is more dense than mineral oil but less dense than water.

**Page 78**

21. **a.** chemical; **b.** physical; **c.** physical; **d.** chemical
22. Burning.
23. The metal combined with a substance in the air.

**Page 80**

24. A rock is called an ore when it can be used as a source of a useful metal.
25. Carbon.
26. These elements have been known since the early days of chemistry.
27. There are one or two letters in a symbol. The first letter is capitalized.

## Chapter Review

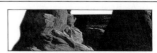

Page 81, Content Review

1. Three ways of describing the quantity of matter in a given sample are its mass, volume, and weight.

2. Mass is a description of the quantity of matter that is not affected by temperature or location.

3. An element cannot be broken down into other substances by an ordinary chemical change, but a compound can.

4. $? \text{ g sodium} = \dfrac{39.3 \text{ g sodium}}{100 \text{ g salt}} \times 168 \text{ g salt} =$
   $66.0 \text{ g sodium} = 6.60 \times 10^{1} \text{ g sodium}$

5. **a.** $? \text{ g carbon} = \dfrac{74.9 \text{ g carbon}}{100 \text{ g methane}} \times 225 \text{ g methane}$
   $= 168 \text{ g carbon}$

   **b.** $? \text{ g hydrogen} = \dfrac{25.1 \text{ g hydrogen}}{100 \text{ g methane}} \times$
   $66.0 \text{ g methane} = 16.6 \text{ g hydrogen}$

6. Besides elements, the groups into which matter can be classified are compounds and mixtures.

7. Elements and compounds can be classified as substances.

8. Four examples of liquid mixtures might include the following: shampoo, milk, perfume, sea water, ketchup, gasoline. (Other answers are possible.)

9. Mixtures differ from substances in three ways: (1) A mixture retains the properties of each of its constituents; a substance has only one set of properties. (2) The composition of a mixture is not fixed; the composition of a substance is. (3) Mixtures can be either homogeneous or heterogeneous; substances are always homogeneous.

10. A pizza is a heterogeneous mixture.

11. Three extensive properties are volume, mass, and weight. Intensive properties include density, color, odor, taste, and boiling and melting points.

12. The mass and volume of the candy are extensive properties. Its color and taste are intensive properties.

13. Density is the mass of a substance in a given unit volume. It is expressed in units such as $g/cm^3$, $g/L$, and $kg/m^3$.

14. Density is an intensive property because it is independent of the size of the sample.

15. When temperature increases, a typical solid expands. This increase in volume, at constant mass, causes a decrease in density.

16. $\text{Density} = \dfrac{\text{mass}}{\text{volume}} = \dfrac{75.6 \text{ g}}{8.50 \text{ cm}^3} = 8.89 \text{ g/cm}^3$

17. $\text{Volume} = \dfrac{\text{mass}}{\text{density}} = \dfrac{58.0 \text{ g}}{18.9 \text{ g/cm}^3} = 3.07 \text{ cm}^3$

18. $\text{Mass} = \text{density} \times \text{volume}$
    $= 10.5 \text{ g/cm}^3 \times 24.0 \text{ cm}^3$
    $= 252 \text{ g}$
    $= 2.52 \times 10^2 \text{ g}$

19. **a.** $\text{mass} = \text{density} \times \text{volume}$
    $\text{mass of piece 1} = 2.70 \text{ g/cm}^3 \times \;\; 5.0 \text{ cm}^3 = 14 \text{ g}$
    $\text{mass of piece 2} = 2.70 \text{ g/cm}^3 \times \;\; 9.2 \text{ cm}^3 = 25 \text{ g}$
    $\text{mass of piece 3} = 2.70 \text{ g/cm}^3 \times 12.5 \text{ cm}^3 = 33.8 \text{ g}$
    $\text{mass of piece 4} = 2.70 \text{ g/cm}^3 \times 17.0 \text{ cm}^3 = 45.9 \text{ g}$

    **b.** See Figure 4-2 (on this page).

    **c.** The slope of the line is

    $\dfrac{49 \text{ g}}{18 \text{ cm}^3} = 2.7 \text{ g/cm}^3$ (the density of aluminum)

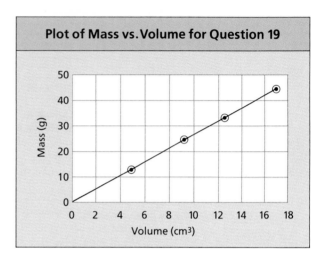

Plot of Mass vs. Volume for Question 19

**Figure 4-2**

   **d.** Figures 4-15 (student text) and 4-2 (on this page) are the same in that both are straight lines that go through the origin. The slope of the line for each graph is the density of the metal whose mass is being plotted against its volume. The two slopes are numerically different because lead is more dense than aluminum. Hence, the slope of the line in text Figure 4-15 (the density of lead) is greater than the slope of the line in Teacher's Guide Figure 4-2 (the density of aluminum).

20. Changes in phase are physical because a substance has the same composition in all phases.

21. Physical properties are characteristics that can be observed without the production of new substances. Examples are color, odor, taste, solubility, density, and melting point.

22. Chemical properties are characteristics that describe how the substance interacts with other substances to produce new substances (or fails to interact).

23. If the nail is bent or broken, it has undergone a physical change. If it rusts, it has undergone a chemical change.

24. Chemical changes are usually accompanied by greater energy changes than physical changes.

25. **a.** Baking of bread is a chemical change.
   **b.** Melting of iron is a physical change.
   **c.** Dissolving of sugar in water is a physical change.
   **d.** Tarnishing of silver is a chemical change.

26. Lavoisier heated tin in a sealed container of air. After cooling the container, he weighed it and found no change in mass. The tin had lost its luster and turned to an ash. When the container was opened, air rushed in, and the container then showed a gain of mass. Evidently, something in the air had combined with the tin.

27. The most common element in the earth is oxygen, at 46.7% by mass. The second most common is silicon, at 27.7%. The total percentage of these elements is 74.4%.

28. In the free, or elemental, state, an element exists alone and uncombined. In the combined state, an element is combined with other elements as part of a compound.

29. The symbols for these elements are: **a.** iron, Fe; **b.** hydrogen, H; **c.** carbon, C; **d.** nitrogen, N; **e.** sulfur, S.

30. The elements represented by these symbols are: **a.** O, oxygen; **b.** Na, sodium; **c.** Ne, neon; **d.** Hg, mercury; **e.** Si, silicon.

## Page 82, Content Mastery

31. Density $= \dfrac{\text{mass}}{\text{volume}} = \dfrac{833 \text{ g}}{378 \text{ cm}^3} = 2.20 \text{ g/cm}^3$

32. $42.1\% \times 45 \text{ g} = 19 \text{ g carbon}$

33. The symbols for these elements are: sodium, Na; potassium, K; silicon, Si; sulfur, S; phosphorus, P; iron, Fe; iodine, I; cobalt, Co; copper, Cu; argon, Ar; silver, Ag; nitrogen, N; nickel, Ni; tin, Sn; lead, Pb; mercury, Hg.

34. Physical properties can be observed without changing the chemical nature of a substance. However, chemical properties involve interactions between substances to form a new substance, or the failure of a substance to interact with other substances.

35. Length, area, volume, and mass are extensive properties. Color, melting point, density, boiling point, and temperature are intensive properties.

36. Density $= \dfrac{\text{mass}}{\text{volume}}$ therefore volume $= \dfrac{\text{mass}}{\text{density}}$

   volume $= \dfrac{17.2 \text{ kg}}{5.75 \text{ g/cm}^3} \times \dfrac{10^3 \text{ g}}{1 \text{ kg}} \times \dfrac{1 \text{ dm}^3}{10^3 \text{ cm}^3}$
   $= 2.99 \text{ dm}^3$

37. The law of conservation of mass states that the total mass at the end of a reaction equals the total mass at the start of the reaction. Because the oxygen and hydrogen reacted completely, the mass of the water must equal the original mass of the oxygen and hydrogen. Therefore the mass of the water is 48.0 kg + 6.0 kg = 54.0 kg.

38. *Physical changes:*
   **a.** freezing of milk;
   **c.** drawing copper into a wire;
   **d.** melting of solder;
   **f.** heating a copper wire until it glows;
   **j.** dissolving sugar in water;
   **k.** hammering of aluminum into a sheet;
   **l.** melting of ice.
   *Chemical changes:*
   **b.** souring of milk;
   **e.** frying an egg;
   **g.** rusting of an iron hammer;
   **h.** decomposing water into hydrogen and oxygen;
   **i.** burning of wood.

39. Density $= \dfrac{\text{mass}}{\text{volume}} = \dfrac{8.54 \text{ g}}{0.442 \text{ cm}^3} = 19.3 \text{ g/cm}^3$
   Therefore gold is 19 times as heavy as an equal volume of water.

40. Mass = density × volume
   $= 10.5 \text{ g/cm}^3 \times 0.987 \text{ dm}^3 \times 10^3 \text{ cm}^3/\text{dm}^3$
   $= 10.4 \times 10^3 \text{ g} = 10.4 \text{ kg}$

41. The volume of water displaced would be equal to the volume of the copper.
   Volume $= \dfrac{\text{mass}}{\text{density}} = \dfrac{46 \text{ kg}}{8.92 \text{ g/cm}^3} \times \dfrac{10^3 \text{ g}}{1 \text{ kg}}$
   $= 5.2 \times 10^3 \text{ cm}^3$

42. $\dfrac{16.0 \text{ g oxygen}}{18.0 \text{ g water}} \times 1.00 \text{ kg water} \times 10^3 \text{ g/kg}$
   $= 0.889 \times 10^3 \text{ kg oxygen} = 8.89 \times 10^2 \text{ kg oxygen}$

43. If a silver spoon were pure silver it would be composed of only the element silver, Ag, but it is more likely either a homogeneous mixture of silver with another element or a heterogeneous mixture: a thin plating of silver on another metal. Ice is solid water, a compound of the elements hydrogen and oxygen. The water in the beaker is also a compound. Vinegar-and-oil salad dressing is a mixture that separates into two separate liquids unless it is shaken. Even when it is mixed, different parts of the dressing have a different composition, so it is a heterogeneous mixture. The glass beaker is a homogeneous liquid, a mixture of metal and non metal oxides.

## Page 83, Concept Mastery

44. **Concept:** *A Substance has one set of physical properties, such as one melting point.*

*Solution:* Butter and margaine are not substances because when heated they gradually soften rather than melt at one definite temperature. Both are mixtures of substances that have a variety of melting points. At some temperatures some of the substances are solid and some are liquid.

**45.** *Concept:* *Conservation of mass.*
*Solution:* Even though a solid is formed, the mass of the substances present after the reaction must be equal to the mass of the substances present before the reaction, because no atoms are gained or lost.

**46.** *Concept:* *Conservation of mass.*
*Solution:* Although a gas is formed, it does not escape into the atmosphere. The mass after the reaction is equal to the mass before the reaction.

**47.** *Concept:* *Volume is not conserved.*
*Solution:* Mass is more predictable because it is conserved, so the combined mass would be 100.0 g. Volume is not always conserved, so the combined volume would not necessarily be 100 $cm^3$; in fact, it would be slightly less.

**48.** *Concept:* *Density.*
*Solution:* Sample A has the larger volume because mass = density × volume.

**49.** *Concept:* *Density.*
*Solution:* As in problem 48, the substance with the lower density, substance Y, would have a greater volume. Thus all of the sample of Y could not fit into the tube.

**50.** *Concept:* *Density.*
*Solution:* No water will run over the top. The part of the ice below the water displaces a mass of water equal to the mass of the ice. As the ice melts, its density will increase, causing the water that was in the ice to occupy a smaller volume.

**51.** *Concept:* *The difference between mass and weight.*
*Solution:* The mass of the gold would remain 4.2 kg since mass is independent of gravity.

## Page 84, Cumulative Review

**52. c.** $45.3 \text{ g} \times \dfrac{1 \text{ kg}}{1000 \text{ g}} = 0.0453 \text{ kg}$

**53. b.** $42.5 \times 10^{-3} = 4.25 \times 10^{-2}$

**54. c.** $V = 14.32 \text{ cm} \times 2.18 \text{ cm} \times 0.52 \text{ cm} = 16 \text{ cm}^3$.

The answer should have two significant figures because 0.52 cm has two significant figures.

**55. d.** $A = 14.4 \text{ m} \times 8.1 \text{ m} = 1.2 \times 10^2 \text{ m}^2$. The answer should have two significant figures because 8.1 m has two significant figures.

**56.** The example shows both good accuracy, because the balance has an accuracy of a thousandth of a gram, and good precision, because the values from the four weighings are very close to each other.

**57. a.** $\begin{array}{l} 4.21 \times 10^3 = \phantom{-}4.21 \times 10^3 \\ -2.1 \times 10^2 = -0.21 \times 10^3 \\ \hline \phantom{-4.21 \times 10^2 =}4.00 \times 10^3 \end{array}$  Powers must be equal before subtracting.

**b.** $3 \times 10^{+2}$
**c.** $2 \times 10^{-1}$
**d.** $2 \times 10^0$

**58. a.** $4.5 \times 10^7$;  **b.** $2.50 \times 10^{-5}$;
**c.** $7.21 \times 10^3$;  **d.** $5.0 \times 10^{-2}$

**59.** $5.0 \times 10^2 \text{ cm}^3 \times \dfrac{1 \text{ dm}^3}{10^3 \text{ cm}^3} = 5.0 \times 10^{-1} \text{ dm}^3$
$= 0.50 \text{ dm}^3$

% error $= \dfrac{0.45 \text{ dm}^3 - 0.50 \text{ dm}^3}{0.50 \text{ dm}^3} \times 100\% = -10\%$

The minus sign means that the measured value is smaller than the true value.

**60. a.** $5.4 \text{ cm} \times 1 \text{ m}/1000 \text{ cm} = 0.054 \text{ m}$
**b.** $8.1 \text{ mm} \times 1 \text{ cm}/10 \text{ mm} = 0.81 \text{ cm}$
**c.** $50 \text{ cm}^3 \times 1 \text{ dm}^3/1000 \text{ cm}^3 = 0.050 \text{ dm}^3$
**d.** $0.25 \text{ m} \times 1000 \text{ mm}/1 \text{ m} = 250 \text{ mm}$
**e.** $45.2 \text{ g} \times 1000 \text{ mg}/1 \text{ g} = 45\,200 \text{ mg}$
**f.** $1.3 \text{ dm}^3 \times 1000 \text{ cm}^3/1 \text{ dm}^3 = 1300 \text{ cm}^3$

**61.** The theory stated that all materials contain phlogiston, which they lose during burning until the air is full of phlogiston, which causes the fire to go out. Lavoisier showed that a burning substance actually removed something (oxygen) from the air, rather than added something (phlogiston).

## Page 84, Critical Thinking

**62.** *Similarities between elements and compounds:* A pure sample of an element or compound has the same intensive properties as any other pure sample of that element or compound; some elements and some compounds are not found in nature and are made only by people.
*Differences:* An element cannot be broken down chemically, but a compound can be broken down into the elements of which it was formed; the chemical and physical properties of a compound are different from the properties of the elements of which it was formed.

**63. a.** salt: compound; **b.** mercury: element; **c.** carbon: element; **d.** hydrochloric acid: compound; **e.** lime:

compound; **f.** fertilizer: compound; **g.** coal: mixture; **h.** aluminum: element

**64.** Technician B's answer is more likely correct because B used the substance's intensive properties, which provide reliable data for identifying substances.

**65. a.** Instant coffee and water form a mixture, so this is a physical change.
   **b.** The properties are changed, suggesting that the red substance is not iron, so the change is chemical.
   **c.** Melting is a physical change.
   **d.** Steam (a form of water) and the black solid (carbon) have very different properties from sugar, so a chemical change has occurred.

**66.** Both iron and steel are metals that are solid at room temperature, but iron is an element and steel is an alloy (a mixture of iron and one or more other elements). Iron has a specific set of properties, but the properties of steel vary according to the components and proportions of the mixture.

**67.** The fact that the mass has not changed indicates that the gas has not escaped. It has probably changed to a liquid or a solid, either by condensation (a physical change) or by a chemical reaction. (This phenomenon occurred in 1938 when the gas formed a solid polymer, leading research chemist Roy J. Plunkett to discover Teflon.)

**Page 85, Challenge Problems**

**68.** The density of the bracelet can be calculated:

$$\frac{45 \text{ g}}{(11.7 \text{ cm}^3 - 9.2 \text{ cm}^3)} = \frac{45 \text{ g}}{2.5 \text{ cm}^3} = 18 \text{ g/cm}^3$$

This density is much closer to that of gold than to that of copper. (See text Figure 4-14.)

**69.** Students should note chemical changes in their bodies (e.g., respiration, digestion), in things they use (e.g., cooking food, combustion in a car engine), and in the environment (e.g., photosynthesis, formation of acid rain). For each change they should explain the effect on their lives if it did not occur, and suggest an alternative. For example, without photosynthesis we would lose our source of oxygen; one possible alternative might be electrolysis of water, using solar power.

**70.** Compounds that have improved daily life include plastics and medicines. Examples of ultimate compounds could include a drug that kills cancerous cells without harming normal cells, a fertilizer that prevents erosion while it helps plant growth, ad a compound that is a superconductor at room temperature.

**71.** Add water to dissolve the salt but not the sand. Stir and filter. Rinse the sand a few times, saving all of the liquid. Let the sand dry. Evaporate the water (heat if necessary) to leave the salt dry.

**72.** Volume of sheet $= 50.0 \text{ kg} \times \dfrac{10^3 \text{ g}}{1 \text{ kg}} \times \dfrac{1 \text{ cm}^3}{7.86 \text{ g}}$

$$= 6.36 \times 10^3 \text{ cm}^3$$

Volume $=$ length $\times$ width $\times$ thickness

$6.36 \times 10^3 \text{ cm}^3 =$ length $\times 120.00 \text{ cm} \times 2.00 \text{ cm}$

length $= 26.5 \text{ cm}$

# Energy

5

## Chapter Planning Guide

| Text Section | Labs (Lab Manual) and Demonstrations (TE) | Supplementary Materials (Teacher's Resource Book) |
|---|---|---|
| **5-1** The Concept of Energy, p. 87 <br> **5-2** Forms of Energy, pp. 88-89 | Demo 5-1: Ethanol Cannon, p. TG-99 | |
| **5-3** Conversion of Energy and Its Conservation, pp. 90-91 <br> **5-4** Energy and Chemical Reactions, pp. 91-92 | Demo 5-2: Cold "Milk," p. TG-99 <br> Demo 5-3: Unclogging Your Pipes, p. TG-100 <br> Demo 5-4: Activation Energy, p. TG-100 | Critical and Creative Thinking: Judging Things and Ideas, p. CCT-59 |
| **5-5** Heat Energy and Temperature, pp. 92-95 | | Transparency Master: Making a Celsius Thermometer, p. 5-2 <br> Transparency Master: A Comparison of Three Temperature Scales, p. 5-3 <br> Review Activity: Temperature, p. 5-7 |
| **5-6** Heat and Its Measurement, pp. 95-99 | Lab 7: Calorimetry: Heat of Fusion of Ice <br> Lab 8: Calorimetry: Heat of Crystallization of Wax | Open-Ended Experiment: How Fattening Is a Peanut, p. 5-4 <br> Open-Ended Experiment: Relative Temperature in a Bunsen Burner Flame, p. 5-5 <br> Non-SI Supplementary Problems, p. 5-9 <br> Review Activity: Calorimetry, p. 5-8 |
| **Career** Chemical Sales Representative, p. 98 | | |
| **Application** The Energy Values of Different Foods, p. 100 | | |
| **5-7** The Kinetic Theory of Heat and Temperature, p. 101 | | |
| **5-8** Interactions Between Electric Charges, pp. 102-103 | | Societal Issues: Alternative Sources of Energy, p. SI-18 |
| | | Test—Form A, p. AT-17 <br> Alternate Test—Form B, p. BT-17 |

☐ Core  ☐ Advanced  ☐ Optional

# Chapter Overview

In Chapter 5 we define energy, describe its forms, and state how it can be converted from one form to another. Exothermic chemical reactions are contrasted to endothermic chemical reactions. Students learn the difference between heat energy and temperature. They convert temperatures from the Celsius to the Kelvin scale, and vice versa, and solve problems in calorimetry. Heat and temperature are explained in terms of the kinetic theory. The chapter ends with a discussion of electric charges, including the nature of positive and negative charges, electrostatic forces, electric current, and electric conductors.

# Chapter Objectives

After students have completed this chapter, they will be able to:

1. Identify various forms of energy.    *5-1* and *5-2*
2. Describe changes in energy that take place during a chemical reaction.    *5-3* and *5-4*
3. Distinguish between heat energy and temperature.    *5-5* to *5-7*
4. Solve calorimetry problems.    *5-6*
5. Describe the interactions that occur between electrostatic charges.    *5-8*

# Teaching Suggestions

## 5-1 The Concept of Energy, p. 87, and

## 5-2 Forms of Energy, pp. 88-89

| Planning Guide | |
| --- | --- |
| Labs (Lab Manual) and Demonstrations (TE) | Supplementary Materials (Teacher's Resource Book) |
| Demo 5-1: Ethanol Cannon, p. TG-99 | |

■ Start the chapter with a "bang" by doing Demonstration 5-1, "Ethanol Cannon," a dramatic example of energy being converted from one form to another (electrical to mechanical) and doing work (a stopper pops with explosive force from a bottle). Then discuss the scientific definition of energy, the classes and forms of energy, and the ways in which energy is transformed.

■ Help students to distinguish between kinetic and potential energy as headings under which all forms of energy can be classified. Energy that is in evidence when a force is moving through a distance (i.e., when

work is being done) is *kinetic energy.* When an object is in position to move through a distance, it possesses *potential energy.* Ask students to state examples of different forms of energy, including those observed in the demonstration, and to classify them as kinetic or potential.

■ You may wish to preview the role of energy in chemical reactions by giving students who already have some knowledge of chemistry the following information. In chemical reactions, energy is often used to remove electrons from the attractive force of the positive nucleus. For example, when sodium and chlorine atoms combine, energy is used to remove electrons from the sodium atoms, and a greater amount of energy is released when electrons join the chlorine atoms. The net result is a reaction that releases energy.

■ **Application.** When discussing forms of energy, be sure that your students are made aware of the harmful effect on the skin of exposure to ultraviolet light, a form of electromagnetic energy that is part of the radiation we receive from the sun. Although exposure to ultraviolet light has been linked to skin cancer, acquiring a suntan is still a popular activity in our society. Inform students that they can protect themselves by using a sunscreen preparation of the appropriate SPF (sun protective factor) for the individual's type of skin and the length of exposure.

## 5-3 Conversion of Energy and Its Conservation, pp. 90-91, and

## 5-4 Energy and Chemical Reactions, pp. 91-92

| Planning Guide | |
| --- | --- |
| Labs (Lab Manual) and Demonstrations (TE) | Supplementary Materials (Teacher's Resource Book) |
| Demo 5-2: Cold "Milk," p. TG-99 Demo 5-3: Unclogging Your Pipes, p. TG-100 Demo 5-4: Activation Energy, p. TG-100 | Critical and Creative Thinking: Judging Things and Ideas, p. CCT-59 |

■ Expand the law of conservation of mass to include energy. In any reaction where energy is released or absorbed, the amount of mass or energy, measured separately, will not be constant. However, the *total* quantity of mass plus energy does remain constant. You may wish to look ahead to the discussion of the Einstein equation in Chapter 26 in order to help clarify this point.

■ To help students to distinguish between reactions in which energy is absorbed and those in which energy is released, do Demonstration 5-2 "Cold 'Milk'" (an endothermic reaction) and Demonstration 5-3 "Unclogging Your Pipes" (an exothermic reaction). Because energy is released, students may wonder if exothermic reactions proceed spontaneously. Explain that activation energy is needed to loosen the bonds sufficiently to form new ones. After the reaction starts, the formation of stronger bonds releases enough energy to make the reaction self-sustaining. Use Demonstration 5-4 "Activation Energy" to illustrate the point vividly.

■ **Application.** You may want to point out to students that as the amount of energy required to heat and cool our homes and other buildings increases, the cost of that energy becomes an important issue. Preventing energy loss is the major concern of many industries, such as those that manufacture thermal windows and insulating materials.

■ **Concept Mastery.** Many students think of both heat and cold as physical things. To help correct this misconception, you may use Concept Mastery question 35 (chapter-end question). Point out that the beaker feels cold when the substance dissolves because heat is absorbed in the dissolving process, not because the physical entity "cold" enters the substance.

■ **Critical Thinking.** In the Critical and Creative Thinking worksheet "Judging Things and Ideas" students are asked to consider the utility of methanol as an automobile fuel. The worksheet provides practice in making judgments and addresses the need for thorough evaluation of the pros and cons of an idea. This can help students to avoid snap judgments, in both chemistry and everyday decisions.

## 5-5 Heat Energy and Temperature, pp. 92-95

| Planning Guide | |
|---|---|
| Labs (Lab Manual) and Demonstrations (TE) | Supplementary Materials (Teacher's Resource Book) |
| | Transparency Master: Making a Celsius Thermometer, p. 5-2 Transparency Master: Comparison of Three Temperature Scales, p. 5-3 Review Activity: Temperature, p. 5-7 |

■ **Concept Mastery.** Students often memorize the formula for the conversion of temperature from the Fahrenheit to the Celsius scale, and vice versa, without understanding it. To help students see how these temperature scales are derived and how arbitrary the scales actually are, you may wish to discuss Concept Mastery question 36 (chapter-end question). Students can derive the answer to the question pictorially. Then

have them derive the formula relating temperature in degrees Celsius to temperature on the new scale:

Temp. on new scale = 3(°C) + 100

Have students relate this formula to the one for converting temperatures from Fahrenheit to Celsius.

## 5-6 Heat and Its Measurement, pp. 95-99

| Planning Guide | |
|---|---|
| Labs (Lab Manual) and Demonstrations (TE) | Supplementary Materials (Teacher's Resource Book) |
| Lab 7: Calorimetry: Heat of Fusion of Ice Lab 8: Calorimetry: Heat of Crystallization of Wax | Open-Ended Experiment: How Fattening Is a Peanut, p. 5-4 Open-Ended Experiment: Relative Temperature in a Bunsen Burner Flame, p. 5-5 Non-SI Supplementary Problems, p. 5-9 Review Activity: Calorimetry, p. 5-8 |

■ Be sure students understand the difference between heat and temperature. One way to state that difference is as follows. Heat is a *quantity* of energy and is measured in joules (or calories), while temperature is the *concentration* or *intensity* of heat and is measured in degrees. Ask students for comparisons between the temperature and the amount of heat in a burning match and a burning log of wood. Have them compute and compare the amount of heat required to raise the temperature of 10 cm$^3$ of water from 10°C to 100°C (3.4 kJ) with the amount required to change the temperature of 1000 cm$^3$ of water from 20°C to 21°C (4.2 kJ).

■ Explain that in calorimetry one cannot measure the absolute energy of starting materials, so that the difference in the energies of the initial and final states of a reaction mixture is used.

## 5-7 The Kinetic Theory of Heat and Temperature, p. 101

■ The word kinetic comes from the Greek *kinetikos*, meaning motion. The name of the theory stresses its assumption that particles are in constant motion. To demonstrate the kinetic theory, ask students to rub their hands together briskly and to recall the warmth of a bicycle pump in use or a nail being hammered vigorously. In each of these cases, molecules are given increased velocity and, therefore, increased kinetic energy. This increases the heat content and raises the temperature.

■ **Concept Mastery.** You may wish to use Concept Mastery question 33 (chapter-end questions) to reinforce students' understanding of the distinction between heat and temperature. In discussing these questions, make other comparisons. For example, you may tell students that the amount of heat in an ice cube is probably greater than the amount of heat in the equivalent volume of air because of the larger number of molecules in the solid ice than in the gaseous air. Use question 34 to clarify the point that molecules with a higher kinetic energy will have a higher temperature because temperature is a measure of the average kinetic energy of the molecules.

## 5-8 Interactions between Electric Charges, pp. 102-103

| Planning Guide | |
| --- | --- |
| Labs (Lab Manual) and Demonstrations (TE) | Supplementary Materials (Teacher's Resource Book) |
| | Societal Issues: Alternative Sources of Energy, p. SI-18 |

■ Although most students have probably observed the effects of static electricity, you may open the discussion of electric charges by demonstrating some of those effects. Plastic wrapping can be made to stick to a window against which it has been rubbed. If dry hair is combed (on a day that is cold and dry enough), students can produce a crackling noise because of static electricity.

# Demonstrations

## 5-1 Ethanol Cannon

**Overview:** In this demonstration, electrical energy creates a spark between two iron nails embedded in a polyethylene water bottle containing a milliliter of ethanol. A loud explosion occurs, forcing the stopper out of the bottle. This demonstration shows how energy can be converted from one form to another.

**Materials:** ethanol, 1 mL; tesla coil; ring stand and universal clamp; polyethylene bottle that has two nails inserted into it on opposite sides; cork stopper that fits snugly into the bottle.

**Advance Preparation:** Insert the nails into the polyethylene bottle. The points of the nails should have a gap of about 2 cm between them.

**Safety:** Clamp the bottle so that the cork will be directed upward and away from everyone. Wear goggles.

**Procedure:** 1. Add 1 mL of ethanol to the prepared bottle and insert the stopper. Swirl to coat the sides and to vaporize the alcohol. 2. Clamp the bottle at a

slight angle. 3. Turn on the tesla coil and touch the coil to one of the nails. 4. Ask students what kind of energy is applied to the nail, and have them try to trace the energy conversion. Emphasize the law of conservation of energy. 5. If the demonstration is to be repeated, first wash out the bottle and allow it to dry.

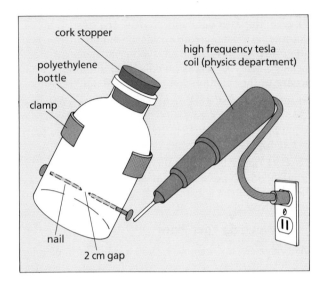

cork stopper

high frequency tesla coil (physics department)

polyethylene bottle

clamp

nail

2 cm gap

**Figure 5-1**

**Results:** A spark that ignites the alcohol will be produced between the two nails. The alcohol will react with oxygen to form water and carbon dioxide gas. This gas will be formed quickly and will force the cork out of the bottle. Electrical energy is applied and is converted to chemical energy, which is converted to mechanical energy.

## 5-2 Cold "Milk"

**Overview:** In this demonstration, equal volumes of two solids are placed into a test tube, and the test tube is stoppered and shaken until reaction occurs. A cold liquid that has the appearance of milk forms. Students observe an endothermic reaction that is similar to the reaction that occurs in cold packs used in hospitals.

**Materials:** ammonium chloride ($NH_4Cl$), reagent grade; barium hydroxide octahydrate crystal ($Ba(OH)_2 \cdot 8H_2O$), reagent grade; large test tube and rubber stopper; thermometer; cold pack (can be obtained from the school nurse or from the athletic department).

**Advance Preparation:** none

**Safety:** Do not pass the test tube containing the reactants around the room because gas is involved and builds up pressure in the tube that can force the stopper out unless you keep your finger over the stopper at all times.

**Procedure:** 1. Working at the fume hood or in a well-ventilated room, place a level teaspoon of each solid into a large test tube. Stopper and shake the test tube with your finger pressed gently over the stopper to hold it in place, until a reaction occurs. 2. While keeping your finger over the stopper, allow students to observe the reaction and to feel the test tube. 3. Determine the temperature of the liquid in the test tube, and carefully wash off the thermometer after the measurement. 4. "Break" a cold pack and relate what occurs to the reaction you just carried out.

**Results:** The test tube will become quite cold, the temperature of its contents falling well below room temperature. The reaction that occurs in the cold pack is also highly endothermic, or energy-absorbing.

**Disposal Tips:** Allow the ammonia gas to escape in the fume hood if possible. Add water to the tube to dissolve all of the substances. Pour into the drain and flush with a great deal of water.

## 5-3 Unclogging Your Pipes

**Overview:** In this demonstration, a solid drain cleaner is added to water to show what happens when the cleaner is placed into a drain. The purpose of each ingredient is discussed. This reaction produces heat and a gas. Together, these help to unclog drains by melting and dislodging grease and bringing about various reactions.

**Materials:** solid drain cleaner (which contains sodium hydroxide, aluminum shavings, coloring matter, and scent); 250-mL tall-form beaker; thermometer.

**Advance Preparation:** none

**Safety:** Wear goggles and rubber gloves when working with the drain cleaner. The reaction container will also become quite hot, and bubbling will occur.

**Procedure:** 1. Fill the beaker half full of water and measure the temperature. 2. Add a scoop of drain cleaner to the water and observe the results. 3. Determine the temperature of the solution now and carefully wash off the thermometer before touching it again. Ask students why they think drain cleaners are effective.

**Results:** The container will become hot, and bubbling will occur. When the sodium hydroxide in the cleaner dissolves, the process is exothermic; that is, heat is released. This heat causes the aluminum to react with the base to produce hydrogen gas and $Al(OH)_4^-$. The combination of the heat and the bubbling inside a drain forces grease to melt and become dislodged, and to react with the sodium hydroxide and move on through the drain.

**Disposal Tips:** Pour the liquid into a large container of dilute HCl to neutralize the sodium hydroxide. Pour the resulting mixture down the drain and flush with a great deal of water.

## 5-4 Activation Energy

**Overview:** In this demonstration, it is shown that a piece of magnesium will not combine with oxygen gas in the air unless a large amount of energy is added to the magnesium. This amount of energy is called the activation energy. Once started, the reaction is highly exothermic.

**Materials:** magnesium ribbon, 3 cm long; long forceps or crucible tongs; burner.

**Advance Preparation:** none

**Safety:** Warn students not to look directly at the burning magnesium, which will give off an amount of light that can be damaging to the eyes.

**Procedure:** 1. Hold the magnesium with the forceps or tongs and place it into the flame on the burner. 2. Point out to the students that a chemical reaction has occurred, and discuss the reaction.

**Results:** The magnesium will combine with atmospheric oxygen to produce magnesium oxide (MgO) and light and heat energy.

# Answers to Questions

### Page 89
1. Energy is the ability to do work.
2. You did no work on the car, because work is done only when a force moves an object through some distance.
3. Potential energy and kinetic energy. Potential energy is stored energy; kinetic energy is energy of motion.
4. Work is required because you use a force to pull an object (the bow string) through a distance.
5. Gasoline has chemical energy, a type of potential energy. This energy is available to do work at a later time.
6. Sound is a form of energy because it does work when it causes matter to vibrate.
7. The joule. Its symbol is J.

### Page 92
8. Electrical energy is converted into heat.
9. In any ordinary energy change, the total amount of energy remains the same.
10. Chemical energy may be changed to heat energy, or heat may be changed to increased chemical energy in the products.
11. In an exothermic reaction, heat is released. In an endothermic reaction, heat is absorbed.

**12.** Activation energy is the minimum energy required to start a chemical reaction.

## Page 95
**13.** The concept of temperature.

**14.** The thermometer is immersed in melting ice and a mark is made. The thermometer is then put into boiling water (at 1 atm) and another mark is made. The scale is then subdivided into 100 equal units (degrees) between the two marks.

**15.** Freezing point of water = 0°C = 273 K. Boiling point of water = 100°C = 373 K.

**16. a.** °C + 273 = K; 10 + 273 = 283 K
**b.** °C + 273 = K; −20 + 273 = 253 K

**17. a.** K − 273 = °C; 25 − 273 = −248°C
**b.** K − 273 = °C; 300 − 273 = 27°C

## Page 99
**18.** The temperature usually rises.

**19.** The colder object gains heat from the hotter one until both reach the same temperature.

**20.** Calorimetry is the measurement of the amount of heat released or absorbed in a chemical reaction.

**21. a.** Heat transferred = mass of water × change in temperature × specific heat of water.
**b.** 5000 g × 60°C × 4.2 J/g-°C = 1.3 × 10⁶ J = 1.3 × 10³ kJ

**22. a.** Heat transferred = mass of water × change of temperature × specific heat of water.
**b.** 2000 g × 30°C × 4.2 J/g-°C = 2.5 × 10⁵ J = 2.5 × 10² kJ

**23.** 500 g × Δt × 4.2 J/g-°C = 1.05 × 10⁴ J
$$\Delta t = \frac{1.05 \times 10^4 \text{ J}}{500 \text{ g} \times 4.2 \text{ J/g-°C}} = 5.0°C$$
Final temperature = 25°C − 5.0°C = 20°C

**24.** The amount of heat would be the same, as shown by the following calculations:
1000 g × 10°C × 4.2 J/g-°C = 4.2 × 10⁴ J
500 g × 20°C × 4.2 J/g-°C = 4.2 × 10⁴ J

## Page 101
**25.** The motion is too rapid for our eyes to detect, and the distances moved are so small. We can only assume that the particles are in motion because the temperature of the wood is above absolute zero.

**26.** The temperature of the body is a measure of the average kinetic energy of its particles.

## Page 103
**27.** The hair and comb acquire opposite electric charges that attract one another with a force called electrostatic attraction.

**28.** In an electrically neutral body, positive and negative charges are present in equal amounts.

**29.** Electrostatic force.

**30.** The energy used to overcome electrostatic force becomes electrical potential energy.

**31.** An electric current is a flow of electrically charged particles.

## Chapter Review   5

### Page 104, Content Review

**1.** The mathematical relationship is: Work = force × distance.

**2.** Six nonmechanical forms of energy associated with submicroscopic particles are chemical, electrical, electromagnetic, magnetic, sound, and heat.

**3.** The energy supplied by a lighted match to a candle is called activation energy.

**4.** The numeric relationship between Kelvin and Celsius temperatures is K = °C + 273.

**5. a.** 0°C + 273 = 273 K;
**b.** 100°C + 273 = 373 K;
**c.** −100°C + 273 = 173 K;
**d.** −273°C + 273 = 0 K

**6. a.** 0 K − 273 = −273°C;
**b.** 100 K − 273 = −173°C;
**c.** 500 K − 273 = 227°C;
**d.** 273 K − 273 = 0°C

**7.** A calorimeter is a device used to measure heat changes in a reaction. It consists of an insulated container, a thermometer, and a known mass of water.

**8.** The mathematical relationship used to calculate the heat absorbed by the water in a calorimeter is
$$\text{Heat} = \frac{\text{mass}}{\text{of water}} \times \frac{\text{temperature change}}{\text{of water}} \times \frac{\text{specific heat}}{\text{of water}}$$

**9.** The joule is the preferred SI derived unit for measuring heat energy.

**10.** Heat = 200 g × 30°C × 4.2 J/g-°C = 25 200 J = 2.5 × 10⁴ J

**11. a.** 8000 J × 1 kJ/1000 J = 8.000 × 10³ J = 8 kJ
**b.** 3.5 × 10⁴ J × 1 kJ/10³ J = 35 kJ
**c.** 2.1 kJ × 1000 J/kJ = 2.1 × 10³ J
**d.** 4.7 × 10⁻¹ kJ × 10³ J/kJ = 4.7 × 10² J

**12.** Temp. change = 2.7 × 10⁴ J ÷ (700 g × 4.2 J/g-°C) = 9.2°C. Therefore, final temperature = 90°C − 9.2°C = 81°C.

**13.** Mass of water = 5.0 × 10⁴ J ÷ (40°C × 4.2 J/g-°C) = 3.0 × 10² g

**14.** Specific heat = 950 J ÷ (20 g × 24°C) = 1.98 J/g-°C = 2.0 J/g-°C

15. Mass = 755 J ÷ (25.0°C × 0.387 J/g-°C) = 78.0 g

16. Specific heat = 428 J ÷ [(215.0°C − 196.0°C) × 93.9 g] = 428 J ÷ (19.0°C × 93.9 g) = 0.24 J/g -°C

17. Energy = 22.8 g × (32.5°C − 16.1°C) × 0.14 J/g-°C = 22.8 g × 16.4°C × 0.14 J/g-°C = 52 J

18. As the temperature increases, the average kinetic energy of the particles increases.

19. At higher temperatures the average kinetic energy of the particles is greater.

20. The sizes of the charges and the distance between the charged objects determine the size of the electrostatic force.

## Page 105, Content Mastery

21. A burning candle converts the stored chemical energy of the wax into heat and light (electromagnetic) energy.

22. Answers will vary. Some possible examples are: **a.** An oil furnace heating air converts chemical energy to heat. **b.** An electric water heater converts electrical energy to heat. **c.** A dry cell converts chemical to electrical energy.

23. Since substance Y has a lower specific heat than substance X, 100 joules of energy will raise Y to a higher temperature.

24. There are 350 Celsius degrees between the freezing point and the boiling point of the liquid. Since a Celsius degree is the same size as a kelvin, this is 350 Kelvin.

25. To keep an object moving at constant speed, more energy must be added to overcome energy losses to the environment in the form of heat and friction.

26. No, the automobile does not violate the law of conservation of energy. The 90% of the energy that is not used to propel the car is released into the environment as heat.

27. Mass needed = $\dfrac{100 \text{ kJ}}{\text{mile}} \times \dfrac{\text{gram hamburger}}{15 \text{ kJ}} \times$

    3.0 miles = 20 g (less than ⅛ of the meat in a quarter pounder)

28. **a.** Burning coal releases heat energy, so it is exothermic. **b.** Boiling water requires addition of heat, so it is endothermic. **c.** Burning of natural gas in a clothes dryer is exothermic. **d.** Drying of clothes (evaporation of water) absorbs heat and therefore is endothermic.

29. Heat = $\dfrac{\text{mass of}}{\text{substance}} \times \dfrac{\text{change in}}{\text{temperature}} \times \dfrac{\text{specific heat}}{\text{of substance}}$

    = 100 g × 14°C × 0.129 J/g-°C

    = $1.8 \times 10^2$ J

30. Charges must always be balanced. If the balloon becomes negatively charged, the flannel must be positively charged.

31. In the illustrated pile driver, the chemical energy of the coal is converted into heat energy, making the gas expand. The expanding gas converts this heat energy into mechanical energy to move the piston and raise the ram.

## Page 106, Concept Mastery

32. **Concept:** *Law of conservation of energy and dependence of heat transfer on mass of substance.*

    *Solution:* Because of the law of conservation of energy, the heat gained by the cooler sample equals the heat lost by the warmer sample. Let $T$ be the temperature of the mixture.

    Heat gained = heat lost

    $$100 \text{ g} \times (T - 20°C) \times \frac{4.2 \text{ J}}{\text{g-}°C} = 50 \text{ g} \times (50°C - T) \times \frac{4.2 \text{ J}}{\text{g-}°C}$$

    $$420(T - 20) = 210(50 - T)$$
    $$420T - 8400 = 10500 - 210T$$
    $$630T = 18900$$
    $$T = 30°C$$

33. **Concept:** *The sense of touch does not give a true comparison of the temperature of objects.*

    *Solution:* The metal and the wood are at the same temperature. The metal feels colder because it conducts heat away from your hand faster than wood does.

34. **Concept:** *Energy is a function of molecular motion, which is a function of temperature and phase.*

    *Solution:* **d, a, b, c.** The mercury vapor has the most kinetic energy. The warmer liquid has more kinetic energy than the colder liquid. The solid has the least kinetic energy.

35. **Concept:** *Cold is not a physical entity but is the absence of heat.*

    *Solution:* A more scientific explanation is that the mixture is absorbing heat.

36. **Concept:** *The scale for measuring temperature is an arbitrary one.*

    *Solution:* On the "New" scale (°N) there are 300 degrees between the freezing point and the boiling point of water. Also, 0°C is equivalent to 100°N. Therefore °C = ⅓(°N − 100). For 250°N:
    °C = ⅓(250°N − 100) = ⅓(150) = 50°C
    K = °C + 273 = 50 + 273 = 323 K

## Page 106, Cumulative Review

**37. a.** $x$ mm = 2.512 m $\times \dfrac{1000 \text{ mm}}{1 \text{ m}}$ = 2512 mm

    **b.** $x$ g = 0.0524 kg $\times \dfrac{1000 \text{ g}}{1 \text{ kg}}$ = 52.4 g

    **c.** $x$ km = 7500 cm $\times \dfrac{1 \text{ m}}{100 \text{ cm}} \times \dfrac{1 \text{ km}}{1000 \text{ m}}$ = 0.075 km

**38.** Volume = $\dfrac{\text{mass}}{\text{density}}$ = $\dfrac{135 \text{ g}}{2.70 \text{ g/cm}^3}$ = 50.0 cm³

**39.** Density = $\dfrac{\text{mass}}{\text{volume}}$ = $\dfrac{52.1 \text{ g}}{30.0 \text{ cm}^3}$ = 1.74 g/cm³

**40. a.** 1.2 cm × 0.487 cm = 0.58 cm²
    **b.** 2.849 g/0.75 cm³ = 3.8 g/cm³
    **c.** 30 cm³ + 8.45 cm³ = 38 cm³
    **d.** 0.97 mm × 1.030 mm = 1.0 mm²

**41. a.** When melting, solid ice changes to liquid water; its volume decreases slightly. When boiling, liquid water changes to gaseous steam; its volume increases greatly. **b.** These changes are physical because the chemical composition of the water does not change.

**42.** Percent error = $\dfrac{(101.5°C - 100°C)}{100°C} \times 100\%$ = 1.5%

**43. a.** 98.6°C has three significant figures.
    **b.** 0.0034 m has two significant figures.
    **c.** 7000.0 cm³ has five significant figures.
    **d.** 10 kg has one or two significant figures.

**44. a.** A sample of matter may undergo a change of weight if its location changes.
    **b.** During the weight change, its mass does not change.

**45.** $\dfrac{(3.0 \times 10^{-2})(2.0 \times 10^3)}{(4.0 \times 10^{-6})(6.0 \times 10^{-7})}$ = 2.5 × 10¹³

**46.** Four examples of physical properties may include the following: color, odor, taste, hardness, density, and melting and boiling points.

## Page 106, Critical Thinking

**47.** *Similarities:* The calorie and the joule are both metric units used to measure energy.
*Differences:* The joule is used to measure all forms of energy, but the calorie usually measures only heat. A calorie is equal to about 4.2 joules. The joule is an SI unit but the calorie is not. Different definitions of the calorie refer to different quantities of energy. A joule refers only to one quantity of energy.

**48. a.** Sulfuric acid has potential energy because it could undergo an exothermic chemical reaction. **b.** A speeding bullet has kinetic energy because it is moving. **c.** Water behind a dam has potential energy that would become kinetic energy if the dam broke. **d.** Fire has kinetic energy because some of the reactants and products (e.g., oxygen and smoke) are in motion. **e.** Lightning has kinetic energy because the charged particles are in motion. **f.** Food has potential energy, some of which is released during digestion.

**49.** The chemist should react C and D because the endothermic reaction will not release heat.

**50.** You are assuming that the solutions have equal specific heats.

**51.** The overall process of photosynthesis is endothermic because energy is absorbed.

**52.** Evaporation is an endothermic process, which absorbs heat. This heat is supplied by your hand.

## Page 107, Challenge Problems

**53. a.** Answers will vary. Typical energy sources include gasoline in a car, food, the sun, and the battery in a calculator.
    **b.** Students should identify the form of energy obtained from each source; for example, gasoline provides chemical energy.
    **c.** Students should list an alternative for each source of energy; for example, riding a bicycle instead of using gasoline in a car.

**54.** Students should realize that they need the mass of water. With the density of water being 1.0 g/cm³, the mass is 200 g.

$$\begin{array}{l}\dfrac{\text{Energy}}{\text{in food}} = \dfrac{\text{mass of}}{\text{water}} \times \dfrac{\text{change in temp.}}{\text{of water}} \times \dfrac{\text{specific heat}}{\text{of water}}\end{array}$$

    = 200 g × (86°C − 21°C) × 4.2 J/g-°C
    = 5.5 × 10⁴ J or 55 kJ

55 kJ in the 10-g sample for the 100-g serving

$\dfrac{55 \text{ kJ}}{10 \text{ g}} \times 100$ g = 550 kJ

**55.** Answers will vary. One possible answer is provided here. "Static cling" is caused by a buildup of charges on clothing. Positively and negatively charged clothing sticks together. In the summer the air contains more water, which prevents this buildup of charges.

5

# Structure of the Atom

## Chapter Planning Guide

| Text Section | | Labs (Lab Manual) and Demonstrations (TE) | Supplementary Materials (Teacher's Resource Book) |
|---|---|---|---|
| 6-1 | Atoms Today, pp. 109-110 | | |
| 6-2 | Historical Background, pp. 110-113 | | Transparency Master: Determining the Composition of Water, p. 6-2 |
| 6-3 | The Law of Multiple Proportions, pp. 113-114 | Lab 9: Conservation of Mass | |
| 6-4 | Dalton's Atomic Theory, pp. 114-115 | Demo 6-1: Making "Cents" out of Dalton's Atomic Theory, p. TG-110 | |
| 6-5 | Updating the Atomic Theory, pp. 115-116 | Demo 6-2: Evidence for the Existence of Electrons, p. TG-110 | |
| 6-6 | Electrons, Protons, and Neutrons, pp. 116-118 | | |
| 6-7 | Charge and Mass of the Electron, pp. 118-119 | | |
| 6-8 | The Rutherford Model of the Atom, pp. 119-121 | Demo 6-3: Black Boxes, p. TG-111 | Transparency Master: The Rutherford Experiment, p. 6-3 |
| Biography | Ernest Rutherford, p. 119 | | |
| 6-9 | Shortcomings of Rutherford's Model, p. 121 | Demo 6-4: Energy Levels in the Bohr Model of the Atom, p. TG-111 | Review Activity: Development of Atomic Theory, p. 6-5 |
| 6-10 | The Bohr Model, pp. 122-123 | | |
| 6-11 | The Charge-cloud Model, pp. 123-124 | | Critical and Creative Thinking: Analyzing Parts-Whole Relationships, p. CCT-11 |
| 6-12 | Scientific Models, pp. 124-125 | | |
| 6-13 | The Nature of Light, pp. 125-127 | Demo 6-5: Making Waves, p. TG-112 Demo 6-6: Acetate Waves, p. TG-112 | |

| Text Section | | Labs (Lab Manual) and Demonstrations (TE) | Supplementary Materials (Teacher's Resource Book) |
|---|---|---|---|
| **6-14** | The Emission and Absorption of Radiation, pp. 127-129 | Lab 10: Emission Spectra and Energy Demo 6-7: Observing Spectra, p. TG-113 | Open-Ended Demonstration: Flame Tests, p. 6-4 |
| **6-15** | Light as Energy, pp. 130-131 | | |
| **6-16** | The Major Nucleons, pp. 131-133 | | |
| **6-17** | Quarks, pp. 133-134 | | |
| **6-18** | The Concept of Atomic Mass, p. 134 | Demo 6-8: Isotopic Pennies, p. TG-113 | |
| **6-19** | Mass Number, pp. 135-136 | | Review Activity: Subatomic Particles, p. 6-6 |
| **6-20** | Modern Standard of Atomic Mass, pp. 136-137 | | |
| **Application** | Mass Spectrometer, pp. 137-138 | | |
| **6-21** | Determining Atomic Masses from Weighted Averages, pp. 138-139 | | |
| | | | Test—Form A, p. AT-21 Alternate Test—Form B, p. BT-21 |

☐ Core　　☐ Advanced　　☐ Optional

## Chapter Overview

After beginning Chapter 6 with a summary of the students' prior learnings about atoms, we look at the development of our model of the atom. We discuss the evidence supporting Democritus's concept of matter as discontinuous and show how Dalton's atomic theory of 1803 is still useful. The major subatomic particles are considered, and their properties are described.

We trace the development of concepts of the nature of the atom from Rutherford's model of a nucleus surrounded by electrons, through Bohr's solar system model, to the charge-cloud model. We show how the study of the emission and absorption of light energy has helped to determine the arrangement of electrons.

An account of quarks gives a glimpse of future elaboration of atomic theory. The concepts of atomic number and atomic mass in relation to protons and neutrons are developed in the final sections.

## Chapter Objectives

After students have completed this chapter, they will be able to:

1. Trace the development of models of the atom through the charge-cloud model.　*6-2 to 6-5, 6-10 to 6-12*

2. Show that the atomic theory is consistent with experimental observations.  *6-3, 6-6 to 6-9*
3. State the properties of atoms and subatomic particles.  *6-1, 6-5, 6-7*
4. Describe the relationship between emission spectra and the structure of atoms.  *6-13 to 6-15*
5. Use the concept of atomic mass.  *6-16 to 6-21*

## Teaching Suggestions

### 6-1 Atoms Today, pp. 109-110, and

### 6-2 Historical Background, pp. 110-113

| Planning Guide | |
|---|---|
| Labs (Lab Manual) and Demonstrations (TE) | Supplementary Materials (Teacher's Resource Book) |
| | Transparency Master: Determining the Composition of Water, p. 6-2 |

■ To get started, prepare a handout and have students complete as much as they can of a blank table like Teacher's Guide Figure 6-1 and then check it against text Figure 6-2. Many students will be able to fill in the table at least partially. Point out how much they already know about the structure of atoms and that they will build on that knowledge in this chapter.

| Properties of Sub-Atomic Particles | | | | |
|---|---|---|---|---|
| | charge | mass | symbol | location |
| proton | | | | |
| electron | | | | |
| neutron | | | | |

**Figure 6-1**

To make atoms less abstract, give everyday examples—or analogies—of continuous and discontinuous matter, such as: mashed potatoes/french fries, ramp/stairway, and riding in a car/walking. Ask students to think of other examples.

■ **Concept Mastery.** Students often do not distinguish between properties due to atoms themselves and properties due to the arrangement of atoms into larger molecules or ionic solids. Use the example shown in Concept Mastery question 49 (chapter-end question) to help students make this distinction.

### 6-3 The Law of Multiple Proportions, pp. 113-114,

### 6-4 Dalton's Atomic Theory, pp. 114-115,

### 6-5 Updating the Atomic Theory, pp. 115-116, and

### 6-6 Electrons, Protons, and Neutrons, pp. 116-118

| Planning Guide | |
|---|---|
| Labs (Lab Manual) and Demonstrations (TE) | Supplementary Materials (Teacher's Resource Book) |
| Lab 9: Conservation of Mass<br>Demo 6-1: Making "Cents" out of Dalton's Atomic Theory, p. TG-110<br>Demo 6-2: Evidence for the Existence of Electrons, p. TG-110 | |

■ Use the class discussion on the law of conservation of mass, the law of definite proportions, and the law of multiple proportions to extend and strengthen earlier study (Chapter 1) on the nature of science and the scientific method. Laws such as these tell "what" happens, not "why" it happens. Hypotheses propose tentative explanations and pose questions that call for testing. A theory, such as the atomic theory, is a general statement that accounts for a variety of observations.

Have students recall the law of conservation of mass from Section 4-9. In Laboratory 9, "Conservation of Mass," students carry out two chemical reactions. They observe that if none of the products escapes from the reaction container, there is no change in mass, and that if a gaseous product does escape, there is a slight loss of mass.

Students usually must work hard at learning the law of multiple proportions. Do not require memorization of any statement of the law, but focus on its understanding. Use text Figure 6-5 to its best advantage. You may want to ask students—especially if they are familiar with the "indirect proof" of geometry—how these observations would be different if matter were continuous.

■ Go through the principles of Dalton's atomic theory from the point of view that Dalton has set out to explain what matter must be like. Does anyone know of any observations that are inconsistent with his explanation? If not, then we will keep his theory because it *satisfactorily* accounts for what we observe. If—before reading Section 6-5—some well-informed students mention observations that are inconsistent with the theory, allow them to put a "patch" on the theory and then proceed.

Demonstration 6-1, "Making 'Cents' out of Dalton's Atomic Theory," uses nickels, pre-1982 pennies, and post-1982 pennies to illustrate Dalton's theory, including its greatest inconsistency with later observations—that not all atoms of an element are identical.

To update Dalton's atomic theory, use a transparency or blackboard version of the theory from Section 6-4. Have students insert the changes that make the theory consistent with discoveries made since 1803.

■ Use Demonstration 6-2, "Evidence for the Existence of Electrons," to show students how a magnet can deflect the path of electrons in a cathode tube. This should help them to think about subatomic particles and their interaction with electrical and magnetic phenomena.

## 6-7 Charge and Mass of the Electron, pp. 118-119

■ You might consider doing Millikan's oil-drop experiment as a demonstration. Or you may describe the experiment, omitting mathematical details. Millikan used X rays to give oil drops a negative charge. The amount of charge on the droplets was determined by measuring the rate of fall of the oil drops between two charged plates and then measuring the rate of rise when the top plate was given a positive charge. The total charge on a drop was always a multiple of $1.60 \times 10^{-19}$ coulomb, indicating that this was the charge of a single electron. Using Thomson's $e/m$ value, Millikan then calculated the mass of an electron.

## 6-8 The Rutherford Model of the Atom, pp. 119-121

| Planning Guide | |
|---|---|
| Labs (Lab Manual) and Demonstrations (TE) | Supplementary Materials (Teacher's Resource Book) |
| Demo 6-3: Black Boxes, p. TG-111 | Transparency Master: The Rutherford Experiment, p. 6-3 |

■ In Demonstration 6-3, "Black Boxes," students determine the nature of the material in a closed container, make mental models of a material based on gathered evidence, and relate their experience to Rutherford's gold-foil experiment. This demonstration also reinforces the correct usage of the terms "law" and "theory."

Use text Figures 6-11 and 6-12 and the Transparency Master "The Rutherford Experiment" to help explain Rutherford's experiment and his interpretation of its results. Here is another chance to ask students what behavior of matter would be observed if atoms did not have dense nuclei but had some other structure, e.g., Thomson's "plum pudding" model.

## 6-9 Shortcomings of Rutherford's Model, p. 121, and

## 6-10 The Bohr Model, pp. 122-123

| Planning Guide | |
|---|---|
| Labs (Lab Manual) and Demonstrations (TE) | Supplementary Materials (Teacher's Resource Book) |
| Demo 6-4: Energy Levels in the Bohr Model of the Atom, p. TG-111 | Review Activity: Development of Atomic Theory, p. 6-5 |

■ Tell students that it is difficult to prove that a theory is "right" and, in fact, research is not intended to *prove* a theory right or wrong. It is the responsibility of the scientific community to scrutinize a theory for consistency and satisfactory performance as a predictor of how matter will behave and to discard it when it does not measure up. Have students recall the rise and fall of the phlogiston theory (Chapter 1).

Use text Figure 6-16 to show students where, according to Bohr, electrons can be located and how energy can be related to the movement of electrons between energy levels. To help explain the excited state—a difficult concept for some students—compare diagrams of several atoms in both an excited state and the ground state. Have students look ahead to text Figure 13-19, showing examples of electron configurations for atoms in both states. You may also have a student volunteer put a book into an "excited state" by moving it from the floor to a table or desk. Then have the student push it off onto the floor. When the book hits the floor (the ground state) sound energy is released just as light energy is released in an atom. Although this is not totally analogous, it should get the idea across.

■ Have students do Demonstration 6-4, "Energy Levels in the Bohr Model of the Atom," in which they observe the relationship between the energy of a ball attached by a rubber band to a paddle and the distance it moves away from the paddle when it is struck. The behavior of the ball is analogous to that of an electron in the Bohr model of the atom.

## 6-11 The Charge-cloud Model, pp. 122-123, and

## 6-12 Scientific Models, pp. 124-125

| Planning Guide | |
|---|---|
| Labs (Lab Manual) and Demonstrations (TE) | Supplementary Materials (Teacher's Resource Book) |
| | Critical and Creative Thinking: Analyzing Parts-Whole Relationships, p. CCT-11 |

■ To introduce the charge-cloud model of the atom, have students examine text Figure 6-16 and locate the nucleus and the area in which the electron is found. If you choose to do more with electron configurations, either directly after Section 6-11 or after completing Chapter 6, consider using Chapter 13 now. It fits quite well. However, for the present, you may prefer to have the charge-cloud model take its place as simply an improved version of the Bohr model.

Many students will have a hard time thinking of a model as something other than a scale model "exact replica." Point out that a model is usually one feature of a theory, and use the succession of atomic models in text Figure 6-19 to help students enlarge their concept of "model."

■ **Application.** You might want to point out to students that atomic theory is still developing and changing, often as part of an interplay between applied science and pure science. For instance, recent developments in the field of superconducting materials have renewed interest in the exact atomic structures of these materials, and there is much current research directed toward determining those structures.

■ **Concept Mastery.** You may wish to use Concept Mastery question 51 (chapter-end question) to help students use a model to form a mental picture of the arrangement of electrons in an atom. You might also use the analogy of the ladder as an example of how analogies eventually break down. Point out that unlike the energy levels of electrons, the rungs of the ladder are evenly spaced and have no sublevels. Then tell students that where one analogy breaks down, another one can often be used. In this case, use the analogy of the rings in the cross section of a tree trunk, which are spaced increasingly closer together as the tree ages. Ask students where, in turn, the tree ring analogy breaks down. (Answer: it looks suspiciously like the Bohr or solar system model, with concentric rings.)

■ **Critical Thinking.** In the worksheet titled "Analyzing Parts-Whole Relationships" students can gain fresh insight into the atom (the whole) by exploring the roles of its parts (subatomic particles). The concepts of atoms, isotopes, and ions are particularly well suited to this topic.

## 6-13 The Nature of Light, pp. 125-127

| Planning Guide | |
|---|---|
| Labs (Lab Manual) and Demonstrations (TE) | Supplementary Materials (Teacher's Resource Book) |
| Demo 6-5: Making Waves, p. TG-112<br>Demo 6-6: Acetate Waves, p. TG-112 | |

■ Have students do Demonstration 6-5, "Making Waves," in which they use a rope or coil to produce standing waves and observe the inverse relationship between wavelength and frequency. Then use Demonstration 6-6, "Acetate Waves," to show that waves of varying frequency and wavelength still move at the same speed.

■ You may wish to have students think about all of the quantitative characteristics of light (wavelength, frequency, and velocity) as various versions and combinations of two units of measurement, length (meters) and time (seconds).

■ **Concept Mastery.** You can reinforce the idea of the electron as having wave properties by using Concept Mastery question 52 (chapter-end question). To help students understand the relationship among wavelength, frequency, and velocity, you may wish to compare each wave to a railroad boxcar. If you know how many cars pass in a given time interval (frequency) and the length of one car (wavelength), you can calculate the speed (velocity) of the train. For example, if cars pass at the rate of three in 10 seconds, and each car is 30 meters long, the train is traveling at 9 meters per second.

## 6-14 The Emission and Absorption of Radiation, pp. 127-129

| Planning Guide | |
|---|---|
| Labs (Lab Manual) and Demonstrations (TE) | Supplementary Materials (Teacher's Resource Book) |
| Lab 10: Emission Spectra and Energy<br><br>Demo 6-7: Observing Spectra, p. TG-113 | Open-Ended Demonstration: Flame Tests, p. 6-4 |

■ Begin with Demonstration 6-7, "Observing Spectra," in which students observe a continuous spectrum and a bright-light spectrum of helium or hydrogen. In addition, or alternatively, show some emission spectra by using discharge tubes and slit diffraction tubes. Cardboard versions of the latter work quite well for simple qualitative demonstration. Students are generally quite amazed to see the breaking up of white light by this crude piece of equipment.

Next, have students do Laboratory 10, "Emission Spectra and Energy Levels," in which they observe and measure spectral lines in hydrogen and mercury and calculate the wavelengths of those lines. Measurements taken in this lab will generate a Bohr-type model for the hydrogen and mercury atoms.

■ You may use the Open-Ended Laboratory Demonstration "Flame Tests" after Section 6-14. Students observe the colors produced in a flame by various metallic ions and by the burning of newspaper printed in black and colored inks. They propose explanations for their observations and suggest ways to test those explanations. Alternatively, this demonstration can be done prior to Lab 25, "Flame Tests," for Chapter 13.

■ **Application.** Students will be interested to know that many professional fireworks and commercial fireplace logs utilize the emission of light of various wavelengths by metallic elements to add attractive colors to the fireworks and log flames. You can also buy crystals to throw on a wood fire to produce colors.

■ **Concept Mastery.** Students sometimes extend a model beyond its usefulness. You might use Concept Mastery question 53 (chapter-end question) as an example of the limitations of models. Point out that one form of sulfur is yellow because of the way the aggregate of sulfur atoms interacts with light, while another form of sulfur with a different arrangement of atoms in the aggregate is dark brown. The individual atoms have no color at all—the concept simply does not apply to single atoms of sulfur or any other element.

### 6-15 Light as Energy, pp. 130-131

■ You may want to use energy calculations in relation to the emission of light. If so, then students will need to practice using the formulas

$$c = f\lambda \text{ or simply } \frac{\text{m}}{\text{s}} = \frac{\text{(wave)}}{\text{s}} \times \frac{\text{m}}{\text{(wave)}}$$

and

$$E = hf \text{ or simply } J = J{\cdot}s \times \frac{1}{\text{s}}$$

Present $c$ (the special symbol for the velocity of light) as the combination of

$$\frac{\text{m}}{\text{(wave)}} \text{ and } \frac{\text{(waves)}}{\text{s}}$$

Present $E$ as "logically" proportional to "how often a wave goes by" (i.e., more often = more energy) and $h$ as simply the constant of proportionality between joules (the SI unit for energy) and hertz (the SI unit for frequency). You may also point out that such constants of proportionality have many uses, such as changing feet into inches or gallons of gasoline into cost of gasoline at the gas pump.

### 6-16 The Major Nucleons, pp. 131-133

■ In discussing nucleons, emphasize the principle that the symbol for an element represents a specific atomic number, hence number of protons (or electrons) in an atom. Give students a great deal of practice using these terms, including locating atomic numbers in the alphabetical list of elements or the periodic table at the end of the book.

■ **Application.** Students, especially those planning careers in the health-related sciences, will be interested in knowing that doctors practicing nuclear medicine use radioactive isotopes of several elements. One example is iodine-131, used to treat an overactive thyroid gland that results from the growth of a tumor in the gland. Another example is phosphorus-32, used to treat leukemia (the overproduction of white blood cells) and polycythemia vera (the overproduction of red blood cells). The treatment is effective because phosphorus is a chemical component of all living cells and thus it freely circulates in the bloodstream.

### 6-17 Quarks, pp. 133-134

■ Tell the students that every year new discoveries give further evidence that atoms are really not indivisible. The study of quarks has provided information about more kinds of subatomic particles.

### 6-18 The Concept of Atomic Mass, p. 134,

### 6-19 Mass Number, pp. 135-136, and

### 6-20 Modern Standard of Atomic Mass, pp. 136-137

| Planning Guide | |
|---|---|
| Labs (Lab Manual) and Demonstrations (TE) | Supplementary Materials (Teacher's Resource Book) |
| Demo 6-8: Isotopic Pennies, p. TG-113 | Review Activity: Subatomic Particles, p. 6-6 |

■ You might like to gather a collection of bolts (or other hardware) of varying sizes and have students weigh them individually. Let each bolt represent an atom and the mass of the smallest bolt be one bolt-mass-unit (bmu), and then express the mass of each bolt in bmu. You could have students determine the mass, in bmu, of a sealed bag of bolts of the same size and then estimate the number of bolts in the bag. If it seems appropriate for your students at this time, encourage the idea of counting by massing. This idea can also be used in Chapter 8.

■ Be sure students can take the ideas and definitions from Sections 6-16 and 6-18 and use them with the concept of mass number in Section 6-19. A mass number must be an integer because it is a counted number of particles. Give students a great deal of practice using various combinations of $A$ (mass number) and $Z$ (atomic number) for many isotopes. Emphasize that atomic mass as given in a reference source is not a mass number for any one particular isotope. Also emphasize that the mass number is not a mass either and that every isotope has an atomic mass with a value that is very close to its mass number.

■ Use Demonstration 6-8, "Isotopic Pennies," to reinforce the concept of isotopes. Students develop a method for finding the average mass or the percent of isotopes in a sample. This demonstration provides a good introduction to the concept of determining atomic mass from weighted averages, in case you plan to teach that topic (Section 6-21).

Students should be able to make use of the concept of atomic mass, discuss the need for a definition of atomic mass unit, and distinguish clearly between atomic mass and mass number.

## 6-21 Determining Atomic Masses from Weighted Averages, pp. 138-139

■ Use the sample problem to explain the concept of using weighted averages to determine atomic mass. If you assume that you have 100 atoms, it should be easy for students to think of approximately 20 atoms (actually 19.78) as weighing 10 (actually 10.013 u) and 80 atoms (actually 80.22) weighing 11 (actually 11.009 u). Some quick thinkers may recognize that the average mass is about 80% toward 11 from 10, or about 10.8. Discuss why simply taking the arithmetic average of the two isotopic masses does not give a true average mass of naturally occurring boron.

# Demonstrations

## 6-1 Making "Cents" out of Dalton's Atomic Theory

**Overview:** In this demonstration, using pennies, nickels, and an overhead projector, the teacher illustrates Dalton's atomic theory. Students develop a better understanding of the statements in the theory by recognizing that atoms are indestructible (in Dalton's view) and that atoms of different elements are different. The different masses of pre- and post-1982 pennies help the students to see how the atomic model was altered to account for the existence of isotopes.

**Materials:** five pre-1982 pennies; five post-1982 pennies; 10 nickels; electronic balance that measures mass to the nearest tenth of a gram (triple-beam balance is also suitable); overhead projector.

**Advance Preparation:** none

**Procedure:** 1. Place five pre-1982 and five post-1982 pennies on the overhead, along with 10 nickels. Point out that these coins are to represent indivisible and indestructible particles. State that the pennies all appear to have the same shape and properties. Find the individual masses of a few pre-1982 pennies. Repeat for the nickels. 2. Place two pre-1982 pennies next to one nickel, to form a "compound." Repeat,

using two post-1982 pennies with the nickel. Reinforce the idea that atoms combine in whole-number ratios. Refer to the formula for water, which has a ratio of two hydrogen atoms to one oxygen atom. 3. Find the mass of one of the "compound" sets of coins and compare it to that of the total of the masses of the two pennies and one nickel weighed separately. 4. Discuss how the preceding illustrates the law of conservation of mass and accounts for the law of definite proportions. 5. By placing two pennies next to two nickels, you can illustrate the law of multiple proportions. Find the mass of two nickels and compare it to the mass of one nickel. 6. Discuss how Dalton's theory had to be altered when new evidence showed that atoms of the same element could have different masses. Take a pre-1982 penny from one "compound" and a post-1982 penny from the other, and tell the class the masses of the two coins. Point out that even though the masses of the pennies ("isotopes") are different, they represent the same element and combine with the nickel in the same manner.

**Results:** In step 1, the mass of each pre-1982 penny will be 3.1 g and the mass of each post-1982 penny will be 2.5 g. Before 1982, pennies were made of 95% copper and 5% tin and zinc. In 1982, the U.S. Mint started making pennies out of copper-coated zinc. The mass of each nickel will be 5.0 g. In step 3, the mass of the "compound" will be equal to the total mass of the individual "atoms" (11.2 g or 10.0 g, depending on the "compound" used), illustrating the law of conservation of mass. Since an individual "compound molecule" is always made up of the same number and kinds of "atoms," the law of definite proportions applies. In step 5, the ratio of the mass of two nickels to the mass of one nickel is 2:1. Dalton's theory had to be altered in terms of the ratio of masses of atoms in a compound, given the existence of isotopes.

## 6-2 Evidence for the Existence of Electrons

**Overview:** In this demonstration, a magnet is placed near a discharge tube. The magnet deflects the path of the electrons. When the poles of the magnet are reversed, the path of electrons is deflected in the opposite direction. This demonstration shows that a magnet can deflect the path of a charged particle in a direction that depends on the charge of the particle.

**Materials:** cathode-ray tube (Crookes tube or some other appropriate type); appropriate high-voltage, low-current power source (can usually be purchased together with the tube); large horseshoe magnet.

**Advance Preparation:** Set up power source, tube.

**Safety:** Be sure to use a safe, low-current power source designed for the purpose.

**Procedure:** 1. Apply a high voltage to the terminals of the tube to produce a straight beam of electrons.

2. Hold the horseshoe magnet in a position near the tube. 3. Reverse the magnet and bring it near the tube. 4. Ask students what they think would happen if a beam of protons were used instead of a beam of electrons.

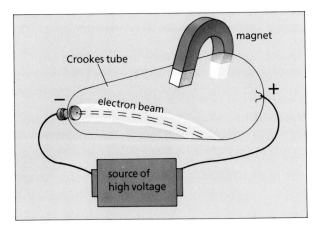

**Figure 6-2**

**Results:** The beam will be deflected by the magnet in opposite directions in steps 2 and 3. A beam of protons would be deflected in a direction opposite to that of a deflected beam of electrons.

## 6-3 Black Boxes

**Overview:** In this demonstration, a procedure that allows students to determine the nature of the material in a closed container is carried out. The students learn how to make mental models of a material, based on gathered evidence. This can be related to Rutherford's gold-foil experiment.

**Materials:** two heavy cardboard boxes similar to old-style cigar boxes; large 1-hole rubber stopper with 10 cm of glass tubing inserted into it; iron cube or sphere, 2–3 cm wide; magnet; bag of Easter-basket "grass"; small lump of clay; metal cube 1–2 cm in width; 5–10 metal-tip darts (or straight needles with wooden or metal handles, from the biology department); dart board, small bulletin board, or empty box.

**Advance Preparation:** Cut the glass tubing to the appropriate length and carefully insert it into the stopper. Place the stopper fitted with the glass tubing inside one of the cigar boxes and tape the box shut. Label it "black box." Repeat, using the iron cube or sphere in the other box. Place a cube of metal onto a horizontally placed dart board or box, and place the Easter basket grass on top of and around it. Make sure the object is not in the center of the grass mound but off to one side, and that it is completely concealed. Make another setup, using a lump of clay inside the grass instead of the metal cube.

**Procedure:** 1. Ask students to distinguish between the terms "law" and "theory." Ask the students to list as many scientific laws as they can. 2. Ask the students to list as many theories as they can. 3. Ask students to determine what sort of question (that is, a "what" question or a "why" question) most laws try to answer. Do the same for theories. 4. Give the two black boxes to two students. Ask them to manipulate the boxes in order to determine information about the material inside. They can tilt the box in different directions, gently shake the box, use a magnet to test for the presence of iron, and so on. Tell the students the purpose is not to identify the object but to describe its properties as to size, shape, and composition. Have each student also tell what evidence supports his or her conclusions. 5. Do not tell students whether they are correct in their descriptions. Instead, give the box to other students and see whether they are in agreement with the first two students. 6. Ask a volunteer to drop darts into the grass mound to determine where an object is located and to determine the nature of the object. The student should hold the darts from a height of about 1 m above the mound and should drop as many as are needed to collect the information. The student should be able to tell whether the object is made of metal, glass, rubber, or clay, and to tell its approximate size and location. 7. Relate this demonstration to Rutherford's gold-foil experiment.

**Results:** Laws generally state what happens (they answer "what" questions) and often relate this information in the form of an equation. Laws tend to be based directly on evidence obtained in the laboratory. Theories tend to tell why something behaves in the way it does. Laws include Newton's laws, the gas laws, Kepler's laws, conservation laws, and the laws of reflection and refraction. Theories include the atomic theory, kinetic molecular theory, Einstein's theory, and Darwin's theory. In Rutherford's gold-foil experiment, evidence was also obtained indirectly, by the use of positively charged "bullets" (analogous to the use of the darts in this demonstration) to gain information about the nature and locations of particles within the atom.

## 6-4 Energy Levels in the Bohr Model of the Atom

**Overview:** In this demonstration, a student uses a toy that consists of a rubber ball attached by a long rubber band to a wooden paddle. The harder he or she hits the ball, the more the rubber band stretches. By analogy, this demonstration helps to suggest that high-energy electrons are found farther away from the nucleus, in higher energy levels.

**Materials:** toy that consists of rubber ball attached by a long rubber band to a paddle.

**Advance Preparation:** none

**Procedure:** 1. Ask a student to try to strike the ball with the paddle. Ask the student to try to use more energy to hit the ball. 2. Have the class note the relationship between the energy with which the ball is struck and the distance the ball moves from the paddle. 3. Relate this to the Bohr concept of the energy level. 4. Ask students to hypothesize about a situation in which a tremendous amount of energy is added to the ball.

**Results:** The harder the ball is struck, the farther it moves from the paddle. In the Bohr model, the more energy the electron has, the farther away it tends to be from the nucleus. Electrons in high-energy levels have more energy associated with them than do the electrons closer to the nucleus. In step 4, students should hypothesize that the ball might come loose and fly off into the room. Note that this sort of situation can exist for atoms also: An ion can form when an electron is removed from an atom.

## 6-5 Making Waves

**Overview:** In this demonstration, using a rope or spring coil, students produce various standing waves and note how the wavelength and frequency change. Students observe that wavelength and frequency are inversely related. They also note that it takes more energy to produce more standing waves, so energy and frequency are directly related. This also gives students a better understanding of Planck's relationship.

**Advance Preparation:** none

**Materials:** spring coil or rope, at least 3 m long.

**Procedure:** 1. Ask for two strong volunteers. Have one student try to produce standing waves by shaking one end of the coil or rope while the other holds onto the other end. Have them try to produce one whole standing wave first. Ask students to observe the positions of the crest and trough of the wave and the length of the wave. 2. Tell the volunteers to try to produce a larger number of standing waves. Have the students note the relationship between the number of waves produced (which is related to the frequency) and the wavelength. Also, have them note the relationship between energy and the number of waves. Ask them how they think energy is related to the frequency of waves and to wavelength. 3. Some students might produce the same number of waves with the same wavelength but larger amplitudes. Tell students that more energy can also be related to larger amplitudes. Refer to sound waves. Point out that if the amplitude of a certain sound wave is increased, the sound becomes louder.

**Results:** As the number of waves produced increases, the wavelength decreases. As energy input increases, the number of waves tends to increase. As energy increases, frequency tends to increase and wavelength tends to decrease.

## 6-6 Acetate Waves

**Overview:** In this demonstration, a transparency marked with a vertical red line is passed underneath a piece of cardboard that has two different wave sets cut out of it. As a result of seeing this demonstration on the overhead projector, the class concludes that although the wavelengths and frequencies of the waves are different, the waves get to the same point at the same time and thus move at the same speed.

**Materials:** half of an 8½-by-11-inch file folder; transparency; masking tape (½-inch wide); scissors or razor; red transparency pen; overhead projector.

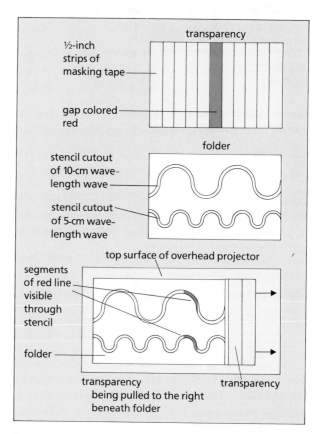

**Figure 6-3**

**Advance Preparation:** 1. Place strips of masking tape across the width of the transparency, leaving a gap of about 1½ cm between strips. 2. Select one gap between the tape strips about 10 cm from the top of the transparency and completely color it in red. 3. Use a pencil to draw a series of waves lengthwise on the folder. The wavelengths should be about 10 cm. On the same folder, draw another series of waves with half the wavelength of the first. These should be about 15 cm below the first set. Make sure the amplitude is the same for both sets of waves. Create a stencil of the waves by using scissors or a razor to cut out the two sets of waves; be careful to leave a 3-cm margin all around the folder. Be sure you cut out enough paper so the waves are visible on the overhead when the stencil is placed on it.

**Procedure:** 1. Turn the transparency horizontally, so that the red line runs vertically, and place it onto the overhead projector. Place the folder over the transparency so that the axis of the waves is perpendicular to the red line. That is, the waves should run horizontally. Hold the folder in place with your left hand and pull the transparency to the right with your right hand. Emphasize that waves in the same medium have a constant speed even though wavelengths and frequencies differ. Refer to the electromagnetic spectrum. Point out that visible light, X rays, ultraviolet light, and so on all travel through space at the same speed: $3.00 \times 10^8$ m/s.

**Results:** The parts of the red line visible in the waves will appear to move along the length of the waves at the same rate in both sets, even though the waves have different wavelengths and frequencies.

## 6-7 Observing Spectra

**Overview:** In this demonstration, using a spectroscope, students observe a continuous spectrum and a bright-line spectrum of hydrogen. Students also observe that red light has a longer wavelength than does violet light, and that, consequently, red light has a lower frequency and lower energy associated with it than does violet light.

**Materials:** incandescent light bulb and lamp; spectrum tube of hydrogen; spectrum-tube power supply; spectroscopes that contain wavelength scale.

**Advance Preparation:** none

**Safety:** Students should not get too close to or touch the tube or power supply when it is turned on.

**Procedure:** 1. Have the students observe through the spectroscope the light coming from a light bulb. 2. Have students observe the bright-line spectrum from a spectrum tube of hydrogen. Point out that the spectrum is like a fingerprint of the element; it can be used to identify the element. 3. Tell students that each line represents the energy given off as electrons move down from a higher energy level to the second energy level of the hydrogen atom. Ask students to hypothesize which line of color represents a transition from the third energy level down to the second.

**Results:** In step 1, students should note the continuous band of colors ("ROYGBIV"), with the violet band on the left near the "4" on the scale (indicating a wave-

length of $4 \times 10^{-7}$ m) and the red band on the right near the "6" (indicating a wavelength of $6 \times 10^{-7}$m). In step 2, a few distinct bright lines of color should be visible. Students should state that the red line is associated with the transition from the third to the second energy level since it represents the lowest amount of energy.

## 6-8 Isotopic Pennies

**Overview:** In this demonstration, the average mass of objects in a sample of a fictitious element, "pennium," is determined using pre-1982 and post-1982 pennies. The concept of isotopes is reinforced, and a method for finding the average mass or the percent of isotopes in a sample is developed.

**Materials:** 10 pre-1982 pennies and 10 post-1982 pennies; balance.

**Advance Preparation:** none

**Procedure:** 1. Find the mass of each type of penny and record it on the board. 2. Make a sample of "pennium" by placing three pre-1982 pennies with seven post-1982 pennies. 3. Have students predict the weighted average mass of the pennies in the sample. If they have difficulty, tell them they can do this by calculating the mass of the three pennies, adding that to the calculated mass of the other seven pennies, and then dividing the sum by 10 to obtain the average. 4. Place the sample of 10 pennies onto the balance and record the total mass on the board. The average mass can be determined by dividing by 10. 5. You can go further by making up a new sample of pennium and asking the class to predict the percentage of each type of penny in it, given the total mass of the 10 pennies and the individual mass of each type. 6. Discuss how the atomic mass of an element is calculated.

**Results:** A pre-1982 penny is made of 95% copper and 5% tin and zinc and has a mass of 3.1 g. A post-1982 penny is made of copper-coated zinc and has a mass of 2.5 g. In step 3, the weighted average mass will be 2.7. In step 4, the actual average mass will be the same as the predicted average mass. In step 5, the percentage will depend on the chosen numbers of each type of penny. The atomic mass of an element is the weighted average of the masses of the individual isotopes of the element as they occur naturally.

## Answers to Questions

### Page 110

1. The three major subatomic particles and their locations are: proton—nucleus, electron—outside the nucleus, and neutron—nucleus.

**2.** A particle that contains 12 protons, 13 neutrons, and 10 electrons has a charge of 2+.

**Page 113**

**3.** No. The composition of a mixture can vary. In fact, variable composition is one of the distinguishing characteristics of mixtures.

**4.** No. There is only one kind of matter in a sample of an element.

**5.** The tiles in a bathroom wall are not always used as indivisible units. At the end of each row or at a wall fixture, a tile is often cut into a smaller piece.

**6.** Hot dogs represent a "discontinuous" version of meat (in comparison with ground beef, which is a "continuous" version). The butcher will not divide a hot dog to give a customer an even pound, so the customer must usually choose between "a little over or a little under" a pound.

**Page 114**

**7. a.**   $\begin{array}{r} 10.00 \text{ g } SO_2 \\ - \ 5.00 \text{ g } S \\ \hline 5.00 \text{ g } O_2 \ \text{ in } SO_2 \end{array}$

　　**b.**   $\begin{array}{r} 8.33 \text{ g } SO_3 \\ -3.33 \text{ g } S \\ \hline 5.00 \text{ g } O_2 \ \text{ in } SO_2 \end{array}$

　　**c.** In $SO_2$: $\dfrac{5.00 \text{ g } S}{5.00 \text{ g } O} = \dfrac{1.00 \text{ g } S}{1.00 \text{ g } O}$

　　In $SO_3$: $\dfrac{3.33 \text{ g } S}{5.00 \text{ g } O} = \dfrac{0.67 \text{ g } S}{1.00 \text{ g } O}$

The fixed mass of oxygen is 1.00 gram for each compound. Therefore the ratio of the masses of sulfur in each compound is $\dfrac{1.00}{0.67}$ or $\dfrac{1.5}{1.0}$ or as simple whole numbers $\dfrac{3}{2}$.

**Page 116**

**8.** The law of conservation of mass, the law of definite proportions, and the law of multiple proportions provide evidence for Dalton's theory.

**9.** (1) All elements are composed of atoms, which are indivisible and indestructible particles.
　　(2) All atoms of the same element are alike.
　　(3) Atoms of different elements are different.
　　(4) Compounds are formed by the joining of atoms.

**10.** (1) Atoms are not indivisible.
　　(2) Atoms can be created and destroyed since some atoms can be changed from atoms of one element to atoms of another.
　　(3) Atoms of the same element are not alike in all ways; they can have different masses.

**Page 118**

**11.** See text Figure 6-7 for a diagram of a Crookes tube. When a high voltage is applied to such a system, a beam of particles travels from the cathode toward the anode.

**12.** Cathode rays are now known as electrons. They were originally known as cathode rays because they were studied as the beams of particles that traveled from the cathode toward the anode in a Crookes tube.

**Page 119**

**13.** "Fundamental" and "indivisible," as used to describe the charge on the electron, mean that no smaller quantity of charge has ever been observed and that all observed charges are a whole-number multiple of this smallest known charge.

**14.** The unit used to measure the quantity of electrical charge is the coulomb.

**Page 121**

**15.** Rutherford described the nucleus of the gold atom as small, positively charged, with relatively great mass.

**16.** Because electrons move in orbits around the nucleus with enough energy of motion to prevent their falling into the positively charged nucleus.

**17.** Negatively charged electrons are attracted to the positively charged nucleus because they have opposite charge.

**18.** If thicker metal foil were used in the Rutherford experiment, fewer alpha particles would pass through, and more would be deflected.

**Page 123**

**19.** Bohr's model proposed certain definite orbits, with a specific energy and no loss of energy from their motion, in which an electron can travel around the nucleus.

**20.** In the Bohr model, higher energy electrons were found at greater distances from the nucleus.

**21.** According to the Bohr theory, electrons move to higher energy levels by absorbing energy.

**22.** An electron in an excited atom loses energy when the atom returns to the ground state.

**23. a.** Three rungs are occupied: two people on each of the first two rungs and one on the third rung.
　　**b.** The first three rungs are occupied and all three are filled.
　　**c.** Only the first two rungs are occupied and both are filled.

**Page 125**

**24.** energy level, energy sublevel, and orbital

**25.** A scientific model helps one to understand something that cannot be seen or experienced directly. Unlike a scale model, it does not provide an actual "picture" of the phenomenon under study.

**26.** During the cooking of food, certain molecules are formed that are given off by the warm food. These molecules move through the air and are detected by the nose of the observer.

## Page 127

27. Both Newton and Planck suggested that light consists of beams of particles. Planck further proposed that the energy of light is quantized; that is, only certain values of these energies exist.
28. Quanta are bundles of energy that make up radiation such as light. A quantum of light is also known as a photon.
29. The Greek letter lambda, $\lambda$, is used to represent the wavelength of light.
30. The wave has a frequency of 5 waves per second or 5 hertz.
31. $v = f\,\lambda$
$$= 550 \text{ Hz} \times 2.40 \times 10^{-3} \text{ m}$$
$$= 550\,\frac{1}{\text{s}} \times 2.40 \times 10^{-3} \text{ m}$$
$$= 1.32 \text{ m/s or } 1.32 \times 10^3 \text{ mm/s or } 1320 \text{ mm/s}$$
32. $f = \dfrac{\text{v}}{\lambda}$
$$= \frac{1.5 \times 10^8 \text{ m/s}}{2.3 \times 10^{-7} \text{ m}}$$
$$= 6.5 \times 10^{14}\,\frac{1}{\text{s}} \text{ or Hz}$$

## Page 129

33. visible light, gamma rays, X rays, radio waves, ultraviolet light, infrared light
34. Among the devices that can detect invisible electromagnetic radiation are radio receivers and photographic film.
35. the continuous spectrum
36. Each element has its own set of characteristic spectral lines. No two elements have the same set of spectral lines.

## Page 131

37. One nanometer is equal to $10^{-9}$ meters.
38. As the wavelength of the radiation increases, its frequency decreases. The velocity remains the same.
39. $E, f; E = hf$. The energy of a quantum of radiation is directly proportional to its frequency.
40. The letter $h$ represents Planck's constant, which has the numerical value of $6.62 \times 10^{-34}$ J/Hz.
41. $f = \dfrac{\text{v}}{\lambda}$
$$= \frac{3.0 \times 10^8 \text{ m/s}}{4.5 \times 10^2 \text{ nm} \times 1 \text{ m}/10^9 \text{ nm}}$$
$$= 6.7 \times 10^{14} \text{ Hz}$$
42. $\lambda = \dfrac{v}{f}$
$$= \frac{3.0 \times 10^8 \text{ m/s}}{8.0 \times 10^{14} \text{ 1/s}}$$

$$= 3.8 \times 10^{-7} \text{ m}$$
43. $E = h\,f$
$$= 6.62 \times 10^{-34} \text{ J·s} \times 8.5 \times 10^{14}\,\frac{1}{\text{s}}$$
$$= 5.6 \times 10^{-19} \text{ J}$$
44. $E = h\,f$ and $f = \dfrac{\text{v}}{\lambda}$

Therefore $E = h\dfrac{v}{\lambda}$
$$= \frac{6.62 \times 10^{-34} \text{ J·s} \times 3.0 \times 10^8 \text{ m/s}}{6.4 \times 10^2 \text{ nm} \times 1 \text{ m}/10^9 \text{ nm}}$$
$$= 3.1 \times 10^{-19} \text{ J}$$

## Page 133

45 Nucleons are the subatomic particles found in the nucleus; the protons and the neutrons.
46. **a.** Compared to the electron, the proton has equal but opposite charge.
    **b.** The proton has much greater mass than the electron. The mass of the proton is about 1840 times the mass of the electron.
47. The atomic number of an atom is the number of protons or electrons it has.
48. **a.** A proton has one unit of elementary positive charge; a neutron has no charge.
    **b.** The mass of a neutron is nearly equal to that of the proton. (The mass of a neutron is slightly greater.)
49. The isotopes of an element are those forms of the element that have the same atomic number (number of protons) but a different number of neutrons.

## Page 136

50. The mass number of an element gives its number of protons and neutrons. The symbol $A$ represents mass number.
51. Each isotope of an element has a different mass number. Since these isotopes have the same number of protons, the mass number identifies their different numbers of neutrons.
52. **a.** The atomic number of any chlorine atom is 17.
    **b.** The mass number of this isotope is $17 + 20$; that is, 37.
53. The symbol $^{17}_{8}\text{O}$ indicates $Z = 8$ and $A = 17$. The number of protons is 8 and the number of neutrons is $(A - Z)$ or 9.
54. The symbol for tritium is $^{3}_{1}\text{H}$.

## Page 137

55. The modern standard for atomic mass is the isotope carbon-12.
56. An atomic mass unit is defined as $\frac{1}{12}$ the mass of a carbon-12 atom.
57. Most elements occur naturally as a mixture of isotopes. Thus, the atomic mass of any element is

the average of the masses of its isotopes, weighted to reflect their relative abundance in nature.

**Page 139**

**58.** Assuming 100 atoms:

$93.12 \times 38.964 = 3628$

$\underline{6.88 \times 40.962 = \quad 281}$

$\qquad\qquad 3909$  the total mass
$\qquad\qquad\qquad$ of 100 atoms

Thus, $\dfrac{3909}{100} = 39.09$ or $39.1$ u
$\qquad\qquad$ the average atomic mass of
$\qquad\qquad$ naturally occurring potassium

## Chapter Review    6

**Page 140, Content Review**

**1. a.** Both the proton and the neutron have a mass of one atomic mass unit; the electron has a mass of $\frac{1}{1837}$ $\mu$, or virtually zero. **b.** The charges are: proton 1+, neutron 0, electron 1−. **c.** Protons and neutrons are located in the nucleus, and electrons are outside the nucleus.

**2.** Neutrons do not contribute to the charge on a particle.
  **a.** 1 proton and 1 electron: $1+ + (1-) = 0$
  **b.** 9 protons and 10 electrons: $9+ + (10-) = 1-$
  **c.** 23 protons and 18 electrons:
    $23+ + (18-) = 5+$

**3.** The continuous theory of matter states that matter can be cut into smaller and smaller pieces without limit. The discontinuous theory states that particles of matter exist that cannot be further subdivided.

**4. a.** The mass of material at the completion of a chemical reaction is equal to the mass before the reaction.
  **b.** Antoine Lavoisier first identified this relationship.
  **c.** The law of conservation of mass explains it.

**5. a.** Yes, samples of ammonia will always contain the same percentage, by mass, of nitrogen.
  **b.** The law of definite proportions explains this.

**6.** Florida sand is 46.8% silicon by mass. Sahara sand is $(0.878 \text{ g Si} \div 1.878 \text{ g sand}) \times 100\% = 46.8\%$ silicon. The samples illustrate the law of definite proportions.

**7.** The law of multiple proportions refers to the relationship of the masses of elements that form more than one compound. The law of definite proportions describes the mass relationship between different elements in the same compound.

**8.** The ratio between the masses of oxygen in carbon monoxide and carbon dioxide is 16.0 g:32.0 g = 1:2.

**9.** Dalton's atomic theory held that in a chemical reaction the atoms, which have definite masses, are simply being rearranged. Therefore there is no loss or gain of mass.

**10. a.** Dalton stated that atoms are indivisible, but we now know that atoms can be divided into subatomic particles such as protons, neutrons, and electrons. **b.** We now know that atoms of the same element may have different numbers of neutrons and therefore slightly different masses.

**11.** The electron was the first subatomic particle to be discovered. It was identified as a distinct particle in 1897.

**12.** Crookes identified the existence of "cathode rays" from his experiments with high voltages applied to evacuated glass tubes. Extending Crookes's experiments, Thomson showed the cathode rays to be streams of negatively charged particles that were attracted to a positive electric field. Thomson is credited with the discovery of the electron.

**13.** Millikan determined the charge of the electron in his oil-drop experiment. He then used Thomson's charge/mass ratio to calculate the mass of the electron.

**14. a.** mass of proton = $(9.11 \times 10^{-28}$ g/electron$)$
    $\times (1837$ electrons/proton$) =$
    $\qquad\qquad 1.67 \times 10^{-24}$ g/proton.
  **b.** charge/mass ratio of proton
    $= (1.60 \times 10^{-19}$ coulomb$) \div (1.67 \times 10^{-24}$ g$)$
    $= 9.58 \times 10^{4}$ coulomb/g
  **c.** $1.00$ g $\div 9.11 \times 10^{-28}$ g/electron $=$
    $\qquad\qquad 1.10 \times 10^{27}$ electrons
  **d.** $1.00$ g $\div 1.67 \times 10^{-24}$ g/proton $=$
    $\qquad\qquad 5.99 \times 10^{23}$ protons

**15.** Rutherford fired alpha particles at thin metal foil surrounded by a screen. When the screen was struck by alpha particles, it emitted light. Most particles passed through as though nothing were there; Rutherford concluded that the atoms in the foil were mostly empty space. A few particles were widely scattered, some were deflected slightly, and a few were deflected back toward their source; Rutherford attributed this to collisions with positively charged central portions, or nuclei.

**16.** The Rutherford model did not adequately explain the movement of electrons around the nucleus.

**17.** Bohr described the energy levels as a set of concentric shells around the nucleus, in which electrons move. The greater the radius of the shell is, the greater the energy level of the electrons is.

18. Electrons in the ground state are occupying the lowest possible energy levels and therefore cannot give off energy by falling to lower levels.

19. Unlike the Bohr model, the charge-cloud model does not show the paths of the electrons. It shows the most probable location of the electrons.

20. A scientific model is a mental picture that helps us to understand something we cannot see or experience directly.

21. **a.** Newton suggested that a beam of light is a stream of particles. Huygens described light as a traveling wave.
    **b.** In the modern theory, light has a dual nature. It can behave both as a wave and as a stream of particles.

22. velocity = frequency × wavelength = 20 Hz × 4.0 m = 20 waves/s × 4.0 m/wave = 80 m/s.

23. frequency = $\dfrac{\text{velocity}}{\text{wavelength}} = \dfrac{3.0 \times 10^8 \text{ m/s}}{3.8 \times 10^{-9} \text{ m/wave}} =$ 7.9 × 10$^{16}$ waves/s = 7.9 × 10$^{16}$ Hz

24. In a continuous spectrum one color blends into the next. In a bright-line spectrum, the lines of color are separated by black spaces.

25. **a.** From red to violet, the wavelength decreases.
    **b.** From red to violet, the frequency increases.

26. **a.** Microwaves have a longer wavelength than radar.
    **b.** Radar beam is nearer to visible light.
    **c.** Radar beam is closer to X rays in frequency value.

27. **a.** wavelength = 518 nm × (1 × 10$^{-9}$ m/nm)
        = 5.18 × 10$^{-7}$ m
    **b.** frequency = velocity ÷ wavelength
        = 3.00 × 10$^8$ m/s ÷ 5.18 × 10$^{-7}$ m
        = 5.79 × 10$^{14}$ s$^{-1}$ = 5.79 × 10$^{14}$ Hz
    **c.** energy = Planck's constant × frequency
        = (6.6 × 10$^{-34}$ J/Hz) × (5.79 × 10$^{14}$ Hz)
        = 3.82 × 10$^{-19}$ J
    **d.** The color is green.

28. **a.** frequency = $E$ ÷ h
        = (4.0 × 10$^{-19}$ J) ÷ (6.6 × 10$^{-34}$ J/Hz)
        = 6.1 × 10$^{14}$ Hz
    **b.** wavelength = velocity ÷ frequency
        = 3.00 × 10$^8$ m/s ÷ 6.1 × 10$^{14}$ Hz
        = 4.9 × 10$^{-7}$ m
    **c.** This radiant energy is in the visible range. Its wavelength, 490 nm, is in the blue-green region.

29. **a.** sodium: Na, $Z = 11$;
    **b.** chromium: Cr, $Z = 24$;
    **c.** arsenic: As, $Z = 33$; **d.** mercury: Hg, $Z = 80$;
    **e.** krypton: Kr, $Z = 36$.

30. **a.** Number of neutrons: protium 0, deuterium 1, tritium 2;
    **b.** Value of $Z$: 1 for all;
    **c.** charge on nucleus: 1+ for all.

31. Two isotopes must have the same number of protons and a different number of neutrons.

32. Quarks are possible particles that would be smaller than protons and neutrons.

33.

| | | I-127 | I-131 |
|---|---|---|---|
| **a.** | Atomic number | 53 | 53 |
| **b.** | Mass number | 127 | 131 |
| **c.** | Number of neutrons | 74 | 78 |
| **d.** | Value of $Z$ | 53 | 53 |
| **e.** | Value of $A$ | 127 | 131 |
| **f.** | Symbol | $^{127}_{53}\text{I}$ | $^{131}_{53}\text{I}$ |

34.

| Symbol | He | Ca | W | Pb | U | Mo |
|---|---|---|---|---|---|---|
| Atomic number | 2 | 20 | 74 | 82 | 92 | 42 |
| Mass number | 4 | 40 | 184 | 210 | 235 | 95 |
| Number of protons | 2 | 20 | 74 | 82 | 92 | 42 |
| Number of neutrons | 2 | 20 | 110 | 128 | 143 | 53 |
| Number of electrons | 2 | 20 | 74 | 82 | 92 | 42 |

35. The atomic mass of 65.39 for zinc represents an average value for all of the naturally occurring isotopes of zinc, weighted according to their different abundances.

36. A mass of an atom having four times the mass of a carbon-12 atom is 4 × 12.0000 u = 48.0000 u.

37. The atomic mass of magnesium is the average of the masses of the naturally occurring isotopes.
    0.7870 × 23.985 = 18.88
    0.1013 × 24.986 =  2.531
    0.1117 × 25.983 =  2.902
    ───────────────────────
               24.31  = atomic mass

### Page 143, Content Mastery

38. If two atoms of oxygen have different numbers of neutrons, they will have different masses. For example, oxygen-17, which has 9 neutrons, has a mass of 17 u, but oxygen-16, which has 8 neutrons, has a mass of 16 u.

39. If two atoms of magnesium have different numbers of electrons, they will have different charges because every magnesium atom has 12 protons. For example, a magnesium atom with 12 electrons has a net charge of 0, but a magnesium atom with 11 electrons has a net charge of 1+.

40. **a.** The mass of $^{12}$C is 12.000 000 000 000 . . . u, by definition.
    **b.** weighted average mass

= (mass of $^{12}$C) (abundance) + (mass of $^{13}$C)
(abundance)
= (12.000 000) (0.9889) + (13.003 354)
(0.0111)
= 11.866 800 0 u + 0.144 337 2 u
= 12.011 137 2 u ≈ 12.01 u

c. Both express the same value, but the periodic table states more significant figures.

**41.** $E = hf$. First calculate frequency from $c = \lambda f$:

$f = \dfrac{c}{\lambda} = \dfrac{3.00 \times 10^8 \text{ m/s}}{4.86 \times 10^2 \times 10^{-9} \text{ m}}$
= 0.617 283 95 × $10^{8-2-(-9)}$ 1/s
≈ 0.617 × $10^{15}$ Hz = 6.17 × $10^{14}$ Hz

$E = hf = (6.6 \times 10^{-34} \text{ J/Hz})(6.17 \times 10^{14} \text{ Hz})$
= 40.74 × $10^{-34+14}$ ≈ 41 × $10^{-20}$ = 4.1 × $10^{-19}$ J

**42.** An electron absorbs light when it moves into an excited state.

**43.** The symbol for any element is $^A_Z[\ ]^{charge}$ where [ ] = symbol for the element (in periodic table), $A$ = mass number (number of nucleons), $Z$ = atomic number (number of protons), and charge = number of protons minus number of electrons. Therefore for $^7_3[\ ]^+$

a. The element is Li, because $Z = 3$.
b. The atomic number, $Z$ (the subscript), is 3.
c. Its mass number, $A$ (the superscript), is 7.
d. It has 7 nucleons because $A = 7$.
e. Number of neutrons = $A - Z = 7 - 3 = 4$.
f. It has 3 protons because $Z = 3$.
g. Number of electrons = number of protons − charge = $3 - (+1) = 2$.
h. The net charge is $1+$, from the + in the symbol.
i. Charge of nucleus = number of protons = $3+$.

**44.** No, excited electrons can emit only light of certain energies. This is supported by the fact that an excited atom emits a line spectrum rather than a continuous spectrum.

**45.** $f = \dfrac{c}{\lambda} = \dfrac{3.00 \times 10^8 \text{ m/s}}{700.0 \times 10^{-9} \text{ m}}$
= 0.004 285 7 × $10^{8-(-9)}$ 1/s
= 0.004 285 7 × $10^{17}$ Hz
≈ 0.004 29 × $10^{17}$ Hz = 4.29 × $10^{-3+17}$ Hz
= 4.29 × $10^{14}$ Hz

**46.** Robert Millikan determined the charge on the electron by stabilizing charged oil drops between two charged plates. Using his calculated charge and Thomson's charge-to-mass ratio, Millikan calculated the mass of the electron:

electron's mass = $\dfrac{\text{electron's charge}}{\text{electron's charge-to-mass ratio}}$
= $\dfrac{1.60 \times 10^{-19} \text{ coulomb}}{1.76 \times 10^8 \text{ coulombs/g}}$ = 9.1 × $10^{-28}$ g

**47.** Wavelength is inversely proportional to frequency, $\lambda = c/f$. Since frequency is directly proportional to energy ($E = hf$), wavelength is inversely proportional to energy.
a. Gamma rays have a higher frequency than visible light, so visible light has a longer wavelength.
b. Ultraviolet light has a shorter wavelength than infrared light, so ultraviolet light has more energy.

**48.** Using the law of definite proportions, we know:
$\dfrac{95.110 \text{ g chlorine}}{200.00 \text{ g KCl}} = \dfrac{\text{unknown g chlorine}}{153.20 \text{ g KCl}}$
Therefore the amount of chlorine is
$\dfrac{95.110 \text{ g chlorine}}{200.00 \text{ g KCl}} \times 153.20 \text{ g KCl} =$
72.854 26 g Cl
≈ 72.854 g Cl = 7.285 4 × $10^1$ g Cl = 72.854 g Cl

## Page 143, Concept Mastery

**49. *Concept:*** *Atomic structure versus molecular arrangement.*
*Solution:* The different properties of graphite and diamonds are due to the arrangements of the carbon atoms. The structures of the atoms themselves are indistinguishable.

**50. *Concept:*** *Electrons in atoms have fixed energy.*
*Solution:* Planets in the solar system travel in definite paths around the sun. Electrons in an atom have fixed energies, but they do not follow fixed paths.

**51. *Concept:*** *Energy of electrons associated with each energy level in an atom varies unevenly.*
*Solution:* Energy levels in an atom are like the rungs of a ladder in that the energy of an electron is fixed according to its energy level. However, the energy levels in an atom are not evenly spaced; higher levels are closer together.

**52. *Concept:*** *Wave theory as applied to matter.*
*Solution:* Electromagnetic waves and "stadium waves" both have a wavelength and a frequency, but "stadium waves" are more like water waves because the people have a vertical motion like water molecules.

**53. *Concept:*** *Atomic structure and color.*
*Solution:* The color of sulfur is due to the atomic arrangement, which determines the molecular arrangement in the macrostructure. The yellow color is due to the

interaction of the electrons with light, not the color of atoms. The wavelength of yellow light is about 560 nm, much longer than the diameter of an atom.

## Page 144, Cumulative Review

**54. c.** The SI unit of energy is the joule.

**55. b.** Burning of wood is exothermic.

**56. c.** Heat = mass × specific heat × $\Delta t$
= 200 g × 4.2 J/g-°C × 30°C = 25 200 J

**57. c.** should be $63.2 \times 10^{-3}$ cm = $6.32 \times 10^{-2}$ cm

**58. b.** $V = \dfrac{\text{M}}{\text{D}} = \dfrac{25.21 \text{ g}}{2.70 \text{ g/cm}^3} = 9.34 \text{ cm}^3$

**59. a.** C: Souring of milk is a chemical change.
   **b.** P: melting of ice is a physical change.
   **c.** C: Tarnishing of silver is a chemical change.
   **d.** C: Cooking a steak is a chemical change.
   **e.** P: Folding paper is a physical change.

**60. a.** M: Milk is a mixture;
   **b.** M: A tree is a mixture;
   **c.** M: Air is a mixture;
   **d.** E: Neon is an element;
   **e.** C: Salt is a compound;
   **f.** M: Lettuce is a mixture.

**61. a.** $(8.1 \times 10^{-3})(4.3 \times 10^{+5}) = 3.5 \times 10^{3}$
   **b.** $\dfrac{27.2 \times 10^{+2}}{3.41 \times 10^{-3}} = 7.98 \times 10^{5}$
   **c.** $\begin{aligned} 6.02 \times 10^{23} &= \quad 6.02 \times 10^{23} \\ + \,4.00 \times 10^{22} &= + \,0.400 \times 10^{23} \\ \hline &\quad\;\, 6.42 \times 10^{23} \end{aligned}$
   **d.** $(0.12)(6.0 \times 10^{23}) = 7.2 \times 10^{22}$

**62.** Heat absorbed = mass × specific heat × $\Delta t$

Specific heat = $\dfrac{\text{heat absorbed}}{\text{mass} \times \Delta t} = \dfrac{500 \text{ J}}{200 \text{ g} \times 30°\text{C}} =$
$0.083 \,\dfrac{\text{J}}{\text{g-}°\text{C}}$

**63.** Answers will vary but may include potential, kinetic, chemical, electrical, electromagnetic, sound, and light.

## Page 144, Critical Thinking

**64.** Energy is directly proportional to frequency, which is inversely proportional to wavelength. Blue light has a shorter wavelength than red light, so blue light has a greater frequency and more energy.

**65.** Heavy water, $^2\text{H}_2\text{O}$, is water in which the hydrogen atoms are deuterium. Because the two isotopes have the same atomic number ($Z = 1$), they have the same properties. Therefore heavy water would taste the same as ordinary water.

**66.** Scientists did not discard the rest of Dalton's theory after the discovery of subatomic particles because the theory explained the chemical behavior of matter.

**67.** Even though matter is mostly empty space, you don't fall through the "holes" in the floor because the repulsion of electron clouds makes matter act as if it were continuous.

**68.** The lowest energy levels are closer to the nucleus because the energy required to separate opposite charges depends on the square of the distance between them.

## Page 145, Challenge Problems

**69.** For the photon with energy $3.76 \times 10^{-19}$ joule:
$f = \dfrac{E}{h} = \dfrac{3.76 \times 10^{-19} \text{ joule}}{6.6 \times 10^{-34} \text{ joule/Hz}} = 5.7 \times 10^{14} \text{ Hz}$
$\lambda = \dfrac{c}{f} = \dfrac{3.00 \times 10^{8} \text{ m/s}}{5.7 \times 10^{14} \text{ Hz}} = 5.3 \times 10^{-7} \text{ m}$
$5.3 \times 10^{-7}$ m × 1 nm ÷ $10^{-9}$ m = $5.3 \times 10^{2}$ nm wavelength 530 nm is yellow-green.

For the photon with energy $2.15 \times 10^{-18}$ joule:
$f = \dfrac{E}{h} = \dfrac{2.15 \times 10^{-18} \text{ joule}}{6.6 \times 10^{-34} \text{ joule/Hz}} = 3.3 \times 10^{15} \text{ Hz}$
$\lambda = \dfrac{c}{f} = \dfrac{3.00 \times 10^{8} \text{ m/s}}{3.3 \times 10^{15} \text{ Hz}} = 9.1 \times 10^{-8} \text{ m}$
$9.1 \times 10^{-8}$ m × 1 nm ÷ $10^{-9}$ m = $9.1 \times 10^{1}$ nm wavelength 91 nm is in the ultraviolet region and not visible.

**70.** Let $x$ = decimal of % by mass of Cu-63 in sample
$1 - x$ = decimal of % by mass of Cu-65
$(x)(62.930 \text{ u}) + (1 - x)(64.928 \text{ u}) = 63.540 \text{ u}$;
$x = 0.6947$,
So the sample is 69.47% Cu-63 and 30.53% Cu-65.

**71.** Answers will vary. One possible answer is that water present as a gas in the air condenses on the windshield as the temperature drops during the night. Students could be challenged to design tests for their models.

6

# Chemical Formulas

**7**

## Chapter Planning Guide

| Text Section | Labs (Lab Manual) and Demonstrations (TE) | Supplementary Materials (Teacher's Resource Book) |
|---|---|---|
| **7-1** Using Symbols to Write Formulas, pp. 147-149 | | |
| **7-2** Kinds of Formulas, pp. 149-151 | | |
| **7-3** Types of Compounds, pp. 151-153 | Demo 7-1: Metals and Nonmetals, p. TG-123 | |
| **7-4** Ionic Substances, pp. 153-154 | | |
| **7-5** Predicting Formulas of Ionic Compounds, pp. 154-159 | Lab 11: Composition of Hydrates | Transparency Master: Names and Charges of Some Common Ions, p. 7-1<br>Review Activity: Formulas of Ionic Compounds, p. 7-7 |
| **Career** Physician, p. 156 | | |
| **7-6** Naming Ionic Compounds, pp. 159-161 | | Transparency Master: Some Binary Compounds with Names that End in *-ide*, p. 7-4<br>Transparency Master: The Traditional System and Stock System for Naming Certain Ions, p. 7-2<br>Open-Ended Demonstration: Differences in the Behavior of Hard and Soft Water, p. 7-5 |
| **Break-through** The Chemical Information System, pp. 162-163 | | |
| **7-7** Formulas of Molecular Compounds, pp. 163-165<br>**7-8** Naming Molecular Compounds, pp. 165-166 | Demo 7-2: Structures of Compounds, p. TG-124<br>Demo 7-3: Chemicals in Everyday Life, p. TG-124 | Review Activity: Empirical and Molecular Formulas, p. 7-8<br>Transparency Master: The Uses of Prefixes in Naming Compounds, p. 7-3<br>Transparency Master: Some Binary Compounds with Names that End in *-ide*, p. 7-4 |
| **7-9** Naming Acids, pp. 166-168 | | Review Activity: Names and Formulas of Compounds, p. 7-9 |
| | | Test—Form A, p. AT-25<br>Alternate Test—Form B, p. BT-25 |

☐ Core  ☐ Advanced  ☐ Optional

**TG-120**

# Chapter Overview

In Chapter 7, we discuss chemical formulas. Three types of chemical formulas are defined and compared: molecular, empirical, and structural. Next we introduce students to the periodic table. We discuss the location of the metals, nonmetals, and semimetals (metalloids) in the periodic table. This information can be used by students to differentiate between the two main classes of compounds that are discussed in this chapter: molecular compounds and ionic compounds. It is important for students to be able to identify a compound as being either molecular or ionic in order for them to name it. The remainder of the chapter presents systematic methods for writing chemical formulas and for naming ionic and molecular compounds.

# Chapter Objectives

After students have completed this chapter, they will be able to:

1. Interpret the information conveyed by chemical formulas.                              *7-1* to *7-4*

2. Derive the formulas for various compounds.
                                         *7-5* and *7-7*

3. Apply the rules for determining the names of compounds.                      *7-6* to *7-9*

# Teaching Suggestions

### 7-1 Using Symbols to Write Formulas, pp. 147-149, and

### 7-2 Kinds of Formulas, pp. 149-151

■ Begin this chapter by reviewing the symbols and names of the most common elements. Emphasize that this knowledge is essential to writing chemical formulas and naming compounds, the subject of Chapter 7. Define chemical formula. Point out that symbols are used to indicate the kind of atoms contained in a unit of a compound and that subscripts are used to indicate the number of atoms in a unit of a compound.

■ Point out to the students that there are different kinds of chemical formulas. Each kind of formula has a particular purpose. Mention the three types of formulas that are discussed in this section: empirical, molecular, and structural.

■ Keep in mind that students often have difficulty in distinguishing between empirical and molecular formulas. Refer students to text Figure 7-5. Have the students construct models of each molecule in the figure if possible. Then, have the students compare the

empirical and molecular formulas of each molecule in turn. Ask the students which molecules have the same empirical and molecular formulas. For a molecule having different empirical and molecular formulas, ask the students how these formulas are related.

■ Compare the formulas of butyl alcohol and ethyl ether, which have identical empirical and molecular formulas. Point out that another type of chemical formula is needed to distinguish between these two compounds. Define structural formula. Compare the structural formulas of butyl alcohol and ethyl ether.

■ **Concept Mastery.** You may want to assign Concept Mastery question 41 (chapter-end question) to check your students' ability to distinguish between symbols and formulas. Discuss other examples such as CO and Co. Another common error is the misuse of subscripts. Students frequently fail to recognize that when a number is not present in a formula, a "1" is understood. You may want to assign Concept Mastery question 43 to check your students' understanding of this convention. In addition, you may want to ask students to make sketches of formulas using circles of various sizes or colors to represent different atoms.

### 7-3 Types of Compounds, pp. 151-153, and

### 7-4 Ionic Substances, pp. 153-154

| Planning Guide | |
|---|---|
| Labs (Lab Manual) and Demonstrations (TE) | Supplementary Materials (Teacher's Resource Book) |
| Demo 7-1: Metals and Nonmetals, p. TG-123 | |

■ Point out to the students that up until now, discussion of compounds has focused only upon molecular compounds, which are represented by molecular formulas. Ionic compounds are introduced in this section. It is important for students to understand the nature of the three classes of elements in order for them to distinguish between these types of compounds. Therefore, remind the students that the elements can be classified as metals, nonmetals, or semimetals (metalloids), based on the properties they exhibit. Demonstration 7-1, "Metals and Nonmetals," can be used to reinforce this concept.

■ There are other major differences between molecular and ionic substances. To discuss these differences it may be necessary to review briefly the structure of the atom. Point out that neutral atoms contain an equal number of protons and electrons, and that a loss or gain of electrons will provide atoms with an excess electrical charge.

■ Explain that unlike molecular substances, ionic substances consist of separate units of positive and

7

negative ions arranged in a structural pattern. Have the students compare the structure of NaCl with that of butyl alcohol. Emphasize that there are no separate "molecules of NaCl." Therefore, a molecular formula cannot be used to represent an ionic compound. Rather, an empirical formula is used.

■ **Concept Mastery.** It is important for students to understand that certain properties of a substance are due to its macrostructure when aggregates of the substance are examined. For example, individual molecules will not have color, be sticky, feel cold, etc. Emphasize that the properties of molecules used to define them are chemical properties. You may want to bring this to the students' attention by assigning Concept Mastery questions 40 and 44 (chapter-end questions).

### 7-5 Predicting Formulas of Ionic Compounds, pp. 154-159

| Planning Guide | |
|---|---|
| **Labs (Lab Manual) and Demonstrations (TE)** | **Supplementary Materials (Teacher's Resource Book)** |
| Lab 11: Composition of Hydrates | Transparency Master: Names and Charges of Some Common Ions, p. 7-1<br>Review Activity: Formulas of Ionic Compounds, p. 7-7 |

■ Explain to the students that a set of rules has been developed to assist them in predicting the formulas of ionic compounds. These rules are based upon the fact that any correct formula for an ionic compound must have a net charge of zero. Walk the students through the three rules discussed in this section. Point out that these rules apply to binary ionic compounds. In regard to Rule 2, point out that the rationale behind the charges on the ions listed in text Figure 7-11 is the loss or gain of electrons by the various atoms. Then discuss the use of the periodic table and text Figure 7-12 to help students infer the charge of an ion.

■ Point out to the students that not all compounds contain only two elements. Some compounds contain polyatomic ions. The three rules for writing formulas of binary compounds can be used to write formulas of compounds containing polyatomic ions if a fourth rule, as described in this section, is added.

■ Have students do Laboratory 11, "Composition of Hydrates." In this lab, students learn that certain ionic compounds, called hydrates, contain water molecules in their ionic structures. This information must also be included in the formula of the compound.

■ **Concept Mastery.** Students frequently write formulas in a very mechanical way without realizing the significance of what they are writing. Concept Mastery

question 42 (chapter-end question) illustrates one of the common mistakes resulting from this approach to writing chemical formulas. Some students will even put coefficients in the middle of formulas, such as Ca2OH. If students are asked to depict these molecules, they may not make these types of mistakes.

### 7-6 Naming Ionic Compounds, pp. 159-161

| Planning Guide | |
|---|---|
| **Labs (Lab Manual) and Demonstrations (TE)** | **Supplementary Materials (Teacher's Resource Book)** |
| | Transparency Master: The Traditional System and Stock System for Naming Certain Ions, p. 7-2<br>Open-Ended Demonstration: Differences in the Behavior of Hard and Soft Water, p. 7-5 |

■ Approach this section in the same way that the previous section is approached. Discuss the naming of binary ionic compounds first. Then move on to a discussion on ternary compounds.

■ Begin by naming a simple binary compound in which the name of the cation is followed by the name of the anion. Then point out the potential confusion resulting from the naming of a compound containing the copper cation. Show the students how to use both the traditional and the Stock system for naming copper compounds.

■ Next, demonstrate the naming of some ternary compounds. Emphasize the similarity between naming binary and ternary compounds.

### 7-7 Formulas of Molecular Compounds, pp. 163-165, and

### 7-8 Naming Molecular Compounds, pp. 165-166

| Planning Guide | |
|---|---|
| **Labs (Lab Manual) and Demonstrations (TE)** | **Supplementary Materials (Teacher's Resource Book)** |
| Demo 7-2: Structures of Compounds, p. TG-124<br>Demo 7-3: Chemicals in Everyday Life, p. TG-124 | Review Activity: Empirical and Molecular Formulas, p. 7-8<br>Transparency Master: The Uses of Prefixes in Naming Compounds, p. 7-3<br>Transparency Master: Some Binary Compounds with Names that End in -ide, p. 7-4 |

■ Explain that predicting formulas for molecular compounds is complicated by the fact that two elements can combine to form many different compounds. Refer to the Transparency Master "The Uses of Prefixes in Naming Compounds," which lists five different compounds of oxygen and nitrogen. Explain that these formulas are determined not through a system like that used for ionic compounds, but rather from experimental data.

■ Explain that the naming of molecular compounds is simplified by a type of bookkeeping system that has been developed. This system is based upon the unequal sharing of electrons in molecular compounds. Define apparent charge or oxidation number. Although oxidation numbers are discussed in detail in Chapter 21, you may find it worthwhile to present a brief explanation of oxidation numbers at this time. Show how apparent charges or oxidation numbers can be derived from the formulas of the five nitrogen oxides in text Figure 7-20. Once the apparent charges are determined, the Stock system can be applied to the naming of molecular compounds. Text Figure 7-21 summarizes the naming of five nitrogen oxides. Refer to text, Figure 7-22, which lists the traditional name and the Stock system name for each of several compounds.

■ Use Demonstration 7-2, "Structures of Compounds," and Demonstration 7-3, "Chemicals in Everyday Life," to summarize all of the material covered so far in this chapter in regard to the writing of chemical formulas and naming of compounds.

■ **Application.** You may want to point out to the students the many places where they encounter the chemical formulas and names of compounds. Many household food items, cleaning agents, and medicines contain a list of ingredients on their labels. These names and formulas should now be more meaningful to the students.

### 7-9 Naming Acids, pp. 166-168

| Planning Guide | |
|---|---|
| **Labs (Lab Manual) and Demonstrations (TE)** | **Supplementary Materials (Teacher's Resource Book)** |
| | Review Activity: Names and Formulas of Compounds, p. 7-9 |

■ Although acids are discussed in detail in Chapters 19 and 20, you may wish to discuss briefly the composition and properties of this class of compounds. Refer to familiar examples of acids such as acetic, hydrochloric, and sulfuric acids. Point out that the pure, undissolved hydrogen compounds that form acids in water solution are named in the same way as other binary and ternary compounds. For example, HCl gas is called hydrogen chloride.

■ Outline the rules for naming acids, and supplement the explanation with many examples.

## Demonstrations

### 7-1 Metals and Nonmetals

**Overview:** In this demonstration, metals and nonmetals are exhibited. Properties of each are discussed.

**Materials:** jars or stoppered test tubes that contain samples of various common metallic and nonmetallic elements; conductivity apparatus; 1 $M$ hydrochloric acid (HCl).

**CAUTION:** *Do not use very reactive metals such as sodium, potassium, and the other alkali metals.*

**Advance Preparation:** 1. Set up the samples of common metallic and nonmetallic elements. You may wish to include elements such as zinc, copper, iron, magnesium, carbon, and sulfur. 2. **1 $M$ HCl:** Prepare a solution that is approximately 1 $M$ by dissolving concentrated HCl in water in a 1:11 ratio. 3. If you do not use a ready-made conductivity apparatus, you can easily construct one by using a low-voltage power source, such as a dry cell, some insulated copper wire, and a low-wattage light bulb and holder, as shown in the accompanying figure.

**Safety:** Be careful in handling the hydrochloric acid, as it is very corrosive. Wear safety goggles and rubber gloves, and when diluting concentrated acid, add the acid to the water, never add the water to the acid.

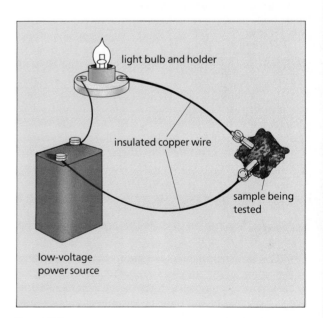

light bulb and holder

insulated copper wire

sample being tested

low-voltage power source

**Figure 7-1**

**Procedure:** 1. Have the students observe the various jars or test tubes and describe properties of metals and nonmetals. 2. Have a student volunteer separate the samples into two main groups: those that are shiny, or lustrous; and those that are dull. 3. Use a conductivity apparatus to test the solids to see which conduct electricity. 4. Add a small piece of each solid separately to HCl solution in a fume hood. 5. Tell students that metals tend to lose electrons during chemical reactions such as the ones involving HCl. Point out that metals form positive ions or cations.

**Results:** Student responses will vary in step 1. Most will focus on the high luster of metals. In step 2, most of the metals will be shiny and most of the nonmetals will be dull. In step 3, most of the metals will be good conductors and most of the nonmetals will be poor conductors. In step 4, many of the metals will react with the HCl, and most of the nonmetals will not.

## 7-2 Structures of Compounds

**Overview:** In this demonstration, models of diatomic molecules of elements and molecular compounds and models of ionic compounds are discussed.

**Materials:** colored Styrofoam balls; colored gumdrops or marshmallows; toothpicks; labeled cards.

**Advance Preparation:** 1. If already colored Styrofoam balls are not available, paint some white ones and allow them to dry. 2. Prepare cards with the following labels: $H_2$, $N_2$, $O_2$, $F_2$, $Cl_2$, $Br_2$, $I_2$, $H_2O$, $CO_2$, $NH_3$, and any others for which you wish to construct models.

**Procedure:** 1. Construct seven models of diatomic elemental molecules, using different-colored and different-sized Styrofoam balls to represent the atoms H, N, O, F, Cl, Br, and I. Place a labeled card in front of each one on the front desk. Tell students that five of the substances are gases, one ($Br_2$) is a liquid, and one ($I_2$) is a solid at room temperature. 2. Make some models of water, carbon dioxide, ammonia, and other simple molecular compounds, using candy and toothpicks. Place a labeled card in front of each structure. Emphasize that the atoms in these compounds are sharing electrons in covalent bonding and form molecules. Ask students what properties these compounds tend to have. 3. Make a model of one unit of ionic crystal of NaCl, using two different colored balls or gumdrops. Use this to discuss the properties of ionic crystals. Ask students to describe these properties.

**Results:** Covalent compounds tend to have low melting and boiling points and to be poor conductors in all phases. Ionic compounds tend to have high melting and boiling points and to be poor conductors as solids but good conductors when molten.

## 7-3 Chemicals in Everyday Life

**Overview:** In this demonstration, large flashcards are used to help students become more familiar with chemical compounds in their lives.

**Materials:** colored index cards; felt-tip marker.

**Advance Preparation:** Write the name and uses of an important chemical substance on one side of each card. Choose substances that are found around the home or that are important in the lives of students. Some examples include: sulfur dioxide, carbon dioxide, carbon monoxide, dinitrogen oxide (laughing gas), iron(III) oxide (rust), calcium oxide (lime), sodium chloride, silicon dioxide (sand), stannous fluoride (tin(II) fluoride), silver sulfide (tarnish), hydrochloric acid (muriatic acid used in swimming pools), sulfuric acid (battery acid), sodium hydroxide (drain cleaner), and sodium bicarbonate (baking soda).

**Procedure:** 1. Show the class each flashcard. Discuss each substance. Ask students to try to come up with the correct formula for each, and write the formulas on the reverse sides of the cards. 2. Use the flashcards for review or in a game involving student teams.

**Results:** The formulas for the examples given are: $SO_2$, $CO_2$, $CO$, $N_2O$, $Fe_2O_3$, $CaO$, $NaCl$, $SiO_2$, $SnF_2$, $Ag_2S$, $HCl$, $H_2SO_4$, $NaOH$, and $NaHCO_3$.

# Answers to Questions

**Page 149**
1. The formula of a molecule of radon is Rn.
2. The formula of a molecule of chlorine is $Cl_2$.
3. Carbon and oxygen are present in $CO_2$.
4. There are two atoms of oxygen for each atom of carbon. Two times $4 \times 10^{20} = 8 \times 10^{20}$

**Page 151**
5. **a.** A chemical formula consists of chemical symbols and subscripts that represent the composition of a substance. **b.** A formula indicates the elements that make up a compound and the ratio of atoms of the elements in the compound. **c.** This formula shows that the compound sulfuric acid consists of the elements hydrogen, sulfur, and oxygen. Moreover, the ratio of the atoms of these elements is 2 (hydrogen) : 1 (sulfur) : 4 (oxygen).
6. A qualitative analysis tells what elements are present in a sample of a compound. A quantitative analysis reveals the mass of each element in a sample of a compound.
7. **a.** An empirical formula shows the simplest ratio of the atoms in a molecule of a compound. **b.** HO is the empirical formula of hydrogen peroxide, $H_2O_2$.
8. Sucrose contains carbon, hydrogen, and oxygen.
9. **a.** The molecular formula is $C_4H_{10}$. **b.** The empirical formula is $C_2H_5$.
10. **a.** No matter what size sample is present, there is always one carbon atom for two oxygen atoms. **b.** It is always 1:2.

**Page 153**

11. $SO_2$ and $CCl_4$ would be molecular rather than ionic because both elements making up each compound are nonmetals.

**Page 154**

12. **a.** Ionic compounds consist of ions. These ions do not form units of covalently bonded molecules but consist of large units of ions in the ratio given in the formula. **b.** A formula unit is different from a molecule in that it represents the lowest whole-number ratio of ions in a compound rather than a discrete particle of a compound.

**Page 158**

13. **a.** An anion is an ion with a negative charge.
   **b.** A cation is an ion with a positive charge.
14. **a.** 1; **b.** 1; **c.** 3
15. **a.** 2+; **b.** 2+; **c.** 6+ because there are three ions each with a charge of 2+.
16. **a.** 2; **b.** 1; **c.** 3
17. **a.** 2−; **b.** 1−; **c.** 3−

**Page 159**

18. **a.** $BaCl_2$; **b.** $Li_2S$; **c.** $Sr_3(PO_4)_2$; **d.** $(NH_4)_2S$; **e.** $Al_2S_3$
19. **a.** $(NH_4)_2CO_3$; **b.** $BaSO_4$; **c.** $Na_3PO_4$; **d.** $AlBr_3$; **e.** $Na_2O_2$

**Page 161**

20. **a.** A binary compound is one that contains two elements. **b.** Sodium chloride, NaCl, and calcium fluoride, $CaF_2$, are examples of binary compounds.
21. **a.** A ternary compound contains three elements. **b.** Ammonium chloride, $NH_4Cl$, is a ternary chloride. Sodium nitrate, $NaNO_3$, is a ternary nitrate.
22. **a.** sodium, $Na^+$; chloride, $Cl^-$
   **b.** barium, $Ba^{2+}$; bromide, $Br^-$
   **c.** calcium, $Ca^{2+}$; sulfate, $SO_4^{2-}$
   **d.** potassium, $K^+$; chloride, $Cl^-$
   **e.** cadmium, $Cd^{2+}$; carbonate, $CO_3^{2-}$
   **f.** cuprous or copper(I), $Cu^+$; chloride, $Cl^-$
   **g.** stannous or tin(IV), $Sn^{4+}$; chloride, $Cl^-$
   **h.** ferrous or iron(II), $Fe^{2+}$; oxide, $O^{2-}$
23. By the traditional system, the names are ferrous chloride and ferric chloride. By the Stock system, they are iron(II) chloride and iron(III) chloride.
24. **a.** cuprous oxide or copper(I) oxide
   **b.** mercurous nitrate or mercury(I) nitrate
25. **a.** FeS; **b.** $Fe_2S_3$; **c.** $Hg_2O$; **d.** HgO

**Page 165**

26. Since oxygen has a charge of 2−, the charge on the carbon must be 2+.

**Page 166**

27. **a.** dinitrogen monoxide, nitrogen(I) oxide; **b.** nitrogen monoxide, nitrogen(II) oxide; **c.** dinitrogen trioxide, nitrogen(III) oxide; **d.** nitrogen dioxide, nitrogen(IV) oxide; **e.** dinitrogen pentoxide, nitrogen(V) oxide

28. If the apparent charge on oxygen is 2− and there are 10 atoms, the total negative charge is 20. The total positive charge must also be 20. Since there are four phosphorus atoms, each must have a charge of 5+.
29. **a.** In CO, the carbon must be 2+ to balance the charge on the oxygen of 2−. In $CO_2$, the charge on the carbon must be 4+ to balance the total negative charge on the oxygen, which is $2 \times 2-$ or 4−.
   **b.** carbon(II) oxide; carbon(IV) oxide

**Page 168**

30. **a.** hydrogen fluoride, hydrofluoric acid
   **b.** hydrogen sulfide, hydrosulfuric acid
   **c.** hydrogen chloride, hydrochloric acid
31. **a.** carbonic acid; **b.** sulfurous acid; **c.** phosphoric acid; **d.** acetic acid
32. **a.** HClO; $HClO_2$; $HClO_3$
   **b.** In HClO, the hydrogen and chlorine each have a positive charge of one, thus balancing the charge of 2− on the oxygen atom. In $HClO_2$, the negative charge is 4 because there are two oxygen atoms each with a charge of 2−. Since the charge on the hydrogen remains at 1+, the charge on the chlorine must be 3+ to form a neutral compound. In $HClO_3$, the charge on the chlorine is 5+.
33. **a.** $ClO_3^-$; $ClO_4^-$; **b.** "Per" means greater than. The chlorine in the perchlorate ion has a higher apparent charge than that in the chlorate ion.
34. The prefix "hypo" means low, and the chlorine atom in hypochlorite compounds has a lower apparent charge than that in chlorite compounds.
35. **a.** HCl; **b.** $H_2SO_3$; **c.** HClO; **d.** $HNO_3$

## Chapter Review  7

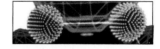

**Page 170, Content Review**

1. The symbols are: helium, He; neon, Ne; hydrogen, H; nitrogen, N; and sulfur, S.

2. The formulas are: helium, He; neon, Ne; hydrogen, $H_2$; nitrogen, $N_2$; and sulfur, $S_8$.

3. In $6 \times 10^{23}$ molecules of sucrose, $C_{12}H_{22}O_{11}$, are: $12 \times 6 \times 10^{23} = 72 \times 10^{23} = 7.2 \times 10^{24}$ carbon atoms; $22 \times 6 \times 10^{23} = 132 \times 10^{23} = 1.32 \times 10^{25}$ hydrogen atoms; and $11 \times 6 \times 10^{23} = 66 \times 10^{23} = 6.6 \times 10^{24}$ oxygen atoms.

4. For cyclobutane: **a.** the molecular formula is $C_4H_8$; **b.** the empirical formula is $CH_2$.

5. Three properties of metals that distinguish them

from nonmetals are malleability, luster, and conductivity (both heat and electrical).

6. Of the listed compounds, MgS and KBr are ionic.

7. A magnesium atom and a magnesium ion each has 12 protons; the number of neutrons varies. A magnesium atom has 12 electrons, but a magnesium ion has 10.

8. When an ionic compound forms, electrons are transferred from the metallic element to the nonmetallic element.

9. Ionic compounds are not made up of molecules. Their formulas, such as $CaCl_2$, are empirical formulas that express the overall ratio of the ions in the substance.

10. For barium iodide, $BaI_2$: **a.** $Ba^{2+}$ is the cation; **b.** $I^-$ is the anion; **c.** the net charge on one formula unit is zero.

11. **a.** The symbols for the ions are: sodium, $Na^+$; sulfur, $S^{2-}$; aluminum, $Al^{3+}$; oxygen, $O^{2-}$; magnesium, $Mg^{2+}$; and chlorine, $Cl^-$. **b.** The formulas for the compounds are: sodium sulfide, $Na_2S$; aluminum oxide, $Al_2O_3$; magnesium chloride, $MgCl_2$; sodium oxide, $Na_2O$; magnesium sulfide, $MgS$; and aluminum chloride, $AlCl_3$.

12. A polyatomic ion is an ion that contains more than one element. The ammonium ion, $NH_4^+$, is a positively charged polyatomic ion listed in text Figure 7-11.

13. The formulas are: **a.** sodium sulfate, $Na_2SO_4$; **b.** magnesium carbonate, $MgCO_3$; **c.** calcium phosphate, $Ca_3(PO_4)_2$; **d.** barium nitrate, $Ba(NO_3)_2$; **e.** ammonium nitrite, $NH_4NO_2$.

14. The names of the compounds are: **a.** KBr, potassium bromide; **b.** $Li_2S$, lithium sulfide; **c.** BaO, barium oxide; **d.** $MgI_2$, magnesium iodide; **e.** $AlF_3$, aluminum fluoride.

15. The names of the compounds are: **a.** $AgClO_3$, silver chlorate; **b.** $NiSO_4$, nickel sulfate; **c.** $AlPO_4$, aluminum phosphate; **d.** $Cs_2CO_3$, cesium carbonate; **e.** $Be(NO_3)_2$, beryllium nitrate.

16. The names, by both the traditional and the Stock system, are: **a.** HgO, mercuric oxide, mercury(II) oxide; **b.** $SnCl_4$, stannic chloride, tin(IV) chloride; **c.** $Cu_2O$, cuprous oxide, copper(I) oxide; **d.** $FeCl_2$, ferrous chloride, iron(II) chloride; **e.** $PbCrO_4$, plumbous chromate, lead(II) chromate.

17. The formulas are: **a.** copper(I) sulfide, $Cu_2S$; **b.** mercury(II) cyanide, $Hg(CN)_2$; **c.** chromium(III) bromide, $CrBr_3$; **d.** aluminum dichromate, $Al_2(Cr_2O_7)_3$; **e.** zinc hydroxide, $Zn(OH)_2$.

18. The sulfur atom in $SO_3$ has an apparent charge of

6+ to balance the three oxygen atoms, which are 2- each.

19. Using the traditional system, the names are: **a.** $SO_2$, sulfur dioxide; **b.** $SiCl_4$, silicon tetrachloride; **c.** $OF_2$, oxygen difluoride; **d.** $N_2S_3$, dinitrogen trisulfide; **e.** CO, carbon monoxide.

20. Using the Stock system, the names are: **a.** $SO_2$, sulfur(IV) oxide; **b.** $SO_3$, sulfur(VI) oxide; **c.** CO, carbon(II) oxide; **d.** $CO_2$, carbon(IV) oxide; **e.** $P_4O_{10}$, phosphorus(V) oxide.

21.

| Formula | Pure Substance | Water Solution |
|---|---|---|
| **a.** HBr | hydrogen bromide | hydrobromic acid |
| **b.** HI | hydrogen iodide | hydroiodic acid |
| **c.** $H_2S$ | hydrogen sulfide | hydrosulfuric acid |

22.

| Formula | Pure Substance | Water Solution |
|---|---|---|
| **a.** $HClO_3$ | hydrogen chlorate | chloric acid |
| **b.** $H_2SO_4$ | hydrogen sulfate | sulfuric acid |
| **c.** $H_2CrO_4$ | hydrogen chromate | chromic acid |
| **d.** $H_2C_2O_4$ | hydrogen oxalate | oxalic acid |
| **e.** $H_2C_4H_4O_6$ | hydrogen tartrate | tartaric acid |

23. Phosphorous acid has the formula $H_3PO_3$, one less oxygen than phosphoric acid, $H_3PO_4$.

24. **a.** hydrochloric acid, HCl; **b.** chloric acid, $HClO_3$; **c.** perchloric acid, $HClO_4$; **d.** hydrosulfuric acid, $H_2S$; **e.** sulfuric acid, $H_2SO_4$.

## Page 171, Content Mastery

25. $HNO_3$, nitric acid; $H_2SO_4$, sulfuric acid; $H_3PO_4$, phosphoric acid; $H_2CO_3$, carbonic acid; HCl, hydrochloric acid.

26. ammonium ion, $NH_4^+$; hydroxide ion, $OH^-$; carbonate ion, $CO_3^{2-}$; nitrate ion, $NO_3^-$; sulfate ion, $SO_4^{2-}$; phosphate ion, $PO_4^{3-}$

27. trisulfur dinitrogen dioxide, $S_3N_2O_2$; sulfur trioxide, $SO_3$; tetraphosphorus triselenide, $P_4Se_3$; phosphorus heptabromide dichloride, $PBr_7Cl_2$; carbon tetraiodide, $CI_4$.

28. nitrous acid, $HNO_2$; sulfurous acid, $H_2SO_3$; perchloric acid, $HClO_4$.

29. Sulfate ion, $SO_4^{2-}$: $x + 4(-2) = -2$, so $x = -2 - (-8) = 6$
Sulfite ion, $SO_3^{2-}$: $x + 3(-2) = -2$, so $x = -2 - (-6) = 4$

30. Nitrate ion, $NO_3^-$: $x + 3(-2) = -1$, so $x = -1 - (-6) = 5$
Nitrite ion, $NO_2^-$: $x + 2(-2) = -1$, so $x = -1 - (-4) = 3$

31. $CF_4$, carbon tetrafluoride; $PBr_5$, phosphorus pentabromide; $N_2S_3$, dinitrogen trisulfide; $SF_6$, sulfur hexafluoride; $S_4N_2$, tetrasulfur dinitride.

**32.** $Al_2(SO_4)_3$ has three units of $SO_4$, so the number of oxygen atoms is $3 \times 4 = 12$.

**33.** The mass of the empirical formula, CH, is $12.011 + 1.008 = 13.019$ g. The actual molecular formula, $(CH)_n$, can be deduced by solving for n:

$$\frac{\text{molecular mass}}{\text{empirical mass}} = \frac{26.04 \text{ g/mol}}{13.02 \text{ g/mol}} = 2.000 \text{ for Chris}$$

$$\frac{78.11 \text{ g/mol}}{13.02 \text{ g/mol}} = 5.999 \approx 6 \text{ for Coleman}$$

Therefore, the molecular formula for Chris is $C_2H_2$; for Coleman, it is $C_6H_6$.

**34.** For both molecules, counting the atoms gives the molecular formula $C_6H_6$, so both have the empirical formula CH.

**35. a.** H—C≡C—H, CH; **b.** $CH_4$, $CH_4$; **c.** $C_6H_6$, CH; **d.** $H_2O$, $H_2O$; **e.** $H_2O_2$, HO; **f.** NaCl, NaCl; **g.** $C_2H_5OH$, $C_2H_6O$; **h.** $C_6H_{12}O_6$, $CH_2O$.

**36.** KCl, potassium chloride; $Al_2O_3$, aluminum oxide; LiH, lithium hydride; $Hg_2Cl_2$, mercury(I) chloride; $HgF_2$, mercury(II) fluoride; CaO, calcium oxide; CuCl, copper(I) chloride; $CuBr_2$, copper(II) bromide; NaI, sodium iodide; MgO, magnesium oxide; CaS, calcium sulfide; $Na_3N$, sodium nitride; FeO, iron(II) oxide; $Fe_2O_3$, iron(III) oxide; PbO, lead(II) oxide; $SnF_2$, tin(II) fluoride; $(NH_4)_2SO_4$, ammonium sulfate.

**37.** The formula for sodium hypochlorite is NaClO.

**38.** $C_2H_3O_2^-$, acetate; $O_2^{2-}$, peroxide; $NO_2^-$, nitrite; $SO_3^{2-}$, sulfite; $ClO_3^-$, chlorate; $HCO_3^-$, hydrogen carbonate (bicarbonate); $ClO_4^-$, perchlorate.

**39.** Calcium nitride, $Ca_3N_2$; stannic oxide, $SnO_2$; lead(II) sulfide, PbS; potassium peroxide, $K_2O_2$; sodium hydride, NaH; ammonium phosphate, $(NH_4)_3PO_4$.

## Page 171, Concept Mastery

**40. Concept:** *Compounds have sets of properties based on molecular structure and how molecules relate to one another.*

**Solution:** A description on the microscopic (atomic) level must include a description of the atoms or ions. Rust (iron oxide) is a lattice of iron ions and oxygen ions.

**41. Concept:** *Formulas and chemical symbols.*

**Solution:** No. the formula NACL for sodium chloride is incorrect. The symbol for an element is either a capital letter or a capital letter with a small letter. The symbols for sodium and chlorine are Na and Cl; the formula for sodium chloride is NaCl.

**42. Concept:** *Formula writing.*

**Solution:** No, the formula $CaOH_2$ for calcium hydroxide is incorrect. It would mean there are two hydrogen atoms and one oxygen atom, but actually there are two hydroxide ($OH^-$) ions. To show this, there should be parentheses around the formula for the ion: $Ca(OH)_2$.

**43. Concept:** *Formula writing.*

**Solution:** No, the number of atoms in the formula $Na_2SO_4$ is not 6. Students frequently fail to realize that a 1 is understood if no subscript is present next to an atom in a formula. The formula indicates that there are two sodium atoms, one sulfur atom, and four oxygen atoms, a total of seven.

**44. Concept:** *Properties of compounds depend on molecular structure.*

**Solution:** The student is confusing microscopic and macroscopic descriptions. On the molecular level there cannot be "a sticky substance"; the properties of the glue are caused by the identity and arrangement of atoms in the molecule.

## Page 172, Cumulative Review

**45. d.** Isotopes differ in the number of neutrons.

**46. b.** The modern standard of atomic mass is C−12.

**47. c.** 10°C is 283 K.

**48. b.** The SI unit of energy is the joule.

**49. c.** A graduated cylinder most precisely measures volume.

**50.**

| Isotope Symbol | At. No. | At. Mass | No. of Prot. | No. of Neut. | No. Elect. |
|---|---|---|---|---|---|
| **a.** $^{27}_{13}Al$ | 13 | 27 | 13 | 14 | 13 |
| **b.** $^{137}_{56}Ba$ | 56 | 137 | 56 | 81 | 56 |
| **c.** $^{35}_{17}Cl$ | 17 | 35 | 17 | 18 | 17 |
| **d.** $^{32}_{16}S^{2-}$ | 16 | 32 | 16 | 16 | 18 |

**51.** A physical change is said to occur if one or more physical properties of a substance are changed but without any change in its chemical properties or composition. A chemical change is any change that results in the production of one or more substances that differ in chemical properties and composition from the original substances. Physical changes include melting, boiling, dissolving, and changes in shape. Chemical changes include burning, rusting of iron, and souring of milk.

**52.** Compounds have definite compositions; mixtures do not. A compound has unique properties, and its constituents lose their properties; in a mixture the constituents retain their properties. Compounds are always homogeneous; mixtures may be heterogeneous. Compounds include salt, sugar, and water. Mixtures include air, seawater, and food.

**53.**

a. $5 \text{ g} \times \dfrac{1 \text{ mol}}{23 \text{ g}} = 0.22 \text{ mol}$

b. $4.0 \times 10^{20} \text{ parts} \times \dfrac{1 \text{ mol}}{6 \times 10^{23} \text{ parts}} \times \dfrac{23 \text{ g}}{1 \text{ mol}} =$
$1.5 \times 10^{-2} \text{ g}$

c. $250 \text{ mL} \times \dfrac{1 \text{ L}}{1000 \text{ mL}} \times \dfrac{1 \text{ mol}}{22.4 \text{ L}} \times \dfrac{23 \text{ g}}{1 \text{ mol}} = 0.26 \text{ g}$

d. $4.7 \text{ mol} \times \dfrac{6 \times 10^{23} \text{ parts}}{1 \text{ mol}} = 2.8 \times 10^{24} \text{ parts}$

**54.**

a. $\dfrac{4.2 \times 10^{3}}{6.0 \times 10^{23}} = 7.0 \times 10^{-21}$

b. $\dfrac{4.0 \times 10^{-15}}{1.2 \times 10^{5}} = 3.3 \times 10^{-20}$

c. $\begin{aligned} 7.2 \times 10^{23} &= \quad 0.72 \times 10^{24} \\ + 4.9 \times 10^{24} &= + 4.9 \ \ \times 10^{24} \\ & \quad\ \ 5.62 \times 10^{24} \approx 5.6 \times 10^{24} \end{aligned}$

**55.** heat $=$ mass $\times$ specific heat $\times \Delta t$
$= 4.00 \times 10^{2} \text{ g} \times 4.20 \text{ J/g-°C} \times 14.0\text{°C}$
$= 2.35 \times 10^{4} \text{ J}$

## Page 173, Critical Thinking

**56.** Metals: Al, Li; nonmetals: H, He, I; semimetals: B, Si, Ge.

**57.** Ionic compounds: KCl, AlF$_3$, CaO, K$_3$N, CaCl$_2$; molecular compounds: CH$_4$, NCl$_3$, CO$_2$, CF$_4$, HCCl$_3$.

**58.** No, you cannot keep a bottle of pure sodium ions on the shelf because it requires too much energy to separate cations from corresponding anions.

**59.** Compounds formed from two nonmetals are molecular because nonmetals are alike enough to share electrons.

**60.** Apparent charge is the number of electrons that one atom shares with another atom in a molecular compound, whereas ionic charge is the number of electrons gained or lost through transfer in the formation of an ionic compound.

## Page 173, Challenge Problems

**61.** The chloride ion has a charge of 1− in sodium chloride and has the same charge in other compounds.

a. In the compound R$_2$Cl$_3$, the chloride ions have a combined charge of 3−. To balance that charge,

the R ions must have a combined charge of 3+. Each R ion would have to have a charge of 1½+, which is impossible. R$_2$Cl$_3$ cannot be an ionic compound.

b. In the compound XCl, the charge of the X ion must be 1+ to balance the 1− charge of the Cl ion. Many ions have a charge of 1+; therefore, XCl could be an ionic compound.

c. In the compound Z$_2$Cl, the combined charge of the Z ions must balance the 1− charge of the Cl ion. For the charges to be balanced, each Z ion would have to have a charge of ½+, which is impossible. Z$_2$Cl cannot be an ionic compound.

**62.** a.

| | Trial 1 | Trial 2 |
|---|---|---|
| mass of container + Mg | 56.55 g | 31.92 g |
| mass of container | − 48.31 g | − 27.73 g |
| mass of Mg | 8.24 g | 4.19 g |
| mass of container + MgO | 62.04 g | 38.20 g |
| mass of container | − 48.31 g | − 27.73 g |
| mass of MgO | 13.73 g | 10.47 g |

Trial 1: $\% \text{ Mg} = \dfrac{8.24 \text{ g}}{13.73 \text{ g}} \times 100\% = 60\%$

Trial 2: $\% \text{ Mg} = \dfrac{4.19 \text{ g}}{10.47 \text{ g}} \times 100\% = 40\%$

The results are inconsistent and do not support the statement.

b. 1) Incomplete burning of the magnesium would yield a smaller mass of MgO, so the percentage of Mg would be larger.
2) Spilling some of the MgO before weighing would yield a smaller mass of MgO, so the percentage of Mg would be larger.
3) If the container was damp before heating, the water would be considered part of the mass of Mg, so the percentage of Mg would be larger. (If a large mass of water evaporated between the first and third weighings, the data might even show a loss of mass as Mg was changed to MgO.)
4) Losing some Mg between weighing and heating would decrease the yield of MgO, so the percentage of Mg would be larger.

c. 1) mass Mg = 42.15 g  mass MgO = 51.66 g
$\phantom{\text{mass Mg} = }$− 27.95 g $\phantom{\text{mass MgO} = }$− 27.95 g
$\phantom{\text{mass Mg} = }$14.20 g $\phantom{\text{mass MgO} = }$23.71 g

$\% \text{ Mg} = \dfrac{14.20 \text{ g}}{23.71 \text{ g}} \times 100\% = 59.89\%$ or 60%

2) Trials 1 and 3 are in agreement.
3) No, the percentage of Mg was the same even though different masses were used. If larger amounts of Mg are used, larger amounts of products result. The percentage is the same.

# The Mathematics of Chemical Formulas

8

## Chapter Planning Guide

| Text Section | Labs (Lab Manual) and Demonstrations (TE) | Supplementary Materials (Teacher's Resource Book) |
|---|---|---|
| **8-1** Stoichiometry, pp. 175-176 | | |
| **8-2** Formula Mass, pp. 176-178 | | Review Activity: Formula Mass, p. 8-6 |
| **8-3** Gram Atomic Mass and Gram Formula Mass, pp. 178-179 | Lab 12: Determining the Gram Atomic Mass of an Element | |
| **8-4** The Mole, pp. 179-182 | Demo 8-1: Mole Jars, p. TG-134 Demo 8-2: Making a Mole of Pencil Marks, p. TG-134 | Stoichiometry Problems: Familiar Quantities of Matter—One-Step Problems, p. SP-3 |
| **8-5** Moles and Atoms, pp. 182-184 | | Stoichiometry Problems: Moles of Elements—One-Step Problems, p. SP-7 |
| **8-6** Moles and Formula Units, pp. 184-186 | | Stoichiometry Problems: Moles of Compounds—One-Step Problems, p. SP-12 Stoichiometry Problems: Interpreting Formulas, p. SP-18 |
| **8-7** Mole Relationships, pp. 186-189 | Demo 8-3: A Gross of Beans, p. TG-134 Demo 8-4: The Molar Volume of a Gas, p. TG-135 | Transparency Master: The Mole Diagram, p. 8-2 Transparency Master: A Mole Diagram for a Sample Problem, p. 8-3 Stoichiometry Problems: —Familiar Quantities of Matter—Two-Step Problems, p. SP-5 —Moles of Elements—Two-Step Problems, p. SP-10 —Moles of Compounds—Two-Step Problems, p. SP-15 —Molar Volume—One-Step Problems, p. SP-30 —Molar Volume—Multi-Step Problems, p. SP-32 Non-SI Supplementary Problems, p. 8-9 Concept Mastery: Moles and Mass Relationships, p. CM-9 |

| Text Section | Labs (Lab Manual) and Demonstrations (TE) | Supplementary Materials (Teacher's Resource Book) |
|---|---|---|
| **8-8** Percentage Composition, pp. 190-191 | Demo 8-5: Percentage of Water in Popcorn, p. TG-135 | Stoichiometry Problems: —Determining the Percentage Composition from a Formula, p. SP-26 —Percentage of Water in a Hydrate, p. SP-28 —Application of Percentage Composition, p. SP-29 Open-Ended Experiment: The Percent of Water in a Tomato, p. 8-4 Review Activity: Quantitative Relationships in Chemistry, p. 8-7 |
| **8-9** Determining the Formula of a Compound, pp. 192-194 | Lab 13: Determining an Empirical Formula | Stoichiometry Problems: —Determining Empirical Formulas, p. SP-19 —Empirical Formulas—An Extra Computation, p. SP-21 —Empirical Formulas of Hydrates, p. SP-23 —Molecular Formulas of Compounds, p. SP-24 |
| **8-10** Another Way to Determine Empirical Formulas, pp. 194-195 | | Practice Problems: p. 8-8 |
| **Biography** Reatha Clark King, p. 191 | | |
| | | Test—Form A, p. AT-28 Alternate Test—Form B, p. BT-28 |

☐ Core     ☐ Advanced     ☐ Optional

## Chapter Overview

In Chapter 8 we introduce one aspect of stoichiometry, the quantitative relationships that can be derived from chemical formulas. This is accomplished by first defining and comparing formula mass and molecular mass. Then, the more useful quantities of gram atomic mass and gram formula mass are defined and related to atomic mass.

Next, Avogadro's number and the mole are presented. The mole is described as the chemical unit used by chemists to "count" particles of matter, to relate the mass of an element or compound to the number of particles in a sample, and to relate the volume of a gas to either the mass of a sample or the number of particles in the sample. The chapter ends with a discussion of percentage composition and three approaches for determining chemical formulas: from percentage composition data, from mass data, or from the number of moles of each element in the compound.

## Chapter Objectives

After students have completed this chapter, they will be able to:

1. Determine the atomic mass of elements and the formula mass of compounds.         *8-1* and *8-2*
2. Determine the gram atomic mass and the gram formula mass of substances.         *8-3*

3. Calculate the mass of a given number of moles of a substance.                              *8-4 to 8-6*
4. Calculate the number of moles in a given mass of a substance.                              *8-4 to 8-6*
5. Calculate the number of molecules in a given number of moles of a substance.          *8-4 to 8-6*
6. Calculate the volume of a given mass of a gaseous substance at STP.                        *8-7*
7. Determine the percentage composition of a substance from its formula.                      *8-8*
8. Determine the empirical and molecular formulas of compounds.                    *8-9 and 8-10*

## Teaching Suggestions

### 8-1 Stoichiometry, pp. 175-176, and

### 8-2 Formula Mass, pp. 176-178

| Planning Guide | |
| --- | --- |
| Labs (Lab Manual) and Demonstrations (TE) | Supplementary Materials (Teacher's Resource Book) |
| | Review Activity: Formula Mass, p. 8-6 |

■ Mention that after the introduction of a quantitative approach to experimentation scientists made great strides in unraveling many of the mysteries of chemistry. Remind the students that the phlogiston theory, supported by a number of prominent scientists, was determined invalid by Lavoisier's quantitative experiments. From then on, rapid progress was made in understanding important chemical reactions.

■ Discuss text Figure 8-2, a review of what the students have learned so far about chemical formulas. Then define stoichiometry. Point out that stoichiometry involves quantitative relationships derived from chemical formulas (the subject of this chapter) and chemical equations (the subject of Chapter 10). Next, stress the importance of stoichiometry to the chemist in the laboratory and in industry.

■ Review the concept of atomic mass. Then introduce the concept of formula mass and relate it to atomic mass. Work out several sample problems where the formula mass is calculated for elements, molecular compounds, and ionic compounds.

■ After the students have mastered the concept of formula mass, introduce the concept of molecular mass. Point out that formula mass, the broader term, applies to both molecular and ionic compounds. Molecular mass, the more restrictive term, applies only to molecular compounds.

### 8-3 Gram Atomic Mass and Gram Formula Mass, pp. 178-179

| Planning Guide | |
| --- | --- |
| Labs (Lab Manual) and Demonstrations (TE) | Supplementary Materials (Teacher's Resource Book) |
| Lab 12: Determining the Gram Atomic Mass of an Element | |

■ Define and discuss gram atomic mass, gram formula mass, and gram molecular mass. Relate these units to atomic mass, formula mass, and molecular mass. Refer students to text Figure 8-9, which summarizes these relationships.

Next, point out that there are several methods for determining the gram atomic mass of an element. Laboratory 12, "Determining the Gram Atomic Mass of an Element," illustrates one method. In this lab, students calculate the gram atomic mass of silver using a compound of known composition ($Ag_2O$).

### 8-4 The Mole, pp. 179-182, and

### 8-5 Moles and Atoms, pp. 182-184

| Planning Guide | |
| --- | --- |
| Labs (Lab Manual) and Demonstrations (TE) | Supplementary Materials (Teacher's Resource Book) |
| Demo 8-1: Mole Jars, p. TG-134 Demo 8-2: Making a Mole of Pencil Marks, p. TG-134 | Stoichiometry Problems: Familiar Quantities of Matter—One-Step Problems, p. SP-3 Stoichiometry Problems: Moles of Elements—One-Step Problems, p. SP-7 |

■ Emphasize that atoms and molecules react with each other in a manner that is related to the number of atoms and molecules present in a sample, rather than to the mass or volume of a sample. The mole is the unit by which we can "count" the number of atoms or molecules present in a sample. The mole enables us to relate mass and volume measurements of a sample to the number of atoms or molecules present. To illustrate this point, do Demonstration 8-1, "Mole Jars." This demonstration helps students to see that one mole of different substances may vary in mass and volume, but not in the number of atoms or molecules present. Emphasize that 1 mole of any substance contains Avogadro's number of atoms or molecules.

To help students realize the magnitude of a mole, you may wish to have students do a few calculations.
1. If you work for $200 per week for 50 weeks per

year, how many years would you have to work to make a mole of pennies? (ans. $6 \times 10^{17}$ years)

2. If a penny is about 2 cm in diameter, how many times would a mole of pennies, lined up next to one another, circle the earth (circumference at equator = 40 074 064 m)? (ans. $3 \times 10^{14}$ times)

■ After the students have mastered the mole concept, move on to stoichiometry problems involving the mole. Point out that the remainder of the chapter deals with different types of problems involving the mole and chemical formulas. Explain that these problems are similar to problems involving the familiar unit *dozen*. After students have solved problems with familiar units and objects, they should be able to solve problems with the mole and chemical substances.

■ Once students have an understanding of the mole as a collection of particles, the mass of a mole can be introduced. Do Demonstration 8-2, "Making a Mole of Pencil Marks." In this demonstration students determine the mass and the number of carbon atoms deposited on a piece of paper from a graphite pencil. They use this information to determine how long it would take them to deposit 1 mole of carbon atoms on a piece of paper in a similar manner.

■ **Application.** You may want to point out the relationship of size of the objects to the magnitude of the unit by which these objects are grouped or packaged. For example, watermelons are purchased in units of one, eggs are bought by the dozen, paper clips come in boxes of 100 or by the gross, and paper is bought in reams. It is therefore appropriate for atoms and molecules to be grouped or "packaged" in a higher-numbered unit—the mole.

## 8-6 Moles and Formula Units, pp. 184-186

| Planning Guide | |
|---|---|
| Labs (Lab Manual) and Demonstrations (TE) | Supplementary Materials (Teacher's Resource Book) |
| | Stoichiometry Problems: Moles of Compounds— One-Step Problems, p. SP-12 |
| | Stoichiometry Problems: Interpreting Formulas, p. SP-18 |

■ Explain that you are now going to move on to mole-mass and mole-particle (molecule or formula units) problems as they relate to compounds. Discuss the Stoichiometry Problems worksheet "Moles of Compounds—One-Step Problems." Finally, summarize the molar interpretation of chemical formulas using the Stoichiometry Problems worksheet "Interpreting Formulas."

■ **Concept Understanding.** Students need to realize that a given quantity of matter can be specified in three different ways—in terms of its number of particles, its mass, or its volume. Therefore 1 mole of an ideal gas at STP contains $6.02 \times 10^{23}$ particles, has a mass equal to its gram molecular mass, and has a volume of 22.4 dm³. You may wish to use Concept Mastery question 39 (chapter-end questions) to reinforce this concept.

## 8-7 Mole Relationships, pp. 186-189

| Planning Guide | |
|---|---|
| Labs (Lab Manual) and Demonstrations (TE) | Supplementary Materials (Teacher's Resource Book) |
| Demo 8-3: A Gross of Beans, p. TG-134 Demo 8-4: The Molar Volume of a Gas, p. TG-135 | Transparency Master: The Mole Diagram, p. 8-2 Transparency Master: A Mole Diagram for a Sample Problem, p. 8-3 Stoichiometry Problems: —Familiar Quantities of Matter—Two-Step Problems, p. SP-5 —Moles of Elements— Two-Step Problems, p. SP-10 —Moles of Compounds— Two-Step Problems, p. SP-15 —Molar Volume— One-Step Problems, p. SP-30 —Molar Volume— Multi-Step Problems, p. SP-32 Non-SI Supplementary Problems, p. 8-9 Concept Mastery: Moles and Mass Relationships, p. CM-9 |

■ Begin by doing Demonstration 8-3, "A Gross of Beans." This demonstration helps to review the relationships between the number of particles in a sample and the mass of the sample. It also illustrates the approach to solving volume problems. Use Demonstration 8-4, "The Molar Volume of a Gas," to introduce the concept of molar volume. Emphasize that the volume of a gas will change with temperature and pressure. Therefore 22.4 dm³ applies only to gases at STP.

■ Discuss the Transparency Master "The Mole Diagram" as a way to organize the relationships between moles and mass, particles, and volume. Show the students how to use this diagram in solving problems by working Sample Problem 9 in the text. This problem is reproduced on the Transparency Master "A Mole Diagram for a Sample Problem." Make sure that the students become thoroughly acquainted with this approach to solving mole problems. They should become

acquainted with the three conversion factors and know when to multiply and when to divide by these factors.
■ **Concept Mastery.** Students often find that the easiest way to solve mole problems is to memorize how to solve them without thinking about what they are actually doing. This can be avoided by making sure that students understand the meaning of a mole on three levels.
1. The macroscopic level: Show students a mole of different substances, or have them use a balance to "weigh" out moles of different compounds and decimal fractions thereof. Have them compare the volumes of these materials.
2. The microscopic level: Have students label the compounds weighed out above in terms of the number of particles present.
3. Number manipulation: Students need practice in converting moles to mass, volume, and particles—and vice versa.

Concept Mastery questions 40–43 in the Chapter Review illustrate these types of conversions.

## 8-8 Percentage Composition, pp. 190-191

| Planning Guide | |
|---|---|
| **Labs (Lab Manual) and Demonstrations (TE)** | **Supplementary Materials (Teacher's Resource Book)** |
| Demo 8-5: Precentage of Water in Popcorn, p. TG-135 | Stoichiometry Problems: —Determining the Percent Composition from a Formula, p. SP-26 —Percentage of Water in a Hydrate, p. SP-28 —Application of Percentage Composition, p. SP-29 Open-Ended Experiment: The Percent of Water in a Tomato, p. 8-4 Review Activity: Quantitative Relationships in Chemistry, p. 8-7 |

■ Once students understand the mole concept, percentage composition problems are an easy application. Chemists are interested in mass percentages as distinguished from number or volume percentages. You may wish to make this distinction by using something familiar to students, such as the seeds in grapes, as illustrated in the Stoichiometry Problems worksheet "Determining the Percent Composition from a Formula."

Next illustrate the calculation of the percentage composition of a substance such as $KClO_3$. Then do Demonstration 8-5, "Percentage of Water in Popcorn."
■ **Application.** It may be helpful to point out that the concept of percent by weight is more familiar to the

students than they might think. This concept is used to express the percent of soap in a bar of soap (i.e., $99^{44}/_{100}$% pure soap) and the percent of water or fat in the human body.

## 8-9 Determining the Formula of a Compound, pp. 192-194

| Planning Guide | |
|---|---|
| **Labs (Lab Manual) and Demonstrations (TE)** | **Supplementary Materials (Teacher's Resource Book)** |
| Lab 13: Determining an Empirical Formula | Stoichiometry Problems: —Determining Empirical Formulas, p. SP-19 —Empirical Formulas— An Extra Computation, p. SP-21 —Empirical Formulas of Hydrates, p. SP-23 —Molecular Formulas of Compounds, p. SP-24 |

■ Explain that empirical formulas are determined from percentage composition data or from mass data. Determining the empirical formula of a compound requires only one step in addition to the steps in a normal mass-mole problem if masses are given in the problem. If percentage composition information is given, two extra steps are required.

First, use an example in which masses are given. Explain the additional step of finding the mole ratio. Second, select a problem in which the mole ratio involves an odd number. Assign Laboratory 13, "Determining an Empirical Formula," in which the students will experimentally determine the empirical formula of MgO.

Now explain a problem in which the given datum is the percentage composition. Point out the importance of this approach when new compounds are discovered and the formula must be determined. Point out the extra step involved. Explain the use of a 100-g sample to simplify the conversion of percentage to grams.

Remind the students of the difference between empirical and molecular formulas. Point out that it is possible to determine the molecular mass of a compound experimentally. Show how these molecular masses can be used to derive molecular formulas from the empirical formulas.
■ **Concept Understanding.** Students need to realize that they are obtaining the molar ratios when they determine the empirical formula of a compound. Because they think science is exact, they fail to recognize the presence of experimental error and to make use of significant figures. Concept Mastery question 44 (chapter-end question) can be used to illustrate this point.

## 8-10 Another Way To Determine Empirical Formulas, pp. 194-195

| Planning Guide | |
| --- | --- |
| Labs (Lab Manual) and Demonstrations (TE) | Supplementary Materials (Teacher's Resource Book) |
| | Practice Problems, p. 8-8 |

■ If you choose to cover this advanced topic, point out that the empirical formula of a compound can be determined if the relative number of moles of each element in the compound can be calculated. Explain how this is accomplished if one of the constituents of the compound is a gas in its elemental form. Discuss Sample Problem 15.

# Demonstrations

## 8-1 Mole Jars

**Overview:** In this demonstration, sealed jars containing 1.00 mole of various elements, molecular compounds, and ionic compounds are displayed. On the label of each is the name of the substance; the mass, in grams, of 1 mole; the general name of the mass (gram formula mass, gram molecular mass, or gram atomic mass); and Avogadro's number of molecules, atoms, or formula units. Students thus become more familiar with the concept of the mole and can see that 1 mole varies in volume and mass for various substances but always contains the same number of units.

**Materials:** sealed jars containing 1.00 mole of a variety of common elements, molecular compounds, and ionic compounds [samples may include: iron filings, carbon, sulfur, water, isopropyl alcohol, silicon dioxide (pure sand), sucrose, sodium chloride, sodium phosphate, and copper(II) sulfate pentahydrate].

**Advance Preparation:** Label each sample with the substance's name and formula; the mass, in grams, of 1 mole; the general name of the mass; and Avogadro's number of units.

**Procedure:** 1. Ask students to observe the jars, each of which represents one mole of substance. Ask them how the volumes compare. 2. Ask students how the masses compare. 3. Ask students to note how the numbers of units in the samples compare.

**Results:** Students should note considerable variation in the volumes and masses. They should also note that the numbers of units in the samples are the same.

## 8-2 Making a Mole of Pencil Marks

**Overview:** In this demonstration, a student places as many graphite (carbon) pencil marks as he or she can in a two-minute period on a preweighed piece of paper. Students then determine the mass and number of carbon atoms placed on the paper in two minutes. The class is asked to determine how long it would take to place a whole mole of carbon on the paper.

**Materials:** graphite pencil; paper; centigram balance; chalk.

**Advance Preparation:** None.

**Procedure:** 1. Ask a volunteer to determine the mass of a piece of paper and then ask him or her to make as many pencil marks on the paper as he or she can in two minutes. 2. Have the volunteer find the mass of paper with the pencil marks and, by subtraction, determine the mass of carbon placed on the paper. 3. Have the class determine how long it would take to place a mole of carbon on the paper. They can do this by dividing the mass deposited per minute into the molar mass, 12.0 g/mole. 4. Carry out a similar procedure with a piece of chalk (calcium carbonate).

**Results:** Depending on the softness of the pencil and the speed with which marks are made, roughly 0.015–0.030 g of carbon should be deposited in 2 minutes. It would take roughly $\dfrac{12 \text{ g}}{0.010 \text{ g/min}} = 1200$ minutes to deposit 1 mole of carbon. Roughly 0.15–0.30 g of $CaCO_3$ should be deposited in 2 minutes. It would take roughly $\dfrac{100 \text{ g}}{0.10 \text{ g/min}} = 1000$ minutes to deposit 1 mole of $CaCO_3$.

## 8-3 A Gross of Beans

**Overview:** In this demonstration, you and your students determine the mass and volume of one gross of beans. Using dimensional analysis and the data obtained, you show students how to calculate the mass and volume of any number of beans and the number of beans in a given mass or volume. This activity lays the groundwork for solving problems involving moles, Avogadro's number of particles, mass, and volume.

**Materials:** 144 dry red beans; 250-mL beaker; balance; 200-mL graduated cylinder; 144 beans of another variety significantly different in mass and volume.

**Advance Preparation:** Count out 144 red beans that are approximately the same size. Do the same for 144 beans of another variety.

**Procedure:** 1. Tell students you are going to collect data on one gross of red beans (144 beans), and ask them for suggestions on specific kinds of data to collect. 2. Find the mass of an empty 250-mL beaker, and record the mass on the board. Place the 144 red beans into the beaker, find the total mass, and record it. Ask students to use the data to calculate the mass of the gross of red beans alone. 3. Determine the volume of the gross of beans by using the water-displacement method. Place about 60 mL of water into a 200-mL graduated cylinder. Record the volume. Add the 144 red beans, and read and record the new volume. Work quickly, as the beans might otherwise begin to absorb a significant amount of water. Have the students use the data to calculate the volume of the one gross of beans alone. 4. On the board, summarize all of the information determined about one gross of beans. Ask students to use this information to determine answers to such questions as: What is the mass of 30 beans? What is the volume of 0.250 gross of beans? Approximately how many beans would be present in a sample whose mass is 800 g? What is the mass of one bean? 5. Repeat steps 2–4, using a different type of bean. Emphasize the fact that one gross of any kind of object contains 144 objects but that the total masses and volumes of one-gross samples of different kinds of objects are generally different.

**Results:** In step 1, students will be likely to suggest collecting mass and volume data. In step 2, the mass of the beans alone is calculated by subtracting the mass of the beaker from the total mass of the beaker and beans. The mass should be roughly 70–90 g. In step 3, the volume of the beans alone is calculated by subtracting the volume of the water from the total volume of the water and beans. The volume should be roughly 80–110 mL. In step 4, calculations should be of the following general forms for the sample questions asked:

$$30.0 \text{ beans} \times \frac{80.0 \text{ g}}{144 \text{ beans}} = 16.7 \text{ g}$$

$$0.250 \text{ gross} \times \frac{95.0 \text{ mL}}{1.00 \text{ gross}} = 23.8 \text{ mL}$$

$$800 \text{ g} \times \frac{144 \text{ beans}}{80.0 \text{ g}} = 1440 \text{ beans}$$

$$\frac{80.0 \text{ g}}{144 \text{ beans}} = 0.556 \text{ g/bean}$$

**Disposal Tips:** Discard the beans in the trash after each demonstration. Use fresh beans for repetitions of the demonstration with other classes.

## 8-4 The Molar Volume of a Gas

**Overview:** In this demonstration, 44 g of carbon dioxide (dry ice) is placed into a large plastic bag in a box that is 22.4 L in volume. After a period of time, the bag expands and fills the entire box. Students can thus visualize the volume of 1 mole of gas.

**Materials:** a cubical box roughly 28 cm on an edge, made from Lucite or cardboard; large plastic garbage bag; 44 g of dry ice.

**Advance Preparation:** Obtain or make a box of the proper size.

**Safety:** Use tongs to handle the dry ice. Do not allow the dry ice to come in contact with your skin.

**Procedure:** 1. Weigh out 44 g of dry ice (solid carbon dioxide) and place it into the plastic garbage bag. Be sure all of the air is pushed out of the bag before adding the dry ice. Tie off the opening of the bag securely. 2. Place the bag and dry ice into the box, and have students observe what happens.

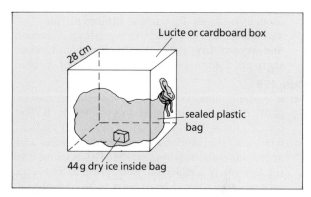

28 cm

Lucite or cardboard box

sealed plastic bag

44 g dry ice inside bag

**Figure 8-1**

**Results:** After a period of time, the dry ice will change into carbon dioxide gas and will fill the bag and, consequently, the box, whose volume is 22.4 L.

## 8-5 Percentage of Water in Popcorn

**Overview:** In this demonstration, the mass of a bag of microwave popcorn is determined. After all of the popcorn has popped, the top is opened to allow the moisture to escape. The percentage of water in the popcorn is then determined.

**Materials:** bag of microwave popcorn; microwave oven; balance.

**Advance Preparation:** none.

**Procedure:** 1. Find the mass of the bag of uncooked popcorn. 2. Cook the popcorn in a microwave oven. 3. Remove the bag from the microwave and carefully open up the bag to allow the vaporized water to escape. 4. Find the mass of the bag and popped corn. 5. Determine the mass of water that was in the popcorn by subtracting the mass of the bag and popped corn from the mass of the bag and uncooked popcorn. 6. Measure the mass of the popped corn alone, and then calculate the percentage of water that was in the corn by dividing the mass of water by the total mass of the popped corn and water, and then multiplying by 100.

**Results:** Actual masses will depend on the amount of popcorn used. Most popcorn is about 11–14% water by mass.

8

# Answers to Questions

**Page 176**

1. Formulas indicate the elements present in a compound and the relative number of atoms of each element in one molecule or formula unit of that compound.

2. The compound $Li_3N$ is made up of the elements lithium and nitrogen. In every sample of the compound, there are three atoms of lithium for each atom of nitrogen. Its name is lithium nitride.

3. The molecular compound $CO_2$ is made up of carbon and oxygen. In every molecule of carbon dioxide, there are 2 atoms of oxygen and 1 atom of carbon.

**Page 178**

4. **a.** Formula mass is the sum of the atomic masses of all of the atoms indicated in the formula. **b.** The formula mass is the same as the molecular mass in molecular substances. **c.** Both formula mass and molecular mass may be applied to $CO_2$ because it is the formula of a molecular substance. **d.** The term formula mass should be applied to KCl because it is an ionic substance.

5.

| Element | Atomic mass | | Atoms per formula | | Product |
|---|---|---|---|---|---|
| Mg | 24 u | × | 1 | = | 24 u |
| N | 14 u | × | 2 | = | 28 u |
| O | 16 u | × | 6 | = | + 96 u |
| | | | Formula mass = | | 148 u |

6.

| Element | Atomic mass | | Atoms per formula | | Product |
|---|---|---|---|---|---|
| N | 14 u | × | 2 | = | 28 u |
| H | 1 u | × | 8 | = | 8 u |
| S | 32 u | × | 1 | = | 32 u |
| O | 16 u | × | 4 | = | + 64 u |
| | | | Formula mass = | | 132 u |

7. **a.** 55.8 g; **b.** 40.1 g; **c.** 24.3 g; **d.** 10.8 g

**Page 179**

8. **a.** 65.4 g; **b.** 31 g; **c.** 35.5 g

9. The same number expressed in grams, 148 g

10. The same number expressed in grams, 132 g

11.

| Element | Atomic mass | | Atoms per formula | | Product |
|---|---|---|---|---|---|
| Al | 27 u | × | 1 | = | 27 u |
| N | 14 u | × | 3 | = | 42 u |
| O | 16 u | × | 9 | = | + 144 u |
| | | | Formula mass = | | 213 u |
| | | | Gram formula mass = | | 213 g |

**Page 184**

12. **a.** Gram atomic mass is that quantity of an element that has a mass in grams equal to its atomic mass.

**b.** The gram atomic mass of hydrogen is 1.0 g; of oxygen, 16.0 g; of chlorine, 35.5 g.

13. A gram-atom of magnesium is 24 g and a gram-atom of carbon is 12 g. Since the ratio of the masses of single atoms of magnesium and carbon is also 24 to 12, we can assume that the gram-atoms of these elements have the same number of atoms.

14. **a.** $6.02 \times 10^{23}$
    **b.** Both a mole of a substance and a gram-atom of an element contain Avogadro's number of unit particles. In the case of an element, these unit particles are atoms.

15. **a.** Four kg of sugar.
    **b.** No, because only relative weights are given.

16. 12 g

17. **a.** A mole of oxygen atoms has a mass of 16.0 g.
    **b.** There are $1.20 \times 10^{24}$ atoms in 2.00 moles of oxygen atoms.

18. **a.** $4.0 \text{ mol Ni} \times \dfrac{58.7 \text{ g Ni}}{\text{mol Ni}} = 2.35 \times 10^2 \text{ g Ni}$

    **b.** $0.50 \text{ mol Ni} \times \dfrac{58.7 \text{ g Ni}}{\text{mol Ni}} = 29.4 \text{ g Ni}$

**Page 185**

19. One mole of $H_2SO_4$ contains 2 moles of H, 1 mole of S, and 4 moles of O.

20. Three moles of $NH_3$ contains 3 moles of N and 9 moles of H.

21. **a.** A mole of oxygen molecules has a mass of 32.0 g.
    **b.** There are $1.2 \times 10^{24}$ atoms in 1 mole of oxygen gas, $O_2$.

**Page 186**

22. $(2 \times 27.0 \text{ g/mol}) + (3 \times 32.1 \text{ g/mol}) = 150 \text{ g/mol } Al_2S_3$

23. $(1 \times 23.0 \text{ g/mol}) + (1 \times 16.0 \text{ g/mol}) + (1 \times 1.00 \text{ g/mol}) = 40.0 \text{ g/mol NaOH}$
    $3.0 \text{ mol} \times 40.0 \text{ g/mol} = 120 \text{ g} = 1.2 \times 10^2 \text{ g NaOH}$

24. $(2 \times 55.8 \text{ g/mol}) + (3 \times 16.0 \text{ g/mol}) = 160 \text{ g/mol } Fe_2O_3$
    $0.005 \text{ mol} \times 160 \text{ g/mol} = 0.8 \text{ g } Fe_2O_3$

25. **a.** $1.00 \times 10^2 \text{ g Cu} \times \dfrac{1 \text{ mol Cu}}{63.5 \text{ g Cu}} = 1.57 \text{ mol Cu}$

    **b.** $1.00 \times 10^2 \text{ g Mg} \times \dfrac{1 \text{ mol Mg}}{24.3 \text{ g Mg}} = 4.12 \text{ mol Mg}$

    **c.** $1.00 \times 10^2 \text{ g } O_2 \times \dfrac{1 \text{ mol } O_2}{32.0 \text{ g } O_2} = 3.13 \text{ mol } O_2$

26. **a.** $1.57 \text{ mol} \times 6.02 \times 10^{23} \text{ atoms Cu/mol} = 9.45 \times 10^{23} \text{ atoms Cu}$

    **b.** $4.12 \text{ mol} \times 6.02 \times 10^{23} \text{ atoms Mg/mol} = 2.48 \times 10^{24} \text{ atoms Mg}$

    **c.** $3.13 \text{ mol} \times \dfrac{6.02 \times 10^{23} \text{ molecules } O_2}{1 \text{ mol } O_2} = 1.88 \times 10^{24} \text{ molecules } O_2 \text{ or } 3.76 \times 10^{24} \text{ atoms O}$

**27. a.** $101 \text{ g } Fe_3O_4 \times \dfrac{1 \text{ mol } Fe_3O_4}{231 \text{ g } Fe_3O_4} = 0.437 \text{ mol } Fe_3O_4$

**b.** $0.437 \text{ mol } Fe_3O_4 \times 6.02 \times 10^{23} \text{ f.u} =$
$$2.63 \times 10^{23} \text{ f.u.}$$

**Page 189**

**28.** $22.0 \text{ g } CO_2 \times \dfrac{1 \text{ mol } CO_2}{44.0 \text{ g } CO_2} \times \dfrac{22.4 \text{ dm}^3 \text{ } CO_2}{1 \text{ mol } CO_2} =$
$$11.2 \text{ dm}^3 \text{ } CO_2$$

**29.** $3.01 \times 10^{23} \text{ molec. } N_2 \times \dfrac{1 \text{ mol } N_2}{6.02 \times 10^{23} \text{ molec. } N_2} \times$
$$\dfrac{28.0 \text{ g } N_2}{1 \text{ mol } N_2} = 14 \text{ g } N_2$$

**30.** $67.2 \text{ dm}^3 \text{ } CH_4 \times \dfrac{1 \text{ mol } CH_4}{22.4 \text{ dm}^3 \text{ } CH_4} \times \dfrac{16.0 \text{ g } CH_4}{1 \text{ mol } CH_4} =$
$$48.0 \text{ g } CH_4$$

**Page 191**

**31. a.** The percentage composition of a compound is the percentage by mass of each of the elements in the compound.

**b.** Percentage composition can be determined from the formula of the compound or by experiment.

**32.** $28 \text{ g} + 12 \text{ g} = 40 \text{ g (total)}$
% iron $= 28 \text{ g}/40 \text{ g} \times 100\% = 70\%$;
% oxygen $= 12 \text{ g}/40 \text{ g} \times 100 = 30\%$

**33.** Formula mass of $Fe_2O_3 = (2 \times 56 \text{ u}) +$
$$(3 \times 16 \text{ u}) = 160 \text{ u}$$
% iron $= 112 \text{ u}/160 \text{ u} \times 100\% = 70\%$;
% oxygen $= 48 \text{ u}/160 \text{ u} \times 100\% = 30\%$

**34.** % sodium $= 53 \text{ g}/90 \text{ g} \times 100\% = 59\%$;
% oxygen $= 37 \text{ g}/90 \text{ g} \times 100\% = 41\%$

**35.** Formula mass of $Na_2O_2 = (2 \times 23 \text{ u}) +$
$$(2 \times 16 \text{ u}) = 78 \text{ u}$$

% sodium $= \dfrac{46 \text{ u}}{78 \text{ u}} \times 100\% = 59\%$

% oxygen $= \dfrac{32 \text{ u}}{78 \text{ u}} \times 100\% = 41\%$

**Page 194**

**36. a.** The empirical formula of a compound may be determined from the percentage composition of the compound. **b.** To determine the molecular formula of a compound, its molecular mass must be known in addition to the information given in **a.**

**37.** Moles of C atoms $= 18 \text{ g C} \times 1 \text{ mol}/12 \text{ g C} =$
$$1.5 \text{ mol C}$$
Moles of N atoms $= 21 \text{ g N} \times 1 \text{ mol}/14 \text{ g N} =$
$$1.5 \text{ mol N}$$
The ratio of C atoms to N atoms is 1:1; therefore, the empirical formula is CN.

**38.** Assuming a 100-g sample,
46.2% of 100 g = 46.2 g C
53.8% of 100 g = 53.8 g N

Moles of C atoms $= 46.2 \text{ g} \times 1 \text{ mol}/12.0 \text{ g} =$
$$3.85 \text{ mol}$$
Moles of N atoms $= 53.8 \text{ g} \times 1 \text{ mol}/14.0 \text{ g} =$
$$3.84 \text{ mol}$$
The ratio of C atoms to N atoms is 1:1; therefore, the empirical formula is CN.

**39.** Some possible molecular formulas are
CN (molecular mass = 26 u),
$C_2N_2$ (molecular mass = 52 u), and
$C_3N_3$ (molecular mass = 78 u).
The molecular formula is $C_2N_2$.

**40. a.** In a 100-g sample, there are 80 g C and 20 g H.
80 g C $\times$ 1 mol/12 g = 6.7 mol C;
20 g H $\times$ 1 mol/1.0 g = 20 mol H
The ratio of the C atoms to the H atoms is 1:3; therefore the empirical formula is $CH_3$.

**b.** If the molecular mass is 30.0 u, the molecular formula is $C_2H_6$.

**Page 195**

**41.** The empirical formula is NO. It is unnecessary to use 22.4 dm³ because if 100 cm³ of each gas forms, there must be equal numbers of diatomic molecules in each volume according to Avogadro's hypothesis. The ratio must be 1:1.

**42.** $1.134 \text{ g } I_2 \times \dfrac{1 \text{ mol}}{254 \text{ g } I_2} = 4.46 \times 10^{-3} \text{ mol } I_2$

$100.0 \text{ cm}^3 \text{ } H_2 \times \dfrac{1 \text{ dm}^3}{1000 \text{ cm}^3} \times \dfrac{1 \text{ mol}}{22.4 \text{ dm}^3} =$
$$4.46 \times 10^{-3} \text{ mol } H_2$$

The empirical formula is HI.

## Chapter Review   ⑧

**Page 196, Content Review**

**1.** The formula $C_6H_{12}O_6$ tells you that one molecule of glucose contains 6 carbon atoms, 12 hydrogen atoms, and 6 oxygen atoms.

**2.** The formula mass is the sum of all of the atomic masses in the formula.
**a.** $MgBr_2$: 24.3 u + 2(79.9 u) = 184 u
**b.** $NaClO_3$: 23.0 u + 35.5 u + 3(16.0 u) = 106 u
**c.** $Zn_3(PO_4)_2$: 3(65.4 u) + 2(31.0 u) + 8(16.0 u)
$$= 386 \text{ u}$$

**3.** The gram formula mass is the formula mass in grams instead of atomic mass units.
**a.** 184 g; **b.** 106 g; **c.** 386 g

**4.** The gram atomic mass is the quantity of an element that has a mass in grams numerically equal

to its atomic mass in atomic mass units.
**a.** 35.5 g; **b.** 200.6 g; **c.** 107.9 g; **d.** 4.0 g

5. 1.00 mole of F contains $6.02 \times 10^{23}$ fluorine atoms. 1.00 mole of $F_2$ contains $1.20 \times 10^{24}$ fluorine atoms.

6. 1.00 mole of pencils contains $6.02 \times 10^{23}$ pencils. 0.25 mole of pencils contains $1.5 \times 10^{23}$ pencils.

7. Multiply number of moles by gram atomic mass.

$$7.5 \text{ mol Fe} \times \frac{55.8 \text{ g Fe}}{1 \text{ mol Fe}} = 4.2 \times 10^2 \text{ g Fe}$$

8. Find the number of moles by multiplying the mass by the gram atomic mass. Find the number of atoms by multiplying the number of moles by Avogadro's number.

$$295 \text{ g Au} \times \frac{1 \text{ mol Au}}{197 \text{ g Au}} = 1.50 \text{ mol Au}$$

$$1.50 \text{ mol Au} \times \frac{6.02 \times 10^{23} \text{ atoms Au}}{\text{mol Au}} =$$
$$9.03 \times 10^{23} \text{ atoms Au}$$

9. Find the mass of 1.00 mole of each substance by adding the gram atomic masses of each atom in the substance.
   **a.** N: 14.0 g/mol;
   **b.** $N_2$: 2(14.0 g) = 28.0 g/mol;
   **c.** $NH_3$: 14.0 g + 3(1.01 g) = 17.0 g/mol
   **d.** $N_2H_4$: 2(14.0 g) + 4(1.01 g) = 32.0 g/mol
   **e.** $HNO_3$: 1.01 g + 14.0 g + 3(16.0 g) = 63.0 g/mol

10. To find the gram molecular mass of $NH_4CN$, add the gram atomic masses of 2 nitrogens, 4 hydrogens, and 1 carbon.
    $NH_4CN$: 2(14.01 g) + 4(1.01 g) + 12.01 g = 44.1 g

11. First, find the mass of 1.00 mole. Then, multiply by 0.0250 mole.
    **a.** $Mg(OH)_2$: 24.3 g + 2(16.0 g) + 2(1.01 g) = 58.3 g/mol

$$0.0250 \text{ mol Mg(OH)}_2 \times \frac{58.3 \text{ g}}{1 \text{ mol}} = 1.46 \text{ g Mg(OH)}_2$$

    **b.** $Na_3PO_4$: 3(23.0 g) + 31.0 g + 4(16.0 g) = 164 g/mol

$$0.0250 \text{ mol NaPO}_4 \times \frac{164 \text{ g}}{\text{mol}} = 4.10 \text{ g NaPO}_4$$

12. Divide the mass by the gram molecular mass to find the number of moles.
    **a.** $Ba(NO_3)_2$: 137.3 g + 2(14.0 g) + 6(16.0 g) = 261.3 g/mol

$$500 \text{ g Ba(NO}_3)_2 \times \frac{1 \text{ mol}}{261.3 \text{ g}} = 1.91 \text{ mol Ba(NO}_3)_2$$

    **b.** $SnCl_2$: 118.7 g + 2(35.5 g) = 189.7 g/mol

$$500 \text{ g SnCl}_2 \times \frac{1 \text{ mol}}{189.7 \text{ g}} = 2.64 \text{ mol SnCl}_2$$

13. STP is 0°C and 101.3 kPa.

14. The molar volume is the volume occupied by 1.00 mole of gas. Most gases occupy 22.4 $dm^3$ at STP.

15. Multiply the number of moles by Avogadro's number to find the number of molecules.

$$42.0 \text{ g N}_2 \times \frac{1.00 \text{ mol}}{28.0 \text{ g}} \times \frac{6.02 \times 10^{23} \text{ molecules}}{\text{mol}} =$$
$$9.03 \times 10^{23} \text{ molecules}$$

16. Find the volume of gas from the number of moles and the molar volume at STP.
    **a.** $14.0 \text{ g CO} \times \frac{1.00 \text{ mol}}{28.0 \text{ g}} \times \frac{22.4 \text{ dm}^3}{\text{mol}} = 11.2 \text{ dm}^3$
    **b.** $16.0 \text{ g SO}_2 \times \frac{1.00 \text{ mol}}{64.0 \text{ g}} \times \frac{22.4 \text{ dm}^3}{\text{mol}} = 5.60 \text{ dm}^3$
    **c.** $1.50 \text{ mol CH}_4 \times 22.4 \text{ dm}^3/\text{mol} = 33.6 \text{ dm}^3$
    **d.** $3.01 \times 10^{24} \text{ molec. UF}_6 \times \frac{1 \text{ mol}}{6.02 \times 10^{23} \text{ molec.}} \times$
$$\frac{22.4 \text{ dm}^3}{\text{mol}} = 112 \text{ dm}^3$$
    **e.** $1.20 \times 10^{23} \text{ molec. NO}_2 \times \frac{1 \text{ mol}}{6.02 \times 10^{23} \text{ molec.}} \times$
$$\frac{22.4 \text{ dm}^3}{\text{mol}} = 4.47 \text{ dm}^3$$

17. First, find the gram molecular mass of silver nitrate.
    $AgNO_3$: 107.9 g + 14.0 g + 3(16.0 g) = 169.9 g/mol
    Every 169.9 g of silver nitrate contains 107.9 g of silver, so the percent silver is 63.5%.

$$\% \text{ Ag} = \frac{107.9 \text{ g Ag}}{169.9 \text{ g AgNO}_3} \times 100\% = 63.5\%$$

    Find the percentages for the other elements as well.

$$\% \text{ N} = \frac{14.0 \text{ g N}}{169.9 \text{ g AgNO}_3} \times 100\% = 8.2\%$$

$$\% \text{ O} = \frac{48.0 \text{ g O}}{169.9 \text{ g AgNO}_3} \times 100\% = 28.3\%$$

    Check: 63.5% + 8.2% + 28.3% = 100.0%

18. $\% \text{ C} = \frac{72.0 \text{ g C}}{88.0 \text{ g compound}} \times 100\% = 81.8\%$

$$\% \text{ H} = \frac{16.0 \text{ g H}}{88.0 \text{ g compound}} \times 100\% = 18.2\%$$

    Check: 81.8% + 18.2% = 100.0%

19. Find the relative number of moles of carbon and hydrogen in the compound.

$$\text{mol C} = 72.0 \text{ g} \times \frac{1 \text{ mol C}}{12 \text{ g C}} = 6.0 \text{ mol C}$$

$$\text{mol H} = 16.0 \text{ g} \times \frac{1 \text{ mol H}}{1 \text{ g H}} = 16.0 \text{ mol H}$$

    mole ratio = 16.0 mol H/6.0 mol C = 8/3
    empirical formula: $C_3H_8$

20. From the mass of each element, find the number of moles.

$$14.0 \text{ g N} \times \frac{1 \text{ mol N}}{14.0 \text{ g N}} = 1.0 \text{ mol N}$$

$$8.0 \text{ g H} \times \frac{1 \text{ mol H}}{16.0 \text{ g O}} = 0.50 \text{ mol O}$$

mole ratio = 1.0 mol N/0.50 mol O = 2/1
empirical formula: $N_2O$

21. From the mass of each element, find the number of moles and then the relative mole ratio.

$$68.4 \text{ g Cr} \times \frac{1 \text{ mol Cr}}{52.0 \text{ g Cr}} = 1.32 \text{ mol Cr}$$

$$31.6 \text{ g O} \times \frac{1 \text{ mol O}}{16.0 \text{ g O}} = 1.98 \text{ mol O}$$

mole ratio = 1.98 O/1.32 Cr = 3/2
empirical formula: $Cr_2O_3$

22. **a.** Use the percent composition to find the relative number of moles of each element in nicotine and then the mole ratio. Since nicotine is 74.0% C, 100.0 g of nicotine contains 74.0 g C.

$$74.0 \text{ g C} \times \frac{1 \text{ mol C}}{12.0 \text{ g C}} = 6.17 \text{ mol C}$$

$$8.7 \text{ g H} \times \frac{1 \text{ mol H}}{1.01 \text{ g H}} = 8.6 \text{ mol H}$$

$$17.3 \text{ g N} \times \frac{1 \text{ mol N}}{14.0 \text{ g N}} = 1.24 \text{ mol N}$$

Divide the number of moles by 1.24 to get the ratio.
mole ratio = 5 C/7 H/1 N
empirical formula: $C_5H_7N_1$

**b.** Find the empirical formula mass for $C_5H_7N_1$.
5(12.0 g) + 7(1.01 g) + 14.0 g = 81.1 g
Since the molecular mass of nicotine (162.1 g) is twice the empirical formula mass (81.1 g), the molecular formula is twice the empirical formula, or $C_{10}H_{14}N_2$.

23. Find the number of formula units in the molecular formula by dividing the molecular mass by the empirical formula mass.
CH: 1(12.0 u) + 1(1.01 u) = 13.0 u

$$\frac{\text{number of}}{\text{formula units}} = \frac{\text{molecular mass}}{\text{empirical mass}} = \frac{78 \text{ u}}{13 \text{ u}} = 6$$

molecular formula: $C_6H_6$

24. Find the number of moles from the mass and the volume.

$$0.800 \text{ g S} \times \frac{1 \text{ mol S}}{32.1 \text{ g S}} = 0.0249 \text{ mol S}$$

$$0.560 \text{ dm}^3 \text{ H}_2 \times \frac{1 \text{ mol H}_2}{22.4 \text{ dm}^3} \times \frac{2 \text{ mol H}}{1 \text{ mol H}_2} =$$
$$0.0500 \text{ mol H}$$

mol ratio = 2 H/1 S
empirical formula: $H_2S$

25. $$4.80 \text{ g C} \times \frac{1 \text{ mol C}}{12.0 \text{ g C}} = 0.400 \text{ mol C}$$

$$11.2 \text{ dm}^3 \text{ H}_2 \times \frac{1 \text{ mol H}_2}{22.4 \text{ dm}^3} \times \frac{2 \text{ mol H}}{1 \text{ mol H}_2} = 1.00 \text{ mol H}$$

mole ratio = 2 C/5 H
empirical formula: $C_2H_5$

## Page 197, Content Mastery

26. Multiply the number of moles by Avogadro's number to get the number of molecules. Then multiply by 3 atoms per molecule to get the number of atoms.
(17.0 mol)(6.02 × 10²³ molec./mol) =
$$1.02 \times 10^{25} \text{ molec.}$$
(17.0 mol)(6.02 × 10²³ molec./mol) ×
$$3 \text{ atoms/molec.} = 3.07 \times 10^{25} \text{ atoms}$$

27. Multiply the number of moles by the gram molecular mass.
$C_2H_5OH$: 2(12.0 g) + 6(1.0 g) + 16.0 g = 46.0 g
0.498 mol × 46.0 g/mol = 22.9 g

28. Divide the number of grams by the gram molecular mass to find the number of moles.
$CCl_4$: 12.0 g + 4(35.5 g) = 154.0 g

$$1.00 \text{ g CCl}_4 \times \frac{1 \text{ mol CCl}_4}{154.0 \text{ g CCl}_4} = 6.50 \times 10^{-3} \text{ mol} =$$
$$6.50 \text{ mmol}$$

29. 100.0 g of this substance contains 40.0 g C, 53.3 g O, and 100.0 − 40.0 − 53.3 = 6.7 g H.

$$40.0 \text{ g C} \times \frac{1 \text{ mol C}}{12.0 \text{ g C}} = 3.33 \text{ mol C}$$

$$53.3 \text{ g O} \times \frac{1 \text{ mol O}}{16.0 \text{ g O}} = 3.33 \text{ mol O}$$

$$6.7 \text{ g H} \times \frac{1 \text{ mol H}}{1.01 \text{ g H}} = 6.7 \text{ mol H}$$

mole ratio = 1 C/1 O/2 H
empirical formula: $CH_2O$
formula mass = 12.0 g + 2(1.01 g) + 16.0 g =
$$30.0 \text{ g}$$

Since the molecular mass (180 g/mol) is six times the formula mass, the molecular formula is $C_6H_{12}O_6$.

30. Divide the grams by the gram molecular mass to find the number of moles of nitrogen molecules. Multiply this by the number of nitrogen atoms per nitrogen molecule to find the number of atoms.

$$\text{moles N}_2 = 98.2 \text{ g} \times \frac{1 \text{ mol}}{28.0 \text{ g}} = 3.51 \text{ mol N}_2$$

$$\text{moles N} = 98.2 \text{ g} \times \frac{1 \text{ mol}}{28.0 \text{ g}} \times \frac{2 \text{ atoms}}{\text{molecule}} =$$
$$7.01 \text{ mol N}$$

31. The formula mass is the sum of all of the atomic masses in the formula.
Oxygen gas is $O_2$. Its mass is 2(16.0 u) = 32.0 u.
He: 4.00 u; $NH_3$: 14.0 u + 3(1.01 u) = 17.0 u;
$Mg(OH)_2$: 24.3 u + 2(16.0 u) + 2(1.01 u) =
58.3 u; KCl: 39.1 u + 35.5 u = 74.6 u; $Al_2(SO_4)_3$:
2(27.0 u) + 3(32.1 u) + 12(16.0 u) = 342 u

32. Multiply the number of moles by the molar volume at STP to get the volume of gas, and multiply by

Avogadro's number to get the number of atoms.

$$91.2 \text{ g} \times \frac{1 \text{ mol}}{4.00 \text{ g}} = 22.8 \text{ mol of helium}$$

$$22.8 \text{ mol} \times \frac{22.4 \text{ dm}^3}{1 \text{ mol}} = 511 \text{ dm}^3$$

$$22.8 \text{ mol} \times \frac{6.02 \times 10^{23} \text{ atoms}}{1 \text{ mol}} = 1.37 \times 10^{25} \text{ atoms}$$

33. To find the percentage composition, divide the number of grams of each element by the number of grams of ammonia, and multiply by 100%.
$NH_3$: 14.0 g + 3(1.0 g) = 17.0 g

$$\% \text{ N} = \frac{14.0 \text{ g}}{17.0 \text{ g}} \times 100\% = 82.4\%$$

$$\% \text{ H} = \frac{3(1.0 \text{ g})}{17.0 \text{ g}} \times 100\% = 17.6\%$$

Check: 82.4% + 17.6% = 100.0%

34. Convert grams to moles, moles to number of molecules, and molecules to number of oxygen atoms. Once you have the gram molecular mass, you can do the rest of the calculation in one step.
$Ca(NO_3)_2$: 40.1 + 2(14.0) + 6(16.0) = 164

$$98.2 \text{ g} \times \frac{1 \text{ mol}}{164 \text{ g}} \times \frac{6.02 \times 10^{23} \text{ molec.}}{\text{mol}} \times \frac{6 \text{ O atoms}}{\text{molec.}}$$

$$= 21.6 \times 10^{23} \text{ O atoms}$$
$$= 2.16 \times 10^{24} \text{ O atoms in}$$
$$98.2 \text{ g } Ca(NO_3)_2 \text{ molecules}$$

35. Look up the gram atomic masses of these elements in the periodic table. The gram atomic mass of nitrogen is 14.0067, which rounds off to 14.0 g/mol. The gram atomic mass of chlorine is 35.453, which rounds off to 35.5 g/mol. The formula for nitrogen gas is $N_2$. The gram formula mass is 2(14.0067) = 28.0134 or 28.0 g/mol. The formula for chlorine gas is $Cl_2$, and its gram formula mass is 2(35.453) = 70.906 or 70.9 g/mol.

36. First, find the formula mass of $NaC_{12}H_{11}N_2O_3$.
23.0 + 12(12.0) + 11(1.0) + 2(14.0) + 3(16.0) =
    23.0 + 144 + 11 + 28 + 48 = 254 g/mol
Now, convert grams of compound to moles of compound, then convert to moles of Na, and finally to grams of Na.

$$1.00 \text{ g} \times \frac{1 \text{ mol}}{254 \text{ g}} \times \frac{1 \text{ mol Na}}{1 \text{ mol cmpd.}} \times \frac{23 \text{ g Na}}{1 \text{ mol Na}} =$$
$$0.0905 \text{ g} = 9.05 \times 10^{-2} \text{ g or } 90.5 \text{ mg}$$

37. Since the mass of nitrogen is 14.0 u, the mass of 1.00 mole of nitrogen atoms is 14.0 grams. The mass of 1.00 mole of nitrogen molecules, which have 2 atoms per molecule, is 2(14.0 g) or 28.0 grams. The mass of 1.00 mole of nitric acid, $HNO_3$, is the sum of the masses of 1 hydrogen, 1 nitrogen, and 3 oxygens, or 1.00 + 14.0 + 3(16.0) = 63.0 g.

38. Set up the problem as if you were going to convert

the volume of each gas to number of moles in order to find the mole ratio.

$$\frac{\text{moles } O_2}{\text{moles } Cl_2} = \frac{\dfrac{97.9 \text{ dm}^3}{22.4 \text{ dm}^3/\text{mol}}}{\dfrac{49.0 \text{ dm}^3}{22.4 \text{ dm}^3/\text{mol}}}$$

If you cancel 22.4 dm³/mol out of the numerator and the denominator, the arithmetic is simpler. Since both gases are produced at STP, the ratio of their volumes is equal to the ratio of the number of moles.

$$\frac{\text{moles } O_2}{\text{moles } Cl_2} = \frac{97.9}{49.0} = \frac{2}{1}$$

empirical formula: $ClO_2$

## Page 198, Concept Mastery

39. **Concept:** *Moles consist of mass, volume, and particles.*
    **Solution:** When "a" is given in a problem, some students do not realize that it stands for "1." Enough information is given in the problem if students realize they can calculate the gram molecular mass of $CO_2$ from the atomic mass table.
    molecular mass of $CO_2$ = 12 + 2(16) = 44 g/mol

$$\frac{44 \text{ g}}{\text{mol } CO_2} \times \frac{1 \text{ mol}}{6.02 \times 10^{23} \text{ molec.}} = 7.3 \times 10^{-23} \text{ g/molecule}$$

40. **Concept:** *Moles consist of mass, volume, and particles.*
    **Solution:** At STP, the solid dry ice evaporates. The gas fills a volume proportional to the number of moles present. The gram molecular mass of $CO_2$ is 44 g/mol, and the molar volume at STP is 22.4 dm³.

$$5.0 \text{ g} \times \frac{1 \text{ mol}}{44 \text{ g}} \times \frac{22.4 \text{ dm}^3}{\text{mol}} = 2.5 \text{ dm}^3$$

Rearrange the formula for the volume of a sphere to solve for r. The value of $\pi$ is 22/7.

$$V = \frac{4}{3} \pi r^3$$

$$r^3 = \frac{3\,V}{4\,\pi} = \frac{3(2.5 \text{ dm}^3)}{4\,\pi} = 0.62 \text{ dm}^3$$

$$r = (0.62 \text{ dm}^3)^{1/3} = 0.85 \text{ dm}$$

The diameter is twice the radius of the sphere.
d = 2r × 2(0.85 dm) = 1.7 dm

41. **Concept:** *Moles consist of mass, volume, and particles.*
    **Solution:** Multiply the number of moles by Avogadro's number.

$$5.0 \text{ g} \times \frac{1 \text{ mol}}{44 \text{ g}} \times \frac{6.02 \times 10^{23} \text{ molec.}}{\text{mol}} =$$
$$6.8 \times 10^{22} \text{ molec.}$$

42. ***Concept:*** *Moles consist of mass, volume, and particles.*

    *Solution:*

    $$\frac{5.0 \text{ g}}{6.8 \times 10^{22} \text{ molecules}} \times \frac{1 \text{ cm}^3}{2.0 \text{ g}} =$$
    $$3.7 \times 10^{-23} \text{ cm}^3/\text{molecule}$$

43. ***Concept:*** *Moles consist of mass, volume, and particles.*

    *Solution:* Total volume of sample of gas from question 40 is:

    $$2.6 \text{ dm}^3 \times \frac{1000 \text{ cm}^3}{1 \text{ dm}^3} = 2500 \text{ cm}^3$$

    Using the density of the solid in question 42, the volume of the particles is:

    $$5.0 \text{ g} \times \frac{1 \text{ cm}^3}{2.0 \text{ g}} = 2.5 \text{ cm}^3$$

    Ratio = $2500 \text{ cm}^3/2.5 \text{ cm}^3 = 1000:1$
    The particles occupy only 1/1000th of the available space.

44. ***Concept:*** *There is an experimental error in determining formulas.*

    *Solution:* The correct formula is $CH_4$. The student failed to consider the experimental error involved in the mass measurements.

## Page 198, Cumulative Review

45. **c.** The number of neutrons is equal to the atomic mass minus the number of protons, or $137 - 56 = 81$.

46. **e.** The sum of the charges on the elements in a neutral compound is zero. The charge on Zn is $2+$ and that on Cl is $1-$. Therefore, there must be 2 Cl atoms per molecule. The correct formula is $ZnCl_2$. The charge on Na is $1+$ and that on Cl is $1-$, so NaCl is correct. K is $1+$, C is $4+$, and 3 O are $3(2-)$, which equals $6-$. This does not add up to zero. The correct formula is $K_2CO_3$. When Fe has a charge of $2+$, it can combine with 1 O to make FeO. Mg is $2+$ and OH is $1-$. The correct formula has parentheses around the OH: $Mg(OH)_2$.

47. **b.** The pointer points at the scale between 5 g and 6 g, so the mass is greater than 5 g and less than 6 g. The scale is further divided into tenths. Since the pointer points at the third line between 5 g and 6 g, the mass is 5.3 g.

48. **d.** The charge on Br is $1-$. Since the compound $MBr_2$ is neutral, M must have a charge of $2+$. M could be any element in Group 2, such as magnesium.

49. **a.** The $SO_4^{2-}$ ion has a charge of $2-$, 3 of them contribute $6-$, which must be balanced by 2 ytterbium ions. Therefore, each Yb must have a charge

of $3+$. Thus, 1 Yb must have a charge of $3+$. Thus, 1 Yb forms a neutral compound with 3 Cl atoms (charge of $1-$).

50. Metal B. The specific heat is the number of joules required to raise by 1°C the temperature of 1.00 gram of a substance. Since the specific heat of metal B is lower than that of metal A, metal B requires less energy than metal A to raise its temperature by a constant amount. Similarly, when both metals absorb the same amount of energy, the temperature of metal B increases more than that of metal A.

51. If the products have more potential energy than the reactants, then they have absorbed energy. A reaction in which energy is absorbed is endothermic.

52. The key idea in Bohr's model of the atom is that there are certain definite orbits in which an electron can travel around the nucleus without radiating energy. Each orbit represents a particular energy level of electrons. Electrons can move from one orbit to another by absorbing or releasing just the right amount of energy, thus accounting for bright-line and absorption spectra.

53. The velocity equals the frequency times the wavelength.
    $v = f\lambda = 10 \text{ m} \times 15 \text{ Hz} = 150 \text{ m/sec}$

54. **a.** Examples of monatomic molecules are the noble gases: helium (He), neon (Ne), argon (Ar), krypton (Kr), xenon (Xe), and radon (Rn).
    **b.** Examples of diatomic molecules are hydrogen ($H_2$), fluorine ($F_2$), chlorine ($Cl_2$), nitrogen ($N_2$), and oxygen ($O_2$).

55. Look at the position of the elements in the periodic table. Ionic compounds form between a metal and a nonmetal. Molecular compounds form between nonmetals.

56. **a.** $KClO_3$; **b.** NaOH; **c.** HCl; **d.** $Pb(NO_3)_2$; **e.** $Na_2SO_4$; **f.** $Br_2$; **g.** $Al_2(SO_4)_3$; **h.** $CaCl_2$; **i.** $BaCO_3$; **j.** $CO_2$

57. **a.** sulfuric acid; **b.** zinc chloride; **c.** magnesium chloride; **d.** calcium oxide; **e.** chlorine gas; **f.** silver nitrate; **g.** copper(II) nitrate; **h.** nitric acid; **i.** iron(II) oxide; **j.** aluminum sulfite

## Page 199, Critical Thinking

58. **d.** The smallest value given is half of Avogadro's number, which equals $3.01 \times 10^{23}$. **b.** Then, 1.5 N, which equals $9.03 \times 10^{23}$, is less than 2 mol (**a**), which equals $12.06 \times 10^{23}$. **c.** The largest value given is $15.05 \times 10^{23}$ atoms.

8

**59.** There are several possible causes. If the samples were not homogeneous, one sample could release more of gas C than the other sample. If one decomposition reaction went to completion and the other did not, a different number of moles of gas C would be produced. John would record different volumes under different conditions of temperature or pressure or both. Perhaps one set of measurements was not accurate.

**60.** The empirical formula of a compound shows the simplest ratio in which the atoms combine to form the compound. The molecular formula of a compound is a whole-number multiple of the empirical formula. It shows the actual number of atoms of each element in one molecule of the compound.

**61.** No, the densities of gases are not all the same at STP. Density is mass per unit volume. If the volume of 1 mole is the same for all gases, then all gases must have the same molecular mass to have equal densities. But gases have different molecular masses. Therefore, they have different densities.

## Page 199, Challenge Problems

**62. a.** Find the mass of each reactant.
given: 2.92 g C

$$7.32 \times 10^{22} \text{ molec. } O_2 \times \frac{1 \text{ mol}}{6.02 \times 10^{23}} \times \frac{32.0 \text{ g}}{1 \text{ mol}} = 3.89 \text{ g O}$$

$$5.45 \text{ dm}^3 \text{ H}_2 \times \frac{1 \text{ mol}}{22.4 \text{ dm}^3} \times \frac{2.00 \text{ g}}{1 \text{ mol}} = 0.487 \text{ g H}$$

mass of compound = 3.89 g + 0.487 g + 2.92 g
= 7.30 g

$$\% \text{ C} = \frac{2.92}{7.30} \times 100 = 40.0\%$$

$$\% \text{ O} = \frac{3.89}{7.30} \times 100 = 53.3\%$$

$$\% \text{ H} = \frac{0.487}{7.30} \times 100 = 6.67\%$$

Check: 40.0% + 53.3% + 6.67% = 99.97%, which rounds off to 100%

**b.** From the percent composition, find the mole ratios and the empirical formula.

$$2.92 \text{ g C} \times \frac{1 \text{ mol C}}{12.0 \text{ g C}} = 0.243 \text{ mol C}$$

$$3.89 \text{ g O}_2 \times \frac{1 \text{ mol O}_2}{32.0 \text{ g O}_2} \times \frac{2 \text{ mol O}}{1 \text{ mol O}_2} = 0.243 \text{ mol O}$$

$$0.487 \text{ g H}_2 \times \frac{1 \text{ mol H}_2}{2.00 \text{ g H}_2} \times \frac{2 \text{ mol H}}{1 \text{ mol H}_2} = 0.487 \text{ mol H}$$

mole ratio = 1 C/1 O/2 H

empirical formula: $CH_2O$
empirical formula mass = 12.0 + 2(1.01) + 16.0
= 30.0
Since the molecular mass, 180 g, is six times the empirical formula mass, 30.0 g, the molecular formula contains six empirical formula units.
$(CH_2O)_6 = C_6H_{12}O_6$

**63. a.** Find the mass of copper, of sulfur, and of the compound.
mass Cu = 30.25 g − 28.71 g = 1.54 g Cu
mass S = 30.64 g − 30.25 g = 0.39 g S
mass compound = 30.64 g − 28.71 g = 1.93 g

$$\% \text{ Cu} = \frac{1.54}{1.93} \times 100 = 80.0\%$$

$$\% \text{ S} = \frac{0.39}{1.93} \times 100 = 20\%$$

Check: 80.0% + 20% = 100%

**b.** Find the mole ratio.

$$1.54 \text{ g Cu} \times \frac{1 \text{ mol Cu}}{64.0 \text{ g Cu}} = 0.0241 \text{ mol Cu}$$

$$0.39 \text{ g S} \times \frac{1 \text{ mol S}}{32.0 \text{ g S}} = 0.012 \text{ mol S}$$

mole ratio = 2 Cu/1 S
empirical formula: $Cu_2S$

**c.** The compound is ionic because it is formed from a metal (Cu) and a nonmetal (S).

**d.** The name of the compound is copper(I) sulfide or cuprous sulfide.

**64.** Use the molar volume at STP to find the number of moles of chlorine gas, fluorine gas, and hydrogen gas.

$$2.24 \text{ dm}^3 \text{ Cl}_2 \times \frac{\text{mol Cl}_2}{22.4 \text{ dm}^3} \times \frac{2 \text{ atoms}}{\text{molec.}} = 0.200 \text{ mol Cl}$$

$$1.12 \text{ dm}^3 \text{ H}_2 \times \frac{\text{mol H}_2}{22.4 \text{ dm}^3} \times \frac{2 \text{ atoms}}{\text{molec.}} = 0.100 \text{ mol H}$$

$$1.12 \text{ dm}^3 \text{ F}_2 \times \frac{\text{mol F}_2}{22.4 \text{ dm}^3} \times \frac{2 \text{ atoms}}{\text{molec.}} = 0.100 \text{ mol F}$$

To find the number of moles of carbon, find the mass of carbon by subtracting the masses of chlorine, hydrogen, and fluorine from the mass of the compound.
mass Cl = 0.200 mol × 35.5 g/mol = 7.10 g
mass H = 0.100 mol × 1.01 g/mol = 0.101 g
mass Fl = 0.100 mol × 19.0 g/mol = 1.90 g
total = 9.10 g

mass C = 10.3 g − 9.10 g = 1.2 g

$$1.2 \text{ g C} \times \frac{1 \text{ mol C}}{12.0 \text{ g C}} = 0.10 \text{ mol C}$$

mole ratio = 1 C/1 H/2 Cl/1 F
empirical formula: $Cl_2CHF$

# Chemical Equations

## Chapter Planning Guide

| Text Section | Labs (Lab Manual) and Demonstrations (TE) | Supplementary Materials (Teacher's Resource Book) |
|---|---|---|
| **9-1** Word Equations, pp. 201-202 | | |
| **9-2** Interpreting Formula Equations, pp. 202-206 | Demo 9-1: Atom Accounting, p. TG-147 | |
| **9-3** Determining Whether an Equation Is Balanced, p. 207 | | |
| **9-4** Balancing Chemical Equations, pp. 208-211 | | |
| **9-5** Showing Energy Changes in Equations, p. 211   **9-6** Showing Phases in Chemical Equations pp. 212-213 | | Transparency Master: The Use of Phase Notation in Formulas, p. 9-1  Transparency Master: The Reaction of Solid Zinc with Hydrochloric Acid, p. 9-2  Concept Mastery: Balancing Equations, p. CM-10 |
| **9-7** Ions in Water Solution, pp. 213-215 | | Concept Mastery: Conservation of Mass, p. CM-11 |
| **9-8** Classifying Chemical Reactions, pp. 215-216   **9-9** Direct Combination or Synthesis Reactions, p. 216   **9-10** Decomposition or Analysis, pp. 216-218 | Lab 14: Types of Chemical Reactions  Demo 9-2: Direct Combination Reactions, p. TG-148  Demo 9-3: Decomposition Reactions, p. TG-149 | |
| **9-11** Single Replacement Reactions, pp. 218-220 | Demo 9-4: Single Replacement Reactions, p. TG-149 | |
| **9-12** Double Replacement Reactions, pp. 220-224 | Demo 9-5: Double Replacement Reactions, p. TG-150 | Review Activity: Categories of Chemical Reactions, p. 9-3  Concept Mastery: Types of Chemical Reactions, p. CM-12 |

| Text Section | Labs (Lab Manual) and Demonstrations (TE) | Supplementary Materials (Teacher's Resource Book) |
|---|---|---|
| **9-13** Writing Ionic Equations, pp. 224-226 | | Review Activity: Chemical Changes, p. 9-4<br>Practice Problems, p. 9-5<br>Concept Mastery: Ionic Equations, p. CM-13 |
| **Career** Chemical Engineer, p. 225 | | |
| | | Test—Form A, p. AT-32<br>Alternate Test—Form B, p. BT-32 |

☐ Core    ☐ Advanced    ☐ Optional

## Chapter Overview

In Chapter 9 we investigate chemical equations. We define word equation and formula equation and point out the information they provide. Then we move on to balanced equations and discuss their relationship to the law of conservation of mass. A three-step approach for balancing equations is presented, as well as opportunities for students to balance equations using this approach. Additional information about how to indicate energy changes and the phases of the reactants and products in equations is also presented.

We present a classification scheme for chemical reactions to assist the student in predicting the products of reactions. The four categories of reactions included in this scheme are: direct combination or synthesis, decomposition or analysis, single replacement, and double replacement. The chapter ends with an advanced topic on ionic equations and presents a four-step approach for writing net ionic equations.

## Chapter Objectives

After students have completed this chapter, they will be able to:
1. Interpret the information in chemical equations.                    *9-1, 9-2, 9-5 to 9-7*
2. Balance chemical equations; relate this process to the law of conservation of mass.    *9-2 to 9-4, 9-13*
3. Classify many reactions as belonging to one of four categories.                    *9-8 to 9-12*
4. Predict the products of single and double replacement reactions.          *9-11 and 9-12*

## Teaching Suggestions

### 9-1 Word Equations, pp. 201-202

■ Emphasize the importance of a chemical equation, explaining that it condenses the qualitative and quantitative information about a chemical reaction. Point out that the first step in writing an equation is to write the word equation—the qualitative description of a reaction.

■ Tell the students that writing a word equation can be an involved task. To write a word equation the reactants and products must be known. Sometimes the products may be difficult to detect if they escape into the atmosphere or dissolve in one of the reactants or other products. Explain that there are other factors to consider when preparing to write a word equation. For example, extra substances that do not react, such as air or water, might be present. These substances are not apparent in a word equation.

### 9-2 Interpreting Formula Equations, pp. 202-206

| Planning Guide | |
|---|---|
| Labs (Lab Manual) and Demonstrations (TE) | Supplementary Materials (Teacher's Resource Book) |
| Demo 9-1: Atom Accounting, p. TG-147 | |

■ Show how a formula equation is derived from a word equation. Then introduce the relationship between the law of conservation of mass and chemical reactions by doing Demonstration 9-1, "Atom Accounting." In this demonstration students begin to "see" that mass is conserved in chemical reactions. Then indicate that the reason for this is that in chemical reactions, atoms are neither lost nor gained but are merely rearranged. You may want to use molecular models, Tinker Toy pieces, or Lego blocks to reinforce this point by allowing the students to make different objects from the same set of pieces.

■ Next, discuss text Figures 9-3 through 9-7 and walk the students through the discussion in the text regarding the reaction of 5.0 g of $H_2$ with 40 g of $O_2$. This discussion illustrates the very important relationships among the law of conservation of mass, the number of moles, the number of particles, and the coefficients in a balanced chemical equation.

■ Present the class with a number of balanced equations and have the students interpret them both qualitatively and quantitatively. Ask them how these equations confirm the validity of the law of conservation of mass. Then ask why the number of moles on each side of the equation may not be equal.

■ **Application.** You may want to indicate to the students that the reaction of hydrogen with oxygen is not just a textbook preparation of water. The second- and third-stage engines of the Apollo launch vehicles were powered by the burning of liquid hydrogen and liquid oxygen.

### 9-3 Determining Whether an Equation Is Balanced, p. 207

■ Emphasize that determining whether or not an equation is balanced is quite simple if you approach it systematically. Point out that, at least in the beginning, it is helpful to set up a table similar to that shown in Sample Problem 3. Present numerous balanced and unbalanced equations and instruct the students to ascertain whether or not they are balanced. Encourage them to fill in a table similar to that in Sample Problem 3.

### 9-4 Balancing Chemical Equations, pp. 208-211

■ Once students can determine whether an equation is balanced, move on to the topic of balancing chemical equations. The ideal way to begin this discussion is to have students observe a simple chemical reaction, such as (1) observing the flame of a bunsen burner, (2) mixing $AgNO_3$ with $NaCl$, or (3) mixing $Zn$ with $HCl$. Then illustrate what is happening on the microscopic level using molecular models. Next, balance the equation using the three-step approach outlined in the text. Repeat this with several different reactions.

■ Be sure to emphasize that this process for balancing equations is a trial and error approach. In addition to the three steps discussed in the text, point out the following rules to help simplify the process:

1. Balance first those elements that appear in the least number of formulas.

2. After a coefficient is written, check its effect upon other formulas.

3. Check the final result to make sure the equation is actually balanced.

■ **Concept Mastery.** Research has shown that half of the students in an average high school chemistry course who demonstrate that they can balance equations do so in a rote manner. When these same students are asked to represent the atoms and molecules of the substances involved using molecular models, they make no distinction between such species as $4H$ and $2H_2$. Many students cannot understand the basis for balancing equations because they do not understand the difference between conservation of atoms and conservation of molecules. This points to the necessity of using models to help students understand the meaning of the symbols in a balanced equation. With sufficient practice in manipulating models of the species involved in a chemical reaction, students should be able to answer Concept Mastery questions 34 through 37 at the end of the chapter.

### 9-5 Showing Energy Changes in Equations, p. 211, and

### 9-6 Showing Phases in Chemical Equations, pp. 212-213

| Planning Guide | |
|---|---|
| Labs (Lab Manual) and Demonstrations (TE) | Supplementary Materials (Teacher's Resource Book) |
| | Transparency Master: The Use of Phase Notation in Formulas, p. 9-1 |
| | Transparency Master: The Reaction of Solid Zinc with Hydrochloric Acid, p. 9-2 |
| | Concept Mastery: Balancing Equations, p. CM-10 |

■ Point out that in chemical equations, additional information may be conveyed by using certain conventions established by scientists to indicate energy changes and the phases of the reactants and products. Explain the convention for indicating exothermic and endothermic reactions. Next, use the Transparency Masters "The Use of Phase Notation in Formulas," which indicates the symbols used for the phases of reactants and products, and "The Reaction of Solid Zinc with Hydrochloric Acid."

■ **Concept Mastery.** Students often memorize the rules for balancing equations without understanding the different possible interpretations for the coefficients. The Concept Mastery worksheet "Balancing Equations" in the *Teacher's Resource Book* can help students to visualize equations at the molecular level.

## 9-7 Ions in Water Solution, pp. 213-215

| Planning Guide | |
| --- | --- |
| **Labs (Lab Manual)**<br>**and Demonstrations (TE)** | **Supplementary Materials**<br>**(Teacher's Resource Book)** |
| | Concept Mastery:<br>Conservation of Mass,<br>p. CM-11 |

■ Begin by reviewing the differences between ionic and molecular compounds. Discuss several equations showing the formation of ions from ionic compounds such as $MgCl_2$ and $Na_2SO_4$. Call attention to the fact that ions are present in the solid phase as well as in solution. Explain that the ions in a solid are held together by electrostatic attraction. In solution, however, these same ions are separated from each other and free to move throughout the solution. Next, compare the dissociation of some molecular compounds, such as acids, when they are dissolved. Emphasize that these molecular substances do not consist of ions in the pure state. Only when dissolved in water do they form ions by interaction with the water. Ask the students to write equations for the dissociation of acids and for the ionization of soluble ionic compounds dissolved in water.

■ **Concept Mastery.** Students often forget that the law of conservation of mass applies to reactions that produce a solid or a gas. The Concept Mastery worksheet "Conservation of Mass" in the *Teacher's Resource Book* addresses this misconception, and can be used to test students' understanding of this law.

## 9-8 Classifying Chemical Reactions, pp. 215-216,

## 9-9 Direct Combination or Synthesis Reactions, p. 216, and

## 9-10 Decomposition or Analysis, pp. 216-218

| Planning Guide | |
| --- | --- |
| **Labs (Lab Manual)**<br>**and Demonstrations (TE)** | **Supplementary Materials**<br>**(Teacher's Resource Book)** |
| Lab 14: Types of Chemical<br>  Reactions<br>Demo 9-2: Direct<br>  Combination Reactions,<br>  p. TG-148<br>Demo 9-3: Decomposition<br>  Reactions, p. TG-149 | |

■ Explain that it is often possible to predict the products of a particular combination of reactants. Organizing chemical reactions into classes makes it easier to do this. Tell the students that there are various classification schemes, none of which is entirely satisfacto-ry. However, the most useful scheme, presented in the text, divides reactions into four classes. Use Laboratory 14, "Types of Chemical Reactions," to introduce the classes of chemical reactions.

■ Point out that combination and decomposition reactions are two of the easiest classes of reactions to identify, to predict products for, and to balance. Therefore, it is best to concentrate on these types first. Do Demonstration 9-2, "Direct Combination Reactions." Ask the students to predict the products of these various combination reactions and then to balance the resulting equations. Next, do Demonstration 9-3, "Decomposition Reactions," where students investigate a particular type of decomposition reaction, namely electrolysis. Ask the students to predict the products of various other decomposition reactions and to balance these equations.

■ Students tend to make two types of errors when predicting the products of combination and decomposition reactions. In combination reactions, they tend to combine the two reactants without considering the correct formula of the compound. For example, they may write $Mg + O_2 \rightarrow MgO_2$. In decomposition reactions, they decompose the compound further than it actually decomposes under the specified reaction conditions. For example, $NH_4OH$ does not ordinarily decompose to nitrogen, oxygen, and hydrogen.

■ **Concept Mastery.** You may wish to use Concept Mastery question 33 (chapter-end question) to make a very important point. We often use words in a nontechnical sense, thereby making it more difficult to understand the technical meaning of a word. For example, fish do not have the mechanism to decompose water into hydrogen and oxygen. Rather, fish make use of the oxygen that is dissolved in the water. No decomposition reaction is needed to obtain this oxygen.

Other processes are also deceptive. Ask students what type of reaction is occurring when their toast is exposed to too much heat and turns black. Point out that the process of burning is actually a combination reaction. However, when toast burns, in a nontechnical sense it "decomposes" even though no decomposition reaction is involved.

## 9-11 Single Replacement Reactions, pp. 218-220

| Planning Guide | |
| --- | --- |
| **Labs (Lab Manual)**<br>**and Demonstrations (TE)** | **Supplementary Materials**<br>**(Teacher's Resource Book)** |
| Demo 9-4: Single<br>  Replacement Reactions,<br>  p. TG-149 | |

■ Begin the discussion of single replacement reactions by doing Demonstration 9-4, "Single Replacement Reactions." In this demonstration students can observe two single replacement reactions and test the products. Show the students that there are three general types of replacement reactions: replacement of hydrogen from acids and water, replacement of a metal by another metal, and replacement of a nonmetal by another nonmetal.

## 9-12 Double Replacement Reactions, pp. 220-224

| Planning Guide | |
|---|---|
| Labs (Lab Manual) and Demonstrations (TE) | Supplementary Materials (Teacher's Resource Book) |
| Demo 9-5: Double Replacement Reactions, p. TG-150 | Review Activity: Categories of Chemical Reactions, p. 9-3<br>Concept Mastery: Types of Chemical Reactions, p. CM-12 |

■ Do Demonstration 9-5, "Double Replacement Reactions." In this demonstration students observe a double replacement reaction in which a gaseous product is formed and one in which a precipitate is formed. Point out that double replacement reactions occur only if one of the products is removed from the solution. Explain how this is accomplished by the formation of a gas, a precipitate, or water. Point out that the formation of a precipitate can be predicted by consulting the Table of Solubilities in Appendix D.

■ **Application.** You may want to call the students' attention to the following reaction sequence, which is one noncommercial method for recycling copper metal. This sequence provides an interesting framework to review word equations, formula equations, balancing equations, types of chemical reactions, and the activity series.

**a.** impure copper + nitric acid →
copper(II) nitrate + nitrogen dioxide + water
**b.** copper(II) nitrate + sodium hydroxide →
copper(II) hydroxide + sodium nitrate
**c.** copper(II) hydroxide + heat →
copper(II) oxide + water
**d.** copper(II) oxide + sulfuric acid →
copper(II) sulfate + water
**e.** copper(II) sulfate + zinc → copper + zinc sulfate

■ **Concept Mastery.** The Concept Mastery worksheet "Types of Chemical Reactions" in the *Teacher's Resource Book* can be used after Section 9-12 to test the students' understanding of a variety of reactions. Students are given several pictorial models of reaction products and are asked to identify the possible types of reactions that produced each set of products. The students are then given several sets of reactants and asked to match them to the products.

## 9-13 Writing Ionic Equations, pp. 224-226

| Planning Guide | |
|---|---|
| Labs (Lab Manual) and Demonstrations (TE) | Supplementary Materials (Teacher's Resource Book) |
| | Review Activity: Chemical Changes, p. 9-4<br>Practice Problems, p. 9-5<br>Concept Mastery: Ionic Equations, p. CM-13 |

■ If you choose to teach this advanced topic, begin by reviewing how to write equations for the ionization and dissociation of various substances. Then refer to the four steps listed in the text for writing balanced ionic equations. Call students' attention to those ions that are referred to as spectator ions. Finally, show the students how to check to see that both conservation of charge as well as conservation of atoms are maintained.

■ **Concept Mastery.** The Concept Mastery worksheet "Ionic Equations" in the *Teacher's Resource Book* can be used for review after Section 9-13. The worksheet helps students to visualize what happens to the particles involved in an ionic reaction.

## Demonstrations

### 9-1 Atom Accounting

**Overview:** In this demonstration, using various coins and the overhead projector, you demonstrate what happens to the atoms in a chemical reaction. You also try to discover the "recipe" for making ammonia from hydrogen and nitrogen gases. Students learn the meaning of the law of conservation of mass as well as the significance of the coefficients in a balanced equation.

**Materials:** 24 pennies and 8 quarters.

**Advance Preparation:** none

**Procedure:** 1. Place the coins onto the overhead projector and tell students to help you determine how to make ammonia ($NH_3$) from hydrogen ($H_2$) and nitrogen ($N_2$) gases. 2. On the right, make one ammonia "molecule" by placing three pennies (hydrogen atoms) around a quarter (nitrogen atom). Make three more ammonia molecules. Ask the students how many coins should be placed on the left (reactant side) in order to make these four product units. Remind them that both of the reactant gases are diatomic. Place the suggested number of pairs of pennies on the left. Repeat for the pairs of quarters. 3. Show how the coins can be rearranged to make some new molecules without loss of any atoms or gain of new ones. Emphasize the law of conservation of mass. 4. Ask students to state the simplest whole-number "recipe" for making the ammonia molecules. 5. Write the balanced equation on an overhead transparency or on the board. Emphasize that the coefficients represent the correct ratio in which the molecules combine to form a product.

**Results:** In step 2, six pairs of pennies ($H_2$) and two pairs of quarters ($N_2$) are needed to make four product units ($NH_3$). In step 4, one nitrogen molecule and three hydrogen molecules produce two ammonia molecules. the balanced equation is $N_2 + 3H_2 \rightarrow 2NH_3$.

## 9-2 Direct Combination Reactions

**Overview:** In this demonstration, students observe reactions in which only one product is formed. They also learn how to test for the presence of acids and bases.

**Materials:** bottle of concentrated hydrochloric acid; bottle of concentrated ammonia; strip of magnesium metal, 3 cm long; Bunsen burner; tweezers or crucible tongs; red and blue litmus paper; small piece of dry ice; test tubes in test-tube rack; wash bottle containing distilled water.

**Advance Preparation:** none

**Safety:** The concentrated hydrochloric acid and ammonia are both quite corrosive, so be careful in handling them. Warn students not to look directly at the burning magnesium, which can produce a dangerously bright light. Be careful when you use the dry ice, which is at a very low temperature; use tongs in handling it.

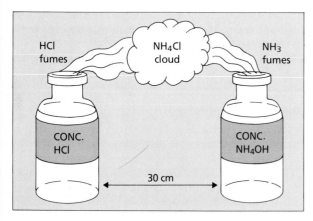

Figure 9-1

**Procedure:** 1. Place the bottles of hydrochloric acid and ammonia about 30 cm apart in the fume hood. 2. Remove the caps from the hydrochloric acid and the ammonia bottles, and carefully fan the HCl and $NH_3$

gases together. Replace both caps. 3. Have a student volunteer try to write the balanced equation for this reaction on the board. 4. Show students a piece of magnesium ribbon. Tell them you are going to heat it in a flame and allow it to react with oxygen gas in the air. Use tweezers or tongs to hold the magnesium in the hottest part of the burner flame. Once the magnesium

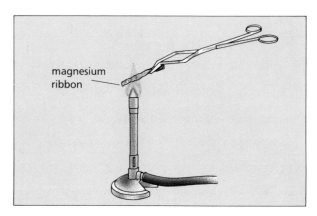

Figure 9-2

begins to react, remove it from the flame and allow the reaction to continue. 5. Have students observe the differences in properties of the reactant and product. 6. Have another volunteer write the balanced equation for this reaction on the board. 7. Add the powder that was produced in the magnesium reaction to distilled water. Cork and shake the powder and water. Test the solution with litmus paper. Ask students to try to write an equation for the reaction between the powder and water. 8. Fill a large test tube half full of distilled water. Test the water with red and blue litmus paper. 9. Using tweezers, add a small piece of dry ice (solid carbon dioxide) to the water. Test the solution with litmus paper. Ask students to try to write an equation for the reaction between the dry ice and water.

**Results:** In step 2, a white cloud of powdery ammonium chloride ($NH_4Cl$) will form. The equation is $HCl(g) + NH_3(g) \rightarrow NH_4Cl(s)$. In step 4, the magnesium will burn with a brilliant light. The gray metallic magnesium will produce a powdery white solid. The equation is $2Mg + O_2 \rightarrow 2MgO$. In step 7, the MgO reacts with water to form $Mg(OH)_2$, a base, which turns litmus blue. The equation for the reaction is $MgO + H_2O \rightarrow Mg(OH)_2$. In step 8, the water, which is neutral, will not change the color of litmus. In step 9, the dry ice reacts with the water to form $H_2CO_3$, an acid, which turns litmus red. The equation is $CO_2 + H_2O \rightarrow H_2CO_3$.

**Disposal Tips:** All of the solutions just mentioned can be poured directly into the drain and flushed with water. Solids should be placed into the trash can.

## 9-3 Decomposition Reactions

**Overview:** In this demonstration, students observe the decomposition of a substance through electrolysis. They also learn how to test for the presence of a free halogen.

**Materials:** 6-volt battery; electrolysis cell containing carbon electrodes; 0.2 $M$ solution of copper(II) bromide ($CuBr_2$); TTE (1,1,2-trichloro-1,2,2-trifluoroethane) or 1,1,1-trichloroethane; long eyedropper; test tubes in a rack; fume hood.

**Advance Preparation: 0.2 $M$ $CuBr_2$:** Prepare a solution that is approximately 0.2 $M$ by dissolving 5 g $CuBr_2$ in enough water to make 100 mL of solution.

**Safety:** Do not allow the TTE to spatter or come into contact with the skin; if this does occur, wash the skin immediately with soap and water. Also be careful in handling the bromine. This demonstration should be done in a.properly functioning fume hood.

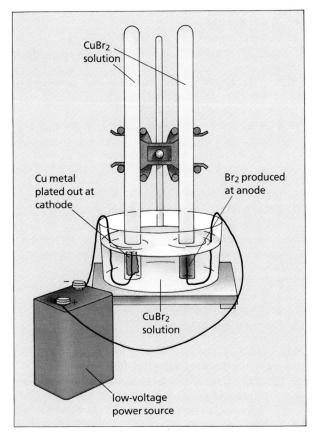

CuBr$_2$ solution

Cu metal plated out at cathode

Br$_2$ produced at anode

CuBr$_2$ solution

low-voltage power source

**Figure 9-3**

**Procedure:** 1. Ask students to predict the products of the electrolysis of aqueous copper(II) bromide and ask them to propose a method to test their hypothesis.

2. Students should be reminded that bromine exists as a diatomic molecule. Point out that when a free halogen is added to TTE, the resulting color can be used to identify the halogen: iodine produces a pink or violet liquid, bromine produces an amber or reddish-brown liquid, and chlorine produces a nearly colorless liquid. 3. In the fume hood, set up the electrolysis apparatus for the copper(II) bromide solution, and allow the reaction to occur for about three minutes. Have students come up to the demonstration table to observe. 4. Squeeze all of the air out of a long eyedropper and take a sample from the yellowish or reddish area in the chamber. Add this to about 1 mL of TTE in a test tube. Cork and agitate carefully. 5. Have a volunteer write the equation on the board. Save the bromine–TTE mixture for the following demonstration.

**Results:** In step 1, some students should correctly predict that copper will form at one electrode, and they will suggest looking for a copper-colored solid. The copper will indeed plate out at the negative electrode, or cathode. At the positive electrode, or anode, dense yellowish or reddish liquid bromine should form and flow to the bottom of the reaction chamber. In step 4, the bottom TTE layer should be amber, indicating the presence of bromine. The equation is $CuBr_2(aq) \rightarrow Cu(s) + Br_2(l)$.

**Disposal Tips:** Save the bromine–TTE mixture for Demonstration 9-4. The water solutions can be poured down the drain and flushed with additional water.

## 9-4 Single Replacement Reactions

**Overview:** In this demonstration, students observe some single replacement reactions and learn how to test for hydrogen gas.

**Materials:** bromine in TTE from the previous demonstration; 0.2 $M$ potassium iodide (KI); 2-cm strip of magnesium ribbon; 0.5 $M$ hydrochloric acid (HCl); small test tubes in a rack, with corks; wooden splints; tweezers.

**Advance Preparation:** 1. **0.2 $M$ KI:** mix 3.3 g of KI in enough water to make 100-mL solution. 2. **0.5 $M$ HCl:** carefully mix concentrated HCl and water in a 1:22 ratio by volume.

**Safety:** Be careful in handling the hydrochloric acid and the bromine–TTE mixture. In step 4, do not push the cork tightly into the tube, as the gases will force the cork to pop out violently or cause the tube to shatter. Wear goggles.

**Procedure:** 1. Place about 2 mL of KI solution into a test tube. 2. Add to the KI solution some of the bromine–TTE from the previous demonstration. Cork and agitate carefully, and ask students to observe the result. 3. Have a student volunteer attempt to write the equation for the reaction on the board. 4. Place about 4 mL of HCl solution into a small test tube and add a small strip of magnesium ribbon to it. Gently set a cork on top of the tube to keep most of the gas that is produced trapped inside the tube. 5. Light a wooden splint and carefully bring it over the mouth of the tube after removing the cork. 6. A volunteer should attempt to write the equation for the reaction between the acid and the magnesium.

**Results:** In step 2, iodine will be produced and will cause the TTE layer to turn pink or violet. The equation is $2KI + Br_2 \rightarrow 2KBr + I_2$. In step 4, hydrogen gas will be produced and will burn with a popping sound when the splint is brought over the mouth of the tube. The reaction is $Mg + 2HCl \rightarrow MgCl_2 + H_2$.

**Disposal Tips:** The TTE should be placed into a specially marked container for soluble organic waste. The other water solutions can be poured down the drain and the drain flushed with water.

## 9-5 Double Replacement Reactions

**Overview:** In this demonstration, students observe double replacement reactions in which a gas or precipitate forms.

**Materials:** 0.2 *M* sodium hydrogen carbonate ($NaHCO_3$); 0.5 *M* hydrochloric acid (HCl); 0.2 *M* aluminum chloride ($AlCl_3$); test tubes in rack; cork.

**Advance Preparation:** 1. **0.2 *M* NaHCO₃**: mix 8.4 g of $NaHCO_3$ in enough water to make 100-mL solution. 2. **0.5 *M* HCl:** carefully mix concentrated HCl and water in a 1:22 ratio by volume. 3. **0.2 *M* AlCl₃:** mix 13.3 g of $AlCl_3$ in enough water to make 100-mL solution.

**Safety:** Be careful in handling the hydrochloric acid. In step 2, do not push the cork tightly into the tube.

**Procedure:** 1. Place about 5 mL of sodium hydrogen carbonate solution into a test tube and add 2 mL of hydrochloric acid solution. Ask students what gas has been produced. 2. Place a cork gently on top of the tube to trap some of the gas. Bring a burning splint to the mouth of the tube as the cork is removed. 3. Tell students that $CO_2$ is the gas produced. Ask them to write the equation. 4. Add 3 mL of sodium hydrogen carbonate solution to 3 mL of aluminum chloride solution in a test tube. Ask students to write the equation.

**Results:** In step 1, carbon dioxide gas will be produced. The splint will go out, but no popping sound will be heard, so the gas cannot have been hydrogen. The equation is $NaHCO_3 + HCl \rightarrow NaCl + H_2O + CO_2$. In step 4, students will observe a white solid forming in the solution. This precipitate is aluminum hydrogen carbonate. The equation is: $3NaHCO_3 + AlCl_3 \rightarrow 3NaCl + Al(HCO_3)_3$.

# Answers to Questions

**Page 202**

1. A chemical equation is a condensed statement that describes the facts about a chemical reaction.
2. Reactants are the substances that exist before a chemical reaction occurs. Products are the substances that are formed during a chemical reaction.
3. Copper plus silver nitrate yields silver plus copper nitrate.
4. **a.** water = reactant; hydrogen and oxygen = products
   **b.** sodium and chlorine = reactants; sodium chloride = product
5. **a.** water → hydrogen gas + oxygen gas
   **b.** sodium + chlorine gas → sodium chloride

**Page 206**

6. The symbol of the element oxygen (O) represents one atom of that element. The formula of oxygen gas ($O_2$) represents the composition of a molecule of oxygen gas.
7. 2CO represents two molecules of carbon monoxide. $CO_2$ represents one molecule of carbon dioxide.
8. **a.** Two atoms of sodium plus one molecule of chlorine gas produce two formula units of sodium chloride.
   **b.** Two formula units of potassium chlorate produce two formula units of potassium chloride and three molecules of oxygen gas.

**Page 207**

9. A balanced equation is one in which there are the same number of atoms of each element on both sides of the equation.
10. A balanced equation conforms to the law of conservation of mass. All atoms of the reactants must be accounted for in the products.
11. **a.** 5 nitrogen, 15 hydrogen
    **b.** 4 calcium, 8 oxygen, 8 hydrogen
    **c.** 3 barium, 3 sulfur, 12 oxygen
12. Equation **a** is balanced.

**Page 211**

13. (1) Write the word equation for the reaction.
    (2) Write the correct formulas for all of the reactants and products.
    (3) Balance the equation.
14. **a.** $4Na + O_2 \rightarrow 2Na_2O$; **b.** $2Cu + S \rightarrow Cu_2S$; **c.** balanced; **d.** balanced
15. $2Cu + S \rightarrow Cu_2S$
    ○ ○ ●   ○●○
16. **a.** iron + oxygen → iron(III) oxide
    **b.** $Fe + O_2 \rightarrow Fe_2O_3$
    **c.** $4Fe + 3O_2 \rightarrow 2Fe_2O_3$

17. **a.** sodium + water → sodium hydroxide
                                    + hydrogen gas
    **b.** $Na + H_2O → NaOH + H_2$
    **c.** $2Na + 2H_2O → 2NaOH + H_2$
18. **a.** copper + sulfuric acid →
            copper(II) sulfate + water + sulfur dioxide
    **b.** $Cu + H_2SO_4 → CuSO_4 + H_2O + SO_2$
    **c.** $Cu + 2H_2SO_4 → CuSO_4 + 2H_2O + SO_2$

**Page 213**

19. **a.** gas; **b.** solid; **c.** liquid
20. Many substances will not react unless they are dissolved in water.
21. **a.** hydrogen bromide dissolved in water (hydrobromic acid); **b.** solid carbon dioxide (dry ice); **c.** carbon dioxide gas
22. $NaCl(aq)$ means that sodium chloride is in water solution. $NaCl(l)$ indicates liquid sodium chloride (melted sodium chloride).
23. To indicate that heat is released, put the term "energy" on the right side of the equation.
24. solid sodium + liquid water → sodium hydroxide
                        solution + hydrogen gas + energy.

**Page 215**

25. $Ca(NO_3)_2$ (**a**) and $MgI_2$ (**d**) are ionic substances. HCl (**b**) and $H_2SO_4$ (**c**) are molecular substances.
26. **a.** 1 calcium ion, 2 nitrate ions; **b.** 1 hydrogen ion, 1 chloride ion; **c.** 2 hydrogen ions, 1 sulfate ion; **d.** 1 magnesium ion, 2 iodide ions; **b** and **c** are molecules and form ions only in water solutions.

**Page 217**

27. The four types of chemical reactions are: direct combination, decomposition, single replacement, and double replacement.
28. **a.** single replacement; **b.** direct combination (synthesis); **c.** decomposition; **d.** double replacement; **e.** direct combination (synthesis)
29. Another name for a direct combination reaction is a synthesis reaction.
30. A decomposition reaction is also called analysis.
31. A catalyst is a substance that speeds up a chemical reaction without being permanently altered.

**Page 218**

32. **a.** $2H_2 + O_2 → 2H_2O$
    **b.** $2Na + Cl_2 → 2NaCl$
    **c.** $N_2 + 2O_2 → 2NO_2$
    **d.** $NH_3 + HCl → NH_4Cl$
33. **a.** $2CO → 2C + O_2$
    **b.** $2AlCl_3 → 2Al + 3Cl_2$
    **c.** $CCl_4 → C + 2Cl_2$
    **d.** $NH_4OH → NH_3 + H_2O$

**Page 220**

34. The general equation of a single replacement reaction is: A + BC → B + AC.
35. **b** and **c** occur.

36. **b.** potassium + water → potassium hydroxide +
                                    hydrogen gas
    **c.** zinc + silver nitrate → zinc nitrate + silver

**Page 223**

37. **b.** $2K + 2H_2O → 2KOH + H_2$
    **c.** $Zn + 2AgNO_3 → Zn(NO_3)_2 + 2Ag$
38. A double replacement reaction is also called an exchange of ions.
39. One of the products must be separated or removed from the solution in order for a double replacement reaction to occur.
40. A precipitate is a solid substance formed by a physical or a chemical change in a liquid or gaseous medium. It is often formed in double replacement reactions.
41. A precipitate is indicated by (s).
42. Reactions **b**, **c**, and **d** occur.

**Page 224**

43. **b.** lead(II) nitrate + zinc chloride →
                        lead(II) chloride + zinc nitrate
    **c.** sodium hydroxide + phosphoric acid →
                        sodium phosphate + water
    **d.** potassium sulfate + calcium chloride →
                        potassium chloride + calcium sulfate
44. **b.** $Pb(NO_3)_2(aq) + ZnCl_2(aq) →$
                        $PbCl_2(s) + Zn(NO_3)_2(aq)$
    **c.** $3NaOH(aq) + H_3PO_4(aq) →$
                        $Na_3PO_4(aq) + 3H_2O(l)$
    **d.** $K_2SO_4(aq) + CaCl_2(aq) → CaSO_4(s) + 2KCl(aq)$

**Page 226**

45. **a.** An ionic equation is one in which aqueous ionic substances are written as ions. A net ionic equation shows only ions that react.
    **b.** A spectator ion is one that is present in the reacting vessel but does not react.
46. The reactants and the products are electrically neutral. The positive charges are balanced by the negative charges on the spectator ions that are not shown in the net ionic equation.
47. **a.** Reactant ions are $2H^+$; **b.** product ions are $Zn^{2+}$; **c.** spectator ions are $2Cl^-$.
48. **a.** $2Na^+(aq) + 1SO_3^{2-}(aq)$
    **b.** $2Al^{3+}(aq) + 3SO_4^{2-}(aq)$
    **c.** $2Na^+(aq) + 2OH^-(aq)$
    **d.** $6K^+(aq) + 3SO_4^{2-}(aq)$
49. **a.** single replacement; **b.** single replacement; **c.** double replacement; **d.** double replacement
50. **a.** $2Na(s) + 2H_2O(l) →$
                        $2Na^+(aq) + 2OH^-(aq) + H_2(g)$
    **b.** $Ca(s) + Mg^{2+}(aq) → Ca^{2+}(aq) + Mg(s)$
    **c.** $Ba^{2+}(aq) + SO_4^{2-}(aq) → BaSO_4(s)$
    **d.** $CO_3^{2-}(aq) + Ca^{2+}(aq) → CaCO_3(s)$
51. **a.** no spectator ions; **b.** $SO_4^{2-}$; **c.** $K^+$, $Cl^-$; **d.** $Na^+$, $OH^-$

## Chapter Review

1. A word equation is an equation in which the reactants and products are represented by their names.

   zinc + copper(II) chloride →

   copper + zinc chloride

2. The law of conservation of mass states that matter cannot be created or destroyed by a chemical change. Therefore, the total mass of the substances that exist before a chemical reaction is equal to the total mass of the substances after the reaction.

3. **a.** This reaction says that 2 atoms of sodium react with 2 molecules of water to form 2 formula units of sodium hydroxide and 1 molecule of hydrogen.
   **b.** This reaction says that 1 formula unit of calcium carbonate reacts with 2 formula units of hydrogen chloride to form 1 molecule of carbon dioxide, 1 formula unit of calcium chloride, and 1 molecule of water.

4. **a.** This equation is not balanced because the number of H atoms on both sides of the equation is different. The reactants contain 4 H atoms, whereas the products contain 6 H atoms. The balanced equation follows.
   $N_2 + 3H_2 \rightarrow 2NH_3$
   **b.** This equation is not balanced in $SO_4$ ions nor in H atoms. The balanced equation follows.
   $Ca(OH)_2 + H_2SO_4 \rightarrow CaSO_4 + 2H_2O$
   **c.** This equation is balanced, with 4 C, 4 H, and 10 O on both sides of the equation.

5. **a.** $2NaCl \rightarrow 2Na + Cl_2$
   **b.** $3Ti + 2N_2 \rightarrow Ti_3N_4$
   **c.** $2Al + 3ZnCl_2 \rightarrow 2AlCl_3 + 3Zn$

6. **a.** aluminum + oxygen → aluminum oxide
   **b.** $Al + O_2 \rightarrow Al_2O_3$
   **c.** $4Al + 3O_2 \rightarrow 2Al_2O_3$

7. An endothermic reaction absorbs energy as the reaction proceeds, whereas an exothermic reaction releases energy.

8. **a.** $HClO_4$ is molecular because all of the elements are nonmetals. **b.** $NH_4NO_3$ is ionic because it is made up of the polyatomic ions and nitrate ions. **c.** $Na_2S$ is ionic because Na is a metal and S is a nonmetal. **d.** HBr is molecular because both elements are nonmetals.

9. **a.** $HClO_4$ contains 1 $H^+$ and 1 $ClO_4^-$.
   **b.** $NH_4NO_3$ contains 1 $NH_4^+$ and 1 $NO_3^-$.
   **c.** $Na_2S$ contains 2 $Na^+$ and 1 $S^{2-}$.
   **d.** HBr contains 1 $H^+$ and 1 $Br^-$.

10. **a.** Reaction is a decomposition: 1 compound breaks down to produce 2 new compounds.
    **b.** This reaction is a single replacement, in which the chlorine replaces the bromine in the compound, forming a new compound and elemental bromine.
    **c.** This reaction is a direct combination or synthesis, in which two elements combine to form a compound.
    **d.** This reaction is a double replacement, in which two compounds exchange their ions to form two new compounds.

11. **a.** $CaCO_3 \rightarrow CaO + CO_2$
    **b.** $2KBr + Cl_2 \rightarrow 2KCl + Br_2$
    **c.** $Sn + O_2 \rightarrow SnO_2$
    **d.** $Zn(NO_3)_2 + H_2S \rightarrow ZnS + 2HNO_3$

12. **a.** $N_2 + 3H_2 \rightarrow 2NH_3$
    **b.** $2SO_2 + O_2 \rightarrow 2SO_3$
    **c.** $2H_2 + O_2 \rightarrow 2H_2O$
    **d.** $4Fe + 3O_2 \rightarrow 2Fe_2O_3$

13. A catalyst is a substance that increases the rate of reaction without itself being permanently altered.

14. **a.** $2KClO_3 \rightarrow 2KCl + 3O_2$
    **b.** $2CuO \rightarrow 2Cu + O_2$
    **c.** $2NO \rightarrow N_2 + O_2$
    **d.** $2HI \rightarrow H_2 + I_2$

15. **a.** Because copper is more reactive than zinc, copper will replace zinc in a single replacement reaction. This reaction does go as written. **b.** Lithium is more reactive than sodium, so sodium cannot replace lithium in a compound. This reaction does not go as written. **c.** Because lithium is more reactive than sodium, this reaction does go as written. **d.** Because bromine is more reactive than iodine, bromine will replace iodine in a compound. This reaction does go as written.

16. Double replacement reactions go as written if one of the products is removed. **a.** This reaction goes as written because a product, $CaCO_3$, forms a white precipitate. **b.** This reaction does not go because all four of the ions remain dissolved in aqueous solution. **c.** This reaction forms water as a product, removing $H^+$ and $OH^-$ from solution. **d.** All of these ions remain in solution, so the reaction does not go as written.

17. **a.** $(NH_4)_2CO_3(aq) + CaCl_2(aq) \rightarrow$
    $CaCO_3(s) + 2NH_4Cl(aq)$
    **c.** $2KOH(aq) + H_2SO_4(aq) \rightarrow$
    $K_2SO_4(aq) + 2H_2O(l)$

**18. a.** $Ca^{2+}(aq) + CO_3^{2-}(aq) \rightarrow CaCO_3(s)$
   **b.** $Ag^+(aq) + Cl^-(aq) \rightarrow AgCl(s)$
   **c.** $Zn(s) + 2Ag^+(aq) \rightarrow Zn^{2+}(aq) + 2Ag(s)$
   **d.** $Ba^{2+}(aq) + SO_4^{2-}(aq) \rightarrow BaSO_4(s)$

**19.** The spectator ions are all of the ions in the molecular formula that cancel out of the ionic formula. **a.** $Na^+$ and $Br^-$; **b.** $Na^+$ and $NO_3^-$; **c.** $NO_3^-$; **d.** $H^+$ and $Cl^-$

**Page 229, Content Mastery**

**20.** nitrogen gas + hydrogen gas → (ammonia)

**21.** potassium hydroxide + sulfuric acid → ?
   potassium hydroxide + sulfuric acid →
                  potassium sulfate + water
   $2KOH(aq) + H_2SO_4(aq) \rightarrow K_2SO_4(aq) + 2H_2O(l)$
   This reaction follows the general form for double replacement reactions.
   AB + CD → AD + BC.

**22.** $2OH^-(aq) + 2H^+(aq) \rightarrow 2H_2O(l)$

**23.** The law of conservation of mass states that matter cannot be created or destroyed in a chemical reaction. Thus, the complete reaction of 870.6 g of reactants must produce 870.6 g of products for any reaction.

**24.** $135.0 \text{ g Al} \times \dfrac{1 \text{ mol Al}}{26.98 \text{ g Al}} \times \dfrac{3 \text{ mol H}_2\text{SO}_4}{2 \text{ mol Al}} =$
                  $7.506 \text{ mol H}_2\text{SO}_4$

**25.** hydrogen gas + chlorine gas → ?
   $H_2(g) + Cl_2(g) \rightarrow 2HCl(l)$
   This follows the general form for a direct combination or synthesis reaction.
   A + B → AB

**26.** calcium + phosphoric acid → ?
   $3Ca(s) + 2H_3PO_4(aq) \rightarrow Ca_3(PO_4)_2(aq) + 3H_2(g)$

**27.** An endothermic reaction absorbs energy. If energy is listed as a reactant, the reaction is endothermic. If energy is listed as a product, however, the reaction is exothermic. Reaction **b** is endothermic; the rest are exothermic.

**28.** Exothermic reactions are sources of heat. Reactions **a**, **c**, and **d** release energy and, therefore, are exothermic.

**29.** magnesium metal + nitric acid → ?
   $Mg(s) + 2HNO_3(aq) \rightarrow Mg(NO_3)_2(aq) + H_2(g)$
   This follows the general form for a single replacement reaction.
   A + BC → AC + B

**30.** paraffin + oxygen → carbon dioxide + water
   $C_{25}H_{52}(s) + 38O_2(g) \rightarrow 25CO_2(g) + 26H_2O(g)$

**31.** aluminum chloride $\xrightarrow{\text{electrolysis}}$ ?
   $2AlCl_3(l) + \text{energy} \rightarrow 2Al(s) + 3Cl_2(g)$

This reaction follows the general form for a decomposition reaction.
AB → A + B

**32.** silver metal + hydrochloric acid → ? $(s)$
   $2Ag(s) + 2HCl(aq) \rightarrow 2AgCl(s) + H_2(g)$

**Page 229, Concept Mastery**

**33. *Concept:*** *Decomposition reactions.*
   *Solution:*  Fish breathe oxygen gas dissolved in the water. They do not decompose the water into hydrogen and oxygen.

**34. *Concept:*** *Balancing equations.*
   *Solution:*  Even though the student has balanced the number of atoms of each element, the student did not balance the equation correctly. In adding the subscript 2, the student changed the chemical composition of the product to $MgO_2$, which does not exist. The correct product is MgO. In balancing equations, adjust the coefficients that indicate stoichiometry. Do not change the subscripts. The correct equation is $2Mg + O_2 \rightarrow 2MgO$.

**35. *Concept:*** *Formulas represent reality.*
   *Solution:*  The hydrogen is incorrectly represented. There is a distinction between $H_4$ and $2H_2$. The student has represented $H_4$. The correct representation is shown in Figure 9-4.

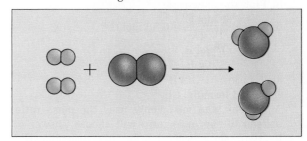

**Figure 9-4**

**36. *Concept:*** *Balancing equations.*
   *Solution:*  The formula for the product, $Zn2C_2H_3O_2$, is incorrect. Equations cannot be balanced by writing coefficients in the middle of a formula. The student is using a mechanical approach and does not realize the meaning of the formula as representing a chemical entity. The convention for showing 2 units of $C_2H_3O_2$ is to put the unit in parentheses and put a subscript 2 after the closing parenthesis. When the

product is correctly written as $Zn(C_2H_3O_2)_2$, the equation is balanced.

37. **Concept:** *Balancing equations.*
    **Solution:** The student probably added 2 (the co-efficient for silver nitrate) plus 2 (the coefficient for silver chloride) to get 4. The student forgot to add in the coefficients for the calcium chloride and for the calcium nitrate, both of which are 1. When there is only 1 molecule of a substance in the balanced equation, the coefficient 1 is not written but understood. The correct sum of the coefficients is $1 + 2 + 2 + 1 = 6$.

## Page 229, Cumulative Review

38. **c.** Iron oxide is incorrect. Iron can form 2 ions, $Fe^{2+}$ and $Fe^{3+}$. The correct name of compound **c** is iron(II) oxide. The others are correct.

39. **d.** There are 2 atoms of chlorine in each molecule of calcium chloride: $CaCl_2$. There is only 1 atom of magnesium in a molecule of magnesium oxide: $MgO$. The other formulas are correct.

40. **c.** The mass of $Cu = 85.78 - 60.28 = 25.50$ g

$$25.50 \text{ g} \times \frac{1 \text{ mol}}{63.540 \text{ g}} = 0.4013 \text{ mol Cu}$$

41. **e.** The atomic number gives the number of protons in the nucleus. In a neutral atom, the number of protons equals the number of electrons.

42. **b.** Find the mole ratio.

$$6.0 \text{ g C} \times \frac{1 \text{ mol C}}{12 \text{ g C}} = 0.50 \text{ mol C}$$

$$1.0 \text{ g H} \times \frac{1 \text{ mol H}}{1.0 \text{ g H}} = 1.0 \text{ mol H}$$

mole ratio = 1 C/2 H
empirical formula: $CH_2$
A student who mistakenly uses the mass ratio instead of the mole ratio will choose answer **c**. Reinforce the concept that formulas depend on the relative number of moles, not the relative mass.

43. Assume a sample of 100 g.

$$49.4 \text{ g K} \times \frac{1 \text{ mol K}}{39.1 \text{ g K}} = 1.26 \text{ mol K}$$

$$20.2 \text{ g S} \times \frac{1 \text{ mol S}}{32.1 \text{ g S}} = 0.629 \text{ mol S}$$

$$30.4 \text{ g O} \times \frac{1 \text{ mol O}}{16.0 \text{ g O}} = 1.90 \text{ mol O}$$

mole ratio = 2 K/1 S/3 O
empirical formula: $K_2SO_3$

44. The mass of 1.0 mol of calcium phosphate is the sum of the masses of all of the atoms in the molecule.

$Ca_3(PO_4)_2$: $3(40) + 2(31) + 8(16) = 310$ g

45. $10 \text{ mol H}_2O \times \dfrac{6.02 \times 10^{23} \text{ molec.}}{\text{mol}} \times \dfrac{3 \text{ atoms}}{\text{molec.}} =$
    $180.6 \times 10^{23} \text{ atoms} = 1.8 \times 10^{25} \text{ atoms}$

46. A substance that has equal numbers of C and H atoms has a mole ratio of 1 C/1 H. Therefore, the empirical formula is CH. The empirical formula mass for CH is $12.0 + 1.0 = 13$ g. Since the molecular mass, 78 g, is six times the empirical formula mass, 13 g, there are six formula units in the molecular formula: $C_6H_6$.

47. The 2 chlorine isotopes have the same atomic number because they have the same number of protons in the nucleus. They are both chlorines, after all. They also have the same number of electrons. They are different isotopes because they have different atomic masses due to different numbers of neutrons in the nucleus.

48. $1 \text{ atom Ag} \times \dfrac{\text{mol}}{6.02 \times 10^{23} \text{ atoms}} \times \dfrac{108 \text{ g}}{1 \text{ mol}} =$
    $17.9 \times 10^{-23} \text{ g} = 1.79 \times 10^{-22} \text{ g}$

49. Equal volumes of all gases at STP contain the same number of moles, and hence the same number of molecules. Therefore, $20.00 \text{ dm}^3$ of carbon dioxide contains the same number of molecules as $20.00 \text{ dm}^3$ of chlorine gas at the same temperature and pressure.

50. The bowl of cereal and fruit is a mixture because the constituents are not combined in a definite proportion, as they are in a compound. Also, the constituents retain their individual properties and can be separated by physical means.

51. Specific heat is the number of joules required to raise 1.00 gram of the substance by 1°C. The specific heat of water is 4.2 J/g–°C. The heat lost by the water ($H_w$) equals the heat gained by the metal ($H_m$).
    $H_w = (4.2 \text{ J/g–°C}) (200 \text{ g}) (80.0°C - 75.0°C)$
    $\quad\quad = (4.2 \text{ J/g–°C}) (200 \text{ g}) (5°C)$
    $\quad\quad = 4200 \text{ J} = H_m$
    Specific heat metal =
    $$\frac{4200 \text{ J}}{(200 \text{ g}) (75°C - 20°C)} = \frac{4200 \text{ J}}{(200 \text{ g}) (55°C)} =$$
    $$0.382 \text{ J/g–°C}$$

## Page 230, Critical Thinking

52. The production of smog is a two-step process. In the first step, the automobile engine produces enough heat for the nitrogen and oxygen in the air to combine.
    $N_2(g) + O_2(g) + \text{heat} \rightarrow 2NO(g)$
    Sunlight provides the energy to make the reddish-brown product.

$2NO(g) + O_2(g) + \text{sunlight} \rightarrow 2NO_2(g)$
Since both of these reactions have a form of energy on the left side of the equation, they are both endothermic.

**53.** Souring milk and burning paper are both chemical changes in which an intrinsic property (odor or color) changes. Grinding limestone is a physical change.

**54.** These compounds that form ions in water are water soluble. That does not mean that all water-soluble compounds form ions in water.

**55. a.** double replacement; **b.** decomposition or analysis; **c.** synthesis; **d.** single replacement

**56.** Most decomposition reactions are endothermic, requiring energy to go as written. If they were exothermic, compounds would be unstable, breaking down spontaneously.

**Page 230, Challenge Problems**

**57. a.** $Zn(s) + 2HCl(aq) \rightarrow ZnCl_2(aq) + H_2(g)$
This single replacement reaction does occur because zinc is more active than hydrogen.
**b.** $Ba(NO_3)_2(aq) + Na_2SO_4(aq) \rightarrow$
$$BaSO_4(s) + 2NaNO_3(aq)$$
This double replacement reaction does occur because a precipitate is formed.
**c.** $AgNO_3(aq) + KCl(aq) \rightarrow AgCl(s) + KNO_3(aq)$
This double replacement reaction does occur because a precipitate is formed.
**d.** $NH_4Cl + NaC_2H_3O_2(aq) \rightarrow NaCl(aq) +$
$$NH_4C_2H_3O_2(aq)$$
This double replacement reaction does not go

because there is no gas, water, or precipitate formed, so there is nothing to pull the reaction to completion.
**e.** $Mg(s) + H_2SO_4 \rightarrow MgSO_4(s) + H_2(g)$
This single replacement reaction occurs because magnesium is more active than hydrogen.

**58. a.** sodium carbonate$(s)$ + hydrochloric acid$(aq)$
$\rightarrow$ carbon dioxide$(g)$ + water$(l)$ +
$$\text{sodium chloride}(aq)$$
$Na_2CO_3(s) + 2HCl(aq) \rightarrow$
$$CO_2(g) + H_2O(l) + 2NaCl(aq)$$
**b.** $4.00 \times 10^{23} \, Na_2CO_3 \times \dfrac{2HCl}{Na_2CO_3} =$
$$8.00 \times 10^{23} \, HCl$$
**c.** $4.00 \times 10^{23} \, Na_2CO_3 \times \dfrac{1 \, mol}{6.02 \times 10^{23}} =$
$$0.67 \, mol \, Na_2CO_3$$
$8.00 \times 10^{23} \, HCl \times \dfrac{1 \, mol}{6.02 \times 10^{23}} = 1.33 \, mol \, HCl$
**d.** $Na_2CO_3$: $2(23.0) + 12.0 + 3(16.0) = 106$ g
$10.0 \, g \, Na_2CO_3 \times \dfrac{1 \, mol \, Na_2CO_3}{106 \, g \, Na_2CO_3} \times \dfrac{2 \, mol \, HCl}{1 \, mol \, Na_2CO_3}$
$$\times \dfrac{36.5 \, g \, HCl}{1 \, mol \, HCl} = 6.89 \, g \, HCl$$

**59. a.** Zinc is less active than sodium, so no reaction occurs. For **b, c,** and **d,** write the molecular equation, balance it, write the ionic equation, and cancel the spectator ions from both sides of the equation.
**b.** $2Al(s) + 3Fe^{2+}(aq) \rightarrow 2Al^{3+}(aq) + 3Fe(s)$
**c.** $Ag^+(aq) + Cl^-(aq) \rightarrow AgCl(s)$
**d.** $NH_4Cl(s) + OH^-(aq) \rightarrow$
$$NH_3(g) + H_2O(l) + Cl^-(aq)$$

# The Mathematics of Chemical Equations

## Chapter Planning Guide

| Text Section | Labs (Lab Manual) and Demonstrations (TE) | Supplementary Materials (Teacher's Resource Book) |
|---|---|---|
| **10-1** The Importance of Mathematics in Chemistry, p. 233<br><br>**10-2** Coefficients and Relative Volumes of Gases, pp. 234-238 | Demo 10-1: Changing a Recipe, p. TG-160<br>Lab 15: Relating Moles to Coefficients of a Chemical Equation | Transparency Master: The Mole Diagram (from Chapter 8), p. 8-2<br>Stoichiometry Problems: Interpreting Equation Coefficients as Numbers of Molecules, p. SP-39<br>Stoichiometry Problems: Interpreting Equation Coefficients as Moles, p. SP-41<br>Stoichiometry Problems: Interpreting Equation Coefficients as Gas Volumes, p. SP-43<br>Concept Mastery: Avogadro's Hypothesis, p. CM-14<br>Concept Mastery: Mole-Mole and Mole-Particle Problems, p. CM-15 |
| **Career** Agricultural Chemist, pp. 237 | | |
| **10-3** Mass-Mass Relationships, pp. 239-243 | Lab 16: Mole and Mass Relationships<br>Lab 17: Mass-Mass Relationships in Reactions | Transparency Master: The Expanded Mole Diagram, p. 10-1<br>Transparency Master: An Expanded Mole Diagram of a Sample Problem, p. 10-2<br>Stoichiometry Problems: The Expanded Mole Diagram, p. SP-45<br>Stoichiometry Problems: Mass-Mass Problems, p. SP-46<br>Concept Mastery: Mass-Mass Problems, p. CM-16 |
| **10-4** Mixed Mass-Volume-Particle Relationships, pp. 243-249 | | Stoichiometry Problems: Mass-Volume Problems, p. SP-48<br>Stoichiometry Problems: Molecule-Mass-Volume Problems, p. SP-50<br>Non-SI Supplementary Problems, p. 10-7 |

| Text Section | Labs (Lab Manual) and Demonstrations (TE) | Supplementary Materials (Teacher's Resource Book) |
|---|---|---|
| **10-5** Limiting Reactant Problems, pp. 249-252 | Demo 10-2: Making Cookies, p. TG-160 | Open-Ended Demonstration: Limiting Quantities, p. 10-3<br>Stoichiometry Problems: Limiting Reactant Problems, p. SP-55<br>Review Activity: The Mathematics of Chemical Equations, p. 10-5<br>Practice Problems, p. 10-6<br>Concept Mastery: Limiting Reactant Problems, p. CM-17 |
| | | Test—Form A, p. AT-36<br>Alternate Test—Form B, p. BT-36 |

☐ Core   ☐ Advanced   ☐ Optional

## Chapter Overview

In Chapter 8, we discussed one aspect of stoichiometry—quantitative relationships derived from chemical formulas. In Chapter 10, we introduce another aspect of stoichiometry—quantitative relationships derived from balanced chemical equations. The importance of reaction stoichiometry in the laboratory and in industry is emphasized. Then we discuss the molar volume of a gas and its usefulness in solving stoichiometry problems involving gases.

The remainder of the chapter focuses upon solving various types of reaction stoichiometry problems. The five types of problems described are: particle-particle, mole-mole, volume-volume, mass-mass, and mixed mass-volume-particle problems. In the last section we move from these theoretical stoichiometry problems to real laboratory situations by presenting the concepts of limiting reactant and excess reactant.

## Chapter Objectives

After students have completed this chapter, they will be able to:

1. Derive quantitative information about reactants and products in a chemical reaction.   *10-1* to *10-4*

2. Solve problems based upon mass-mass, volume-volume, and mass-volume relationships in equations.   *10-2* to *10-4*

3. Determine the limiting reactant when given data about reacting substances.   *10-5*

## Teaching Suggestions

**10-1 The Importance of Mathematics in Chemistry, p. 233, and**

**10-2 Coefficients and Relative Volumes of Gases, pp. 234-238**

| Planning Guide | |
|---|---|
| Labs (Lab Manual) and Demonstrations (TE) | Supplementary Materials (Teacher's Resource Book) |
| Demo 10-1: Changing a Recipe, p. TG-160<br>Lab 15: Relating Moles to Coefficients of a Chemical Equation | Transparency Master: The Mole Diagram (from Chapter 8), p. 8-2<br>Stoichiometry Problems: Interpreting Equation Coefficients as Numbers of Molecules, p. SP-39<br>Stoichiometry Problems: Interpreting Equation Coefficients as Moles, p. SP-41<br>Stoichiometry Problems: Interpreting Equation Coefficients as Gas Volumes, p. SP-43<br>Concept Mastery: Avogadro's Hypothesis, p. CM-14<br>Concept Mastery: Mole-Mole and Mole-Particle Problems, p. CM-15 |

■ Review the meaning of the mole and review the Transparency Master "The Mole Diagram" introduced in Chapter 8. Give the students a few sample conversion problems to check their understanding of the mole concept as it applies to chemical formulas. Emphasize the importance of quantitative information to the chemist. Explain that quantitative techniques are needed in order for the chemist to be able to control reactions and ensure the maximum yield of a product. This chapter shows how quantitative information may be obtained from chemical equations. Do Demonstration 10-1, "Changing a Recipe," to relate the change of a recipe to calculations involving the coefficients of a balanced chemical equation.

■ Point out to the students that the coefficients of a balanced chemical equation can express three things about the quantities of reactants and products in a reaction: (1) the relative number of particles, (2) the relative number of moles, and (3) the relative volume of gases when all of the gases are at the same temperature and pressure.

■ Once the students understand the molar interpretation of coefficients, assign Laboratory 15, "Relating Moles to Coefficients of a Chemical Equation." In this laboratory, the students experimentally determine the ratio of moles of a reactant to moles of product for a chemical reaction. This ratio is then related to the coefficients of a chemical equation.

■ Introduce Avogadro's hypothesis and tie it in with the mole concept. Ask the students to inspect the balanced equations in Section 10-2 that include at least two gases. Ask them to justify, using Avogadro's hypothesis, the fact that the coefficients express the relative number of particles, the relative number of moles, and finally, the relative volumes of the gases involved.

■ **Application.** It may be helpful to point out to your students that the questions answered by stoichiometry calculations are not as unfamiliar to them as they may think. How much do I need? How much do I want? How much will I get? We ask ourselves these questions quite frequently. How much candy must your club sell to raise $1000 if a 1-dollar sale yields $.32 profit? How many cases of soda must be bought for a party of 30 people, if each person drinks three cans?

■ **Concept Mastery.** Students often fail to see the physical reality of what equations represent and therefore fail to solve problems correctly. To compensate for this lack of understanding, students frequently memorize how to solve problems involving moles without understanding what they are actually doing and why they are doing it.

The Concept Mastery worksheet "Avogadro's Hypothesis" (TRB) can help students to visualize the relationship between the particles and the volume of a gas. You may wish to use Concept Mastery question 27 (chapter-end question) to check your students' understanding of the volume interpretation of equations

involving gases at STP. If your students understand that an equation can represent moles, particles, and volumes at constant conditions of temperature and pressure, they will not set up the problem as shown in question 27, which contains unnecessary steps.

The Concept Mastery worksheet "Mole-Mole and Mole-Particle Problems" (TRB) can be used to test the students' understanding of these kinds of problems.

## 10-3 Mass-Mass Relationships, pp. 239-243

| Planning Guide | |
| --- | --- |
| Labs (Lab Manual) and Demonstrations (TE) | Supplementary Materials (Teacher's Resource Book) |
| Lab 16: Mole and Mass Relationships<br>Lab 17: Mass-Mass Relationships in Reactions | Transparency Master: The Expanded Mole Diagram, p. 10-1<br>Transparency Master: An Expanded Mole Diagram of a Sample Problem, p. 10-2<br>Stoichiometry Problems: The Expanded Mole Diagram, p. SP-45<br>Stoichiometry Problems: Mass-Mass Problems, p. SP-46<br>Concept Mastery: Mass-Mass Problems, p. CM-16 |

■ Introduce the discussion of mass-mass relationships by doing Laboratory 16, "Mole and Mass Relationships." This lab illustrates the usefulness of a balanced equation in determining mass relationships among reactants and products. Refer to text Figure 10-9, which summarizes the strategy for solving the problems posed in Laboratory 16 and other mass-mass problems.

■ Instruct the students to use the expanded mole diagram to solve other mass-mass problems. Either leave the expanded mole diagram transparency on while students do the problems or pass out individual copies of the expanded mole diagram. The Stoichiometry Problems worksheet "Mass-Mass Problems" provides a number of such problems from which to choose. The students should understand the reasons for all of the steps illustrated in the expanded mole diagram. Check the students at each step for their understanding of the basic theory involved. This will help them to solve problems of the mixed mass-volume type introduced in the next section.

■ Assign Laboratory 17, "Mass-Mass Relationships in Reactions," to emphasize the importance of mass-mass calculations in the chemistry laboratory.

■ **Concept Mastery.** Students often have difficulty with multi-step stoichiometry problems, especially if they have simply memorized the solution procedures.

The Concept Mastery worksheet "Mass-Mass Problems" (TRB) can help students to visualize the equations in terms of particles and macroscopic quantities.

## 10-4 Mixed Mass-Volume-Particle Relationships, pp. 243-249

| Planning Guide | |
| --- | --- |
| **Labs (Lab Manual) and Demonstrations (TE)** | **Supplementary Materials (Teacher's Resource Book)** |
| | Stoichiometry Problems: Mass-Volume Problems, p. SP-48 Stoichiometry Problems: Molecule-Mass-Volume Problems, p. SP-50 Non-SI Supplementary Problems, p. 10-7 |

■ Explain to the class how the expanded mole diagram can be used to solve various types of problems including mass-particle, volume-mass, mole-volume, particle-volume, etc. Use the expanded mole diagram to show students the general strategies for solving these types of problems. Point out that it is not always necessary to change the given quantities to moles. For example, if volumes of gases are given in the problem and temperature and pressure do not change, the solution may be obtained directly from the coefficients in the equation. This is often the case since volumes of gases are more easily obtained than their masses.

■ Before asking students to actually determine answers to various problems, list several problems on the board and ask the students to determine the steps needed to solve the problem. The Stoichiometry Problems worksheets "Mass-Volume Problems" and "Molecule-Mass-Volume Problems" provide a wide assortment of problems from which to choose. Ask other students if there are alternate routes to solve the problem. Then, calculate the answers.

■ **Concept Mastery.** Too often students memorize a set procedure to solve chemistry problems and use it without thinking. Concept Mastery question 28 (chapter-end problem) includes a correct setup for solving the problem. Ask your students if they can explain the purpose or significance of each step indicated. It is important that they note that 1 mole of a gas at STP contains $6.02 \times 10^{23}$ molecules and occupies 22.4 dm$^3$. Therefore, $6.023 \times 10^{23}/22.4$ dm$^3$ is a necessary and a correct conversion factor. However, in Concept Mastery question 29, the students must realize that water is a liquid at STP, so 22.4 dm$^3$ of water vapor will condense and form a very small volume of liquid. If a student can explain the strategy for solving these two problems, he or she has a good understanding of the principles involved.

## 10-5 Limiting Reactant Problems, pp. 249-252

| Planning Guide | |
| --- | --- |
| **Labs (Lab Manual) and Demonstrations (TE)** | **Supplementary Materials (Teacher's Resource Book)** |
| Demo 10-2: Making Cookies, p. TG-160 | Open-Ended Demonstration: Limiting Quantities, p. 10-3 Stoichiometry Problems: Limiting Reactant Problems, p. SP-55 Review Activity: The Mathematics of Chemical Equations, p. 10-5 Practice Problems, p. 10-6 Concept Mastery: Limiting Reactant Problems, p. CM-17 |

■ Point out that the law of definite proportions limits how much product or products are yielded by a chemical reaction. Therefore, at the conclusion of a chemical reaction, an excess of a reactant may be found together with the product or products. Perform Demonstration 10-2, "Making Cookies." This demonstration helps students to understand the concept of limiting reactant by first focusing upon more familiar examples before moving on to examples involving chemicals. Ask the students to identify the reactants in excess and the limiting reactants in all of the examples discussed in the demonstration. Explain why it is necessary or advantageous to have a reactant in excess.

■ Do the Open-Ended Demonstration "Limiting Quantities." This demonstration can serve as a very good transition from limiting reactants of familiar materials to limiting reactants involving chemicals. Students can view the reaction of various amounts of magnesium with a constant amount of hydrochloric acid and compare the amounts of hydrogen gas produced.

■ Assign the Stoichiometry Problems worksheet "Limiting Reactant Problems" to provide an assortment of problems for the students to solve.

■ For a review of all of the various problems introduced in this chapter, use the Practice Problems (TRB) and the Review Activity "The Mathematics of Chemical Equations."

■ **Applications.** You may want to point out that limiting reactant applies to areas outside the chemistry laboratory. The distance you travel in an automobile is limited by the amount of gas in the car or the amount of money in your pocket. The amount of weight you gain depends (at least in part) on the amount of food you eat.

10

■ **Concept Mastery.** Very few students are able to solve limiting reactant problems when they are retested several weeks after they have been introduced to this material. This is probably because they do not fully understand the physical significance of limiting reactants. They fail to see why they must first determine which is the limiting reactant before calculating the amount of product theoretically produced. The Concept Mastery worksheet "Limiting Reactant Problems" (TRB) will help students to visualize the quantities involved. You may want to assign Concept Mastery question 31 (chapter-end question) to check your students' understanding of the principle of a limiting reactant.

# Demonstrations

## 10-1 Changing a Recipe

**Overview:** In this demonstration, you show students how to change the quantities in a list of ingredients for a three-bean-salad recipe for one person into quantities that will produce enough salad to feed a larger number of people.

**Materials:** ingredients list for three-bean salad to feed one person, written on a transparency; ingredients list for three-bean salad to feed 200 people, written on another transparency; overhead projector.

**Advance Preparation:** Write out the following two lists of ingredients on separate transparencies: three-bean salad for one person: 72 red beans (canned), 72 French-cut green beans (canned), 72 yellow wax beans (canned), 25 mL of salad oil, 25 mL of vinegar, ⅛ cup of chopped onion, ⅛ cup of sugar; three-bean salad for 200 persons: 100 gross of red beans (canned), 100 gross of French-cut green beans (canned), 100 gross of yellow wax beans (canned), 5 L of salad oil, 5 L of vinegar, 25 cups of chopped onion, 25 cups of sugar.

**Procedure:** 1. Show the class the ingredients list for three-bean salad for one person. (You might even want to consider making this salad in front of the class!) 2. Ask the students to work in small groups to develop an ingredients list for a recipe that would feed 200 people, and that would make use of larger units (liters instead of milliliters, gross of beans instead of number of beans). 3. Have the members of one group present their list to the class and discuss it. 4. Show your previously prepared transparency that contains the list for the recipe for 200 people, and have students compare it with the list prepared by their group. 5. Relate the technique of changing a recipe to working with coefficients in a balanced equation.

On the board write out the balanced equation for the formation of ammonia from hydrogen and nitrogen: $3H_2 + N_2 \rightarrow 2NH_3$. Ask students to tell you how many molecules of nitrogen gas would be needed to react completely with 6 molecules of hydrogen gas. Relate this process of adapting an equation to the doubling of a recipe. 6. Ask students to predict how many molecules of nitrogen gas would be needed to react with $18.1 \times 10^{23}$ molecules of hydrogen gas. Mention that it is more convenient to use moles in this case, and have students calculate the number of moles involved. 7. Tell students that coefficients in an equation represent a ratio of reacting molecules or moles. 8. State Avogadro's hypothesis: Equal volumes of gases at the same temperature and pressure contain the same number of molecules. Explain that it can be stated another way: Equal numbers of gas molecules at the same temperature and pressure have the same volume. Thus, the coefficients in a balanced equation involving gases under those conditions can also represent a ratio of reacting gas volumes.

**Results:** The student ingredients lists should match your list. In step 5, 2 molecules of nitrogen would be needed. In step 6, $6.02 \times 10^{23}$ molecules (1 mole) of nitrogen would be needed.

## 10-2 Making Cookies

**Overview:** In this demonstration, you give students a listing of the ingredients needed to make one batch of 48 chocolate-chip cookies, as well as a listing of the quantities of ingredients actually available to make the cookies. You then ask the students to determine how many cookies could be made from the given amounts available. This is an interesting way to introduce the concept of a limiting reactant.

**Materials:** list of ingredients needed to make a batch of 48 cookies; list of available quantities of ingredients.

**Advance Preparation:** Prepare copies of the following lists of ingredients and of quantities available.

| Ingredients to Make 48 Cookies | Quantities Available |
|---|---|
| ½ cup (1 stick) butter | 10 sticks butter |
| ¼ cup brown sugar | 3 cups brown sugar |
| ½ cup sugar | 4¼ cups sugar |
| 1 teaspoon vanilla | one 2-ounce bottle vanilla |
| 1½ cups flour | 7½ cups flour |
| ½ teaspoon baking soda | 1.0-lb box baking soda |
| ½ teaspoon salt | 1 cup salt |
| 8 ounces chocolate chips | 4 pounds chocolate chips |

**Procedure:** 1. Give each small group of students a copy of the ingredients list for the cookies and a list of the quantities available to make the cookies. Have the students in each group decide how many cookies could be made from the quantities available. (You might have to give the groups some information on food conversion: 3 teaspoons = 1 tablespoon, 16 tablespoons = 1 cup, 16 ounces = 1 pound). Have students write their answer on a piece of paper, together with an explanation of how they arrived at it. 2. When all of the groups have turned in their answers, give the correct answer and the proper method for arriving at it. 3. Ask students to name the ingredient that limited the amount of cookies that could be made. Call this ingredient the limiting reactant. Discuss other limiting-reactant-type situations—for example: How many boy–girl couples could dance at the same time, given 10 boys and 12 girls? How many sandwiches could be made from 9 slices of bread, a large jar of peanut butter, and a large jar of jelly? 4. Ask students to determine which is the limiting reactant when 10 molecules of hydrogen gas are added to three molecules of nitrogen gas to make ammonia gas.

**Results:** The flour is the limiting reactant because the smallest number of batches—five—can be made using it (5 × 1.5 cups = 7.5 cups), whereas the other ingredients are all in excess. Thus, 5 batches × 48 cookies/batch = 240 cookies can be made. Ten dance couples and four sandwiches can be formed in step 3. In step 4, $N_2$ is the limiting reactant; $H_2$ is in excess since there are 10 molecules of it, one more than the number needed to react with the three molecules of $N_2$, according to the equation $N_2 + 3H_2 \rightarrow 2NH_3$, or $3N_2 + 9H_2 \rightarrow 6NH_3$.

## Answers to Questions

**Page 238**

1. The coefficients in a balanced equation can stand for moles, molecules, or formula units (depending on the substance). They can also stand for relative volumes of gases.

2. Coefficients represent relative volumes of gases if they are at the same temperature and pressure.

3. One mole of a gas has a volume of 22.4 $dm^3$ if the gas is at STP (0°C and 101.3 kPa).

4. It is not possible for 100 atoms of sodium to react with 100 molecules of chlorine. According to the balanced equation, 2 atoms of sodium react with 1 molecule of chlorine. Therefore, 100 atoms of sodium react with 50 molecules of chlorine.

5. **a.** The ratio of $H_2:O_2:H_2O$ is 2:1:2. Five moles of water is produced from 5 moles of $H_2$ and 2.5 moles of $O_2$.

   **b.** The ratio of $H_2$ to $O_2$ is 2:1. Therefore, 124 $dm^3$ of oxygen reacts with 248 $dm^3$ of hydrogen.

   **c.** The ratio of $O_2$ to $H_2O$ is 1:2. If 100 molecules of $O_2$ react with sufficient $H_2$, 200 molecules of water are produced.

**Page 242**

6. By using the coefficients in the balanced chemical equation to derive the appropriate mole ratio. Multiply by the ratio of the coefficients.

7. Mass and atoms are conserved in a balanced chemical equation.

8. The three steps needed to solve mass-mass problems are:
   (1) Change the given mass to moles.
   (2) Use the mole ratio from the equation to change moles of substance given to moles of substance sought.
   (3) Change moles of substance sought to mass.

**Page 243**

9. **a.** $23 \text{ g Na} \times \dfrac{1.0 \text{ mole Na}}{23 \text{ g Na}} = 1.0 \text{ mol Na}$

   **b.** 2 mol of Na produces 1 mol of $H_2$. Therefore, 1.0 mol Na will produce 0.50 mol $H_2$.

   **c.** $0.50 \text{ mol } H_2 \times \dfrac{2.02 \text{ g } H_2}{1.0 \text{ mol } H_2} = 1.0 \text{ g } H_2$

10. $29.4 \text{ g } H_2SO_4 \times \dfrac{1 \text{ mol } H_2SO_4}{98.1 \text{ g } H_2SO_4} \times \dfrac{1 \text{ mol } Ca(OH)_2}{1 \text{ mol } H_2SO_4} \times$

   $\dfrac{74.1 \text{ g } Ca(OH)_2}{1 \text{ mol } Ca(OH)_2} = 22.2 \text{ g } Ca(OH)_2$

11. $NaCl(aq) + AgNO_3(aq) \rightarrow NaNO_3(aq) + AgCl(s)$

   $8.50 \text{ g } AgNO_3 \times \dfrac{1 \text{ mol } AgNO_3}{170 \text{ g } AgNO_3} \times \dfrac{1 \text{ mol } AgCl}{1 \text{ mol } AgNO_3} \times$

   $\dfrac{143.5 \text{ g } AgCl}{1 \text{ mol } AgCl} = 7.18 \text{ g } AgCl$

**Page 249**

12. **a.** To find moles B from moles A requires 1 step.
    **b.** To find mass C from mass A requires 3 steps.
    **c.** To find molecules D from molecules B requires 1 step.
    **d.** To find volume C from mass B requires 3 steps.

13. A three-step alternative is:

   Mass A $\xrightarrow{1}$ moles A $\xrightarrow{2}$ molecules A $\xrightarrow{3}$ molecules C

14. $2.80 \text{ dm}^3 \text{ } NH_3 \times \dfrac{1 \text{ mol } NH_3}{22.4 \text{ dm}^3 \text{ } NH_3} \times \dfrac{2 \text{ mol } NH_4Cl}{2 \text{ mol } NH_3} \times$

   $\dfrac{53.5 \text{ g } NH_4Cl}{1 \text{ mol } NH_4Cl} = 6.69 \text{ g } NH_4Cl$

15. $3.27 \text{ g Zn} \times \dfrac{1 \text{ mol Zn}}{65.4 \text{ g Zn}} \times \dfrac{1 \text{ mol } H_2}{1 \text{ mol Zn}} \times \dfrac{22.4 \text{ dm}^3 \text{ } H_2}{1 \text{ mol } H_2} =$

   $1.12 \text{ dm}^3 \text{ } H_2$ at STP

16. $98.0 \text{ g } KClO_3 \times \dfrac{1 \text{ mol } KClO_3}{122.6 \text{ g } KClO_3} \times \dfrac{3 \text{ mol } O_2}{2 \text{ mol } KClO_3} \times$

   $\dfrac{22.4 \text{ dm}^3 \text{ } O_2}{1 \text{ mol } O_2} = 26.9 \text{ dm}^3 \text{ } O_2$

17. Use the first two steps of problem 16 to find moles of $O_2$. This equals 1.20 mol $O_2$.

10

$$1.20 \text{ mol } O_2 \times \frac{6.02 \times 10^{23} \text{ molec. } O_2}{1 \text{ mol } O_2} =$$
$$7.22 \times 10^{23} \text{ molec. } O_2$$

**Page 252**

**18.** The mole ratio $CH_4:O_2:CO_2:H_2O$ is 1:2:1:2.
 **a.** $O_2$ is the limiting reactant.
 **b.** 25 molecules of $CO_2$ are formed.
 **c.** 50 molecules of $H_2O$ are formed.
 **d.** $CH_4$ is in excess by 25 molecules.
**19. a.** $O_2$ is the limiting reactant.
 **b.** 3 moles of $CO_2$ is formed.
 **c.** 6 moles of $H_2O$ is formed.
 **d.** $CH_4$ is in excess by 5 moles.
**20. a.** $50.0 \text{ g } CH_4 \times \dfrac{1 \text{ mol } CH_4}{16.0 \text{ g } CH_4} = 3.13 \text{ mol } CH_4$

$$100 \text{ dm}^3 O_2 \times \frac{1 \text{ mol } O_2}{22.4 \text{ dm}^3 O_2} = 4.46 \text{ mol } O_2$$

In the comparison of the moles calculated to the mole ratio, $CH_4$ is in excess and $O_2$ is the limiting reactant.
 **b.** $4.46 \text{ mol } O_2 = 4.46 \text{ mol } H_2O$
$$4.46 \text{ mol } H_2O \times \frac{18.0 \text{ g } H_2O}{1 \text{ mol } H_2O} = 80.3 \text{ g } H_2O$$
 **c.** $4.46 \text{ mol } O_2 \times \dfrac{1 \text{ mol } CO_2}{2 \text{ mol } O_2} \times \dfrac{22.4 \text{ dm}^3 CO_2}{1 \text{ mol } CO_2} =$
$$50.0 \text{ dm}^3 CO_2$$
 **d.** $4.46 \text{ mol } O_2 \times \dfrac{1 \text{ mol } CH_4}{2 \text{ mol } O_2} = \dfrac{2.23 \text{ mol } CH_4}{\text{required}}$
$3.13 \text{ mol } CH_4 - 2.23 \text{ mol } CH_4 = 0.90 \text{ mol } CH_4 \text{ in excess}$
$0.90 \text{ mol } CH_4 \times \dfrac{16.0 \text{ g } CH_4}{1 \text{ mol } CH_4} = \dfrac{14.4 \text{ g } CH_4}{\text{in excess}}$

## Chapter Review    10

**Page 253, Content Review**

1. The mathematics of chemistry enables chemists to understand chemical changes better. In industry, it helps them to control the quantities of substances used in chemical reactions.

2. $0.6 \text{ mol } H_2O \times \dfrac{2 \text{ mol } H_2}{2 \text{ mol } H_2O} = 0.6 \text{ mol } H_2$

$0.6 \text{ mol } H_2O \times \dfrac{1 \text{ mol } O_2}{2 \text{ mol } H_2O} = 0.3 \text{ mol } O_2$

3. $500 \text{ dm}^3 NH_3 \times \dfrac{3 \text{ dm}^3 H_2}{2 \text{ dm}^3 NH_3} = 750 \text{ dm}^3 H_2 =$
$$7.5 \times 10^2 \text{ dm}^3 H_2$$

**4.** $2.2 \times 10^{20} \text{ molec. } SO_2 \times \dfrac{1 \text{ molec. } O_2}{2 \text{ molec. } SO_2} =$
$1.1 \times 10^{20} \text{ molec. } O_2 \times \dfrac{1 \text{ mol } O_2}{6.02 \times 10^{23} \text{ molec. } O_2} =$
$$1.8 \times 10^{-4} \text{ mol } O_2$$

**5.** Since all 1-mole samples of gases contain the same number of molecules, Avogadro's number, they must also have the same volumes under the same conditions. This follows from Avogadro's hypothesis, which says that equal volumes of gases at the same conditions have the same number of molecules. This volume at STP is $22.4 \text{ dm}^3$ and is called the molar volume.

**6. a.** If two samples of gases are at the same temperature and pressure and are made up of an equal number of molecules, the volumes are equal.
 **b.** The coefficients of gases in equations express the relative numbers of molecules of these gases and their relative volumes under the same conditions.

**7.** $? \text{ g } BaCl_2 = \dfrac{188 \text{ g } Al_2(SO_4)_3}{342 \text{ g/mol}} \times \dfrac{3 \text{ mol } BaCl_2}{1 \text{ mol } Al_2(SO_4)_3} \times$
$\dfrac{208.3 \text{ g } BaCl_2}{\text{mol } BaCl_2} = 343.5 \text{ g} \approx 344 \text{ g } BaCl_2$

**8.** $2CuO(s) \rightarrow 2Cu(s) + O_2(g)$
$? \text{ g } Cu = \dfrac{95.4 \text{ g } CuO}{79.5 \text{ g/mol}} \times \dfrac{2 \text{ mol } Cu}{2 \text{ mol } CuO} \times \dfrac{63.5 \text{ g } Cu}{\text{mol } Cu} =$
$$76.2 \text{ g } Cu$$
$? \text{ g } O_2 = \dfrac{95.4 \text{ g } CuO}{79.5 \text{ g/mol}} \times \dfrac{1 \text{ mol } O_2}{2 \text{ mol } CuO} \times \dfrac{32 \text{ g } O_2}{\text{mol } O_2} =$
$$19.2 \text{ g } O_2$$

**9.** $2KOH(aq) + H_2SO_4(aq) \rightarrow K_2SO_4(aq) + 2H_2O(l)$
$? \text{ g } K_2SO_4 = \dfrac{19.6 \text{ g } KOH}{56.1 \text{ g/mol}} \times \dfrac{1 \text{ mol } K_2SO_4}{2 \text{ mol } KOH} \times$
$\dfrac{174.2 \text{ g } K_2SO_4}{\text{mol } K_2SO_4} = 30.4 \text{ g } K_2SO_4$
$? \text{ g } H_2O = \dfrac{19.6 \text{ g } KOH}{56.1 \text{ g/mol}} \times \dfrac{2 \text{ mol } H_2O}{2 \text{ mol } KOH} \times \dfrac{18 \text{ g } H_2O}{\text{mol } H_2O} =$
$$6.29 \text{ g}$$

**10.** $4Fe(s) + 3O_2(g) \rightarrow 2Fe_2O_3(s)$
$? \text{ dm}^3 O_2 = \dfrac{15.0 \text{ g } Fe}{55.8 \text{ g/mol}} \times \dfrac{3 \text{ mol } O_2}{4 \text{ mol } Fe} \times \dfrac{22.4 \text{ dm}^3}{\text{mol}} =$
$$4.52 \text{ dm}^3$$

**11.** $4.52 \text{ dm}^3 O_2 \times \dfrac{1 \text{ mol}}{22.4 \text{ dm}^3} \times \dfrac{6.02 \times 10^{23} \text{ molecules}}{1 \text{ mol}} =$
$$1.21 \times 10^{23} \text{ molecules } O_2$$

**12.** $? \text{ dm}^3 NO_2 = \dfrac{9.6 \text{ g } Cu}{63.5 \text{ g/mol}} \times \dfrac{2 \text{ mol } NO_2}{1 \text{ mol } Cu} \times \dfrac{22.4 \text{ dm}^3}{\text{mol}}$
$$= 6.8 \text{ dm}^3$$

**13.** $? \text{ g FeS} = 100 \text{ cm}^3 \text{ H}_2\text{S} \times \dfrac{1 \text{ mol}}{22\,400 \text{ cm}^3} \times$

$\dfrac{1 \text{ mol FeS}}{1 \text{ mol H}_2\text{S}} \times \dfrac{87.8 \text{ g FeS}}{\text{mol FeS}} = 0.392 \text{ g FeS}$

**14. a.** The limiting reactant is HCl.

**b.** $? \text{ ZnCl}_2 \text{ molecules} = 100 \text{ molecules HCl} \times$

$\dfrac{1 \text{ molecule ZnCl}_2}{2 \text{ molecules HCl}} = 50$

**c.** $\text{H}_2 \text{ molecules} = 100 \text{ molecules HCl} \times$

$\dfrac{1 \text{ molecule H}_2}{2 \text{ molecules HCl}} = 50$

**d.** $100 \text{ molecules HCl} \times \dfrac{1 \text{ molecule Zn}}{2 \text{ molecules HCl}} =$

50 molecules Zn used

$100 - 50 = 50$ molecules Zn in excess

**15. a.** The limiting reactant is HCl.

**b.** $? \text{ g ZnCl}_2 = \dfrac{36.5 \text{ g HCl}}{36.5 \text{ g/mol}} \times \dfrac{1 \text{ mol ZnCl}_2}{2 \text{ mol HCl}} \times$

$\dfrac{136.4 \text{ g ZnCl}_2}{\text{mol}} = 68.2 \text{ g}$

**c.** $? \text{ dm}^3 \text{ H}_2 = \dfrac{36.5 \text{ g HCl}}{36.5 \text{ g/mol}} \times \dfrac{1 \text{ mol H}_2}{2 \text{ mol HCl}} \times$

$\dfrac{22.4 \text{ dm}^3}{\text{mol}} = 11.2 \text{ dm}^3$

**d.** $? \text{ g Zn} = \dfrac{36.5 \text{ g HCl}}{36.5 \text{ g/mol}} \times \dfrac{1 \text{ mol Zn}}{2 \text{ mol HCl}} \times \dfrac{65.4 \text{ g Zn}}{\text{mol}}$

$= 32.7 \text{ g Zn used}$

$73.0 - 32.7 = 40.3 \text{ g Zn in excess}$

**16.** First determine the limiting reactant.

$2.0 \text{ g H}_2 \times \dfrac{1 \text{ mol H}_2}{2.0 \text{ g H}_2} = 1.0 \text{ mol H}_2$

$10.0 \text{ g O}_2 \times \dfrac{1 \text{ mol O}_2}{32 \text{ g O}_2} = 0.31 \text{ mol O}_2$

The balanced equation requires ½ mole $\text{O}_2$ for every mole $\text{H}_2$. Therefore, $\text{O}_2$ is the limiting reactant.

$? \text{ H}_2\text{O} = 10.0 \text{ g O}_2 \times \dfrac{1 \text{ mol O}_2}{32.0 \text{ g O}_2} \times \dfrac{2 \text{ mol H}_2\text{O}}{1 \text{ mol O}_2} \times$

$\dfrac{18.0 \text{ g H}_2\text{O}}{1 \text{ mol H}_2\text{O}} = 11.3 \text{ g H}_2\text{O}$

**17.** $\text{H}_2$ is in excess.

$? \text{ g H}_2 = \dfrac{10.0 \text{ g O}_2}{32 \text{ g/mol}} \times \dfrac{2 \text{ mol H}_2}{1 \text{ mol O}_2} \times \dfrac{2 \text{ g H}_2}{\text{mol}} = 1.25 \text{ g}$

$2.0 - 1.25 = 0.75 \text{ g H}_2 \text{ in excess}$

**Page 254, Content Mastery**

**18.** $2.0 \text{ kg ore} \times 3.5\% \text{ SnO}_2 = 70 \text{ g SnO}_2$

$? \text{ g Sn} = 70 \text{ g SnO}_2 \times \dfrac{1 \text{ mol SnO}_2}{150.7 \text{ g SnO}_2} \times \dfrac{118.7 \text{ g Sn}}{1 \text{ mol Sn}}$

$= 55 \text{ g Sn}$

**19.** First, find the number of moles of $\text{SO}_2$:

$1.00 \times 10^6 \text{ g} \div 64.1 \text{ g/mol} = 1.56 \times 10^4 \text{ mol} =$

15.6 kmol

The ratio of $\text{SO}_2$ to $\text{O}_2$ in the reaction is 2:1, so $\text{SO}_2$ is the limiting reactant. The number of moles of $\text{H}_2\text{SO}_4$ produced is the same as the number of moles of $\text{SO}_2$, 15.6 kmol.

**20. a.** $1 \text{ mol C}_{25}\text{H}_{52} = 12(12.011) + 52(1.0079) =$

352.7 g

$? \text{ mol CO}_2 = \dfrac{25 \text{ mol CO}_2}{1 \text{ mol C}_{25}\text{H}_{52}} \times \dfrac{1 \text{ mol C}_{25}\text{H}_{52}}{352.7 \text{ g C}_{25}\text{H}_{52}} \times$

$23.4 \text{ g C}_{25}\text{H}_{52} = 1.66 \text{ mol CO}_2$

$? \text{ dm}^3 \text{ CO}_2 = 1.66 \text{ mol} \times 22.4 \text{ dm}^3/\text{mol} =$

$37.2 \text{ dm}^3 \text{ CO}_2$

**b.** $? \text{ mol H}_2\text{O} = \dfrac{26 \text{ mol H}_2\text{O}}{1 \text{ mol C}_{25}\text{H}_{52}} \times \dfrac{1 \text{ mol C}_{25}\text{H}_{52}}{352.7 \text{ g C}_{25}\text{H}_{52}} \times$

$23.4 \text{ g C}_{25}\text{H}_{52} = 1.72 \text{ mol H}_2\text{O}$

$? \text{ cm}^3 \text{ H}_2\text{O} = 1.72 \text{ mol H}_2\text{O} \times \dfrac{18.0 \text{ g H}_2\text{O}}{1 \text{ mol}} \times$

$\dfrac{1 \text{ cm}^3 \text{ H}_2\text{O}}{1 \text{ g H}_2\text{O}} = 31.2 \text{ cm}^3 \text{ H}_2\text{O}$

**21.** See Figure 10-1.

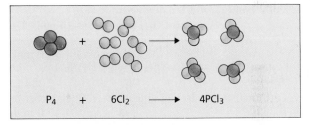

$P_4 \quad + \quad 6Cl_2 \quad \longrightarrow \quad 4PCl_3$

**Figure 10-1**

**22. a.** *2 moles HCl* reacting with 2 moles MgO: The mole ratio for HCl:MgO is 2:1. Therefore, the 2 moles of HCl will be used up reacting with just 1 mole of MgO.

**b.** *7 moles HCl* reacting with 5 moles MgO: The 7 moles of HCl will be used up reacting with 3.5 moles of MgO.

**c.** 4 grams HCl reacting with *2 grams MgO:* The mass ratio is $2 \text{ mol} \times 36.5 \text{ g/mol}$ HCl to $1 \text{ mol} \times 40.3 \text{ g/mol}$ MgO, or 1.8:1. Therefore, the 2:1 mass ratio given means the HCl is in excess and MgO is the limiting reactant.

**23.** The balanced equation is $2\text{H}_2 + \text{O}_2 \rightarrow 2\text{H}_2\text{O}$, so one water molecule is formed for each hydrogen molecule that reacts.

$? \text{ moles H}_2 = \dfrac{33.2 \text{ kg}}{2.016 \text{ g/mol}} = \dfrac{33.2 \times 10^3 \text{ g}}{2.016 \text{ g/mol}} =$

$1.65 \times 10^4 \text{ mol}$

**10**

? molecules = $1.65 \times 10^4$ mol $\times 6.02 \times 10^{23}$ molecules/mole = $9.93 \times 10^{27}$ molecules of water

24. The balanced equation is $C_3H_8 + 5O_2 \rightarrow 3CO_2 + 4H_2O$, so four water molecules are formed for each propane molecule.

? moles $C_3H_8$ = 188 g ÷ 44.096 g/mol = 4.26 mol $C_3H_8$

? moles $O_2$ = 185 dm³ $O_2 \times \dfrac{1 \text{ mol } O_2}{22.4 \text{ dm}^3}$ = 8.26 mol $O_2$

21.3 mol $O_2$ is required to react with the 4.26 mol $C_3H_8$. Therefore, $O_2$ is the limiting reactant.

185 dm³ $O_2 \times \dfrac{1 \text{ mol } O_2}{22.4 \text{ dm}^3\ O_2} \times \dfrac{4 \text{ mol } H_2O}{5 \text{ mol } O_2} \times$

$\dfrac{6.02 \times 10^{23} \text{ molec. } H_2O}{1 \text{ mol } H_2O}$ = $3.98 \times 10^{24}$ molec. $H_2O$

25. The balanced equation is Mg + $2HNO_3 \rightarrow Mg(NO_3)_2 + H_2$, so one molecule of $H_2$ is formed for each atom of Mg.

? mol Mg = 46.3 g ÷ 24.3 g/mol = 1.91 mol Mg
? g $H_2$ = 1.91 mol $\times$ 2.01 g/mol = 3.84 g

26. **a.** $6CO_2(g) + 6H_2O(l)$ + energy $\rightarrow C_6H_{12}O_6(s) + 6O_2(g)$

**b.** 6 molecules of water are needed to make 1 molecule of glucose.

**c.** ? mol $CO_2$ = 2.5 mol glucose $\times$ (6 $CO_2$/1 glucose) = 15 mol $CO_2$

**d.** ? mol $O_2$ = 2.50 mol glucose $\times$ (6 $O_2$/1 glucose) = 15.0 mol
? L $O_2$ (at STP) = 15 mol $\times$ 22.4 L/mol = 336 L

**e.** ? mol C = 2.50 mol glucose $\times$ (6 C/1 glucose) = 15.0 mol
? atoms C = 15.0 mol $\times$ $6.02 \times 10^{23}$ atoms/mole = $9.03 \times 10^{24}$ atoms

**f.** Using coefficients as relationships between volumes:
? dm³ $O_2$ = 9.32 dm³ $CO_2 \times$ (6 $O_2$/6 $CO_2$) = 9.32 dm³ $O_2$

## Page 255, Concept Mastery

27. ***Concept:*** *Stoichiometry problem solution.*
*Solution:*  The problem is solved correctly but in a roundabout way, indicating that the student used a mechanical approach. A more direct approach would be to notice that the number of molecules of $CO_2$ is the same as the number of molecules of CO, so the volume is the same.

28. ***Concept:*** *Stoichiometry problems can be solved in a variety of ways.*
*Solution:*  The problem is set up correctly, using a correct shortcut in the last step; the student will get the correct answer.

29. ***Concept:*** *The volume of 1 mole as 22.4 dm³ holds only for gases at STP.*
*Solution:*  The problem is not set up correctly because water is a liquid at STP, so the volume of 1 mole is not 22.4 dm³.

30. ***Concept:*** *The volume of the molecules of a gas is negligible in relation to the total volume occupied by the gas.*
*Solution:*  Equal volumes of hydrogen and oxygen gas, under the same conditions, contain the same number of molecules. The volume of a molecule of a gas is negligible compared with the space surrounding it. Equal volumes contain the same number of molecules according to Avogadro's hypothesis.

31. ***Concept:*** *Substances react in definite ratios, which can be determined from the balanced equation.*
*Solution:*  Unless the masses of the reactants are in the correct ratio, one will be the limiting reactant and the other will not react completely. The student should have compared the ratio of the masses available with the ratio that would actually react.

## Page 255, Cumulative Review

32. **e.** Rutherford's experiments pointed up the existence of the nucleus.

33. **c.** mass $CO_2$ = $\dfrac{28 \text{ g/mol } CO_2}{18 \text{ g/mol } H_2O} \times$ 50.0 g $H_2O$ = 77.8 g $CO_2$

34. **d.** The empirical formula shows the atoms present and the simplest atom ratio.

35. **c.** Air is a mixture.

36. **a.** $H_2O$, FeO, and $NH_4C_2H_3O_2$ are all compounds.

37. **b.** To balance the equation, $H_2O$ should be inserted.

38. An ion is charged, but an atom is neutral.

39. **a.** The empirical formula for $C_2H_6O$ is $C_2H_6O$.
**b.** The empirical formula for $H_2O_2$ is HO.
**c.** The empirical formula for $C_6H_6$ is CH.

40. **a.** The apparent charge on N in $NO_2$ is 4+.
**b.** The apparent charge on C in $CO_2$ is 4+.
**c.** The apparent charge on P in $P_2O_5$ is 5+.
**d.** The apparent charge on C in CO is 2+.

41. **a.** HClO: hypochlorous acid
**b.** HBr: hydrobromic acid
**c.** $H_2SO_4$: sulfuric acid
**d.** $HClO_4$: perchloric acid

| Text Section | | Labs (Lab Manual) and Demonstrations (TE) | Supplementary Materials (Teacher's Resource Book) |
|---|---|---|---|
| **11-10** | Vapor Pressure and Boiling, pp. 277-279 | | Transparency Master: Measuring the Vapor Pressure of a Liquid, p. 11-8 Transparency Master: Vapor Pressure of $H_2O$ at Various Temperatures, p. 11-9 Transparency Master: Vapor Pressure Curves for Three Substances, p. 11-10 Review Activity: Vapor Pressure and Boiling, p. 11-18 |
| **11-11** | Liquefaction of Gases, p. 279 | Demo 11-4: Distillation, p. TG-173 | Critical and Creative Thinking: Identifying Assumptions, p. CCT-31 |
| **11-12** | Heat of Vaporization, pp. 280-281 | | |
| **11-13** | Distillation, pp. 282-283 | | |
| **11-14** | Solids and the Kinetic Theory, p. 283 | | Non-SI Supplementary Problems, p. 11-21 |
| **11-15** | Melting and the Heat of Fusion, pp. 283-285 | | |
| **11-16** | Sublimation, pp. 285-286 | Demo 11-5: Properties of Hydrates, p. TG-173 Demo 11-6: Densities of Solids and Liquids, p. TG-174 | Review Activity: Processes Involving Liquids and Solids, p. 11-19 Practice Problems, p. 11-20 Concept Mastery: Density, p. CM-21 |
| **11-17** | Crystals, p. 286 | | |
| **11-18** | Water of Hydration in Crystals, pp. 287-288 | | |
| **11-19** | Hygroscopic and Deliquescent Substances, p. 288 | | |
| **11-20** | Densities of the Solid and Liquid Phases, pp. 288-290 | | |
| **Can You Explain This?** | "Double Boiler," p. 290 | | |
| | | | Test-Form A, p. AT-40 Alternate Test—Form B, p. BT-40 |

☐ Core  ☐ Advanced  ☐ Optional

## Chapter Overview

In Chapter 11, we describe the behavior of matter in each of the three physical phases and during changes of phase, and we explain that behavior in terms of the kinetic theory. Among the topics dealing with matter in the gas and liquid states are: the measurement of pressure, boiling point and melting point, vapor pressure, evaporation, vapor-liquid equilibrium, heat of vaporization, and liquefaction. We describe how the kinetic theory explains the properties of each phase in terms of molecular motion. Among the topics dealing with matter in the solid state are: heat of fusion, sublimation, crystals, and water of hydration. The chapter ends with a comparison of the densities of substances in the solid and liquid phases.

## Chapter Objectives

After students have completed this chapter, they will be able to:

1. Explain gas pressure. *11-1 to 11-3*
2. Describe the uses and operation of mercury barometers and manometers. *11-3 and 11-4*
3. Relate boiling to the air pressure. *11-5 and 11-10*
4. Explain the properties of gases, liquids, and solids in terms of the kinetic theory.
   *11-6 to 11-8, 11-11 to 11-14*
5. Compare the properties of liquids and solids.
   *11-14 to 11-20*
6. Describe equilibria in mixtures of different phases. *11-9*

## Teaching Suggestions

### 11-1 The Study of Phases, p. 259, and

### 11-2 The Meaning of Pressure, pp. 259-260

■ Review the properties of the three phases of matter. Compare the relative arrangement of the particles that compose each of these phases. Point out that this chapter explores these phases in more detail, explaining the observed properties of solids, liquids, and gases in terms of the arrangement of their particles.

■ One property of matter that needs to be elaborated upon is pressure. Point out that pressure is the force per unit area. Explain that for a substance on earth, the force an object exerts is the product of its mass and the acceleration of gravity. Because gravity is constant at any one location, the force of gravity on an object (the weight of the object) at any one location may be considered to be proportional to its mass. The SI unit of force is the newton. The SI unit of area is the square meter. Therefore, the SI unit of pressure, called a pascal, is 1 newton per square meter. Refer to text Figure 11-1 to reinforce this concept.

■ **Application.** You may want to introduce the students to a fourth phase of matter—plasma. The plasma phase is similar to the gas phase, but plasma particles are electrically charged. Plasma is found in

the ionosphere. Interest in the plasma phase has increased with the desire to control nuclear fusion reactions. The extremely high temperatures required to initiate a nuclear fusion reaction are needed to completely ionize gases into plasma, a mixture of atomic nuclei and electrons. One attempt to control fusion reactions is based on the possibility of confining the superhot plasma in a strong magnetic field.

### 11-3 Atmospheric Pressure, pp. 261-263

| Planning Guide | |
|---|---|
| **Labs (Lab Manual) and Demonstrations (TE)** | **Supplementary Materials (Teacher's Resource Book)** |
| Demo 11-1: Orange Crush, p. TG-172 | Societal Issues: Mercury in the Environment, p. SI-22 |
| Demo 11-2: Cartesian Diver, p. TG-172 | |

■ An exciting way to begin this lesson is to perform Demonstration 11-1, "Orange Crush." This demonstration illustrates the tremendous force that can be exerted by our atmosphere. Ask the students why we are not particularly aware of this atmospheric pressure although it is continuously pressing down on our bodies to the extent of about 1 kilogram per square centimeter (about 10 newtons per square centimeter).

■ Do Demonstration 11-2, "Cartesian Diver." Use this demonstration and text Figure 11-5 as a basis for discussion of the mercury barometer. Then, demonstrate the mercury barometer and its use in measuring atmospheric pressure. Discuss standard pressure and its SI equivalent. Next discuss the Societal Issue "Mercury in the Environment." This article points out that mercury is toxic. Emphasize that mercury and equipment containing it should be handled with care.

### 11-4 Measuring Gas Pressure, pp. 263-265

| Planning Guide | |
|---|---|
| **Labs (Lab Manual) and Demonstrations (TE)** | **Supplementary Materials (Teacher's Resource Book)** |
| | Transparency Master: U-Tube Manometer, Problem 1, p. 11-4 |
| | Transparency Master: U-Tube Manometer, Problem 2, p. 11-5 |
| | Transparency Master: U-Tube Manometer, Problem 3, p. 11-6 |
| | Review Activity: Measuring Pressure, p. 11-15 |

■ Point out that, so far, we have discussed measuring atmospheric pressure. In the chemistry laboratory it is often necessary to measure the pressure of a container of gas. Refer to text Figure 11-6, which illustrates the design and use of a manometer for measuring gas pressure. To explain the principle of the manometer, walk the students through Sample Problem 2 in the text. The three Transparency Masters "U-Tube Manometer, Problem 1," "U-Tube Manometer, Problem 2," and "U-Tube Manometer, Problem 3" are useful for reviewing variations of the open-ended manometer problems. You may wish to use the Review Activity "Measuring Pressure" to summarize the material related to this topic.

## 11-5 Boiling and Melting, p. 265, and

## 11-6 Theory of Physical Phase, pp. 266-267

| Planning Guide | |
|---|---|
| **Labs (Lab Manual) and Demonstrations (TE)** | **Supplementary Materials (Teacher's Resource Book)** |
| Demo 11-3: Boiling Warm Water, p. TG-172 | Open-Ended Demonstration: Boiling an Egg in a Vaccum, p. 11-11 Concept Mastery: Kinds of Matter, p. CM-18 |

■ Students are familiar with the concept of boiling. However, there are certain aspects of boiling that need to be emphasized. First, point out that boiling is not the same process as evaporation. Evaporation occurs at the surface of a liquid, and at various temperatures. Boiling occurs throughout the liquid, usually, but not always, when it is being heated. Second, emphasize that boiling is dependent upon pressure.

■ Perform Demonstration 11-3, "Boiling Warm Water." This demonstration provides a very striking illustration that the boiling point of a liquid is dependent upon pressure. Then discuss the principle of the pressure cooker. Define boiling point and normal boiling point. Explain that these definitions are refined in Section 11-10 along with the discussion of vapor pressure.

■ Define and discuss melting point, freezing point, and normal melting point. Explain that the effect of changes in pressure on the melting points of solids is very slight in comparison to the effect of changes in pressure on the boiling points of liquids.

■ Explain that many of the properties of solids, liquids, and gases are a direct consequence of the distances between particles and the forces of attraction among the particles. Use text Figure 11-10 to explain how these two factors affect such properties as volume, compressibility, particle velocity, and density.

■ **Application.** You may want to discuss the process of fractional distillation. Separation of crude oil into fractions based on boiling point differences is an example of a useful application of this technique.

■ **Concept Mastery.** Concept Mastery question 46 (chapter-end question) can help you to determine if your students understand the definitions of melting point and boiling point. In this question, they are asked to determine which substances are solids, liquids, or gases at various temperatures based upon the melting and boiling points of the substances. In addition, ask whether all substances exist in the three phases. Do all elements exist in three phases? Do all compounds exist in three phases? Can sugar be a gas?

The Concept Mastery worksheet "Kinds of Matter" (TRB) is a challenging exercise that requires students to visually connect particle representations with macroscopic descriptions of substances in different phases. This may be used to review or to test the students' mastery of these concepts.

## 11-7 Temperature and Phase Change, pp. 267-270

| Planning Guide | |
|---|---|
| **Labs (Lab Manual) and Demonstrations (TE)** | **Supplementary Materials (Teacher's Resource Book)** |
| Lab 18: Heating and Cooling Curves | Computer Experiment: Preparing a Cooling Curve, p. 11-13 Review Activity: A Heating Curve, p. 11-16 Concept Mastery: Phase Changes, p. CM-20 |

■ Discuss the relationship between temperature and phase changes. Examine what is taking place at the macroscopic level as a phase change occurs. Use text Figure 11-11 to guide this discussion. Define heating curve. Emphasize that an energy change occurs during any phase change. Students might not understand that an energy change is occurring during a phase change even though there is no change in temperature. Explain that when liquid water is converted to a vapor, the energy supplied to the system is being used to overcome the attractive forces among the molecules.

■ Next, have the students do Laboratory 18, "Heating and Cooling Curves," in which they gain experience with the heating and cooling curves of a substance other than water. Emphasize that when a substance undergoes a phase change in the process of cooling, energy is given off. For additional reinforcement of this concept, assign Computer Experiment "Preparing a Cooling Curve." In this experiment the students gener-

11

ate a cooling curve for paradichlorobenzene using a microcomputer and an attached temperature probe.

■ **Concept Mastery.** You may want to discuss Concept Mastery question 44 (chapter-end problem), as students are often surprised by the response of the thermometer when measuring the temperature of a substance undergoing a change in phase. Even though they know that most substances have a definite melting and boiling point, they do not connect this with the thermometer reading in an experiment.

The Concept Mastery worksheet "Phase Changes" (TRB) helps students to relate the particle representations of different phases of a substance with the difference in volume of each phase.

## 11-8 The Kinetic Theory of Gases, pp. 271-274

■ Explain that the kinetic theory is a conceptual scheme that enables us to imagine what is happening to solids, liquids, and gases at the microscopic or particle level. Discuss the five assumptions of the kinetic theory listed in the text. The third assumption involving elastic collisions may need elaboration as students are probably only familiar with inelastic collisions. Point out that gas molecules undergo elastic collisions, in that they do not lose energy when they collide with other gas molecules or the walls of the container. They may transfer energy to other gas molecules, but the overall energy of the system remains constant. The proof of this behavior is the fact that a closed container of a gas does not "settle out" or lose pressure with time, which you would expect to happen if the molecules of the gas lost energy upon collision. The molecules of a gas continue to move about the container, filling the entire volume.

■ Point out that a gas that conforms to all five assumptions of the kinetic theory is called an ideal gas. Tell students that real gases, which deviate slightly from ideal behavior, are discussed in Chapter 12.

■ Next move on to discuss liquids in terms of the kinetic theory. Ask the class how the kinetic theory accounts for the volume, shape, density, diffusibility, and compressibility of liquids relative to gases. Discuss evaporation and condensation in terms of the kinetic theory. Then ask why a liquid cools slightly upon evaporation. Ask how the rates of evaporation and condensation can be increased. Finally, ask why the process of condensation favors an increase in temperature.

■ **Concept Mastery.** The collapsing can, described in Concept Mastery question 48 (chapter-end question), is a good illustration of some of the principles related to the kinetic theory of gases. Ask students to explain what is happening at the molecular level in this demonstration.

## 11-9 Vapor-Liquid Equilibrium, pp. 274-277, and
## 11-10 Vapor Pressure and Boiling, pp. 277-279

| Planning Guide | |
|---|---|
| Labs (Lab Manual) and Demonstrations (TE) | Supplementary Materials (Teacher's Resource Book) |
| | Transparency Master: Equilibrium between the Vapor Phase and the Liquid Phase, p. 11-7 Transparency Master: Measuring the Vapor Pressure of a Liquid, p. 11-8 Transparency Master: Vapor Pressure of $H_2O$ at Various Temperatures, p. 11-9 Transparency Master: Vapor Pressure Curves for Three Substances, p. 11-10 Review Activity: Vapor Pressure and Boiling, p. 11-18 |

■ You are now going to introduce the students to the very important concept of equilibrium. Point out that there are two types of equilibrium: physical equilibrium discussed here and chemical equilibrium discussed in Chapter 18.

Define vapor pressure. Point out that vapor pressure changes when the temperature changes. Redefine boiling point in terms of vapor pressure. Use the Transparency Master "Vapor Pressure Curves for Three Substances" to compare the vapor pressures of three substances as a function of temperature. Indicate the boiling points of the substances on the graph. To conclude this section, assign the Review Activity "Vapor Pressure and Boiling."

## 11-11 Liquefaction of Gases, p. 279,
## 11-12 Heat of Vaporization, pp. 280-281, and
## 11-13 Distillation, pp. 282-283

| Planning Guide | |
|---|---|
| Labs (Lab Manual) and Demonstrations (TE) | Supplementary Materials (Teacher's Resource Book) |
| Demo 11-4: Distillation, p. TG-173 | Critical and Creative Thinking: Identifying Assumptions, p. CCT-31 |

■ Begin by defining liquefaction. Explain why it is easier to liquefy a vapor than a gas. For most gases, both a temperature decrease and a pressure increase are needed. For a vapor, a temperature decrease will usually suffice. Discuss the effects of changes in temperature and pressure on intermolecular attractions. Next, define critical temperature and critical pressure. Point out that at temperatures above the critical temperature, gas molecules have enough kinetic energy to withstand liquefaction regardless of the pressure.

■ Introduce the topic of heat of vaporization by asking why a steam burn is more severe than one by an equal mass of boiling water. Point out that since the temperatures of the steam and boiling water are the same, they must have equal amounts of kinetic energy. The steam, however, has added potential energy. Mention the relationship of heat of vaporization to heat of condensation. Finally, emphasize the relationship of heat of vaporization to intermolecular forces.

■ Tell the students that the processes of vaporization and condensation are combined in the process of distillation. Perform Demonstration 11-4, "Distillation," in which a mixture of alcohol, water, and food coloring is separated by this technique. Point out the usefulness of distillation in separating the components of many different mixtures.

■ **Critical Thinking.** In the Critical and Creative Thinking worksheet "Identifying Assumptions" (TRB) students analyze the logic used by scientists investigating an explosion in a prototype ammonia synthesis plant. The worksheet gives students practice in identifying assumptions that are taken for granted and recognizing the consequences of these assumptions. Students who master this skill can use it to evaluate decisions and judgments that affect their lives.

## 11-14 Solids and the Kinetic Theory, p. 283, and

## 11-15 Melting and the Heat of Fusion, pp. 283-285

| Planning Guide | |
| --- | --- |
| Labs (Lab Manual) and Demonstrations (TE) | Supplementary Materials (Teacher's Resource Book) |
| | Non-SI Supplementary Problems, p. 11-21 |

■ Remind the students that so far gases and liquids have been discussed in terms of the kinetic theory. Solids can be discussed in a similar fashion. Discuss the properties of solids. Compare them to the properties of liquids and gases. Explain the properties of solids in terms of the arrangement of their particles. Be sure to point out that although the particles in solids are held in fixed positions, they are not immobile. They actually vibrate about fixed positions.

■ Discuss the macroscopic and microscopic behavior of solids undergoing phase changes (solids to liquids and liquids to solids). Define heat of fusion and heat of

crystallization. Explain the relationship of bonding forces to melting points. Ask why heats of fusion are small compared with heats of vaporization.

■ Explain that some of the materials that we think of as being solids are really not true solids. Glass is one example. It is not a solid but rather a very viscous liquid. Ask if anyone has ever noticed the glass window panes on very old buildings. The flowing of the glass leaves a distinct pattern in the panes of glass.

■ If you want your students to practice using non-SI units, you may assign Chapter 11 Non-SI Supplementary Problems.

■ **Concept Mastery.** You may want to discuss Concept Mastery question 45 (chapter-end question). Students are often confused by the fact that ice and liquid water can exist at the same temperature: 0°C. This confusion may be caused by students' lack of understanding of the distinction between heat and temperature. Ask students to describe what is happening on the molecular level and in terms of heat and temperature as ice is heated from −20°C to 125°C.

## 11-16 Sublimation, pp. 285-286,

## 11-17 Crystals, p. 286,

## 11-18 Water of Hydration in Crystals, pp. 287-288,

## 11-19 Hygroscopic and Deliquescent Substances, p. 288, and

## 11-20 Densities of the Solid and Liquid Phases, pp. 288-290

| Planning Guide | |
| --- | --- |
| Labs (Lab Manual) and Demonstrations (TE) | Supplementary Materials (Teacher's Resource Book) |
| Demo 11-5: Properties of Hydrates, p. TG-173 Demo 11-6: Densities of Solids and Liquids, p. TG-174 | Review Activity: Processes Involving Liquids and Solids, p. 11-19 Practice Problems, p. 11-20 Concept Mastery: Density, p. CM-21 |

■ Explain that the remainder of this chapter focuses upon some unusual properties of certain solids. Define and discuss sublimation, decrepitation, efflorescence, and deliquescence. Point out ways that solids exhibiting these properties are made use of in the home, in the laboratory, and in industry. For example, dry ice is used as a refrigerant and iodine vapor is used as a stain for chromatographic plates. Deliquescent materials are packed in vitamin containers.

■ Crystals can prove to be a very interesting subject for many students. Exhibit samples of crystals. You may even want to grow copper(II) sulfate or alum crystals in the classroom. Do Demonstration 11-5, "Properties of Hydrates," to initiate the discussion of a special group of crystals called hydrates.

■ Next, point out that since the particles in most solids are held more closely than those in liquids, solids are ordinarily denser than liquids. Water is an exception. Demonstration 11-6, "Densities of Solids and Liquids," reinforces this concept. Explain the lower density of the ice in terms of the open structure of ice crystals. Ask the students why water pipes may crack in freezing weather and what would happen to fish life in a lake if ice were denser than water.

■ **Application.** You may want to point out to the students that household mothball crystals and solid air fresheners are examples of materials that sublime. If students look into a storage box of woolens on a hot summer day, they will not find the woolens soaked in melted mothball crystals.

■ **Concept Mastery.** Students can often become confused about density if they think of it as an extensive property of matter similar to the concept of mass. On the other hand, density does vary with the temperature and phase of a substance, and so might confuse students who think of intensive properties as invariant. The Concept Mastery worksheet "Density" helps to overcome these misconceptions using a particle approach to the concept of density.

# Demonstrations

## 11-1 Orange Crush

**Overview:** In this demonstration, water is placed into an empty soft-drink can that is then heated until the water evaporates. Students observe that when the can is turned upside down and placed into a container of crushed ice and water, the can collapses.

**Materials:** empty soft-drink can; large beaker or other container filled with crushed ice and water; beaker tongs; hot plate or burner.

**Advance Preparation:** Fill the beaker or other container about three-fourths full with the crushed ice and water.

**Procedure:** 1. Place a few milliliters of water into an empty soft-drink can. Using a hot plate or burner, heat the can until some water vapor escapes from it. 2. Remove the can with beaker tongs and immediately plunge it, upside down, into the ice water. Continue to hold the can under water until the result is evident. Ask students for an explanation.

**Results:** The can will collapse because the vaporized water molecules slow down and condense, causing the

pressure to decrease inside the can and allowing the outside pressure to push in the can.

## 11-2 Cartesian Diver

**Overview:** In this demonstration, students observe that when the pressure over the surface of water in a plastic bottle is increased, a half-filled eyedropper "dives," or sinks, to the bottom of the container. The water is forced into the eyedropper, making the object as a whole more dense and causing it to sink.

**Materials:** 2000-mL plastic soft-drink bottle with screw-on top; eyedropper fitted into a screw-on cap; plastic cup full of water; drinking straws.

**Advance Preparation:** none

**Procedure:** 1. Have a student volunteer drink water from a plastic cup by using a straw. Ask the class to explain the result. 2. Ask another volunteer to place two straws into his or her mouth; the other end of the first straw should be placed into the cup of water and the other end of the second straw should be exposed to the atmosphere. Ask the student to try to draw water up the first straw. Ask for an explanation of the result. 3. Fill a 2000-mL plastic soft-drink bottle with tap water until the water level is within 3–5 cm of the top of the bottle. Squeeze the air out of the eyedropper and fill it half full of water. Place the eyedropper carefully into the bottle, so that it floats in a vertical position because of the air trapped inside it. 4. Squeeze the bottle. Have students observe and explain the result. 5. Point out to students that what they have observed in this demonstration is related to the fact that an increase in air pressure forces mercury up into a barometer tube.

**Results:** In step 1, the water rises in the straw when air is drawn out of it. The pressure over the water is reduced inside the straw as compared with the outside pressure. This causes the outside air to force the water up into the straw. In step 2, the student will be unable to draw water up the straw. Any attempt to do so will simply cause air to be drawn in through the second straw. In step 4, the increase in pressure forces water up into the eyedropper, making it more dense as a whole and causing it to sink, or "dive."

## 11-3 Boiling Warm Water

**Overview:** In this demonstration, students observe that water at about 60°C boils under reduced pressure. This shows that water can boil at different temperatures and that boiling point is related to the pressure over the water surface.

**Materials:** 250-mL Erlenmeyer flask, one-third full of warm distilled water; thermometer; vacuum pump and bell jar.

**Advance Preparation:** Set up the vacuum pump and

bell jar, and warm some distilled water to below boiling.

**Procedure:** 1. Determine the temperature of the water in the flask. It should be around 60–65°C. 2. Set up the vacuum pump apparatus and place the flask inside the bell jar. Allow the pump to run for a few minutes, until the result is evident. Ask students to explain what has occurred. It would be appropriate to refer to a graph of water vapor pressure versus temperature. 3. Ask students to guess whether it would take more or less time to hard-boil an egg in Denver, Colorado, which is at a high altitude, as compared with the amount of time required in a coastal city.

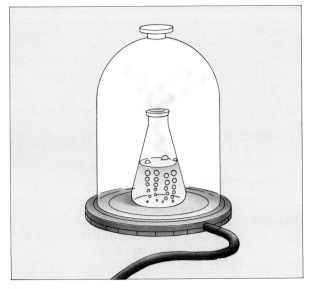

**Figure 11-1**

**Results:** The water will boil, since its vapor pressure is equal to that of the low-pressure atmosphere above it. The egg will take longer to cook in Denver, since the boiling point of water is lower there and less heat energy is present to cook the egg.

## 11-4 Distillation

**Overview:** In this demonstration, a mixture of red dye, water, and alcohol is distilled. This demonstration shows students how to separate a mixture. It also shows that a liquid changes to a gas when heated and that the gas is changed back to a liquid when cooled.

**Materials:** distillation apparatus; mixture of red food coloring, ethyl alcohol, and water; hot plate; thermometer.

**Advance Preparation:** Mix together ethyl alcohol and water in equal proportions and add a few drops of red food coloring.

**Procedure:** 1. Place the mixture of red dye and liquids into the distillation flask, and tell the class what the

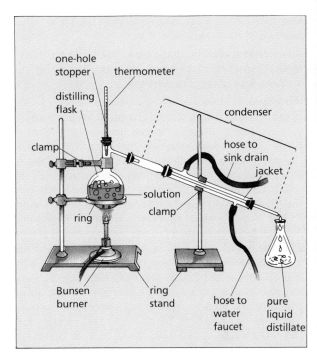

**Figure 11-2**

components of the mixture are. Insert the thermometer into the stopper of the flask. Assemble the rest of the distillation apparatus and start the water running through the condenser. 2. Heat the mixture until it boils. Collect the liquid that condenses first. Determine whether it has an odor. Ask students what they think the liquid is. 3. Continue to heat the rest of the mixture until the temperature stabilizes at a higher value. Collect a sample of this liquid, and ask students what they think it is. 4. Do not heat the flask to dryness. Ask students to draw a conclusion about the red coloring material.

**Results:** The alcohol will begin to boil out first. The water will boil out next. The red coloring material, which is solid in the pure state, is not volatile and remains in the distillation flask.

## 11-5 Properties of Hydrates

**Overview:** In this demonstration, samples of hydrates are heated to produce the corresponding anhydrous solids. The properties of deliquescence and efflorescence are exhibited.

**Materials:** copper(II) sulfate pentahydrate crystals ($CuSO_4 \cdot 5H_2O$); cobalt(II) chloride hexahydrate ($CoCl_2 \cdot 6H_2O$); calcium chloride, anhydrous powder ($CaCl_2$); sodium hydrogen phosphate heptahydrate ($Na_2HPO_4 \cdot 7H_2O$); watch glasses; hot plate; bag of silica gel; two salt shakers, one containing sodium chloride and a trace of magnesium chloride, and the other containing those salts and rice.

**Advance Preparation:** Place some NaCl and a trace of $MgCl_2$ into each of two salt shakers. To one of the shakers, add some uncooked rice.

**Procedure:** 1. Place a scoop of copper(II) sulfate pentahydrate onto a watch glass. Have students observe the blue crystals. 2. Place the watch glass onto a warm hot plate. Have students observe what occurs. 3. Remove the watch glass and allow it to cool. Add one drop of water to the powder. 4. Repeat the procedure with the cobalt(II) chloride hexahydrate. Ask students whether they know the principal commercial uses of this solid. 5. Fill a watch glass about two-thirds full of anhydrous calcium chloride. Find the total mass and record it on the board. About 30 minutes later, find the mass again and record it. 6. Leave the solid out overnight, and observe it and find its mass the next day. 7. Show the class the two salt shakers you prepared. Ask: From which of the shakers would you expect the salts to come out more easily? What is the role of the rice? Demonstrate by shaking out some salt. 8. Show the class a small bag of silica gel of the sort that is usually found in vitamin or pill bottles, new-camera boxes, and so on. Ask: What is the purpose of the solid?

**Results:** In step 2, the blue crystals will turn whitish as the water of hydration is driven off. In step 3, the powder should become warm and turn blue as the hydrate is re-formed. In step 4, the pink crystals will turn to anhydrous blue ones. Materials coated commercially with this substance will change color depending on the amount of moisture in the air. In step 5, the mass will increase, since the hygroscopic solid absorbs moisture from the air. In step 6, the mass will increase further, and so much moisture will be absorbed that a solution will form. In step 7, the salts will come out more easily from the shaker containing the rice, which absorbs moisture and prevents the salts from caking. In step 8, the silica gel absorbs moisture and helps to keep the material with which it is packed dry.

## 11-6 Densities of Solids and Liquids

**Overview:** In this demonstration, a piece of solid water (ice) is added to a beaker of liquid water, and a piece of solid paraffin is added to a beaker of melted paraffin. Students observe that the ice floats in the liquid water but that the solid paraffin sinks in the liquid paraffin.

**Materials:** ice cubes; beaker of water; piece of paraffin; small beaker of paraffin melted over a hot plate.

**Advance Preparation:** Carefully melt some paraffin in a small beaker over a hot plate.

**Procedure:** 1. Add a piece of ice to water and have

students note whether the ice sinks or floats. Ask them to explain the result, on the basis of crystal structure. 2. Add a piece of paraffin to the beaker of melted paraffin, which should be kept on a hot plate set on low. Have students observe and explain the result.

**Results:** The ice floats in the water because the density of ice is lower. The ice crystal contains a good deal of empty space because of its open hexagonal packing. The solid paraffin sinks in the liquid paraffin because the former is more dense, its molecules being packed more closely together.

## Answers to Questions

**Page 260**
1. Pressure is the force per unit area.
2. Because the same force is applied to both areas, the force per unit area (the pressure) is greater for the smaller area.
3. $\dfrac{5.0 \times 10^{-2}\ \text{N}}{6.0 \times 10^{-7}\ \text{m}^2} = 8.3 \times 10^4\ \text{N/m}^2$, or $8.3 \times 10^4$ Pa
4. $\dfrac{5.0 \times 10^{-2}\ \text{N}}{6.0 \times 10^{-4}\ \text{m}^2} = 8.3 \times 10\ \text{N/m}^2$, or $8.3 \times 10$ Pa
5. $\dfrac{\text{Pressure exerted by nail}}{\text{Pressure exerted by wood}} = \dfrac{8.3 \times 10^4\ \text{Pa}}{8.3 \times 10\ \text{Pa}} =$
$$1.0 \times 10^3$$

**Page 262**
6. Atmospheric pressure is caused by the weight and kinetic energy of the air molecules.
7. The pressure of a liquid increases as the depth increases.
8. The air pressure pressing down on the mercury in the container prevents the mercury in the tube from running out into the container.
9. One atmosphere of pressure is equal to
   **a.** 760 mm Hg; **b.** 101.3 kPa

**Page 263**
10. $1.50\ \text{atm} \times 760\ \text{mm Hg/atm} = 1140\ \text{mm Hg}$
11. $\dfrac{1.00\ \text{mm Hg}}{760\ \text{mm Hg}} \times 101.3\ \text{kPa} = 0.133\ \text{kPa} = 133\ \text{Pa}$

**Page 264**
12. **a.** The pressure of the gas in the container, which is greater than air pressure, causes the level of the mercury to move upward in the open arm against the smaller pressure of the air.
    **b.** The pressure difference is 4.7 kPa. This is equivalent to
    $$4.7\ \text{kPa} \times \dfrac{760\ \text{mm Hg}}{101.3\ \text{kPa}} = 35\ \text{mm Hg}$$

**Page 265**

**13.** 30 mm Hg is equivalent to

$$30 \text{ mm Hg} \times \frac{101.3 \text{ kPa}}{760 \text{ mm Hg}} = 4.0 \text{ kPa}$$

gas pressure = 102 kPa + 4.0 kPa = 106 kPa

**Page 267**

**14.** The statement should include the air pressure.

**15.** The normal boiling point of water is 100°C at 760 mm Hg or 101.3 kPa.

**16.** **a.** melting point; **b.** freezing point

**17.** It must have a definite melting point.

**18.** Temperature is a measure of the average kinetic energy of particles no matter what the phase is. Therefore, the average kinetic energies of these phases are equal.

**Page 270**

**19.** The added heat is used to change the solid to the liquid phase.

**20.** The added heat is used to change the liquid to the gas phase rather than to raise the temperature.

**21.** **a.** While melting, paradichlorobenzene does not change its temperature. The melting point is the temperature corresponding to the horizontal portion of the graph—54°C.

   **b.** The change of phase from liquid to gas would be indicated by a horizontal line. This is not shown on the graph.

   **c.** After 20 minutes of heating, it is in the liquid phase, as shown by the portion of the graph slanting upward.

**22.** 500 g × 5.0°C/min × 2.1 J/g-°C =

$$5.3 \times 10^3 \text{ J/min}$$

**Page 274**

**23.** Molecules of a liquid are held together by intermolecular attractions.

**24.** The molecules of a liquid have more restricted motion than the molecules of a gas. In a liquid, the molecules are held together by intermolecular forces that are strong enough to keep the molecules from separating but are weak enough to allow the liquid to assume the shape of its container.

**25.** A vapor is the term used for the gas phase of substances that exist as liquids or solids at ordinary conditions.

**26.** The molecules with higher kinetic energies leave the liquid first during evaporation.

**27.** Increasing the temperature raises the average kinetic energy. The rate of evaporation increases because more molecules acquire enough energy to enable them to leave the liquid phase.

**28.** The high-energy molecules remain in the vapor phase and the lower-energy molecules condense. Therefore, the temperature of the vapor increases.

**Page 279**

**29.** Equilibrium between evaporation and condensation is a balance in the rates of opposing physical changes.

**30.** As the temperature increases, the average kinetic energy of the vapor molecules increases. This results in an increased vapor pressure.

**31.** In order for bubbles of vapor to form, the vapor pressure of the water must be equal to the opposing atmospheric pressure. At standard pressure, this occurs at 100°C.

**32.** The liquid will boil.

**33.** With lower pressure on the surface, the bubbles of gas will form at lower temperatures; therefore, the liquid will boil at a lower temperature.

**34.** Pressure of $H_2$ = 99.4 kPa − water vapor pressure = 99.4 kPa − 2.81 kPa = 96.6 kPa

**Page 282**

**35.** Under high pressures the molecules are forced closer together. When the molecules are closer, the intermolecular attractions are greater.

**36.** Decreasing the temperature is another factor favoring liquefaction.

**Page 283**

**37.** Above the critical temperature, a gas cannot be liquefied regardless of how great the pressure is.

**38.** As the temperature of a liquid increases, the heat of vaporization of most liquids decreases.

**39.** A large heat of vaporization indicates large intermolecular forces of attraction.

**40.** During a distillation, a liquid is first changed to a gas by heating it. The gas is then condensed by cooling it.

**41.** 250 g × (2.3 × 10³ J/g) = 5.8 × 10⁵ J

**42.** $\dfrac{1.8 \times 10^5 \text{ J}}{2.3 \times 10^3 \text{ J/g}} = 79 \text{ g}$

**Page 285**

**43.** Molasses has a high viscosity when it is cold and therefore flows very slowly.

**44.** The molecules of a solid vibrate about fixed positions forming a regular geometric pattern.

**45.** The melting point and freezing point of a pure substance are the same.

**46.** If no energy is added or removed, the solid and liquid will remain in equilibrium so that the mass of each remains constant.

**47.** *Heat of fusion* is the term for the heat required to melt a unit mass of a solid at a constant temperature.

**48.** At constant pressure, the quantity of heat absorbed by a gram of ice as it melts is the same as the quantity of heat released when a gram of liquid water freezes.

11

**49.** $44 \text{ g water} \times \dfrac{3.4 \times 10^2 \text{ J}}{1 \text{ g water}} = 1.5 \times 10^4 \text{ J}$

**50.** $\dfrac{1.18 \times 10^4 \text{ J}}{3.4 \times 10^2 \text{ J/g}} = 35 \text{ g}$

## Page 290

**51.** Sublimation is the change of a substance directly from the solid phase to the gas phase without first passing through the liquid phase.

**52.** The solid has weak intermolecular attractive forces and a resulting high vapor pressure.

**53.** The arrangement of molecules in a crystal is called a crystal lattice.

**54.** The shape of a solid is determined by the relative sizes of the particles and the nature of the binding forces.

**55.** Slower evaporation produces larger crystals.

**56.** A hydrate is a crystalline compound in which the solid substance combines chemically with water in a definite ratio.

**57.** In efflorescence, a hydrate loses some or all of its combined water without being heated. In deliquescence, a solid absorbs moisture from the air and may eventually dissolve in the absorbed moisture.

**58.** For most substances, the solid phase has a greater density than the liquid phase.

**59.** For the solid phase, from −10°C up to 0°C, the volume *increases* slightly, causing the density to *decrease* slightly. During melting at 0°C, the volume *decreases*, causing the density to *increase*. The maximum density is reached at 4°C. From 4°C to 10°C, the volume *increases* slightly, causing the density to *decrease*.

## Page 290, "Double Boiler"

**1.** The temperature of the water inside the flask falls below 100°C as ice water is poured over the flask.

**2.** As ice water is poured over the flask, some of the vapor inside the flask condenses. This decreases the pressure over the water inside the flask. The decreased pressure on the water allows it to boil at a temperature below its normal boiling point at 100°C.

# Chapter Review    11

## Page 292, Content Review

**1.** The SI unit of force is the newton. It symbol is N.

**2.** Pressure = force ÷ area.

**3.** Pressure = $9.0 \text{ N} \div 2.0 \text{ m}^2 = 4.5 \text{ N/m}^2 = 4.5 \text{ Pa}$

**4.** The atmosphere exerts pressure because of its weight and because of the kinetic energy of its moving molecules.

**5. a.** 955 mm Hg × 1 atm/760 mm Hg = 1.26 atm
**b.** 955 mm Hg × 101.3 kPa/760 mm Hg = 127 kPa
**c.** 127 kPa × 1000 Pa/1.00 kPa = 127 000 Pa
**d.** 127 000 Pa = $1.27 \times 10^5$ Pa = $1.27 \times 10^5 \text{ N/m}^2$

**6. a.** The mercury in the open arm would move down if the air pressure increased. **b.** To make the levels of mercury the same in both arms, the level in the closed arm would have to rise. This would decrease the volume of the gas in the container, so its pressure would increase.

**7.** With increasing altitude, the atmospheric pressure decreases. This causes a decrease in the boiling point of a liquid.

**8.** The melting point of ice and the freezing point of water are the same temperature.

**9.** The attractive forces between particles are strongest in solids, weaker in liquids, and weakest in gases.

**10.** The ice absorbs heat until it reaches the melting point. Additional heat causes melting until all of the sample becomes liquid. Its temperature rises until it reaches the boiling point. The temperature of the liquid remains constant until all of the water becomes steam.

**11.** The graph should be similar to text Figure 11-12, with the plateau at 80°C.

**12.** During evaporation, the more energetic molecules escape. This lowers the average kinetic energy and therefore the temperature of the liquid.

**13.** Evaporation rate is affected by temperature, surface area, and air currents.

**14.** Pressure of $N_2$ = 95.6 kPa − pressure of water vapor = 95.6 kPa − 2.1 kPa = 93.5 kPa.

**15.** Water will boil at temperatures below its normal boiling point if the external pressure is reduced.

**16.** In a pressure cooker, the increased pressure forces the water to reach a higher temperature before it can boil. Food cooks faster in this hotter water.

**17.** A gas liquefies more easily at low temperatures because the molecules have less kinetic energy and are less able to overcome the attractive forces that exist between the particles.

**18.** heat required = mass × heat of vaporization
600 g × $2.26 \times 10^3$ J/g = $1.36 \times 10^6$ J

**19.** mass = heat released ÷ heat of vaporization
$6.50 \times 10^4$ J ÷ $2.26 \times 10^3$ J/g = 28.8 g

**20.** During distillation, any dissolved solid remains in the distilling flask.

21. Glass is not a true solid because it does not have a definite melting point.

22. heat released = mass × heat of fusion
85.0 g × 3.4 × 10² J/g = 2.9 × 10⁴ J

23. mass = heat required ÷ heat of fusion
6.8 × 10⁴ J ÷ 3.4 × 10² J/g = 2.0 × 10² g

24. A solid with a high vapor pressure sublimes at room temperature.

25. A slow evaporation rate gives dissolved particles time to find existing crystals on which to attach, so larger crystals form.

26. As a hydrate is heated, it loses its water of hydration and becomes anhydrous.

27. Efflorescence is the spontaneous loss of water of hydration. This would cause a loss in mass.

28. Deliquescence makes a substance hygroscopic.

29. It is unique that ice floats in water because most substances are more dense as solids than they are as liquids.

## Page 293, Content Mastery

30. heat required = 25.0 g × 5.0°C × 2.1 J/g-°C = 260 J

31. $P_{\text{dry } O_2} = P_{\text{wet } O_2} - P_{H_2O} = 97.90 \text{ kPa} - P_{H_2O}$
From text Figure 11-18, $P_{25°C} = 3.17$ kPa and
$P_{26°C} = 3.36$ kPa
Interpolation yields (0.2) (3.36 − 3.17) kPa = 0.038 kPa
Therefore $P_{25.2°C} = 3.17$ kPa + 0.04 kPa = 3.21 kPa
Thus $P_{\text{dry } O_2} = P_{\text{wet } O_2} - P_{H_2O} = 97.90 - 3.21 = 94.69$ kPa

32. The temperature at which steam liquefies is that at which water boils: 100.0°C at 101.3 kPa.

33. See Figure 11-3.

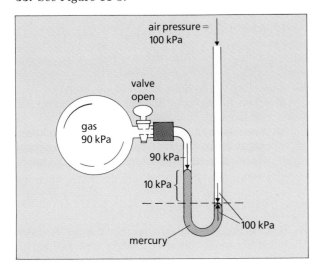

**Figure 11-3**

34. To increase evaporation: heat the liquid, increase its surface area, or supply air currents across its surface to prevent condensation. To promote boiling: heat the liquid to its boiling point or reduce the external pressure to equal the liquid's vapor pressure.

35. Heat of vaporization = $\dfrac{\text{energy to vaporize}}{\text{mass vaporized}}$ =
$$\frac{4.53 \times 10^7 \text{ J}}{3.33 \times 10^3 \text{ g}} = 1.36 \times 10^4 \text{ J/g}$$

36. To remove salt and other impurities from seawater, set up distillation equipment and boil the seawater. The pure water leaves the seawater and condenses into another container. This distilled water will be free of salt and other impurities.

37. Evaporation occurs at the surface of a liquid at temperatures below the liquid's boiling point. Boiling occurs throughout the liquid at the liquid's boiling point.

38. mass = 20.0 L × (1 dm³/L) × (10³ g/dm³) = 2.00 × 10⁴ g
heat = mass × heat of fusion = 2.00 × 10⁴ g × 0.34 kJ/g = 6.8 × 10³ kJ

39. Formula for sodium sulfate decahydrate: $Na_2SO_4 \cdot 10H_2O$.
Formula mass
= 2(Na) + S + 4(O) + 10(water)
= 2(22.990) + 32.06 + 4(15.999) + 10(18.0152)
= 45.98 + 32.06 + 63.996 + 180.152
= 322.2 g/mol

40. 755 mm × (101.3 kPa/760 mm) = 100.63 kPa ≈ 101 kPa

41. Pressure = weight/area, so weight = pressure × area.
pressure = 101.3 kPa = 101.3 × 10³ Pa = 1.013 × 10⁵ Pa
weight = 1.013 × 10⁵ Pa × 1.00 m² = 1.01 × 10⁵ N

42. $P_{\text{man}}$ = 89 N ÷ 1.00 m² = 89 N/m²
$P_{\text{child}}$ = 8.9 N ÷ 100 cm² = 8.9 ÷ 0.01 m² = 890 N/m²
The child exerts more pressure.

43. Critical temperature is the temperature above which no amount of pressure can turn a gas into a liquid.

## Page 293, Concept Mastery

44. **Concept:** *Temperature is constant during phase changes.*
*Solution:* The constant temperature means that the solid must be melting or subliming at 92°C. The heat is being used to cause

the phase change rather than to increase the temperature of the substance.

**45. Concept:** *Freezing and melting points are identical.*

    **Solution:** At 0°C, both liquid and solid water would be present. If heat is being removed, ice is forming. If heat is being added, liquid water is being formed.

**46. Concept:** *Melting and boiling points determine whether a substance is a solid, liquid, or gas at a given temperature.*

    **Solution:**
  **a.** At 90°C, water and mercury are liquids. At −200°C, oxygen and nitrogen are liquids.

  **b.** At 90°C, oxygen and nitrogen are gases. At −200°C, none of these substances is a gas.

  **c.** At 90°C, iron is solid. At −200°C, water, mercury, and iron are solids.

**47. Concept:** *Water in the air can condense as a liquid.*

    **Solution:** Water from the air condenses on the outside of the glass because the cold glass cools the air, so the air cannot hold as much water.

**48. Concept:** *Changes from gas to liquid leave fewer molecules in the gas state, causing a decrease in pressure.*

    **Solution:** Air is driven from the can and replaced by water molecules as the water boils. After the can is sealed, the water vapor is cooled by the cold water. The water vapor changes back to liquid, leaving very few molecules in the upper part of the can. This causes reduced pressure within the can. The pressure of the air molecules outside the can is then greater than the pressure inside the can, so the can collapses until the internal and external pressures are equal.

**49. Concept:** *Boiling is a physical change in which molecules remain intact.*

    **Solution:** The bubbles that form are made of water vapor. The air has been forced out as the water was heated. There is not enough heat to cause the water molecules to decompose into hydrogen and oxygen.

**50. Concept:** *Evaporation results when a liquid gradually changes into vapor.*

    **Solution:** The liquid water has changed to a gas that has mixed with the air. Eventually it may change back to liquid or solid water as rain, frost, etc.

**51. d.** $6 \text{ mol C}_4\text{H}_{10} \times \dfrac{8 \text{ mol CO}_2}{2 \text{ mol C}_4\text{H}_{10}} = 24 \text{ mol CO}_2$

**52. a.** $4 \text{ g CH}_4 \times \dfrac{1 \text{ mol CH}_4}{16 \text{ g CH}_4} \times$

$\dfrac{6.02 \times 10^{23} \text{ molecules}}{1 \text{ mol CH}_4} = 1.5 \times 10^{23} \text{ molecules}$

**53. b.** The precipitate is barium sulfate.

**54. b.** Single replacement occurs in reactions between an element and a compound.

**55. c.** 1.580 g compound − 0.948 g Mg = 0.632 g O
0.948 g Mg × (1 mol Mg/24.3 g Mg) =
                 0.0390 mol Mg
0.632 g O × (1 mol O/16.0 g O) =
                 0.0395 mol O
The empirical formula is MgO.

**56. a.** sulfuric acid, $H_2SO_4$; **b.** sodium phosphate, $Na_3PO_4$; **c.** zinc nitrite, $Zn(NO_2)_2$; **d.** potassium bromide, KBr; **e.** ammonium hydrogen carbonate, $NH_4HCO_3$.

**57.** $10.0 \text{ g KClO}_3 \times \dfrac{1 \text{ mol KClO}_3}{122 \text{ g KClO}_3} \times \dfrac{3 \text{ mol O}_2}{2 \text{ mol KClO}_3} \times$

$\dfrac{22.4 \text{ dm}^3 \text{ O}_2}{1 \text{ mol O}_2} = 2.73 \text{ dm}^3 \text{ O}_2 \text{ at STP}$

**58.**

| Isotope Symbol | At. No. | At. Mass | No. of Prot. | No. of Neut. | No. of Elect. |
|---|---|---|---|---|---|
| **a.** $^{208}_{82}\text{Pb}^{2+}$ | 82 | 208 | 82 | 126 | 80 |
| **b.** $^{80}_{35}\text{Br}^{-1}$ | 35 | 80 | 35 | 45 | 36 |
| **c.** $^{23}_{11}\text{Na}$ | 11 | 23 | 11 | 12 | 11 |

**59.** molecular mass of $CCl_4$ = 12 + 4(35) = 152

$100 \text{ cm}^3 \text{ CCl}_4 \times \dfrac{1.8 \text{ g}}{1 \text{ cm}^3} \times \dfrac{1 \text{ mol}}{152 \text{ g}} \times$

$\dfrac{6.02 \times 10^{23} \text{ molecules}}{1 \text{ mol}} = 7.1 \times 10^{23} \text{ molecules}$

**60.** According to the Bohr model of the atom:
  **a.** When an electron absorbs enough energy, it can move up to a higher energy level.

  **b.** When an excited electron goes down to a lower energy level, it emits definite quanta of energy, which, if visible, make up a bright-line spectrum.

**61.** By crawling out onto the ice, the rescuer spreads his or her weight out over a larger area so that the pressure on any one part of the ice is less than it would be if the rescuer stood up.

**62.** The atmospheric pressure in Death Valley should be greater than that at sea level, due to the greater height in the atmosphere and the greater density of the air. Therefore, water would need to be above 100°C before it could boil.

**63.** Mercury is a better choice than water in a barometer because mercury has a much greater density, so it requires more pressure to elevate it in the glass tube. Water would require a much longer glass tube, which would be inefficient and harder to use.

**64.** Water has the least kinetic energy at the time of vaporization; alcohol, more; and chloroform, the most.

**65.** Although all may indicate the presence of a crystal, X rays provide the most accurate data.

**66.** From the data, one could generalize that as the temperature increases, so does the vapor pressure.

### Page 295, Challenge Problems

**67. a.** Mass of hydrated crystal:

$$105.76 \text{ g}$$
$$-\ 88.25 \text{ g}$$
$$17.51 \text{ g}$$

Mass of water in crystal:

$$105.76 \text{ g}$$
$$-\ 97.92 \text{ g}$$
$$7.84 \text{ g}$$

% water = $(7.84 \text{ g} \div 17.51 \text{ g}) \times 100\% = 44.8\%$

% $NiSO_4$ = $100\% - 44.8\% = 55.2\%$

**b.** $9.67 \text{ g } NiSO_4 \times \dfrac{1 \text{ mol } NiSO_4}{155 \text{ g } NiSO_4} =$

$$0.0624 \text{ mol } NiSO_4$$

$$7.84 \text{ g } H_2O \times \dfrac{1 \text{ mol } H_2O}{18.0 \text{ g } H_2O} = 0.436 \text{ mol } H_2O$$

Ratio of mol units:

$0.0624 \text{ mol } NiSO_4/0.0624 = 1.00 \text{ mol } NiSO_4$

$0.436 \text{ mol } H_2O/0.0624 = 6.99 \text{ mol } H_2O$

Formula: $NiSO_4 \cdot 7H_2O$

**68.** The heating curve in text Figure 11-11 shows that the substance goes through four separate processes; the heat for each is calculated separately.

**(a)** Heat to raise temperature of ice from $-20°C$ to 0°C:

heat = mass × specific heat of ice × $\Delta T$

= 200 g × 2.1 J/g-°C × 20°C = 8400 J

**(b)** Heat to melt the ice at 0°C:

heat = mass × heat of fusion

= 200 g × $3.4 \times 10^2$ J/g = $680 \times 10^2$ J

**(c)** Heat to raise temperature of water from 0°C to 100°C:

heat = mass × specific heat of water × $\Delta T$

= 200 g × 4.2 J/g-°C × 100°C = 84 000 J

**(d)** Heat to change water from liquid to gas at 100°C:

heat = mass × heat of vaporization

= 200 g × $2.3 \times 10^3$ J/g = $460 \times 10^3$ J

Total heat = 8400 J + $680 \times 10^2$ J + 84 000 J + $460 \times 10^3$ J

= $(0.084 + 0.68 + 0.84 + 4.60) \times 10^5$ J

= $6.2 \times 10^5$ J

**69.** Answers will vary, depending on estimated skin area. If the estimated area is 20 000 cm², the force is equal to the weight of 20 000 kg, or 20 metric tons.

11

# The Gas Laws

12

## Chapter Planning Guide

| Text Section | Labs (Lab Manual) and Demonstrations (TE) | Supplementary Materials (Teacher's Resource Book) |
|---|---|---|
| **12-1** Development of the Kinetic Theory of Gases, p. 297 **12-2** Relationship Between the Pressure and the Volume of a Gas—Boyle's Law, pp. 298-303 | Demo 12-1: The Exploding and Shrinking Marshmallows, p. TG-185 Lab 19: Boyle's Law | Transparency Master: Boyle's Law—Table of Data, p. 12-5 Review Activity: Boyle's Law, p. 12-15 Concept Mastery: Pressure and Volume Changes, p. CM-22 |
| **12-3** Relationship Between the Temperature and the Volume of a Gas—Charles's Law, pp. 303-309 | Demo 12-2: Ballooning, p. TG-186 Lab 20: Charles's Law (demonstration) | Transparency Masters: —Charles's Law—Data Table 1, p. 12-6 —Plotting the Temperature of a Gas against Its Volume at Constant Pressure, p. 12-7 —Plotting the Temperature of a Gas against Its Volume at Constant Pressure (*answer*), p. 12-8 —Charles's Law: A Graphical Representation, p. 12-9 —Charles's Law Data: The Constant *V/T* Ratio, p. 12-10 Review Activity: Charles's Law, p. 12-16 Open-Ended Demonstration: Differences in the Behavior of Rubber and Mylar Balloons, p. 12-13 |
| **12-4** Relationship Between the Temperature and the Pressure of a Gas, pp. 310-311 | Demo 12-3: Water Balloon in the Bottle, p. TG-186 Demo 12-4: The Handboiler, p. TG-187 | Concept Mastery: Temperature Changes, p. CM-23 |
| **12-5** The Combined Gas Law, pp. 311-313 **Application** Self-cooling Cans, p. 313 | Lab 21: The Molar Volume of a Gas | Critical and Creative Thinking: Conditional Arguments, p. CCT-55 |
| **12-6** The Densities of Gases, pp. 314-315 | Lab 22: Determining the Molecular Mass of a Gas | Stoichiometry Problems: Density of Gases, p. SP-34 Stoichiometry Problems: Determining Molecular Mass from Density, p. SP-35 |

| Text Section | Labs (Lab Manual) and Demonstrations (TE) | Supplementary Materials (Teacher's Resource Book) |
|---|---|---|
| **12-7** Volume as a Measure of the Quantity of a Gas, pp. 315-317 | | Concept Mastery: Densities of Gases, p. CM-24 Transparency Master: Same Gas, Volume, and Temperature, but . . . , p. 12-11 |
| **12-8** Mass-Volume Problems at Non-standard Conditions, pp. 317-318 | | Stoichiometry Problems: Molar Volume at Non-STP Conditions, p. SP-37 Stoichiometry Problems: Gases at Non-standard Conditions, p. SP-52 |
| **12-9** Dalton's Law of Partial Pressures, pp. 318-320 **12-10** Graham's Law of Diffusion, pp. 320-321 | Lab 23: Mass-Volume Relationships in Reactions Lab 24: Graham's Law of Diffusion | Concept Mastery: Dalton's Law of Partial Pressures, p. CM-26 Review Activity: The Gas Laws, p. 12-17 |
| **12-11** The Kinetic Theory and the Gas Laws, pp. 322-324 | | |
| **12-12** Deviations from Ideal Behavior, pp. 324-326 | | Transparency Master: Deviations from Ideal Gas Behavior, p. 12-12 |
| **12-13** The Ideal Gas Law, pp. 326-328 | | Computer Experiment: The Gas Laws, p. 12-14 Practice Problems, p. 12-18 Non-SI Supplementary Problems, p. 12-19 Societal Issues: Air Pollution, p. SI-26 |
| **Career** Chemistry Teacher, p. 328 | | |
| | | Test—Form A, p. AT-44 Alternate Test—Form B, p. BT-44 |

☐ Core   ■ Advanced   ☐ Optional

## Chapter Overview

The ideal gas laws are developed using the kinetic theory. We discuss the individual work of Boyle, Charles, Dalton, and Graham and provide opportunities for students to solve problems based on the laws these scientists developed. We also discuss the formula derived from Boyle's and Charles's laws, the combined gas law. The gas laws are based on the behavior of ideal gases, but real gases do not behave ideally. Therefore, in this chapter, we discuss deviations from ideal behavior. The chapter ends with a discussion of the ideal gas law ($PV = nRT$) and the calculations that can be made using this relationship.

## Chapter Objectives

After students have completed this chapter, they will be able to:

1. Understand the ideal gas laws formulated by Boyle, Charles, Dalton, and Graham and solve problems based on these laws. *12-1* to *12-5, 12-9,* and *12-10*

2. Use the kinetic theory to explain the theoretical basis for the gas laws. *12-11*

3. Show how the absolute temperature scale is derived. *12-3*

4. Find the mass of a sample of gas if its molecular mass and volume at STP are known. *12-7*

5. Determine the density of a gas at a particular temperature and pressure if the density of the gas at another temperature and pressure is known. *12-6*

6. Solve mixed mass-volume problems when there are non-standard conditions of temperature and pressure. *12-8*

7. Use the ideal gas law to solve gas problems. *12-12* and *12-13*

## Teaching Suggestions

### 12-1 Development of the Kinetic Theory of Gases, p. 297, and

### 12-2 Relationship Between the Pressure and the Volume of a Gas—Boyle's Law, pp. 298-303

| Planning Guide | |
|---|---|
| **Labs (Lab Manual) and Demonstrations (TE)** | **Supplementary Materials (Teacher's Resource Book)** |
| Demo 12-1: The Exploding and Shrinking Marshmallows, p. TG-185<br>Lab 19: Boyle's Law | Transparency Master: Boyle's Law—Data Table, p. 12-5<br>Review Activity: Boyle's Law, p. 12-15<br>Concept Mastery: Pressure and Volume Changes, p. CM-22 |

■ Point out that the investigation of the nature of gases that led to the formulation of the kinetic molecular theory of gases illustrates how theories are developed. Many observations regarding the macroscopic behavior of gases were reported. Based upon these observations, the kinetic molecular theory of gases was formulated to explain this behavior in terms of what is taking place at the atomic level.

■ Introduce the discussion of Boyle's law by doing Demonstration 12-1, "The Exploding and Shrinking Marshmallows." In this dramatic demonstration, the students see the effect of a change in pressure on the volume of a marshmallow, a balloon, and some shaving cream. Each of these materials contains trapped air that expands and contracts in response to pressure changes. Then explain that as early as 1660, Robert Boyle noticed this property of gases. In later experiments, Boyle used quantitative data to express the relationship between the volume and pressure of a gas. This relationship is called Boyle's law. Emphasize that Boyle's law is logical since reducing the volume of a gas increases the concentration of the particles, resulting in more frequent collisions. Point out that the reverse is also true. Assign Laboratory 19, "Boyle's Law," in which the students observe the usefulness of Boyle's law in the chemistry laboratory.

■ **Application.** You may want to mention that a respirator is an application of Boyle's law. When the pressure in the unit is decreased, the air volume in the patient's lungs increases, forcing the chest to expand. The reverse occurs when the pressure in the unit is increased. The alternate expansion and contraction of the chest enables the patient to breathe even though he or she cannot control the movement of the diaphragm.

■ **Concept Mastery.** Students often memorize the equations for gas laws without attempting to understand the physical implications of the laws. The Concept Mastery worksheet "Pressure and Volume Changes" (TRB) helps students to visualize the ramifications of Boyle's law at both the molecular and the macroscopic level.

### 12-3 Relationship Between the Temperature and the Volume of a Gas—Charles's Law, pp. 303-309

| Planning Guide | |
|---|---|
| **Labs (Lab Manual) and Demonstrations (TE)** | **Supplementary Materials (Teacher's Resource Book)** |
| Demo 12-2: Ballooning, p. TG-186<br>Lab 20: Charles's Law (demonstration) | Transparency Masters:<br>—Charles's Law—Data Table 1, p. 12-6<br>—Plotting the Temperature of a Gas against Its Volume at Constant Pressure, p. 12-7<br>—Plotting the Temperature of a Gas againsts Its Volume at Constant Pressure (*answer*), p. 12-8<br>—Charles's Law: A Graphical Representation, p. 12-9<br>—Charles's Law Data: The Constant $V/T$ Ratio, p. 12-10<br>Review Activity: Charles's Law, p. 12-16<br>Open-Ended Demonstration: Differences in the Behavior of Rubber and Mylar Balloons, p. 12-13 |

■ Do Demonstration 12-2, "Ballooning," in which the students can see the effect of temperature on the volume of a gas in qualitative terms. Use this demonstration to begin discussion of Charles's law. Tell the students that around 1780 Charles and Gay-Lussac, French scientists, investigated the relationship between volume of a gas and temperature. In their work with hot-air balloons, they found that any gas sample, at constant pressure, expands to $\frac{1}{273}$ of its volume for every degree rise in temperature. A century after Charles reported his findings, scientists realized that this observation could be used as a basis for the absolute temperature scale.

■ Work through Sample Problems 4 and 5 to show the types of calculations that can be done using Charles's law. Do Laboratory 20, "Charles's Law," as a teacher demonstration to eliminate the risk of the students handling mercury. The students can record the data as you perform the demonstration/experiment. Then they can do calculations and construct a graph, thereby verifying the relationship between the temperature and the volume of a gas at constant pressure.

■ **Application.** You may want to point out to your students that they may have experienced a qualitative application of Charles's law at the beach. The air over the hot sands is heated, expands, and rises. As it moves away from the warm surface of the earth, it cools, contracts, and falls down over the cooler water. This produces the convection current called a sea breeze. The same principle allows birds to glide above a highway.

■ **Concept Mastery.** You may wish to assign Concept Mastery question 37 (chapter-end question) to check that your students understand that the size of the molecule does not affect the pressure. Review the kinetic molecular theory in Section 12-11. Students need to understand that the heavier particles move at slower velocities and this compensates for their larger masses when they strike the walls of the container.

### 12-4 Relationship Between the Temperature and the Pressure of a Gas, pp. 310-311

| Planning Guide | |
| --- | --- |
| Labs (Lab Manual) and Demonstrations (TE) | Supplementary Materials (Teacher's Resource Book) |
| Demo 12-3: Water Balloon in the Bottle, p. TG-186<br>Demo 12-4: The Handboiler, p. TG-187 | Concept Mastery: Temperature Changes, p. CM-23 |

■ Remind the students that heating a gas increases molecular velocities and the number of impacts per unit time (i.e., pressure). Then do Demonstration 12-3, "Water Balloon in the Bottle." In this demonstration the students can see the effect of a change in tempera-

ture on the pressure in a sealed container. Once the students understand the principle of this demonstration, do Demonstration 12-4, "The Handboiler." This is another demonstration illustrating the qualitative relationship between temperature and pressure of a gas at constant volume. Discuss the apparatus shown in text Figure 12-15. Explain that keeping the volume of a gas constant, while heating it, results in an increase in pressure. Ask the students to compare this relationship to the relationship of temperature and volume of a gas at constant pressure. Discuss Equation 6 in the text.

■ **Application.** You may want to make the students aware of the danger associated with heating closed containers such as a stoppered test tube or an aerosol can. Even if the material inside does not vaporize, the response of the enclosed air to a temperature increase can result in an explosion.

■ **Concept Mastery.** If students are having difficulty answering Concept Mastery question 35 (chapter-end question), you may want to take a piece of dry ice and let it expand in a balloon. Students need to visualize gases on the particle level. They need to be able to relate the size of the individual molecules to the spaces between the molecules. Then, the students can explain what is happening at the molecular level when a gas is being heated. They can understand that the gas particles are moving farther apart rather than expanding in size. The Concept Mastery worksheet "Temperature Changes" (TRB) can be used to test the students' comprehension of the effects of changing the temperature of a gas.

### 12-5 The Combined Gas Law, pp. 311-313

| Planning Guide | |
| --- | --- |
| Labs (Lab Manual) and Demonstrations (TE) | Supplementary Materials (Teacher's Resource Book) |
| Lab 21: The Molar Volume of a Gas | Critical and Creative Thinking: Conditional Arguments, p. CCT-55 |

■ Point out that in most situations, chemists work with volumes of gases where both the temperature and the pressure change. For these situations, Boyle's law and Charles's law are combined to enable the chemist to determine the effect of these changes on the volume. Emphasize that in solving problems where both pressure and temperature are changed, the student should first try to visualize the effect of the individual changes on the system and then write the appropriate fractions. For example, if the pressure is increased ($P_2 > P_1$), the volume will decrease. Therefore, the pressure fraction should have a value less than one ($P_1/P_2$).

If the temperature is increased ($T_2 > T_1$), the volume is increased. Therefore, the temperature fraction should have a value greater than one ($T_2/T_1$). Caution the students to use only Kelvin temperatures in these fractions. Once students can visualize these relationships, they do not have to memorize Equation 7 in the text in order to solve combined gas law problems.

■ Have the students do Laboratory 21, "The Molar Volume of a Gas." In this lab, the students use the combined gas law to determine experimentally the molar volume of a gas.

■ **Critical Thinking.** In the Critical and Creative Thinking worksheet "Conditional Arguments" students evaluate the conclusions and validity of several conditional arguments. This thinking skill is an excellent tool for helping the students to decide when conditions are appropriate for applying a particular gas law.

## 12-6 The Densities of Gases, pp. 314-315, and

## 12-7 Volume as a Measure of the Quantity of a Gas, pp. 315-317

| Planning Guide | |
|---|---|
| **Labs (Lab Manual) and Demonstrations (TE)** | **Supplementary Materials (Teacher's Resource Book)** |
| Lab 22: Determining the Molecular Mass of a Gas | Stoichiometry Problems: Density of Gases, p. SP-34<br>Stoichiometry Problems: Determining Molecular Mass from Density, p. SP-35<br>Concept Mastery: Densities of Gases, p. CM-24<br>Transparency Master: Same Gas, Volume, and Temperature, but . . . , p. 12-11 |

■ Remind the students that the density of a gas varies with temperature and pressure. Therefore, when scientists report the density of a gas, they must specify the temperature and pressure at which the density was determined. Explain that the gas laws enable us to convert the density of a gas measured at one temperature and pressure to its density at another temperature and pressure. Discuss Sample Problem 8.

■ Point out that when dealing with gases, it is often convenient to use the volume of a gas sample as a measure of quantity. Remind the students that this volume varies with temperature, pressure, and mass. Then point out that the mass of a sample of gas can be calculated if the density of the gas is known. This gas density must be measured under the same conditions

of temperature and pressure as those for which the volume is measured. If the conditions are not identical, the combined gas law can be used to convert the volume to the same conditions under which the density was measured. Assign Laboratory 22, "Determining the Molecular Mass of a Gas," in which the students experimentally determine the molecular mass of a substance from measurements of density.

■ **Application.** You may want to discuss how a hot-air balloon rises. A gas burner heats the air in the balloon, causing the air to expand and become less dense than the air outside the balloon.

■ **Concept Mastery.** Students often have difficulty with the concept of density, particularly when applied to gases. The Concept Mastery worksheet "Densities of Gases" (TRB) can help students to visualize density at the particle level.

## 12-8 Mass-Volume Problems at Non-standard Conditions, pp. 317-318

| Planning Guide | |
|---|---|
| **Labs (Lab Manual) and Demonstrations (TE)** | **Supplementary Materials (Teacher's Resource Book)** |
| | Stoichiometry Problems: Molar Volume at Non-STP Conditions, p. SP-37<br>Stoichiometry Problems: Gases at Non-standard Conditions, p. SP-52 |

■ Tell the students that, so far, stoichiometry problems involving gases have dealt with volumes at STP. Not all volumes are measured at standard conditions. Therefore, the volumes of the gases must be converted to non-standard conditions using the combined gas law.

## 12-9 Dalton's Law of Partial Pressures, pp. 318-320, and

## 12-10 Graham's Law of Diffusion, pp. 320-321

| Planning Guide | |
|---|---|
| **Labs (Lab Manual) and Demonstrations (TE)** | **Supplementary Materials (Teacher's Resource Book)** |
| Lab 23: Mass-Volume Relationships in Reactions<br>Lab 24: Graham's Law of Diffusion | Concept Mastery: Dalton's Law of Partial Pressures, p. CM-26<br>Review Activity: The Gas Laws, p. 12-17 |

■ John Dalton was interested in weather phenomena, and his experiments with humidity led him to the law of partial pressures. Explain the law of partial pressures. Discuss Sample Problems 11 and 12 and then assign Laboratory 23, "Mass-Volume Relationships in Reactions." In this lab, students collect $CO_2$ by water displacement. They use the law of partial pressures to obtain the pressure of the dry $CO_2$ produced.

■ Assign Lab 24, "Graham's Law of Diffusion," to introduce the concept of diffusion. In this lab the students observe that the gas molecules of HCl and $NH_3$ diffuse or spread out within a glass tube. They eventually diffuse close enough to react and form $NH_4Cl$. Explain that Graham's law is based on the fact that the average kinetic energy of the molecules is the same for all gases at the same temperature. Using the $\frac{1}{2}mv^2$ formula for kinetic energy, show that, for these gases, the velocities of diffusion are inversely proportional to the square roots of their molecular masses or their densities. In this lab, the students can experimentally verify Graham's law by measuring the distances traveled by HCl and $NH_3$ gas molecules.

■ **Concept Mastery.** You may want to use Concept Mastery question 39 (chapter–end question) to check students' understanding of the particle nature of gases and Dalton's law of partial pressures. Present the experimental evidence first, showing that the pressure is independent of the kind of molecule present. Then explain this in more detail when discussing the kinetic molecular theory. The Concept Mastery worksheet "Dalton's Law of Partial Pressures" (TRB) can be used to give students further practice in developing a molecular-level understanding of partial pressures.

## 12-11 The Kinetic Theory and the Gas Laws, pp. 322-324

■ Review the main assumptions of the kinetic theory of gases discussed in Section 11-8. Then discuss Boyle's law, Charles's law, Dalton's law of partial pressures, and Graham's law of diffusion in terms of the kinetic theory.

■ **Concept Mastery.** It is very important that students understand the kinetic molecular theory and its significance in everyday life. Concept Mastery questions 36 and 38 pose situations that many students may have encountered. Discuss these questions in terms of the kinetic molecular theory. Understanding the answers to these questions will be a great aid in solving gas–law problems.

## 12-12 Deviations from Ideal Behavior, pp. 324-326

| Planning Guide | |
|---|---|
| Labs (Lab Manual) and Demonstrations (TE) | Supplementary Materials (Teacher's Resource Book) |
| | Transparency Master: Deviations from Ideal Gas Behavior, p. 12-12 |

■ Discuss the Transparency Master "Deviations from Ideal Gas Behavior," which compares the $PV$ product for an ideal gas and for two real gases (nitrogen and carbon dioxide). Explain that there is no gas that is ideal, nor one that obeys the gas laws at all temperatures and pressures. Explain the large deviations from ideal behavior at extreme conditions of temperature and pressure. Point out that for real gases, the intermolecular attractions at high pressures and low temperatures account for smaller volumes than those predicted by the gas laws.

## 12-13 The Ideal Gas Law, pp. 326-328

| Planning Guide | |
|---|---|
| Labs (Lab Manual) and Demonstrations (TE) | Supplementary Materials (Teacher's Resource Book) |
| | Computer Experiment: The Gas Laws, p. 12-14 Practice Problems, p. 12-18 Non-SI Supplementary Problems, p. 12-19 Societal Issues: Air Pollution, p. SI-26 |

■ Chemists do not have to convert gas volumes to STP when they are interested in the number of moles of gas involved. This can be found more easily by using the ideal gas equation, $PV = nRT$. Point out that this equation can be used to find the molecular masses of gases, to calculate the volume occupied by a given mass of a gas at stated conditions, or to calculate the mass of a gas in a sample for which the volume is given at specified conditions. The advantage of the ideal gas equation is that the conversion to STP is embodied in the value of $R$. This saves time and provides a direct and less complicated method for solving gas problems. To illustrate this point, discuss Sample Problems 14 and 15.

■ After reading the Societal Issues article "Air Pollution" students may appreciate how the gas laws can help them to understand an important issue that affects their daily lives. The critical thinking questions at the end of the article are designed to develop the skills necessary for forming an educated opinion.

## Demonstrations

### 12-1 The Exploding and Shrinking Marshmallows

**Overview:** In this demonstration, you place a small balloon, marshmallows, and shaving cream inside a bell jar connected to a vacuum pump. As air is drawn out of the bell jar, the items—all of which contain trapped air—expand, suggesting that pressure is inversely related to volume of a gas. This is an exciting way to develop Boyle's law.

**Materials:** vacuum pump and bell jar; balloon blown up to 8 cm in diameter; adhesive tape; fresh marshmallows; shaving cream; small beaker.

**Advance Preparation:** 1. Blow up a balloon and let the air out until the diameter is about 8 cm. Tie off the neck of the balloon and place on its end a piece of tape that can be attached to the side of the bell jar during the demonstration. 2. Set up the vacuum pump and bell jar and be sure the apparatus is working properly.

**Procedure:** 1. Tape the inflated balloon to the upper side of the bell jar and place the jar securely on the vacuum-pump apparatus. Turn on the vacuum pump and ask students to observe and explain what happens. 2. Turn off the pump and allow air back into the bell jar. 3. Place several marshmallows beneath the bell jar, being careful not to cover the opening through which the air is drawn out. Replace the jar and turn on the pump. Tell students to observe and explain what happens. 4. Stop the pump, allow air to flow into the jar, and have students observe what happens to the marshmallows. 5. Place a small amount of shaving cream into the bottom of a beaker, and place the beaker inside the bell jar. Turn on the pump and have students observe what happens. 6. Allow air to re-enter the jar, and have students observe what happens to the shaving cream. 7. In each case, relate the volume of the trapped gas to the pressure. Refer to the charts and graphs of pressure and volume in the student text, and discuss Boyle's law.

**Results:** In all cases, the pressure will decrease on the objects as air molecules are withdrawn from the bell jar. The pressure outside the objects will be less than the pressure of air trapped inside the objects. The air molecules inside the objects can spread farther apart and create an increase in the volume of the objects. The balloon will expand and then will return to its original size when the pump is turned off. After the marshmallows increase in size as the air molecules in them expand, some of the molecules will escape, and the marshmallows will seem to "explode" or deflate at that point. When air is allowed into the jar, the marshmallows will shrink to a size that is smaller than their initial size because there will be fewer air molecules inside the marshmallows. The shaving cream, after it inflates, will start to deflate as soon as the pump is turned off because it does not have a relatively firm structure like that of the marshmallows.

## 12-2 Ballooning

**Overview:** In this demonstration, you place three identical balloons into environments of different temperatures. The volume of the balloons should change depending on the temperature. This demonstration can be used to discuss direct relationships between two variables and to develop Charles's law.

**Materials:** 3 small latex balloons blown up to the same size; 2 identical large, wide-mouth jars, one containing several small chunks of dry ice and the other containing water at about 60°–70°C.

**Advance Preparation:** 1. Blow up three balloons to the same size (about 3–5 cm in diameter) and tie off each one. 2. Obtain some dry ice and a large, wide-mouth jar. Shortly before the demonstration, place chunks of the dry ice into the jar to a depth that is one-eighth of the jar's total depth. 3. Shortly before carrying out the demonstration, heat some water to about 70°C. Fill a jar to about one-eighth full with this hot water, and replace the lid.

**Safety:** Use gloves and tongs when working with dry ice.

**Procedure:** 1. Ask the students to try to predict what will happen to the volume of a sealed balloon at room temperature when it is placed into a warmer or cooler environment. 2. Place a balloon into each of the two jars, and place a third balloon on your desk, at room temperature, as a reference. Have students observe what happens to the balloons. 3. Tell the students that temperature is directly related to volume when the pressure remains constant. Refer to the charts and graphs in the student text and discuss Charles's law.

**Results:** The balloon expands at a higher temperature and contracts at a lower temperature.

## 12-3 Water Balloon in the Bottle

**Overview:** In this demonstration, you place a water balloon with a diameter of about 6 cm over the mouth of a bottle that has an opening about 4 cm wide, and cause the balloon to enter the bottle without breaking. The demonstration suggests a direct relationship between temperature and pressure.

**Materials:** water balloon, about 6 cm in diameter; wide-mouth bottle, about 25 cm tall with an opening about 4 cm wide; matches; piece of newspaper; plastic straw.

**Advance Preparation:** Prepare a water-filled balloon that is about 6 cm in diameter.

**Safety:** Handle the matches and burning newspaper carefully.

**Procedure:** 1. Tell the students you will make the water balloon go into the bottle without breaking the balloon. Place the balloon on top of the bottle to show them the difference in size. 2. Lift the balloon. Light a small piece of newspaper and drop it into the bottle. Immediately place the balloon over the mouth of the bottle, and have students observe and explain what happens. 4. Tell the students you want to remove the balloon from the bottle, and ask for suggestions on how to do so. Place a sturdy plastic straw between the balloon and the side of the bottle. Gently tug on the balloon until it comes out. Ask students to explain what has happened. 5. Relate the temperature of a gas to its pressure. Discuss the direct relationship between the two variables.

**Results:** As the temperature of the hot gas inside the bottle decreases, so does the molecular motion and, thus, so does the pressure of the trapped gas. Since the pressure outside is greater than the pressure inside, the balloon is pushed into the bottle. In order to get the balloon out of the bottle, the pressures have to be kept equal. The straw allows air to enter the bottle as the balloon is gently tugged and released from the bottle.

### 12-4 The Handboiler

**Overview:** In this demonstration, a glass handboiler (or the glass part of the "drinking bird" from Demonstration 1-4) is held in the palm of the hand, which causes the colored liquid inside it to move up the tube and appear to boil. This helps to show the direct relationship between the temperature and pressure of a gas.

**Materials:** handboiler (can be purchased at science-museum gift shops for about $5 or from Fascinations, P.O. Box 60548, Fairbanks, AK 99701) or "drinking bird" (see Demonstration 1-4).

**Advance Preparation:** none

**Procedure:** 1. Ask a student volunteer to hold the bottom bulb of the handboiler or "drinking bird" in the palm of his or her hand. Ask students to observe and explain what happens. 2. Have another student hold the top bulb of the handboiler, and have students observe and attempt to explain what happens. Ask them to describe the relationship between temperature and pressure of a gas.

**Results:** In step 1, the heat from the hand will increase the temperature of the vapor inside the bulb, which increases the pressure of this vapor against the volatile liquid beneath it. This increase in pressure will force liquid up into the tube and top bulb so quickly that the liquid will appear to boil. The heat from the hand will also make the liquid in the lower bulb evaporate faster, which will force more molecules into the gas phase, increasing the pressure and forcing liquid up into the tube. In step 2, the heat of the hand will have a similar effect on the contents of the upper bulb, this time causing liquid to be pushed down the tube. As the temperature of a gas increases, so does its pressure.

## Answers to Questions

**Page 302**
1. The value of $B$ is decreased by one-fifth.
2. Their product is a constant.
3. **a.** $AB = K$
   **b.** See Figure 12-2.

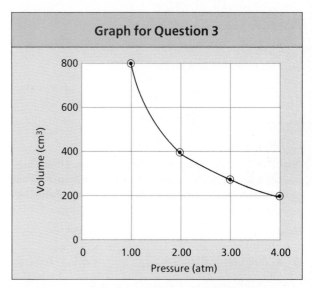

Figure 12-2

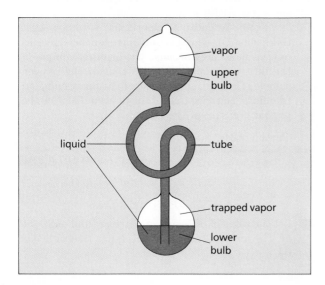

Figure 12-1

**4.** $PV = 2.0 \times 10^2$ atm-cm$^3$

**5.** The pressure will be decreased.

**6. a.** 1/7; **b.** 3/1; **c.** $1/0.28 = 3.6$

## Page 303

**7.** $600 \text{ cm}^3 \times \dfrac{302 \text{ kPa}}{604 \text{ kPa}} = 300 \text{ cm}^3 = 3.00 \times 10^2 \text{ cm}^3$

**8.** $862 \text{ kPa} \times \dfrac{752 \text{ cm}^3}{624 \text{ cm}^3} = 1.04 \times 10^3 \text{ kPa}$

## Page 309

**9.** The factors that cause a weighted piston to produce a downward pressure are the weight of the piston, the total weight resting on the piston, and the air pressure.

**10.** The volume will increase.

**11.** There will be no change in the downward force exerted by the piston because the weight of the piston, the weight of the mass, and the atmospheric pressure will not have changed. Under these conditions, heating merely causes the volume of the gas to increase.

**12. a.** Line A; **b.** Line C

**13.** Charles's law states that, at constant pressure, the volume of a sample of gas is directly proportional to its Kelvin temperature.

**14.** The constant $K$ will change if there are changes in the quantity, kind, or pressure of the gas.

**15.** A gas will cease to follow Charles's law when it changes from a gas to a liquid.

**16.** The value of $B$ becomes ⅓ as great.

**17.** $A = 0.12 \dfrac{\text{dm}^3}{\text{K}} \times B$

**18.** $102 \text{ cm}^3 \times \dfrac{402 \text{ K}}{201 \text{ K}} = 204 \text{ cm}^3$

**19.** $400 \text{ K} \times \dfrac{603 \text{ cm}^3}{804 \text{ cm}^3} = 300 \text{ K, or } 27°\text{C}$

## Page 310

**20.** The pressure will be increased.

**21.** $(273 + -33°\text{C})\text{K} \times \dfrac{133 \text{ kPa}}{53.3 \text{ kPa}} = 599 \text{ K, or } 326°\text{C}$

**22.** $33.5 \text{ kPa} \times \dfrac{250 \text{ K}}{290 \text{ K}} = 28.9 \text{ kPa}$

## Page 313

**23.** In most experiments involving gases, there are changes in both temperature and pressure. The combined gas laws can be used to calculate the effect of both of these changes on volume.

**24.** $212 \text{ dm}^3 \times \dfrac{42.4 \text{ kPa}}{33.3 \text{ kPa}} \times \dfrac{307 \text{ K}}{311 \text{ K}} = 266 \text{ dm}^3$

**25. a.** $850 \text{ cm}^3 \times \dfrac{273 \text{ K}}{300 \text{ K}} \times \dfrac{85 \text{ kPa}}{101.3 \text{ kPa}} = 6.5 \times 10^2 \text{ cm}^3$

    **b.** $6.5 \times 10^2 \text{ cm}^3 \times \dfrac{1 \text{ dm}^3}{10^3 \text{ cm}^3} \times \dfrac{1.52 \text{ g}}{\text{dm}^3} = 0.99 \text{ g}$

## Page 315

**26.** $1.00 \text{ cm}^3 \times \dfrac{273 \text{ K}}{294 \text{ K}} \times \dfrac{102.2 \text{ kPa}}{101.3 \text{ kPa}} = 0.937 \text{ cm}^3$

$\dfrac{1.68 \times 10^{-3} \text{ g}}{0.937 \text{ cm}^3} = 1.79 \times 10^{-3} \text{ g}$

## Page 317

**27.** The volume varies with changes in temperature and pressure.

**28.** $1.24 \text{ dm}^3 \times \dfrac{293 \text{ K}}{333 \text{ K}} \times \dfrac{202.5 \text{ kPa}}{101.3 \text{ kPa}} = 2.18 \text{ dm}^3$

$2.18 \text{ dm}^3 \times 0.166 \text{ g/dm}^3 = 0.362 \text{ g}$

## Page 318

**29.** $3.22 \text{ dm}^3 \times \dfrac{273 \text{ K}}{313 \text{ K}} \times \dfrac{120.2 \text{ kPa}}{101.3 \text{ kPa}} =$

$3.33 \text{ dm}^3 \text{ (volume at STP)}$

$\dfrac{3.33 \text{ dm}^3}{22.4 \text{ dm}^3} = 0.149 \text{ mol of NH}_3, 0.149 \text{ mol of NH}_4\text{Cl}$

$\dfrac{53.5 \text{ g NH}_4\text{Cl}}{\text{mol NH}_4\text{Cl}} \times 0.149 \text{ mol NH}_4\text{Cl} = 7.97 \text{ g NH}_4\text{Cl}$

## Page 321

**30. a.** The total pressure of the mixture is equal to the pressure of the dry air plus the pressure of the water vapor. This equals 96 kPa. **b.** The dry air pressure is 93 kPa. The water vapor pressure is 2.8 kPa.

**31.** According to Graham's law, a denser gas diffuses more slowly. Therefore, the $H_2S$ (molecular mass = 34 u) will reach you before the $CO_2$ (molecular mass = 44 u) does.

**32.** Before the 2 dm$^3$ of nitrogen and 1 dm$^3$ of oxygen are put into the same container, the gases occupy a total volume of 3 dm$^3$. Because the gases are being put into a container with a 3-dm$^3$ volume, the pressure after mixing the gases remains the same, i.e., 101.3 kPa.

    From Avogadro's hypothesis, we know that there must be twice as many nitrogen molecules as oxygen molecules because the original volume of the nitrogen sample is twice that of the oxygen sample. The partial pressure of the nitrogen must, therefore, be twice that of the oxygen. Let $x$ be the partial pressure of the $O_2$.

Partial press. $N_2$ + partial press. $O_2$ = 101.3 kPa

$2x + x = 101.3 \text{ kPa}$

$x = 33.77 \text{ kPa (partial press. O}_2)$

$2x = 67.53 \text{ kPa (partial press. N}_2)$

**33.** Let the rates of diffusion of $CH_4$ be $v_1$ and of $SO_2$ be $v_2$. The molecular mass of $CH_4$ is 16; that of $SO_2$ is 64.

$$\dfrac{v_1}{v_2} = \sqrt{\dfrac{64}{16}}$$

$$\frac{\text{rate of diffusion } CH_4}{\text{rate of diffusion } SO_2} = \frac{2}{1}$$

Our result tells us that $CH_4$ diffuses at twice the rate of $SO_2$.

**Page 324**

**34. a.** Increasing the volume decreases the number of molecules per unit volume. The number of impacts per unit area of surface is decreased, causing the pressure to decrease.

**b.** An increase in temperature increases the speeds of the molecules of gas and their number of impacts per unit volume. In order for the pressure to remain constant, however, the number of impacts per unit volume must not increase. Therefore, volume must increase.

**35.** The number and intensity of molecular impacts per unit area do not change because of large spaces between molecules.

**36.** At the same temperature, gases have the same average kinetic energies. From the equation, it can be seen that molecules with smaller masses must have greater velocities.

**Page 326**

**37.** An ideal gas follows all of the gas laws perfectly.

**38.** High pressures and low temperatures cause real gases to deviate from ideal behavior.

**39. a.** Intermolecular forces of attraction cause their volumes to be less than that of an ideal gas.

**b.** The molecules are so close that their volume is a significant part of the total volume.

**Page 328**

**40.** $\frac{48.0 \text{ g}}{16.0 \text{ g/mol}} = 3.00 \text{ mol } CH_4$

$$\frac{3.00 \text{ mol} \times 273 \text{ K} \times 8.31 \frac{\text{kPa-dm}^3}{\text{mol-K}}}{101.3 \text{ kPa}} = 67.2 \text{ dm}^3$$

**41.** $\frac{50.6 \text{ kPa} \times 0.750 \text{ dm}^3}{8.31 \frac{\text{kPa-dm}^3}{\text{mol-K}} \times 373 \text{ K}} = 0.01224 \text{ mol}$

$FM = \frac{0.490 \text{ g}}{0.01224 \text{ mol}} = 40.0 \text{ g/mol}$

**42. a.** $\frac{20.0 \text{ dm}^3 \times 94.2 \text{ kPa}}{8.31 \frac{\text{kPa-dm}^3}{\text{mol-K}} \times 294 \text{ K}} = 0.771 \text{ mol}$

**b.** $\frac{0.771 \text{ mol} \times 8.31 \frac{\text{kPa-dm}^3}{\text{mol-K}} \times 358 \text{ K}}{35.0 \text{ dm}^3} =$
65.5 kPa

**43. a.** $\frac{10.0 \text{ dm}^3 \times 125.8 \text{ kPa}}{8.31 \frac{\text{kPa-dm}^3}{\text{mol-K}} \times 308 \text{ K}} = 0.492 \text{ mol}$

**b.** $\frac{8.4 \text{ dm}^3 \times 174.2 \text{ kPa}}{8.31 \frac{\text{kPa-dm}^3}{\text{mol-K}} \times 0.492 \text{ mol}} = 358 \text{ K} = 85°C$

## Chapter Review   12

**Page 329, Content Review**

**1.** The kinetic theory of gases ties together the work of Boyle, Charles, Dalton, and Graham.

**2.** Temperature must be kept constant when considering the relationship between volume and temperature of a fixed mass of gas.

**3.** $V = 380 \text{ dm}^3 \times \frac{106.6 \text{ kPa}}{101.3 \text{ kPa}} = 400 \text{ dm}^3$

**4.** $P_2 = \frac{P_1V_1}{V_2} = \frac{93.3 \text{ kPa} \times 120 \text{ dm}^3}{30 \text{ dm}^3} = 370 \text{ kPa}$

**5.** Pressure must be kept constant when considering the relationship between the temperature and volume of a fixed mass of gas.

**6.** The volume of a gas will increase by $^{50}/_{273}$ of its value if the temperature changes from 0°C to 50°C.

**7.** The volume of a gas will double if the temperature is raised from 0°C to 273°C at constant pressure.

**8.** $300 \text{ dm}^3 = 150 \text{ dm}^3 \times \frac{T}{293 \text{ K}}$; $T = 586 \text{ K or } 313°C$

**9.** At constant volume, the pressure of a gas is directly proportional to the Kelvin temperature.

**10.** $98.6 \text{ kPa} \times (265 \text{ K}/295 \text{ K}) = 88.6 \text{ kPa}$

**11.** The increase in pressure of the gas, produced by the temperature increase, may cause the flask to explode.

**12.** $500 \text{ dm}^3 \times (101.3 \text{ kPa}/93.3 \text{ kPa}) = 543 \text{ dm}^3$

**13.** $150 \text{ dm}^3 = 200 \text{ dm}^3 \times \frac{106.6 \text{ kPa}}{98.6 \text{ kPa}} \times \frac{T}{290 \text{ K}}$;
$T = 201 \text{ K or } -72°C$

**14.** Density is inversely proportional to volume.
$V_2 = V_1 \times \frac{P_1}{P_2} \times \frac{T_2}{T_1} = 1 \text{ cm}^3 \times \frac{101.3 \text{ kPa}}{100.5 \text{ kPa}} \times \frac{294 \text{ K}}{273 \text{ K}} =$
1.09 cm³
$D = \frac{M}{V} = \frac{3.12 \times 10^{-3} \text{ g}}{1.09 \text{ cm}^3} = 2.87 \times 10^{-3} \text{ g/cm}^3$

**15.** $V = 0.73 \text{ dm}^3 \times \frac{102.5 \text{ kPa}}{101.3 \text{ kPa}} \times \frac{273 \text{ K}}{294 \text{ K}} = 0.67 \text{ dm}^3$
$M = V \times D = 0.67 \text{ dm}^3 \times 0.90 \text{ g/dm}^3 = 0.60 \text{ g}$

16. 132 g FeS ÷ 87.8 g/mol = 1.50 mol FeS
From the equation, 1.50 mol $H_2S$ will be produced.
At STP: (1.50 mol $H_2S$) × (22.4 $dm^3$) = 33.6 $dm^3$
$$V = 33.6 \text{ dm}^3 \times \frac{101.3 \text{ kPa}}{95.1 \text{ kPa}} \times \frac{303 \text{ K}}{273 \text{ K}} = 39.7 \text{ dm}^3$$

17. **a.** When the oxygen is transferred to the container of nitrogen, the nitrogen will exert the same pressure as before, 101.3 kPa. **b.** The oxygen will have twice as much volume, so its pressure will be halved to 101.3 kPa. The total pressure of the mixture is the sum, 202.6 kPa.

18. The molecular mass of a gas determines the rate at which it diffuses. Under the same conditions of temperature and pressure, gases diffuse at a rate inversely proportional to the square roots of their molecular masses.
$$\frac{V_1}{V_2} = \sqrt{\frac{M_2}{M_1}}$$

19. **a.** In a gas at STP, about 99.95% of the volume is empty space, so the volume of the molecules is 0.05% or ½₀₀₀ of the total volume. Taking the cube root of this shows that the diameter of a molecule is about ⅓ of the distance between molecules. **b.** The pressure of a confined gas is due to the number and intensity of the impacts of the molecules on a unit area of the surface.

20. The Kelvin temperature determines the average kinetic energy of the molecules of a gas.

21. In an ideal gas, the molecules are points without volume and do not exert any force of attraction for one another.

22. **a.** ? mol $= \dfrac{120.0 \text{ kPa} \times 2.00 \text{ dm}^3}{8.31 \text{ kPa-dm}^3/\text{mol-K} \times 300 \text{ K}} =$
                                           0.0963 mol
**b.** $0.0963 \times 6.02 \times 10^{23} = 5.80 \times 10^{22}$ molecules

Page 330, Content Mastery

23. By Dalton's law, the total pressure is the sum of the individual pressures. Thus at STP, 101.3 kPa = 20.1 kPa + 81.1 kPa + $P_{unknown}$, so $P_{unknown} =$
                                           0.1 kPa.

24. $\dfrac{P_1V_1}{T_1} = \dfrac{P_2V_2}{T_2}$ so $P_2 = \dfrac{P_1V_1T_2}{T_1V_2} =$
$$\frac{(101.3 \text{ kPa})(0.952 \text{ dm}^3)(2T_1)}{(0.225 \text{ dm}^3)(T_1)} = 857 \text{ kPa}$$

25. $P_2 = \dfrac{P_1T_2}{T_1} = \dfrac{(202.5 \text{ kPa})(348 \text{ K})}{(254 \text{ K})} = 277 \text{ kPa}$
% incr. $= \dfrac{(277 - 202.5) \text{ kPa}}{202.5 \text{ kPa}} \times 100 = 36.8\%$

26. $Zn(s) + 2HCl(aq) \rightarrow ZnCl_2(aq) + H_2(g)$

$n_{Zn} = 38.2 \text{ g} \div 65.4 \text{ g/mol} = 0.584 \text{ mol}$; 1 Zn atom produces 1 $H_2$ molecule, so $n_{H_2} = 0.584$ mol
At STP, $V = (0.584)(22.4 \text{ dm}^3) = 13.1 \text{ dm}^3$
At the given conditions, $V =$
$$\frac{(13.1 \text{ dm}^3)(101.3 \text{ kPa})(298 \text{ K})}{(98.3 \text{ kPa})(273 \text{ K})} = 14.7 \text{ dm}^3$$

27. $n = \dfrac{PV}{RT} = \dfrac{(94.2 \text{ kPa})(5.544 \text{ m}^3)}{\left(8.312 \dfrac{\text{kPa-dm}^3}{\text{mol-K}}\right)(298 \text{ K})} \times \dfrac{\text{dm}^3}{10^{-3} \text{ m}^3} =$
                                           $210.8 \text{ mol} \approx 211 \text{ mol}$

28. $V_2 = \dfrac{P_1V_1}{T_1} \times \dfrac{T_2}{P_2} = \dfrac{V_1P_1T_2}{P_2T_1} =$
$$\frac{(0.857 \text{ dm}^3)(101.3 \text{ kPa})(296 \text{ K})}{(48.3 \text{ kPa})(310 \text{ K})} =$$
                                           $1.716 \text{ dm}^3 \approx 1.72 \text{ dm}^3$

29. From Charles's law,
$$V_2 = \frac{V_1T_2}{T_1} = \frac{(3.44 \text{ dm}^3)(343 \text{ K})}{(273 \text{ K})} = 4.32 \text{ dm}^3$$

30. From Boyle's law,
$$P_2 = \frac{P_1V_1}{V_2} = \frac{(101.3 \text{ kPa})(0.952 \text{ dm}^3)}{(0.225 \text{ dm}^3)} = 429 \text{ kPa}$$

31. $\dfrac{v_1}{v_2} = \sqrt{\dfrac{m_2}{m_1}}$
$m_1$ = molecular mass of $H_2$ = 2(1.0079) =
                                           2.0158 g/mol
$m_2$ = molecular mass of $UF_6$ =
          238.029 g/mol + 6(18.9984 g/mol) =
          238.029 + 113.9904 = 352.019 g/mol
$\dfrac{v_1}{v_2} = \sqrt{\dfrac{352.019 \text{ g/mol}}{2.0158 \text{ g/mol}}} = \sqrt{174.630} = 13.2148 \approx$
                                           13.21 times faster

32. $m$ of $N_2$ = 2(14.007) g/mol = 28.014 g/mol
molecular volume at STP = 22.4 $dm^3$/mol.
density $= \dfrac{\text{molecular mass}}{\text{molecular volume}} = \dfrac{28.014 \text{ g/mol}}{22.4 \text{ dm}^3/\text{mol}} =$
                                           $1.25 \text{ g/dm}^3 = 1.25 \text{ kg/m}^3$

33. $V_1 = \dfrac{V_2P_2T_1}{P_1T_2} = \dfrac{(3.34 \text{ dm}^3)(98.7 \text{ kPa})(273 \text{ K})}{(101.3 \text{ kPa})(310 \text{ K})}$
                                           = 2.866 $dm^3$
Therefore, mass = (density)(volume) =
          $(3.17 \text{ g/dm}^3)(2.866 \text{ dm}^3) = 9.09 \text{ g}$

34. **a.** Squeezing a balloon decreases the volume, so the molecules hit the wall of the balloon more often, increasing the pressure. **b.** Heating a balloon gives the molecules more energy, so they travel faster, striking the wall with more force, expanding the balloon's volume. **c.** Adding more air molecules to a tire means that more molecules bounce off the walls of the tire, increasing the pressure.

**Page 331, Concept Mastery**

35. **Concept:** *Gases expand on heating.*
    *Solution:* When gases are heated, the molecules move faster and the space between molecules increases. Thus the gas takes up more space. The molecules themselves do not expand.

36. **Concept:** *Pressure of gases is due to the frequency and the kinetic energy with which the particles strike the walls of the container.*
    *Solution:* When the football is inflated, the pressure exerted by the molecules within the football is greater than the external pressure. This is because the molecules within the football are closer together than those on the outside. As time passes, some air leaks out of the football until the frequency of molecules striking the football on the inside and outside is identical; that is, the internal and external pressures are identical.

37. **Concept:** *Pressure of gases depends on kinetic energy.*
    *Solution:* Both gases would have the same kinetic energy if they were at the same temperature. There would be an equal number of molecules in each container, and they would exert the same pressure. Heavier molecules would be moving at a slower rate; the faster moving particles would have less impact.

38. **Concept:** *Volume of gases is dependent on temperature.*
    *Solution:* As the balloon becomes warm, the molecules move at faster rates, become farther apart, and therefore occupy more space. The phenomenon has nothing to do with hot air rising.

39. **Concept:** *The pressure of each gas is independent of the mass of the particles. It is dependent on the number of particles and their kinetic energy.*
    *Solution:* **a.** Since there are five gases, each has a partial pressure of one-fifth of the total pressure, or 20 kPa. **b.** Each has the same pressure, so each has the same number of molecules. **c.** The molecules of each gas have the same kinetic energy because they are at the same pressure and temperature. **d.** The molecules of each gas do not have the same velocity; the less massive particles move faster. **e.** See Figure 12-3.

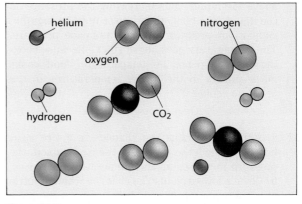

**Figure 12-3**

**Page 332, Cumulative Review**

40. **d.** No reaction occurs when copper is placed in HCl.

41. **b.** Forming iron oxide in moist air is a chemical property of iron.

42. **d.** 1 g of O contains twice as many atoms as 1 g of S.

43. **b.** mass of oxygen in oxide = 5.42 g − 1.48 g = 3.94 g
    moles of carbon: 1.48 g ÷ 12.01 = 0.123 mol
    moles of oxygen: 3.94 g ÷ 16.00 = 0.246 mol
    ratio O:C = 0.246:0.123 = 2:1; formula = $CO_2$

44. **a.** $10.0 \text{ g Cu} \times \dfrac{1 \text{ mol Cu}}{64.0 \text{ g Cu}} \times \dfrac{1 \text{ mol Pb}}{2 \text{ mol Cu}} \times \dfrac{207 \text{ g Pb}}{1 \text{ mol Pb}}$
    $= 16.17 \text{ g Pb} \approx 16.2 \text{ g Pb}$

45. **a.** $2Na(s) + 2H_2O(l) \rightarrow 2NaOH(aq) + H_2(g)$
    **b.** No reaction: no gas, water, or precipitate is formed. No ions are removed from the solution.
    **c.** $2Mg(s) + O_2(g) \rightarrow 2MgO(s)$
    **d.** $NH_4OH(aq) \rightarrow NH_3(g) + H_2O(l)$

46. $(C_2H_5)_x = 87$; $29x = 87$; $x = 3$; $(C_2H_5)_3 = C_6H_{15}$

47. When water boils, the heat energy becomes potential energy that overcomes the attractive forces between the molecules, allowing them to break free as gas molecules.

48. Boiling occurs when equilibrium vapor pressure equals the atmospheric pressure. According to text Figure 11-20, the vapor pressure will be 80 kPa at approximately 94°C.

49. $25.0 \text{ g Na}_2SO_4 \times \dfrac{1 \text{ mol Na}_2SO_4}{142 \text{ g Na}_2SO_4} \times \dfrac{1 \text{ mol BaSO}_4}{1 \text{ mol Na}_2SO_4} \times$
    $\dfrac{233.3 \text{ g BaSO}_4}{1 \text{ mol BaSO}_4} = 41.1 \text{ g BaS}$

50. As water evaporates in the pressure cooker, it increases the number of particles in the space

above the liquid, thus increasing the pressure on the liquid. The temperature rises until the equilibrium vapor pressure equals this inside pressure. The temperature goes above 100°C. Because cooking speed depends on temperature, food cooks more quickly in the higher temperatures in the pressure cooker.

## Page 332, Critical Thinking

**51. a.** $P/T = K$ explains the changes in a tire as it heats up. Since the volume of the tire is fixed, the pressure increases as the temperature increases. **b.** Boyle's law explains the changes when a bottle of room-temperature soda is opened. As the pressure decreases, the volume of gas increases. **c.** $P/T = K$ explains the changes when a bottle of cold soda is warmed but not opened. The volume is fixed, so the pressure increases as the temperature increases. **d.** The combined gas law explains the changes when a bottle of soda is warmed and opened. The temperature increases and the pressure decreases, so the volume of the gas increases. **e.** The combined gas law explains the changes when a weather balloon rises. If the amount of gas in the balloon remains constant, the external pressure decreases with increasing altitude, and the temperature decreases. More information would be needed to calculate the effect of these changes on the volume of the balloon. **f.** Charles's law explains the changes when an inflated balloon is cooled. The pressure on the balloon is constant, so as temperature decreases, volume decreases.

**52.** The molecules of a liquid are much closer together than the molecules of a gas, so two basic assumptions of the kinetic theory are not true for liquids: Liquid molecules occupy a volume that is not negligible compared to the volume of a liquid. Molecules of a liquid attract one another.

**53.** Unlike liquids and solids, gases cannot conveniently be weighed on a scale. Therefore, it is useful to be able to determine the mass of a gas sample from its volume, temperature, and pressure.

**54.** If gases in a container reacted, Dalton's law of partial pressures would apply only if the number of moles of the products equaled the number of moles of the reactants.

**55.** The kinetic theory assumes that the molecules of

an ideal gas occupy a point volume; that they have no attraction for one another; and that each molecule acts independently, as if it were the only molecule present in that sample of gas.

## Page 333, Challenge Problems

**56. a.** Helium at STP:
$$20.0 \text{ g He} \times \frac{1 \text{ mol He}}{4.00 \text{ g He}} \times \frac{22.4 \text{ dm}^3}{1 \text{ mol}} = 112 \text{ dm}^3$$

Pressure of He in container:
$$P_{He} = 1.00 \text{ atm} \times \frac{293 \text{ K}}{273 \text{ K}} \times \frac{112 \text{ dm}^3}{50.0 \text{ dm}^3} = 2.40 \text{ atm He}$$

Oxygen at STP:
$$70.0 \text{ g O}_2 \times \frac{1 \text{ mol O}_2}{32.0 \text{ g O}_2} \times \frac{22.4 \text{ dm}^3}{1 \text{ mol}} = 49.0 \text{ dm}^3$$

Pressure of $O_2$ in container:
$$P_{O_2} = 1.00 \text{ atm} \times \frac{293 \text{ K}}{273 \text{ K}} \times \frac{49.0 \text{ dm}^3}{50.0 \text{ dm}^3} = 1.05 \text{ atm O}_2$$

**b.** Total pressure = $P_{He} + P_{O_2}$ =
2.40 atm + 1.05 atm = 3.45 atm

**57.** Find the empirical formula, assuming a 100-g sample:
C = 82.8 g × (1 mol C/12.0 g C) = 6.90 mol
H = 17.2 g × (1 mol H/1.00 g H) = 17.2 mol
Ratio of H:C = 17.2:6.90 = 5:2,
empirical formula $C_2H_5$.
Find the molecular mass, using Graham's law:
$$\frac{R_{gas X}}{R_{O_2}} = \sqrt{\frac{m_{O_2}}{m_X}} \quad \frac{3.7 \text{ cm}^3/s}{5.0 \text{ cm}^3/s} = \sqrt{\frac{32}{X}}$$

$$0.74 = \sqrt{\frac{32}{X}} \quad 0.55 = \frac{32}{X} \quad X = 58$$

$(C_2H_5)_y = 58$; $29n = 58$; $n = 2$; formula = $C_4H_{10}$

**58. a.** $PV = nRT$ where $n$ = moles = $\dfrac{\text{mass}}{\text{molecular mass}}$
$$PV = \frac{\text{mass}}{\text{molecular mass}} \times RT$$
$$\frac{(P)(\text{molecular mass})}{RT} = \frac{\text{mass}}{V} = \text{density}$$

**b.** molecular mass = $\dfrac{(\text{mass})(RT)}{PV}$

**59.** The lighter $NH_3$ (17 u/molecule) will travel faster than HCl (36.5 u/molecule) and therefore farther in the same length of time, so the $NH_4Cl$ will form at point C.

# Electron Configurations

## Chapter Planning Guide

| Text Section | Labs (Lab Manual) and Demonstrations (TE) | Supplementary Materials (Teacher's Resource Book) |
|---|---|---|
| **13-1** Wave Mechanics, pp. 335-337 <br> **13-2** Probability and Energy Levels, pp. 337-338 | Demo 13-1: The Heisenberg Uncertainty Principle, p. TG-197 <br> Demo 13-2: Standing Waves, p. TG-197 | |
| **Biography** Neils Bohr, p. 336 | | |
| **13-3** Energy Levels of the Wave-Mechanical Model of the Atom, pp. 339-341 <br> **13-4** Orbitals, pp. 341-343 | Lab 25: Flame Tests | Transparency Master: Sublevels Available in Each Principal Energy Level, p. 13-1 <br> Transparency Master: The First Four Principal Energy Levels and Their Sublevels, p. 13-2 <br> Transparency Master: Principal Energy Level and the Maximum Number of Orbitals and Electrons, p. 13-3 |
| **13-5** The Shapes of Orbitals, pp. 343-345 <br> **13-6** Electron Spin, pp. 345-346 | Demo 13-3: Shapes of Orbitals, p. TG-197 | |
| **13-7** Quantum Numbers, p. 346 | | |
| **13-8** Notation for Electron Configurations, p. 347 <br> **13-9** Electron Configurations for the First 11 Elements, pp. 347-349 <br> **13-10** Electron Configurations for Elements of Higher Atomic Numbers, pp. 349-350 <br> **13-11** Significance of Electron Configurations, pp. 350-352 | | Review Activity: Writing Electron Configurations, p. 13-4 <br> Review Activity: Quantum Mechanics and Electron Configurations, p. 13-5 |

13

| Text Section | Labs (Lab Manual) and Demonstrations (TE) | Supplementary Materials (Teacher's Resource Book) |
|---|---|---|
| **13-12**  Electron Configurations for Atoms in the Excited State, pp. 352-353 | | |
| | | Test—Form A, p. AT-48 Alternate Test—Form B, p. BT-48 |

☐ Core    ■ Advanced    ☐ Optional

## Chapter Overview

We begin Chapter 13 with the application of wave mechanics to atomic theory and then continue with an explanation of the charge-cloud model of the atom. This currently accepted model is based on plots of electron probability, with electrons being assigned to energy levels, sublevels, and orbitals. The orientation and shape of orbitals and the spin property of electrons are also considered. Students use orbital notation and orbital diagrams to determine the electron configurations of atoms in the ground state. We describe both the valence shell and the individual valence electrons of an atom and note their importance in chemical bonding. A discussion of the electron configurations of atoms that are in the excited state ends the chapter.

## Chapter Objectives

After students have completed this chapter, they will be able to:

1. Explain the use of wave mechanics in atomic theory.                    *13-1* and *13-2*

2. Describe the wave-mechanical model of the atom.                    *13-3* to *13-7*

3. Locate electrons in energy levels, sublevels, and orbitals according to the wave-mechanical model.                    *13-3* to *13-7*

4. Construct orbital diagrams and write electron configurations for elements with atomic numbers 1 through 38.                    *13-8* to *13-12*

## Teaching Suggestions

### 13-1 Wave Mechanics, pp. 335-337, and

### 13-2 Probability and Energy Levels, pp. 337-338

| Planning Guide | |
|---|---|
| Labs (Lab Manual) and Demonstrations (TE) | Supplementary Materials (Teacher's Resource Book) |
| Demo 13-1: The Heisenberg Uncertainty Principle, p. TG-197 Demo 13-2: Standing Waves, p. TG-197 | |

■ You may begin by giving some examples of the motion of objects that can be described by classical mechanics: the legendary apples that Newton watched dropping from a tree, colliding marbles or billiard balls, the use of a block and tackle to lift a piano, etc. In this space age, students are usually aware that laws of motion govern the behavior of objects. Therefore, they can accept the idea that laws govern the behavior of electrons in atoms, even though these laws depart radically from those of classical mechanics. Review Sections 6-10 and 6-11, which describe how the Bohr model of the atom gave way to the charge-cloud model as a result of the introduction of quantum mechanics.

■ To help students understand quantization, have them recall (Section 6-2) the concept of continuous versus discontinuous matter and the conclusion, based on experimental evidence, that matter is discontinuous, i.e., it consists of discrete entities or atoms. In other words, matter is quantized. The energy associated with electrons is also quantized. As an analogy, point out that a multistory building with elevators has "quantized" movement between floors. Ask students to think about using a stairway ("quantized" movement) versus using a ramp (continuous or non-quantized movement) in the building.

■ Use Demonstration 13-1, "The Heisenberg Uncertainty Principle," to suggest the idea that one cannot know both the location and the velocity of a subatomic particle at the same time.

Without the mathematics of physics, the concept of wave behavior will remain elusive, but students do not need the calculations to apply many of the conclusions reached through their use. For a qualitative account of standing waves, walk students through the rope model in text Figure 13-3. Then do Demonstration 13-2, "Standing Waves," using a spring coil model to show that wavelength depends on energy input.

### 13-3 Energy Levels of the Wave-Mechanical Model of the Atom, pp. 339-341, and

### 13-4 Orbitals, pp. 341-343

| Planning Guide | |
|---|---|
| Labs (Lab Manual) and Demonstrations (TE) | Supplementary Materials (Teacher's Resource Book) |
| Lab 25: Flame Tests | Transparency Master: Sublevels Available in Each Principal Energy Level, p. 13-1 |
| | Transparency Master: The First Four Principal Energy Levels and Their Sublevels, p. 13-2 |
| | Transparency Master: Principal Energy Level and the Maximum Number of Orbitals and Electrons, p. 13-3 |

■ Many students come to chemistry with a solar-system model of the atom in mind. To help them replace that model with the wave-mechanical model, use analogies such as the following. Describe the behavior of hummingbirds, which move so fast that we cannot determine the paths by which they travel between feeding stops. All we can do is to plot their feeding locations and compare the distances of those locations from the nest.

For another analogy, you can make a line drawing of a bird's-eye view of a basketball court and ask students to shade the drawing with denser shading for locations of high probability of finding the ball. As students will recall from participating in or watching basketball games, the areas of high probability will be the rim, backboard, and foul line.

■ While discussing energy levels and sublevels, you may want to tell students the origin of the letters used to designate the energy sublevels, which are derived from the descriptions of the nature of certain lines in the emission spectra of elements studied during early research. These letters originated as: *s*, sharp; *p*, principal; *d*, diffuse; and *f*, fundamental.

■ In doing Laboratory 25, "Flame Tests," students make use of the fact that electrons of atoms of metals can become excited in the flame of a laboratory burner. Students observe the characteristic colors associated with the wavelengths of the electromagnetic energy emitted as the excited electrons return to the ground state, and they use the colors to identify the metals.

■ Explain that energy levels, sublevels, and orbitals are a lot like hotels. Energy levels are like floors, sublevels are like wings of rooms on a floor, and orbitals are like the rooms themselves. There is a large difference in elevation off the ground among floors. You, or an elevator, must work harder (put in more energy) to get to the higher floors. On a given floor of a large hotel, one wing is likely to be just a little bit higher or lower than the others. Finally, in this hotel each room is equipped with twin beds and thus can hold only two guests—so that a room can be empty, half full, or full.

To extend the hotel analogy, point out that the twin beds are arranged head-to-foot, so that when two people (like electrons) occupy a room they must sleep in opposite directions (opposite spin, according to the Pauli exclusion principle). Furthermore, when several people are first assigned to a wing, they may occupy separate rooms (Hund's rule) in that wing. Only after each room has one occupant is the second bed in each room filled with additional guests.

■ **Concept Mastery.** In addition to the analogies of the basketball game and hummingbirds described, you may wish to use Concept Mastery questions 37 and 38 (chapter-end questions) to help students overcome earlier misconceptions about the structure of the atom and to learn the quantum-mechanical model.

### 13-5 The Shapes of Orbitals, pp. 343-345, and

### 13-6 Electron Spin, pp. 345-346

| Planning Guide | |
|---|---|
| Labs (Lab Manual) and Demonstrations (TE) | Supplementary Materials (Teacher's Resource Book) |
| Demo 13-3: Shapes of Orbitals, p. TG-197 | |

■ Students are often troubled by the shapes of orbitals. Remind them that the "shape" of an orbital is a three-dimensional version of the charge-cloud plot. It is not a path for an electron—the wave-mechanical model does not include any account of paths for the

13

movement of electrons. Using plastic or wooden models of the orbitals is helpful here. In addition, or alternatively, do Demonstration 13-3, "Shapes of Orbitals," which uses balloons as models. Be sure your technique for drawing $x$, $y$, and $z$ axes on the chalkboard, projector, or paper looks believable to students.

■ Magnetic fields are associated with those kinds of atoms that have electrons in half-filled orbitals. One way to account for these fields is to assign spin—either clockwise or counterclockwise—to electrons. In a filled orbital, the electrons have opposite spin, cancelling out any magnetic field. Where there are half-filled orbitals the field persists and can be detected experimentally.

### 13-7 Quantum Numbers, p. 346

■ Quantum numbers are used to locate electrons. If you have students who are able to understand this topic, you may tell them that the first three quantum numbers are numerical solutions to the Schrödinger wave equation. Use text Figure 13-13 to show how quantum numbers correspond to energy level, sublevel, and orbital identifications in the charge-cloud model. The range of values for each quantum number is:

$$n = 1, 2, 3, \ldots$$
$$l = 0, 1, 2, \ldots, n - 1$$
$$m = -l, \ldots, -1, 0, +1, \ldots, +l \text{ (sometimes the symbol } m_l \text{ is used instead of } m\text{)}$$
$$s = +\tfrac{1}{2}, -\tfrac{1}{2} \text{ (sometimes the symbol } m_s \text{ is used instead of } s\text{)}$$

### 13-8 Notation for Electron Configurations, p. 347,

### 13-9 Electron Configurations for the First 11 Elements, pp. 347-349,

### 13-10 Electron Configurations for Elements of Higher Atomic Numbers, pp. 349-350, and

### 13-11 Significance of Electron Configurations, pp. 350-352

| Planning Guide | |
|---|---|
| Labs (Lab Manual) and Demonstrations (TE) | Supplementary Materials (Teacher's Resource Book) |
| | Review Activity: Writing Electron Configurations, p. 13-4 Review Activity: Quantum Mechanics and Electron Configurations, p. 13-5 |

■ Emphasize to students that the buildup of electrons in atoms represents an orderly filling of energy levels, sublevels, and orbitals. It does not show how atoms are actually formed.

Students need to know how to generate an electron configuration for an atom simply by knowing its atomic number. They should memorize the sequence of energy levels and sublevels for $Z = 1$ through 36. Text Figure 13-6 shows one way to remember this. Assign the Review Activity "Writing Electron Configurations" to reinforce this skill.

■ Be sure that students can match orbital diagrams to electron configurations. For a given atom in the ground state, ask them to count the numbers of:

. . . filled energy levels      . . . occupied energy levels
. . . filled sublevels          . . . occupied sublevels
. . . filled orbitals           . . . occupied orbitals
    . . . half-filled orbitals     . . . empty orbitals
    . . . empty orbitals
      in occupied sublevels
. . . paired electrons          . . . unpaired electrons
. . . kernel electrons          . . . valence electrons

■ **Concept Mastery.** You may wish to use Concept Mastery question 41 (chapter-end question) to help students compare the structures of the kernels of atoms with those of whole atoms. Students may think of atoms as being neutral objects, but if only the kernel is being considered, point out that this is not the case. Have students draw the kernels of atoms.

### 13-12 Electron Configurations for Atoms in the Excited State, pp. 352-353

■ If you elect to teach this section, the hotel analogy can be used to help develop the concept of the excited state. A hotel guest can get to a higher floor (an excited state) by doing some work—climbing the stairs or taking the elevator (energy input). If the person makes such a move, he or she will leave a vacancy behind on a lower floor (lower energy level). Help students to look for atoms in an excited state by comparing given electron configurations to the lowest energy levels and sublevels available. Here are some examples that may be helpful:

(1) $1s^2 2s^2 2p^4 3s^1$: one of many possible excited states of an atom of fluorine. The configuration is for *fluorine*, because 9 electrons are specified. The configuration is for an atom in the *excited* state because the 9 electrons are not arranged in the lowest levels and sublevels, which would be: $1s^2 2s^2 2p^5$

(2) [Ar]$3d^8 4s^1 5p^1$: an excited state of an atom of nickel

■ **Concept Mastery.** If students think of the energy levels of atoms as the paths that they make around the nucleus, they may not understand Concept Mastery questions 38 and 39 (chapter-end questions). Be sure students avoid showing energy levels as concentric circles. Instead, have them use diagrams like those in text Figure 13-16.

# Demonstrations

## 13-1 The Heisenberg Uncertainty Principle

**Overview:** In this demonstration, a double transparency containing the words "location" and "velocity" is placed onto the overhead projector. As the word "location" is focused, the word "velocity" goes increasingly out of focus. This demonstration helps to suggest the idea that it is impossible to know both the location and the velocity of a subatomic particle at the same time.

**Materials:** two transparencies; strips of cardboard about 25 cm × 5 cm; transparency-marking pen.

**Advance Preparation:** Write the word "location" in large letters across the top third of a transparency. Write the word "velocity" across the bottom third of another transparency. Separate the two transparencies with a double thickness of cardboard strips between their edges. This can be glued or taped to the transparencies.

**Procedure:** 1. Place the transparency setup onto the overhead projector. Focus the word "location." Have students observe what happens to the other word. 2. Focus the word "velocity," and have students note what happens to the other word. 3. Tell the students that Heisenberg's uncertainty principle states that it is impossible to know the precise location and velocity of a subatomic particle at the same time: The more that is known about the one, the less that is known about the other.

**Results:** When one word is focused, the other will go out of focus.

## 13-2 Standing Waves

**Overview:** In this demonstration, students use a spring coil to make standing waves. They observe that when a certain amount of energy is used to produce the standing waves, only a certain number of the waves form. The wavelength depends on the energy input.

**Materials:** spring coil; rope.

**Advance Preparation:** none

**Procedure:** 1. Have two students hold the ends of the coil. While the end of the coil is held fixed by one student, the other student should try to vary the energy input to make various numbers of standing waves. Have students observe the relationship between energy input and number of waves and wavelength. 2. Have students note whether any energy input—or only certain energies—will produce the standing waves. Relate this to the energy associated with energy levels in the atom. 3. Have students use a rope to produce standing waves. Students should note whether a different amount of energy is needed to produce the same number of standing waves as were produced using the coil. This helps to suggest whether an electron in a given energy level of one kind of atom might have a different amount of energy associated with it than would an electron in the same energy level in another kind of atom.

**Figure 13-1**

**Results:** In step 1, as energy input increases, the number of waves will increase and the wavelength will decrease. In step 2, only certain energies will produce the standing waves. In step 3, a different amount of energy is needed.

## 13-3 Shapes of Orbitals

**Overview:** In this demonstration, students use different-shaped balloons to better understand $s$ and $p$ orbitals.

**Materials:** balloons, round and elongated.

**Advance Preparation:** Be sure that all of the elongated balloons are of the same size and that they can be twisted at the halfway point without breaking.

**Procedure:** 1. Blow up several round balloons to different diameters. Ask students which kind of orbitals these represent. 2. Blow up three elongated balloons of different colors. Twist each elongated balloon in half, and twist all three together so each balloon lies on a different axis, perpendicular to the others. Make sure that students note that all three balloons are equal in size and differ only in their orientation around the center. Ask the students what these balloons represent.

**Results:** In step 1, the balloons represent $s$ orbitals in various energy levels. In step 2, the balloons represent the three $p$ orbitals in a particular energy level, which have the same amount of energy associated with them.

13

# Answers to Questions

## Page 337

1. The study of mechanics is concerned with qualitative and quantitative descriptions of bodies in motion under the influence of forces.
2. The major shortcoming of the Bohr model was that it could not predict energy levels for atoms with more than one electron.

## Page 338

3. **a.** The equations of wave mechanics describe what the probability is of finding an electron with specified energy at a particular location and how this probability changes from location to location.
   **b.** Wave mechanics describes the most probable locations of electrons. It does not describe how electrons move from one location to another.
4. A standing wave is a wave that meets itself without any overlap.
5. A navigator could locate the harbor by shining a searchlight in many directions from the boat until the familiar features of the harbor could be seen. Also, a radar or radio beam received from the harbor shore might guide the boat in the direction of strongest reception. The navigator could also listen for a foghorn or follow lighted markers.

    Someone on shore could use the same techniques, that is, observing wave phenomena such as sound, radio, or light. These could be detected unaided (sight, hearing) or aided by such devices as radio or radar transmitters and receivers.

## Page 343

6. The theory of wave mechanics (quantum mechanics) was developed to account for the behavior of small particles such as electrons.
7. The principal quantum number of an electron gives the principal energy level of the electron.
8. The wave-mechanical model provides for sublevels within the energy levels proposed by Bohr.
9. The number of sublevels in an energy level is given by the number $n$ (principal quantum number) of that energy level.
   **a.** In the third principal energy level, there are three sublevels ($s, p, d$).
   **b.** In the sixth principal energy level, there are six sublevels ($s, p, d, f, g, h$). After the $f$ sublevel, additional sublevels are assigned letters in alphabetical order beginning with $g$.
10. **a.** An orbital is a region within the probability plot of a sublevel where one or two electrons may be found. An orbital may, of course, also be unoccupied.
    **b.** One or two electrons can occupy an orbital.

11. **a.** $3s \rightarrow 2s$    **c.** $3s \rightarrow 1s$
    **b.** $4s \rightarrow 4p$    **d.** $1s \rightarrow 2s$
12. The element with the smallest $Z$ that has a $5s$ electron as its highest energy electron is $_{37}$Rb ($Z = 37$). Since there are only two electrons permitted in the $5s$ sublevel, the element with the largest $Z$ is $_{38}$Sr ($Z = 38$).

## Page 346

13. **a.** The shape of an $s$ orbital is spherical.
    **b.** The shape of a $p$ orbital is that of a figure eight or a dumbbell.
14. **a.** A $1s$ orbital differs from a $2s$ orbital in that a $1s$ orbital has electrons with less energy that are located, on average, closer to the nucleus.
    **b.** A $2s$ orbital differs from a $2p$ orbital in that the $2s$ orbital has electrons with *slightly* less energy. The $s$ orbital is spherical, whereas the $p$ orbital is in the shape of a figure eight.
15. Wave mechanics does not account for the path of an electron. Hence, it does not give information about how the path of a $3s$ electron differs from the path of a $3p$ electron.
16. The $n$ quantum number identifies the principal energy level of the electron. The $l$ quantum number identifies the energy sublevel. The $m$ quantum number identifies the specific orbital within the energy sublevel. The $s$ quantum number identifies the direction of spin of the electron.

## Page 349

17. The electrons in an atom in the ground state possess the lowest possible energy. They are located in the lowest possible energy levels and sublevels.
18. The electron configuration of an atom refers to the arrangement of its electrons among its energy levels, sublevels, and orbitals.
19. **a.** The symbol $3p_x{}^1$ refers to or stands for the one electron in the $p_x$ *orbital of the* $p$ sublevel of the third principal energy level.
    **b.** The symbol $2s^2$ refers to the two electrons in the only orbital of the $s$ sublevel of the second principal energy level. On occasion, it may also refer only to the second of those two electrons.
20. According to the electron configuration given, there are 4 electrons: 2 in the $1s$ sublevel plus 2 in the $2s$ sublevel. Thus, $Z = 4$.
21. An atom with the given configuration has 4 orbital pairs of electrons. This is shown best in an orbital diagram. (See text Figure 13-16 for the element with $Z = 9$, fluorine.)
22. The notation given, intended for $_7$N, is incorrectly written. It shows 6 electrons but should show 7 electrons and be written as $1s^2 2s^2 2p_x{}^1 2p_y{}^1 2p_z{}^1$.

**Page 352**

**23.** The next electron is assigned to the *s* orbital of next higher principal energy level.

**24.** The valence shell is the outer principal energy level of an atom that has at least one electron. When the valence shell is the first energy level, its electron capacity is 2. For each of the remaining valence shells, each has a capacity of 8 electrons.

**25.** The atom specified is an aluminum atom ($Z = 13$). The third energy level is the valence shell. It contains 3 electrons.

**26.** The kernel refers to an atom's nucleus and inner energy levels of electrons. Only the valence shell of electrons is excluded from the kernel.

**Page 353**

**27.** Atoms in the excited state contain more energy than atoms in the ground state. In the excited state, one or more electrons occupy "positions" above the lowest available energy level/sublevel. In the ground state, electrons occupy the lowest available energy levels and sublevels.

**28.** The electron configuration for an atom of aluminum in an excited state is $1s^2 2s^2 2p^6 4s^1 4p^1 4d^1$. Its orbital diagram is:

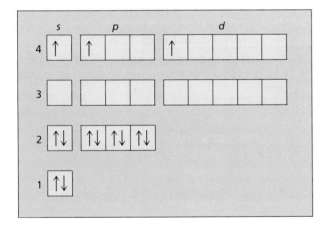

**29.** The electron configuration given does not represent an excited state because the sublevels $p_x$, $p_y$, and $p_z$ have the same energy. All electrons are in the lowest available energy levels and sublevels.

## Chapter Review   13

**Page 354, Content Review**

**1.** Classical mechanics refers to the laws of motion described by Isaac Newton.

**2.** The classical laws successfully explain the motion of objects on the earth, the motion of the earth's moon, and the motion of planets. They also explain the properties and behavior of gases.

**3. a.** Einstein's relativity theory is used to explain the motion of objects traveling at speeds close to the speed of light.

   **b.** Wave mechanics is used to explain the motion of subatomic particles.

**4.** As the mass of an object increases, the wavelength of the waves associated with that object decreases.

**5.** To have its location or velocity measured, an electron must be "seen." To be seen, it must interact with photons of light. During this interaction, the photon transfers some of its energy to the electron, thus changing the electron's position or velocity or both.

**6.** The equations give the probability of finding an electron in a particular region of space at a particular time, but they cannot be used to calculate exact orbits for electrons.

**7.** In the Bohr model, an electron emits energy when it falls from its orbit to one of lower energy. The wavelength depends on the magnitude of the energy jump; the wavelength is shorter for larger energy jumps.

**8.** The Bohr model allows electrons to exist only in the principal energy levels. This model could not account for the abundance of lines in the spectra of atoms. The wave model allows electrons to occupy sublevels of slightly different energies within the principal energy levels. The existence of these sublevels can account for the abundance of lines in atomic spectra.

**9.** An atom with three principal energy levels full of electrons has the configuration $1s^2 2s^2 2p^6 3s^2 3p^6$. The total number of electrons is $2 + 2 + 6 + 2 + 6 = 18$. Since the $3d$ sublevel is at a higher energy than the $4s$ sublevel, it is empty.

**10.** The fourth principal energy level has $1\,s + 3\,p + 5\,d + 7\,f = 16$ orbitals.

**11.** Four of the *d* orbitals look like 2 dumbbells crossed in the middle and at right angles to each other. The other *d* orbital looks like 1 dumbbell with a doughnut around its middle.

**12.** An orbital pair is 2 electrons with opposite spins in the same orbital.

**13.** In an electron configuration, the coefficient gives the principal energy level, the letter gives the sublevel, the superscript gives the number of electrons in that sublevel.

13

14. Since the sum of the superscripts in the electron configuration is $2 + 2 + 3 = 7$, this neutral atom has 7 electrons, so its atomic number ($Z$) is also 7. Since the 3 electrons in the $2p$ orbital are unpaired, the atom has only 2 orbital pairs, one in the $1s$ and the other in the $2s$ sublevel.

15. Start filling sublevels in the proper order until the total number of electrons in a neutral atom equals its atomic number.
    **a.** $1s^2 2s^1$
    **b.** $1s^2 2s^2 2p^6$
    **c.** $1s^2 2s^2 2p^6 3s^2 3p^1$
    **d.** $1s^2 2s^2 2p^6 3s^2 3p^6 4s^2$ or $[Ar]4s^2$

16. Add up the superscripts to find the total number of electrons, which equals the atomic number of a neutral atom. Use the periodic table to find the name of the element from the atomic number.
    **a.** $Z = 2 + 1 = 3$, lithium
    **b.** $Z = 2 + 2 + 2 + 1 + 1 = 8$, oxygen
    **c.** $Z = 2 + 2 + 6 + 2 + 4 = 16$, sulfur
    **d.** $Z = 18 + 2 = 20$, calcium

17. Electrons fill the $4s$ orbital before they fill the $3d$ orbital because the $4s$ is at a lower energy level than the $3d$. This orbital overlap means that the next higher energy level is started when the current level has full $s$ and $p$ orbitals. Therefore, the valence shell (the outermost shell) never has more than 8 electrons in it.

18. The kernel is the nucleus plus the inner levels of electrons, excluding the valence shell. The atomic number of sodium (11) minus the number of valence electrons (1) equals the number of electrons in the kernel (10). Thus, the configuration of the kernel is $1s^2 2s^2 2p^6$.

19. The valence shell is the shell with the highest principal quantum number. Even though $3d$ electrons are at a higher energy level than $4s$ electrons, the electrons in the $4s$ orbital are the valence electrons because their principal quantum number 4 is larger than the other principal quantum number, 3. Because of this orbital overlap, electrons in the $d$ and $f$ orbitals can never be valence electrons.
    **a.** and **b.** The electrons in the $4s$ orbital are the valence electrons for both atoms, and not the 10 or 5 electrons in the $3d$ orbitals, respectively.

20. In an excited atom, at least 1 electron moves from its ground-state orbital to a higher energy level. The empty space in the ground-state orbital shows in the electron configuration of an excited atom as a missing or partially filled orbital at a lower energy level than the highest occupied orbital.
    **a.** This atom is in the ground state because the only partially filled orbital is the $2p$, which is also at the highest energy level.
    **b.** This atom is excited because the $2p$ orbital is only partially filled, and it is not the highest orbital. A $2p$ electron has jumped to the $3s$ level. Because the neutral element has 8 electrons, it must be oxygen.
    **c.** The only partially filled orbital is the $3p$. Because this is also the highest energy level, this atom is in the ground state.

## Page 355, Content Mastery

21. Si $= 1s^2 2s^2 2p^6 3s^2 3p^2$
    K $= 1s^2 2s^2 2p^6 3s^2 3p^6 4s^1$
    Cu $= 1s^2 2s^2 2p^6 3s^2 3p^6 4s^1 3d^{10}$
    Br $= 1s^2 2s^2 2p^6 3s^2 3p^6 4s^2 3d^{10} 4p^5$

22. The Pauli exclusion principle says that 2 electrons that occupy the same orbit must have opposite spins. No 2 electrons in the same atom can have the same set of quantum numbers ($n$, $l$, $m$, and $s$).

23. The first shell ($n = 1$) has only 1 $s$ orbital and no $p$ orbitals. The second shell ($n = 2$) is the lowest shell for which $p$ orbitals exist.

24. An orbital can hold 0 electrons, 1 electron, or 2 electrons of opposite spins.

25. For any energy level with principal quantum number $n$, the values of $l$ range from 0 to $n - 1$.

26. An orbital diagram uses arrows to show paired and unpaired electrons in boxes representing the orbitals.
    Al: $Z = 13$

    | $1s^2$ | $2s^2$ | $2p^6$ | $3s^2$ | $3p^1$ |
    |---|---|---|---|---|
    | ↑↓ | ↑↓ | ↑↓ ↑↓ ↑↓ | ↑↓ | ↑ _ _ |

    P: $Z = 15$

    | $1s^2$ | $2s^2$ | $2p^6$ | $3s^2$ | $3p^3$ |
    |---|---|---|---|---|
    | ↑↓ | ↑↓ | ↑↓ ↑↓ ↑↓ | ↑↓ | ↑ ↑ ↑ |

    Cl: $Z = 17$

    | $1s^2$ | $2s^2$ | $2p^6$ | $3s^2$ | $3p^5$ |
    |---|---|---|---|---|
    | ↑↓ | ↑↓ | ↑↓ ↑↓ ↑↓ | ↑↓ | ↑↓ ↑↓ ↑ |

    Zn: $Z = 30$

    | $1s^2$ | $2s^2$ | $2p^6$ | $3s^2$ | $3p^6$ |
    |---|---|---|---|---|
    | ↑↓ | ↑↓ | ↑↓ ↑↓ ↑↓ | ↑↓ | ↑↓ ↑↓ ↑↓ |

    | $4s^2$ | $3d^{10}$ |
    |---|---|
    | ↑↓ | ↑↓ ↑↓ ↑↓ ↑↓ ↑↓ |

27. **a.** $2s \rightarrow 3p$ The energy change is greater between orbitals that are farther apart.
    **b.** The energy change in jumping from $1s \rightarrow 2p$ equals the energy change in falling from $2p \rightarrow 1s$.

28. The principal quantum number $n$ can have values 1, 2, 3, 4, 5 . . .

29. The motion of an electron that is part of an atom is best described by wave mechanics.

30. The electron configuration in **a** is excited because the $3p$ level is only partially filled and a higher level ($4s$) contains an electron. Since the neutral atom has 16 electrons, it must be sulfur. The configurations in **b** and **c** are ground state.

31. Chromium has 24 electrons. If the electrons filled the orbitals in the proper order, the electron configuration would be $[Ar]4s^23d^4$. Chromium gains symmetry and, therefore, stability by promoting 1 of its $4s$ electrons to make the $3d$ level half full: $[Ar]4s^13d^5$.

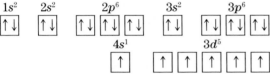

32. Since the first shell has only 2 valence electrons, the first 3 elements with 7 valence electrons are fluorine, chlorine, and bromine.
   F: $[He]2s^22p^5$
   Cl: $[Ne]3s^23p^5$
   Br: $[Ar]4s^23d^{10}4p^5$

33. The third shell ($n = 3$) is the lowest shell for which $d$ orbitals exist. The first shell ($n = 1$) has only $s$ orbitals, the second shell ($n = 2$) has only $s$ and $p$ orbitals.

34. Because the two electrons are in the same orbital, they have the same values for $n$, $l$, and $m$, but different values for $s$. Thus, the quantum numbers for Electron A must be 4, 2, 1, $-\frac{1}{2}$.

35. The atomic number of calcium is 20. Its configuration is $[Ar]4s^2$. It has 2 valence electrons, and $20 - 5 = 18$ electrons in its kernel.

36. The fourth shell has 4 sublevels—$s$, $p$, $d$, and $f$.

Page 356, Concept Mastery

37. **Concept:** *An orbital represents the particular region of space where the electron is most likely to be found. It represents a probability, not a certainty.*
   *Solution:* This student is mistaken in thinking that the electron spends ALL of its time inside its own orbital. The probability of finding it inside its own orbital is greater than the probability of finding it elsewhere. The probability of finding an electron outside its orbital is small but finite.

38. **Concept:** *An orbital represents the particular region of space where the electron is most likely to be found. It represents a probability, not a definite path.*

*Solution:* This student is also mistaken. An electron does not travel in a definite orbital around the nucleus the way planets travel around the sun. Because of its wave nature, an electron is spread throughout the atom. Its orbital is the region of space inside the atom where the electron is most likely to be found.

39. **Concept:** *The sublevels that the electrons occupy are actually different energy levels.*
   *Solution:* No, this is false. The 2 electrons in the $1s$ sublevel have less energy than the 2 electrons in the $2s$ sublevel, which have less energy than the 6 electrons in the $2p$ sublevel, which have less energy than the electron in the $3s$ sublevel.

40. **Concept:** *An electron jumps from the ground state to an excited state by absorbing a discrete amount (or quanta) of energy. If the electron absorbs enough energy to be removed completely from that atom, the atom is said to be ionized.*
   *Solution:* No, this statement is false. An excited electron is still attracted to the nucleus of the atom because it occupies an orbital around that nucleus. Only when a positive ion is formed does the attraction between the nucleus and the electron completely disappear.

41. **Concept:** *The kernel of an atom includes the nucleus and the inner shells of electrons, excluding the electrons in the valence shell.*
   *Solution:* If an atom contains only kernel electrons, it has lost all of the electrons in its valence shell and must be a cation. If it loses 1 electron (alkali metals), its cation has a charge of 1+. If it loses 8 electrons (noble gases), its cation has a charge of 8+.

Page 356, Cumulative Review

42. The total heat required is the heat needed to raise the liquid to 100.0°C plus the heat needed to turn the liquid to steam.
   $100.0°C - 20.0°C = 80.0°C$
   Heat required to raise the liquid to 100.0°C:
   $$250 \text{ g} \times \frac{4.19 \text{ J}}{\text{g-°C}} \times 80°C = 83.8 \times 10^3 \text{ J}$$
   Heat required to turn the liquid into steam:
   $250 \text{ g} \times 2.26 \times 10^3 \text{ J/g} = 565 \times 10^3 \text{ J}$
   Total heat $= 83.8 \times 10^3 \text{ J} + 565 \times 10^3 \text{ J} =$
   $648.8 \times 10^3 \text{ J} = 6.48 \times 10^5 \text{ J}$

13

**43. c.** $20°C = 293$ K; $40°C = 313$ K

$$2.7 \text{ dm}^3 \times \frac{313 \text{ K}}{293 \text{ K}} = 2.9 \text{ dm}^3$$

**44. b.** $54.0 \text{ g H}_2\text{O} \times \dfrac{1 \text{ mol}}{18.0 \text{ g}} \times \dfrac{40.7 \text{ kJ}}{\text{mol}} = 122 \text{ kJ}$

**45. d.** Since ammonia is the lightest of the four gases, it diffuses the fastest.

**46. c.** $KClO_3$: $39 + 35 + 3(16) = 122$ g

$$5.00 \text{ g KClO}_3 \times \frac{1 \text{ mol KClO}_3}{122 \text{ g}} \times \frac{3 \text{ mol O}_2}{2 \text{ mol KClO}_3} \times$$

$$\frac{22.4 \text{ dm}^3}{1 \text{ mol O}_2} = 1.38 \text{ dm}^3$$

**47. d.** A neutral magnesium atom, Mg, loses 2 electrons to form a cation, $Mg^{2+}$. An anion has more electrons, a different element has more protons, and a different isotope has more neutrons.

**48. a.** $4.2 \text{ dm}^3 \times \dfrac{204 \text{ kPa}}{102 \text{ kPa}} = 8.4 \text{ dm}^3$

**49.** The total pressure of a gas collected over water equals the partial pressure of the gas plus the vapor pressure of water at that temperature. The vapor pressure of water at $15°C$ is 1.7 kPa.
$P_{neon} = 108.2 \text{ kPa} - 1.7 \text{ kPa} = 106.5 \text{ kPa}$

**50. a.** $Zn(s) + Cu(NO_3)_2(aq) \rightarrow Cu(s) + Zn(NO_3)_2(aq)$
   **b.** $BaCl_2(aq) + Na_2SO_4(aq) \rightarrow 2NaCl(aq) +$
$$BaSO_4(s)$$
   **c.** $2Fe(s) + 6HCl(aq) \rightarrow 2FeCl_3(aq) + 3H_2(g)$
   **d.** $NaOH(aq) + HCl(aq) \rightarrow NaCl(aq) + H_2O(l)$

**51.** The gas pressure is greater than atmospheric pressure. The mercury in the U-tube is pushed down by the gas, so it rises in the column that is open to the atmosphere. The gas pressure equals atmospheric pressure plus the manometer reading, or 770 mm Hg + 25 mm Hg = 795 mm Hg.

**52.** In 100.0 g of this compound, there are 47.3 g of Cu and 52.7 g of Cl.

$$47.3 \text{ g Cu} \times \frac{1 \text{ mol Cu}}{63.5 \text{ g Cu}} = 0.745 \text{ mol Cu}$$

$$52.7 \text{ g Cl} \times \frac{1 \text{ mol Cl}}{35.5 \text{ g Cl}} = 1.48 \text{ mol Cl}$$

mole ratio = 1 Cu/2 Cl
empirical formula = $CuCl_2$

## Page 357, Critical Thinking

**53.** The 3 orbitals have to get as far away from each other as they can in order to minimize the repulsion between negatively charged electrons in each orbital. They cannot be 3 different spheres with different radii because they are all at the same energy level. They cannot be 3 spheres with the same radii because 3 different orbitals cannot occupy the same space.

**54.** The $2p_x$ and the $2p_y$ orbitals have the same shape and are at the same energy level. The only difference is their orientation in space.

**55.** The electron configuration of the next element would probably be $[Rn]7s^2 5f^{14} 6d^8$.

**56.** The kernel is a convenient abbreviation for the nucleus plus all of the inner electrons. It also emphasizes the valence electrons, which are used to predict chemical reactivity.

**57.** The elements in Group 1 easily lose the lone electron in the $s$ orbital in their valence shell to form cations with a charge of 1+. H loses its $1s$ electron; Li loses its $2s$ electron; Na, its $3s$ electron; and so on.

## Page 357, Challenge Problems

**58.** One solution is to allow the fourth quantum number, $s$, to have 4 values instead of just 2. The spin could be up, down, left, or right, for example. Another solution is to create a fifth quantum number (call it $t$) that has 2 allowable values (such as forward and backward).

**59.** $Z = 8$: $1s^4 2s^4$
$Z = 10$: $1s^4 2s^4 2p^2$
$Z = 14$: $1s^4 2s^4 2p^6$
$Z = 20$: $1s^4 2s^4 2p^{12}$

The elements with $Z$ equal to 8 and 20 would be stable because of filled $2s$ or $2p$ levels. The element with $Z$ equal to 14 would be somewhat stable because the $2p$ level is half filled. The element with $Z$ equal to 10 would be unstable and very likely to form a 2+ cation.

# The Periodic Table

14

## Chapter Planning Guide

| Text Section | Labs (Lab Manual) and Demonstrations (TE) | Supplementary Materials (Teacher's Resource Book) |
|---|---|---|
| **14-1** Origin of the Periodic Table, pp. 359-363 | | |
| **14-2** Reading the Periodic Table, pp. 364-365 **14-3** Periods of Elements, pp. 365-367 **14-4** Groups of Elements, pp. 367-368 | Lab 26: Group 2—The Alkaline Earth Metals Lab 27: Group 17—The Halogens | Reference Tables: Periodic Table, Blank Version, p. RT-18 Color Periodic Table Poster, front pocket |
| **14-5** Periodicity in Properties, pp. 368-369 | Demo 14-1: What's the Trend?, p. TG-207 | |
| **14-6** Ionization Energy and Periodicity, pp. 369-371 **14-7** Electronegativity and Periodicity, pp. 371-372 **14-8** Position of Electrons, pp. 372-373 | | Transparency Master: Periodicity of Ionization Energy, p. 14-1 Reference Tables: Ionization Energies and Electronegativities, p. RT-8 |
| **14-9** Atomic Radius and Periodicity, pp. 374-378 | | Reference Tables: Radii of Atoms, p. RT-13 Transparency Master: Covalent Radius vs. Atomic Number, p. 14-2 Transparency Master: Summary of Periodic Trends in Properties, p. 14-3 Review Activity: Graphing Covalent Atomic Radii, p. 14-5 |
| **14-10** Ionic Radius, pp. 378-379 | | |
| **14-11** Isoelectronic Species, p. 380 | | |
| **14-12** Metals, Nonmetals, and Semimetals in the Periodic Table, pp. 381-382 | Demo 14-2: Which Is More Metallic?, p. TG-207 Demo 14-3: Which Is More Nonmetallic?, p. TG-208 | Transparency Master: Properties of Metals and Nonmetals, p. 14-4 Review Activity: The Periodic Table, p. 14-7 Review Activity: Characteristics of Elements, p. 14-8 Reference Tables: Periodic Table: One-Page Version, p. RT-20 Societal Issues: Fluoridation, p. SI-29 |

TG-203

| Text Section | Labs (Lab Manual) and Demonstrations (TE) | Supplementary Materials (Teacher's Resource Book) |
|---|---|---|
| | | Test—Form A, p. AT-52<br>Alternate Test—Form B, p. BT-52 |

☐ Core  ☐ Advanced  ☐ Optional

## Chapter Overview

Chapter 14 begins on an historical note that focuses on Mendeleev's periodic table as the forerunner of the modern form established after Moseley's discovery of atomic numbers. We describe the arrangement of the elements into periods and groups and the relationship between electron configurations of the elements and their positions in the periodic table. Students see how the periodic table represents systematically the observed periodicity of many properties of the elements. These include ionization energy, electronegativity, atomic radius, and ionic radius. The chapter concludes with a description of the position of elements in the periodic table with respect to their metallic and nonmetallic character.

## Chapter Objectives

When students have completed this chapter, they will be able to:

1. Describe the origin of the periodic table. *14-1*
2. State the periodic law. *14-1*
3. Explain the relationship between electron configurations and the locations of the elements in the periodic table. *14-2 to 14-4*
4. Describe the nature of periods and groups of elements in the periodic table. *14-2 to 14-5*
5. State the definitions of some properties of the elements that exhibit periodicity, and describe the trends of those properties within periods and groups of elements. *14-6 to 14-12*

## Teaching Suggestions

### 14-1 Origin of the Periodic Table, pp. 359-363

■ The history of the periodic table is an interesting journey through the annals of chemistry. If you like to use biographical material, the stories of the scientists who participated in the development of the periodic table are especially colorful. Johann Döbereiner (in 1829) studied triads of elements arranged in order of increasing mass and found that the properties of the middle element were intermediate between those of the other two. John Newlands (in 1864) arranged the known elements in the order of increasing atomic masses and noted that every eighth element had properties similar to the first. Working independently, Lothar Meyer and Dmitri Mendeleev (in 1869) discovered that the properties of the elements are periodic functions of their atomic masses. While Newlands tried to force elements into groups where they did not belong, Mendeleev left gaps for elements not yet discovered. For this and other reasons the major credit for classifying the elements has gone to Mendeleev. In 1914, Henry Moseley found that when the elements were arranged in order of their atomic numbers the elements that seemed out of place in Mendeleev's arrangement (K and Ar; Co and Ni; I and Te) fell into their correct family groups.

### 14-2 Reading the Periodic Table, pp. 364-365,

### 14-3 Periods of Elements, pp. 365-367, and

### 14-4 Groups of Elements, pp. 367-368

| Planning Guide | |
|---|---|
| **Labs (Lab Manual) and Demonstrations (TE)** | **Supplementary Materials (Teacher's Resource Book)** |
| Lab 26: Group 2—The Alkaline Earth Metals<br>Lab 27: Group 17—The Halogens | Reference Tables: Periodic Table, Blank Version, p. RT-18<br>Color Periodic Table Poster, front pocket |

■ Be sure that you have the large periodic table from the *Teacher's Resource Book* in a prominent position on the wall at or near the front of the classroom. Use a pointer to walk your students through the periodic table, outlining:

—groups/periods and their numbers
—the step-like line
—metals/nonmetals/semimetals

—actinoids/lanthanoids

—alkali metals/alkaline earth metals/halogens/ noble gases

■ Displaying samples of the elements embedded in plastic mounts helps to bring reality to this topic. These samples work best if you design a series of questions that match the elements that you intend to use. Your questions should concern obvious properties such as phase (solid, liquid, gas), luster, color, etc.

■ To help students understand the meaning of family resemblances among elements, have them do Laboratory 26, "Group 2—The Alkaline Earth Metals," in which they investigate reactions of some members of a family of metals and note trends in that family. Then have students do Laboratory 27, "Group 17—The Halogens," which is a similar investigation into a family of nonmetals.

■ To incorporate an understanding of electron configuration into your presentation of the periodic table, call attention to the $s$, $p$, $d$, and $f$ blocks of elements as shown in text Figure 14-9. Have students record valence shell electron configurations on a copy of the "Periodic Table: Blank Version" (TRB). Then have them relate the table of configurations to similarities in properties.

■ **Concept Mastery.** Impress upon students that they should not memorize the characteristic relationships within families and periods in the periodic table. Explain that if they understand the table, they will be able to synthesize many concepts in chemistry. You may want to use Concept Mastery questions 29, 30, and 31 (chapter-end questions) to help make the point. These questions require students to have and be able to apply a conceptual understanding of some of the fundamental relationships within the periodic table.

■ **Application.** If you or one of your students know anyone who is traveling to the Soviet Union, you might want to try to obtain a copy of a Russian periodic table. Students are always surprised to see that the same table, including the symbols in English, is used worldwide.

## 14-5 Periodicity in Properties, pp. 368-369

| Planning Guide | |
| --- | --- |
| Labs (Lab Manual) and Demonstrations (TE) | Supplementary Materials (Teacher's Resource Book) |
| Demo 14-1: What's the Trend?, p. TG-207 | |

■ The use of the term "periodic" to describe properties may be strange to students, but the concept itself is familiar. If you push them a bit, most students can come up with some illustrations of an everyday, commonplace periodic property that is a function of time.

Some are obvious—the rising of the sun, the phases of the moon, the chimes of Westminster. Less obvious are periodic functions of other variables. Mileposts on highways often have a special shape or symbol every tenth of a mile and/or every full mile. Encourage students to think of other illustrations.

■ Even though you may not want to define covalent atomic radius yet, it may be helpful to refer to the illustration of this property in text Figure 14-19 as you begin to consider periodicity. The same suggestion applies to Figure 14-14, which shows a small portion of the periodic relationship associated with ionization energy.

■ As background for the discussion of trends in the periodic table introduced in this section and developed in the remainder of the chapter, Demonstration 14-1 "What's the Trend?" is appropriate for use at this time.

## 14-6 Ionization Energy and Periodicity, pp. 369-371,

## 14-7 Electronegativity and Periodicity, pp. 371-372, and

## 14-8 Position of Electrons, pp. 372-373

| Planning Guide | |
| --- | --- |
| Labs (Lab Manual) and Demonstrations (TE) | Supplementary Materials (Teacher's Resource Book) |
| | Transparency Master: Periodicity of Ionization Energy, p. 14-1 Reference Tables: Ionization Energies and Electronegativities, p. RT-8 |

■ You can use the Transparency Master "Periodicity of Ionization Energy" to help students visualize the concept of periodicity. Hand out copies of the Reference Table "Ionization Energies and Electronegativities," which shows the data used to construct this graph.

■ You may want to develop a diagram of all of the periodic trends discussed in the chapter as you explain each one in class. To do this, you can give students copies of the "Periodic Table, Blank Version." As you discuss each property have the students add arrows showing the direction of a trend. Be sure students can tell *why* the trend exists as indicated. Pose many questions for class discussion that require comparing several atoms in terms of the magnitude of these properties. Use Section 14-8 to increase student understanding of the relationship between some of these properties.

14

## 14-9 Atomic Radius and Periodicity, pp. 374-378

| Planning Guide | |
|---|---|
| Labs (Lab Manual) and Demonstrations (TE) | Supplementary Materials (Teacher's Resource Book) |
| | Reference Tables: Radii of Atoms, p. RT-13 Transparency Master: Covalent Radius vs. Atomic Number, p. 14-2 Transparency Master: Summary of Periodic Trends in Properties, p. 14-3 Review Activity: Graphing Covalent Atomic Radii, p. 14-5 |

■ Emphasize the point that in the wave-mechanical model, atoms are not ball-like spheres. Use text Figure 14-18 to help your students sort out the three types of atomic radius. You may use the Transparency Master "Covalent Radius vs. Atomic Number" as the basis for a discussion to make sure that students can account for the trend within a period. The trend within a group is somewhat less obvious. Ask students to lay a straight edge across the curves so that it lies on the values for members of the same group. Students should be able to account for the positive slope that appears.

## 14-10 Ionic Radius, pp. 378-379

■ It should be easy for students to think of ions as being derived from atoms. Point out the changes in size associated with the formation of ions, as shown in text Figures 14-22 and 14-23. In general, these changes seem quite logical to students. To test mastery of these principles, ask students to choose the ions that are the largest, smallest, or most similar in size from lists you prepared. Text Figure 14-20 gives a good overall view of atomic and ionic radii.

Ask students to describe group and periodic trends in ionic radius using Figure 14-20. They will probably note that the group trend for ionic radius matches that for atomic radius. However, the periodic trend is not so clear, because the smallest ion in a period is probably found in Group 13 or 14. Attention to this matter leads into the next section, an advanced topic.

## 14-11 Isoelectronic Species, p. 380

■ To cut the phrase "isoelectronic species" down to size for your students, divide it into three parts:
*iso-* means equal or the same, as in isosceles triangle

*electronic* means related to electrons
*species* means kind of thing
Thus, isoelectronic species are those kinds of things that have the same electronic structures. Tell students that in this case we are considering ions that are isoelectronic with some of the atoms of the noble gases, i.e., those atoms that have 10, 18, and 36 electrons. The example in the text covers the atoms and ions with 10 electrons. You may wish to have students construct a diagram like text Figure 14-24 to cover the 18-electron and 36-electron species, using information found in Figure 14-20.

## 14-12 Metals, Nonmetals, and Semimetals in the Periodic Table, pp. 381-382

| Planning Guide | |
|---|---|
| Labs (Lab Manual) and Demonstrations (TE) | Supplementary Materials (Teacher's Resource Book) |
| Demo 14-2: Which Is More Metallic?, p. TG-207 Demo 14-3: Which Is More Nonmetallic?, p. TG-208 | Transparency Master: Properties of Metals and Nonmetals, p. 14-4 Review Activity: The Periodic Table, p. 14-7 Review Activity: Characteristics of Elements, p. 14-8 Reference Tables: Periodic Table: One-Page Version, p. RT-20 Societal Issues: Fluoridation, p. SI-29 |

■ Use Demonstration 14-2, "Which Is More Metallic?," to show that the elements with the most metallic properties are located in the lower left portion of the periodic table. Then use Demonstration 14-3, "Which Is More Nonmetallic?," to show that the elements with the most nonmetallic properties are—if we do not count the noble gases—located at the upper right portion of the periodic table.
■ Your students may want to put each element into one of two categories: metal or nonmetal. For some elements, such as calcium or chlorine (and the other elements used in the demonstrations for this section), there is no uncertainty. Explain why some elements, especially those in Groups 14 and 15, must be classified as semimetals (or metalloids).

Emphasize the ways in which the properties of metals and nonmetals can be compared. Help students to account for each property and its comparison in terms of electron structure and bond strength.
■ You may want to use the Societal Issue "Fluoridation" in connection with your discussion of the position of fluorine in the periodic table.
■ The Review Activities "The Periodic Table" and "Characteristics of Elements" are both appropriate for use after Section 14-12.

# Demonstrations

## 14-1 What's the Trend?

**Overview:** In this demonstration, you place onto the overhead projector eight rectangles made from a transparency and ask students to help you arrange the rectangles in some logical order so that trends can be observed among them. The students are then asked to make predictions about a missing rectangle. This provides a background for discussing trends in the periodic table.

**Materials:** 9 rectangles made out of a transparency sheet; red, green, blue, and black transparency-marking pens; overhead projector.

**Advance Preparation:** 1. Cut a transparency into nine rectangles, each about 6 cm × 9 cm. 2. Using marking pens, draw a red border around three of them, a green one around another three, and a blue one around the last three, as shown in the accompanying figure. Using a black marker, place a whole number, a decimal number, and one to three stars on each, also as shown.

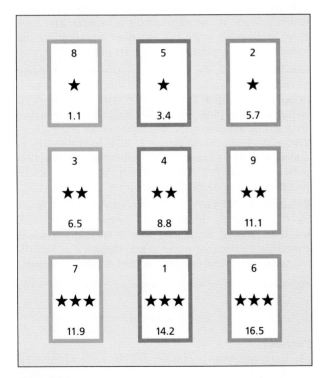

**Figure 14-1**

**Procedure:** 1. Mix up the rectangles and place all but the one marked with the whole number "9" onto the overhead projector. Tell students you would like them to help you arrange the rectangles in some logical pattern that is three rectangles wide and three rectangles high, counting a ninth rectangle, which you

should tell them is missing. Also, tell them that the whole numbers correspond only to a random order in which you marked the rectangles. 2. After a student-suggested pattern has been constructed on the overhead projector, tell students to describe consistent trends for color, difference in decimal-number value, and number of stars in the pattern. Also, ask them to describe the placement and characteristics of the missing rectangle. If they are unable to do these things given their suggested pattern, ask them to suggest a more suitable one. Do this until the correct pattern is established. 3. After the correct pattern has been constructed, add the missing rectangle to it, and have students compare its characteristics to those they predicted it would have. 4. Tell students that the periodic table of chemical elements has been set up logically by increasing atomic number and by characteristic trends, and that many properties of once-discovered elements were predicted by examination of these trends and the gaps within them.

**Results:** The correct pattern is shown in Figure 14-1. Note that the rectangles in different (vertical) columns have different-color borders. Also, the decimal numbers increase by 2.3 for each rectangle, moving across a row. They increase by 5.4 for each rectangle, moving down a column. They increase as a whole, as the entire pattern is scanned, line by line. The number of stars is 1 for each member of row 1, 2 for each member of row 2, and 3 for each member of row 3.

## 14-2 Which Is More Metallic?

**Overview:** In this demonstration, you add various metals to water and to dilute hydrochloric acid to determine which of the metals are more reactive. The results indicate that the most metallic elements are in the lower left portion of the periodic table.

**Materials:** magnesium turnings; calcium turnings; aluminum turnings; 0.2 $M$ hydrochloric acid (HCl); 6 50-mL or 100-mL beakers; forceps; overhead projector; safety goggles.

**Advance Preparation: 0.2 $M$ HCl:** Mix concentrated HCl and water in a 1:60 ratio by volume.

**Safety:** Do not allow acid to come into contact with your body or clothing. In diluting, add the acid to the water. Reaction of the metals (especially Ca) with the dilute acid may produce spattering, so wear goggles and do not permit students to sit or stand near the reacting mixtures. Do not handle the calcium with your fingers; use forceps instead.

**Procedure:** 1. Briefly discuss the properties of metals, and remind students that metals tend to lose electrons in chemical reactions. Point out that one can assume that the greater tendency an element has to lose

14

electrons, the more metallic the element is.

2. Ask students to predict whether Al, Ca, or Mg would tend to lose valence electrons most easily. Place three beakers onto the overhead projector. Add a small amount of water and a different metal (Al, Ca, Mg) to each. Ask students to observe the reactions and to conclude which metal is the most reactive.

3. Repeat step 2, using 0.2 $M$ HCl instead of water. Ask students to state where the most active metals are located in the periodic table.

**Results:** Only the Ca will react to any observable degree with the water. Bubbles of hydrogen gas will be released. The reaction is: $Ca + 2H_2O \rightarrow H_2 + Ca(OH)_2$. All three of the metals should react with the HCl solution to produce the corresponding chlorides and hydrogen gas. Ca will react most rapidly, and Al will react least rapidly. Students should be able to conclude that metals become more reactive toward the left in the periodic table (Ca and Mg are to the left of Al), and that they also become more reactive downward in the table (Ca is below Mg). The most active metals (those that tend most readily to lose electrons) are located in the lower left portion of the table.

**Disposal Tips:** If all of the metal has been consumed, pour the solutions down the drain and flush the drain with water. Do not put Ca metal into the sink, as it will continue to react with water and form hydrogen gas, which is flammable and potentially explosive.

## 14-3 Which Is More Nonmetallic?

**Overview:** In this demonstration, you add two free halogens dissolved in TTE to solutions of halides and determine which of the halogens is more reactive (more nonmetallic). The results indicate that iodine is less reactive than bromine.

**Materials:** bromine water (buy already prepared solution); iodine (solid); 0.5 $M$ potassium iodide (KI); 0.5 $M$ potassium bromide (KBr); TTE (1,1,2-trichloro-1,2,2-trifluoroethane) or 1,1,1-trichloroethane; long eyedropper; test tubes and stoppers.

**Advance Preparation:** 1. **0.5 $M$ KI:** mix 8.3 g of KI in enough water to make 100 mL of solution. 2. **0.5 $M$ KBr:** mix 5.9 g of KBr in enough water to make 100 mL of solution.

**Safety:** Avoid touching the halogens or breathing their vapors. Also, take care in handling the TTE or 1,1,1-trichloroethane. As you carry out the procedure, you should mix all solutions in a properly functioning fume hood.

**Procedure:** 1. Ask students to predict which halogen is more reactive: iodine or bromine? Remind them that nonmetals tend to gain electrons in reactions. The more reactive a nonmetal is, the greater is its tendency

to gain electrons and the greater is its ability to displace other halogens from their halide compounds.

2. Place about 1 mL of the bromine water into a test tube, and add 1 mL of TTE (or 1,1,1-trichloroethane). Have the students notice that the TTE sinks to the bottom of the tube, because it is more dense than water. Stopper the test tube and carefully shake to mix the two layers. Tell students that bromine is more soluble in TTE than in water, so most of the bromine moves to the TTE layer. Have them observe the resulting color of this bromine–TTE layer. Use an eyedropper to remove the top, aqueous layer and dispose of this liquid. 3. Place about 1 mL of TTE into another test tube, and add a few iodine crystals. Stopper the test tube and shake carefully. Have students observe the resulting color of this iodine–TTE layer. 4. Place a few milliliters of 0.5 $M$ KI into a test tube, and add to it the 1 mL of bromine–TTE solution you prepared in step 2. Place a few milliliters of 0.5 $M$ KBr into another test tube, and add to it 1 mL of the iodine–TTE solution you prepared in step 3. Stopper the test tubes and agitate each until reaction occurs. Have students note any changes in the bottom TTE layers. Ask them which halogen is the more active nonmetal, and have them attempt to write the balanced equation for the halogen–halide reaction that occurred.

**Results:** In step 2, the $Br_2$–TTE solution will be reddish or yellowish. In step 3, the $I_2$–TTE solution will be pink or purple. In step 4, the yellowish or reddish $Br_2$–TTE will change to pink or purple, indicating a reaction with iodide ion to form $I_2$. The equation is: $Br_2 + 2I^- \rightarrow 2Br^- + I_2$. The pink or purple $I_2$–TTE to which KBr is added will not change color, indicating no reaction between $I_2$ and $Br^-$. Thus, bromine is a more active halogen and nonmetal than is iodine.

**Disposal Tips:** The water solutions can be poured down the drain and the drain flushed with water. The TTE solutions should be placed into a specially marked container for organic solvents and disposed of according to the guidelines of your school district or state.

## Answers to Questions

**Page 361**

1. Early attempts to classify the elements were based on chemical similarities and atomic mass (atomic weight).

2. **a.** Mendeleev arranged most of the elements in his table in order of increasing atomic mass (weight).

   **b.** The empty spaces in Mendeleev's table represented elements not yet discovered.

3. Mendeleev placed iodine after tellurium because he wanted to show similarities between the chemi-

cal properties of iodine and those of chlorine and bromine.

4. Moseley contributed to the modern periodic law and table by discovering the characteristic of atomic number. Atomic number was proposed as a replacement in the statement of the periodic law for atomic mass (weight).

5. **a.** The modern periodic law states that the chemical and physical properties of the elements are periodic functions of their atomic numbers.
   **b.** The modern periodic law places the elements in increasing order of their atomic numbers rather than their atomic masses.

**Page 365**

6. **a.** On the periodic table, each horizontal row is called a period.
   **b.** On the periodic table, each vertical column is called a group or a family.

7. The number of valence electrons (electrons in the outer energy level) for each of these elements is
   **a.** sulfur—6 **b.** calcium—2 **c.** nickel—2
   **d.** arsenic—5

8. Three elements in Period 4 have one valence electron: K, Cr, and Cu. Nine elements in Period 4 have two valence electrons: Ca, Sc, Ti, V, Mn, Fe, Co, Ni, and Zn.

9. **a.** In Period 4, one element, As, has a half-filled $p$ sublevel.
   **b.** Eight elements in Period 4 have a filled $3d$ sublevel: Cu, Zn, Ga, Ge, As, Se, Br, and Kr.
   **c.** In Period 4, two elements, Cr and Mn, have a half-filled $3d$ sublevel.

**Page 368**

10. The distribution of electrons in an atom of an element is related to the number, $n$, of the period in which the element is located. There are $n$ occupied (but not necessarily filled) energy levels. The valence electrons are found in the $n$th energy level where $n$ is equal to the number of the period in which the element is located.

11. **a.** The three short periods are numbered 1, 2, 3.
    **b.** The three short periods (1, 2, and 3) contain 2, 8, and 8 elements, respectively.

12. **a.** Periods 4 and 5 contain 18 elements each.
    **b.** Periods 6 and 7 each contain a maximum of 32 elements. Whereas Period 6 is full, only 23 elements are presently known for Period 7.

13. The transition elements differ from other elements in that they have partly filled $(n-1)d$ sublevels or give rise to a cation or cations with incomplete $d$ sublevels.

14. The transition elements are not placed in vertical columns with nontransition elements because they have different electron configurations with resulting different chemical and physical properties.

15. The transition elements of the lanthanoid series differ from the other transition elements of Period 6 because the $(n-2)$ energy level of the lanthanoid transition elements have a partly filled $f$ sublevel.

16. **a.** The alkaline earth metals (group 2).
    **b.** The halogens (group 17).

**Page 371**

17. The strength of attraction between two oppositely charged bodies is determined by the quantity of charge on each and the distance separating them.

18. Within Period 2, as atomic number ($Z$) increases, the ionization energy of the element generally increases. Boron and oxygen are exceptions.

19. In text Figure 14-15:
    **a.** The top pair has the greater attraction because of the greater charge on the negative particle.
    **b.** The bottom pair has the greater attraction because of the smaller distance between particles.
    **c.** The bottom pair has the greater attraction because of both the greater charge on the negative particle and the smaller distance between particles.

20. These atoms are listed according to increasing kernel charge: Zn, Al, C, S. Their net kernel charges are $Zn^{2+}$, $Al^{3+}$, $C^{4+}$, $S^{6+}$.

21. **a.** The charge on the kernel of an atom can never be negative because all of the protons of an atom are found in its kernel. An atom never has more electrons than protons. Most atoms have one or more valence electrons that are not included when determining the net charge on the kernel.
    **b.** The charge on the kernel of any atom can never be greater than 8+ because the valence shell never has more than 8 electrons. The charge on the kernel of an atom is always positive and equal to the number of valence electrons.

**Page 373**

22.

| electronegativity: | 0.9 | 1.0 | 1.5 | 2.9 | 3.5 |
|---|---|---|---|---|---|
| element: | Na | Ca | Al | Br | O |

23. For all three pairs of atoms listed, the electron pair is more strongly attracted to the oxygen atom. In each case, oxygen has the higher electronegativity.

$$3.5 \quad 2.2 \qquad 3.5 \quad 2.2 \qquad 3.5 \quad 2.9$$
$$O \leftarrow H \qquad O \leftarrow P \qquad O \leftarrow Br$$

24. The electron pair is more strongly attracted to the nitrogen atom only in N:H. The electronegativity of nitrogen is greater than that of H. In the other pairs, the other nonmetal has greater electronegativity than the nitrogen atom:

$$3.2 \quad 2.2 \qquad 2.2 \quad 3.5 \qquad 2.2 \quad 3.2$$
$$N \leftarrow H \qquad N \rightarrow O \qquad N \rightarrow Cl$$

**Page 379**

25. The covalent atomic radius of an atom is the effective distance between the nucleus and the valence shell of the atom when that atom has formed a covalent bond by sharing a pair of electrons.

26. The shielding effect decreases the attraction of the nucleus for the outer electrons so that the radius of the atom increases.

27. **a.** Generally, as nuclear charge increases within a period (proceeding from left to right), atomic radius decreases due to increased attraction between the increasingly positive nucleus and the negative electrons.

    **b.** Generally, as the number of occupied energy levels increases, atomic radius increases because the attractive force of the positive nucleus for the negative valence electrons is somewhat shielded by electrons in the intervening energy levels.

28. **a.** Reading across a period from left to right, nuclear charge increases and therefore atomic radius decreases.

    **b.** Reading from top to bottom in a group, the number of occupied energy levels increases and therefore the atomic radius increases.

29. **a.** The ionic radii of metals are smaller than their atomic radii because metals lose valence electrons as they form positive ions.

    **b.** The ionic radii of nonmetals are greater than their atomic radii because nonmetals gain valence electrons as they form negative ions.

**Page 380**

30. **a.** These ions are isoelectronic with argon and are listed in order of increasing ionic radius:
    $P^{3-}$, $S^{2-}$, $Cl^-$, $K^+$, $Ca^{2+}$, $Sc^{3+}$, $Ti^{4+}$, $V^{5+}$, $Cr^{6+}$
    (Students may list any six in order.)

    **b.** The kernel charge increases because the number of protons in the nucleus increases.

    **c.** There is no change in the number of electrons or in their arrangement. The number remains 18. The arrangement is the electron configuration of the argon atom.

**Page 382**

31. A metal is a substance that loses electrons and forms positive ions during chemical reactions.

32. The metallic character of the elements in a period decreases from left to right across the period because ionization energy increases with similar regularity. Ionization energy measures the energy required to form a positive ion. When more energy is required, the element is less metallic.

33. The metallic character of the elements in a group increases as you move down the group from top to bottom because ionization energy decreases with similar regularity. (See also question 32.)

34. A nonmetal is a substance that gains electrons and forms negative ions during a chemical reaction.

35. A semimetal is a substance that has some properties of both metals and nonmetals. Semimetals are also known as metalloids.

## Chapter Review   14

**Page 384, Content Review**

1. In addition to Dmitri Mendeleev, three other scientists who made significant contributions to the classification of the elements were Johann Döbereiner, John Newlands, and Lothar Meyer.

2. **a.** From the periodic table, the elements with atomic numbers 8, 10, and 36 are neon (Ne), argon (Ar), and krypton (Kr), respectively.

    **b.** All three elements are in Group 18. Ne is in Period 2, Ar in Period 3, and Kr in Period 4.

3. Chemical properties are determined by the electron configuration. Elements in the same group (not the same period) have the same configuration in the valence shell. Strontium is closer chemically to calcium (same group) than it is to rubidium (same period).

4. Period 4 is longer than Period 3 because 10 additional electrons are needed to fill the $3d$ orbitals.

5. Both the actinoids and the lanthanoids are filling the $f$ orbitals.

6. Group 1 (alkali metals) and Group 17 (halogens) contain elements that are found in nature only in the combined state. These elements are too reactive to exist uncombined.

7. **a.** The elements that have an $s^1$ configuration have 1 electron in the valence shell. These elements are in Group 1 and are called alkali metals.

    **b.** The three lightest members are lithium, sodium, and potassium.

    **c.** Although hydrogen has an $s^1$ configuration, it is not an alkali metal.

8. Electronegativity and ionization energy are related to the attraction between the nucleus and the electrons.

9. **a.** Each noble gas is a peak on the graph of ionization energy versus atomic number. It is more difficult to remove an electron from a

noble gas because its full valence shell is particularly stable.

**b.** As atomic number increases, the ionization energy of the noble gases decreases. This trend results from an increase in the atomic radius and an increase in the shielding effect of the inner (kernel) electrons.

**10. a.** Fluorine has the highest electronegativity: 4.0.
   **b.** The electronegativities of oxygen and chlorine are 3.5 and 3.2, respectively.

**11.** In order of increasing electronegativity, the elements are K (potassium = 0.8), Na (sodium = 0.9), Br (bromine = 2.9), and Cl (chlorine = 3.2).

**12.** The electron pair is more strongly attracted to the element with the higher electronegativity. The electron pair is attracted to the bromine more strongly than it is to the other element only in **b** (BrI) and **c** (BrS). The electronegativity of Br (2.9) is greater than the electronegativity of I (2.7) or S (2.6). In compounds **a** and **d**, the electronegativity of Br is less than that of the other element: Cl = 3.2, O = 3.5.

**13. a.** As the atomic number increases, the atomic radius increases.
   **b.** Yes, the same trend is evident in the halogens.
   **c.** As atomic number increases, the atomic radius increases because the valence electrons are in higher energy levels, which are farther away from the nucleus, making the atom bigger.

**14.** In **a** through **d**, both species have the same configuration in their valence shell. The larger species is the one with the valence electrons in a higher shell. For example, S has 6 electrons in the third shell, so it is larger than O, with 6 electrons in the second shell. In **e** and **f**, the larger species is the one with more electrons.
   **a.** S is larger than O.
   **b.** $S^{2-}$ is larger than $O^{2-}$.
   **c.** K is larger than Na.
   **d.** $K^+$ is larger than $Na^+$.
   **e.** Ca is larger than $Ca^{2+}$.
   **f.** $F^-$ is larger than F.

**15.** Isoelectronic means having the same electronic configuration. $As^{3-}$, $Se^{2-}$, $Br^-$, $Rb^+$, $Sr^{2+}$, and $Y^{3+}$ are all isoelectronic with Kr: $1s^2 2s^2 2p^6 3s^2 3p^6 4s^2 3d^{10} 4p^6$.

**16.** The correct answer is **a, c,** and **d.** Metals have a low ionization energy, are solid at ordinary conditions, and are malleable. Metals form positive (not negative) ions and have a low (not a high) electronegativity.

**Page 384, Content Mastery**

**17.** Electronegativity is the ability of an atom to pull an electron in a shared pair toward itself.

**18.** Two elements belong to the same period if they are in the same horizontal row in the periodic table. The only pair in which both elements are in the same row is **a**, Na and Cl (in this case, Period 3).

**19. a.** $Ca^{2+}$ is smaller than $K^+$ because its increased nuclear charge attracts the electrons more strongly.
   **b.** $C^{4+}$ is smaller than $C^{4-}$ because it has the same nuclear charge and 8 fewer electrons.
   **c.** $F^-$ is smaller than $O^{2-}$ because of its increased nuclear charge.
   **d.** $F^-$ is smaller than $Cl^-$ because its valence shell is 2. Chloride's valence shell is 3.
   **e.** $F^-$ is smaller than $S^{2-}$ because its valence shell is 2, not 3.

**20.** Two elements belong to the same family if they are in the same vertical column. The only pair in which both elements are in the same column is **c**, C and Pb (in this case, Group 14).

**21. a.** Since the electronegativity of nitrogen (3.1) is greater than that of hydrogen (2.2), the electrons are most attracted to the nitrogen in the N:H bond.
   **b.** Both fluorine (4.0) and chlorine (3.2) pull electrons away from nitrogen (3.1), but fluorine pulls harder.

**22.** The trends are opposite in both cases.
   **a.** Metallic character decreases and electronegativity increases across a period.
   **b.** Metallic character increases and electronegativity decreases down a group.

**23.** Atomic weight increases across a period and down a group.
   **a.** Lithium is the lightest alkali metal (elements in Group 1 except hydrogen). Fluorine is the lightest halogen (elements in Group 17).
   **b.** Radon is the heaviest noble gas (Group 18). Radium is the heaviest alkaline earth metal (Group 2).

**24.** The energy required to remove an electron from an atom in the gas phase is called the ionization energy.

**25.** Ionization energy increases across a period and decreases down a group. Since sulfur (S) is above and to the right of both arsenic (As) and tin (Sn), its ionization energy is highest.

**26.** Dmitri Mendeleev's periodic table is based on atomic mass, whereas Henry Moseley's periodic table is based on atomic number.

14

**27. a.** Cesium (Cs) is the alkali metal (Group 1) in Period 6 (row 6).

**b.** Bromine (Br) is the halogen (Group 17) in Period 4 (row 4).

**28.** Silver (Ag) is at the intersection in the periodic table of Period 5 (fifth horizontal row) and group 11 (eleventh column).

### Page 385, Concept Mastery

**29. *Concept:*** *Periodic arrangements of elements show trends in physical properties, such as color, hardness, and melting point.*

*Solution:* The first arrangement might look like the table that follows. Notice that melting point increases across a period and down a group, whereas hardness decreases. (At this stage, it is equally valid to arrange the elements so that melting point decreases across a row or down a group.)

The elements on the left are all silvery and black; those in the middle, darkly colored; and those on the right, brightly colored. (With the given information, element J could also be put in the right group, either above or below C.)

| | | | | | |
|---|---|---|---|---|---|
| B | −333 | H | 300 | I | 900 |
| G | −200 | D | 400 | C | 1000 |
| F | −100 | J | 1000 | A | 1050 |
| | | | | E | 1200 |

**30. *Concept:*** *Periodic arrangements also show trends in chemical properties.*

*Solution:* The following table reflects similarities in chemical properties. Since B, G, and F show the same chemical properties, the left group formed in Question 29 remains intact. The middle group is split in two, with H on the left because its chemical properties are identical to those of the elements in the left group. D and J do not react with water, so they are closer to the elements in the right group.

| | | | | |
|---|---|---|---|---|
| B | H | D | I | C |
| G | | J | A | E |
| F | | | | |

**31. *Concept:*** *Periodic arrangements can be refined using information about relative masses.*

*Solution:* **a.** Notice that the brightly colored elements are now on the left side of the table.

| | | | | | |
|---|---|---|---|---|---|
| C | I | | | | B |
| | A | J | D | | G |
| E | | | | H | F |

**b.** Xeno's unreactive elements (C and E) are on the left side of the table, whereas earth's noble gases are on the right. Xeno's hard, silvery elements are gases at 25°C and are on the right, whereas earth's metals are solid at 25°C and are on the left side of the table.

**c.** This table now has 3 periods and 6 families (groups).

**d.** This table has places for 18 elements, 10 of which are known. The properties of a missing element should follow the trends in properties within its period and its group.

**e.** Although it is easy to record the physical properties given in stage 1, these properties by themselves do not give enough information to build a periodic table. The chemical properties from stage 2 are very useful, but the best information is the relative atomic masses from stage 3.

Notice the similarities between this process of building your table for the elements on Xeno and the historical development of the periodic table on earth.

### Page 386, Cumulative Review

**32. c.** $T_1 = 273 + 20 = 293$ K

$T_2 = 273 + 40 = 313$ K

$$V_2 = V_1 \times \frac{T_2}{T_1} = \frac{(5.0 \text{ dm}^3)(313 \text{ K})}{293 \text{ K}} = 5.3 \text{ dm}^3$$

**33. a.** Oxygen has an apparent charge of 2−, so 10 oxygens contribute $(10)(2-) = 20-$ in $P_4O_{10}$. Since the compound is neutral, the 4 phosphorus atoms must contribute 20+ to cancel out the 20− from the oxygens. Each phosphorus has an apparent charge of 20+/4= 5+.

**34. d.** density = mass/volume
volume = mass/density

$$\text{volume of silver} = \frac{41.9 \text{ g silver}}{10.5 \text{ g/cm}^3} = 3.99 \text{ cm}^3$$

**35. b.** $2.20 \text{ dm}^3 \times \dfrac{1 \text{ mol}}{22.4 \text{ dm}^3} \times \dfrac{39.948 \text{ g}}{1 \text{ mol}} = 3.92 \text{ g}$

**36.** The correct answer is **c**, neutrons. An isotope differs from another isotope of that element in the number of neutrons in the nucleus. An atom that has a different number of electrons is an ion. An atom that has a different number of protons is an atom of a different element. Quarks are hypothetical, basic particles from which many of the elementary particles in an atom may be made. Nucleons are thought to be made of 3 quarks.

**37.** In the first 4 periods, energy levels are filled with electrons in the following order: $1s^2 2s^2 2p^6 3s^2 3p^6 4s^2 3d^{10} 4p^6$. Below are the electron configurations of some elements.

   **a.** fluorine             $1s^2 2s^2 2p^5$
   **b.** chlorine             $1s^2 2s^2 2p^6 3s^2 3p^5$
   **c.** bromine            $1s^2 2s^2 2p^6 3s^2 3p^6 4s^2 3d^{10} 4p^5$
   **d.** lithium              $1s^2 2s^1$
   **e.** sodium              $1s^2 2s^2 2p^6 3s^1$
   **f.** potassium        $1s^2 2s^2 2p^6 3s^2 3p^6 4s^1$

**38.** $C_2H_5OH$

Calculate the molecular mass.
2 C = 2(12.0 g) = 24.0 g
6 H = 6(1.0 g)  =  6.0 g
1 O = 1(16.0 g) = 16.0 g
                  46.0 g/mol

Next, calculate the percent by mass for each element in the compound.

$$C = \frac{24.0 \text{ g}}{46.0 \text{ g}} \times 100\% = 52.2\%$$

$$H = \frac{6.0 \text{ g}}{46.0 \text{ g}} \times 100\% = 13.0\%$$

$$O = \frac{16.0 \text{ g}}{46.0 \text{ g}} \times 100\% = 34.8\%$$

Finally, make sure the percentages add up to 100%. They do. 52.2% + 13.0% + 34.8% = 100.0%

**39. a.** The atom is in the ground state because the energy levels are filled with electrons in the order of increasing energy.

   **b.** The 2 electrons in the 1s orbital form 1 pair; the 8 electrons in the 2s and 2p orbitals form 4 pairs; and the 2 electrons in the 3s orbital form 1 pair, for a total of 1 + 4 + 1 = 6 pairs. The 3 electrons in the 3p orbitals are unpaired.

   **c.** Three of the four electrons go into the 3p orbitals. The fourth goes into the 4s orbital. The new electron configuration is $1s^2 2s^2 2p^6 3s^2 3p^6 4s^1$.

**40. a.** $N_2 + H_2 \rightarrow NH_3$       2 N means $2NH_3$
       $N_2 + H_2 \rightarrow 2NH_3$      6 H means $3H_2$
       $N_2 + 3H_2 \rightarrow 2NH_3$

   **b.** $Al_2(SO_4)_3 + BaCl_2 \rightarrow AlCl_3 + BaSO_4$
                         2 Al means $2AlCl_3$
       $Al_2(SO_4)_3 + BaCl_2 \rightarrow 2AlCl_3 + BaSO_4$
                         6 Cl means $3BaCl_2$
       $Al_2(SO_4)_3 + 3BaCl_2 \rightarrow 2AlCl_3 + BaSO_4$
                         3 Ba means $3BaSO_4$
       $Al_2(SO_4)_3 + 3BaCl_2 \rightarrow 2AlCl_3 + 3BaSO_4$
                       3 $SO_4$ agrees with 3 $SO_4$

   **c.** $CuO \rightarrow Cu + O_2$        2 O means 2CuO
       $2CuO \rightarrow Cu + O_2$     2 CuO means 2Cu
       $2CuO \rightarrow 2Cu + O_2$

   **d.** $C_6H_{12}O_6 + O_2 \rightarrow CO_2 + H_2O$
                         6 C means $6CO_2$
       $C_6H_{12}O_6 + O_2 \rightarrow 6CO_2 + H_2O$
                        12 H means $6H_2O$
       $C_6H_{12}O_6 + O_2 \rightarrow 6CO_2 + 6H_2O$
                     18 O means 6 O + $6O_2$
       $C_6H_{12}O_6 + 6O_2 \rightarrow 6CO_2 + 6H_2O$

**41.** The standard for modern tables of atomic masses is carbon-12.

## Page 386, Critical Thinking

**42.** An element can be classified as a metal, nonmetal, or semimetal depending on its position in the periodic table. Sodium and tin are metallic. Boron, aluminum, and silicon are semimetallic. Carbon and bromine are nonmetallic.

**43.** Metallic character decreases across a period and increases down a group. The strongest metals are in the lower left, the weakest metals in the upper right corner of the table. In order of increasing metallic character, the elements are fluorine, phosphorus, copper, potassium, and cesium.

**44.** Mendeleev assumed that there was a reason for the regular variation of chemical properties with the atomic mass. In other words, he assumed that some feature of the structure of the atoms (atomic mass) determined their behavior (properties).

**45.** Yes, the actinoids should and do resemble the lanthanoids because their structures (electronic configurations) are similar to those of the lanthanoids. The lanthanoids have $6s^2$ valence electrons and are filling the $4f$ sublevel, whereas the actinoids have $7s^2$ valence electrons and are filling the $5f$ sublevel. Their chemistry is similar because the chemistry depends more on the $2s$ electrons in the valence shell than on the number of $f$ electrons being added to an inner shell.

**46.** It is true that energy is required to form a cation. Once that ion is formed, however, it is highly reactive and undergoes reactions that a neutral atom would not undergo (such as solvation). Much energy is subsequently released in these reactions, pulling the ionization reaction forward. See the discussion of activation energy and equilibrium in Chapter 18.

**47.** Britain thought scientists should be protected and changed its policy after Moseley was killed. Students' answers to this question will vary, reflecting their position on basic, democratic values.

14

For those who think scientists should be protected, ask whether there are other groups of people who should also be protected. Does the student who thinks so belong to one of those groups?

For those who think scientists should be treated like everyone else, ask whether a scientist is not more valuable to the government than an unskilled worker. A scientist can, with one discovery, change the course of history, whereas one soldier is unlikely to have much of an effect on the outcome of a war.

48. So far, the total number of orbitals in a given level is equal to the square of the principal quantum number. There is 1 orbital in the first shell ($1\,s$), $2^2 = 4$ orbitals in the second ($1\,s + 3\,p$), $3^2 = 9$ in the third ($1\,s + 3\,p + 5\,d$), and $4^2 = 16$ in the fourth ($1\,s + 3\,p + 5\,d + 7\,f$).

If this relationship held true, then the total number of orbitals in level 5 would be $5^2 = 25$, 9 of which would be $5g$ orbitals holding a total of 18 electrons. The last element in Period 8 would have the electronic configuration $[?]8s^2 5g^{18} 6f^{14} 7d^{10} 8p^6$. There would be 50 elements ($2 + 18 + 14 + 10 + 6 = 50$) in Period 8.

## Page 387, Challenge Problems

49. Mendeleev's predictions were remarkably accurate, usually with less than 3% error. "True" values are in the CRC Handbook.

To find the error in both the molecular mass and the density, find the difference between the true value and Mendeleev's value. Divide this difference by the true value, and multiply by 100%. Do this for each of the elements. Mass is reported in g/mol, density in g/mL.

|  | True value | Mende-leev's value | % error |
|---|---|---|---|
| **Gallium** | | | |
| mass | 70 | 68 | $\frac{70-68}{70} \times 100\% = 2.9\%$ |
| density | 5.9 | 6.0 | $\frac{6.0-5.9}{5.9} \times 100\% = 1.7\%$ |
| **Scandium** | | | |
| mass | 45 | 44 | $\frac{45-44}{45} \times 100\% = 2.2\%$ |
| density of oxide | 3.9 | 3.5 | $\frac{3.9-3.5}{3.9} \times 100\% = 10\%$ |
| **Germanium** | | | |
| mass | 73 | 72 | $\frac{73-72}{73} \times 100\% = 1.4\%$ |
| density | 5.4 | 5.5 | $\frac{5.5-5.4}{5.4} \times 100\% = 1.9\%$ |

50. Answers will vary. Students are not expected to know the elements in many of the compounds listed as ingredients. Some common elements are sodium, potassium, calcium, iron, carbon, hydrogen, and oxygen.

51. If each orbital held 4 electrons instead of 2, then the energy levels would accommodate exactly twice as many electrons. There would be twice as many groups in the $s$, $p$, and $d$ blocks. A table with five periods would hold all of the known 109 elements. The $f$ orbitals would be empty. See the diagram in Figure 14-2.

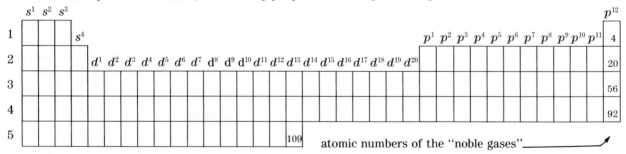

**Figure 14-2**

# Chemical Bonding

**15**

## Chapter Planning Guide

| Text Section | | Labs (Lab Manual) and Demonstrations (TE) | Supplementary Materials (Teacher's Resource Book) |
|---|---|---|---|
| **15-1** | The Attachment Between Atoms, pp. 389-391 | | Transparency Master: Electron Distributions of the Noble Gases, p. 15-5 |
| **15-2** | Ionic Bonding, pp. 391-395 | | Societal Issue: Asbestos, p. SI-32 |
| **Break-through** | Smudgeless Newspaper Ink, p. 395 | | |
| **15-3** | Covalent Bonding, pp. 396-400 | | Transparency Master: The Formation of the Chlorine Molecule by Covalent Bonding, p. 15-6<br>Review Activity: Bonding, p. 15-11<br>Critical and Creative Thinking: Comparing and Contrasting, p. CCT-15 |
| **15-4** | Hybridization, pp. 400-402 | | |
| **15-5** | Dot Diagrams for Molecules and Polyatomic Ions, pp. 402-406 | | |
| **15-6** | The Shapes of Molecules—the VSEPR Model, pp. 406-409 | | Review Activity: Orbital and Dot Diagrams and Molecular Shape, p. 15-12 |
| **15-7** | Exceptions to the Rule of Eight, pp. 410-412 | Demo 15-1: Paramagnetism, p. TG-221 | |
| **15-8** | Polar Bonds and Polar Molecules, pp. 412-416 | Demo 15-2: Attractive Liquids, p. TG-221<br>Lab 28: Three-Dimensional Models of Covalent Molecules | Transparency Master: Electronegativities of Some Common Elements, p. 15-7<br>Computer Experiment: Chemical Bonding, p. 15-9<br>Critical and Creative Thinking: Reasoning by Analogy, p. CCT-43 |

| Text Section | Labs (Lab Manual) and Demonstrations (TE) | Supplementary Materials (Teacher's Resource Book) |
|---|---|---|
| **15-9** Hydrogen Bonding, pp. 416-419 | Demo 15-3: Hydrogen Bonding in Liquids, p. TG-222 | Review Activity: Hydrogen Bonding and Boiling Point, p. 15-14 |
| **15-10** Metallic Bonding, pp. 419-420 | | |
| **15-11** Molecular Substances, pp. 421-422 | | |
| **15-12** Network Solids, p. 423 | | |
| **15-13** Ionic Crystals, pp. 423-425 | Demo 15-4: Ionic Crystals, p. TG-223 Demo 15-5: Ionic versus Covalent Properties, p. TG-223 | Transparency Master: The Arrangement of Ions in a Crystal of NaCl, p. 15-8 Review Activity: Types of Bonds, p. 15-16 |
| **15-14** Bond Energy—The Strength of a Chemical Bond, pp. 425-426 | | |
| **Biography** Emma Carr, p. 426 | | |
| | | Test—Form A, p. AT-56 Alternate Test—Form B, p. BT-56 |

☐ Core  ☐ Advanced  ☐ Optional

## Chapter Overview

In Chapter 15, we discuss the three major types of chemical bonds: ionic, covalent, and metallic. We discuss how atoms combine, the reason they combine, and the properties of the substances resulting from their combination. Several concepts related to covalent bonding are also introduced in this chapter, including hybridization, electron-dot diagrams, molecular shape, the rule of eight, and bond and molecular polarity. The last section deals with the energy changes accompanying the making and breaking of chemical bonds.

## Chapter Objectives

After students have completed this chapter, they will be able to:

1. Describe the nature of the chemical bond and its relationship to valence electrons.  *15-1*

2. Compare ionic and covalent bonding.  *15-2* to *15-4*

3. Use dot diagrams to represent ionic and covalent compounds.  *15-5* and *15-7*

4. Describe the relationship between molecular polarity and bond polarity.  *15-6* and *15-8*

5. Account for the nature and effects of metallic bonding, hydrogen bonding, and van der Waals forces.  *15-9* and *15-10*

6. Compare the structure and properties of polar and nonpolar molecules.  *15-6, 15-8,* and *15-11*

7. Compare the four classes of solids: ionic, molecular, metallic, and network.  *15-12* and *15-13*

8. Explain the role of energy in simple chemical reactions.  *15-14*

# Teaching Suggestions

## 15-1 The Attachment Between Atoms, pp. 389-391, and

## 15-2 Ionic Bonding, pp. 391-395

| Planning Guide | |
| --- | --- |
| **Labs (Lab Manual) and Demonstrations (TE)** | **Supplementary Materials (Teacher's Resource Book)** |
| | Transparency Master: Electron Distributions of the Noble Gases, p. 15-5 Societal Issue: Asbestos, p. SI-32 |

■ Remind the students that more than 100 elements are known. From these elements thousands of compounds are formed. In other words, most compounds do not consist of individual, isolated atoms, but of aggregates of atoms. Define chemical bond. Ask the students what the driving force is for the formation of chemical bonds. Explain that atoms with complete valence shells possess stability, which other atoms strive to acquire. Depending upon the type of element, this stability is acquired through sharing, losing, or gaining electrons. Next, introduce the three types of bonds: ionic, covalent, and metallic.

■ Discuss the "octet rule" or "rule of eight." Emphasize that many atoms tend to undergo chemical reactions so that electrons can be rearranged to attain this octet. Use the electron structures of the valence shells in products of chemical reactions to show that reacting atoms have acquired the stable octet.

■ Emphasize the difference between atoms and ions. Discuss what happens to an atom in the process of forming an ion. Point out that an ionic bond is the result of an electrostatic attraction between oppositely charged ions. Be sure students can clearly distinguish between the formation of simple monatomic ions and the formation of an ionic bond. Next, discuss the quantitative energy changes that occur as electrons are transferred in the process of forming ionic bonds.

■ Discuss several examples of ionic bond formation. Sodium chloride, magnesium fluoride, and potassium chloride are appropriate examples to discuss in detail. Use electron configurations to show how and where on the atoms electrons can be added or removed to achieve stable octets of electrons in these compounds. Then illustrate the usefulness of orbital diagrams to show the gain and loss of electrons.

■ Emphasize that when bonds form between ions, no molecules are produced.

■ **Concept Mastery.** The charges on ions that result from the loss or gain of electrons are particularly confusing for some students. Students must have a clear mental image of the structure of an atom to fully understand ionization. They must realize that the nucleus is the central core and that the protons and neutrons within it are tightly bound. The electrons that are lost to form ions are those that are most distant from the nucleus. In addition, electrons that are gained by an atom are added to the outermost region of the atom. You may want to assign Concept Mastery question 41 (chapter-end question) to check your students' understanding of ionization.

## 15-3 Covalent Bonding, pp. 396-400

| Planning Guide | |
| --- | --- |
| **Labs (Lab Manual) and Demonstrations (TE)** | **Supplementary Materials (Teacher's Resource Book)** |
| | Transparency Master: The Formation of the Chlorine Molecule by Covalent Bonding, p. 15-6 Review Activity: Bonding, p. 15-11 Critical and Creative Thinking: Comparing and Contrasting, p. CCT-15 |

■ Use the formation of the $H_2$ molecule to introduce the concept of covalent bonding. Emphasize orbital overlap, the resulting increase in stability, the electrostatic attractions of the two nuclei for the electrons, and the delocalized nature of the shared electrons.

■ Define polyatomic ion and discuss the bonding in these ions. Then explain that there are multiple covalent bonds and coordinate covalent bonds. Refer to text Figure 15-11 to illustrate an example of a polyatomic ion formed via a coordinate covalent bond. Refer to Figure 15-12 when discussing multiple bonds.

■ **Critical Thinking.** The Critical and Creative Thinking worksheet "Comparing and Contrasting" is intended as a laboratory investigation. Be sure to read through the worksheet and prepare the lab in advance. Students compare and contrast the properties of ionic and covalent solids and propose generalizations about the properties of each class. In the process, students will practice analytic skills that can be used in many areas of chemistry.

## 15-4 Hybridization, pp. 400-402

■ Point out that hybridization is a model that was developed to explain many observations. This model provides a way to explain what we know about the bonds and the relationships between atoms in some molecules.

15

■ Your more insightful students may be skeptical about the intellectual honesty of the concept of hybridization. Make good use of this skepticism by saying that chemists know that this model has some weak points. Point out that another theory that is more sophisticated has been proposed. This theory is called molecular orbital theory.

■ Discuss a simple case of hybridization, such as the hybridization of the carbon atom in methane. Then discuss the $sp$ and $sp^2$ hybridization of Be and B, respectively.

■ **Application.** You may want to stress that orbital hybridization is one way in which elements change in order to form more stable compounds. From their biology classes, most students can recall that hybrid flowers and fruits are developed so that more desirable and hardier plants are produced.

## 15-5 Dot Diagrams for Molecules and Polyatomic Ions, pp. 402-406

■ If you plan to cover the Advanced Topic of dot diagrams, begin by discussing $CH_4$ and $NH_3$. Then choose examples of molecules from the following list that are appropriate for your class.

| Easier | Moderate | Challenging |
|--------|----------|-------------|
| $H_2O$ | $HClO_4$ | $NH_4^+$ |
| $CH_2Cl_2$ | $H_2SO_4$ | $HPO_4^{2-}$ |
| $PH_3$ | $C_2H_6$ | $NO_2^-$ |
| $ClBr$ | $HCN$ | $ClO^-$ |
| $H_2S$ | $C_2H_4$ | $H_2CO_3$ |

## 15-6 The Shapes of Molecules—The VSEPR Model, pp. 406-409

| Planning Guide | |
|---|---|
| **Labs (Lab Manual) and Demonstrations (TE)** | **Supplementary Materials (Teacher's Resource Book)** |
| | Review Activity: Orbital and Dot Diagrams and Molecular Shape, p. 15-12 |

■ Emphasize that the key to understanding the VSEPR model for molecular geometry is remembering that electrostatic repulsions between electrons cause them to be oriented as far apart as possible. Illustrate this point by discussing the geometry of a linear molecule such as $BeF_2$. Then discuss $BF_3$ and $CH_4$. Explain the effect of unshared pairs of electrons on the shape of the molecule. Illustrate this point by discussing the geometry of a molecule of $NH_3$ and $H_2O$. Refer to text Figure 15-29 and show the students how to use the information in this table to predict molecular geometry. It is generally desirable to have space-filling models as well as ball-and-stick models available to represent the five molecular shapes listed in Figure 15-29. Ask the class to make predictions about the geometry of molecules such as $C_2H_2$, $HgCl_2$, $SnCl_2$, $BCl_3$, and $SF_6$.

■ **Concept Mastery.** Because the content of this chapter is so theoretical, students need visual representations of the shapes of molecules. Molecular model kits or Styrofoam balls of different colors and sizes are particularly helpful in answering Concept Mastery question 43 (chapter-end question). (You might wish to use the materials from Demonstration 7-2 here.) Students can see that no amount of manipulation of a three-atom molecule will yield a shape other than a bent or linear one.

## 15-7 Exceptions to the Rule of Eight, pp. 410-412

| Planning Guide | |
|---|---|
| **Labs (Lab Manual) and Demonstrations (TE)** | **Supplementary Materials (Teacher's Resource Book)** |
| Demo 15-1: Paramagnetism, p. TG-221 | |

■ If you plan to cover this Advanced Topic, begin by doing Demonstration 15-1, "Paramagnetism." In this demonstration you lead the students to the conclusion that certain molecules with an even number of electrons may have some unpaired electrons. The explanation for paramagnetism points to the fact that some compounds have valence shells that do not conform to the rule of eight.

■ Point out that there are other exceptions to the rule of eight. Emphasize that the rule of eight is not "wrong"—it is simply inadequate. The common substances described in this chapter that are exceptions to the rule of eight are noteworthy partly because there are so few exceptions.

■ Define and discuss resonance. Use the $SO_2$ molecule to illustrate this concept. Then discuss the bonding in boron compounds that have fewer than four pairs of electrons around the central atom. Discuss the compounds of the elements in Groups 13, 15, 16, and 17 that have more than four pairs of electrons around the central atom.

■ **Concept Mastery.** Students frequently memorize the definition of a new term, such as paramagnetism, but do not really understand the physical significance of the term. Concept Mastery question 45 (chapter-end question) describes an experiment that can be performed to determine whether or not a compound is paramagnetic. In order to understand the experiment, students should draw dot diagrams for an oxygen molecule.

## 15-8 Polar Bonds and Polar Molecules, pp. 412-416

| Planning Guide | |
|---|---|
| Labs (Lab Manual) and Demonstrations (TE) | Supplementary Materials (Teacher's Resource Book) |
| Demo 15-2: Attractive Liquids, p. TG-221 Lab 28: Three-Dimensional Models of Covalent Molecules | Transparency Master: Electronegativities of Some Common Elements, p. 15-7 Computer Experiment: Chemical Bonding, p. 15-9 Critical and Creative Thinking: Reasoning by Analogy, p. CCT-43 |

■ Tell the students that the concept of electronegativity is useful even though it is not quite exact because there is no simple, direct way to measure it. Pauling's electronegativity values are the ones usually used and they are derived from bond energy values.
■ Explain how to use electronegativity values to predict the type of bond formed between two elements—that is, whether a bond is polar or nonpolar, covalent or ionic. Show the students how to use differences in electronegativity and text Figure 15-37 to ascertain the type of bond formed between two elements. Use this figure for the bonding in the following series of compounds: $H_2$, HCl, $Cl_2$, BrCl, ICl, and NaCl. Have students fill in a table similar to this one:

| Bond | $E_{neg}$ diff. | Bond type |
|---|---|---|
| H-H | 0 | nonpolar |
| H-Cl | 1.0 | polar |
| Cl-Cl | 0 | nonpolar |
| Br-Cl | 0.3 | polar |
| I-Cl | 0.5 | polar |
| Na-Cl | 2.3 | ionic |

Ask the students to list the bonds according to increasing polarity. Then do Demonstration 15-2, "Attractive Liquids," which demonstrates the ability of a polar liquid to be attracted by a charged rod.
■ Explain that polar molecules are formed when polar bonds are asymmetrically distributed in a molecule. Therefore, a polar molecule has at least one polar bond, but the presence of polar bonds does not necessarily mean that the molecule is polar. Reinforce this concept by discussing the sequence of molecules shown in accompanying Figure 15-1. Ask the students to identify those molecules that are polar and those that are nonpolar. Ask them to explain their answers. Assign Laboratory 28, "Three-Dimensional Models of Covalent Molecules." In this lab the students predict the shape and polarity of various compounds.
■ **Concept Mastery.** You may need to emphasize that there are two conditions that must be met for a

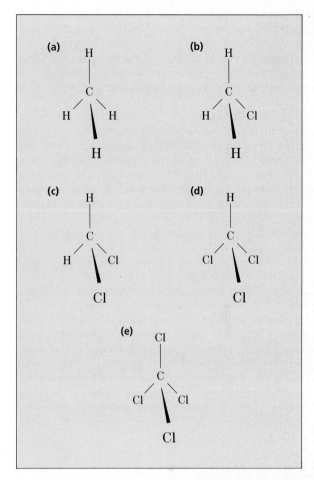

Figure 15-1

molecule to be polar. The molecule must have polar bonds, and these bonds must be arranged asymmetrically. You may wish to assign Concept Mastery question 42 (chapter-end question) to check your students' understanding of this principle. Demonstration 15-2 also reinforces this principle.
■ **Critical Thinking.** Models are very important in the study of chemistry. The Critical and Creative Thinking worksheet "Reasoning by Analogy" uses the familiar water molecule to focus on how models work. Students will better understand both the usefulness and limitations of models of chemical bonding.

## 15-9 Hydrogen Bonding, pp. 416-419

| Planning Guide | |
|---|---|
| Labs (Lab Manual) and Demonstrations (TE) | Supplementary Materials (Teacher's Resource Book) |
| Demo 15-3: Hydrogen Bonding in Liquids, p. TG-222 | Review Activity: Hydrogen Bonding and Boiling Point, p. 15-14 |

■ Explain hydrogen bonding in terms of the difference in electronegativity between the hydrogen atom and the element with which it is combined. Point out that a hydrogen atom acts almost like a proton and, with this high concentration of positive charge, is attracted by a pair of electrons on the electronegative atom of a neighboring molecule. Do Demonstration 15-3, "Hydrogen Bonding in Liquids," in which students observe the properties of various liquids and relate them to the degree of hydrogen bonding in the liquids. Point out that hydrogen bonding affects properties in addition to those discussed in Demonstration 15-3. Then mention that hydrogen bonding also leads to high melting points, low vapor pressures, and high heats of vaporization. Ask the students to explain why these properties are affected in this manner. Discuss examples of hydrogen bonding in $H_2O$, $NH_3$, and HF.

■ Emphasize that many organic compounds exhibit hydrogen bonding because of their —OH and —$NH_2$ groups. Then discuss the importance of hydrogen bonding in biological systems.

■ **Concept Mastery.** You may want to assign Concept Mastery question 44 (chapter-end question), which points out that water does not follow the general pattern of most substances in that the solid phase is less dense than the liquid phase. Ask students to illustrate matter at the molecular level in all three phases. Then ask them if they would expect matter to become more dense as it changed from the solid phase to the liquid phase.

## 15-10 Metallic Bonding, pp. 419-420

■ Introduce the third major type of bonding—metallic bonding. Discuss the "diffuse cloud of electrons" model. Explain the most common properties of metals in terms of this model.

## 15-11 Molecular Substances, pp. 421-422

■ Emphasize the two levels of interaction in molecules:
1. covalent bonding between atoms to form molecules
2. van der Waals forces between molecules to yield the condensed phases of matter (liquids and solids)

Explain to the students that if covalent bonding was the only type of force in molecular substances, all molecular substances would be gases. Ask the students to explain the difference in phase in carbon dioxide, alcohol, and glucose. All of these compounds are covalent structures. For gases such as carbon dioxide, the molecules are nonpolar and the intermolecular forces are weak. The intermolecular attractions of the polar alcohol molecules are strong enough to produce the liquid phase. In glucose, the attractions

of polar molecules are supplemented by van der Waals forces, which are greater in glucose than in smaller molecules. The net result is that glucose is in the solid phase.

■ Explain that van der Waals forces are electrostatic in nature and are due to the shifts in the positions of the electrons, creating an uneven charge distribution. Point out that the forces increase with the number of electrons in the molecule. Ask the class to relate the boiling points and freezing points of the noble gases to the number of electrons in an atom of each noble gas. Ask the class to relate the phases of the halogens to the number of electrons in each.

## 15-12 Network Solids, p. 423

■ Tell the students that network solids, like molecular solids, are bonded by covalent bonds. However, there is one important difference. In network solids, covalent bonds extend from atom to atom in a continuous three-dimensional pattern. In a sense, the entire mass of a network solid may be considered to be a single, giant molecule. Explain that in this type of structure, only the solid phase is possible. The strong bonds in network solids also account for their high melting points, insolubility in ordinary solvents, and poor conductivity.

## 15-13 Ionic Crystals, pp. 423-425

| Planning Guide | |
| --- | --- |
| Labs (Lab Manual) and Demonstrations (TE) | Supplementary Materials (Teacher's Resource Book) |
| Demo 15-4: Ionic Crystals, p. TG-223<br>Demo 15-5: Ionic versus Covalent Properties, p. TG-223 | Transparency Master: The Arrangement of Ions in a Crystal of NaCl, p. 15-8<br>Review Activity: Types of Bonds, p. 15-16 |

■ Begin this section by doing Demonstration 15-4, "Ionic Crystals." In this demonstration you make a model of the ionic crystal lattice of NaCl. Use this model to emphasize the absence of discrete molecules of NaCl. Ask the students to construct models of other ionic crystals such as $CaCl_2$ and $CaCO_3$. Calcium carbonate is useful in showing how polyatomic ions fit into a crystal lattice. Students may not understand the nature of an ionic solid until they really grasp the process of ion formation. You may have to keep referring to this process. Understanding this concept is a major accomplishment for many students.

■ Next, move on to discuss the properties of ionic crystals in terms of the lattice structure. Then do Demonstration 15-5, "Ionic versus Covalent Properties." In this demonstration you compare the properties of selected ionic and molecular substances.

■ Summarize the information about the four classes of solids by referring to text Figure 15-53.

■ **Application.** You may want to have the students grow various ionic crystals in the classroom. Have them vary the growing conditions so that they can discover the process that produces the best crystals. Using a magnifying lens, the students can then classify the crystals by shape.

### 15-14 Bond Energy—The Strength of a Chemical Bond, pp. 425-426

■ The vocabulary of this section is used in many subsequent chapters. The principles of energy in chemical reactions are most thoroughly presented in Chapter 17. However, some of these principles can be presented now while the concepts of bond formation, bond breaking, and the related electron rearrangements are fresh in the minds of your students.

■ Compare exothermic and endothermic processes. Define bond energy. Stress that the higher the bond energy is, the greater the stability is of that bond. Describe the role of stored energy. Trace the energy change as sodium chloride is formed from its elements. Repeat this process for the formation of water from hydrogen and oxygen.

## Demonstrations

### 15-1 Paramagnetism

**Overview:** In this demonstration, you hold a powerful magnet near dangling test tubes that contain different salts of transition metals. Those test tubes containing salts that are paramagnetic will be slightly attracted to the magnet, whereas those with salts that are diamagnetic will not be attracted and may be slightly repelled by it.

**Materials:** 4 medium-size test tubes; anhydrous copper(II) sulfate ($CuSO_4$); zinc sulfate ($ZnSO_4$); manganese(II) sulfate ($MnSO_4$); calcium sulfate ($CaSO_4$); 4 ring stands, each with a universal clamp or ring attached; thread; powerful magnet.

**Advance Preparation:** Place a different solid into each test tube, filling each one-fourth full. Tie a piece of thread, about 25 cm long, to each test tube. Tie the other end of the thread to a clamp or ring, so that the tube hangs freely.

**Procedure:** 1. Ask students to consider the electron configurations for $Ca^{2+}$, $Cu^{2+}$, $Mn^{2+}$, and $Zn^{2+}$. Have students try to tell the number of unpaired electrons in each metal ion and predict which ions will be attracted to the magnet. 2. Bring one end of the magnet very

near the lower part of one of the filled test tubes. Make sure the tube is absolutely motionless before you begin, and be careful not to touch it. Move the magnet around and try to cause the tube to move toward it. 3. Repeat with the other tubes.

**Results:** $Ca^{2+}$ and $Zn^{2+}$ have completely filled $s$ and $p$ orbitals, and $Zn^{2+}$ also has completely filled $d$ orbitals. Since there are no unpaired electrons in these ions, they are diamagnetic. The test tubes containing them will not be attracted by the magnet and may even be slightly repelled by it, if the magnet is powerful enough. $Cu^{2+}$ has nine electrons in its $d$ orbitals; thus, it has one unpaired electron and is paramagnetic and will be attracted by the magnet. $Mn^{2+}$ has five electrons in its $d$ orbitals, each in a half-filled orbital. Consequently, it is paramagnetic and will be attracted by the magnet.

### 15-2 Attractive Liquids

**Overview:** In this demonstration, you bring a charged rod near streams of a polar liquid and a nonpolar liquid. The polar liquid is attracted to the rod, whereas the nonpolar liquid is not.

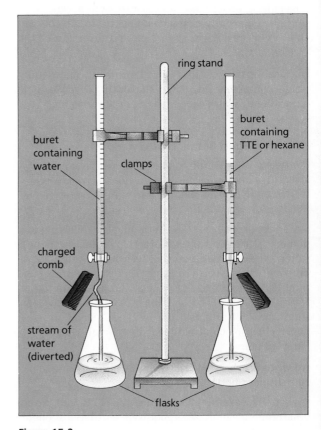

**Figure 15-2**

**Materials:** 2 50-mL burets; TTE (1,1,2-trichloro-1,2,2-trifluoroethane) or hexane; 2 flasks; plastic or rubber comb or rod; ring stand and buret clamps.

**Advance Preparation:** Fill one buret to the 25-mL mark with water. Fill a second buret to the same level with TTE or hexane. Attach each to a ring stand, using clamps. Place a flask beneath each.

**Safety:** Be careful in handling the TTE and hexane, and avoid breathing their vapors. Work in a well-ventilated room or at a fume hood.

**Procedure:** 1. Ask a student who has long, non-oily hair to comb his or her hair, using the plastic or rubber comb. Open the stopcock of the water-filled buret to allow a thin, steady stream of water to flow into the flask below it. Have the student hold the comb close to the stream, and have the class observe and explain the result. 3. Have the student repeat step 1, this time using a stream of TTE or hexane instead of the water. Again have students observe and try to explain the result.

**Results:** The TTE (or hexane) molecule is essentially nonpolar, and thus does not have charged ends that can be attracted to the charged comb. The water molecule is polar, and can turn in such a way as to place its oppositely charged end nearer to the charged comb. This results in attraction and diversion of the stream of water.

**Disposal Tips:** Place the TTE or hexane into an organic-waste container, not down the drain. Dispose of it according to your school-district or state policy.

## 15-3 Hydrogen Bonding in Liquids

**Overview:** In this demonstration, you compare the structures and properties of four liquids, some characterized by hydrogen bonding and one characterized by London forces acting between molecules.

**Materials:** dropper bottles containing the following five liquids: TTE (1,1,2-trichloro-1,2,2-trifluoroethane); water; ethanol; 1,2-ethanediol (ethylene glycol); 1,2,3-propanetriol (glycerin or glycerol); test tube rack containing 3 medium-size test tubes and placed on top of several paper towels; iron filings; 2–3 glass microscope slides; small clear plastic cup or glass; 3 small boxes of paper clips; piece of cardboard or metal, roughly 10 cm × 10 cm.

**Advance Preparation:** Place the five liquids into separate dropper bottles.

**Safety:** Be careful in handling the TTE and avoid breathing its vapor. Work in a well-ventilated room or at a fume hood.

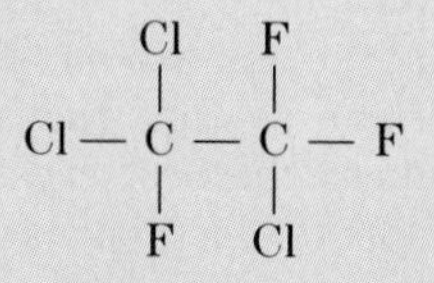

1,1,2-trichloro -1,2,2-trifluoroethane (TTE)

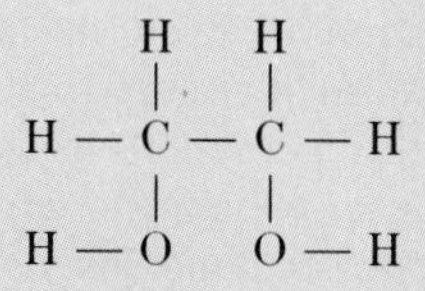

1,2-ethanediol (ethylene glycol)

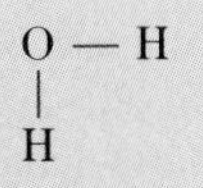

Water

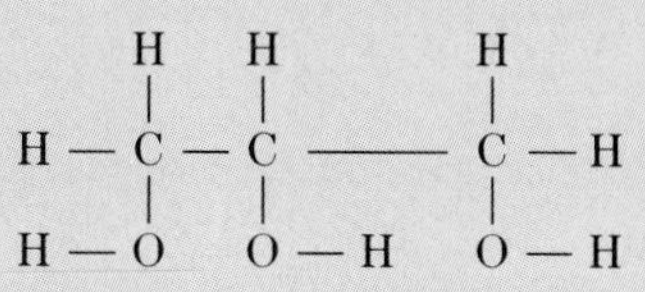

1,2,3-propanetriol (glycerin)

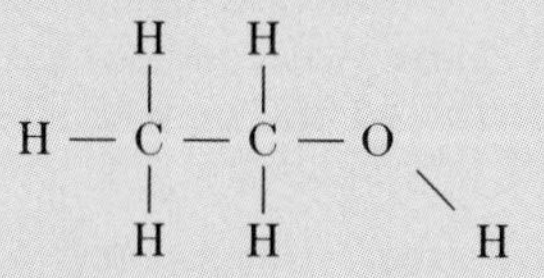

Ethanol

Figure 15-3

**Procedure:** 1. Show students the structures (see accompanying figure) of the five compounds in the dropper bottles, and have the students predict which one is characterized by the highest attractive forces between molecules. 2. Fill the first tube almost to the rim with TTE. Continue to add drops of TTE just until the liquid starts to run over the sides of the tube. Do the same with the ethanol and water. Ask students to compare the surfaces of the three liquids and account for the differences. Sprinkle some iron filings onto each of the three surfaces, and ask students to observe and explain what happens. 3. Ask a student to fill the cup or glass as full as possible with water until the water runs over the sides. Take a piece of cardboard or metal, and slide it across the top of the cup or glass to remove the excess water, so that the water level comes only to the top of the rim. Ask students to predict how many paper clips could be added to the water before it ran over the sides of the container. Start adding the clips one at a time, until the water runs over. 4. Compare the viscosities of the five liquids by placing one large drop of each onto a separate glass slide. Have students observe the size and curvature of the drops. Tilt the plate to allow the drops to flow downward. Have students observe which drop moved the fastest and which moved the slowest. Ask them how this is related to the forces between molecules.

**Results:** In step 2, the TTE surface will be flat, that of the alcohol will be slightly rounded, and that of the water will bulge markedly. TTE is essentially nonpolar and is characterized by weak forces of attraction (London dispersion forces) between its molecules, whereas alcohol and water are characterized by hydrogen bonding. Water, with its strong intermolecular attractions and high surface tension, can support the most filings. In step 3, a very large number of clips can be added to the water before it overflows. In step 4, viscosity depends on forces of attraction between molecules and on the ability of the molecules to become "entangled" in each other. Glycerin has the greatest viscosity, followed by ethylene glycol, water, ethanol, and, finally, TTE.

**Disposal Tips:** Pour all of the organic liquids into an organic-waste container, not down the drain, and dispose of them in the appropriate way.

## 15-4 Ionic Crystals

**Overview:** In this demonstration, you make lattice models of ionic crystals, using gumdrops and toothpicks.

**Materials:** gumdrops; toothpicks.

**Advance Preparation:** Make a model of a simple cubic crystal of sodium chloride (NaCl) by using gumdrops of two different colors and toothpicks. Start by placing four or five alternating-colored gumdrops in a row and then complete several more rows, and connect the rows to each other, to make a plane of them. Make several such planes, and attach them as shown in the accompanying figure. Make another row and leave it detached from the others.

**Procedure:** 1. Show the model of the NaCl lattice structure. Point out a unit cell and tell the students that the force of attraction between the ions is a very strong electrostatic force, involving oppositely

charged particles. Ask the students to predict whether NaCl has a relatively low or relatively high melting point. 2. Place the separate row of ions next to the crystal structure, in normal position, with positive ions near negative ones. Next, move it down one row, so that same-colored gumdrops are next to each other. Ask students what would happen to an actual crystal of NaCl in such a case. 3. Ask students whether NaCl could be expected to conduct electricity well and, if so, under what conditions.

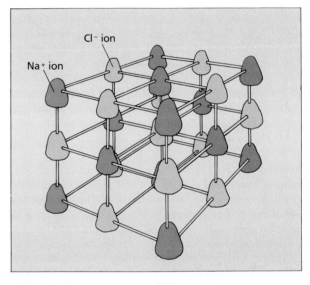

**Figure 15-4**

**Results:** NaCl has a high melting point, due to the very strong forces of attraction between the ions in the crystal. When like ions are moved next to each other, repulsion results and an entire plane of ions repels the adjacent plane, resulting in clean splitting, or cleavage, along the boundary of the planes.

## 15-5 Ionic versus Covalent Properties

**Overview:** In this demonstration, you compare and contrast properties of ionically bonded compounds with those of covalently bonded compounds. Melting point, combustibility, solubility in water, and conductivity are the properties compared.

**Materials:** paraffin; sucrose ($C_{12}H_{22}O_{11}$); sodium chloride (NaCl); potassium iodide (KI); ice; hot plate; top lid removed from a tin can; forceps; conductivity apparatus; 3 150-mL or 250-mL beakers; distilled water; 5 test tubes, half filled with water; Bunsen burner.

**Advance Preparation:** 1. Use a can opener to cut the lid from a tin can. 2. Set up the conductivity apparatus. 3. Fill five test tubes halfway with water.

**Safety**: Be careful in using the heat sources and conductivity apparatus. (Use only a low-power electricity source, such as a dry cell.)

**Procedure**: 1. Place separate small quantities of paraffin, sucrose, NaCl, KI, and ice onto a tin can lid placed on a hot plate. Heat gently, and have students note how quickly each substance melts. Ask them to draw conclusions relating the type of bonding in a substance to the substance's melting point. 2. Using forceps, hold a small piece of each of the five solids in the flame of a burner and have students note whether the substance melts, burns, and/or produces a characteristic flame color. 3. Place pieces, each about the size of the head of a pin, of each solid into a test tube that is half full of water. Cork and shake, and have students observe whether the solids dissolve. 4. Cover the bottom of one 150-mL or 250-mL beaker with sugar crystals, the bottom of another beaker of the same size with sodium chloride crystals, and the bottom of a third beaker with potassium iodide crystals. Use a conductivity apparatus to test the conductivity of the solid crystals. Add distilled water to each, and again test each solution for conductivity.

**Results**: In step 1, paraffin, sucrose, and ice will melt readily (have low melting points) and are covalently bonded, whereas NaCl and KI will not melt under the given conditions and are ionically bonded. In step 2, paraffin and sucrose should melt and burn in the burner flame and leave a black carbon residue, whereas the ice will melt and turn to steam. NaCl and KI will produce characteristic flame colors of yellow and violet, respectively. In step 3, the paraffin will not dissolve appreciably in water, but the ice cube, sucrose, NaCl, and KI will dissolve in water. In step 4, none of the substances will conduct in the solid phase. The solutions of the ionic substances NaCl and KI will conduct, but the solutions of the three covalently bonded substances will not.

# Answers to Questions

## Page 390

1. A chemical bond is a force of attraction that holds two atoms together.
2. Chemical bonds are formed when valence electrons are shared by atoms or transferred from one atom to another.
3. Compounds are formed by ionic bonds when electrons are transferred from one atom to another, a process that forms positive and negative ions. Compounds are formed by covalent bonds when electrons are shared between atoms.

4. When a chemical bond is formed, energy is given off.

## Page 394

5. The term *stable octet of electrons* refers to the eight electrons found in the valence (outer) shells of the atoms of the noble gases. It also refers to the eight valence electrons found in most covalently bonded atoms and most monatomic ions.
6. An ion is an atom that has acquired a charge by the gain or loss of one or more electrons.
7. During the process of ionic bonding, one electron or more is transferred from the metal atom to the nonmetal atom.
8. The process of ionic bonding (transfer of electrons) has no effect on the nucleus.
9. A neutral atom becomes an ion with a charge of 2+ by losing two electrons.
10. The number of electrons found most often in the outer shell of an ion is eight.
11. A dot diagram shows the symbol of an element and its valence electrons.
12. The dot diagram for a sulfur atom is $\cdot\ddot{S}\!:$
13. Nonmetals tend to form negative ions because nonmetal atoms attract electrons more strongly than metal atoms do.
14. The "rule of eight" summarizes the tendency of valence electrons to rearrange themselves during bonding so that each atom in a molecule has eight electrons through the sharing of 2 to 6 electrons. (The most frequent exception is the hydrogen atom, which, because of its small size, can accommodate only two electrons in its valence shell.)
15. Dot diagrams for this question are:

    a. $\ddot{Be}$     b. $\ddot{B}\!\cdot$     c. $\cdot\ddot{O}\!:$     d. $\ddot{Si}\cdot$

16. Dot diagrams for this question are:

    a. $\left[ Ca \right]^{2+}$   b. $\left[ :\!\overset{x}{\underset{\cdot\cdot}{Br}}\!: \right]^{-}$   c. $\left[ :\!\overset{\cdot\cdot}{\underset{x\times}{O}}\!: \right]^{2-}$   d. $\left[ Ga \right]^{3+}$

17. a. When aluminum reacts with chlorine gas to form $AlCl_3$, three valence electrons of aluminum are transferred to three chlorine atoms, forming one $Al^{3+}$ ion and three $Cl^-$ ions.
    b. The symbol for the aluminum ion is $Al^{3+}$. It has a charge of 3+ because it has lost three electrons.
    c. The symbol for the chloride ion is $Cl^-$. The ion has a charge of 1− because it has gained one electron.

## Page 400

18. A covalent bond is the force of attraction between two atoms that are sharing valence electrons.

19. Molecular substances differ from ionic substances in that molecular substances contain no ions, whereas ionic substances contain no molecules. As a result of these differences, ionic and molecular compounds are distinctly different in their properties.

20. Noble gases do not readily combine with each other or with atoms of other elements because the atoms of noble gases have stable octets of electrons.

21. The bonds between atoms in polyatomic ions are covalent bonds, many of which are coordinate covalent bonds.

22. A coordinate covalent bond is one in which both members of the shared electron pair come from the same atom.

23. A double bond is a force of attraction resulting from the sharing of two pairs of electrons. A triple bond is the result of sharing three pairs of electrons. An example of a triple bond is:

$$H - C \equiv C - H \qquad \text{acetylene}$$

24. Of the species listed, only $CO_3^{2-}$, $OH^-$, and $C_2H_3O_2^-$ are polyatomic ions. $H_2O$, $CO_2$, and $H_2SO_4$ are molecules. $Br^-$ and $Mg^{2+}$ are monatomic ions.

25. The diagram for $Cl_2$ is similar to text Figure 15-8 (page 397) except that the shared pair of electrons is in the third energy level.

## Page 402

26. Hybridization, which occurs during the formation of some bonds, is the rearrangement of electrons within the valence orbitals of an atom.

27. One might expect the formula for the compound between carbon and hydrogen to be $CH_2$ because an unbonded carbon atom has two half-filled orbitals. However, the true formula is $CH_4$. By promoting one electron from the $2s$ to the $2p$ sublevel, carbon has four half-filled orbitals, thus accounting for the formation of four covalent bonds in $CH_4$.

28. The number of orbitals resulting from hybridization is:
    a. two orbitals for $sp$ hybridization
    b. three orbitals for $sp^2$ hybridization
    c. four orbitals for $sp^3$ hybridization

29. The electrons of beryllium before and after hybridization are:

|  | $1s$ | $2s$ | $2p$ |
|---|---|---|---|
| Before hybridization: | ↑↓ | ↑↓ | ☐ ☐ ☐ |

|  | $1s$ | $sp$ | $p$ |
|---|---|---|---|
| After hybridization: | ↑↓ | ↑ ↑ | ☐ ☐ |

## Page 406

30. Dot diagrams for the answers to this question are:

**a.** H:Br:   **b.** H:P:H   **c.** H:C:::N:   **d.** :F:O:F:
                    H

31. Dot diagrams for the answers to this question are:

**a.** H:Cl:O:

**b.** $\begin{bmatrix} :O: \\ :O: P :O: \\ :O: \end{bmatrix}^{3-}$

**c.** $\begin{bmatrix} :O: \\ :O:N:O: \end{bmatrix}^{-}$

**d.** $\begin{bmatrix} H \\ H:O:H \end{bmatrix}^{+}$

Each arrow points to a coordinate covalent bond.

## Page 409

32. In order to form a bond angle, there must be at least three atoms in a molecule.

33. Any molecule with a 180° bond angle is a linear molecule. Any two-atom molecule is also classified as a linear molecule.

34. All molecules with $sp^3$ hybridization have the tetrahedral shape, with a bond angle of 109.47°.

35. The letters in the term *VSEPR* refer to *Valence-Shell Electron-Pair Repulsion*.

36. The tetrahedral angle is the bond angle in a regular tetrahedron, 109.47°.

37. Trigonal planar is the shape of a molecule that contains three total pairs of electrons, with all three pairs shared as covalent bonds.

38. Predicted shapes for some molecules:
    a. $H_2Se$—bent       c. $CH_2Cl_2$—tetrahedral
    b. $Cl_2O$—bent       d. $PCl_3$—trigonal pyramid

39. Predicted shapes for some polyatomic ions:
    a. $SO_4^{2-}$—tetrahedral       c. $NO_2^+$—linear
    b. $ClO_3^-$—trigonal pyramid       d. $NH_2^-$—bent

## Page 412

40. Resonance refers to a particular arrangement of electrons. In this arrangement, electrons form bonds even though the electrons are not shared as pairs. The electrons are spread across the locations of two or more bonds.

41. The concept of resonance is used when the octet rule does not adequately describe the electron arrangement and corresponding bond formation in a molecule.

42. The boron atom is an exception to the octet rule because it can hold only three electron pairs in its valence shell. Hence, it can form only three bonds and does not form an octet in its valence shell.

43. **a.** A trigonal bipyramid is shown in Figure 15-5 (a). **b.** Phosphorous pentachloride, $PCl_5$, has the

15

shape of a trigonal bipyramid. **c.** The structural formula of PCl₅ is shown in Figure 15-5(b).

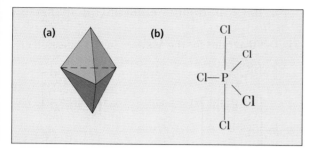

**Figure 15-5**

**44.** Paramagnetism is the term applied to a weak interaction between a molecule or atom and a magnetic field. It is caused by the presence in the molecule of unpaired electrons.

**45.** In order for an atom or a molecule to exhibit paramagnetism, it must have one or more unpaired electrons. That is, it must have at least one half-filled orbital.

**Page 416**

**46.** The electrons in a covalent bond are shared unequally when one atom has a higher electronegativity than the other atom.

**47.** A covalent bond is generally considered to be polar when the difference in electronegativity values of the bonded atoms is between 0.8 and 1.7.

**48.** A polar molecule behaves as if it has a positive end and a negative end.

**49.** A molecule can be nonpolar even though its bonds are polar if the polar bonds are distributed symmetrically throughout the molecule.

**50.** Electronegativity values are not given for the Group 18 elements because those elements do not attract electrons readily. This lack of attraction is the result of the valence shells of those elements being filled with eight electrons (two electrons for helium).

**51.** $NH_3$ is likely to be a polar molecule because it has three polar bonds that are unevenly distributed within the molecule.

**52.** $BH_3$ is not likely to be a polar molecule because its three bonds are not polar and are distributed symmetrically within the molecule. (The molecule lies in a plane.)

**53.** These bonds are listed in order of decreasing polarity:
**a.** C-F, C-Cl, C-H, C-Br, C-I
**b.** As-Cl, P-Cl, H-Cl, N-Cl
**c.** P-O, S-O, C-O, N-O

**54.** These bonds are listed in order of increasing ionic character:
**a.** Ca-I, Ca-Br, Mg-Cl, Mg-F
**b.** H-Cl, Al-Cl, Ca-Cl, K-Cl
**c.** Sb-H, As-H, Ge-H, Al-H

**Page 419**

**55.** The amount of effective positive charge on the hydrogen end of a molecule that forms hydrogen bonds is greater than the corresponding amount of positive charge on the end of an ordinary polar molecule.

**56.** The presence of hydrogen bonds accounts for higher boiling points.

**57.** The presence of hydrogen bonds also accounts for lower vapor pressure, higher heat of vaporization, and higher melting point—all properties associated with stronger forces of attraction between molecules.

**58.** A hydrogen atom in a molecule resembles an exposed proton when that hydrogen atom is bonded to a small, highly electronegative atom. The strong attraction for electrons exhibited by that electronegative atom pulls most of the electron cloud away from the hydrogen atom.

**Page 420**

**59.** In a metallic bond, the positive ions of the metal are held in place within a diffuse cloud of electrons.

**60.** A substance can be classified as a metal when it conducts heat and electricity as a solid and as a liquid, when it possesses a shiny luster, and when it is malleable.

**Page 422**

**61.** Van der Waals forces are those weak forces of attraction that exist between all molecules.

**62.** Van der Waals forces are much weaker than ionic, covalent, and hydrogen bonds.

**63. a.** The strength of van der Waals forces increases as the number of electrons in a molecule increases.
**b.** The effectiveness of van der Waals forces increases as the distance between molecules decreases.

**64.** A molecule is a cluster of atoms held together by covalent bonds. A molecule is also the smallest particle capable of independent motion or existence.

**65.** In molecular substances, the molecules align themselves so that ends with opposite charges are attracted to each other.

**Page 425**

**66.** Substances that exist as ionic crystals are not considered to be made up of molecules because each lattice point is occupied by a discrete, charged particle—an ion. No particles matching the definitions given in the answer to question 64 can be found in ionic crystals.

**67.** In a network solid, covalent bonds extend from one atom to another in a continuous pattern.

**68.** Network solids are typically hard and brittle. They are poor conductors of electricity and have high melting points.

**69.** In a crystal lattice of sodium chloride, ions of sodium and chlorine are found in a regular cubic array.

**70.** Molecular solids and ionic solids are similar in that both represent regular geometric arrays of molecules and ions, respectively. Their differences include:
- Ionic solids conduct current when dissolved or melted, are brittle, and have high melting points.
- Molecular solids are good insulators, are soft, and have low melting points.

**Page 426**

**71.** Bond energy is the energy required to break a chemical bond.

**72.** Molecules that are stable have greater bond strength.

**73.** When sodium and chlorine combine to form the compound sodium chloride, energy is released. The net output of energy is greater than the net input of energy.

**74.** In an endothermic reaction, the net input of energy is greater than the net output of energy.

# Chapter Review    15

## Page 428, Content Review

**1.** Atoms combine to form compounds in two general ways: formation of a covalent bond or formation of an ionic bond.

**2.** Electrons that are shared between atoms are in a lower energy state than when they are attracted to just one nucleus.

**3.** The attraction between oppositely charged anions and cations is the force that makes up an ionic bond.

**4. a.** An argon atom has eight valence electrons, so there are 8 dots around its symbol in the dot diagram.
  **b.** The eight valence electrons fill the valence shell, so argon is stable. It is a noble gas.

**5.**  $\ddot{\text{Mg}}$     $\cdot\ddot{\text{P}}\cdot$     $\cdot\ddot{\text{S}}\colon$     $\colon\ddot{\text{Ne}}\colon$

**6.** Hydrogen atoms are bonded together covalently in a hydrogen molecule. The bond comes from the electrostatic attraction between the positive nuclei and the negative electrons.

**7.** In a covalent bond, both atoms contribute one electron to the pair of shared electrons. In a coordinate covalent bond, both electrons are donated by the same atom.

**8.** In methane, one $2s$ orbital and three $2p$ orbitals of carbon combine to form four identical $sp^3$ orbitals. The $sp^3$ orbitals are called hybrids because each has some $s$ character and some $p$ character.

**9. a.**  H:F̈:    **c.**  H:S̈:H

  **b.**  H:C̈:H     **d.**  :F̈:C̈:F̈:
      with H above and below C on b

**10.** The valence-shell electron-pair repulsion model is a way of predicting the shapes of molecules. The model indicates that electron pairs repel each other because they are all negatively charged, so the electron pairs try to get as far away from each other as they can.

**11.** Hybridization refers to a rearrangement of the valence electrons in the orbitals just before bonding so that the resulting orbitals are at equal energy levels. In methane, for example, one of the $2s$ electrons in the C atom is promoted to the empty $2p$ orbital, so that each of the valence orbitals now has one electron in it. Each orbital has ¼ $s$ character and ¾ $p$ character. They are at the same energy level and form identical bonds with hydrogen.

**12. a.** Since C uses $sp^3$ hybridization to bond to four Cl atoms, the molecule is a regular tetrahedron.
  **b.** Since B uses $sp^2$ hybridization to bond to three F atoms, the molecule is trigonal planar with the B at the center and an F at each corner.
  **c.** The S has six valence electrons and each H adds one. Therefore, there are two shared pairs and two unshared pairs of electrons. The S uses four $sp^3$ hybrid orbitals to accommodate all of these electrons. The S is at the center of an irregular tetrahedron with the two H atoms at two of the corners, so the molecule is bent. The other two corners of the tetrahedron are occupied by unshared pairs of electrons.
  **d.** Since each S is double bonded to the C and there are no unshared pairs of electrons occupying other orbitals, the C uses $sp$ hybridization. The molecule is linear.

**13.** The shared electrons spread out across the atoms that are involved in resonance.

14. Electronegativity is the attraction of an atom for electrons in a covalent bond. Chemically active metals have a low attraction for such electrons, so their electronegativities are low.

15. A polar bond is a covalent bond in which the electrons are attracted to one of the atoms more than the other.

16. The difference in the electronegativities of the atoms in MgO $(3.5 - 1.2 = 2.3)$ is greater than 1.7, so the covalent bond is predominantly ionic.

17. The boiling point of $H_2O$ is the highest because extra energy is needed to break the hydrogen bonds holding the molecules together.

18. This is a good description of metals.

19. Van der Waals forces depend on the electrostatic attraction between positive and negative charges and, therefore, increase as the charges get closer together. As a result, van der Waals forces are strongest in the solid phase and weakest in the gas phase.

20. Many nonpolar covalent substances are gases at room temperature because the forces of attraction between the molecules are too weak to hold the molecules in the liquid phase.

21. In a network solid, covalent bonds extend from atom to atom in a continuous, three-dimensional pattern. There is no "edge" to the molecule.

22. Ionic substances are made of ions.

23. The bond energy is the energy required to break a chemical bond. Stronger bonds have higher bond energies.

24. Energy is required to break a bond, so the process is endothermic.

## Page 429, Content Mastery

25. Hydrogen bonds exist only in compounds in which the hydrogen is bonded to a small, highly electronegative atom. The polarity of the covalent bond allows the positive hydrogen to partially bond to the negative end of a neighboring molecule, forming a hydrogen bond. If the covalent bond between hydrogen and the other atom is not polar enough, the hydrogen is not free to form a weak bond with another molecule.

26. The valence shell of He is the first shell, which is full with two $1s$ electrons. This electron configuration is stable. The valence shell of Mg is the third shell, which takes eight electrons to fill, not two. Mg is active chemically because its valence shell is not full.

27. 1. Metals are good conductors because of the mobility of their valence electrons. 2. Metals are hard because of the strong binding forces of the electrons. These forces draw the kernels of the atoms closer together. 3. Their luster comes from the way the mobile electrons absorb and re-emit the light that strikes them. 4. The malleability, ductility, and sectility come from the uniform attraction between the electrons and the ions. Because there are no strongly preferred positions, the particles can move easily into other positions.

   (Malleable means capable of being rolled or hammered into thin sheets. Ductile means capable of being drawn out into wires. Sectile means capable of being cut smoothly.)

28. **a.** :N⋮⋮N:

    **b.** Ö⋮⋮Ö

    **c.** S̈⋮⋮C⋮⋮S̈

    **d.** H:C⋮⋮C:H [or H:C⋮⋮C:H]

29. Polyatomic ions are species that carry a charge and contain more than one atom. The polyatomic ions are **a.** $C_2H_3O_2^-$, **c.** $HSO_4^-$, **d.** $CN^-$, and **f.** $MnO_4^-$. $Ca^{2+}$ is an ion but it is not polyatomic; it contains only calcium. $CH_4$ is polyatomic, but it is a molecule, not an ion; it carries no net charge.

30. Hybridization is the rearrangement of electrons within the valence orbitals of an atom during a reaction, resulting in a number of equivalent orbitals, each at the same energy level, and each with partial $s$ and partial $p$ character. The possible hybrids from $s$ and $p$ orbitals are $2sp$, $3sp^2$, and $4sp^3$ orbitals.

31. **a.**    :Ö:
            H:C̈l:Ö:
              :Ö:

    **b.** $\left[\begin{array}{c} :Ö: \\ :Ö:S:Ö: \\ :Ö: \end{array}\right]^{2-}$

    **c.**    :Ö:H
            :Ö:P:Ö:H
              :Ö:H

    **d.** $\left[\begin{array}{c} :Ö: \\ :Ö ⋮C⋮ :Ö: \end{array}\right]^{2-}$

    **e.**    :Ö:
            :Ö⋮⋮N:Ö:H

32. An ionic bond is the electrostatic force of attraction that bonds anions to their neighboring cations in an ionic crystal. For example, $MgCl_2$ con-

tains one cation and two anions per formula unit.

**33.** To predict the shape of a molecule, find the hybridization used by the central atom, which must have enough orbitals to hold all of the shared and unshared pairs of electrons. Remember that double (and triple) bonds are made of one hybrid orbital plus one (or two) unhybridized $p$ orbital(s) that point in the same direction as the hybrid orbital. The $p$ orbitals that form double and triple bonds cannot be used to make hybrid orbitals.

**a.** $CBr_4$, $sp^3$, regular tetrahedron

**b.** $NCl_3$, $sp^3$, pyramid (One corner of the tetrahedron has an unshared electron pair.)

**c.** $OF_2$, $sp^3$, bent (Two corners of the tetrahedron have unshared pairs.)

**d.** $CS_2$, $sp$, linear (Each double bond in $S = C = S$ consists of one $sp$ hybrid orbital and one unhybridized $p$ orbital.)

**e.** HCN, $sp$, linear (The triple bond between the C and N uses one hybrid $sp$ orbital and two unhybridized $p$ orbitals.)

**f.** $BF_3$, $sp^2$, trigonal planar (The B has only three pairs of valence electrons.)

**34. Group  dot diagram      where M is**

| | Group | dot diagram | where M is |
|---|---|---|---|
| **a.** | 1 | $\dot{M}$ | H, Li, Na, K, Rb, Cs, or Fr |
| **b.** | 2 | $\ddot{M}$ | Be, Mg, Ca, Sr, Ba, or Ra |
| **c.** | 13 | $\ddot{M}\cdot$ | B, Al, Ga, In, or Tl |
| **d.** | 14 | $\ddot{M}\cdot$ | C, Si, Ge, Sn, or Pb |

**35.** Refer to the answers for questions 31 and 33 for the dot diagrams and shapes of these molecules.

**a.** Since $CBr_4$ is a regular tetrahedron, the bond angle is 109.47°.

**b.** Since the unshared pair in $NCl_3$ occupies more space than the three bonded pairs of electrons, the bond angles are a little less than 109.47° (actually about 107°).

**c.** In $CO_3^{2-}$, one of the O is double bonded to the C, so the C uses $sp^2$ hybridization, which means the molecule is trigonal planar. Since resonance spreads that double bond equally among all three oxygen atoms, the bond angles are equal: 120°.

**d.** $OF_2$ has two unshared pairs, so the bond angles are a little less than 109.47° (actually about 105°).

**e.** Linear molecules like HCN have a bond angle of 180°.

**36.** Polar molecules have polar bonds arranged asymmetrically in the molecule. (Symmetrically arranged polar bonds cancel each other out, so the molecule itself is nonpolar.) A polar bond is one in

which the difference in electronegativities is 0.8 to 1.7 (text Figure 15-36).

**a.** $NCl_3$ is nonpolar because the $N - Cl$ bonds are not polar $(3.2 - 3.1 < 0.8)$.

**b.** $H_2S$ is nonpolar because the $H - S$ bonds are not polar $(2.6 - 2.2 < 0.8)$.

**c.** HCl is polar because the $H - Cl$ bond is polar $(3.2 - 2.2 \doteq 1.0)$. Since there is only one bond in the molecule, it is asymmetrical.

**d.** $NH_3$ is polar $(3.1 - 2.2 > 0.8)$. The three slightly polar $N - H$ bonds pull toward three corners of a tetrahedron, so the molecule is asymmetrical.

**e.** $H_2O$ is polar because the polar bonds $(3.5 - 2.2 > 0.8)$ are at an angle to each other and, thus, asymmetrical.

**f.** $CH_4$ is nonpolar. The $C - H$ bond is nonpolar $(2.6 - 2.2 < 0.8)$ and the molecule is symmetrical.

**g.** CO is polar because the one bond is polar $(3.5 - 2.5 > 0.8)$.

**h.** $BCl_3$ is nonpolar, even though the bonds are polar $(3.2 - 2.0 > 0.8)$, because the molecule is trigonal planar and, therefore, symmetrical. The polar bonds pull toward corners of an equilateral triangle and cancel each other out.

**37. a.** $[Ba]^{2+}$

**b.** $[\ddot{\underset{..}{S}}]^{2-}$

**38.** Hydrogen bonding only occurs when hydrogen is bonded to a small, electronegative element: F, O, or N. Hydrogen bonding happens in **a.** $H_2O$, **b.** $H_2O_2$, **e.** $CH_3NH_2$, **f.** $CH_3OH$, and **g.** HF. Hydrogen bonding does NOT happen in **c.** $H_2S$, because the sulfur is not electronegative enough. It does NOT happen in **d.** $H_3CF$, because the H is bonded directly to the C, not to the F.

**39.** In the dot diagrams for the most common kind of resonance, a central atom bonds to two atoms of the same element, one with a single and the other with a double bond. Since these bonds are equivalent, the double bond is really spread out across all three of the atoms involved.

**a.** $CBr_4$, **b.** $SO_4^{2-}$, and **d.** $OF_2$ have no resonance structures because they have only single bonds.

$$\ddot{:}\underset{}{Br}\ddot{:} \\ :\overset{..}{Br}:\overset{..}{C}:\overset{..}{Br}: \\ :\underset{..}{Br}:$$

$$\left[\begin{array}{c} :\ddot{O}: \\ :\overset{..}{O}:\overset{..}{S}:\overset{..}{O}: \\ :\underset{..}{O}: \end{array}\right]^{2-}$$

$$:\overset{..}{F}:\overset{..}{\underset{..}{O}}:\overset{..}{F}:$$

**c.** $CO_3^{2-}$ has three resonance structures because it has three equivalent C-O bonds. Each has $\frac{1}{3}$ double-bond character.

40. Bonds with high bond energies are more stable than those with low bond energies because the bond energy is the amount of energy that is required to break a chemical bond.

## Page 429, Concept Mastery

41. **Concept:** *Ions are formed by the loss or gain of valence electrons.*

    *Solution:* No, protons cannot be lost from the nucleus in an ordinary CHEMICAL reaction, which involves the loss or gain of electrons. The number of protons can change during NUCLEAR reactions, but the number of electrons also changes. The result is a neutral atom of a different element, not a negative ion.

42. **Concept:** *Water is a polar molecule and, as such, responds to a magnetic field.*

    *Solution:* The physical act of combing your hair strips some anions and cations from your hair and leaves them on the comb. These charged particles are attracted to each other and move toward each other. This movement of charge creates a small magnetic field around the comb. It is this field that causes the polar water molecules to move with respect to the comb.

43. **Concept:** *The shape of the molecule depends on the number of shared and unshared pairs of electrons surrounding the central atom.*

    *Solution:* Three atoms can be arranged either in a straight line or in a bent line. If the central atom has no unshared pairs of electrons, it only needs two orbitals, so it uses *sp* hybridization, and the molecule is linear. The presence of double or triple bonds does not affect the shape of the molecule. If the central atom has one or two unshared pair of electrons, it needs three or four orbitals, so it uses $sp^2$ or $sp^3$ hybridization, and the molecule is bent (at an angle of $< 120°$ or $< 109.47°$, respectively).

44. **Concept:** *Water contracts when it melts and expands when it freezes. Ice floats because it is less dense than liquid water.*

    *Solution:* The hydrogen bonds between water molecules in the solid phase (ice) hold the molecules in a crystal structure with many hexagonal openings. When ice melts, water molecules are released from the crystal structure and move freely into these hexagonal holes, making liquid water denser than ice.

45. **Concept:** *The lone pairs of electrons in oxygen make oxygen paramagnetic.*

    *Solution:* The nitrogen molecule is $:N:::N:$. It has no lone electrons, so it is not significantly affected by a magnetic field. The oxygen molecule is $:\ddot{O}::\ddot{O}:$, which contains four unshared electrons. These unshared electrons make oxygen paramagnetic, so it is attracted to a magnet just like iron filings are.

## Page 429, Cumulative Review

46. **a.** Na. Atomic radii decrease across a period because of the increased nuclear charge.

47. **b.** $0.100 \text{ mol KClO}_3 \times \dfrac{3 \text{ mol O}_2}{2 \text{ mol KClO}_3} \times \dfrac{22.4 \text{ dm}^3}{1 \text{ mol O}_2} = 3.36 \text{ dm}^3$

48. **b.** electrons; The number and arrangement of electrons in the valence shell determines chemical reactivity.

49. **c.** Particle motion stops at 0 K, not 0°C.

50. **c.** $Mg^{2+}$, which has the electron configuration of neon.

51. $45.0°C - 20.0°C = 25°C$

    $1.00 \text{ kg H}_2\text{O} \times \dfrac{1000 \text{ g}}{1 \text{ kg}} \times 4.2 \text{ J/g·°C} \times 25.0°C = 105 \times 10^3 \text{ J} = 105 \text{ kJ}$

    $2.00 \text{ g hydrocarbon} \times \dfrac{1 \text{ mol}}{100 \text{ g}} = 2.00 \times 10^{-2} \text{ mol}$

    $\dfrac{105 \text{ kJ}}{2.00 \times 10^{-2} \text{ mol}} = 52.5 \times 10^2 \text{ kJ/mol} = 5250 \text{ kJ/mol}$

52. **a.** $K^+(aq)$ and $OH^-(aq)$
    **b.** $Zn^{2+}(aq)$ and $NO_3^-(aq)$
    **c.** $Mg^{2+}(aq)$ and $Br^-(aq)$
    **d.** $Na^+(aq)$ and $S^-(aq)$

53. Mass iron = $35.21 \text{ g} - 27.85 \text{ g} = 7.36 \text{ g Fe}$
    Mass oxygen = $38.02 \text{ g} - 35.21 \text{ g} = 2.81 \text{ g O}$

    $7.36 \text{ g Fe} \times \dfrac{1 \text{ mol Fe}}{55.8 \text{ g Fe}} = 0.132 \text{ mol Fe}$

    $2.81 \text{ g O} \times \dfrac{1 \text{ mol O}}{16.0 \text{ g O}} = 0.176 \text{ mol O}$

mole ratio = 0.132 Fe/0.176 O = 1 Fe/1.33 O =

3 Fe/4 O

empirical formula = $Fe_3O_4$

**54. a.** sodium chlorite
   **b.** mercury(I) nitrate
   **c.** aluminum sulfate
   **d.** silver carbonate
   **e.** ammonium hydroxide
   **f.** chloric acid (or hydrogen chlorate if not in water)
   **g.** iron(II) phosphate
   **h.** potassium dichromate

**55. a.** $Zn(s) + Pb(NO_3)_2(aq) \rightarrow Pb(s) + Zn(NO_3)_2(aq)$
   Zn is more active than Pb.
   **b.** $CaCO_3(s) + 2HCl(aq) \rightarrow$
$$CaCl_2(aq) + CO_2(g) + H_2O(l)$$
   Gas and liquid water are produced.
   **c.** $Mg(s) + H_2SO_4(aq) \rightarrow MgSO_4(aq) + H_2(g)$
   Mg is more active than H.
   **d.** $2AgNO_3(s) + Na_2S(aq) \rightarrow$
$$2NaNO_3(aq) + Ag_2S(s)$$
   Solid precipitate is formed.
   **e.** There is no reaction because H is less reactive than Cu and will not replace Cu.

**Page 430, Critical Thinking**

**56.** Electronegativity increases across a period and up a group. See text Figure 15-36.

| Cs | K | Ca | Ga | Si | P | O | F |
|----|----|----|----|----|----|----|----|
| 0.7 | 0.8 | 1.0 | 1.6 | 1.9 | 2.2 | 3.5 | 4.0 |

**57.** In ionic bonds (diagrams b and c), electrons are transferred from one atom to another to form cations and anions. In covalent bonds (diagrams a and d), the electrons are shared by both atoms.

**58. a.** B is a metal.    **d.** Fe is a metal.
   **b.** Cl is a nonmetal.    **e.** Mg is a metal.
   **c.** Ne is a noble gas.    **f.** S is a nonmetal.

**59.** Multiple bonds are stronger than single bonds, and covalent bonds are usually stronger than ionic bonds. Based on these generalizations, a student might predict that the covalent bonds in $C_2H_2$, $CO_2$, and $O_2$ are stronger than the ionic bond in NaCl. Students also may predict that the triple bond in $C_2H_2$ is stronger than the double bonds in $O_2$ and $CO_2$. In fact, the correct order of increasing bond strength is: NaCl, $O_2$, $CO_2$, $C_2H_2$.

**60.** The electrostatic forces of attraction between polar molecules are stronger than those between nonpolar molecules, so polar molecules generally melt and boil at higher temperatures.
   **a.** $CHCl_3$, because the chlorines make it polar. $CH_4$ is nonpolar because it is symmetrical.
   **b.** $H_2O$, because it is polar. $CO_2$ is linear and nonpolar.
   **c.** $Cl_2$, because it is nonpolar. The forces of attraction between molecules are weak, so the vapor pressure is high. HCl is polar, the intermolecular forces of attraction are stronger; the vapor pressure is lower.

**Page 431, Challenge Problems**

**61.**
$$:\ddot{O}:\ddot{O}::\ddot{O}: \leftrightarrow :\ddot{O}::\ddot{O}:\ddot{O}:$$

or

$$O-O=O \leftrightarrow O=O-O$$

**62.** A hydrogen bond forms between the H bonded to an electronegative O on one molecule and the O that is double-bonded to the C on another molecule.

**63.** Answers will vary widely. Physical properties that might be described are phase at ordinary temperatures, melting and boiling points, hardness, density, malleability, color, luster, odor, taste, and electrical conductivity. Most of the substances are likely to be complex mixtures of substances. Most of the elements the students might list probably will not be pure: He in a helium balloon, C in the graphite in lead pencils, C in a diamond ring, Ne in a neon sign, Al in storm doors or siding, Fe in nails, Cu in pennies, Ag and Au in jewelry, Hg in a thermometer.

15

# Solutions

## Chapter Planning Guide

| Text Section | | Labs (Lab Manual) and Demonstrations (TE) | Supplementary Materials (Teacher's Resource Book) |
|---|---|---|---|
| **16-1** | Mixtures, p. 433 | Demo 16-1: Solutions, Colloids, and Suspensions, p. TG-237 | Concept Mastery: Types of Solutions, p. CM-27 |
| **16-2** | Solutions, pp. 434-435 | | |
| **16-3** | Types of Solutions, pp. 435-436 | | |
| **16-4** | Antifreeze, pp. 436-437 | Demo 16-2: What a Gas!, p. TG-238 | Open-Ended Experiment: The Solubility of a Solid in Aqueous Solution, p. 16-7 |
| **16-5** | Degree of Solubility, pp. 437-438 | Demo 16-3: Factors Affecting the Rate of Dissolving, p. TG-238 | |
| **16-6** | Factors Affecting the Rate of Solution, pp. 438-440 | | |
| **16-7** | Solubility and the Nature of a Solvent and a Solute, pp. 440-441 | Demo 16-4: The Disappearing Cup, p. TG-239 | Transparency Master: The Hydration of Ions, p. 16-3 |
| **16-8** | Energy Changes During Solution Formation, p. 442 | Lab 29: Bonds, Polarity, and Solubility | Concept Mastery: Dissolving Ionic and Molecular Solids, p. CM-28 |
| **16-9** | Solubility Curves and Solubility Tables, pp. 442-444 | Lab 30: Solubility of a Salt | Transparency Master: Solubility Curves for a Number of Water Soluble Inorganic Substances, p. 16-4 |
| | | Lab 31: Precipitates and Solubility Rules | Review Activity: Solubility Curves, p. 16-11 |
| | | | Critical and Creative Thinking: Generalization, p. CCT-35 |
| **16-10** | Saturated, Unsaturated, and Supersaturated Solutions, pp. 444-446 | | Open-Ended Experiment: Crystallization of Alum, p. 16-9 |
| **16-11** | Dilute and Concentrated Solutions, pp. 446-448 | | |
| **Break-through** | Synthetic Diamonds, p. 447 | | |
| **16-12** | Expressing Concentration—Molarity, pp. 449-451 | | Non-SI Supplementary Problems, p. 16-15 |
| | | | Concept Mastery: Making Molar Solutions, p. CM-29 |
| | | | Concept Mastery: Changing Solution Concentrations, p. CM-30 |

| Text Section | Labs (Lab Manual) and Demonstrations (TE) | Supplementary Materials (Teacher's Resource Book) |
|---|---|---|
| **16-13** Expressing Concentration—Molality, pp. 452-453 | | Review Activity: Solution Vocabulary, p. 16-12 |
| **16-14** Freezing Point Depression, pp. 453-457  **16-15** Boiling Point Elevation, pp. 457-458 | | Transparency Master: Vapor Pressure Curves for Pure Water and for Ice, p. 16-5  Transparency Master: Vapor Pressure Curves for a Water Solution, for Pure Water, and for Ice, p. 16-6  Practice Problems, p. 16-14 |
| | | Test—Form A, p. AT-60  Alternate Test—Form B, p. BT-60 |

■ Core     ■ Advanced     ■ Optional

## Chapter Overview

In Chapter 16, we discuss the properties of solutions as homogeneous mixtures, classify solutions into types according to physical phase, and describe the factors that affect solubility and rate of solution. We also distinguish among solutions that are saturated, unsaturated, or supersaturated, and solutions that are dilute or concentrated. Students interpret data in solubility curves and tables and solve problems relating to solutions with concentrations expressed in molarity and in molality. The final sections of the chapter discuss freezing point depression and boiling point elevation and the application of these concepts to solving problems.

## Chapter Objectives

After students have completed this chapter, they will be able to:
1. Describe the various types of solutions.
*16-1* to *16-3*
2. Discuss the factors affecting the solubility of a solute in a given solvent and its rate of solution.
*16-5* to *16-8*
3. Interpret the data in solubility curves and tables.
*16-9*
4. Understand the terms *saturated, unsaturated, supersaturated, dilute,* and *concentrated* as they pertain to solutions.
*16-10* and *16-11*

5. Solve problems that concern the concentrations of solutions.
*16-12* and *16-13*
6. Describe the effects of dissolved substances on the freezing points and boiling points of solutions, and solve problems related to these effects.
*16-4, 16-14,* and *16-15*

## Teaching Suggestions

### 16-1 Mixtures, p. 433

### 16-2 Solutions, pp. 434-435, and

### 16-3 Types of Solutions, pp. 435-436

| Planning Guide | |
|---|---|
| Labs (Lab Manual) and Demonstrations (TE) | Supplementary Materials (Teacher's Resource Book) |
| Demo 16-1: Solutions, Colloids, and Suspensions, p. TG-237 | Concept Mastery: Types of Solutions, p. CM-27 |

■ As a solution is a type of mixture, discuss the nature of homogeneous mixtures and compare them to heterogeneous mixtures. Point out that the uniformity with which the particles are spread throughout a mixture is apt to be greater as the particle size decreases. Define solution. Remind students that the definition of solution is not limited to aqueous solutions. However, because this is the type of solution that the students

16

are most familiar with, begin discussing the properties of this type of solution. Explain that the properties of solutions result from a mixture of rapidly moving, extremely small particles. Then define solute and solvent. Explain that where the components of a solution are originally in different phases, the solution itself is in a single phase, that of the solvent. Where both components are originally in the same phase, the component in the smaller amount is the solute. Mention examples of various solutions such as seltzer water, sterling silver, tincture of iodine, etc., and ask the students to identify the solute and solvent in each example.

■ Explain that because of the wide variety of solutions known, it is useful to classify them. The simplest classification scheme includes three types based upon the phase of the solvent: gaseous, liquid, and solid solutions. Ask the students to identify and discuss solvent systems found in their environment such as vinegar, beverages, gasoline, salt water, brass, the atmosphere, coins, and gold jewelry. Point out that the solid solution does not have the obvious properties of gaseous and liquid solutions, but that it is a homogeneous mixture of molecules or atoms.

■ At some point your students may suggest that milk or blood are examples of solutions. Milk and blood are examples of colloids. You may want to do Demonstration 16-1, "Solutions, Colloids, and Suspensions," to illustrate the differences among these three types of liquid mixtures.

■ **Application.** You might want to make students aware of the fact that clean, dry air is a solution. It consists of the following components:

| Component | Percentage by mass |
|---|---|
| Nitrogen | 78.1 |
| Oxygen | 20.8 |
| Argon | 0.93 |
| Carbon dioxide | 0.03 |
| Neon, helium, krypton, and hydrogen | ~.003 |

In fact, these gases can be isolated by liquefying the air. Once the gases are liquefied, they can be separated from each other by fractional distillation.

■ **Concept Mastery.** It is important to have the students distinguish between substances and mixtures, and homogeneous and heterogeneous mixtures. Both the macroscopic and the microscopic distinction should be made. Concept Mastery questions 43 through 46 (chapter-end questions) should help you to determine if your students understand these concepts. The Concept Mastery worksheet "Types of Solutions" (TRB) can be used to test the students' ability to visualize the particles in various kinds of solutions.

## 16-4 Antifreeze, pp. 436-437,

## 16-5 Degree of Solubility, pp. 437-438, and

## 16-6 Factors Affecting the Rate of Solution, pp. 438-440

| Planning Guide | |
|---|---|
| **Labs (Lab Manual) and Demonstrations (TE)** | **Supplementary Materials (Teacher's Resource Book)** |
| Demo 16-2: What a Gas!, p. TG-238<br>Demo 16-3: Factors Affecting the Rate of Dissolving, p. TG-238 | Open-Ended Experiment: The Solubility of a Solid in Aqueous Solution, p. 16-7 |

■ Tell the students that the freezing point of a liquid solution is always less than that of the pure solvent. Section 16-14 explains this phenomenon in more detail. To prevent the water in a car's radiator from freezing during cold weather, ethylene glycol (antifreeze) and water are mixed to form a solution that freezes at a much lower temperature than pure water. Explain that it is important to determine if sufficient ethylene glycol is present in the solution to prevent it from freezing. This is accomplished by using an instrument called a hydrometer. Refer to and discuss text Figure 16-6. You may want to demonstrate the use of a hydrometer and measure the specific gravities of some common liquid solutions.

■ Define solubility and discuss the three factors that affect the degree of solubility: nature of solute and solvent, temperature, and pressure. Emphasize that the degree of solubility measures the maximum mass of solute that can be dissolved in a given quantity of solvent at specified conditions. Then emphasize that degree of solubility is different from rate of solubility. The rate of solubility measures the quantity of material dissolving per unit time. Students often have difficulty differentiating between degree and rate of solubility. To help reinforce the difference between these two concepts, do Demonstration 16-2, "What a Gas!", and Demonstration 16-3, "Factors Affecting the Rate of Dissolving." Demonstration 16-2 stresses that the effect of temperature on the solubility of gases is opposite the effect of temperature on the solubility of solids. Demonstration 16-3 illustrates the effects of agitation, crushing, temperature, and nature of solvent on the rate of dissolving.

■ **Application.** You may want to point out the effect of pressure on the solubility of a gas in a liquid, as manifested by opening a can of soda. While under pressure, the soda remains carbonated indefinitely. But the soda loses its carbonation (goes flat) when the pressure is reduced by opening the can. In fact, few students realize that a large degree of the enjoyment they get from drinking carbonated beverages comes from the tingling sensation they feel as they drink a cold liquid from which carbon dioxide is escaping.

## 16-7 Solubility and the Nature of Solvent and Solute, pp. 440-441,

## 16-8 Energy Changes During Solution Formation, p. 442, and

## 16-9 Solubility Curves and Solubility Tables, pp. 442-444

| Planning Guide | |
| --- | --- |
| Labs (Lab Manual) and Demonstrations (TE) | Supplementary Materials (Teacher's Resource Book) |
| Demo 16-4: The Disappearing Cup, p. TG-239<br>Lab 29: Bonds, Polarity, and Solubility<br>Lab 30: Solubility of a Salt<br>Lab 31: Precipitates and Solubility Rules | Transparency Master: The Hydration of Ions, p. 16-3<br>Concept Mastery: Dissolving Ionic and Molecular Solids, p. CM-28<br>Transparency Master: Solubility Curves for a Number of Water Soluble Inorganic Substances, p. 16-4<br>Review Activity: Solubility Curves, p. 16-11<br>Critical and Creative Thinking: Generalization, p. CCT-35 |

■ A stimulating way to begin this section is to do Demonstration 16-4, "The Disappearing Cup." In this demonstration a Styrofoam cup "disappears" in a small amount of solvent (acetone). Ask the students to explain what is taking place. Then review the concept of polarity. Ask the students why a symmetrical arrangement of bonds results in a nonpolar molecule. Have the students visualize the dissolving process as a series of steps. In this process attractive forces between molecules or ions must be overcome. Assign Laboratory 29, "Bonds, Polarity, and Solubility," which leads to an understanding of the expression "like dissolves like."

■ Emphasize that the solution process involves an energy change. Discuss examples of endothermic and exothermic energy changes during solution formation.

■ Review the general nature of graphs and tables. Assign Laboratory 30, "Solubility of a Salt," in which the students collect experimental data necessary to construct the solubility curve for potassium nitrate.

■ Refer the class to the solubility table in Appendix D of the text. Explain how to use this table to extract information useful in the chemistry laboratory. Then assign Laboratory 31, "Precipitates and Solubility

Rules." This lab illustrates how the information in the solubility tables is experimentally determined and how this information can be used to formulate general rules of solubility.

■ **Concept Mastery.** Often students do not correctly predict the behavior of solutions because they fail to consider whether the solute is an ionic or a molecular substance. The Concept Mastery worksheet "Dissolving Ionic and Molecular Solids" (TRB) can help to overcome confusion by directing students to draw the molecules of the solute before and after dissolving.

■ **Critical Thinking.** In the Critical and Creative Thinking worksheet "Generalization" students use a table of solubilities to make generalizations about the solubility of various anion-cation combinations. This skill focuses not on making generalizations, but rather on assessing whether the sample of data used is sufficiently representative to make a particular generalization probable.

## 16-10 Saturated, Unsaturated, and Supersaturated Solutions, pp. 444-446, and

## 16-11 Dilute and Concentrated Solutions, pp. 446-448

| Planning Guide | |
| --- | --- |
| Labs (Lab Manual) and Demonstrations (TE) | Supplementary Materials (Teacher's Resource Book) |
| | Open-Ended Experiment: Crystallization of Alum, p. 16-9 |

■ Emphasize that, with the exception of completely miscible liquids, there is an upper limit to how much solute can be dissolved in a specific amount of solvent. Define saturated solution and solution equilibrium. Ask the students to explain the effect of a temperature change on the solution equilibrium of a system. Then define unsaturated solution and supersaturated solution. Ask the students to name the type of solution that remains after excess crystals are precipitated from a supersaturated solution and to state why heat is produced during precipitation.

■ Discuss the meaning of the terms *concentration, dilute solution*, and *concentrated solution*. Using the solubility curves in text Figure 16-13, ask the students the following questions:

1. What kind of solution is obtained when 100 g of $NaNO_3$ is dissolved in 100 g of water at 50°C? (unsaturated and concentrated)
2. What happens if the solution is cooled to 35°C?
3. Using 100 g of water as solvent, what are the temperature and the quantity of solute that may be present in a solution of $KNO_3$ that is **a.** concentrated

16

and unsaturated, **b.** dilute and saturated, and **c.** concentrated and saturated.

■ **Concept Mastery.** You may wish to use Concept Mastery questions 39 through 42 to determine your students' understanding of dilute and concentrated solutions. If they are having difficulty, you may wish to have the students make some solutions of sugar or lemonade. Ask the students what happens when these solutions are heated to the boiling point. Do both the solvent and the solute leave the beaker? What happens to the concentrations of the solutions as they continue to boil? Have students describe these solutions on the microscopic level. It is unrealistic to think that students can master the concept of molarity if they do not understand the concept of concentration as it relates to solutions.

## 16-12 Expressing Concentration—Molarity, pp. 449-451

| Planning Guide | |
| --- | --- |
| Labs (Lab Manual) and Demonstrations (TE) | Supplementary Materials (Teacher's Resource Book) |
| | Non-SI Supplementary Problems, p. 16-15 Concept Mastery: Making Molar Solutions, p. CM-29 Concept Mastery: Changing Solution Concentrations, p. CM-30 |

■ Point out that the terms *dilute* and *concentrated* are actually qualitative terms for describing the concentration of a solution. In certain circumstances, a more quantitative term is needed. There are several quantitative terms for expressing the concentration of a solution. One such term is *molarity*. Define molarity. Explain that this concentration unit is convenient to use because it involves mass and volume, quantities that can be measured directly.

■ Remind the students that when discussing chemical reactions, the number of reacting atoms, molecules, or ions (not their mass or volume) is important. Explain that the concentration unit molarity is the chemist's way of "counting" the number of reacting species in a solution. Discuss Sample Problems 5 and 6.

■ **Concept Mastery.** If students are unable to understand the qualitative terms *dilute* and *concentrated*, they will not be able to understand *molarity*. They will instead memorize the definition of molarity and work problems in a rote fashion. In presenting the concept of molarity, you may wish to use something familiar to students such as sugar water or lemonade

powder. Concept Mastery questions 47 through 50 can be used to introduce the concept of molarity by comparing "normal" to molar, in this instance.

The Concept Mastery worksheet "Making Molar Solutions" (TRB) can be used to help students visualize the concept of molarity. In the Concept Mastery worksheet "Changing Solution Concentrations" (TRB) students work out problems that cannot be solved using simple formulas.

## 16-13 Expressing Concentration—Molality, pp. 452-453

| Planning Guide | |
| --- | --- |
| Labs (Lab Manual) and Demonstrations (TE) | Supplementary Materials (Teacher's Resource Book) |
| | Review Activity: Solution Vocabulary, p. 16-12 |

■ Define the concentration unit molality. Discuss Sample Problems 7 and 8. Be aware of the fact that students have a great deal of difficulty in distinguishing between molarity and molality. Compare the definitions of molarity and molality, emphasizing that the former is based upon moles per cubic decimeter of solution, and the latter is based upon moles per kilogram of solvent. Explain that equal volumes of solutions of the same molarity have the same number of moles of solute and, therefore, the same number of solute particles. However, in these solutions, the number of solvent molecules is different. In equal volumes of solutions of the same molality, both the number of solute molecules and the number of solvent molecules are the same. In such solutions, the mole fractions (moles solute divided by moles solvent) of the solute are the same.

## 16-14 Freezing Point Depression, pp. 453-457, and

## 16-15 Boiling Point Elevation, pp. 457-458

| Planning Guide | |
| --- | --- |
| Labs (Lab Manual) and Demonstrations (TE) | Supplementary Materials (Teacher's Resource Book) |
| | Transparency Master: Vapor Pressure Curves for Pure Water and for Ice, p. 16-5 Transparency Master: Vapor Pressure Curves for a Water Solution, for Pure Water, and for Ice, p. 16-6 Practice Problems, p. 16-14 |

■ Freezing points and boiling points of solutions are better understood if the effect of a solute on vapor pressure is discussed. Define vapor pressure as the pressure of a vapor in equilibrium with a liquid at a given temperature. Ask the students to visualize what happens to the concentration of the liquid molecules when a nonvolatile solid is dissolved. Since the vapor pressure is proportional to the molecular concentration of the solvent, the decrease in this concentration causes a lowering of the vapor pressure. Point out the resulting decrease in the freezing point. Explain that the boiling point is increased because, starting with a lowered vapor pressure, a higher temperature is needed to bring the vapor pressure up to atmospheric pressure. Emphasize that all of these effects depend on the concentration of solute particles in a given concentration of solvent molecules, or the molality.

Assign a number of problems in which the freezing points of aqueous solutions of different molalities can be calculated. Assign similar problems in which the solvent is not water. Also, have the class solve for molecular masses of solutes when they are given the solute mass, the solvent mass, and the freezing point of the solution.

Assign problems requiring the determination of boiling points of various solutions. Ask why the solute must be a nonvolatile substance as well as a nonelectrolyte. Explain briefly why solutions of electrolytes have higher boiling points and lower freezing points than solutions of nonelectrolytes of the same molality.

## Demonstrations

### 16-1 Solutions, Colloids, and Suspensions

**Overview:** In this demonstration, you use filtration and other methods to illustrate the differences among solutions, colloids, and suspensions.

**Materials:** table salt (sodium chloride, NaCl) in water; starch in water; potting soil in water; 3 stirring rods; 3 filtration setups; flashlight and cardboard cover; gelatin in water; egg white; vinegar; concentrated hydrochloric acid (HCl); dilute solution of sodium thiosulfate ($Na_2S_2O_3$); saturated solution of salt (NaCl) water; test-tube rack and 6 medium test tubes.

**Advance Preparation:** 1. Place 150 mL of water into each of three 250-mL beakers. Add about one-half teaspoonful of table salt (NaCl) to one, of starch to the next, and of potting soil to the third. Heat the starch mixture until all of the starch dissolves. Allow the mixture to cool. 2. Cut a circular piece of cardboard to fit over the top of the flashlight. Poke a small hole, about 2–3 mm in diameter, in the middle of the cardboard and tape the cardboard over the top of the

flashlight. 3. **$Na_2S_2O_3$ solution:** Dissolve about one-half teaspoonful of the sodium thiosulfate in 100 mL of water in a beaker. 4. Following package directions, prepare some colored gelatin ahead of time in a beaker or large test tube. 5. Separate the egg white from the yolk, and divide the egg white between two test tubes. 6. Saturated NaCl solution: Place about 50 mL of water into a beaker and add enough NaCl so that some of the salt remains on the bottom of the beaker after thorough stirring. 7. Set up three filtration apparatuses, using filter paper, funnels, and rings and ring stands. (See the accompanying figure.)

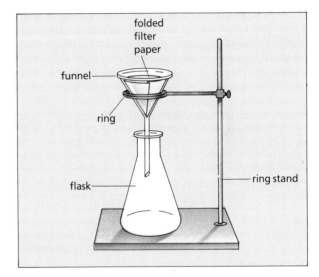

**Figure 16-1**

**Safety:** Pour the concentrated acid into a dropper bottle in the fume hood. Avoid breathing the HCl vapor, and do not allow the acid to come into contact with your body or clothing.

**Procedure:** 1. Place the three beakers containing the salt water, starch and water, and soil and water next to each other. Stir the contents of each beaker, and ask students to note differences among the three. 2. Pour some liquid from each of the beakers through separate filtration apparatuses, and have students observe which liquid leaves a residue on the paper. 3. Use a covered flashlight to shine a narrow beam of light through the contents of each of the three beakers, and have students compare the results of this test for the Tyndall effect. 4. Fill a large test tube half full of the sodium thiosulfate solution. Shine a narrow light beam through this solution, and have students observe what happens. Add a few drops of concentrated hydrochloric acid to the test tube and agitate the tube carefully. Shine the light beam through the tube until a change is observed. 5. Test for the Tyndall effect by shining the beam of light through each of the following: colored gelatin, egg white, and white vinegar. Ask students to tell which are colloids and which are solutions. 6. Add a few drops of concentrated hydrochloric acid to a test tube containing egg white, and have students note the results. Repeat by adding a milliliter of saturated salt water to the other sample of egg white.

**Results:** In step 1, after the contents of the three beakers have been stirred, the soil will begin to settle out, whereas the contents of the other two will continue to appear to be homogeneous. In step 2, only the soil will remain on the filter paper. In step 3, the beam of light will be visible in the starch–water colloid and in the soil–water suspension. In step 4, the hydrochloric acid will react with the sodium thiosulfate slowly to form colloidal sulfur, and the beam will eventually become visible in the mixture. In step 5, the gelatin and the egg white will exhibit the Tyndall effect (the scattering of light in all directions) and are thus colloids, whereas the white vinegar is a solution. In step 6, the strong electrolytes HCl and NaCl will help to neutralize repelling charges on the colloidal particles, which will then coagulate.

## 16-2 What A Gas!

**Overview:** In this demonstration, you shake up hot and cold bottles of club soda whose mouths are covered by balloons. The expansion of the balloon is related to the change in gas solubility. You also prepare hard-boiled eggs, and relate color change of the yolks to temperature and solubility of gases.

**Materials:** 3 10-oz bottles of club soda; bottle opener; 2 latex balloons; bucket of hot water; bucket of ice water; 2 raw eggs; pan of water with cover; hot plate.

**Advance Preparation:** Place one bottle of club soda into the bucket of hot water and a second bottle of the soda into the ice water for at least 15 minutes before the demonstration. Start cooking the two eggs about 10 minutes before you need them in the demonstration. Heat them to boiling, and turn the heat down and allow them to cook for about another 8 minutes.

**Procedure:** 1. Shake up a bottle of club soda and remove the cap over a sink or a surface covered with a towel. Ask students to observe the result. 2. Carefully remove the two bottles from the buckets, and place a balloon over the mouth of each bottle as soon as you remove the caps. Shake each bottle and have students observe the results. Ask them how temperature affects the solubility of a gas. 3. Remove the two cooked eggs from the pan after 8 minutes of cooking at a low heat. Place one into ice water and the other onto the table to cool. After a few minutes, cut each egg open and have students observe and attempt to explain the difference in the color of the outer surfaces of the two yolks.

**Results:** When the cap is removed from the first bottle, in step 1, a great deal of dissolved carbon dioxide gas will escape. The pressure over the soda will decrease from about 4 atmospheres to about 1 atmosphere when the cap is removed, and the gas escapes because gas solubility is directly related to pressure, according to Henry's law. When the balloons are placed over the top of the hot and cold bottles of soda, the balloons will become inflated with the carbon dioxide gas that escapes. Because gases are less soluble at high temperatures, more gas will escape from the warm solution and will inflate the balloon to a much greater volume than will the gas from the colder solution. In step 3, when the two eggs are cut open, the yolk of the one that cooled slowly at room temperature should have a greenish surface, whereas that of the one cooled in ice water should be bright yellow. As the eggs cook in boiling water, some of the proteins and other substances will decompose, producing a variety of products, including hydrogen sulfide gas. As this gas forms, it moves toward the coolest part of the egg—which, in the case of the slowly cooled egg, is the yolk—because gases are more soluble at low-temperature conditions than at high-temperature conditions. The yolk is rich in iron, which reacts with the gas to form iron sulfides, which are responsible for the greenish film around the yolk. In the egg that is immersed in cold water after cooking, the hydrogen sulfide gas diffuses outward toward the shell, which is cooler than the yolk.

## 16-3 Factors Affecting Rate of Dissolving

**Overview:** In this demonstration, you prepare solutions of a colored substance and determine factors that affect the rate of dissolving.

**Materials:** copper(II) sulfate pentahydrate ($CuSO_4 \cdot 5H_2O$) crystals; mortar and pestle; 5 petri dishes; stirring rod; cooking oil; large test tube and cork.

**Advance Preparation:** none

**Procedure:** 1. Place a small crystal of copper(II) sulfate into water in a petri dish on the overhead projector. Have students observe what happens to the undisturbed crystal. After a few minutes, agitate the dish. 2. Place water into two more petri dishes. Add one large crystal of copper(II) sulfate to one dish. Crush another large crystal of copper(II) sulfate in a mortar and pestle, and add the powder to the other dish. Have students note in which dish the dissolving occurs faster. 3. Place cold tap water into one petri dish and hot tap water into another. Add a crystal of copper(II) sulfate to each and note which dissolves faster. 4. Place some water into a large test tube and add an equal amount of cooking oil. Cork and shake the test tube, and have students observe what happens.

**Results:** The copper(II) sulfate will dissolve faster when it has been agitated (step 1), crushed (step 2), or placed into hot water (step 3). In step 4, the shaking of the oil-and-water mixture will not produce appreciable dissolving. After the shaking, two layers will again form.

### 16-4 The Disappearing Cup

**Overview:** In this demonstration, you add a Styrofoam (polystyrene) cup and then a large quantity of Styrofoam peanuts to a container of acetone. Students watch in amazement as the Styrofoam quickly disappears as it dissolves in a relatively small amount of solvent.

**Materials:** large jar with screw-top lid; 200 mL of acetone; about 1 cubic foot (roughly 0.036 $m^3$) of Styrofoam peanuts or small pieces; Styrofoam cup that will fit through the mouth of the jar.

**Safety:** Acetone is a flammable and volatile liquid and should be kept away from any flames. Work at a fume hood or in a well-ventilated room.

**Procedure:** 1. Place about 200 mL of acetone into a large jar. Add the Styrofoam cup to the acetone. Have students observe what happens and give an explanation for it. 2. Add the small Styrofoam pieces, a handful at a time, to the acetone. 3. Discuss everyday situations in which "like dissolves like" plays an important part: removing fingernail polish with polish remover, removing paint with solvents, soaking onion halves in water before dicing them (since the substance that is responsible for tearing is soluble in water), taking certain vitamins on a daily basis (since they are water soluble and do not remain in the body).

**Results:** The acetone and the Styrofoam will dissolve in each other to a considerable extent, causing the cup to apparently disappear. As the Styrofoam dissolves, the air that is trapped between the polymer molecules escapes as a gas and causes some fizzing. In step 2, not all of the material will dissolve, since a large excess of solute is added. A white "glob" of Styrofoam will appear in the bottom of the beaker. This material can be washed and allowed to reharden.

**Disposal Tips:** Pour the acetone into a flammable-waste container, and dispose of it as directed by your school district.

## Answers to Questions

### Page 436

1. **a.** In a heterogenous mixture, the particles are not spread uniformly throughout the mixture. In a homogeneous mixture, the particles are spread uniformly.

   **b.** Generally, the smaller the particle size of the components of a mixture is, the easier it is to make a homogeneous mixture.

2. A solution is homogeneous, does not settle on standing, is clear and transparent, is a single phase, and cannot be separated into its components by filtration.

3. **a.** The solute is the dissolved substance.

   **b.** The solvent is the dissolving medium of a solution.

   **c.** An aqueous solution is one in which the solvent is water.

4. 

| Solution | Solute |
|---|---|
| **a.** salt water | salt |
| **b.** ammonia water | ammonia |
| **c.** water vapor in the air | water vapor |
| **d.** brass alloy (75% Cu; 25% Zn) | zinc |
| **e.** 40 g alcohol + 60 g water | alcohol |

5. **a.** A tincture is a solution in which the solvent is alcohol.

   **b.** An amalgam is an alloy containing mercury mixed with one or more other metals.

   **c.** iodine

   **d.** mercury

6. **a.** A gas solution is one in which both solute and solvent are gases or vapors. Air is a gas solution.

   **b.** A liquid solution is one in which a gas, a liquid, or a solid is dissolved in a liquid. Salt water and antifreeze are examples.

   **c.** A solid solution is one in which two or more solids are uniformly spread throughout one another. An alloy is an example of a solid solution.

### Page 440

7. Solubility expresses the maximum quantity of solute that can dissolve in a given quantity of solvent or solution at a specified temperature.

8. **a.** The solubility of a solid is affected by the temperature and the nature of the solvent.

   **b.** The solubility of a gas is affected by the temperature, the pressure, and the nature of the solvent.

9. A rise in temperature **a** increases the solubility of most solids, and **b** decreases the solubility of all gases.

10. **a.** The rate of solution describes the speed with which a solute dissolves in a solvent. Solubility refers to how much solute will dissolve in a given amount of solvent.

   **b.** The rate of solution is determined by

■ the size of the solute particles (smaller particles dissolve faster),

■ stirring (stirring increases the rate),

**16**

- quantity of solute already in the solution (rate decreases with increased quantity), and
- temperature (see question 9).

**11. a.** $2.00 \times 10^2$ g sucrose will dissolve in $1.00 \times 10^2$ g water.

  **b.** $\dfrac{4.00 \times 10^2 \text{ g sucrose}}{2.00 \times 10^2 \text{ g H}_2\text{O}} =$

  $$2.00 \text{ g sucrose per } 1.00 \text{ g H}_2\text{O}$$

**12.** For each of the four pieces, total area is:

  4 sides × 1.0  cm × 0.50 cm = 2.0 cm²
  + 2 sides × 0.50 cm × 0.50 cm = $\underline{0.5 \text{ cm}^2}$
  2.5 cm²

  (2.5 cm²/piece) × 4 pieces = 10 cm²
  This 10 cm² is 4 cm² greater than the surface area of the original cube (with a surface area of 6 cm²).

## Page 444

**13.** The sodium and chloride ions are hydrated—i.e., the positive ends of the polar $H_2O$ molecules are attracted to the negative $Cl^-$ ions, and the negative ends of the water molecules are attracted to the positive $Na^+$ ions.

**14.** Fat molecules are nonpolar and are, therefore, not attracted to either of the ends of a polar water molecule.

**15.** Both fat and benzene are nonpolar. Therefore, the forces of attraction between benzene molecules and between fat molecules are weak, permitting the molecules of one of the substances to intermingle freely with the molecules of the other substance.

**16.** In the process of dissolving a solid in water, energy is absorbed because it is needed to break the intermolecular forces holding the particles of the solid together.

**17. a.** Barium chloride is soluble.
  **b.** Copper(II) hydroxide is nearly insoluble.
  **c.** Lead iodide is slightly soluble.

**18.** According to the curves in text Figure 16-13,
  **a.** the solubility of $KNO_3$ at 70°C is 140 g/100 g $H_2O$;
  **b.** the solubility of NaCl at 100°C is 40 g/100 g $H_2O$;
  **c.** the solubility of $NH_4Cl$ at 90°C is 72 g/100 g $H_2O$.

**19.** The solute, referred to in question 18, that is most soluble at 15°C is NaCl.

## Page 448

**20. a.** A saturated solution is one that has dissolved in it all of the solute that it can normally hold at the given conditions.
  **b.** To a given quantity of water, add salt slowly and stir until no more salt dissolves and a slight excess remains undissolved.
  **c.** The rate at which solid goes into solution is equal to the rate at which solute in the aqueous phase comes out of solution and enters the solid phase.
  **d.** An unsaturated solution is generally produced when a saturated solution is heated.

**21. a.** To produce a supersaturated solution, prepare a saturated solution using warm water and let it cool without disturbing it.
  **b.** The excess solute will crystallize, leaving behind a saturated solution.

**22.** When crystals of salt are stirred into a saturated solution of sugar, the salt will dissolve because the solution is saturated only with respect to the sugar.

**23. a.** Because $Ag_2SO_4$ is only slightly soluble, all of its solutions are dilute.
  **b.** For the same reason as that given in **a** no solution of $Ag_2SO_4$ can be concentrated.
  **c.** A saturated solution can be prepared. It will be dilute.
  **d.** An unsaturated solution can be prepared by using less solute than that required to make a saturated solution.

**24.** According to text Figure 16-13, at 10°C the solubility of KI is 135 g/100 g $H_2O$. In 50 g $H_2O$, only half as much KI is required to make a saturated solution:
  ½ × 135 g KI/100 g $H_2O$ = 68 g KI

## Page 451

**25.** Molarity is the number of moles of solute per cubic decimeter of solution (per liter of solution).

**26.** A mole of $CaCl_2$ consists of 1 mole of $Ca^{2+}$ ions and 2 moles of $Cl^-$ ions. Hence, in 1.0 dm³ of a 1.0 *M* solution, there are 1.0 mol $Ca^{2+}$ and 2.0 mol $Cl^-$. In 1.0 dm³ of solution of 1.0 *M* $CaCl_2$, there are $6.02 \times 10^{23}$ formula units of $CaCl_2$.

**27.** The number of molecules of the one substance is equal to the number of molecules of the other substance.

**28. a.** $152 \text{ cm}^3 \times \dfrac{1 \text{ dm}^3}{1000 \text{ cm}^3} \times \dfrac{0.364 \text{ mol NaCl}}{1 \text{ dm}^3} =$
  $$0.0553 \text{ mol NaCl}$$
  **b.** $0.0553 \text{ mol NaCl} \times \dfrac{58.5 \text{ g NaCl}}{1 \text{ mol NaCl}} = 3.24 \text{ g NaCl}$

**29. a.** $\dfrac{0.258 \text{ mol dextrose}}{1.00 \text{ dm}^3} \times 325 \text{ cm}^3 \times \dfrac{1.00 \text{ dm}^3}{1000 \text{ cm}^3} =$
  $$0.0839 \text{ mol dextrose}$$
  **b.** 0.0839 mol dex. × 180 g dex./mol dex. =
  $$15.1 \text{ g dextrose}$$

**30.** $\dfrac{1.00 \text{ dm}^3}{0.50 \text{ mol H}_2\text{SO}_4} \times \dfrac{1.00 \text{ mol H}_2\text{SO}_4}{98 \text{ g H}_2\text{SO}_4} \times 98 \text{ g H}_2\text{SO}_4 =$
  $$2.0 \text{ dm}^3$$

**31.** $\dfrac{53 \text{ g Na}_2\text{CO}_3}{215 \text{ cm}^3} \times \dfrac{1.0 \text{ mol Na}_2\text{CO}_3}{106 \text{ g Na}_2\text{CO}_3} \times \dfrac{1000 \text{ cm}^3}{1.0 \text{ dm}^3} =$
  2.3 mol $Na_2CO_3$/dm³ = 2.3 *M* $Na_2CO_3$

**32.** $\dfrac{12.6\ \text{g HNO}_3}{5.00 \times 10^2\ \text{cm}^3} \times \dfrac{1.00\ \text{mol HNO}_3}{63.0\ \text{g HNO}_3} \times \dfrac{1000\ \text{cm}^3}{1.00\ \text{dm}^3} =$

$0.400\ \text{mol HNO}_3/\text{dm}^3 = 0.400\ M\ \text{HNO}_3$

### Page 453

**33. a.** Molality expresses the number of moles of solute in 1 kilogram of solvent.
   **b.** Molality is indicated by the symbol $m$.
   **c.** Molarity is the number of moles of solute per *cubic decimeter of solution*. Molality is the number of moles of solute per *kilogram of solvent*.

**34.** $\dfrac{2.05\ \text{g Ca(NO}_3)_2}{252\ \text{g solvent}} \times \dfrac{1\ \text{mol Ca(NO}_3)_2}{164\ \text{g Ca(NO}_3)_2} \times \dfrac{1000\ \text{g solv.}}{1\ \text{kg solv.}} =$

$0.0496\ \text{mol Ca(NO}_3)_2\ \text{per kg solvent} = 0.0496\ m$

**35.** $\dfrac{1.00\ \text{kg water}}{2.5\ \text{mol Ca(NO}_3)_2} \times \dfrac{1.0\ \text{mol Ca(NO}_3)_2}{164\ \text{g Ca(NO}_3)_2} \times$

$8.2\ \text{g Ca(NO}_3)_2 = 0.020\ \text{kg water, or 20 g water}$

### Page 456

**36. a.** The molal freezing point constant is the number of degrees that the freezing point of a solvent is depressed by a 1-molal solution of a nonelectrolyte.
   **b.** 1.86°C/molal;
   **c.** −1.86°C.

**37.** $\Delta T_f = Km$
$\Delta T_f = 0.24\ \text{molal} \times 1.86°\text{C/molal} = 0.45°\text{C}$
The freezing point of the solution is −0.45°C.

### Page 457

**38.** $\Delta T_f = 0.850\ \text{molal} \times 1.86°/\text{molal} = 1.58°\text{C}$
The freezing point of the solution is −1.58°C.

**39.** $68.4\ \text{g sucrose} \times \dfrac{1\ \text{mol sucrose}}{342\ \text{g sucrose}} =$

$0.200\ \text{mol sucrose}$

$\dfrac{0.200\ \text{mol sucrose}}{1.00 \times 10^2\ \text{g water}} \times \dfrac{1000\ \text{g water}}{1.00\ \text{kg water}} = 2.00\ \text{molal}$

$\Delta T_f = 2.00\ \text{molal} \times 1.86°\text{C/molal} = 3.72°\text{C}$
The freezing point of the solution is −3.72°C.

**40.** $\dfrac{0.310°\text{C}}{1.86°\text{C}/m} = 0.167\ m$

$\dfrac{4.50\ \text{g}}{225\ \text{g H}_2\text{O}} \times 1000\ \text{g H}_2\text{O} = 20.0\ \text{g}$

$\text{formula mass} = \dfrac{20.0\ \text{g}}{0.167\ \text{mol}} = 120\ \text{g/mol}$

**41.** $\dfrac{2.79°\text{C}}{1.86°\text{C}/m} = 1.50\ m$

$\dfrac{18.0\ \text{g}}{2.00 \times 10^2\ \text{g H}_2\text{O}} \times 1000\ \text{g H}_2\text{O} = 90.0\ \text{g}$

$\text{formula mass} = \dfrac{90.0\ \text{g}}{1.50\ m} = 60.0\ \text{g/mol}$

### Page 458

**42. a.** The molal boiling point constant is the rise in boiling point of a solvent in a 1-molal solution of a nonvolatile nonelectrolyte.
   **b.** 0.52°C/molal
   **c.** 100.52°C

**43. a.** 5.03°C/molal
   **b.** $\Delta T_b = 78.4°\text{C} − 76.8°\text{C} = 1.6°\text{C}$

$\dfrac{1.6°\text{C}}{5.03°\text{C/molal}} = 0.318\ m$

$\dfrac{8.10\ \text{g solute}}{300\ \text{g CCl}_4} \times 1000\ \text{g CCl}_4 = 27.0\ \text{g solute}$

$\text{gram molecular mass} = \dfrac{27.0\ \text{g solute}}{0.318\ \text{mol}} = 85\ \text{g/mol}$

**44.** $\dfrac{1.4°\text{C}}{1.22°\text{C}/m} = 1.15\ m$

$\dfrac{14.2\ \text{g solute}}{264\ \text{g alcohol}} \times 1000\ \text{g alcohol} = 53.8\ \text{g solute}$

$\text{gram molecular mass} = \dfrac{53.8\ \text{g solute}}{1.15\ \text{mol}} = 47\ \text{g/mol}$

## Chapter Review    **16**

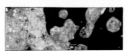

### Page 460, Content Review

**1.** A solution is a homogeneous mixture.

**2. a.** The sugar in a sugar solution is a solute.
   **b.** The water in a sugar solution is a solvent.
   **c.** Iodine in alcohol is a tincture.
   **d.** Salt water is an aqueous solution.

**3.** Liquid solutions are more common than solid solutions and gas solutions.

**4.** Antifreeze prevents the radiator coolant from freezing and from boiling over.

**5. a.** Three factors that generally determine the degree of solubility of a substance are the nature of the solute and solvent, the temperature, and the pressure.
   **b.** The solubility of most solids increases with temperature.
   **c.** The solubility of gases decreases as temperature increases. The solubility increases as pressure increases.

**6.** To dissolve large potassium nitrate crystals as quickly as possible, the crystals should be ground to powder and stirred into hot water.

**7.** As KCl dissolves in $H_2O$, its ions are surrounded by water molecules. The positive ends of the polar water molecules are attracted to the $Cl^-$ ions, while the negative ends of the water molecules are

16

attracted to the $K^+$ ions. These forces of attraction overcome the forces between the ions, and the ions are pulled into solution.

8. In both oil and benzene, the molecules are held together by weak forces that allow the molecules to intermingle freely to form a solution.

9. When a solid dissolves in a liquid, the change is generally endothermic.

10. **a.** The solubility of KCl at 80°C is 50 g/100 g $H_2O$.
    **b.** The solubility of $KClO_3$ at 90°C is 49 g/100 g $H_2O$.
    **c.** The solubility of $NaNO_3$ at 10°C is 80 g/100 g $H_2O$.

11. **a.** Calcium hydroxide is slightly soluble.
    **b.** Barium carbonate is nearly insoluble.
    **c.** Aluminum sulfate is soluble.

12. Since the solubility of KCl increases with temperature, heating a saturated solution makes it unsaturated.

13. Solution A is unsaturated, solution B is saturated, and solution C is supersaturated.

14. **a.** The solutions of ammonia and sodium nitrate are concentrated. The solutions of potassium chlorate and potassium nitrate are dilute.
    **b.** The solution of potassium chlorate is least concentrated.

15. Formula mass of NaOH: $23.0 + 16.0 + 1.0 = 40.0$ g/mol

$$M = \frac{\text{mol solute}}{\text{dm}^3 \text{ solution}} = \frac{19.2 \text{ g NaOH}}{40.0 \text{ g/mol}} \times \frac{1}{160 \text{ cm}^3} \times$$

$$\frac{1000 \text{ cm}^3}{1 \text{ dm}^3} = 3.00 \text{ M NaOH}$$

16. Molecular mass of HCl: $1.0 + 35.5 = 36.5$ g/mol.

$$M = \frac{\text{mol solute}}{\text{dm}^3 \text{ solution}} = \text{g solute} \times \frac{\text{mol solute}}{\text{g solute}}$$

$$\text{g solute} = M \times \text{dm}^3 \text{ solution} \times \frac{\text{g solute}}{\text{mol solute}}$$

$$= (0.300 \text{ M}) (0.150 \text{ dm}^3) (36.5 \text{ g/mol})$$
$$= 1.64 \text{ g}$$

17. Volume $= (62.2 \text{ cm}^3) (1 \text{ dm}^3) \div (10^3 \text{ cm}^3) =$ 0.0622 dm$^3$
$n = (4.54 \text{ M}) (0.0622 \text{ dm}^3) = 0.282$ mol

18. Formula mass of $NaNO_3$
    $= 23.0 + 14.0 + 3(16.0) = 85.0$ g/mol
$$m = \frac{\text{mol solute}}{\text{kg solute}} = \frac{34 \text{ g}}{100 \text{ g}} \times \frac{\text{mol}}{85 \text{ g}} \times \frac{10^3 \text{ g } H_2O}{1 \text{ kg } H_2)} =$$
$$4.0 \ m$$

19. Formula mass of $AgNO_3 = 107.9 + 14.0 + 3(16.0) = 169.9$ g/mol
$$m = \frac{\text{mol solute}}{\text{kg solute}} = \frac{\text{g solute}}{\text{kg solvent}} \times \frac{\text{mol solute}}{\text{g solute}}$$

g solute $= m \times$ kg solvent $\times$ (g solute/mol solute)
$= (0.300 \ m) (0.200 \text{ kg}) (169.9 \text{ g/mol})$
$= 10.2$ g

20. Molecular mass of $C_2H_5OH = 2(12.0) + 6(1.0) + 16.0 = 46.0$ g/mol

$$\Delta T_f = K_f m = K_f \times \frac{\text{g solvent}}{\text{g/mol solute} \times \text{kg solvent}} =$$
1.86°C/mol $\times$ 20 g $\div$ (46.0 g/mol) (0.250 kg) = 3.23°C
Freezing point = 0°C − 3.23°C = −3.23°C

21. Molecular mass of $C_2H_4(OH)_2 = 2(12.0) + 6(1.0) + 2(16.0) = 62.0$ g/mol

$$\text{g solute} = \frac{\Delta T}{K_f} \times \text{kg solvent} \times \frac{\text{g solute}}{\text{mol}} = 7.44°C \times$$
0.500 kg $H_2O$ $\times$ 62.0 g/mol $\div$ 1.86°C/m = 124 g

22. $$\frac{\text{g}}{\text{mol}} = \frac{(K_f)(\text{g solute})}{(\Delta T)(\text{kg solvent})} = \frac{(0.52°C/m)(51 \text{ g})}{(0.78°C)(0.500 \text{ kg})} = 68 \text{ g/mol}$$

23. The molality of the solution and the nature of the solvent determine the magnitude of freezing point depression and boiling point elevation.

## Page 461, Content Mastery

24. Ammonium nitrate absorbs energy from its surroundings as it dissolves. The solution becomes cold enough to freeze the puddle of water under the beaker.

25. From text Figure 16-13, the amount of $KNO_3$ that dissolves in 100 g $H_2O$ at 50°C is about 85 g.
$$\frac{255 \text{ g } KNO_3}{85 \text{ g } KNO_3/100 \text{ g } H_2O} = 300 \text{ g} = 3.0 \times 10^2 \text{ g } H_2O$$

26. An alloy is a solid-solid solution.

27. You could increase the rate at which a solute dissolves by reducing the size of the particles, stirring the solution, or reducing the amount of solute already in solution. Except for gases, increasing the temperature would also work.

28. Molecular mass of $HNO_3 = 1.0 + 14.0 + 3(16.0) = 63.0$ g/mol
$n = 46.6$ g $\div$ 63.0 g/mol = 0.7397 mol
$M = n/V = 0.7397$ mol/0.7500 dm$^3$ = 0.986 M

29. $\Delta T = K_f m = 1.86°C/m \times 4.88$ mol/2.00 kg = 4.54°C
Freezing point of solution = 0°C − 4.54°C = −4.54°C

30. **a** and **b** apply colligative properties; **c** does not.
    **a.** The salt raises the boiling point of the water, so the vegetables cook faster.
    **b.** The $CaCl_2$ lowers the freezing point of water, thus melting some of the ice.
    **c.** The sugar only sweetens the fruit.

**31.** $\Delta T_f = K_f \times m = K_f \times \dfrac{\text{g solute}}{\text{kg solvent}} \times \dfrac{\text{mol solute}}{\text{g solute}}$

$\dfrac{\text{g solute}}{\text{mol solute}} = \dfrac{K_f \times \text{g solute}}{\text{kg solute} \times \Delta T_f} = \dfrac{6.8°C/m \times 52.3 \text{ g}}{0.505 \text{ kg} \times 8.8°C} =$

$80.03 \approx 80 \text{ g/mol}$

**32. a.** At 30°C, the solubility of $NaNO_3$ is about 96 g in 100 g of $H_2O$, or 960 g in 1000 g $H_2O$. This solution is saturated.

   **b.** At 20°C, the solubility of $NH_3$ is about 570 g/1000 g $H_2O$. Because the solution contains only 411 g, it is unsaturated.

   **c.** At 50°C, the solubility of $NH_4Cl$ is about 520 g/1000 g $H_2O$. Because the solution contains 611 g, it is supersaturated.

**33.** Benzene is the only solvent listed that is nonpolar and therefore would dissolve grease, which is also nonpolar.

**34.** Formula mass of NaCl = 23.0 + 35.5 = 58.5 g/mol

$M = \dfrac{\text{mol solute}}{\text{dm}^3 \text{ solution}} = \dfrac{\text{g}}{\text{dm}^3 \text{ solution}} \times \dfrac{1}{\text{g/mol}}$

$\text{g} = M \times \text{dm}^3 \text{ solution} \times \text{g/mol solute}$
$= 6.6 \, M \times 0.231 \text{ dm}^3 \times 58.5 \text{ g/mol} = 89 \text{ g}$

**35.** Formula mass of NaCl = 23.0 + 35.5 =
58.5 g/mol

$m = \dfrac{\text{mol solute}}{\text{kg solvent}} = \dfrac{31 \text{ g}}{0.559 \text{ kg}} \times \dfrac{1 \text{ mol}}{58.5 \text{ g}} = 0.95 \, m$

**36.** 1.00 mol of ethylene glycol and 1.00 mol of ethyl alcohol would lower the freezing point of water by the same amount, since freezing point depression depends only on the number of moles of solute.

**37.** Formula mass of NaCl = 23.0 + 35.5 = 58.5 g/mol

$\text{g solute} = \dfrac{\Delta T}{K_b} \times \text{kg solvent} \times \dfrac{\text{g solute}}{\text{mol}}$

$= (1.5°C \div 0.52°C/\text{mol}) \times 1.00 \text{ kg } H_2O \times$
58.5 g/mol

$= 168.75 \text{ g} \approx 1.7 \times 10^2 \text{ g}$

**38.** Formula mass of NaOH = 23.0 + 16.0 + 1.0 =
40.0 g/mol

$M = \dfrac{\text{mol solute}}{\text{dm}^3 \text{ solution}} = \dfrac{\text{mol solute}}{\text{dm}^3 \text{ solution (g solute/mol solute)}}$

$\text{cm}^3 = \dfrac{47.1 \text{ g}}{40.0 \text{ g/mol}} \times \dfrac{1000 \text{ cm}^3}{1 \text{ dm}^3} \times \dfrac{\text{dm}^3}{3.00 \text{ mol}} = 393 \text{ cm}^3$

## Page 461, Concept Mastery

*Concept (questions 39-42): Molarity (moles of solute per volume of solution) is a measure of concentration, independent of the amount of solution present.*

**39.** *Solution:* The most concentrated solutions are **(b)** (12 sucrose molecules in a unit volume) and **(c)** (6 sucrose molecules in

half a unit volume). **(b)** and **(c)** have the same concentration.

**40.** *Solution:* Solution **(c)** has the smallest volume, half that of the other solutions.

**41.** *Solution:* Solutions **(b)** and **(c)** have the same molarity, that is, the same number of moles of sucrose per unit volume.

**42.** *Solution:* The molarity of solution **(a)** is half that of **(b)** and **(c)**, and twice that of **(d)**.

*Concept (questions 43-46): Solids, liquids, and gases differ on the microscopic level.*

**43.** *Solution:* Picture **(a)** shows a gas. Pictures **(b)**, **(c)**, and **(d)** show solids.

**44.** *Solution:* **(b)** is homogeneous. **(a)** and **(d)** are homogeneous on the macroscopic level but heterogeneous on the microscopic level. **(c)** shows a mixture of solids and is heterogeneous.

**45.** *Solution:* **(b)** and **(d)** are both substances. **(a)** is a gas solution. **(c)** is neither; it is a heterogeneous mixture.

**46.** *Solution:* **(b)** is an element, and **(d)** is an ionic compound. **(a)** and **(c)** are mixtures.

*Concept (questions 47-50): The concentration of a solution can be expressed in terms of the concentration of a standard, or "normal," solution.*

**47.** *Solution:* Five grams of powder is half the normal mass, but the volume is the normal volume. Thus, the concentration is half normal.

**48.** *Solution:* Half of the normal mass of powder is dissolved in half of the normal volume of water. The concentration would be the same as the original solution, so this solution is normal.

**49.** *Solution:* 1.5 times the normal mass of powder is dissolved in three times the normal volume of water. This solution is 1.5 ÷ 3 = 0.5, or half normal.

**50.** *Solution:* Twice the normal mass of powder is dissolved, and the volume is reduced to the normal volume. This solution is twice normal.

## Page 462, Cumulative Review

**51. b.** The $3p$ sublevel becomes filled when a $Cl^-$ ion is formed.

**52. b.** An alkali metal is the element with the lowest ionization energy within a given period of the periodic table.

**53. c.** When atoms A and B form ions, $A^+$ is smaller than A; $B^-$ is larger than B.

16

**54. c.** $0.40 \text{ mol CaCO}_3 \times \dfrac{1 \text{ mol CO}_2}{1 \text{ mol CaCO}_3} \times \dfrac{22.4 \text{ dm}^3}{1 \text{ mol}} \times$

$\dfrac{293 \text{ K}}{273 \text{ K}} \times \dfrac{101.3 \text{ kPa}}{104.0 \text{ kPa}} = 9.367 \text{ dm}^3 \approx 9.4 \text{ dm}^3 \text{ of CO}_2$

**55. a.** Ethyl alcohol boils at 78°C at sea level, 101.3 kPa.
   **b.** Ethyl alcohol boils at 72°C on a mountaintop, 80.0 kPa.
   **c.** Ethyl alcohol boils at 80°C in a deep mine, 105 kPa.

**56.** Unlike a real gas, an ideal gas would have no forces of attraction between molecules and no molecular volume.

**57. a.** A gas has no definite volume or shape.
   **b.** A solid has a definite volume and shape.
   **c.** A liquid has a definite volume but no definite shape.

**58. a.** Anhydrous crystals have no water in their composition.
   **b.** Hydrated crystals have water in their composition.
   **c.** Efflorescent crystals lose water of hydration spontaneously at room temperature.
   **d.** Hygroscopic crystals absorb moisture from the air.
   **e.** Deliquescent crystals absorb so much moisture that they dissolve in it.

**59.** Metals are reflective, are good conductors of electricity and heat, and are malleable. Non-metals are not.

**60.** $2\text{Al}(s) + 6\text{HCl}(aq) \rightarrow 2\text{AlCl}_3(aq) + 3\text{H}_2(g)$

$5.0 \text{ dm}^3 \times \dfrac{273 \text{ K}}{313 \text{ K}} \times \dfrac{98.2 \text{ kPa}}{101.3 \text{ kPa}} \times \dfrac{1 \text{ mol H}_2}{22.4 \text{ dm}^3} \times$

$\dfrac{2 \text{ mol Al}}{3 \text{ mol H}_2} \times \dfrac{27 \text{ g Al}}{1 \text{ mol Al}} = 3.4 \text{ g Al}$

## Page 463, Critical Thinking

**61.** Forming an alloy, or solid solution, requires complete mixing at the atomic level. This complete mixing is possible in the molten phase, in which the atoms are free to move.

**62.** $m = \dfrac{\Delta T}{K_f} \, m_1 = \dfrac{-37°C}{-1.86°C/\text{molal}} = 19.89 \text{ molal} \approx$

$20 \text{ molal}$

If a solution that is ½ ethylene glycol is 20 molal, a solution that is ⅛ ethylene glycol is 5 molal.

$\Delta T = m \times K_f = 5 \text{ molal} \times (-1.86°C/\text{molal}) = -9.3°C$

**63.** Solute Q could not have been potassium nitrate **(b)**, because dissolving of potassium nitrate is endothermic.

**64.** As temperature increases, solubility of most solids increases.

**65.** Both molarity and molality are ways of expressing the concentration of solutions. Molarity is the number of moles of solute in 1 liter of solution, whereas molality is the number of moles of solute in 1 kilogram of solvent.

**66.** From text Figure 16-13, the solubility of $KClO_3$ at 20°C is about 8 g/100 g $H_2O$, or 16 g/200 g $H_2O$. Since the analyzed solution contains 28 g/200 g $H_2O$, it is supersaturated.

## Page 463, Challenge Problems

**67.** To grow copper sulfate crystals: (1) Make a solution of $CuSO_4$ that is saturated (with excess solid in the bottom of the beaker). (2) Heat the solution to boiling to dissolve as much excess $CuSO_4$ as possible. There should still be solid in the beaker. (3) Pour the hot saturated solution into a clean beaker without transferring any of the solid. (4) Let the solution cool undisturbed. (5) If crystals do not form as the solution cools, add a tiny seed crystal of $CuSO_4$.

**68.** Answers will vary. A few possible responses are given.

| Solution | Solute | Solvent | Concentration | Phase |
|---|---|---|---|---|
| air | oxygen and other gases | nitrogen | unsaturated | gas |
| club soda | $CO_2$ | water | saturated | liquid |
| steel | carbon | iron | dilute | solid |

**69.** $\text{Mg} + 2\text{HCl} \rightarrow \text{MgCl}_2 + \text{H}_2$

**a.** $0.750 \text{ dm}^3 \times \dfrac{0.200 \text{ mol HCl}}{1 \text{ dm}^3 \text{ HCl}} \times \dfrac{1 \text{ mol Mg}}{2 \text{ mol HCl}} \times$

$\dfrac{24.3 \text{ g}}{1 \text{ mol Mg}} = 1.82 \text{ g Mg}$

**b.** $0.750 \text{ dm}^3 \times \dfrac{0.200 \text{ mol HCl}}{1 \text{ dm}^3 \text{ HCl}} \times \dfrac{1 \text{ mol H}_2}{2 \text{ mol HCl}} \times$

$\dfrac{22.4 \text{ dm}^3}{1 \text{ mol H}_2} \times \dfrac{295 \text{ K}}{273 \text{ K}} \times \dfrac{101.3 \text{ kPa}}{98.7 \text{ kPa}} = 1.86 \text{ dm}^3 \text{ H}_2$

# Chemical Kinetics and Thermodynamics

17

## Chapter Planning Guide

| Text Section | | Labs (Lab Manual) and Demonstrations (TE) | Supplementary Materials (Teacher's Resource Book) |
|---|---|---|---|
| **17-1** | Two Major Topics in Chemistry, pp. 465-466 | Demo 17-1: Effective Collisions, p. TG-252 | |
| **17-2** | Rate of Reaction and the Collision Theory, pp. 466-467 | | |
| **17-3** | Reaction Mechanisms, pp. 467-469 | | |
| **17-4** | The Nature of the Reactants and Reaction Rate, pp. 469-470 | Demo 17-2: Collisions and Temperature, p. TG-253 | |
| **17-5** | Temperature and Reaction Rate, pp. 470-471 | | |
| **17-6** | Concentration of Reactants and Reaction Rate, pp. 471-473 | Demo 17-3: Collisions and Concentration, p. TG-254 | |
| **17-7** | Pressure and Reaction Rate, p. 473 | Lab 32: Rates of Reaction | |
| **17-8** | Catalysts and Reaction Rate, pp. 474-475 | Demo 17-4: Colliding Particles, p. TG-254 | |
| **17-9** | Activation Energy and the Activated Complex, pp. 475-476 | | Review Activity: Reaction Mechanisms, p. 17-14 |
| **17-10** | Reaction Mechanisms and Rates of Reaction, pp. 476-477 | | |
| **17-11** | Potential Energy Diagrams, pp. 477-479 | | Transparency Master: Potential Energy Diagram for the Reaction between Substances $A$ and $B$ to Produce Substance $C$, p. 17-4<br>Transparency Master: Potential Energy Diagram for the Decomposition of Substance $C$ to Produce Substances $A$ and $B$, p. 17-5<br>Transparency Master: Identifying Energies on a Potential Energy Diagram, p. 17-6 |

| Text Section | Labs (Lab Manual) and Demonstrations (TE) | Supplementary Materials (Teacher's Resource Book) |
|---|---|---|
| **17-12** Activation Energy: Temperature and Concentration, pp. 479-481 <br><br> **17-13** Activation Energy and Catalysts, p. 482 | | Transparency Master: Potential Energy Diagram Showing the Effect of a Catalyst, p. 17-7 <br> Computer Experiment: First Order Kinetics, p. 17-12 <br> Review Activity: Reaction Rate, p. 17-16 <br> Review Activity: Potential Energy Diagrams, p. 17-17 |
| **17-14** Heat Content, or Enthalpy, pp. 482-484 | Lab 33: Heats of Reaction (demo.) | |
| **17-15** Heat of Formation, pp. 484-487 <br><br> **17-16** Stability of Compounds, pp. 487-488 | | Transparency Master: Standard Heats of Formation for Some Selected Compounds, p. 17-8 |
| **17-17** Hess's Law of Constant Heat Summation, pp. 488-491 | | |
| **17-18** The Direction of Chemical Change, pp. 491-492 <br><br> **17-19** Entropy, pp. 492-494 <br><br> **17-20** The Effect of Changes in Entropy on the Direction of Spontaneous Change, pp. 494-496 | Demo 17-5: 52 Pickup: An Abbreviated Version, p. TG-255 | Transparency Master: The Effect of the Sign of $\Delta H$ and $\Delta S$ on Spontaneous Change, p. 17-9 |
| **17-21** The Gibbs Free Energy Equation, pp. 496-500 | | Transparency Master: The Effect of Changes in Enthalpy and Changes in Entropy on the Change in Free Energy, p. 17-10 |
| **Career** Food Scientist, p. 497 | | |
| **17-22** Application of the Gibbs Equation to a Physical Change, pp. 500-502 <br><br> **17-23** Free Energy of Formation, pp. 502-505 | | Transparency Master: Standard Heats of Free Energy for Some Selected Compounds, p. 17-11 <br> Review Activity: Enthalpy and Entropy, p. 17-18 <br> Practice Problems, p. 17-19 <br> Non-SI Supplementary Problems, p. 17-20 |
| **Can You Explain This?** A Glowing Platinum Wire, p. 505 | | |

| Text Section | Labs (Lab Manual) and Demonstrations (TE) | Supplementary Materials (Teacher's Resource Book) |
|---|---|---|
|  |  | Test—Form A, p. AT-64<br>Alternate Test—Form B, p. BT-64 |

■ Core   ■ Advanced   ■ Optional

## Chapter Overview

In Chapter 17, we introduce two very important concepts: chemical kinetics and thermodynamics. Chemical kinetics is presented first and is explained in terms of the collision theory. We emphasize that reactions take place at different rates and point out the factors that can affect these rates, including the nature of reactants, their surface area, their concentrations, the temperature of the reaction system, and the presence of a catalyst. Next, we define reaction mechanism and discuss some examples.

The remaining part of this chapter focuses on thermodynamics. Energy and entropy, the two factors that determine physical and chemical changes, are defined and discussed. Various problems for calculating changes in enthalpy are illustrated, as well as the relationship of heat of formation to stability of compounds. We state Hess's law and illustrate its use in calculating heats of reaction. The chapter ends with a discussion on the Gibbs free energy equation and its use in determining which physical and chemical changes can occur.

## Chapter Objectives

After students have completed this chapter, they will be able to:

1. Explain the collision theory of reactions.
   *17-1* and *17-2*
2. Describe what is meant by a reaction mechanism, a rate-determining step, an activated complex, and activation energy.   *17-3, 17-4,* and *17-9*
3. Account for the effect on reaction rates of the nature of the reactants, their surface area, their concentrations, the temperature of the reaction system, and the presence of a catalyst.
   *17-5* to *17-8, 17-10, 17-12,* and *17-13*
4. Interpret potential energy diagrams and energy distribution diagrams.   *17-11*
5. Interpret the significance of changes in enthalpy in chemical or physical changes.
   *17-14* to *17-16* and *17-18*

6. Use Hess's law for calculations related to heats of reaction and heats of formation.   *17-15* and *17-17*
7. Describe the role of changes in entropy on chemical and physical changes.   *17-18* to *17-20*
8. Determine values for changes in free energy and use them to predict spontaneous reactions.
   *17-21* to *17-23*

## Teaching Suggestions

### 17-1 Two Major Topics in Chemistry, pp. 465-466, and

### 17-2 Rate of Reaction and the Collision Theory, pp. 466-467

| Planning Guide | |
|---|---|
| Labs (Lab Manual) and Demonstrations (TE) | Supplementary Materials (Teacher's Resource Book) |
| Demo 17-1: Effective Collisions, p. TG-252 |  |

■ The topics in the previous chapter on solutions are essentially descriptive. This chapter is highly theoretical. Therefore, you may want to present to your students the following list of the topics covered in this chapter, for use as an advanced organizer. This list could be written on a large poster that is visible during class, on a transparency, or as a notebook page to be handed out to the students.

| Kinetics | |
|---|---|
| Reaction Rate | Discussed in Terms of |
| Nature of reactants | Mechanism with simple steps |
| Temperature | Activation energy ($E_{ACT}$) |
| Concentration | Activated complex |
| Pressure | Potential energy diagrams |
| Catalysts | Potential energy diagrams |

| Thermodynamics | |
|---|---|
| Heat of Reaction | Driving Force |
| Enthalpy change ($\Delta H$) | Free energy change ($\Delta G$) |
| Heat of formation ($\Delta H$) | Entropy change ($\Delta S$) |
|  | Free energy of formation |

17

This brief overview helps students to organize and relate these very theoretical concepts. As you work through this chapter, refer occasionally to this overview to help students monitor their progress.

■ Define chemical kinetics, reaction rates, reaction mechanism, and thermodynamics. Point out that the rate of a chemical reaction may be observed by noting the disappearance of one or more reactants or the formation of one or more products. Therefore, the progress of a reaction can be monitored by measuring changes in gas pressure, thermal conductivities, electrical conductivities, densities, or masses of reactants and products.

■ Emphasize that collisions of reacting species play an important role in the progress of a reaction. Explain thoroughly the collision theory, which forms the theoretical basis for understanding the material in this chapter. Emphasize the two main points about collisions that affect the rate of a reaction: effectiveness of collision and frequency of collision. Do Demonstration 17-1, "Effective Collisions," to illustrate the difference between an effective collision and one that is ineffective. Next, discuss frequency of collision. Explain how frequency of collision influences the rate of a chemical reaction. List the five factors that affect the frequency of collisions: nature of reactants, temperature, concentration of the reactants, pressure, and catalysts. Point out that each of these factors is explained in detail in later sections.

## 17-3 Reaction Mechanisms, pp. 467-469

■ Point out that chemical reactions can be broken down into a series of simple steps. Generally, the fewer the steps, the faster the reaction is. When more than two particles react, a two-particle collision forms an intermediate particle. This reacts with a third particle to form another intermediate particle or perhaps the final product. Explain that a reaction mechanism shows the exact sequence of steps by which a reaction occurs. Refer to text Figure 17-3 to illustrate the progress of a theoretical reaction through several simple steps. Emphasize the higher probability of a two-particle collision occurring as compared to a random, simultaneous three-particle collision. Then discuss an example of a specific reaction mechanism, such as the burning of hydrogen. The probability of two hydrogen molecules meeting an oxygen molecule at one point and at precisely the same instant is extremely low. Experimental evidence indicates that about seven different steps occur in which atomic hydrogen, atomic oxygen, and hydroxide radicals are involved, leading to the formation of water.

## 17-4 The Nature of the Reactants and Reaction Rate, pp. 469-470, and

## 17-5 Temperature and Reaction Rate, pp. 470-471

| Planning Guide | |
|---|---|
| Labs (Lab Manual) and Demonstrations (TE) | Supplementary Materials (Teacher's Resource Book) |
| Demo 17-2: Collisions and Temperature, p. TG-253 | |

■ Explain that the next five sections focus on the factors that affect the frequency of collisions, and that these factors are discussed in terms of the collision theory. Be sure to relate these factors not only to frequency of collision but also to the effectiveness of collision.

■ Explain why the nature of a bond in the reacting species is a factor in determining the rate of reaction. Then point out that, in general, reactions of ions in solution take place rapidly because the oppositely charged ions are readily attracted to each other. Discuss examples of rapid reactions between ions. Two examples of these rapid reactions are:

$NaCl(aq) + AgNO_3(aq) \rightarrow AgCl(s) + NaNO_3(aq)$

$2KI(aq) + Pb(NO_3)_2(aq) \rightarrow PbI_2(s) + 2KNO_3(aq)$

Explain that simple reactions involving covalent bonds proceed much more slowly because the atoms are arranged in stable molecules. These arrangements of molecules must be disturbed in the course of the reaction. Burning and other strongly exothermic reactions are exemptions to this generalization about covalent compounds. Once started, burning reactions generally occur rapidly even though many covalent bonds must be rearranged. The energy given off in these types of reactions is utilized in rearranging the bonds. Slower reaction rates can be demonstrated by placing 3-mm or 4-mm pellets of NaOH in separate 5-cm³ samples of primary, secondary, and tertiary butanol. The class can observe the rate at which bubbles of gas form. (CAUTION: Hydrogen gas is generated.)

■ Do Demonstration 17-2, "Collisions and Temperature," to illustrate that the speed and kinetic energy of reacting particles affect the frequency of collisions between them. Then refer to text Figure 17-6, which illustrates the relationship of the temperature to the kinetic energy of the particles. Emphasize that the increase in temperature causes the reactants to move more rapidly and thus increases the number of collisions per unit time. This increase in energy results in a higher percentage of effective collisions.

## 17-6 Concentration of Reactants and Reaction Rate, pp. 471-473,

## 17-7 Pressure and Reaction Rate, p. 473, and

## 17-8 Catalysts and Reaction Rate, pp. 474-475

| Planning Guide | |
|---|---|
| Labs (Lab Manual) and Demonstrations (TE) | Supplementary Materials (Teacher's Resource Book) |
| Demo 17-3: Collisions and Concentration, p. TG-254<br>Lab 32: Rates of Reaction<br>Demo 17-4: Colliding Particles, p. TG-254 | |

■ Do Demonstration 17-3, "Collisions and Concentration," to illustrate the relationship between concentration and the frequency of collision. Define homogeneous reaction and heterogeneous reaction. Discuss the effect of concentration on these two types of reactions. Emphasize that for heterogeneous reactions, the effect of change in surface area is similar to the effect of change in concentration for homogeneous systems.

■ Assign Laboratory 32, "Rates of Reaction." In this lab the students study the effects of concentration (Part A) and temperature (Part B) on the rate of a chemical reaction.

■ Do Demonstration 17-4, "Colliding Particles," to illustrate the effect of a larger number of particles on the number of collisions between particles. Ask the students to relate this demonstration to reacting gas molecules in a closed system. Point out that for gas phase systems, pressure is actually an expression of concentration. Remind the students that since $PV = nRT$, then $P = nRT/V$ and that $n/V$ is moles per cubic decimeter, an expression of concentration. The usual way to change the pressure in a gas phase system is to change the number of molecules or to change the volume, either one of which changes the concentration. Discuss the effect of a change in pressure on the frequency and on the effectiveness of collisions.

■ Catalysts have a quality that captures the imagination of some students. To supplement the text discussion of catalysts, you may wish to explain the specific means by which some catalysts increase reaction rates. For example, finely divided platinum, acting as a contact catalyst for hydrogen, adsorbs large quantities of the gas. The platinum holds the hydrogen in a highly reactive atomic form.

■ **Application.** You may want to ask your students whether they have ever had trouble lighting a Bunsen burner. The difficulty may have arisen from an insufficient amount of reactants (air and gas) to allow the reaction to take place. If the amount of air fed into the burner mixture is too great (or the amount of gas is too small), the burner will not light. Another example of the effect of concentration on a chemical reaction involves the hydrogen/oxygen mixture in air. Hydrogen is a component of air. Fortunately, the concentration of hydrogen in the air is low enough to prevent hydrogen and oxygen from reacting together in the presence of an open flame.

■ **Concept Mastery.** You may wish to determine whether your students understand the meaning of reaction mechanism and the meaning of catalyst by using Concept Mastery questions 48 through 50 (chapter-end questions). Students may be able to predict a reaction mechanism on paper, but they may not realize how difficult it is for chemists to actually determine a mechanism for a specific reaction. To reinforce this point, you may want to have your students determine the mechanism of the "Blue Bottle Experiment," which was first described in the November 1969 issue of the *Journal of Chemical Education*. In that demonstration students observe an experiment and then are asked to determine the mechanism. The article gives some typical responses made by the students and how they can be verified.

## 17-9 Activation Energy and the Activated Complex, pp. 475-476, and

## 17-10 Reaction Mechanisms and Rates of Reaction, pp. 476-477

| Planning Guide | |
|---|---|
| Labs (Lab Manual) and Demonstrations (TE) | Supplementary Materials (Teacher's Resource Book) |
| | Review Activity: Reaction Mechanisms, p. 17-14 |

■ If you choose to cover these Advanced Topics, begin by explaining them in terms of the collision theory. According to the collision theory, a molecule-like particle called an activated complex is formed when two particles collide. For most reactions, it is difficult to identify the activated complex because it is short-lived. Emphasize the principle that an activated complex is a reactive intermediate. It can come apart to re-form the original reactants or it can come apart to form the final product(s). An effective collision occurs when reactant particles collide with enough energy and with the proper geometry to form an activated complex in which the bonds can be rearranged to form a molecule of product.

A good analogy of activated complex formation is the moment of contact between the foot of a kicker and the football or between the bat and the baseball. In this context, at the instant of contact between the foot and football or the bat and baseball, the activated complex is formed.

■ Use the analogies in the text to help explain the concept of rate-determining step. Most students quickly see the logic of this concept in the mailing process described. Explain how experiments can be designed to keep all conditions constant except for the concentration of one reactant. Changes in the concentration of this reactant become the independent variable. The rate of the reaction, observed as the rate at which product is formed or reactant consumed, is the dependent variable. In this situation, the role of one reactant in the reaction mechanism can be determined.

■ **Application.** You may want to use the Bunsen burner as a tool to illustrate the principle of activation energy. No matter how long the gas jet is turned on, the air and gas mixture does not ignite. It requires activation energy before it can burn, even though burning is an exothermic reaction.

■ **Concept Mastery.** To help students distinguish between the activation energy and endothermic reactions, discuss Concept Mastery question 46 (chapter-end question). Students should understand that even endothermic reactions need activation energy to get them started. An interesting compound that illustrates this fact is nitrogen triiodide. Upon drying, this compound can explode if jarred. In fact, when a small amount of $NI_3$ is placed on a piece of filter paper and left to dry, it will explode if it is touched by a feather attached to the end of a meter stick.

## 17-11 Potential Energy Diagrams, pp. 477-479

| Planning Guide | |
|---|---|
| Labs (Lab Manual) and Demonstrations (TE) | Supplementary Materials (Teacher's Resource Book) |
| | Transparency Master: Potential Energy Diagram for the Reaction between Substances $A$ and $B$ To Produce Substance $C$, p. 17-4 |
| | Transparency Master: Potential Energy Diagram for the Decomposition of Substance $C$ To Produce Substances $A$ and $B$, p. 17-5 |
| | Transparency Master: Identifying Energies on a Potential Energy Diagram, p. 17-6 |

■ If you choose to cover this Advanced Topic, point out that it is difficult to portray the transition-state theory clearly without the use of potential energy diagrams.

Discuss the Transparency Master "Potential Energy Diagram for the Reaction between Substances $A$ and $B$ To Produce Substance $C$." It is important for students to understand each labeled feature in this diagram. Explain how potential energy increases as particles move on a collision path. As their velocities decrease, becoming a minimum at the instant of collision, kinetic energy is converted to potential energy. Point out the relative positions of reactant particles heading toward each other before collision, contacting each other as the activated complex is formed, and moving apart after the collision. Emphasize the time character of the $x$-axis. Show how $E_{ACT}$ on the potential energy diagram is related to $E_{ACT}$ on the energy distribution curve.

## 17-12 Activation Energy: Temperature and Concentration, pp. 479-481, and

## 17-13 Activation Energy and Catalysts, p. 482

| Planning Guide | |
|---|---|
| Labs (Lab Manual) and Demonstrations (TE) | Supplementary Materials (Teacher's Resource Book) |
| | Transparency Master: Potential Energy Diagram Showing the Effect of a Catalyst, p. 17-7 |
| | Computer Experiment: First Order Kinetics, p. 17-12 |
| | Review Activity: Reaction Rate, p. 17-16 |
| | Review Activity: Potential Energy Diagrams, p. 17-17 |

■ Remind the students that temperature is a measure of average kinetic energy. Refer to text Figure 17-16 to show that an increase in temperature increases the number of reactant particles possessing energies greater than the activation energy. Discuss text Figure 17-17 and point out that this also happens when concentrations of reactants are increased.

■ Remind the students of the definition of a catalyst. Give examples of catalysts and describe their effects on the reactions catalyzed.

## 17-14 Heat Content, or Enthalpy, pp. 482-484

| Planning Guide | |
|---|---|
| Labs (Lab Manual) and Demonstrations (TE) | Supplementary Materials (Teacher's Resource Book) |
| Lab 33: Heats of Reaction (demonstration) | |

■ Point out that the rest of the chapter deals with thermodynamics. Discuss the concept of enthalpy before the other topics in thermodynamics. Emphasize that the exact enthalpy of a substance or a system cannot be calculated or measured directly. Only the change in enthalpy of a substance or system can be calculated. For example, when carbon burns to carbon dioxide, releasing energy, we can conclude that the enthalpy of the $CO_2$ is less than the total enthalpy of the carbon and oxygen. The enthalpy of the $CO_2$ is quite low, making it a stable compound. Relate the sign of $\Delta H$ values to the terms exothermic and endothermic as follows:

exothermic—energy lost by the system to the outside world — $\Delta H$ is negative

endothermic—energy gained by the system from the outside world — $\Delta H$ is positive

■ Generally, the calorie as a unit of energy is familiar to students—at least in the context of diet if not from their earlier work with phase changes and cooling and warming curves. Consider assigning students to bring in food labels or newspaper recipes showing calories (actually kilocalories). Ask them to convert these values to kilojoules (4.18 kJ/kcal).

■ Laboratory 33, "Heats of Reaction," can be done here. However, because of the potential hazard of handling sodium hydroxide, it is recommended that this lab experiment be done as a teacher demonstration. This lab can also be done in conjunction with Section 17-17, as the results are consistent with Hess's law. In Laboratory 33, students determine heats of reaction for three related exothermic reactions.

■ **Concept Mastery.** Sometimes students think that chemical reactions happen and then no more chemical activity occurs. The burning of a gas in a laboratory burner is a familiar example. After burning begins, a steady state is reached. You may want to assign Concept Mastery question 47 to review the difference between heat and temperature. Even though the temperature of the laboratory burner is constant, the reaction is still proceeding.

### 17-15 Heat of Formation, pp. 484-487, and

### 17-16 Stability of Compounds, pp. 487-488

| Planning Guide | |
| --- | --- |
| Labs (Lab Manual) and Demonstrations (TE) | Supplementary Materials (Teacher's Resource Book) |
| | Transparency Master: Standard Heats of Formation for Some Selected Compounds, p. 17-8 |

■ Distinguish between heat of reaction and heat of formation. Mention that the unit for the heat of reaction is the kilojoule whereas the unit for the heat of formation is kilojoule per mole. Refer to text Figure 17-21 to illustrate the symbolism for heat of formation. Ask the class to explain the difference in the heats of formation of water in the gas and liquid phases. Point out that the standard heat of formation gives an indication of the stability of a compound. Use potential energy diagrams to illustrate this difference in stability.

### 17-17 Hess's Law of Constant Heat Summation, pp. 488-491

■ This Advanced Topic is likely to be difficult reading for some students. Mention that Hess's law follows as a consequence of the law of conservation of energy. Explain that you can apply Hess's law by either of two methods: adding the heats of reaction for the partial equations, or subtracting the heat(s) of formation of the reactant(s) from the heat(s) of formation of the products. Illustrate the use of both methods.

### 17-18 The Direction of Chemical Change, pp. 491-492,

### 17-19 Entropy, pp. 492-494, and

### 17-20 The Effect of Changes in Entropy on the Direction of Spontaneous Change, pp. 494-496

| Planning Guide | |
| --- | --- |
| Labs (Lab Manual) and Demonstrations (TE) | Supplementary Materials (Teacher's Resource Book) |
| Demo 17-5: 52 Pickup: An Abbreviated Version, p. TG-255 | Transparency Master: The Effect of the Sign of $\Delta H$ and $\Delta S$ on Spontaneous Change, p. 17-9 |

■ As you begin this Advanced Topic, help students to acquire an appropriate understanding of "spontaneous" as used in the context of thermodynamics. Use some everyday examples of changes that occur spontaneously. Then point out that spontaneous change, as used by the chemist, refers not only to reactions that occur suddenly, but also to any reaction that can occur under existing conditions. For example, the decomposition of water is spontaneous under the conditions of electrolysis. Remind the students that chemical changes tend to proceed in a direction in which the change is exothermic and the products have relatively strong bonds. However, change to a lower energy condition does not tell the whole story. Describe some endothermic reactions that are spontaneous, emphasizing the

17

conditions under which they occur. The phase change of ice to water is a familiar example that illustrates the change from lower potential energy to higher potential energy. Use this example to illustrate that another factor (entropy) influences the direction of a chemical change.

■ The concept of disorder or randomness is interesting to most students. Do Demonstration 17-5, "52 Pickup: An Abbreviated Version." Then define entropy. Refer to text Figure 17-27 and discuss the checker analogy to reinforce this concept. Discuss the change in entropy associated with each of these processes:

dissolving: $NaCl(s) \rightarrow Na^+(aq) + Cl^-(aq)$
sublimation: $CO_2(s) \rightarrow CO_2(g)$
decomposition: $2KClO_3(s) \rightarrow 2KCl(s) + 3O_2(g)$

Emphasize that changes in entropy play a role in determining the direction of spontaneous change. Use text Figures 17-28 and 17-29 to illustrate changes in entropy and the corresponding change in a system to the more probable, less ordered arrangement. Discuss the Transparency Master "The Effect of the Sign of $\Delta H$ and $\Delta S$ on Spontaneous Change." This table helps to summarize the role of energy change and entropy change in determining the direction of spontaneous change.

## 17-21 The Gibbs Free Energy Equation, pp. 496-500

| Planning Guide | |
|---|---|
| Labs (Lab Manual) and Demonstrations (TE) | Supplementary Materials (Teacher's Resource Book) |
| | Transparency Master: The Effect of Changes in Enthalpy and Changes in Entropy on the Change in Free Energy, p. 17-10 |

■ Show how the Gibbs free energy equation gives a quantitative description of reaction spontaneity. Free energy change, $\Delta G$, is the balance struck between the two fundamental driving forces in any chemical or physical change. The tendency toward lower energy, negative $\Delta H$, and the tendency toward higher entropy, positive $\Delta S$, are combined as $\Delta G$ in the relationship

$$\Delta G = \Delta H - T\Delta S$$

The effect of $\Delta H$ and $\Delta S$ on the change in free energy is summarized in the Transparency Master "The Effect of Changes in Enthalpy and Changes in Entropy on Changes in Free Energy."

## 17-22 Application of the Gibbs Equation to a Physical Change, pp. 500-502, and

## 17-23 Free Energy of Formation, pp. 502-505

| Planning Guide | |
|---|---|
| Labs (Lab Manual) and Demonstrations (TE) | Supplementary Materials (Teacher's Resource Book) |
| | Transparency Master: Standard Heats of Free Energy for Some Selected Compounds, p. 17-11 Review Activity: Enthalpy and Entropy, p. 17-18 Practice Problems, p. 17-19 Non-SI Supplementary Problems, p. 17-20 |

■ Apply the Gibbs equation to the freezing of water and the melting of ice. Point out that freezing is favored by the enthalpy change and opposed by the entropy change. The reverse is true for the melting of ice. Ask the students to write a brief summary of this section to promote their understanding of the Gibbs equation as it applies to physical changes.

■ Explain that the standard free energy of formation is an indication of the spontaneity of a formation reaction at 298 K. It gives the best estimate of the stability of a compound. Point out that a compound is more stable when its $\Delta G_f^\circ$ is negative and larger than that of another compound. Show how an unknown term in either of the following equations can be determined when the other terms are known.

$$\Delta G_f^\circ = \Delta H_f^\circ + T_{298}\Delta S_f^\circ$$
$$\Delta G_f^\circ = \Delta G_{f\ prod}^\circ - \Delta G_{f\ react}^\circ$$

## Demonstrations

### 17-1 Effective Collisions

**Overview:** In this demonstration, you cause effective and ineffective collisions to occur between objects. An effective collision is one in which the colliding particles approach each other with the proper angle and energy. The effectiveness and the frequency of collisions determine the rate of a chemical reaction.

**Materials:** 6 large spheres (20–30 cm) and 3 smaller spheres (5–15 cm) made of foam rubber or Styrofoam; Velcro; pins or glue.

**Advance Preparation:** Secure Velcro to the spheres, using pins or glue. Approximately 25% of the surface of the first large and the first small sphere should be covered with Velcro. Approximately 50% of the surface of the second large and the second small sphere should be covered with Velcro. The surface of the third large and the third small sphere should be covered completely with Velcro. Do not be concerned if the attached Velcro does not form a perfect sphere. Three large spheres should be left uncovered.

**Procedure:** 1. Ask your students how easy it is for two particles in space to collide. Ask them to consider how easy it would be for two students throwing two spheres to bring about mid-air collisions between the spheres. 2. Choose two students at random and give each a large sphere that is not covered with Velcro. Position them about 4 m apart, away from breakable objects, and ask them to throw the spheres so that the spheres will collide with each other in midair. Allow the students to come closer together and try again. 3. Choose three other students and challenge them to bring about a three-sphere simultaneous collision in space. Ask students why most reaction mechanisms tend to take into consideration collisions between no more than two spheres. 4. Show students the spheres that have the Velcro attached to them. Explain that the Velcro area represents an active chemical site for the occurence of an effective collision and bonding. Point out that the chance for the occurrence of the Velcro "bonding" is related to the Velcro's surface area on the sphere. 5. Demonstrate, with the spheres at short range, that when the spheres collide with the Velcro in the correct orientation, they stick together. Demonstrate that nearly every collision is effective when the two spheres covered entirely with the Velcro are used. This situation represents one in which there is a high probability of an effective molecular collision at all angles. Repeat, using the spheres that are covered with Velcro in more limited proportions. 6. By very lightly touching two spheres together, demonstrate that if a collision does not have enough force, "bonding" does not tend to occur. 7. Give a pair of students the large and small spheres that are covered 25% with Velcro. Allow the students to stand relatively close together and to try to bring about mid-air collisions that will cause the spheres to stick together. Allow the same two students or a different pair of students to attempt the same thing, using the spheres that are covered 50% with Velcro. Also, allow the students to vary the distances between them.

**Results:** In step 1, students will be likely to think that it is very easy to throw the Styrofoam spheres in such a way as to bring about a midair collision. In step 2, students will be very surprised to discover that at 4 m the likelihood of a collision between two spheres is quite low. As the distance between the individuals decreases, the frequency of two-sphere collisions will increase. Simultaneous collisions between two spheres will occur much more frequently than the simultaneous collisions between three spheres that are attempt-

ed in step 3. In reaction mechanisms, one usually deals with collisions between a maximum of two particles because collisions involving more particles are much less likely to occur. In step 5, the lower the percentage of coverage by Velcro is, the lower the likelihood of effective collision will be. This helps to suggest that a molecule or ion with a large reaction site will tend to be more reactive than one with a small site, other factors being equal. In step 7, as the percentage of coverage increases, or as the distance decreases, the likelihood of effective collision will increase.

## 17-2 Collisions and Temperature

**Overview:** In this demonstration, you show that as the speed and kinetic energy of particles increase, so does the frequency of collisions between them.

**Materials:** collision-theory apparatus; overhead projector; 5 opaque and 5 clear marbles.

**Advanced Preparation:** Construct the collision-theory apparatus. (See Figure 17-1.)

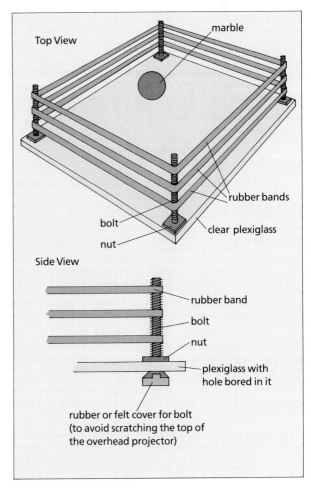

**Figure 17-1**

**Procedure:** 1. Place the collision-theory apparatus on top of the overhead projector. Place one marble into the apparatus. Gently shake the apparatus with a random motion, and have students observe the motion of the marble. Next, shake the apparatus with more force, and have students again observe the motion of the marble. 2. Place five clear marbles and five opaque marbles into the apparatus. Gently shake the apparatus, and have students observe the collisions and get a sense of the frequency of them. Next, shake the apparatus again, but this time with more force. Have students again observe the collisions. Ask them to relate their overall observations to collisions of molecules and to temperature and reaction rate.

**Results:** Students should observe a higher velocity and a higher frequency of collisions as the force applied to the apparatus is increased. An increase in the number of molecules also increases the frequency of collisions. The students should relate what they have observed to the fact that the collision rate of molecules and the reaction rate increase as average kinetic energy, or temperature, increases.

## 17-3 Collisions and Concentration

**Overview:** In this demonstration, you illustrate, via an inexpensive mechanical model, the effect of concentration on the number of collisions that particles undergo in a closed system.

**Materials:** overhead projector; collision-theory apparatus; 10 opaque and 10 clear marbles.

**Advance Preparation:** If you have not already done so, construct the collision-theory apparatus shown in Figure 17-1.

**Procedure:** 1. Set the apparatus on top of the overhead projector. 2. Place one marble into the apparatus. 3. Gently shake the apparatus from side to side, using a gentle, random motion. Have students observe the random path of the marble as it strikes the sides defined by the rubber bands. 4. Place one opaque marble and one clear marble into the apparatus and again shake the apparatus. Have students observe the collisions between the marbles and get a sense of the frequency of the collisions. 5. Place one opaque marble and five clear marbles into the apparatus and shake as just described. Have students again observe the collisions between the marbles and get a sense of the frequency of collisions. 6. Place 10 opaque marbles and 10 clear marbles into the apparatus and gently shake as described. Again have students observe the collisions. Ask them to relate their overall observations to collisions of molecules and to concentration and reaction rate.

**Results:** Students should observe a higher frequency of collisions as the number of marbles is increased (in steps 5 and 6). The students should relate what they have observed to the fact that the collision rate of molecules is dependent upon concentration, and that reaction rate depends, in general, on concentration.

## 17-4 Colliding Particles

**Overview:** In this demonstration, the number of particles and the velocity of the particles are kept constant while the area of a collision-theory apparatus is varied. The effect of area on the number of collisions between particles is observed.

**Materials:** overhead projector, 3 transparent marbles; 3 opaque marbles; 2 collision-theory apparatuses.

**Advance Preparation:** Construct the two collision-theory apparatuses. (See Figure 17-1, the illustration for Demonstration 17-2.) The two apparatuses should be identical in all ways except for area. The areas should be in the ratio of two to one. (Be sure that the larger apparatus can fit on your overhead projector.)

**Procedure:** 1. Discuss the collision-theory apparatuses with the class, pointing out the limitations of the model, which include the difficulty of maintaining a constant random shaking motion, the effect of friction, the inelasticity of collisions, the difficulty of keeping track of the collisions quantitatively, and the fact that the motion is limited to two dimensions. 2. By placing the smaller one into the larger one, demonstrate that the only difference in the construction of the apparatuses is the area. If you wish, you can divide the larger apparatus's surface area by the smaller one's surface area, to show the 2:1 ratio. 3. Place the smaller collision-theory apparatus onto the overhead projector, and place one marble into the apparatus. Shake the apparatus with your hand, using a random motion of constant magnitude, and have students observe the velocity of the marble. Repeat this procedure, using the larger collision-theory apparatus and the same marble. 4. Place three transparent and three opaque marbles into the smaller collision-theory apparatus, and shake the apparatus, using a random motion of constant magnitude. Have students observe and get a sense of how frequently the marbles collide. Place three transparent and three opaque marbles into the larger apparatus, and shake the apparatus, using a similar motion. Have students again observe the frequency of collisions and have them compare the frequencies for the two apparatuses. 5. Ask students what this demonstration suggests about a three-dimensional situation involving reacting gas particles.

**Results:** In step 3, students should observe that the marble's velocities in the two apparatuses will be about the same, indicating equal kinetic energies. In step 4, students should observe that the frequency of collisions in the larger apparatus will be less than that in the smaller apparatus. The spaces between the particles will be greater in the larger apparatus, and the marbles will have to travel longer distances in order to participate in a collision. The demonstration suggests that an increase in the volume of reacting gases produces a decrease in frequency of collisions and, therefore, a decrease in reaction rate.

### 17-5 52 Pickup: An Abbreviated Version

**Overview:** In this demonstration, you show that systems tend to move spontaneously from order to disorder, often with release of energy in either a useful or a nonuseful form.

**Materials:** 13 playing cards of a single suit.

**Advance Preparation:** Place the cards in order of rank, from ace (1) through king.

**Procedure:** 1. Show the students that the cards are in order. 2. Hold the set of cards high above the desk or the floor and let go of them, allowing them to fall onto the desk or floor. Have students observe the degree of orderliness of the cards on the floor. 3. Pick up each card individually, and put the cards back into order. 4. Discuss with the class which process expended more of your energy: changing the cards from an ordered to a disordered state or changing them from a disordered back to an ordered state.

**Results:** The cards will assume a disordered state when dropped to the desk or floor, and energy will be given off in the process (some of it detectable as sound). The energy input involved in placing the cards back into an ordered state will exceed the energy expended when the cards are dropped.

## Answers to Questions

### Page 467

1. **a.** The rate of a reaction is the measure of the number of moles of product formed or of reactant consumed per unit time.
   **b.** One example of a slow reaction is the decomposition of hydrogen peroxide, $H_2O_2$:
   $$2H_2O_2(l) \rightarrow 2H_2O(l) + O_2(g)$$
   An example of a rapid reaction is the precipitation of AgCl from solution when some $AgNO_3$ is added to a solution of NaCl($aq$):
   $$AgNO_3(aq) + NaCl(aq) \rightarrow$$
   $$AgCl(s) + NaNO_3(aq)$$

2. An effective collision between reacting particles is one in which the particles have enough energy and approach each other at the proper angle so that the reactants are converted to products.

3. The four chief factors that affect the rate of a chemical reaction are the nature of the reactant, concentration, temperature, and the presence of catalysts.

### Page 469

4. **a.** Most effective collisions are collisions between two particles. In order for a chemical change to occur, a series of such collisions is usually necessary. Collisions between more than two particles simultaneously are extremely unlikely.
   **b.** A reaction mechanism is the series of steps by which reacting particles are rearranged to form products.

5. **a.** A possible reaction mechanism is:
   $$C + S \rightarrow Int$$
   $$Int + S \rightarrow CS_2$$
   **b.** The same mechanism may *not* fit all reactions of the form $2A + B \rightarrow C$. Other kinds of steps are possible.
   **c.** The only way to determine the mechanism for a reaction is to perform carefully controlled experiments.

### Page 471

6. **a.** In a rapid reaction, the nature of the reactants is such that only a few electrons/bonds must be rearranged in order for the reactants to be converted to products.
   **b.** In a slow reaction, the nature of the reactants is such that many rearrangements of chemical bonds are necessary for conversion of the reactants to products.

7. An increase in temperature increases the average kinetic energy of the reacting particles. This increase in kinetic energy is manifested by an increase in the average speed of the particles, causing them to collide more frequently and with more energy.

8. When the speed of a molecule increases, its kinetic energy increases.

### Page 475

9. A homogeneous reaction system contains one phase. A heterogeneous reaction system contains more than one phase.

10. When the concentration of the reactants increases, the speed of a homogeneous reaction generally increases.

11. When a given mass of iron is broken into small pieces, the iron rusts faster because the increased surface area enables more iron atoms to contact oxygen.

12. **a.** The concentration of two reacting gases can be increased by adding gas or by decreasing the volume of the system.

17

**b.** The concentration of two reacting solutions can be increased by adding solute or by removing some of the solvent.

13. An increase in the concentration of reactants usually causes an increase in the reaction rate because at higher concentrations, collisions will occur more frequently.

14. A catalyst is a substance that speeds up chemical change without itself being permanently changed.

15. When $MnO_2$ is added to $KClO_3$, the thermal decomposition occurs at a lower temperature and at a higher rate. Since the $MnO_2$ is not consumed, it is classified as a catalyst.

**Page 477**

16. The slowest step in a reaction mechanism is the rate-determining step.

17. **a.** An increase in the concentration of $A$ will increase the rate of the first step. This has no effect on the overall rate of reaction since this is a fast step. However, an increase in the concentration of $A$ will also increase the rate of step 2, the rate-determining step. Therefore, increasing the concentration of $A$ will increase the overall reaction rate.

    **b.** An increase in the concentration of $B$ will increase the rate of the first step and will have the same effect as an increase in the concentration of $A$. Therefore, the overall reaction rate will increase.

    **c.** When the concentration of $C$ increases, the rate of reaction is not affected. Substance $C$ is used after the slow step. Substance $C$ is always "waiting" for $Int_2$, the product of the slow step.

18. **a.** A collision between molecules of $A$ and $B$ may be ineffective if the molecules collide at a speed that is too slow (energy too low) or at an unfavorable angle.

    **b.** An activated complex is an unstable molecule or ion that is formed as an intermediate particle in a chemical reaction. It has a chemical formula and distinct geometry (bond lengths and angles).

    **c.** When an activated complex breaks up, it may either re-form the reactants or form the new products.

    **d.** The activation energy is the energy required to form the activated complex.

**Page 479**

19. **a.** In text Figure 17-15, the forward reaction is exothermic. The reverse is endothermic.

    **b.** The energy of activation for the forward reaction, $E_{ACT,FWD}$, is less than the energy of activation for the reverse reaction, $E_{ACT,REV}$.

20. See Figure 17-2.

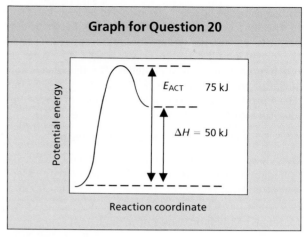

**Graph for Question 20**

Potential energy — Reaction coordinate

$E_{ACT}$   75 kJ

$\Delta H = 50$ kJ

**Figure 17-2**

**Page 481**

21. **a.** The temperature of a system is proportional to its average kinetic energy. Kinetic energy is given by $\frac{1}{2}mv^2$, where $v$ stands for the average velocity of the particles in the system.

    **b.** An increase in temperature causes an increase in the rate of reaction because at higher temperatures collisions between molecules become more frequent and occur with higher energy.

22. See Figure 17-3. At lower temperatures, fewer molecules meet the activation energy requirement; hence, the reaction rate is lower.

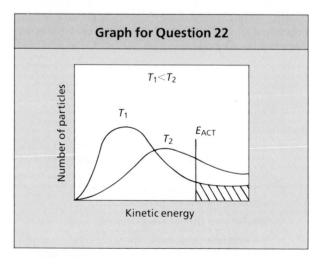

**Graph for Question 22**

Number of particles — Kinetic energy

$T_1 < T_2$

$T_1$   $T_2$   $E_{ACT}$

**Figure 17-3**

23. Molecules with greater average kinetic energy (molecular velocity) can produce an activated complex with greater potential energy because, upon collision, more kinetic energy is available to be converted to potential energy in the activated complex.

## Page 482

**24. a.** The presence of a catalyst lowers the energy of activation, $E_{ACT}$. The catalyst creates a new reaction mechanism that has a lower energy of activation than the non-catalyzed reaction.

**b.** The presence of a catalyst has no effect on the net energy change of a reaction.

**25.** The proposed existence of a "negative catalyst" that produces a reaction mechanism with a higher energy of activation would not account for a decreased reaction rate. If such a negative catalyst were introduced into a system, the reaction would proceed at the original and faster "non-catalyzed" rate; thus, such a "negative catalyst" would have no effect on reaction rate.

## Page 484

**26. a.** The enthalpy or heat content of a substance is the total energy in that substance.

**b.** The symbol $H_{H_2O(s)}$ is used to represent the enthalpy of ice.

**c.** The symbol $\Delta H$ is used to represent the change in enthalpy.

**27. a.** The equation $\Delta H = H_{H_2O(s)} - H_{H_2O(l)}$ represents the change in enthalpy that occurs when water is frozen into ice: $H_2O(l) \rightarrow H_2O(s)$.

**b.** This is a negative change in enthalpy because energy is removed from the system as the ice is formed.

**28.** The SI unit used to measure change in enthalpy is kJ.

## Page 486

**29. a.** The heat of formation, $\Delta H_f$, is the energy change for a reaction in which a compound is formed from its elements.

**b.** The heat of formation is measured in kJ/mol.

**c.** The heat of formation for a substance will change if the reaction is carried out at a different temperature, pressure, or phase.

**30. a.** Standard heat of formation, $\Delta H_f^\circ$, applies to the formation of a compound with reactants and products in their standard states at 298 K and 1 atm (101.3 kPa) of pressure.

**b.** $\Delta H_f^\circ$ for $H_2O(l)$ is $-286$ kJ/mol.

**c.** $\Delta H_f^\circ$ for $H_2O(g)$ is $-242$ kJ/mol. Note that less energy is given off when water is formed in the gas phase.

**d.** $H_2(g) + \frac{1}{2}O_2(g) \rightarrow H_2O(l) + 286$ kJ

**31.** The reaction for the formation of $Al_2O_3$ is given by the equation:
$$2Al(s) + \tfrac{3}{2}O_2(g) \rightarrow Al_2O_3(s) + 1676 \text{ kJ}$$

**32.** $11.5 \text{ g C}_2\text{H}_5\text{OH} \times \dfrac{1 \text{ mol C}_2\text{H}_5\text{OH}}{46.0 \text{ g C}_2\text{H}_5\text{OH}} \times \dfrac{9.50 \times 10^2 \text{ kJ}}{1 \text{ mol C}_2\text{H}_5\text{OH}} =$
$$2.38 \times 10^2 \text{ kJ}$$

**33.** $33.0 \text{ g C}_3\text{H}_8 \times \dfrac{1 \text{ mol C}_3\text{H}_8}{44.0 \text{ g C}_3\text{H}_8} \times \dfrac{-2.22 \times 10^3 \text{ kJ}}{1 \text{ mol C}_3\text{H}_8} =$
$$-1.67 \times 10^3 \text{ kJ}$$

## Page 488

**34.** Compounds with values for $\Delta H_f^\circ$ that are large and negative tend to have high stability.

**35. Stability:**

| | MgO | > | CO$_2$ | > | NH$_3$ | > | NO |
|---|---|---|---|---|---|---|---|
| $\Delta H_f^\circ$: | $-602$ | | $-394$ | | $-46$ | | $+90.4$ |

(in kJ/mol)

This sequence of decreasing relative stability matches the sequence of increasing standard heats of formation.

**36.** A positive value for $\Delta H_f^\circ$ indicates an endothermic reaction.

## Page 491

**37.** The heat of formation for a compound has the opposite sign of its heat of decomposition.

**38.** $\Delta H_{f, HgO(s)}^\circ = -91.0$ kJ/mol

Use the reverse of the given equation to show the formation of 2 mol of HgO. It is an exothermic reaction. Thus, the heat of formation is

$\frac{1}{2} \times -182$ kJ/mol or $-91$ kJ/mol

**39.** $\Delta H_{f, Fe_2O_3(s)}^\circ = -822$ kJ/mol

The equation as written shows the formation of 2 mol of $Fe_2O_3$. Thus the heat of formation is

$\frac{1}{2} \times -1643$ kJ/mol $= -822$ kJ/mol

**40.** Applying Hess's law:

$$\Delta H = [2(\Delta H_{f, HCl}^\circ) + \Delta H_{f, Br_2}^\circ] - [\Delta H_{f, Cl_2}^\circ + 2(\Delta H_{f, HBr}^\circ)]$$
$$= [2(-92.0 \text{ kJ}) + 0 \text{ kJ}] - [0 \text{ kJ} + 2(-36.4 \text{ kJ})]$$
$$= -111 \text{ kJ}$$

**41.** Applying Hess's law:

$$\Delta H = [\Delta H_{f, CHCl_3}^\circ + 3(\Delta H_{f, HCl}^\circ)] - [\Delta H_{f, CH_4}^\circ + 3(\Delta H_{f, Cl_2}^\circ)]$$
$$= [-132 \text{ kJ} + 3(-92.0 \text{ kJ})] - [-74.8 \text{ kJ} + 3(0 \text{ kJ})]$$
$$= -333 \text{ kJ}$$

**42.** Applying Hess's law:

$$\Delta H = -137 \text{ kJ/mol} = [\Delta H_{f, C_2H_6}^\circ] - [\Delta H_{f, C_2H_4}^\circ + \Delta H_{f, H_2}^\circ]$$
$$= [\Delta H_{f, C_2H_6}^\circ] - [52.3 \text{ kJ/mol} + 0 \text{ kJ/mol}]$$
$$\Delta H_{f, C_2H_6}^\circ = -137 \text{ kJ/mol} + 52.3 \text{ kJ/mol}$$
$$= -84.7 \text{ kJ/mol}$$

## Page 496

**43. a.** Compounds with large and negative heats of formation are very stable because the heat of reaction for the reverse reaction (decomposition) is large and positive; thus, the compound is not easily decomposed, because a very large input of energy would be required.

**b.** Chemical reactions tend to move toward the formation of stronger bonds because, once stronger bonds are formed, they are less likely

17

to become broken. In addition, the formation of stronger bonds is accompanied by the release of more energy.

44. **a.** The term *entropy* refers to the randomness or disorder of a system.

  **b.** The evaporation of water is an example of increasing entropy because molecules in the gas phase are more disordered than those in the liquid phase.

  **c.** The decomposition of $MgCO_3$ is an example of increasing entropy because a solid is converted into another solid (MgO) and a gas ($CO_2$).

  **d.** The dissolving of sugar is also an example of increasing entropy because these molecules leave the highly ordered solid crystalline state to become more disordered as dissolved and hydrated molecules.

  **e.** When air is heated, its entropy increases. At a higher temperature, molecular motion, hence disorder, increases.

45. The gases become mixed uniformly because that kind of mixture is the most random mixture possible with those components. The gas molecules move with sufficient velocity and have sufficient open space to permit rapid uniform mixing.

46. Processes with positive $\Delta H$ and negative $\Delta S$ (increase in enthalpy and a decrease in entropy) cannot occur spontaneously.

## Page 500

47. **a.** The Gibbs free energy equation is:
  $\Delta G = \Delta H - T\Delta S$, where
  $\Delta G$ = free energy change
  $\Delta H$ = enthalpy change
  $T$ = temperature (K)
  $\Delta S$ = entropy change

  **b.** The change in free energy is sometimes called the net driving force of a reaction, because it gives the combined effect of changes in enthalpy and entropy.

  **c.** negative values

48. **Algebraic signs**

| | $\Delta H$ | $-T\Delta S$ |
|---|---|---|
| **a.** | − | − |
| **b.** | − | + |
| **c.** | + | − |

49. **a.** The effectiveness of changes in entropy depends on temperature, because the effect of entropy changes on $\Delta G$ is given by the term $T\Delta S$ in the Gibbs equation.

  **b.** Mercury combines with oxygen at temperatures below 400°C but not at higher temperatures. For the reaction
  $Hg(l) + \frac{1}{2}O_2(g) \rightarrow HgO(s)$
  both $\Delta H$ and $\Delta S$ are negative. In terms of the

Gibbs equation, $\Delta G = \Delta H - T\Delta S$, at high temperatures, the unfavorable $\Delta S$ effect predominates and $\Delta G$ becomes positive. At lower temperatures, the favorable (negative) $\Delta H$ effect predominates, $\Delta G$ is negative, and the reaction can proceed. $\Delta S$ is unfavorable because HgO($s$) has less entropy than Hg($l$) and $O_2(g)$.

## Page 504

50. **a.** A sample of ice melts at temperatures of more than 273 K. $\Delta H$ and $\Delta S$ are both positive for this change. $\Delta G$ can be negative only when the temperature is high enough to cause the favorable entropy effect to predominate over the unfavorable enthalpy effect. The temperature is high enough at 273 K and above. Thus, ice melts only at temperatures above 273 K.

  **b.** For the freezing of water, both $\Delta H$ and $\Delta S$ are negative. At higher temperatures, the unfavorable entropy effect predominates, $\Delta G$ is positive, and the change does not occur. At a low enough temperature, the favorable enthalpy effect can predominate and water can freeze. Thus, $\Delta G$ is negative and the freezing of water can occur only when the temperature is 273 K or lower.

51. $\Delta G = [\Delta G^\circ_{f,\,C_2H_4Cl_2} + 2(\Delta G^\circ_{f,\,HCl})] -$
$$[\Delta G^\circ_{f,\,C_2H_6} + 2(\Delta G^\circ_{f,\,Cl_2})]$$
$= [-80.3 \text{ kJ} + 2(-95.2 \text{ kJ})] -$
$$[-32.9 \text{ kJ} + 2(0 \text{ kJ})]$$
$= -238 \text{ kJ}$

52. $\Delta G = [2(\Delta G^\circ_{f,\,Fe}) + 3(\Delta G^\circ_{f,\,CO_2})] -$
$$[\Delta G^\circ_{f,\,Fe_2O_3} + 3(\Delta G^\circ_{f,\,CO})]$$
$-31.3 \text{ kJ/mol} = [2(0 \text{ kJ/mol}) + 3(-394 \text{ kJ/mol})] -$
$$[\Delta G^\circ_{f,\,Fe_2O_3} + 3(-137 \text{ kJ/mol})]$$
$\Delta G^\circ_{f,\,Fe_2O_3} = -742 \text{ kJ/mol}$

53. $\Delta H = 2 \times \Delta H^\circ_f = -870 \text{ kJ}$
  $\Delta G = 2 \times \Delta G^\circ_f = -818 \text{ kJ}$
  $\Delta G = \Delta H - T\Delta S$
  $-818 \text{ kJ} = -870 \text{ kJ} - 298 \text{ K}(\Delta S)$
  $\Delta S = -\dfrac{52 \text{ kJ}}{298 \text{ K}} = -0.17 \text{ kJ/K}$

54. $\Delta H = -2218 \text{ kJ}$
  $\Delta S = 0.101 \text{ kJ/K}$
  $\Delta G = \Delta H - T\Delta S$
  $= -2218 \text{ kJ} - 298 \text{ K}(0.101 \text{ kJ/K})$
  $= -2248 \text{ kJ}$

55. **a.** At 298 K:
  $\Delta G = \Delta H - T\Delta S$
  $-50.2 \text{ kJ} = -92.0 \text{ kJ} - 298 \text{ K}(\Delta S)$
  $\Delta S = -\dfrac{41.8 \text{ kJ}}{298 \text{ K}} = -0.140 \text{ kJ/K}$

**b.** At 500 K:

$$\Delta G = \Delta H - T\Delta S$$
$$= -92.0 \text{ kJ} - 500 \text{ K}(-0.140 \text{ kJ/K})$$
$$= -22.0 \text{ kJ}$$

### Page 505, A Glowing Platinum Wire

When the hot platinum is lowered into the beaker, contact is made between the platinum metal and methyl alcohol vapor from the liquid. The platinum is a catalyst for the formation of formaldehyde and hydrogen gas from methyl alcohol. Since the reaction is exothermic, the released heat keeps the platinum wire hot for as long as the platinum is close enough to the methyl alcohol for the reaction to continue vigorously.

## Chapter Review     17

### Page 507, Content Review

1. Kinetics is the study of rates and mechanisms of chemical reactions. Thermodynamics is the study of changes in energy in chemical reactions and the influence of temperature on those changes.

2. According to the collision theory of reaction, molecules must collide in order for chemical change to occur. The colliding particles must meet at the proper angles and have sufficient energy.

3. In a chemical reaction, the rate of reaction depends on the *frequency* of collisions and the *effectiveness* of them.

4. The probable steps are: $Br_2 \rightarrow 2Br$; $Br + H_2 \rightarrow HBr + H$; $Br_2 + H \rightarrow HBr + Br$. In this chain mechanism, the second and third steps are repeated until they are terminated by the combination of single atoms to form $H_2$ or $Br_2$.

5. An ionic replacement reaction generally occurs faster than a molecular rearrangement reaction, which requires breaking bonds.

6. Compared to 0°C, a reaction at 10°C would be twice as fast, at 20°C it would be four times as fast, and at 30°C it would be eight times as fast.

7. A mixture of hydrogen and chlorine will react faster if the volume is decreased, because smaller spaces between molecules result in more frequent collisions.

8. For a system in which all of the reactants are gases, increased pressure increases the rate of reaction because smaller spaces between molecules result in more frequent collisions.

9. A catalyst speeds up a reaction without itself being permanently altered. An inhibitor slows down a reaction by "tying up" reactants in other side reactions.

10. In the decomposition of $H_2O_2$, **a.** $IO^-$ behaves as an activated complex and **b.** $I^-$ acts as a catalyst.

11. Activation energy is the minimum amount of energy needed to form the activated complex.

12. The rate-determining step is taking orders and making change, so two employees should be assigned to this step. (This assumes that an employee can do only one step.)

13. The reaction shown is endothermic. **a.** 2 is the activation energy; **b.** 1 is the potential energy of the reactant; **c.** 3 is the potential energy of the activated complex.

14. An increase in temperature increases the kinetic energy of the molecules. This enables the reactants to acquire the activation energy to form the activated complex. Also, with this increase in energy, a greater percentage of the activated complex units will change to the products instead of returning to the form of the reactants.

15. **a.** A catalyst changes the reaction mechanism of a reaction.
    **b.** This change decreases the activation energies of the steps in the mechanism.
    **c.** The net energy change represents the difference between the potential energies of the reactants and the products of the reaction. This is the same whether a catalyst is used or not.

16. **a.** $\Delta H$ is negative in an exothermic reaction.
    **b.** $\Delta H$ is positive in an endothermic reaction.

17. The heat of reaction is usually measured in kilojoules.

18. Formula mass of NaCl = 22.99 + 35.45 = 58.44 g/mol

    $n$NaCl = 14.4 g ÷ 58.44 g/mol = 0.246 mol

    $\Delta H_f^\circ = -411$ kJ/mol (from text Figure 17-22)
    Therefore, $\Delta H$ = (0.246 mol)(−411 kJ/mol) = −101 kJ

19. −892 kJ/mol ÷ 16.0 g/mol = −55.75 kJ/g, so 55.8 kJ of heat is given off.

20. **a.** NO is the least stable of the compounds in text Figure 17-22.
    **b.** $Al_2O_3$ is the most stable.

21. −132 kJ/mol − (−75.0 kJ/mol) = −57.0 kJ

22. −636.5 kJ + (−394.1 kJ) − (−1208 kJ) = 177.4 kJ

23. $4(-394.1 \text{ kJ}) + 2(-286.2 \text{ kJ}) - 2(\Delta H_{f, \ C_2H_2}) = -2604 \text{ kJ}$

$\Delta H_f$ of $C_2H_2$ = 227.6 kJ/mol

24. Chemical changes tend to proceed spontaneously from systems of higher energy to those of lower energy. In releasing energy, exothermic reactions produce substances with lower potential energy.

25. The oxidation of mercury is spontaneous at temperatures below 400°C but not above this temperature.

26. **a.** When an explosive detonates, entropy increases. The rise in temperature and the change of a solid to a gas produce less restriction on molecular arrangements, resulting in less organization and greater disorder.
    **b.** When a sugar solution is separated, entropy decreases. Sugar molecules in solution have greater randomness in motion. Solid sugar has an ordered molecular arrangement.
    **c.** When a gas expands into a vacuum, entropy increases. The molecules have more space in which to move.
    **d.** When $NO_2$ decomposes into NO and $O_2$, entropy increases. Each of the products has a simpler structure than $NO_2$.
    **e.** When $H_2$ and $O_2$ combine to form liquid water, entropy decreases. The motion of the molecules is more restricted in a liquid than in a gas, and the atoms of hydrogen and oxygen are restricted in a molecule of greater complexity.
    **f.** When water is heated from 20°C to 50°C, entropy increases. The increase in molecular velocities increases random motion and disorder.

27. Potassium nitrate dissolves in water, even though $\Delta H$ for this reaction is positive, because the increase in entropy when KOH separates into ions is sufficient to counteract the unfavorable change in enthalpy.

28. An endothermic reaction may occur spontaneously if $\Delta S$ is positive and favors the reaction enough to counteract the effect of $\Delta H$ being positive.

29. The decomposition of $KClO_3$ into KCl and $O_2$ is endothermic; $\Delta H$ is positive. The entropy change is positive; that is, entropy increases and favors the reaction. At temperatures above 370°C the $-T\Delta S$ term has a large enough negative value that the free energy change becomes negative in spite of the unfavorable $\Delta H$. At temperatures below 370°C, the $-T\Delta S$ term is not negative enough to overcome the positive $\Delta H$.

30. Water is in a higher entropy state as a liquid than as a solid. Ice has a rigid, orderly array, but liquid water has random molecular arrangements. Therefore when ice melts, $\Delta S$ is positive. As the change is endothermic, $\Delta H$ is also positive. $\Delta G$ must be negative because the change is spontaneous. Despite the positive $\Delta H$, the value of the $-T\Delta S$ term is sufficiently negative to make $\Delta G$ negative.

31. **a.** $\Delta G$ = 3(−395 kJ/mol) − (−742 kJ/mol) − 3(−137 kJ/mol) = −32.0 kJ/mol
    **b.** Before the reaction can proceed spontaneously at 298 K, the activation energy must be supplied.

## Page 509, Content Mastery

32. Hydrochloric acid and zinc react more slowly if the acid is dilute, because in the more dilute acid there is a lower concentration of dissolved hydrogen chloride and, therefore, of reacting hydrogen ions.

33. Hydrochloric acid reacts faster with sodium hydroxide than with ethyl alcohol because sodium hydroxide is an ionic solid and ethyl alcohol is covalent. In solution, sodium ions and hydroxide ions separate and move about rapidly, causing frequent and effective collisions. Breaking the covalent bonds in ethyl alcohol requires energy, resulting in a slower reaction.

34. **a.** $\Delta G$ = −125.7 kJ − 298 K(−0.34 kJ/K) = −24 kJ
    **b.** $\Delta G$ = −125.7 kJ − 500 K(−0.34 kJ/K) = +44.3 kJ; not spontaneous at 500 K

35. Atomic mass of Al = 27.0 u; mass of 2 mol = 54.0 g
    Energy = (6.75 g ÷ 54.0 g) × 1670 kJ = 209 kJ

36. The change in heat content values, $\Delta H$, is used instead of total heat content because it is not possible to measure or calculate all of the potential and kinetic components that are incorporated into heat content.

37. **a.** For $\Delta G° < 0$, a spontaneous reaction is favored.
    **b.** For $\Delta G° = 0$, the system is in equilibrium.
    **c.** For $\Delta G° > 0$, a spontaneous reaction is not favored.

38. From text Figure 17-22 we get:
    (1) $\frac{1}{2}N_2(g) + \frac{1}{2}O_2(g) \rightarrow NO(g)$: $\Delta H$ = +90.4 kJ/mol
    (2) $\frac{1}{2}N_2(g) + O_2(g) \rightarrow NO_2(g)$: $\Delta H$ = +33.1 kJ/mol
    Rewriting equation (1) in reverse order yields
    (3) $NO(g) \rightarrow \frac{1}{2}N_2(g) + \frac{1}{2}O_2(g)$: $\Delta H$ = −90.4 kJ/mol
    Add the equations (2) and (3), cancel, and use Hess's law:
    $NO(g) + \frac{1}{2}O_2(g) \rightarrow NO_2(g)$: $\Delta H$ = −57.3 kJ/mol

39. No, it is not possible to determine the mechanism of a chemical reaction by looking at the net equation, because there may be numerous intermediate steps that cancel in the net equation.

**40.** From text Figure 17-22; $\Delta H$ for the reaction is $-1676$ kJ/mol. From text Figure 17-36, $\Delta G$ for the reaction is $-1577$ kJ/mol.
$\Delta G = \Delta H - T\Delta S$ and $T = 298$ K so
$\Delta S = (\Delta G - \Delta H) \div 298$
$\Delta S = [-1577 - (-1675)] \div 298 = -0.33$ kJ/K

**41.** From text Figure 17-22 we get:
(1) $\frac{1}{2}N_2(g) + \frac{3}{2}H_2(g) \rightarrow NH_3(g)$: $\Delta H = -46.0$ kJ/mol
(2) $\frac{1}{2}N_2(g) + O_2(g) \rightarrow NO_2(g)$: $\Delta H = +33.1$ kJ/mol
(3) $H_2(g) + \frac{1}{2}O_2(g) \rightarrow H_2O(g)$: $\Delta H = -242$ kJ/mol
Rewriting equation (1) in reverse order yields:
(4) $NH_3(g) \rightarrow \frac{1}{2}N_2(g) + \frac{3}{2}H_2(g)$: $\Delta H = +46.0$ kJ/mol
To get 4 $NH_3$ molecules, multiply equation (4) by 4:
(5) $4NH_3(g) \rightarrow 2N_2(g) + 6H_2(g)$: $\Delta H = +184.0$ kJ/mol
To get 4 $NO_2$ molecules, multiply equation (2) by 4:
(6) $2N_2(g) + 4O_2(g) \rightarrow 4NO_2(g)$: $\Delta H = +132.4$ kJ/mol
To get 6 $H_2O$ molecules, multiply equation (3) by 6:
(7) $6H_2(g) + 3O_2(g) \rightarrow 6H_2O(g)$: $\Delta H = -1452$ kJ/mol
Add equations (5) + (6) + (7), cancel, and use Hess's law:
$4NH_3(g) + 7O_2(g) \rightarrow 4NO_2(g) + 6H_2O(g)$:
$$\Delta H = -1136 \text{ kJ}$$

**42.** From text Figure 17-36 we get:
(1) $C(s) + O_2(g) \rightarrow CO_2(g)$: $\Delta G° = -395$ kJ/mol
(2) $C(s) + \frac{1}{2}O_2(g) \rightarrow CO(g)$: $\Delta G° = -137$ kJ/mol
Rewriting equation (2) in reverse order:
(3) $CO(g) \rightarrow C(s) + \frac{1}{2}O_2(g)$: $\Delta G° = +137$ kJ/mol
Add equations (1) and (3), cancel, and use Hess's law:
$CO(g) + \frac{1}{2}O_2(g) \rightarrow CO_2(g)$: $\Delta G° = -258$ kJ/mol

**43.** The rate of a reaction can generally be increased by increasing the temperature, increasing the concentration, or adding a catalyst.

**44.** A catalyst does not affect $\Delta H$.

**45.** From $\Delta G = \Delta H - T\Delta S$ we see that when $\Delta H$ and $\Delta S$ "oppose" each other (have the same sign), $\Delta H$ generally prevails at very high temperatures and $\Delta S$ at low temperatures. A spontaneous reaction is favored if $\Delta G$ is negative.

| $\Delta H$ | $\Delta S$ | Temperature | Favors spontaneous reaction? |
|---|---|---|---|
| + | − | high | no |
| + | − | low | no |
| − | + | high | yes |
| − | + | low | yes |
| + | + | high | yes |
| + | + | low | no |
| − | − | high | no |
| − | − | low | yes |

**46. Concept:** *In an endothermic reaction, heat must continuously be supplied for the reaction to continue.*
**Solution:** Although heat must be supplied to start a candle burning, the heat produced by the reaction will keep the reaction going. As the net effect is the evolution of heat, the reaction is exothermic.

**47. Concept:** *A constant temperature gives no indication of whether a reaction is endothermic or exothermic.*
**Solution:** The temperature of the Bunsen burner flame is constant because the burning gases are released into the air at a constant rate. The reaction is continuously giving off heat and is exothermic.

**48. Concept:** *The overall reaction is the sum of the reactions in the reaction mechanism.*
**Solution:** The overall reaction is $A_2(g) + C_2(g) \rightarrow 2AC(g)$.

**49. Concept:** *Reaction rates can be increased by changing the concentration of substances.*
**Solution:** Adding $A_2$ will not increase the overall reaction rate because $A_2$ reacts in a fast reaction. B is a solid, so its concentration would not be increased; therefore, adding B will probably not help unless it is finely divided. Adding $C_2$ would probably have the greatest effect. $C_2$ is a gas, so adding $C_2$ would increase the pressure. The reaction in which $C_2$ is used is slow, so it would be speeded up. Because there is another slow reaction in the mechanism, however, one cannot be sure that the overall reaction would be speeded up.

**50. Concept:** *A catalyst takes part in a reaction but is not used up.*
**Solution:** B is a catalyst. It is regenerated in the reaction and undergoes no permanent change.

**51. c.** $25.0 \text{ g AgNO}_3 \times \dfrac{1 \text{ mol AgNO}_3}{170 \text{ g AgNO}_3} \times \dfrac{2 \text{ mol AgCl}}{2 \text{ mol AgNO}_3} \times \dfrac{143 \text{ g AgCl}}{1 \text{ mol AgCl}} = 21.0 \text{ g}$

**52. c.** A bond between phosphorus and oxygen would be polar covalent.

17

**53. a.** $PH_3$ is a polar molecule.

**54. c.** $\dfrac{6.0 \text{ g C}}{12.0 \text{ g/mol}} = 0.5 \text{ mol C}; \dfrac{1.0 \text{ g H}}{1.0 \text{ g/mol}} = 1.0 \text{ mol H}$

C:H = 0.5:1.0 = 1:2, empirical formula $CH_2$.

**55. d.** Mg forms $Mg^{2+}$ ions, has a low ionization energy, and is in the same period as chlorine.

**56. a.** $MgCl_2$

:Cl:
:Mg → $[Mg]^{2+}$ $[:\!\ddot{C}l\!:]^{1-}$
.Cl: $[:\!\ddot{C}l\!:]^{1-}$

**b.** HCl H:Cl:

**d.** CO :C:::O:

**c.** $NH_3$ H:N:H
H

**e.** $O_2$ :O::O:

**57.** Water has very strong hydrogen bonding between molecules because the molecules are very polar.

**58. a.** No, only about 48 g of $KNO_3$ will dissolve in 100 g of water at 30°C.

**b.** The solution would be saturated at about 48°C.

**c.** At 60°C, 112 g will dissolve, so an additional 112 g − 80 g = 32 g must be added.

**59.** $10.0 \text{ g KClO}_3 \times \dfrac{1 \text{ mol KClO}_3}{122 \text{ g KClO}_3} \times \dfrac{3 \text{ mol O}_2}{2 \text{ mol KClO}_3} \times$

$\dfrac{22.4 \text{ dm}^3}{1 \text{ mol O}_2} \times \dfrac{293}{273} \times \dfrac{101.3 \text{ kPa}}{103.5 \text{ kPa}} = 2.89 \text{ dm}^3$

**60.** An ionic solid dissolves in water, is hard, conducts electricity when melted or in solution, and has a high melting point. A molecular solid is insoluble or slightly soluble in water, is relatively soft, does not conduct, and has a relatively low melting point.

## Page 510, Critical Thinking

**61.** The constant manufacture of enzymes by organisms is not necessary because enzymes are catalysts and are not used up during the reactions they catalyze.

**62.** Chemists must indicate the phase of a compound when they give its $\Delta H_f^\circ$ because it takes energy to melt a compound from solid to liquid, so the standard heat of formation is less for a solid than for a liquid.

**63.** Hess's law allows chemists to calculate the enthalpy of any reaction from known heats of formation, so they do not have to measure each unknown enthalpy experimentally.

**64. a. and b.** Melting ice and evaporating water show an increase in entropy because water molecules have more freedom of motion in the liquid phase than in the solid phase, and more in the gas phase than in the liquid phase.

**c.** A crowd of people forming a line represents an increase in order, or a decrease in entropy.

**d.** The periodic table has more order, or less entropy, than a random list of elements.

**e.** Mixing any materials, such as NaCl solution and water, represents an increase in entropy.

**65.** Sugar is oxidized in the body at a much lower temperature than is necessary outside the body because enzymes are used in the body to lower the activation energy of the reaction.

## Page 511, Challenge Problems

**66.** Because changing the concentration of a reactant in the rate-determining step affects the overall rate of reaction, the rate-determining step can be identified by changing the concentrations of A (or B), D, and Y, one at a time. If changing the concentration of A changes the reaction rate, then the first step is the rate-determining step, and so on.

**67. a.** For the entire reaction,
$\Delta H = 200 \text{ kJ} - 320 \text{ kJ} = -120 \text{ kJ}$

**b.** The rate-determining step for this three-step reaction is the one with the highest activation energy, step 1.

**c.** $E_{ACT}$ for the rate-determining step is 80 kJ.

**d.** $E_{ACT}$ for the reverse direction of the rate-determining step is 120 kJ.

**e.** $\Delta H$ for the entire reaction in the reverse direction is +120 kJ.

# Chemical Equilibrium

## Chapter Planning Guide

| Text Section | Labs (Lab Manual) and Demonstrations (TE) | Supplementary Materials (Teacher's Resource Book) |
|---|---|---|
| **18-1** Reversible Reactions, pp. 513-514 <br><br> **18-2** Characteristics of an Equilibrium, pp. 514-516 | | Concept Mastery: Characteristics of Equilibrium, p. CM-31 |
| **18-3** The Mass-Action Expression, pp. 516-517 | | |
| **18-4** The Equilibrium Constant, pp. 518-521 | | Transparency Master: Starting and Equilibrium Concentrations for the Reaction Between Hydrogen and Iodine at 490°C, p. 18-3 <br> Transparency Master: The Significance of the Relative Length of Double Arrows, p. 18-4 |
| **18-5** Applications of $K_{eq}$, pp. 521-523 | | |
| **Biography** Luis W. Alvarez, p. 524 <br><br> **18-6** Effects of Stresses on Systems at Equilibrium: Le Chatelier's Principle, pp. 524-527 | Demo 18-1: The Effect of Concentration on Equilibrium, p. TG-267 <br> Lab 34: Chemical Equilibrium and Le Chatelier's Principle | Societal Issues: Chelation Therapy, p. SI-35 |
| **18-7** The Role of the Equilibrium Constant, pp. 527-529 | | |
| **18-8** Le Chatelier's Principle: Changing Temperature or Pressure, Adding a Catalyst, pp. 529-531 <br><br> **Application** The Haber Process, pp. 531-532 | Demo 18-2: The Effect of Temperature on Equilibrium, p. TG-268 | Review Activity: Le Chatelier's Principle, p. 18-10 <br> Concept Mastery: Changing the Equilibrium, p. CM-32 <br> Critical and Creative Thinking: Causal Explanation, p. CCT-39 <br> Computer Experiment: The Industrial Synthesis of Ammonia, p. 18-7 |

18

| Text Section | Labs (Lab Manual) and Demonstrations (TE) | Supplementary Materials (Teacher's Resource Book) |
|---|---|---|
| **18-9** Solubility Equilibrium, pp. 533-537 | Lab 35: Solubility Product Constant | Transparency Master: Solubility Equilibrium in a Saturated Solution of AgCl, p. 18-5<br>Transparency Master: Selected Solubility Product Constants, $K_{sp}$, at Room Temperature, p. 18-6<br>Review Activity: Equilibrium, p. 18-11 |
| **18-10** The Common-Ion Effect, pp. 538-539 | | Practice Problems, p. 18-12 |
| **Can You Explain This?** Expanding Balloons, p. 539 | | |
| | | Test—Form A, p. AT-68<br>Alternate Test—Form B, p. BT-68 |

☐ Core     ☐ Advanced     ☐ Optional

## Chapter Overview

In this chapter we explain how to recognize equilibrium systems and how to account for the behavior of a system at equilibrium. The mass-action expression and its numerical value at equilibrium, the equilibrium constant, are derived, interpreted, and used in solving problems. Next, three types of stresses that can disturb equilibrium are discussed: a change in concentration of reactants or products, a change in temperature, and a change in pressure. The effects of these stresses on a system at equilibrium are described in terms of the rates of opposing reactions, of the mass-action expression, and of Le Chatelier's principle. The chapter ends with a discussion on solubility equilibrium. The solubility product constant, $K_{sp}$, is defined. Attention is given to methods of calculating $K_{sp}$ from the given concentrations and calculating concentrations when $K_{sp}$ and other information are given.

## Chapter Objectives

After students have completed this chapter, they will be able to:
1. Distinguish between a reversible reaction that is in equilibrium and one that is not.     *18-1* and *18-2*
2. Derive mass-action expressions.     *18-3*

3. Calculate equilibrium constants and apply them to reversible reactions.     *18-4, 18-5,* and *18-7*
4. Explain and apply Le Chatelier's principle.     *18-6, 18-8,* and *18-10*
5. Derive solubility product expressions.     *18-9*
6. Determine solubilities from solubility products. *18-9*
7. Calculate solubility products from solubilities. *18-9*

## Teaching Suggestions

### 18-1 Reversible Reactions, pp. 513-514, and

### 18-2 Characteristics of an Equilibrium, pp. 514-516

| Planning Guide | |
|---|---|
| Labs (Lab Manual) and Demonstrations (TE) | Supplementary Materials (Teacher's Resource Book) |
| | Concept Mastery: Characteristics of Equilibrium, p. CM-31 |

■ Define reversible reaction. Refer to text Figure 18-1, which illustrates an interesting example of a reversible reaction, the reaction between hydrogen gas and iron oxide. Use this example to emphasize that when two reactions in the same reaction vessel are in opposition, they approach a state of equilibrium. Emphasize that an equilibrium is a dynamic state in which microscopic changes are occurring even though there are no macroscopic changes in the system. Refer to Equation 3 in the text and point out that the double arrow is the customary way to indicate a reversible reaction when writing an equation for one.

■ Distinguish between a physical equilibrium and a chemical equilibrium. Point out that although an equal sign is sometimes used in place of the double arrow, it is misleading. Emphasize that the reactants do not equal the products. Nor does the mass of the reactants equal the mass of the products. What is equal at equilibrium are the rates of the opposing reactions. Discuss text Figure 18-2. The concept of equal and opposing rates is one of the major principles of this chapter.

■ **Concept Mastery.** Students often fail to understand the distinction between a steady state situation and a system at equilibrium. You may want to discuss Concept Mastery question 37 (chapter-end question) to check your students' understanding of the difference between these two very important concepts.

Students often think that nothing happens once a solution has reached equilibrium, or that the equilibrium concentrations of the reactants equal the equilibrium concentrations of the products. The Concept Mastery worksheet "Characteristics of Equilibrium" (TRB) addresses these student misconceptions by clarifying what is happening at the molecular level.

## 18-3 The Mass-Action Expression, pp. 516-517

■ Point out that the mass-action expression can be used to describe any chemical system. However, chemists most often use it to describe systems at equilibrium. Be sure that students can formulate mass-action expressions for many different chemical reactions.

## 18-4 The Equilibrium Constant, pp. 518-521

| Planning Guide | |
|---|---|
| Labs (Lab Manual) and Demonstrations (TE) | Supplementary Materials (Teacher's Resource Book) |
| | Transparency Master: Starting and Equilibrium Concentrations for the Reaction Between Hydrogen and Iodine at 490°C, p. 18-3 |
| | Transparency Master: The Significance of the Relative Length of Double Arrows, p. 18-4 |

■ A very effective way to illustrate the significance of the equilibrium constant ($K_{eq}$) is to walk the students through a series of experiments related to a reversible reaction. Use the Transparency Master "Starting and Equilibrium Concentrations for the Reaction Between Hydrogen and Iodine at 490°C," which summarizes the series of experiments discussed in the text. Emphasize the effect of temperature on $K_{eq}$. Once students understand how the equilibrium constant is derived, refer to text Figure 18-6 and discuss the significance of the magnitude of the equilibrium constant. Point out that a large $K_{eq}$ favors formation of products, and a small $K_{eq}$ favors formation of reactants.

## 18-5 Applications of $K_{eq}$, pp. 521-523

■ This section focuses on solving problems related to the equilibrium constant. Discuss Sample Problem 2 in which $K_{eq}$ is calculated from the given equilibrium concentrations of all reactants and products. In Sample Problem 3, $K_{eq}$ is given along with the equilibrium concentrations of the reactants and only one of the products. From this information, students are asked to calculate the equilibrium concentration of the unknown product. Sample Problem 4 is a more difficult problem to solve and may require more discussion. In this problem, the students are asked to calculate $K_{eq}$ from the starting concentration of the only reactant. The equilibrium concentrations of the reactant and product must be determined in order to solve this problem. The tabular format for problem solving, shown in Sample Problem 4, is an especially useful way to keep track of changes in the system based upon the principles of equilibrium. Encourage your students to set up a similar table when solving this type of problem.

■ **Concept Mastery.** You may want to use an analogy which is unrelated to chemistry to give your students a better mental picture of what is involved in an equilibrium situation. This will help them to solve problems related to chemical equilibrium. Consider using the following analogy. A store opens at 9:00 a.m. You focus your attention on the revolving door at the entrance. As the store opens, there is a higher concentration of people outside the store waiting to get in. As people start going into the store, the concentration of people in the store is building up. At some point, a number of people, equal to the number who are entering, begin leaving the store. The concentration of people inside the store, therefore, remains constant. So is the concentration of people outside the store. These two concentrations are not equal. This analogy can be extended to the discussion of Le Chatelier's principle, later in this chapter. Consider what happens when the concentration inside the store increases because of a sale. What would happen if a fire broke out in the store? To check your students' understanding of this very important concept, assign Concept Mastery questions 38 through 40 (chapter-end questions).

**18**

## 18-6 Effects of Stresses on Systems at Equilibrium: Le Chatelier's Principle, pp. 524-527, and

## 18-7 The Role of the Equilibrium Constant, pp. 527-529

| Planning Guide | |
|---|---|
| Labs (Lab Manual) and Demonstrations (TE) | Supplementary Materials (Teacher's Resource Book) |
| Demo 18-1: The Effect of Concentration on Equilibrium, p. TG-267 Lab 34: Chemical Equilibrium and Le Chatelier's Principle | Societal Issues: Chelation Therapy, p. SI-35 |

■ List the possible stresses that can disturb a system at equilibrium:
1. A change in concentration of the reactants or products
2. A change in the temperature of the system
3. A change in pressure for a system involving a gas
The effects of temperature and pressure are discussed in more detail in Section 18-8. Do Demonstration 18-1, "The Effect of Concentration on Equilibrium," to demonstrate that concentration does affect the equilibrium of a system.

   Discuss the effects of a change in concentration in terms of the rates of the opposing reactions. Point out that any stress that affects the equilibrium changes the rate of one of the reactions more than that of the other. Explain that when the temperature is held constant, the effects of changes in concentration can be derived from the mass-action expression. If the rates of the reactions change, the concentrations of the components of the system change as the system approaches a new equilibrium. The value of $K_{eq}$ remains constant as long as the temperature does not change.

   Emphasize the usefulness of Le Chatelier's principle in predicting the effect of changes in concentration on equilibrium. Ask the students to predict the effect of changes in concentration on the following systems:

### System 1

$$CO(g) + Cl_2(g) \rightleftharpoons COCl_2(g) + heat$$

| Stress | Shift in Equilibrium |
|---|---|
| 1. Add $Cl_2$ | $\rightarrow$ |
| 2. Remove CO | $\leftarrow$ |
| 3. Add $COCl_2$ | $\leftarrow$ |

### System 2

$$H_2O(g) + CO(g) \rightleftharpoons H_2(g) + CO_2(g) + heat$$

| Stress | Shift in Equilibrium |
|---|---|
| 1. Add $H_2$ | $\leftarrow$ |
| 2. Remove CO | $\leftarrow$ |
| 3. Add $H_2O$ | $\rightarrow$ |

■ Assign Laboratory 34, "Chemical Equilibrium and Le Chatelier's Principle." In this lab students investigate two equilibrium systems and their response to a stress created by a change in concentration.
■ Show the students how the mass-action expression can be used to predict the effect of a change in concentration. Emphasize that the equilibrium shifts in order to keep the value of the equilibrium constant from changing. Be sure that students understand the logic of the solution to Sample Problem 5.
■ **Application.** You may want to tell your students that the ability of hemoglobin to pick up oxygen in the lungs is based on an equilibrium reaction.

oxygen + hemoglobin $\rightleftharpoons$ oxyhemoglobin

The high concentration of oxygen in the lungs favors the formation of oxyhemoglobin. This is just what would be predicted from Le Chatelier's principle.

## 18-8 Le Chatelier's Principle: Changing Temperature or Pressure, Adding a Catalyst, pp. 529-531

| Planning Guide | |
|---|---|
| Labs (Lab Manual) and Demonstrations (TE) | Supplementary Materials (Teacher's Resource Book) |
| Demo 18-2: The Effect of Temperature on Equilibrium, p. TG-268 | Review Activity: Le Chatelier's Principle, p. 18-10 Computer Experiment: The Industrial Synthesis of Ammonia, p. 18-7 Concept Mastery: Changing the Equilibrium, p. CM-32 Critical and Creative Thinking: Causal Explanation, p. CCT-39 |

■ Extend the use of Le Chatelier's principle to include the effects of changing temperature or pressure. Do Demonstration 18-2, "The Effect of Temperature on Equilibrium," to show students that temperature changes can shift the equilibrium of a system. Explain that to predict the effect of temperature changes you must know whether the forward reaction is endothermic or exothermic. Discuss the effects of a temperature increase and decrease on an exothermic reaction. Ask the students to predict the effect of a temperature increase and decrease on an endothermic reaction.
■ Point out that a change in pressure can also affect a system at equilibrium. This change is negligible when

solids and liquids make up the system, but it is significant when gases are involved. Ask the students to predict the effect of changes in pressure on the following systems (Systems 3 and 4):

**System 3**

$$CO(g) + Cl_2(g) \rightleftharpoons COCl_2(g) + \text{heat}$$

| Stress | Shift in Equilibrium |
|---|---|
| 1. Increase pressure | $\rightarrow$ |
| 2. Decrease pressure | $\leftarrow$ |

**System 4**

$$N_2O_4(g) + \text{heat} \rightleftharpoons 2NO_2(g)$$

| Stress | Shift in Equilibrium |
|---|---|
| 1. Increase pressure | $\leftarrow$ |
| 2. Decrease pressure | $\rightarrow$ |

■ Explain why the addition of a catalyst has no effect on a system at equilibrium.
■ Point out the effect of temperature changes on the value of $K_{eq}$. For an exothermic reaction, the value of $K_{eq}$ generally decreases as temperature increases. For an endothermic reaction, the value of $K_{eq}$ generally increases as temperature increases.
■ **Concept Mastery.** The concept Mastery worksheet "Changing the Equilibrium" (TRB) can help students to visualize what happens at the molecular level when the equilibrium is altered by changes in concentration, pressure, or temperature. It also addresses the typical student misconception that the ratio of equation coefficients equals the ratio of equilibrium concentrations.
■ **Critical Thinking.** In the Critical and Creative Thinking worksheet "Causal Explanation" students explore the possible causes of a decrease in ammonia output at an ammonia-processing plant. This skill, fundamental to scientific inquiry, requires students to generate possible explanations and then to decide which of these are the most likely possiblilities.

### 18-9 Solubility Equilibrium, pp. 533-537

| Planning Guide | |
|---|---|
| **Labs (Lab Manual) and Demonstrations (TE)** | **Supplementary Materials (Teacher's Resource Book)** |
| Lab 35: Solubility Product Constant | Transparency Master: Solubility Equilibrium in a Saturated Solution of AgCl, p. 18-5 Transparency Master: Selected Solubility Product Constants, $K_{sp}$, at Room Temperature, p. 18-6 Review Activity: Equilibrium, p. 18-11 |

■ Emphasize that a solubility equilibrium is also a system with a forward and reverse reaction. Point out that the chemical equation is generally written as a dissolving reaction, implying the stirring of the solid phase into a liquid. Define $K_{sp}$ and compare it to $K_{eq}$.
■ Discuss Sample Problem 6, which shows how to calculate $K_{sp}$ from solubility data. Assign Laboratory 35, "Solubility Product Constant," in which the students experimentally determine the solubility product constant for lead iodide. Plan to spend a great deal of time on Sample Problem 7 (and others like it). Students are likely to have difficulty understanding the role of the coefficient "2" in the dissociation equation and its subsequent use in two places in the solution to the problem. Explain that the "2" plays one role in the solubility product expression. It plays another totally different role in the description of the quantity of $Ag^+$ ions that dissolve when the solution is formed.
■ **Application.** You may want to point out to your students that the ions that cause hard water, usually calcium and magnesium, can be removed from the water by taking advantage of the low solubility product of the salts that these metals form. The salts include magnesium carbonate, calcium carbonate, magnesium phosphate, and calcium phosphate. The substances in household water-softening products used to precipitate these salts are sodium carbonate and trisodium phosphate.

### 18-10 The Common-Ion Effect, pp. 538-539

| Planning Guide | |
|---|---|
| **Labs (Lab Manual) and Demonstrations (TE)** | **Supplementary Materials (Teacher's Resource Book)** |
| | Practice Problems, p. 18-12 |

■ Explain what a common ion is and then discuss the common-ion effect in qualitative terms. Work through Sample Problem 9.

## Demonstrations

### 18-1 The Effect of Concentration on Equilibrium

**Overview:** In this demonstration, you add various solutions to a system that is in equilibrium, in order to shift the equilibrium to the right or to the left.

**Materials:** 0.2 $M$ cobalt(II) chloride hexahydrate ($CoCl_2 \cdot 6H_2O$); concentrated hydrochloric acid (HCl); 3 petri dishes; overhead projector; 0.1 $M$ lead(II) nitrate ($Pb(NO_3)_2$).

**Advance Preparation:** 1. **0.2 $M$ $CoCl_2 \cdot 6H_2O$:** Mix 2.6 g of $CoCl_2 \cdot 6H_2O$ in enough water to make 100 mL of solution. (You may wish to double the amounts, because the $CoCl_2 \cdot 6H_2O$ solution will also be used in Demonstration 18-2.) 2. **0.1 *M* Pb(NO₃)₂:** mix 3.31 g of $Pb(NO_3)_2$ in enough water to make 100 mL of solution.

Safety: Be careful in handling the concentrated hydrochloric acid, which is very corrosive. Avoid breathing its vapors.

**Procedure:** 1. Place the beaker containing the cobalt chloride solution onto the overhead projector. Slowly add concentrated hydrochloric acid to the beaker until the solution turns color. Write the equilibrium equation for this reaction on the front board. It is

$$[Co(H_2O)_6]^{2+}(aq) + 4Cl^-(aq) \rightleftharpoons [CoCl_4]^{2+}(aq) + 6H_2O(l)$$
pink                                           blue

2. Pour some of this solution from step 1 into each of two petri dishes on the overhead projector. Ask students to predict what will happen if more HCl is added to one of the solutions. Add more HCl to the first of the dishes until a shift in color intensity is noticeable. Ask: In which direction did the equilibrium shift? 3. Add water to the second dish from step 2, until a definite color change occurs. Ask: In which direction did the equilibrium shift? 4. Add a few drops of the lead(II) nitrate solution to the first dish until definite changes occur. Ask: In which direction did the equilibrium shift?

**Results:** In step 1, when the concentrated acid is added to the pink solution, the bluish tetrachlorocobalt(II) complex will be formed. The reaction (as just written) will shift to the right in step 2. When water is added, in step 3, the reaction shifts to the left, to produce a pink solution. When the lead(II) nitrate is added, it combines with chloride ions and removes them in the form of a precipitate of $PbCl_2$. The complex reaction shifts to the left, to produce a pink solution. All of the changes are explainable on the basis of LeChatelier's principle.

**Disposal Tips:** Remove the petri dishes from the overhead projector carefully, as they contain hydrochloric acid. Pour all of the liquids into a large container that is three-quarters full of water and pour this liquid mixture down the drain and flush with water. Do not put any lead solids into the drain. Dispose of the small amount of the lead chloride precipitate according to school-district guidelines.

## 18-2 The Effect of Temperature on Equilibrium

**Overview:** In this demonstration, you place a system at equilibrium into hot and cold temperature baths to determine the direction in which the equilibrium will shift.

**Materials:** acidified 0.2 *M* cobalt(II) chloride hexahy-

drate $(CoCl_2 \cdot 6H_2O)$; concentrated hydrochloric acid (HCl); hot plate; 250-mL beaker of ice water; beaker tongs; 250-mL beaker of hot water; 3 large test tubes in a test-tube rack.

**Advance Preparation:** 1. **Acidified 0.2 *M* $CoCl_2 \cdot 6H_2O$:** mix 2.6 g of $CoCl_2 \cdot 6H_2O$ in enough water to make 100 mL of solution; add concentrated hydrochloric acid (as much as 100 mL) to this solution until it just turns blue. 2. Place a 250-mL beaker that is three-quarters full of water onto a hot plate and heat to about 90°C. 3. Place water and ice into another 250-mL beaker.

Safety: Be careful in handling the hydrochloric acid and the hot beaker.

**Procedure:** 1. Fill each of three test tubes half way with some of the blue acidified cobalt chloride solution. Place one tube into the test-tube rack, another into the beaker of hot water, and the third into the beaker of ice water. Have students note the resulting colors of the heated and cooled solutions. Ask them to write a simplified equilibrium equation using only the terms "heat," "pink solution," and "blue solution," to illustrate the effect of temperature on this reaction. Ask them to state whether the forward reaction is endothermic or exothermic. 2. Switch each of the tubes from one bath to the other, and have students observe what happens.

**Results:** In the tube placed into hot water, the equilibrium shifts to the right, to produce a bluer solution. In the tube placed into the cold water the equilibrium shifts to the left, producing a pink solution. (See the balanced equilibrium equation in Demonstration 18-1). The simplified equation is: heat + pink solution $\rightleftharpoons$ blue solution. The forward reaction is endothermic. Switching the tubes will reverse the color changes.

**Disposal Tips:** The tubes can be stoppered and used again. If you wish to dispose of the liquids, add them to a large container of water to dilute the acid, and pour the resulting mixture down the drain and flush with water.

## Answers to Questions

### Page 516
1. In a reversible reaction, products can be directly combined to form reactants. An example is the reaction
$$Fe_3O_4(s) + 4H_2(g) \rightleftharpoons 3Fe(s) + 4H_2O(g)$$
2. A chemical equilibrium occurs in a reversible reaction when the forward reaction and the corresponding reverse reaction are proceeding in the same system at the same rate under the same conditions.

**3.** In a chemical system at equilibrium
$$\text{Rate}_{\text{FWD}} = \text{Rate}_{\text{REV}}$$

**4.** In order to produce the equilibrium
$$A + B \rightleftharpoons C + D$$
A and B can be mixed together, or C and D can be mixed together.

## Page 517

**5.** The mass-action expression for the equilibrium,
$$2HI(g) \rightleftharpoons H_2(g) + I_2(g)$$
is $\dfrac{[H_2]\,[I_2]}{[HI]^2}$

## Page 521

**6.** The law of chemical equilibrium states that the value of the mass-action expression for a reversible reaction is constant at a particular temperature.

**7.** A chemical equilibrium is described as dynamic because at equilibrium opposing reactions are occurring at the same time and at the same rate.

**8.** The equilibrium constant, $K_{eq}$, is obtained directly from the mass-action expression when equilibrium concentrations are used in that expression.

## Page 523

**9.** $K_{eq} = \dfrac{[CO]\,[Cl_2]}{[COCl_2]}$

$= \dfrac{\dfrac{0.76}{2.0}\dfrac{1.50}{2.0}}{\dfrac{1.70}{2.0}}$

$= 0.34$

**10. a.**

|              | **HI**            | **H₂**          | **I₂**          |
|--------------|-------------------|-----------------|-----------------|
| mol avail.   | 1.00              | 0               | 0               |
| change       | −0.28             | +0.14           | +0.14           |
| mol at eq.   | 0.72              | 0.14            | 0.14            |
| conc.        | $\dfrac{0.72}{1}$ | $\dfrac{0.14}{1}$ | $\dfrac{0.14}{1}$ |

**b.** $K_{eq} = \dfrac{[H_2]\,[I_2]}{[HI]^2}$

**c.** $K_{eq} = \dfrac{(0.14)\,(0.14)}{(0.72)^2}$
$= 3.8 \times 10^{-2}$

**11.**

|              | **SO₃**           | **SO₂**           | **O₂**            |
|--------------|-------------------|-------------------|-------------------|
| mol avail.   | 0.60              | 0                 | 0                 |
| change       | −0.24             | +0.24             | +0.12             |
| mol at eq.   | 0.36              | 0.24              | 0.12              |
| conc.        | $\dfrac{0.36}{4}$ | $\dfrac{0.24}{4}$ | $\dfrac{0.12}{4}$ |

$K_{eq} = \dfrac{[SO_2]^2\,[O_2]}{[SO_3]^2}$

$= \dfrac{\left(\dfrac{0.24}{4}\right)^2 \left(\dfrac{0.12}{4}\right)}{\left(\dfrac{0.36}{4}\right)^2}$

$= 1.3 \times 10^{-2}$

## Page 529

**12.** Le Chatelier's principle: When a system at equilibrium is subjected to a stress, the system will shift in the direction that tends to counteract or relieve the effect of the stress.

**13.** When used in a discussion on systems at equilibrium, "stress" refers to a change in a condition such as concentration, temperature, or pressure. A shift refers to the results of a change in the rate of reaction, and, hence, a change in the point of equilibrium and in the equilibrium concentrations. A shift to the left favors the formation of reactants. A shift to the right favors the formation of products.

**14.** For the equilibrium
$$PCl_5(g) \rightleftharpoons PCl_3(g) + Cl_2(g)$$
when $[PCl_3]$ is increased, the reaction shifts left, favoring the reverse reaction. As a result, $[PCl_5]$ increases and $[Cl_2]$ decreases.

**15.** For the equilibrium
$$2HBr(g) \rightleftharpoons H_2(g) + Br_2(g)$$
when $HBr(g)$ is added to the system, the reaction shifts to the right, favoring the forward reaction. As a result, $[H_2]$ increases and $[Br_2]$ increases.

**16.** Addition of $HBr(g)$ to the system described in problem **15** above, causes $[HBr]$ to increase. Some, but not all, of that added HBr is converted to $H_2$ and $Br_2$, thus increasing $[H_2]$ and $[Br_2]$ and causing the value of $K$ to remain constant.

## Page 531

**17. a.** For the equilibrium
$$N_2(g) + O_2(g) \rightleftharpoons 2NO(g)$$
an increase in pressure has no effect because the number of moles of gas is the same on each side of the equation.

**b.** For the equilibrium
$$2SO_3(g) + \text{heat} \rightleftharpoons 2SO_2(g) + O_2(g)$$
an increase in temperature will cause a shift to the right, using up some of the added heat.

**c.** For the equilibrium in **b**, an increase in pressure will cause a shift to the left, favoring the reverse reaction and the formation of fewer moles of gas.

**d.** For the equilibrium
$$CaCO_3(s) \rightleftharpoons CaO(s) + CO_2(g)$$
the removal of $CO_2$ will shift the equilibrium to

**18**

the right, favoring an increase in the formation of $CO_2$.

18. When a catalyst is introduced into a system, equilibrium is reached sooner. There is no effect on the position of the equilibrium.

19. An increase in pressure affects the concentration of the gas molecules. Therefore, the reaction will shift so as to reduce the concentration of the gas molecules.

**Page 537**

20. The solubility product expression for $Ag_2S$:
$$K_{sp} = [Ag^+]^2[S^{2-}]$$

21. The solubility product expression for $Ba_3(PO_4)_2$:
$$K_{sp} = [Ba^{2+}]^3[PO_4^{3-}]^2$$

22. When used in reference to solubility equilibrium, "insoluble" describes a substance that dissolves to only a very slight extent. Thus, a solution saturated with an "insoluble" substance contains a very low concentration of that substance.

23. **a.** The least soluble substance is $PbCrO_4$; it has the smallest $K_{sp}$.
    **b.** The most soluble substance is $PbSO_4$; it has the largest $K_{sp}$.
    **c.** The solubilities of $PbCrO_4$ and $PbCO_3$ are the closest because their $K_{sp}$ values are closest.

24. $[I^-] = 2 \times [Pb^{2+}] = 2.6 \times 10^{-3}$ because $PbI_2$ dissociates according to the equation
$$PbI_2(s) \rightleftharpoons Pb^{2+}(aq) + 2I^-(aq)$$
$$K_{sp} = [Pb^{2+}][I^-]^2$$
$$= (1.3 \times 10^{-3})(2.6 \times 10^{-3})^2$$
$$K_{sp} = 8.8 \times 10^{-9}$$

25. $[Mg^{2+}][CO_3^{2-}] = 2.0 \times 10^{-8}$
$$(X) \quad (X) = 2.0 \times 10^{-8}$$
$$(X)^2 = 2.0 \times 10^{-8}$$
$$X = [Mg^{2+}] = 1.4 \times 10^{-4}$$

**Page 539**

26. A common ion is an ion found in an equilibrium system and in a substance that is to be added to that equilibrium system.

27. The common ion effect is the shift in equilibrium due to the addition of a substance that contains an ion that was present in the original equilibrium.

28. **a.** Dissociation of silver iodide:
$$AgI(s) \rightleftharpoons Ag^+(aq) + I^-(aq)$$
    **b.** When $AgNO_3$ is added, the equilibrium shifts to the left.
    **c.** As a result of the addition of $AgNO_3$ and the subsequent shift in equilibrium, the concentration of $Ag^+$ increases, the concentration of $I^-$ decreases, and the mass of $AgI(s)$ increases.

**Page 539, Expanding Balloons**

1. Granulated magnesium has a large surface area, causing a fast enough reaction for the balloon to fill up with gas in only a few seconds.

2. Magnesium reacts with the hydrogen ion in the acetic acid to produce hydrogen gas, which causes the balloon in photo (b) to enlarge.
$$Mg + 2H^+ \rightarrow Mg^{2+} + H_2$$

3. Sodium acetate was added to the cylinder on the left. The addition of the acetate ions shifted the equilibrium to the left, decreasing the concentration of the hydrogen ion:
$$HC_2H_3O_2 \rightleftharpoons H^+ + C_2H_3O_2^-$$
$$+ \quad \text{addition of}$$
$$\text{acetate ion from}$$
$$C_2H_3O_2^- \quad \text{sodium acetate}$$
The decreased concentration of hydrogen ion causes the hydrogen gas to be produced at a slower rate.

## Chapter Review

**Page 541, Content Review**

1. A closed reaction vessel is necessary to prevent the escape of gaseous reactants and/or products.

2. **a.** The color, pressure, or temperature of a system could change.
   **b.** No. Once equilibrium is reached, these physical properties remain unchanged.

3. **a.** $[CO_2]^4 \times [H_2O]^6/[C_2H_6]^2 \times [O_2]^7$
   **b.** $[P_4] \times [H_2]^6/[PH_3]^4$
   **c.** $[Cl_2]^2 \times [H_2O]^2/[HCl]^4 \times [O_2]$

4. The system must be at equilibrium.

5. A $K_{eq}$ value that is much less than 1.0 indicates a high concentration of reactants compared to the concentration of the products.

6. The value of $K_{eq}$ will remain constant only at a constant temperature.

7. $K_{eq} = [NH_3]^2/[N_2] \times [H_2]^3$
$$= [2.0]^2 / [0.625] \times [4.0]^3$$
$$= 0.100 = 1.0 \times 10^{-1}$$

8. $[COCl_2] = [CO] \times [Cl_2] / K_{eq}$
$$= (1.2 \times 10^{-2})^2 / (8.2 \times 10^{-2})$$
$$= 1.8 \times 10^{-3} \text{ mole/dm}^3$$

9. $[I_2] = 85 \times (1.6 \times 10^{-2})^2 / (1.2 \times 10^{-1})$
$$= 0.18 \text{ } M$$

10. $K_{eq} = (0.010)^2 \times (0.051) / (0.15)^2$
$$= 2.3 \times 10^{-4}$$

11. **a.** $[SO_2] = 2 \times [O_2] = 2 \times 0.300 \text{ } M = 0.600 \text{ } M$
$$[SO_3] = 1.00 \text{ } M - 0.600 \text{ } M = 0.400 \text{ } M$$
    **b.** $K_{eq} = (0.600)^2 \times (0.300) / (0.400)^2$
$$= 0.675$$

12. A change in temperature, pressure, or the concen-

tration of one or more reactants or products are examples of physical stresses that could cause a shift in the position of equilibrium.

**13.** An increase in the concentration of one reactant would cause a shift to the right and
   **a.** an increase in the concentrations of products;
   **b.** an increase in the rate of the forward reaction;
   **c.** an increase in the rate of the reverse reaction;
   **d.** no change in the value of $K_{eq}$, at constant temperature.

**14.** The increase in the concentration of $H_2$ causes an increase in the rate of the forward reaction and, thus, an increase in the concentration of the product, $H_2S$, and a decrease in the concentration of the other reactant, $S_2$. Eventually, the rate of the reverse reaction increases to equal the rate of the forward reaction and equilibrium is re-established.

**15.** See Figure 18-1.

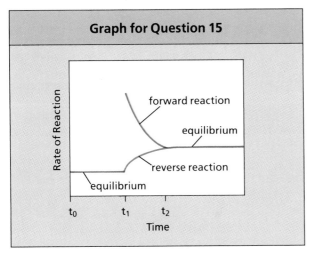

**Graph for Question 15**

Rate of Reaction

forward reaction

equilibrium

reverse reaction

equilibrium

$t_0$    $t_1$    $t_2$

Time

**Figure 18-1**

**16. a.** An increase in temperature causes a stress of additional heat. According to Le Chatelier's principle, the system will shift in the direction to relieve the stress. As the endothermic reaction absorbs heat, a shift in this direction would relieve the stress.
   **b.** A decrease in temperature causes a stress of having too little heat. The system will shift in the direction to produce heat, which is the exothermic direction.
   **c.** An increase in pressure can be relieved by reducing the number of molecules in the container. Thus, this stress would cause the reaction to shift in the direction of producing fewer gas molecules.

**17. a.** An increase in pressure, an increase in the concentration of $SO_2$ or $O_2$, or a decrease in the

concentration of $SO_3$ will result in an increase in the amount of $SO_3$ produced.
   **b.** A rise in temperature will displace the equilibrium point to the left, but equilibrium is attained more rapidly.

**18.** The point of equilibrium is displaced
   **a.** to the left;
   **b.** to the right;
   **c.** to the left.

**19. a.** It increases the rate of the forward reaction.
   **b.** It increases the rate of the backward reaction.
   **c.** $K_{eq}$ remains the same.
   **d.** The concentration of $SO_3$ produced per unit time is increased.

**20. a. and b.** $[Mg^{2+}] \times [OH^-]^2 / [Mg(OH)_2(s)] = K_{eq}$
   **c.** $K_{sp} = [Mg^{2+}] \times [OH^-]^2$
   **d.** 25°C

**21. a.** $K_{sp} = [Fe^{3+}] \times [OH^-]^3$
   **b.** $K_{sp} = [Ag^+]^2 \times [CrO_4^{2-}]$
   **c.** $K_{sp} = [Ca^{2+}] \times [PO_4^{3-}]^2$

**22.** Arranged in order of decreasing solubility, they are: $MgCO_3$, $CaCO_3$, $BaCO_3$, and $PbCO_3$.

**23.** $[Pb^{2+}] = 4.8 \times 10^{-6} M$
   $[OH^-] = 2 \times [Pb^{2+}] = 9.6 \times 10^{-6} M$
   $K_{sp} = [Pb^{2+}] \times [OH^-]^2 = (4.8 \times 10^{-6}) \times$
   $(9.6 \times 10^{-6})^2 = 4.4 \times 10^{-16}$

**24. a.** Molar solubility = $[Cd^{2+}] = [S^{2-}]$
   Let $x = [Cd^{2+}] = [S^{2-}]$
   $x^2 = 1.0 \times 10^{-28}$
   $x = 1.0 \times 10^{-14} M$
   **b.** Molar solubility = $[Ni^{2+}] = [CO_3^{2-}]$
   Let $x = [Ni^{2+}] = [CO_3^{2-}]$
   $x^2 = 1.2 \times 10^{-7}$
   $x = 3.5 \times 10^{-4} M$

**25. a.** The equilibrium shifts toward the barium sulfate.
   **b.** The concentration of barium ions will decrease; the concentration of sulfate ions will not change.
   **c.** The mass of $BaSO_4$ will increase.
   **d.** This shift is called the common-ion effect.

**Page 542, Content Mastery**

**26.** $K_{eq}$ for the reverse reaction is the inverse of the $K_{eq}$ for the forward reaction. $K_{eq} = 1/4.0 \times 10^{-2} = 25$.

**27.** $K_{eq} = [HCl]^2/[H_2] \times [Cl_2]$

**28. a.** The backward (or reverse) reaction would have a much larger $K_{eq}$ value ($1.0 \times 10^{30}$) and would go practically to completion at 25°C.
   **b.** At 2000°C, the $K_{eq}$ of the forward reaction (0.10) is still smaller than the $K_{eq}$ of the reverse

reaction (10). Therefore, the forward reaction goes on to a lesser extent than the reverse reaction.

c. A rise in temperature displaces the reaction to the right.

d. The forward reaction is endothermic because the addition of heat caused a shift to the right.

29. a. 3.50 moles − 0.270 moles = 3.23 moles $PCl_5$.
$[PCl_5]$ = 3.23 moles/0.500 $dm^3$ =
6.46 moles/$dm^3$
$[PCl_3]$ = $[Cl_2]$ = 0.270 mole/0.500 $dm^3$ =
0.540 mole/$dm^3$

b. $K_{eq}$ = $(0.540)^2$/6.46 = 4.51 × $10^{-2}$

30. $[Ce^{3+}]$ = 5.1 × $10^{-6}$ $M$
$[OH^-]$ = 3 × $[Ce^{3+}]$ = 1.53 × $10^{-5}$ $M$
$K_{sp}$ = $[Ce^{3+}]$ × $[OH^-]^3$
= (5.1 × $10^{-6}$) × (1.53 × $10^{-5}$)$^3$
= 1.8 × $10^{-20}$

31. $K_{sp}$ = $[La^{3+}]$ × $[IO_3^-]^3$
the formula mass of $La(IO_3)_3$ is 663.6 g/mol
moles of $La(IO_3)_3$ = 0.457 g/663.6 g/mol
= 6.89 × $10^{-4}$ mol
100 $cm^3$ = 0.100 $dm^3$, therefore
$[La(IO_3)_3]$ = 6.89 × $10^{-4}$ mol/0.100 $dm^3$
= 6.89 × $10^{-3}$ $M$
$[La^{3+}]$ = 6.89 × $10^{-3}$ $M$
$[IO_3^-]$ = 3 × (6.89 × $10^{-3}$ $M$) = 2.07 × $10^{-2}$ $M$
Substituting these values into the first equation yields: $K_{sp}$ = [6.89 × $10^{-3}$] × [2.07 × $10^{-2}$]$^3$
= 6.11 × $10^{-8}$

32. $K_{eq}$ = $[HI]^2$/$[H_2]$ × $[I_2]$
$[HI]$ = ($K_{eq}$ × $[H_2]$ × $[I_2]$)$^{1/2}$
= ([5.1 × $10^1$] × [2.0] × [3.01])$^{1/2}$
= 17 $M$

33. a. The equilibrium will shift to the right.
b. [HCl] will increase.
c. $[Cl_2]$ will decrease.

34. $K_{sp}$ = $[Ni^{2+}]$ × $[OH^-]^2$
$[Ni^{2+}]$ = $x$; $[OH^-]$ = $2x$
Substituting these values yields
1.6 × $10^{-14}$ = [$x$] × [$2x$]$^2$ = $4x^3$
$x$ = 1.6 × $10^{-5}$
Therefore, $[Ni^{2+}]$ = 1.6 × $10^{-5}$ $M$ and $[OH^-]$ = 3.2 × $10^{-5}$ $M$

35. $K_{sp}$ = $[Cu^{2+}]$ × $[OH^-]^2$
$[Cu^{2+}]$ = 1.8 × $10^{-7}$ $M$; $[OH^-]$ = 3.6 × $10^{-7}$
Substituting values yields
$K_{sp}$ = [1.8 × $10^{-7}$] × [3.6 × $10^{-7}$]$^2$
= 2.3 × $10^{-20}$

36. a. If the temperature is increased, $[H_2]$ and $[Cl_2]$ will decrease, and [HCl] will increase.
b. A pressure increase produces no change in the

system's equilibrium because there are equal numbers of gas molecules on both sides of the equation.

37. **Concept:** *Equilibrium occurs when the forward and reverse reactions of a system occur at the same rate. An indication that this has occurred is the constancy of concentration.*

*Solution:* Although the temperature of the flame is constant, this is not a closed system and no reverse reaction is occurring. It is classified as a steady-state reaction.

**Concept (questions 38-40):** *Chemical equilibrium occurs when the forward and reverse reaction rates are equal.*

38. *Solution:* No. Just because the numbers of particles depicted are like that in the equation does not mean the system is at equilibrium.

39. *Solution:* No. Equilibrium means that the forward and reverse reactions are occurring at equal rates. It does not mean equal concentrations.

40. *Solution:* Two pictures are needed to show that there is no change in concentration. The concentrations of each are immaterial. See Figure 18-2.

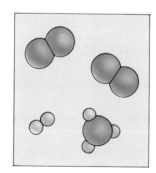 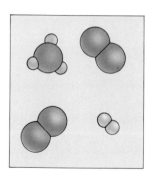

Figure 18-2

**Concept (questions 41 through 44):** *The equilibrium of a system can be shifted to produce more or less of a given product by making changes in the temperature of the system or by modifying the concentrations of the reactants or products.*

41. *Solution:* Increasing the concentration of A should shift the equilibrium to the right, producing more AB.

42. *Solution:* Adding BC should have no effect on the system because BC is a solid, and add-

ing an additional amount does not increase its concentration.

**43. Solution:** Adding a catalyst lowers the activation energy of both the forward and reverse reactions, speeding both of them up equally. Hence, there is no change in the concentrations of any substance in the system.

**44. Solution:** Additional heat would tend to be used up causing an increase in the speed of the reverse reaction. Hence, C would be used up.

**45. Concept:** *In a system at equilibrium, it is the rates of the reactions that are equal.*

**Solution:** It is possible to have these substances at these concentrations and for the reaction to be at equilibrium because it is the rates of the reactions to which equilibrium refers. The reaction does not cease. The forward and reverse reactions occur at the same rate and thus it appears that nothing is happening. If the concentrations remain constant over a period of time, there is an indication that equilibrium has occurred. In some cases, a substance can be tagged with a radioisotope and a comparison can be made in radiation activity of the substances in the system to see if this remains constant over time.

**46. Concept:** *Solution equilibrium occurs when the rates of dissolving and recrystallization are equal.*

**Solution:** The solution is at equilibrium if the total mass of solid that has come out of solution remains constant. In this particular case, part of the crystal went into solution and reformed on the bottom of the jar instead of on the crystal itself.

## Page 544, Cumulative Review

**47. a.** In an endothermic reaction, heat is absorbed and converted to chemical potential energy.

**48. c.** This is a single replacement reaction.

**49. c.** A + BC → B + AC is a general equation for a single replacement reaction.

**50. c.** A 6.8 $m$ solution of NaCl at 20°C is supersaturated.

**51. c.** "Ductile" is not a class of solids.

**52. c.** This equation is unbalanced.

**53.** A catalyst is a substance that speeds up a chemical reaction without itself being permanently altered.

**54.** The state is called physical equilibrium.

**55. a.** hydrosulfuric acid
   **b.** sulfurous acid
   **c.** chloric acid
   **d.** acetic acid

**56.** One mole of $C_2H_6O$ contains: 2.0 mol C × 12.0 g/mol = 24.0 g C; 6.0 mol H × 1.0 g/mol = 6.0 g H; 1.0 mol O = 16.0 g 0; total 46.0 g. 24.0 g / 46.0 g = 52.2% C; 6.0 g / 46.0 g = 13.0% H; 16.0 g / 46.0 g = 34.8% O.

## Page 544, Critical Thinking

**57.** The $K_{eq}$ for the reverse reaction is the reciprocal of the $K_{eq}$ for the forward reaction. 1/0.5 = 2.

**58.** By cooling the system, you remove some of the heat produced as product in an exothermic reaction. Thus, cooling creates a stress (the removal of product) and pulls the reaction forward.

**59.** The equilibrium expression for an ionic solid AB follows:
$K_{eq}$ = [A][B]/[AB]
Rearranging this equation gives the solubility product.
$K_{sp}$ = $K_{eq}$ × [AB] = [A][B]

**60.** The solubility decreases as $K_{sp}$ decreases. Most soluble is $CuCl_2$ = 73.0, then comes $BaCl_2$ = 35.8, $HgCl_2$ = 6.57, and $PbCl_2$ = 1.00, which is the least soluble.

**61.** The rate of reaction would decrease. Because the inhibitor has bound some reactant, fewer molecules can react, so there are fewer collisions.

## Page 545, Challenge Problems

**62.** The dissolving of $CuSO_4$ is endothermic because as the temperature increases, the compound becomes more soluble.

**63.** $K_{eq}$ = [$Pb^{2+}$] [$EDTA^{4-}$]/[Pb-$EDTA^{2-}$] = 5.0 × 10$^{-19}$
[$Pb^{2+}$] = (5.0 × 10$^{-19}$) × [Pb-$EDTA^{2-}$]/[$EDTA^{4-}$]
= (5.0 × 10$^{-19}$) (2.1 × 10$^{-4}$)/(1.8 × 10$^{-2}$)
= 5.8 × 10$^{-21}$ $M$

**64.** $K_{sp}$ = [$Ca^{2+}$]$^3$[$PO_4^{2-}$]$^2$ = 2.0 × 10$^{-29}$
= (1.2 × 10$^{-3}$)$^3$(6.7 × 10$^{-9}$)$^2$ = 7.8 × 10$^{-26}$

A precipitate of $Ca_3(PO_4)_2$ would be expected to form in the blood because its $K_{sp}$ is less in the blood than in water. The precipitate does not form because something in the blood prevents it from forming, perhaps the pH of the blood.

**18**

# Acids, Bases, and Salts

## Chapter Planning Guide

| Text Section | Labs (Lab Manual) and Demonstrations (TE) | Supplementary Materials (Teacher's Resource Book) |
|---|---|---|
| **19-1** The Theory of Ionization, pp. 547-548 <br><br> **19-2** The Dissociation of Ionic Electrolytes, p. 548 <br><br> **19-3** Ionization of Covalently Bonded Electrolytes, pp. 549-550 | Lab 37: Conductivity, Ionization, and Dissociation <br> Demo 19-1: Toying Around with Ionization, p. TG-277 | |
| **19-4** Acids (Arrhenius's Definition), pp. 550-552 <br><br> **19-5** Ionization Constants for Acids, pp. 552-555 | Lab 38: Determining Hydrogen-Ion Concentration of Strong and Weak Acids | Transparency Master: Some Common Acids, p. 19-1 <br> Transparency Master: Ionization of Acids, p. 19-2 <br> Practice Problems, p. 19-9 |
| **19-6** Properties of Acids, pp. 556-557 <br><br> **19-7** Arrhenius Bases and Their Properties, pp. 558-559 <br><br> **19-8** Salts, pp. 559-560 | Lab 36: Properties of Acids and Bases <br> Demo 19-2: Metallic Magic, p. TG-278 | Open-Ended Demonstration: Reactions of Vinegar, p. 19-6 <br> Transparency Master: Names and Formulas of 5 Common Bases, p. 19-3 <br> Transparency Master: Some Neutralization Reactions, p. 19-4 <br> Transparency Master: Formulas, Names of Common Salts, p. 19-5 <br> Review Activity: Reactions Involving Acids and Bases, p. 19-7 |
| **19-9** Brønsted-Lowry Acids and Bases, pp. 560-562 <br><br> **19-10** Conjugate Acid-Base Pairs, p. 563 <br><br> **Career** Chemical Lab Technician, p. 563 <br><br> **19-11** Comparing Strengths of Acids and Bases, pp. 564-566 | Demo 19-3: Acid Concentration and the Great Balloon-Volume Contest, p. TG-279 | Review Activity: Acids and Bases, p. 19-8 <br> Reference Tables: Relative Strengths of Acids in Aqueous Solution, p. RT-9 |
| **19-12** Amphoteric Substances, pp. 566-567 | | |
| **Can You Explain This?** Ammonia Fountain, p. 567 | | |

| Text Section | Labs (Lab Manual) and Demonstrations (TE) | Supplementary Materials (Teacher's Resource Book) |
|---|---|---|
|  |  | Test—Form A, p. AT-72<br>Alternate Test—Form B, p. BT-72 |

■ Core   ■ Advanced   ■ Optional

## Chapter Overview

In Chapter 19 both the classic Arrhenius theory and the modern Brønsted-Lowry concept of acids and bases are presented. We categorize substances as electrolytes and nonelectrolytes. Electrolytes that ionize (Arrhenius acids and some bases) are distinguished from electrolytes that dissociate (salts and most Arrhenius bases). Students solve problems based on the ionization constants for acids. We describe the properties of acids, bases, and salts, and give examples and some uses of each of these classes of compounds. Conjugate acid-base pairs are also discussed. The chapter ends with a discussion of the relative strengths of acids and bases and of amphoteric substances.

## Chapter Objectives

After students have completed this chapter, they will be able to:

1. Distinguish among strong electrolytes, weak electrolytes, and nonelectrolytes.          *19-1*
2. Compare the Arrhenius and Brønsted-Lowry theories of acids and bases.          *19-2 to 19-9*
3. Derive and interpret ionization constants of acids.          *19-5*
4. Describe the properties of acids, bases, and salts.          *19-6 to 19-8*
5. Explain conjugate acid-base pairs and amphoteric substances in terms of the Brønsted-Lowry theory.          *19-10 to 19-12*

## Teaching Suggestions

**19-1 The Theory of Ionization, pp. 547-548,**

**19-2 The Dissociation of Ionic Electrolytes, p. 548, and**

**19-3 Ionization of Covalently Bonded Electrolytes, pp. 549-550**

| Planning Guide | |
|---|---|
| Labs (Lab Manual) and Demonstrations (TE) | Supplementary Materials (Teacher's Resource Book) |
| Lab 37: Conductivity, Ionization, and Dissociation<br>Demo 19-1: Toying Around with Ionization, p. TG-277 |  |

■ As a motivating starter, use Demonstration 19-1, "Toying Around with Ionization," in which you set up a circuit consisting of dry cells, aqueous solutions, and a toy that moves and makes a sound when the solution is a conductor.

■ Although Arrhenius's explanation of the ability of certain solutions to conduct a current was modified by later research, his quantitative experiments were important in establishing a viable theory. If your students have studied depression of freezing points of solutions (Section 16-14), you might have them recall that $1.00 \ m$ solution of a nonelectrolyte (such as sucrose) freezes at $-1.86°C$. Thus, as they can verify by calculation, a $0.100 \ m$ solution of the nonelectrolyte freezes at $-0.186°C$. On the other hand, a $0.100 \ m$ solution of NaCl freezes at $-0.345°C$, which indicates that there are $0.345/0.186 = 1.85$ moles of particles per mole of NaCl. It was from data such as these that Arrhenius assumed that NaCl was composed of molecules that dissociated into $Na^+$ and $Cl^-$ ions in aqueous solution. His calculations led him to believe that a $0.100 \ m$ solution of NaCl was 85% dissociated. The freezing point of a $0.100 \ m$ solution of acetic acid is depressed by about $0.189°C$. Calculations show that the acid is about 1.6% ionized. These figures are consistent with the observations that NaCl is a strong electrolyte and that acetic acid is a weak electrolyte.

Of course, NaCl was later found to be composed of ions, and it is 100% dissociated in solution. You may explain that, at any particular moment, some of the

19

ions are held together by the attraction of their opposite charges. These attractions decrease the effective concentration of the independent particles in solution, so that the freezing point is depressed only to $-0.345°C$, not to $-0.372°C$ as we would expect if all of the ions were separate at all times.

■ In Laboratory 37, "Conductivity, Ionization, and Dissociation," students compare the conductivities of solutions of nonelectrolytes, weak electrolytes, and strong electrolytes.

■ **Concept Mastery.** If students have a good understanding of the difference between ionic and covalent bonding, they will readily grasp the difference between ionization and dissociation. You may use Concept Mastery question 36 (chapter-end question) to determine their comprehension. In addition, you may have students draw pictures representing what happens to ions and molecules when ionic and molecular solids melt and dissolve. Students could also draw pictures of what happens when a gas such as hydrogen chloride dissolves in water.

## 19-4 Acids (Arrhenius's Definition), pp. 550-552, and

## 19-5 Ionization Constants for Acids, pp. 552-555

| Planning Guide | |
|---|---|
| **Labs (Lab Manual) and Demonstrations (TE)** | **Supplementary Materials (Teacher's Resource Book)** |
| Lab 38: Determining Hydrogen-Ion Concentration of Strong and Weak Acids | Transparency Master: Some Common Acids, p. 19-1 Transparency Master: Ionization of Acids, p. 19-2 Practice Problems, p. 19-9 |

■ It is important for students to understand the Arrhenius concept of an acid before the Brønsted-Lowry concept is introduced, later in the chapter. Have them compare text Figure 19-5, showing the process of dissolving HCl gas in water to form hydrochloric acid, with text Figure 19-6, showing an equation and molecular models for the reaction.

■ Use the Transparency Master "Ionization of Acids" to explain ionization constants and their application in the sample problems. Then have students do Laboratory 38, "Determining Hydrogen-Ion Concentration of Strong and Weak Acids." Students use acid-base indicators to determine the hydrogen-ion concentration of a strong acid and a weak acid. They also calculate the ionization constant of a weak acid from experimental data.

## 19-6 Properties of Acids, pp. 556-557,

## 19-7 Arrhenius Bases and Their Properties, pp. 558-559, and

## 19-8 Salts, pp. 559-560

| Planning Guide | |
|---|---|
| **Labs (Lab Manual) and Demonstrations (TE)** | **Supplementary Materials (Teacher's Resource Book)** |
| Lab 36: Properties of Acids and Bases Demo 19-2: Metallic Magic, p. TG-278 | Open-Ended Demonstration: Reactions of Vinegar, p. 19-6 Transparency Master: Names and Formulas of 5 Common Bases, p. 19-3 Transparency Master: Some Neutralization Reactions, p. 19-4 Transparency Master: Formulas, Names of Common Salts, p. 19-5 Review Activity: Reactions Involving Acids and Bases, p. 19-7 |

■ Verbal descriptions of the behavior of acids and bases will be more meaningful after students have done Laboratory 36, "Properties of Acids and Bases," in which they test acids and bases with indicators, react acids with metals and with carbonates, and perform a neutralization. In Demonstration 19-2, "Metallic Magic," you carry out a reactions that is an all-time favorite for students—that of sodium with water to form a base.

■ Have students note that in strong acid-strong base neutralizations, the essential reaction is the combination of hydrogen (hydronium) ions and hydroxide ions to form water. The term *neutralization* is used to indicate an acid-base reaction that results in a neutral solution. Reactions of acids and bases that do not result in neutral solutions are discussed in the next chapter.

■ **Concept Mastery.** Although students may be familiar with the properties of acids and bases from earlier science courses, often they use science vocabulary erroneously in relation to acids and bases. You may wish to use Concept Mastery questions 33 and 34 (chapter-end questions) to help students correctly use the words "react," "dissolve," and "melt."

■ **Application.** You might want to discuss some of the acids that are present in foods and medications and that play a role in life processes. The acid in citric fruits is citric acid. In vinegar, it is acetic acid, and in sour milk, it is lactic acid. Grapes contain tartaric acid. Vitamin C is ascorbic acid, and aspirin is acetylsalicylic acid. The hydrochloric acid found in gastric juice helps to digest proteins, and deoxyribonucleic acid (DNA) is the genetic material in all cells.

Students may also be interested in some of the many industrial processes that use acids. Sulfuric acid is used to make fertilizers, explosives, dyes, and other acids. Hydrochloric acid is used to clean metals, prepare sugar from starch, and manufacture many chemicals. Acetic acid is used in the dyeing of silk and wool and in the manufacture of both rayon and nonflammable film.

## 19-9 Brønsted-Lowry Acids and Bases, pp. 560-562,

## 19-10 Conjugate Acid-Base Pairs, p. 563, and

## 19-11 Comparing Strengths of Acids and Bases, pp. 564-566

| Planning Guide | |
|---|---|
| Labs (Lab Manual) and Demonstrations (TE) | Supplementary Materials (Teacher's Resource Book) |
| Demo 19-3: Acid Concentration and the Great Balloon-Volume Contest, p. TG-279 | Review Activity: Acids and Bases, p. 19-8 Reference Tables: Relative Strengths of Acids in Aqueous Solution, p. RT-9 |

■ In comparing operational and conceptual definitions, emphasize the importance of both, but point out that the conceptual definition has a broader scope. It can be used to predict additional situations and can be extended to include a wider range of substances and chemical changes. A case in point is the extension, in the Brønsted-Lowry theory, of Arrhenius's original conceptual definitions of acids and bases to include substances not covered by those definitions.

■ You may want to show students some ways in which the Brønsted-Lowry theory does not replace the Arrhenius theory but broadens its scope. For example, the Arrhenius hydrogen ion, $H^+$, with its high positive-charge density could not exist in solution—it would be hydrated to form $H_3O^+$. Moreover, the Arrhenius theory did not cover acid-base reactions in nonaqueous media, such as the reaction of ammonium chloride ($NH_4Cl$) and potassium amide ($KNH_2$) in liquid ammonia. The ammonium ion acts as an acid (proton donor) and the amide ion acts as a base (proton acceptor):

$$NH_4^+ + NH_2^- \rightleftarrows NH_3 + NH_3$$

Compare this with the reaction of hydronium and hydroxide ions in water.

■ Demonstration 19-3, "Acid Concentration and the Great Balloon-Volume Contest," compares the production of hydrogen from the reaction of different acids

with zinc in a striking way—the filling of balloons with the gas.

■ Using equations given in Section 19-9, ask students to name the conjugate acid-base pairs and to state, in terms of the Brønsted-Lowry theory, the relative strengths of the acid and base in each pair.

■ **Concept Mastery.** You may wish to use Concept Mastery question 35 (chapter-end question) to draw students' attention to the proper uses of the words *strong*, *weak*, *dilute*, and *concentrated*. Ask students to explain why the familiar use of *weak* attached to beverages such as coffee and tea should, in a chemical context, be replaced by *dilute*.

## 19-12 Amphoteric Substances, pp. 566-567

■ Two equations can conveniently be used to demonstrate the amphoteric nature of water, as defined by the Brønsted-Lowry theory. In the reaction

$$CO_3^{2-} + H_2O \rightleftarrows HCO_3^- + OH^-$$

water gives up a proton, and thus acts as an acid. In the reaction

$$H_2CO_3 + H_2O \rightleftarrows HCO_3^- + H_3O^+$$

water accepts a proton, and thus acts as a base.

■ With above average students, you may wish to discuss the equations showing the amphoteric nature of the hydroxides $Zn(OH)_2$ and $Al(OH)_3$. Explain that while the Arrhenius theory limits amphoteric substances to such hydroxides, the Brønsted-Lowry theory includes these plus many other substances, both ionic and molecular.

## Demonstrations

### 19-1 Toying Around with Ionization

**Overview:** In this demonstration, you observe different aqueous solutions by means of a special conductivity apparatus. This apparatus, which incorporates a battery-operated toy, qualitatively indicates ionization and is used to determine whether a solution conducts electricity.

**Materials:** a battery-operated toy that features movement and sound; 1–4 low-voltage dry cells; 6 alligator clips; knife switch; insulated copper wire; battery holder; two electrodes; clean towel; distilled water; 9 250-mL beakers; tap water; 100 mL of 1 $M$ sucrose ($C_{12}H_{22}O_{11}$) solution; 100 mL of glacial acetic acid ($CH_3COOH$); 100 mL of 1 $M$ acetic acid solution; 100 mL of 1 $M$ sodium chloride ($NaCl$) solution; 100 mL of 1 $M$ sodium hydroxide ($NaOH$) solution; 100 mL of 1 $M$ hydrochloric acid ($HCl$); goggles.

19

**Advance Preparation:** 1. Set up the apparatus and toy as shown in Figure 19-1. 2. **1 _M_ sucrose:** mix 34.2 g of sucrose in enough distilled water to make 100 mL of solution. 3. **1 _M_ acetic acid:** mix glacial (concentrated) acetic acid and distilled water in a 1:17 ratio. 4. **1 _M_ sodium chloride:** mix 5.8 g of NaCl in enough distilled water to make 100 mL of solution. 5. **1 _M_ sodium hydroxide:** mix 4.0 g of NaOH in enough distilled water to make 100 mL of solution. 6. **1 _M_ hydrochloric acid:** mix concentrated hydrochloric acid and distilled water in a 1:11 ratio. 7. Place the five solutions, the distilled water, the tap water, and the glacial acetic acid into eight separate, labeled 250-mL beakers.

**Safety:** Wear goggles and practice the usual safety procedures in preparing and using the solutions. Always add concentrated acid to water, never the reverse.

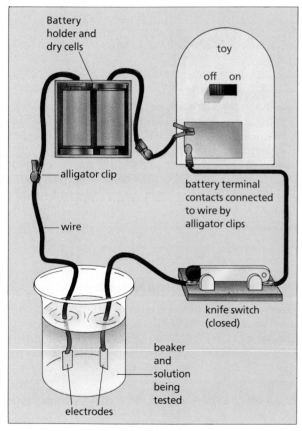

**Figure 19-1**

**Procedure:** 1. With the switch open, connect the two electrode ends of the wires. Close the switch to show that the toy operates when the circuit is completed. Open the switch and separate the two electrode ends of the wires. 2. Test the conductivity of each solution by dipping the electrodes into each of them and closing the switch. Have students observe the operation of the toy each time. Between tests, clean the electrodes by immersing them in a beaker of distilled water (with the switch open) and then wiping them gently with a clean towel. 3. Ask students what enables the solutions to conduct electricity.

**Results:** The following solutions will be good conductors (the toy will operate at essentially full capacity): 1 _M_ NaCl, 1 _M_ NaOH, and 1 _M_ HCl. The following will be relatively poor conductors (the toy will operate at considerably less than full capacity): 1 _M_ acetic acid and tap water (if high in dissolved minerals). The following will be essentially nonconductors (the toy will not operate): distilled water, 1 _M_ sucrose, glacial acetic acid, and tap water (if low in dissolved minerals). The presence of dissolved ions permits the conducting solutions to carry electricity.

## 19-2 Metallic Magic

**Overview:** In this demonstration, a strong base is produced by the highly exothermic reaction between sodium, an active metal from Group 1 of the periodic table, and water. This reaction also illustrates some of the chemical and physical properties of a Group 1 metal.

**Materials:** 1 small piece of freshly cut sodium metal, 1 cm³ in volume (roughly the size of a small pea); glass plate; phenolphthalein indicator solution; metal spatula; forceps; 2 1-L beakers; 2 squares of wire gauze with heat-dispersing centers; test tube, half filled with a 0.1 _M_ hydrochloric acid (HCl) solution; test tube filled with 0.1 _M_ sodium hydroxide (NaOH) solution; safety goggles.

**Advance Preparation:** 1. Fill each beaker to the three-quarters level with water (preferably distilled). Add to one beaker a few drops of phenolphthalein indicator, and stir to mix the indicator with the water. The solution should be colorless. 2. Just before class, cut a 1-cm³ piece of sodium metal. (Do not cut a larger piece. See "Safety.") Return the remaining sodium to its storage bottle, making sure that it remains covered with an appropriate organic liquid, such as kerosene. 3. **0.1 _M_ HCl:** mix concentrated hydrochloric acid and water in a 1:120 ratio by volume. 4. **0.1 _M_ NaOH:** mix 0.4 g NaOH with enough water to make 100 mL of solution. 5. **Phenolphthalein solution:** mix 0.05 g of solid indicator with 50 mL of ethyl alcohol, or use already prepared indicator solution.

**Safety:** Sodium metal reacts violently with water. Wear goggles and use forceps in handling the metal, and be certain that any surface onto which it is placed is completely dry. Do not, under any circumstances, attempt to exceed the specified quantities of sodium.

Use of larger pieces can result in extremely dangerous explosions and fire. Do not allow students access to the metal, and do not allow them to carry out the demonstration or to stand close by while you carry it out. In preparing the acid solutions, observe the usual cautions in working with the highly corrosive acids, and add concentrated acid to water, not water to acid.

**Procedure:** 1. Place a 1-cm$^3$ piece of sodium onto a clean, dry glass plate. Using a metal spatula, cut the sodium into two pieces, each about ½ cm$^3$. Make sure that the students observe how easily you are able to cut the sodium metal. 2. Using forceps and wearing goggles, pick up a ½-cm$^3$ piece of sodium and drop it into the beaker containing pure water. Immediately place a wire-gauze square on top of the beaker, and stand back. Have students record their observations. 3. Repeat the demonstration, but this time place the ½-cm$^3$ piece of sodium into the beaker containing the water and phenolphthalein. Again, have students record their observations, and ask them to explain what has occurred. 4. Add a few drops of phenolphthalein to each of two test tubes, the first filled with 0.1 $M$ HCl solution and the other filled with 0.1 $M$ NaOH.

**Results:** In step 2, addition of sodium to water results in rapid evolution of hydrogen gas and heat. The equation is $2Na(s) + 2H_2O(l) \rightarrow 2Na^+(aq) + 2OH^-(aq) + H_2(g) +$ energy. The rapid release of the hydrogen gas at its surface causes the sodium to float and to move rapidly across the water's surface. The heat released causes the metal to melt and assume a spherical shape. The rapid release of heat can cause the hydrogen gas to combine explosively with oxygen in the air, and a loud popping may occur. The beaker is covered with wire gauze in order to help to prevent this and also to prevent molten sodium from spattering out of the beaker. In step 3, the same results will also be observed, but this time the solution will turn pink, as the phenolphthalein indicator reveals the presence of a base (NaOH). In step 4, the phenolphthalein will cause the NaOH solution to turn pink, but the HCl solution will remain colorless.

## 19-3 Acid Concentration and the Great Balloon-Volume Contest

**Overview:** In this demonstration, samples of four different acids of equal volume and molar concentration are made to react with an excess of zinc. The hydrogen gas that is produced is collected in balloons. The relative magnitudes of the volumes of hydrogen gas that is collected are related to the ability of the acids to produce hydrogen ions.

**Materials:** 4 250-mL Erlenmeyer flasks; 4 large, round balloons (capable of expanding to a diameter of at least 40 cm); 32 g of zinc pellets; 100 mL of 1 $M$ sulfuric acid ($H_2SO_4$); 100 mL of 1 $M$ hydrochloric acid (HCl); 100 mL of 1 $M$ nitric acid ($HNO_3$); 100 mL of 1 $M$ acetic acid ($CH_3COOH$); 4 4–by–6-in. index cards; rubber bands.

**Advance Preparation:** 1. **1 $M$ H$_2$SO$_4$:** mix concentrated sulfuric acid and water in a 1:17 ratio by volume. 2. **1 $M$ HCl:** mix concentrated hydrochloric acid and water in a 1:11 ratio by volume. 3. **1 $M$ HNO$_3$:** mix concentrated nitric acid and water in a 1:14 ratio by volume. 4. **1 $M$ CH$_3$COOH:** mix glacial (concentrated) acetic acid and water in a 1:17 ratio by volume. 5. Pour 100 mL of the acid solutions just described into four separate 250-mL Erlenmeyer flasks. Label the index cards with the names and concentrations of the acids. 6. Place 8 g of zinc pellets into each of four balloons. (A powder funnel may be of assistance in pouring the zinc pellets into the balloon.) 7. Gently squeeze the balloon to remove as much of the air as possible. Be careful not to allow the zinc pellets to cut the balloon. 8. Place a balloon with zinc pellets inside it over the lip of each of the four 250-mL Erlenmeyer flasks. Air should not be trapped inside the balloon. 9. Place a rubber band over the balloon along the lip of the Erlenmeyer flask to hold the balloon on the flask. (See Figure 19-2.)

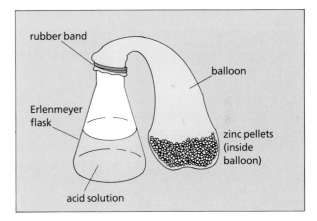

**Figure 19-2**

**Safety:** Be careful in handling the concentrated acids, which are very corrosive. When diluting them, add the acids to the water, not the water to the acids. Be careful not to allow the gas-filled balloons to come into contact with a heat source, as the hydrogen can combine explosively with oxygen in the air. Release the hydrogen into a fume hood, or make certain that the room in which it is released is well ventilated.

**Procedure:** 1. Set the four flasks fitted with the zinc-filled balloons on the demonstration table next to the corresponding index-card labels. 2. Carefully lift the balloons so as to drop the zinc pellets, stored inside them, through the necks of the flasks and into the acid solutions. Have students observe the reactions and qualitatively compare the volumes of the balloons. Ask them to explain their findings.

**Results:** The reactions in all four flasks can be represented by the equation

$$2H^+(aq) + Zn(s) \rightarrow Zn^{2+}(aq) + H_2(g)$$

In each reaction, the zinc is in excess, so essentially all of the hydrogen (or hydronium, $H_3O^+$) ions from the acid will be used up in the production of the hydrogen gas. Thus, the hydronium ion concentration of the acid is the limiting factor. The volumes of gas produced by the hydrochloric acid and nitric acid will be roughly the same. The volume produced by the acetic acid during the observation period may be less, due to the slower rate of reaction of the weak acid. The volume produced by the sulfuric acid will be about twice as great as that produced by the hydrochloric acid or nitric acid. This is because each mole of the diprotic $H_2SO_4$ can produce two moles of $H^+$ ions, whereas the other acids are monoprotic and can produce only one mole of $H^+$ ions.

**Disposal Tips:** Release the highly combustible hydrogen gas you have collected into a fume hood or in a well-ventilated room. Do not store the hydrogen-filled balloons.

# Answers to Questions

## Page 550

1. **a.** The water solution of a strong electrolyte is a good conductor of electricity (e.g., NaCl).
   **b.** The water solution of a weak electrolyte is a poor conductor. Acetic acid is an example.
   **c.** The water solution of a nonelectrolyte is a nonconductor. Sucrose is an example.
2. **a.** Electrolytes break down in solution into ions that conduct the current.
   **b.** *Dissociation* describes what happens when ionic substances dissolve in water.
   **c.** *Ionization* is the term that describes the dissolving of covalent electrolytes in water.
3. **a.** When NaCl dissolves in water, the positive $Na^+$ ions are attracted to the negative ends of the water molecules. The negative $Cl^-$ ions are attracted to the positive ends of the water molecules. The hydrated ions are separated from each other as they are pulled into solution by the water molecules adhering to them.
   **b.** $CaCl_2(s) \rightarrow Ca^{2+}(aq) + 2Cl^-(aq)$
   **c.** $Na_3PO_4(s) \rightarrow 3Na^+(aq) + PO_4^{3-}(aq)$
   **d.** $AlCl_3(s) \rightarrow Al^{3+}(aq) + 3Cl^-(aq)$
   **e.** $(NH_4)_2SO_4(s) \rightarrow 2NH_4^+(aq) + SO_4^{2-}(aq)$

4. **a.** Dry NaCl will not conduct a current because the ions are not mobile. **b.** Melted NaCl will conduct a current because the ions are mobile.
5. **a.** When glacial acetic acid is dissolved in water, a small percentage of the molecules reacts with water to produce hydronium and hydrated acetate ions. The reaction is reversible. The solution is a weak conductor.
   **b.** $HC_2H_3O_2(l) + H_2O(l) \rightleftarrows H_3O^+(aq) + C_2H_3O_2^-(aq)$
   **c.** All acids produce $H^+$ ions when dissolved in water. These ions react with $H_2O$ molecules to form hydronium ions.

## Page 552

6. **a.** An Arrhenius acid is a substance that produces hydrogen ions as the only positive ion in its water solutions.
   **b.** $HCl(g) + H_2O(l) \rightarrow H_3O^+(aq) + Cl^-(aq)$
   **c.** A single arrow is used in the equation in **b** because the reaction is only very slightly reversible. For practical purposes, it goes to completion.
7. **a.** $HNO_3 + H_2O \rightarrow H_3O^+ + NO_3^-$
   **b.** $HC_2H_3O_2 + H_2O \rightleftarrows H_3O^+ + C_2H_3O_2^-$
   **c.** The reaction does not run to completion. An equilibrium is established between the reactants and the products.

## Page 555

8. **a.** $\dfrac{[H^+][C_2H_3O_2^-]}{[HC_2H_3O_2]} = K_a$   **b.** $1.8 \times 10^{-5}$

9. According to text Figure 19-8, of the three acids, HF, $H_2S$, and $HC_2H_3O_2$, **a.** HF (hydrofluoric acid) is the strongest, and **b.** $H_2S$ (hydrosulfuric acid) is the weakest. **c.** None of the three is a strong acid.

10. $\dfrac{3.65 \text{ g HCl}}{2.00 \text{ dm}^3} \times \dfrac{1 \text{ mol HCl}}{36.5 \text{ g HCl}} = 0.0500\, M \text{ HCl}$

   The concentration of the solution is $0.0500\, M$. The concentration of the $H^+$ ion is the same as the concentration of the HCl, i.e., $0.0500\, M$.

11. $\dfrac{3.20 \text{ g HNO}_3}{250 \text{ cm}^3} \times \dfrac{1000 \text{ cm}^3}{1.00 \text{ dm}^3} \times \dfrac{1 \text{ mol HNO}_3}{63.0 \text{ g HNO}_3} =$
   $0.203 \text{ mol HNO}_3/\text{dm}^3 = 0.203\, M \text{ HNO}_3$
   Because $HNO_3$ is a strong acid and because it contains only one ionizable proton per molecule, the concentration of the $H^+$ ions is the same as the concentration of the acid, i.e., $0.203\, M$.

12. In this instance, the concentration of the hydrogen ion is not equal to the concentration of the acid because the acid is weak. Relatively few hydrogen ions are formed from the ionization of the acid.
   Let $x = [H^+] = [C_2H_3O_2^-]$
   $\dfrac{[H^+][C_2H_3O_2^-]}{[HC_2H_3O_2]} = K_a$

   $\dfrac{x^2}{0.25} = 1.8 \times 10^{-5}$

$x^2 = 4.5 \times 10^{-6}$

$x = 2.1 \times 10^{-3} \, M$

13. The concentration of the acetic acid is:

$$\frac{12.0 \text{ g HC}_2\text{H}_3\text{O}_2}{500 \text{ cm}^3} \times \frac{1000 \text{ cm}^3}{1.00 \text{ dm}^3} \times \frac{1 \text{ mol HC}_2\text{H}_3\text{O}_2}{60.0 \text{ g HC}_2\text{H}_3\text{O}_2} =$$

$$0.400 \, M$$

Let $x = [\text{H}^+] = [\text{C}_2\text{H}_3\text{O}_2^-]$

$$\frac{[\text{H}^+][\text{C}_2\text{H}_3\text{O}_2^-]}{[\text{HC}_2\text{H}_3\text{O}_2]} = K_a$$

$$\frac{x^2}{0.400} = 1.8 \times 10^{-5}$$

$x^2 = 7.2 \times 10^{-6}$

$x = 2.7 \times 10^{-3} \, M$

## Page 557

14. **a.** Acids are substances that produce hydrogen (hydronium) ions in aqueous solution, react with active metals to produce hydrogen, neutralize bases, have a sour taste, and give characteristic colors to indicators.
    **b.** red
    **c.** colorless
    **d.** red
15. **a.** $\text{Mg} + 2\text{HCl} \rightarrow \text{MgCl}_2 + \text{H}_2$
    **b.** $\text{Zn} + \text{H}_2\text{SO}_4 \rightarrow \text{ZnSO}_4 + \text{H}_2$
16. **a.** $\text{Mg}(s) + 2\text{H}^+(aq) \rightarrow \text{Mg}^{2+}(aq) + \text{H}_2(g)$
    **b.** $\text{Zn}(s) + 2\text{H}^+(aq) \rightarrow \text{Zn}^{2+}(aq) + \text{H}_2(g)$

## Page 560

17. **a.** A base is a hydroxide that dissolves in water to yield hydroxide ions as the only negative ion.
    **b.** Sodium hydroxide, lye or caustic soda, NaOH; ammonia water, household ammonia, $\text{NH}_3 \cdot \text{H}_2\text{O}$; magnesium hydroxide, milk of magnesia, $\text{Mg(OH)}_2$; calcium hydroxide, slaked lime, $\text{Ca(OH)}_2$.
18. **a.** Bases form solutions containing hydroxide ions, give characteristic colors to indicators, neutralize acids, emulsify fats and oils, and taste bitter.
    **b.** blue, red, and yellow.
19. **a.** $\text{Ca(OH)}_2(s) \rightarrow \text{Ca}^{2+}(aq) + 2\text{OH}^-(aq)$
    **b.** $\text{Ca(OH)}_2 + 2\text{HCl} \rightarrow \text{CaCl}_2 + 2\text{H}_2\text{O}$
    **c.** $\text{KOH} + \text{HC}_2\text{H}_3\text{O}_2 \rightarrow \text{KC}_2\text{H}_3\text{O}_2 + \text{H}_2\text{O}$
20. **a.** Salts are ionic compounds, have high melting points, and conduct a current when molten or dissolved in water.
    **b.** $\text{NaNO}_3$ (Chile saltpeter); $\text{NaHCO}_3$ (baking soda); $\text{NH}_4\text{Cl}$ (sal ammoniac)

## Page 562

21. **a.** An operational definition is based on directly observable properties. A conceptual definition is based on the interpretation of observed facts.
    **b.** A base neutralizes acids, turns litmus blue, tastes bitter, and emulsifies oils.
22. **a.** An Arrhenius acid produces hydrogen ions as the only positively charged ions in its aqueous solutions. An Arrhenius base produces hydroxide ions as the only negatively charged ions in its aqueous solutions. The Brønsted-Lowry definitions of acids and bases include all substances that donate or accept protons.
    **b.** $\text{HCl} + \text{H}_2\text{O} \rightarrow \text{H}_3\text{O}^+ + \text{Cl}^-$
    **c.** $\text{NH}_3 + \text{H}_2\text{O} \rightarrow \text{NH}_4^+ + \text{OH}^-$
    **d.** $\underset{\text{acid}}{\text{NH}^{4+}} + \underset{\text{base}}{\text{OH}^-} \rightarrow \underset{\text{base}}{\text{NH}_3} + \underset{\text{acid}}{\text{H}_2\text{O}}$

    $\underset{\text{base}}{\text{C}_2\text{H}_3\text{O}_2^-} + \underset{\text{acid}}{\text{H}_3\text{O}^+} \rightarrow \underset{\text{acid}}{\text{HC}_2\text{H}_3\text{O}_2} + \underset{\text{base}}{\text{H}_2\text{O}}$

23. **a.** Arrhenius: NaOH is a hydroxide that releases hydroxide ion in aqueous solution as the only negative ion. Brønsted-Lowry: NaOH accepts protons in its chemical reactions.
    **b.** Arrhenius: $\text{CO}_3^{2-}$ is not a hydroxide. Brønsted-Lowry: $\text{CO}_3^{2-}$ accepts protons in its chemical reactions.

## Page 567

24. **a.** The difference in composition is a proton, $\text{H}^+$.
    **b.** A base accepts a proton from the acid or the acid donates a proton to the base.
    **c.** When one is strong, the other is relatively weak.
25. **a.** $\text{SO}_3^{2-}$, $\text{S}^{2-}$, $\text{OH}^-$, $\text{H}_2\text{PO}_4^-$
    **b.** $\text{HNO}_3$, $\text{HCl}$, $\text{HSO}_4^-$, $\text{H}_3\text{O}^+$
26. **a.** $\text{HC}_2\text{H}_3\text{O}_2$ and $\text{C}_2\text{H}_3\text{O}_2^-$; $\text{H}_2\text{O}$ and $\text{H}_3\text{O}^+$
    **b.** $\text{NH}_4^+$ and $\text{NH}_3$; $\text{OH}^-$ and $\text{H}_2\text{O}$
    **c.** $\text{CO}_3^{2-}$ and $\text{HCO}_3^-$; $\text{H}_2\text{O}$ and $\text{OH}^-$
    **d.** $\text{Cl}^-$ and $\text{HCl}$; $\text{H}_3\text{O}^+$ and $\text{H}_2\text{O}$
    **e.** $\text{HPO}_4^{2-}$ and $\text{PO}_4^{3-}$; $\text{H}_2\text{O}$ and $\text{H}_3\text{O}^+$
27. **a.** An amphoteric substance is one that can act as a proton donor or proton acceptor..
    **b.** $\text{HCO}_3^- + \text{H}^+ \rightarrow \text{H}_2\text{CO}_3$; $\text{HCO}_3^- + \text{OH}^- \rightarrow$
    $$\text{CO}_3^{2-} + \text{H}_2\text{O}$$
    **c.** $\text{HS}^- + \text{H}^+ \rightarrow \text{H}_2\text{S}$; $\text{HS}^- + \text{OH}^- \rightarrow \text{S}^{2-} + \text{H}_2\text{O}$

## Page 567, Ammonia Fountain

1. Ammonia water is made by dissolving ammonia ($\text{NH}_3$) gas in water.
2. Heat decreased the solubility of ammonia gas, and the gas was released from the solution.
3. When the ammonia gas was released from solution, it filled the flask and the glass tube leading from the flask as it escaped to the outside. When the flask was inverted and the glass tube immersed in the water, the ammonia in the tube began to dissolve in the water. As the ammonia dissolved in the water, gaseous pressure in the flask dropped below atmospheric pressure. Then, atmospheric pressure was able to push water up

the glass tube into the flask. More ammonia dissolved in the water, decreasing the gaseous pressure in the flask still more.

4. The water solution contains phenolphthalein, which turns red or pink in basic solution. Ammonia dissolved in water is a basic solution.

# Chapter Review

## Page 568, Content Review

1. They form solutions that conduct an electric current because of the presence of mobile ions.

2. **a.** Covalently bonded electrolytes ionize.
   **b.** Ionic electrolytes dissociate.

3. **a.** $Ca(NO_3)_2(s) \rightarrow Ca^{2+}(aq) + 2NO_3^-(aq)$
   **b.** $FeCl_3(s) \rightarrow Fe^{3+}(aq) + 3Cl^-(aq)$
   **c.** $(NH_4)_2SO_4(s) \rightarrow 2NH_4^+(aq) + SO_4^{2-}(aq)$
   **d.** $K_3PO_4(s) \rightarrow 3K^+(aq) + PO_4^{3-}(aq)$

4. **a.** In both of these conditions, the ions are mobile.
   **b.** In solution, the ions are hydrated; they are not hydrated in the molten salt.

5. The $H_3O^+$ ion is called the hydronium ion.

6. **a.** The hydrogen of acetic acid combines with water to form a hydronium ion. The acetate ion is hydrated by water molecules. This happens in a small percentage of the molecules, causing a small degree of ionization.
   **b.** In both cases, hydration takes place. Ions exist in NaCl before solution; hydration causes them to separate. Acetic acid molecules do not contain ions; ions are formed in solution and hydrated.

7. **a.** $HCHO_2 + H_2O \rightleftarrows H_3O^+ + CHO_2^-$
   **b.** $HBr + H_2O \rightleftarrows H_3O^+ + Br^-$
   **c.** $H_2S + 2H_2O \rightleftarrows 2H_3O^+ + S^{2-}$

8. $HCHO_2 + H_2O \rightleftarrows H_3O^+ + CHO_2^-$
   $K_{eq} = [H_3O^+][CHO_2^-] / [HCHO_2][H_2O]$
   Since $[H_2O]$ is a constant, it can be merged with the equilibrium constant, giving a new constant, the ionization constant for formic acid.
   $K_{eq}[H_2O] = [H_3O^+][CHO_2^-] / [HCHO_2] = K_a$

9. Concentration of solution = 6.3 g/0.500 L = 12.6 g/L. Since $HNO_3$ ionizes completely, $[HNO_3]$ = $[H^+]$ = 12.6 g/L × 1 mole $HNO_3$/63 g = 0.20 $M$.

10. The sour taste of many foods, such as citrus fruits, pickles, and vinegar, comes from acid in the food, like citric acid and acetic acid.

11. **a.** $2Al + 6HCl \rightarrow 2AlCl_3 + 3H_2$
    $2Al + 6H_3O^+ \rightarrow 6H_2O + 3H_2 + 2Al^{3+}$
    **b.** $Mg + H_2SO_4 \rightarrow MgSO_4 + H_2$
    $Mg + 2H_3O^+ \rightarrow Mg^{2+} + 2H_2O + H_2$

12. **a.** $Ba(OH)_2(s) \rightarrow Ba^{2+}(aq) + 2OH^-(aq)$
    **b.** $NH_3 + H_2O \rightleftarrows NH_4^+ + OH^-$
    **c.** $3NaOH + H_3PO_4 \rightarrow Na_3PO_4 + 3H_2O$

13. A salt is an ionic compound produced when an acid and base neutralize each other.

14. **a.** The operational definition of an acid is a substance that turns litmus paper red, has a sour taste, and neutralizes bases.
    **b.** The conceptual definition either is a substance that produces hydrogen (hydronium) ions in water solution or is a proton donor.
    **c.** HF should react with water to form hydrated hydrogen ions.

15. The substances are labeled in the order in which they appear in the forward reaction.
    **a.** acid, base, base, acid.
    **b.** acid, base, acid, base.
    **c.** acid, base, acid, base.
    **d.** base, acid, acid, base.

16. **a.** A conjugate acid-base pair is a pair of substances that are formed reversibly from one another by losing or gaining a proton.
    **b.** $H_2O$, $HSO_3^-$, $CO_3^{2-}$, $OCl^-$, $NH_3$
    **c.** $HI$, $HSO_3^-$, $HPO_4^{2-}$, $HC_2H_3O_2$, $H_3BO_3$

17. **a.** Acid: $HClO_4$, base: $ClO_4^-$; acid: $H_3O^+$, base: $H_2O$.
    **b.** $H_2O$ is the stronger base.
    **c.** $HClO_4$ is the stronger acid.

18. Substances that can act either as proton donors or as proton acceptors are called amphoteric or amphiprotic.

## Page 569, Content Mastery

19. The strongest acid is the acid that ionizes the most. The strongest acid has the largest ionization constant, as the concentrations of the ions are in the numerator. Therefore, HCl, with a very large ionization constant, is the strongest acid.

20. NEVER pour water into acid! Step 1 should say "Carefully pour 100 $cm^3$ of concentrated sulfuric acid into 0.5 $dm^3$ of water."

21. Sugar maintains its molecular structure when it dissolves, whereas some molecules of acetic acid ionize in solution.

22. $2H_3PO_4(aq) + 3Ca(OH)_2(aq) \rightarrow$
    $Ca_3(PO_4)_2(aq) + 6H_2O(l)$

23. **a.** Arrhenius defined an acid as a substance that yields $H^+$ ions as the only positive ion when added to water and **b.** a base as a substance that yields $OH^-$ ions as the only negative ion.

**24.** The Brønsted-Lowry definition of an acid as a proton donor is the same as the Arrhenius definition. A Brønsted-Lowry base is a proton acceptor; an Arrhenius base is an OH$^-$ donor.

**25.** Active metals react with acids to produce hydrogen gas.

   **a.** $2Al(s) + 6HNO_3(aq) \rightarrow 2Al(NO_3)_3(aq) + 3H_2(g)$

   **b.** $2Al(s) + 6H^+(aq) + \boxed{6NO_3^-(aq)} \rightarrow$
   $$2Al^{3+}(aq) + \boxed{6NO_3^-(aq)} + 3H_2(g)$$

   **c.** $2Al(s) + 6H^+(aq) \rightarrow 2Al^{3+}(aq) + 3H_2(g)$

**26.** 19.3 g × 1 mol/60 g × 1/1.93 dm$^3$ = $1.67 \times 10^{-1}$ $M$

   **a.** Since acetic acid ionizes only slightly, the concentration of acetic acid molecules is approximately $1.67 \times 10^{-1}$ $M$.

   **b.** $K_a = 1.8 \times 10^{-5} = [H^+][CH_3O_2^-] / [HCH_3O_2] =$
   $$x^2/1.67 \times 10^{-1}$$
   $x^2 = (1.8 \times 10^{-5})(1.67 \times 10^{-1}) = 3.01 \times 10^{-6}$
   $x = 1.73 \times 10^{-3}$ $M$

**27.** $Ba(OH)_2(aq) + H_2SO_4(aq) \rightarrow BaSO_4(s) + 2H_2O(l)$

**28.** **a.** $HPO_4^{2-}(aq) + NaOH(aq) \rightarrow$
   $$Na^+(aq) + PO_4^{3-}(aq) + H_2O(l)$$

   **b.** $HPO_4^{2-}(aq) + HCl(aq) \rightarrow$
   $$H_2PO_4^-(aq) + Cl^-(aq)$$

**29.** **a.** $\boxed{HPO_4^{2-}(aq)} + \boxed{NaOH(aq)} \rightarrow$
   $$Na^+(aq) + \boxed{PO_4^{3-}(aq)} + \boxed{H_2O(l)}$$

   **b.** $\boxed{HPO_4^{2-}(aq)} + \boxed{HCl(aq)} \rightarrow$
   $$\boxed{H_2PO_4^-(aq)} + \boxed{Cl^-(aq)}$$

**30.** $HCl(g) + H_2O(l) \rightarrow H_3O^+(aq) + Cl^-(aq)$
   $HC_2H_3O_2(l) + H_2O(l) \rightleftarrows H_3O^+(aq) + C_2H_3O_2^-(aq)$
   The single arrow in the first equation indicates practically complete ionization. The double arrow in the second equation shows an equilibrium reaction. The shorter arrow points to the right, showing a slight degree of ionization.

**31.** Arrhenius defined a base as a substance that yields hydroxide ions as the only negative ion in water solution. This compound also forms nitrate ions in water solution.
   $Bi(OH)_2NO_3 \rightarrow Bi^{3+} + 2OH^- + NO_3^-$

**32.** The Brønsted-Lowry definition of a base is more inclusive.

| Species | Arrhenius base? | Brønsted-Lowry base? |
|---|---|---|
| KOH | Yes | No |
| PO$_4^{3-}$ | No | Yes |
| SO$_4^{2-}$ | No | Yes |

**Page 570, Concept Mastery**

**33.** ***Concept:*** *Dissolving and reacting are different processes.*

   *Solution:* No. The magnesium disappears because it reacts with the acid, forming magnesium chloride and hydrogen. Evaporating the water yields magnesium chloride, not magnesium. When a substance dissolves, its particles remain in solution and can be recovered by evaporation.

**34.** ***Concept:*** *Melting requires heat, not a solvent.*

   *Solution:* No. Pearls are made of calcium carbonate, which *reacts* with vinegar (acetic acid solution). Melting requires heat, not the presence of a solvent.

**35.** ***Concept:*** *In acid-base chemistry, weak refers to the degree of ionization, dilute, to the concentration.*

   *Solution:* **a.** dilute, strong
   **b.** concentrated, strong
   **c.** dilute, weak
   **d.** concentrated, weak

**36.** ***Concept:*** *Dissociation refers to the separation of already existing ions by a polar substance such as water. Ionization refers to the formation of ions that do not exist in the covalent substance.*

   *Solution:* Ions already exist in NaCl. Therefore, it dissociates in water. HCl is covalently bonded and ionizes in water. NaOH is an ionic compound, so it dissociates.

**37.** ***Concept:*** *Hydronium ions, hydroxide ions, and water molecules are made of hydrogen and oxygen.*

   *Solution:* See Figure 19-3.

**Figure 19-3**

## Page 570, Cumulative Review

**38. c.** Tendency to rust is a chemical property.

**39. a.** *Proton* is another name for the $H^+$ ion.

**40. a.** Pressure does not affect the rate of solution for a solid in a liquid.

**41.** hydrated

**42. a.** sodium peroxide  **d.** sodium bicarbonate
**b.** cadmium carbonate  **e.** silver nitrate
**c.** potassium dichromate  **f.** aluminum cyanide

**43.** $Ca^{2+}(aq) + CO_3^{2-}(aq) \rightarrow CaCO_3(s)$
Spectator ions: $Na^+(aq)$ and $OH^-(aq)$.

**44.** The chemical and physical properties of the elements are periodic functions of their atomic numbers.

**45.** fluorine

**46.** $V_2 = \dfrac{P_1V_1T_2}{P_2T_1} = \dfrac{103.5 \text{ kPa } (0.89 \text{ dm}^3)(273 \text{ K})}{(101.3 \text{ kPa})(294 \text{ K})} =$
$0.84 \text{ dm}^3$

**47.** An ideal gas obeys the gas laws under all conditions of temperature and pressure. Its molecules would be points without volume, and the molecules would have no attraction for one another.

## Page 571, Critical Thinking

**48.** The larger the $K_a$, the stronger the acid: $HClO_4$, $HIO_4$, $HF$, $H_2CO_3$, and $HCN$.

**49.** $Cu(OH)_2$, an ionic compound, dissociates in water.

**50.** $HCl$ and $HCN$ are acids, able to donate $H^+$. $Ca(OH)_2$ is an Arrhenius base containing $OH^-$. $AgCl$, $KNO_3$, $CaO$, and $NaHCO_3$ are salts, containing a metal cation and an anion other than $OH^-$.

**51.** Acids turn litmus paper red. Bases turn litmus paper blue. Therefore, the solution is an acid.

**52.** Since $K_b$ is derived from the equilibrium expression for the ionization of a base, the larger the $K_b$ is, the stronger the base is.

**53.** She assumed that all oxides combine with water to form bases.

## Page 571, Challenge Problems

**54.** $H_3C_6H_5O_7 \rightarrow \quad H^+ + H_2C_6H_5O_7^-$
$H_2C_6H_5O_7^- \rightarrow \quad H^+ + HC_6H_5O_7^{2-}$
$HC_6H_5O_7^{2-} \rightarrow \quad H^+ + C_6H_5O_7^{3-}$
$K_{a_1} = [H^+] [H_2C_6H_5O_7^-] / [H_3C_6H_5O_7]$
$K_{a_2} = [H^+] [HC_6H_5O_7^{2-}] / [H_2C_6H_5O_7^-]$
$K_{a_3} = [H^+] [C_6H_5O_7^{3-}] / [HC_6H_5O_7^{2-}]$
$K_{a_1}$ is the largest; $K_{a_3}$ the smallest.

**55.** The conjugate base is $HC_{20}H_{12}O_4^-$; it has one less proton than the acid. The base present neutralizes phenolphthalein, forming its conjugate base, $HC_{20}H_{12}O_4^-$. This species must be pink because the indicator is pink in basic solution.

**56.** $H_3O^+-H_2O$, $H_2O-OH^-$, $H_2CO_3-HCO_3^-$, $HCO_3^- - CO_3^{2-}$, $NH_4^+-NH_3$, $NH_3-NH_2^-$.

**57.** Molecular weight = 176 g/mol
500 mg $\times$ 1 mol/176 g $\times$ 1 g/$10^3$ mg $\times$
$1/200 \text{ cm}^3 \times 10^3 \text{ cm}^3/1 \text{ dm}^3 =$
$1.42 \times 10^{-2} M$ = concentration of ascorbic acid
$K_a = 8.00 \times 10^{-5} = [H^+] [C_6H_7O_6^-] / [HC_6H_7O_6] =$
$[H^+] [C_6H_7O_6^-] / 1.42 \times 10^{-2}$
$[H^+] = [C_6H_7O_6^-] = x$
$1.14 \times 10^{-6} = x^2$
$x = 1.06 \times 10^{-3} M = [H^+]$

**58.** Molecular weight $HCl$ = 36.5 g/mole
$\dfrac{1/19 \text{ g soln}}{\text{cm}^3 \text{ soln}} \times \dfrac{37 \text{ g HCl}}{100 \text{ g soln}} \times \dfrac{\text{mole HCl}}{36.5 \text{ g HCl}} \times$
$\dfrac{10^3 \text{ cm}^3 \text{ soln}}{\text{L soln}} = 1.2 \times 10^1 M$ HCl

Since $HCl$ is a strong acid, it ionizes completely.
12 $M$ HCl yields 12 $M$ $H_3O^+$.

# Acid-Base Reactions

## Chapter Planning Guide

| Text Section | Labs (Lab Manual) and Demonstrations (TE) | Supplementary Materials (Teacher's Resource Book) |
|---|---|---|
| **20-1** The Self-ionization of Water, pp. 573-576 <br><br> **20-2** The pH of a Solution, pp. 576-578 | Demo 20-1: What's the pH?, p. TG-288 | |
| **20-3** Calculating pH Values, pp. 578-580 | | Skills Development: Logarithms, p. SD-17 <br> Concept Mastery: pH of a Solution, p. CM-33 |
| **20-4** Buffer Solutions, pp. 580-581 | | |
| **20-5** Acid-Base Indicators, pp. 581-583 | | Transparency Master: The pH Range of Common Indicators, p. 20-1 <br> Societal Issues: Acid Rain, p. SI-38 <br> Critical and Creative Thinking: Ordering Information, p. CCT-19 |
| **20-6** Acid-Base Neutralization, p. 584 <br><br> **20-7** Acid-Base Titration, pp. 584-586 | Lab 39: Acid-Base Titration <br> Demo 20-2: A Bright Titration, p. TG-289 | Critical and Creative Thinking: Predicting Consequences, p. CCT-47 <br> Non-SI Supplementary Problems, 20-5 <br> Concept Mastery: Neutralization and Titration, p. CM-34 |
| **20-8** Hydrolysis of Salts, pp. 586-588 <br><br> **20-9** Choice of Indicators, pp. 588-589 | Lab 40: Hydrolysis of Salts <br> Demo 20-3: The Hydrolysis of Salts, p. TG-290 | Transparency Master: The Formation of Salts from Acids and Bases, p. 20-2 |
| **20-10** Gram Equivalent Masses, pp. 589-590 <br><br> **20-11** Normality, pp. 590-593 | | Review Activity: Reactions of Acids and Bases, p. 20-3 <br> Practice Problems, p. 20-4 |
| **Biography** Bert Fraser-Reid, p. 590 | | |
| **Can You Explain This?** Electrolytic Titration, p. 593 | | |

| Text Section | Labs (Lab Manual) and Demonstrations (TE) | Supplementary Materials (Teacher's Resource Book) |
|---|---|---|
|  |  | Test—Form A, p. AT-76 <br> Alternate Test—Form B, p. BT-76 |

■ Core    ■ Advanced    ■ Optional

---

## Chapter Overview

In Chapter 20, we describe the ionization of water and use the ion-product of water to explain the meaning of pH. We then show students how to calculate pH values and hydrogen ion concentrations.

We explain how buffer solutions resist changes in pH, both in the laboratory and in the human body. We then give examples of ways to measure pH values and describe acid-base neutralization. Students solve problems in acid-base titration and learn how to choose indicators for such reactions. The acidic, basic, or neutral character of the solutions of some salts is explained by hydrolysis reactions.

The chapter ends with a discussion on gram equivalent masses and the advantages of using normality to express concentration of solutions employed in acid-base titrations.

## Chapter Objectives

After students have completed Chapter 20, they will be able to:
1. Calculate the hydrogen ion and hydroxide ion concentrations in water or any aqueous solution. *20-1*
2. Calculate pH values.           *20-2* and *20-3*
3. Explain the action of buffer solutions.      *20-4*
4. Explain why indicators change color.      *20-5*
5. Describe how neutralization reactions are used in acid-base titrations.       *20-6* and *20-7*
6. Explain the results of hydrolyses of salt solutions.         *20-8*
7. Select appropriate indicators for acid-base titration.         *20-9*
8. Use normalities in solving titration problems. *20-10* and *20-11*

---

## Teaching Suggestions

### 20-1 The Self-ionization of Water, pp. 573-576, and

### 20-2 The pH of a Solution, pp. 576-578

| Planning Guide | |
|---|---|
| Labs (Lab Manual) and Demonstrations (TE) | Supplementary Materials (Teacher's Resource Book) |
| Demo 20-1: What's the pH?, p. TG-288 |  |

■ Before you discuss how the ion-product constant of water is derived, many students will need to review the multiplication and division of exponential numbers. You may also want to review the effect of temperature changes on chemical equilibria as discussed in Chapter 18.

■ You may wish to do Demonstration 20-1, "What's the pH?", to arouse student interest before discussing the definition of pH and its derivation.

■ If you have average or below-average students who are weak in algebra, you can help them to understand

pH in a less mathematical way than by introducing them to logarithms. You may explain that "pH" originally meant "potenz H ion concentration" or "power of the hydrogen ion concentration," when the concentration was expressed in powers of 10.

■ **Concept Mastery.** You may want to use Concept Mastery question 41 (chapter-end question) to help students understand the reason for an important electrical safety rule. Point out that not only an electrical shock but also death by electrocution can result from using an electrical appliance while any part of the body is in contact with water. Explain that there are enough ions even in pure (distilled) water to conduct a current. Ask students to suggest some additional ions that are likely to be present in water in a bathtub, kitchen sink, swimming pool, or lake.

You can use Concept Mastery question 42 (chapter-end question) to determine if your students understand that a decrease of 1 on the pH scale means that the hydrogen ion concentration has increased by a factor of 10.

■ **Application.** You might want to discuss with students the difference between a pH balanced soap or shampoo and a basic soap or shampoo. Whereas a basic soap may have a pH somewhere between 8 and 10, the pH values of balanced products are slightly acidic, falling in the 4.5 to 5.5 range.

## 20-3 Calculating pH Values, pp. 578-580

| Planning Guide | |
| --- | --- |
| Labs (Lab Manual) and Demonstrations (TE) | Supplementary Materials (Teacher's Resource Book) |
| | Skills Development: Logarithms, p. SD-17 Concept Mastery: pH of a Solution, p. CM-33 |

■ For an understanding of the problems in this section, even above-average students may need a review of logarithms. Use the Skills Development worksheet "Logarithms" to ensure that students understand logarithms and know how to use the log table to find logs and antilogs. If pocket calculators with log functions are available, show students how to use them.

■ **Concept Mastery.** The Concept Mastery worksheet "pH of a Solution" can help students to go beyond the memorization approach to calculating pH values.

## 20-4 Buffer Solutions, pp. 580-581

■ After describing the composition of a buffer system, you may challenge students to suggest the names of substances that might be used in such a solution. Using an example developed in the class discussion, ask students to explain how the solution resists a change in pH upon the addition of a small amount of a strong acid or base. Explain that such a system is delicate, and that the resistance can be overcome if large enough amounts of acid or base are added.

■ You may want to explain that in preparing a buffer system it is best to make the concentration of the basic substance about equal to that of the acidic substance. Thus, in an acetic acid/sodium acetate buffer, the concentration of the acetate ion would be about the same as that of the acetic acid. Equal concentrations of acidic and basic components make the solution equally capable of neutralizing any added acid or base.

■ **Application.** Students may be interested in knowing the difference between buffered aspirin and a chemical buffer. Buffered aspirin contains aspirin (acetylsalicylic acid) and a salt such as sodium bicarbonate that hydrolyzes to form a basic solution. The bicarbonate acts as an antacid, minimizing stomach upset caused by the acidity of the aspirin. The aspirin and the salt are two separate and unrelated substances, and the reaction of one substance does not generate more of the other. By contrast, the two species involved in a chemical buffer system are closely interrelated by

chemical equilibrium. In an acetic acid/acetate ion buffer system the reaction of the acetate ion with an acid increases the acetic acid concentration.

## 20-5 Acid-Base Indicators, pp. 581-583

| Planning Guide | |
| --- | --- |
| Labs (Lab Manual) and Demonstrations (TE) | Supplementary Materials (Teacher's Resource Book) |
| | Transparency Master: The pH Range of Common Indicators, p. 20-1 Societal Issues: Acid Rain, SI-38 Critical and Creative Thinking: Ordering Information, p. CCT-19 |

■ Your class discussion of how indicators work can be used as a review and application of the concepts of conjugate acids-base pairs and of chemical equilibrium. Referring to the equation for the ionization of the indicator HIn, you may ask students to identify the conjugate base (the ion $In^-$) of the weak acid HIn. Then have the students explain the displacement that occurs when the indicator is added to an acid or to a base.

One way to determine student understanding of the action of acid-base indicators is to tell them that some indicators are weak bases that work on the same general principle as weak acid indicators. Based on the general formula of a weak acid indicator (HIn), ask students what would be the general formula of a weak base indicator (InOH) and then use an equilibrium equation to explain how the indicator works.

■ **Critical Thinking.** The Critical and Creative Thinking worksheet "Ordering Information" is appropriate for use with Section 20-5. In this exercise students rank a list of pH indicators according to several criteria. This skill helps students to organize their thoughts when confronted with a large amount of data.

## 20-6 Acid-Base Neutralization, p. 584, and

## 20-7 Acid-Base Titration, pp. 584-586

| Planning Guide | |
| --- | --- |
| Labs (Lab Manual) and Demonstrations (TE) | Supplementary Materials (Teacher's Resource Book) |
| Lab 39: Acid-Base Titration Demo 20-2: A Bright Titration, p. TG-289 | Critical and Creative Thinking: Predicting Consequences, p. CCT-47 Non-SI Supplementary Problems, p. 20-5 Concept Mastery: Neutralization and Titration, p. CM-34 |

- Have students recall (from Chapter 19) that the ability of acids and bases to neutralize each other is one of their properties. Tell them that their study of acid-base reactions in Chapter 20 is quantitative and will show why the products of such reactions may not be exactly neutral.
- You may want to introduce the topic of titration with Demonstration 20-2, "A Bright Titration," in which you monitor an acid-base titration, using a conductivity apparatus and phenolphthalein as the indicator. Students observe neutralization and a titration technique they can apply when they do Laboratory 39, "Acid-Base Titration," in which they use a standard HCl solution to determine the molarity of a NaOH solution.
- **Critical Thinking.** In the Critical and Creative Thinking worksheet "Predicting Consequences" students predict the behavior of malonic acid based on a comparison with other acids. This skill can help students to understand how scientific theories are used to predict experimental results.
- **Concept Mastery.** You can use Concept Mastery question 39 (chapter-end question) to help students visualize what occurs during neutralization. You may wish to give students a neutralization problem in which the concentrations of a strong base and a strong acid are the same but different volumes of each are added to a beaker. Ask students to represent the product pictorially. This would be a good way to reinforce or review their ability to solve limiting reactant problems. The Concept Mastery worksheet "Neutralization and Titration" can then be used to test the students' ability to visualize the molecular view of neutralization.

## 20-8 Hydrolysis of Salts, pp. 586-588, and

## 20-9 Choice of Indicators, pp. 588-589

| Planning Guide | |
|---|---|
| Labs (Lab Manual) and Demonstrations (TE) | Supplementary Materials (Teacher's Resource Book) |
| Lab 40: Hydrolysis of Salts<br>Demo 20-3: The Hydrolysis of Salts, p. TG-290 | Transparency Master: The Formation of Salts from Acids and Bases, p. 20-2 |

- You may wish to begin with Demonstration 20-3, "The Hydrolysis of Salts," in which you use the indicator bromothymol blue to show that some salt solutions are acidic, some are basic, and some are neutral. Students may then do Laboratory 40, "Hydrolysis of Salts," in which they use phenolphthalein and pH paper to determine the relative acidity or basicity of various salt solutions. Note that in the laboratory, the procedure, salts, and indicator are all different from those used in the demonstration. Thus, the two activities do not duplicate but rather complement each other.
- **Application.** You might want to point out to students that some substances used as acid-base indicators in the laboratory have other uses. For example, phenolphthalein is the active ingredient in some commercial laxatives. Congo red is used for dyeing cotton fabrics.

## 20-10 Gram Equivalent Masses, pp. 589-590, and

## 20-11 Normality, pp. 590-593

| Planning Guide | |
|---|---|
| Labs (Lab Manual) and Demonstrations (TE) | Supplementary Materials (Teacher's Resource Book) |
| | Review Activity: Reactions of Acids and Bases, p. 20-3<br>Practice Problems, p. 20-4 |

- If you elect to teach these sections, emphasize that whereas 1 gram equivalent mass of an acid reacts with 1 gram equivalent mass of a base, this simple 1:1 relationship is not always true when the masses are expressed in moles. Students who are planning careers as chemists or technicians in medical laboratories will be interested to know that these workers make use of this simplification. They use normal solutions for many of the titrations that they carry out in the course of their work.

## Demonstrations

### 20-1 What's the pH?

**Overview:** In this demonstration, you prepare a series of solutions of known pH values 1 to 13. Using wide-range pH (Hydrion) paper as indicator, you correlate the actual colors produced by your solutions to the standard colors on the pH-paper package. Using the wide-range indicator, you also determine the pH of common aqueous solutions.

**Materials:** 0.1 $M$ hydrochloric acid (HCl); 0.1 $M$ sodium hydroxide (NaOH); 22 test tubes, with rubber stoppers; 3 test-tube racks; labels; 10-mL pipet; 13 250-mL storage bottles, with stoppers; 100-mL volumetric flask or 100-mL graduated cylinder; distilled water; wide-range pH (Hydrion) paper; soda pop; lemon juice; orange juice; tomato juice; vinegar; milk; shampoo; dish-washing detergent; oven cleaner.

**Advance Preparation:** 1. **0.1 _M_ HCl:** mix distilled water and concentrated hydrochloric acid in an 11:1 ratio. 2. **0.1 _M_ NaOH:** mix 4.0 g of NaOH in enough water to make 100 mL of solution. 3. Pour 100 mL of the 0.1 _M_ HCl solution into a 250-mL storage bottle, and label the bottle "pH 1." 4. Using a 10-mL pipet, transfer 10 mL of the 0.1 _M_ HCl to a 100-mL volumetric flask or 100-mL graduated cylinder. Add enough distilled water to make 100 mL of solution, and mix well. Transfer this solution to a storage bottle, and label it "pH 2." Rinse the 10-mL pipet and 100-mL volumetric flask or graduated cylinder with distilled water. Repeat the 10:1 dilution procedure, using solution at each step to make solution for the following step, until you prepare a solution with a pH of 6. 5. Pour 100 mL of distilled water into a storage bottle marked "pH 7." 6. To make the basic solutions, pour 100 mL of 0.1 _M_ NaOH stock solution into a storage bottle labeled "pH 13." Transfer 10 mL of this 0.1 _M_ NaOH solution to the 100-mL volumetric flask or 100-mL graduated cylinder, using a 10-mL pipet. Add enough distilled water to make 100 mL of solution, and mix well. Transfer this solution to a storage bottle marked "pH 12." Repeat the procedure until you prepare a solution with a pH of 8. Be sure to stopper all of the storage bottles to prevent evaporation. 7. Transfer some of each solution to separate, labeled test tubes, and stopper each test tube. 8. Cut 22 pieces of wide-range pH (Hydrion) paper.

**Safety:** Be careful in handling the hydrochloric acid and sodium hydroxide and their solutions. Also, be careful in handling the oven cleaner.

**Procedure:** 1. Use the pH paper to verify the pH of each solution that was prepared. You can then use each of the resulting pieces of pH paper as color standards against which to measure the pH of other solutions. 2. Use pH paper to measure the pH of lemon juice, vinegar, soda pop, orange juice, tomato juice, milk, shampoo, dish-washing detergent, and oven cleaner.

**Results:** The colors produced in step 1 (red through blue) should match up with the colors on the chart on the pH-paper package. The pH values of the substances in step 2 will be as follows: lemon juice, 2–3; vinegar, 2–4; soda pop, 2–4; orange juice, 2–3; tomato juice, 4–5; milk, 6–7; shampoo, 7–8; dish-washing detergent, 8–12; oven cleaner, 12–13.

## 20-2 A Bright Titration

**Overview:** In this demonstration, you monitor the reaction between HCl and NaOH, using a conductivity apparatus and phenolphthalein as indicator. Students observe the titration and explain their observations in terms of the neutralization reaction.

**Materials:** electrical conductivity apparatus with light bulb and low-power dry cell; 250-mL beaker; 100 mL of 0.1 _M_ sodium chloride (NaCl); 100 mL of distilled water; 100 mL of 0.1 _M_ hydrochloric acid (HCl); 100 mL of 0.1 _M_ sodium hydroxide (NaOH); phenolphthalein solution; 2 burets; wash bottle with distilled water; 2 ring stands; 2 universal clamps.

**Advance Preparation:** 1. **0.1 _M_ NaCl:** mix 5.85 g of NaCl in enough water to make 100 mL of solution. 2. **0.1 _M_ HCl:** mix concentrated hydrochloric acid and water in a 1:11 ratio by volume. 3. **0.1 _M_ NaOH:** mix 4.00 g of NaOH in enough water to make 100 mL of solution.

**Safety:** Be careful in handling the hydrochloric acid and the sodium hydroxide, and in using the conductivity apparatus.

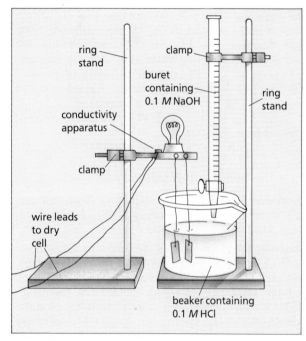

**Figure 20-1**

**Procedure:** 1. Test the conductivity of the 0.1 _M_ HCl, 0.1 _M_ NaOH, and 0.1 _M_ NaCl solutions. After each solution has been tested, remove the leads to the dry cell and conductivity apparatus, and rinse the electrodes with distilled water. 2. Test the conductivity of distilled water. 3. Set up the titration equipment as shown in the accompanying figure. To the beaker in which the conductivity apparatus is placed, add 50 mL of 0.1 _M_ HCl, using a buret. Also, add a few drops of phenolphthalein solution to the beaker. Have students observe the conductivity apparatus and the color of the solution throughout the rest of the demonstration. 4. Using a buret, add 0.1 _M_ NaOH solution to the 0.1 _M_ HCl solution at a moderate rate until about 45 mL has been delivered. From this point onward, the NaOH solution should be added to the HCl solution at a very slow rate, with swirling of the beaker. Ask students to anticipate what they expect to see as the end point is reached. Continue adding the base until the phenolphthalein turns color, indicating that the neutralization point has been reached and passed. Ask students to explain their observations in terms of the neutralization reaction that has occurred.

**Results:** In step 1, the 0.1 $M$ solutions of NaOH, HCl, and NaCl will exhibit high conductivity (the light bulb will glow brightly). The distilled water, in step 2, will be a very poor conductor. In step 4, the colorless solution will turn pink at roughly the end point of the titration. The light bulb of the conductivity apparatus will not dim during the titration, however, not even at the end point. This will indicate that ions are always present in the solution during the neutralization reaction. Although the $H^+$ and $OH^-$ ions combine and produce nonconducting water molecules, the conducting spectator ions $Cl^-$ and $Na^+$ will still be present. The complete equation, including spectator ions, is

$$Na^+(aq) + OH^-(aq) + H^+(aq) + Cl^-(aq) \rightarrow$$
$$H_2O(l) + Na^+(aq) + Cl^-(aq)$$

The net ionic equation is:

$$H^+(aq) + OH^-(aq) \rightarrow H_2O(l)$$

## 20-3 The Hydrolysis of Salts

**Overview:** In this demonstration, you show that certain salts hydrolyze to produce acidic or basic solutions when dissolved in water.

**Materials:** small amounts of the following substances: hydrochloric acid (HCl), sodium hydroxide (NaOH), sodium chloride (NaCl), potassium bromide (KBr), sodium carbonate ($Na_2CO_3$), potassium phosphate ($K_3PO_4$), sodium hydrogen sulfate ($NaHSO_4$), sodium acetate ($NaC_2H_3O_2$); eyedropper, spatula; bromothymol blue indicator solution; distilled water; 9 test tubes and stoppers; test-tube rack.

**Advance Preparation:** none

**Safety:** Be careful in handling the hydrochloric acid, the sodium hydroxide, and the various salts and their solutions.

**Procedure:** 1. Fill three test tubes half full of distilled water. Add 5 drops of bromothymol blue to each test tube. Stopper and shake the first test tube to reveal the color of the indicator in neutral solutions. Add 3 drops of concentrated hydrochloric acid to the second test tube, and using a spatula, drop 1 pellet of NaOH into the third test tube. Shake each to reveal the color of the indicator in acidic and basic solutions. These three samples will serve as color standards in the rest of the demonstration. 2. Fill six other test tubes halfway with distilled water, and add 5 drops of indicator to

each. Using a spatula, add a moderate amount of NaCl to the first of the six tubes, KBr to the second, $Na_2CO_3$ to the third, $K_3PO_4$ to the fourth, $NaHSO_4$ to the fifth, and $NaC_2H_3O_2$ to the sixth. Stopper and shake each. (It is not necessary that all of the salt dissolve.) Compare the resulting colors to those of the three standards to determine whether the resulting solutions are acidic, basic, or neutral. Ask the students to attempt to account for the results in terms of the Brønsted–Lowry concept of acids and bases. Allow them to refer to a chart of acid and base strengths if they wish.

**Results:** In step 1, the indicator will be green in the neutral liquid (distilled water), yellow in the acidic (HCl) solution, and blue in the basic (NaOH) solution. In step 2, the indicator will be green (indicating neutrality) in the solutions of NaCl and KBr, which are the salts of strong acids and strong bases, and, by the Brønsted–Lowry theory, are therefore made up of ions that have a very low ability to cause water to release or accept protons and hydrolyze. The indicator will be yellow (indicating acidity) in the solution of $NaHSO_4$, whose $HSO_4^-$ ions are able to donate protons to water, producing hydronium ($H_3O^+$) ions. The indicator will be blue (indicating basicity) in the solutions of $Na_2CO_3$, $K_3PO_4$, and $NaC_2H_3O_2$, which are the salts of strong bases and weak acids and whose anions are therefore good proton acceptors, and can cause water to hydrolyze, donating protons to them and producing hydroxide ($OH^-$) ions.

## Answers to Questions

**Page 576**

1. $H_2O \rightleftarrows H^+ + OH^-$
2. **a.** $[H^+] \times [OH^-] = K_w$;  **b.** $1.0 \times 10^{-14}$
3. **a.** In pure water, the concentrations of the hydrogen and hydroxide ions are equal: $[H^+] = [OH^-]$
   Therefore, $[H^+] \times [OH^-] = 1.0 \times 10^{-14}$
   $$[H^+]^2 = 1.0 \times 10^{-14}$$
   $$[H^+] = 1.0 \times 10^{-7} \, M$$
   $$[OH^-] = 1.0 \times 10^{-7} \, M$$

   **b.** In a 10 $M$ NaOH solution, $[OH^-] = 10 \, M$.
   $[H^+] \times [OH^-] = 1.0 \times 10^{-14}$
   $$[H^+] \times 10 = 1.0 \times 10^{-14}$$
   $$[H^+] = 1.0 \times 10^{-15} \, M$$

   **c.** In a 1.0 $M$ KOH solution, $[OH^-] = 1.0 \, M$.
   $[H^+] \times 1.0 = 1.0 \times 10^{-14}$
   $$[H^+] = 1.0 \times 10^{-14} \, M$$

   **d.** In a 0.10 $M$ HCl solution, $[H^+] = 0.10 \, M$.

   $0.10 \times [OH^-] = 1.0 \times 10^{-14}$
   $$[OH^-] = 1.0 \times 10^{-13} \, M$$

**e.** In a 10 $M$ HCl solution, [H$^+$] = 10 $M$.
$$10 \times [OH^-] = 1.0 \times 10^{-14}$$
$$[OH^-] = 1.0 \times 10^{-15}\ M$$

**4.** $[KOH] = [OH^-] = \dfrac{1.4\ \text{g KOH}}{0.500\ \text{dm}^3} \times \dfrac{1\ \text{mol KOH}}{56\ \text{g KOH}} =$
$$5.0 \times 10^{-2}\ M$$

At 25°C, [H$^+$] × [OH$^-$] = $1.0 \times 10^{-14}$
$$[H^+] \times 5.0 \times 10^{-2} = 1.0 \times 10^{-14}$$
$$[H^+] = 2.0 \times 10^{-13}\ M$$

**5.** $[NaOH] = [OH^-] = \dfrac{4.0\ \text{g NaOH}}{500\ \text{cm}^3} \times \dfrac{1\ \text{mol NaOH}}{40\ \text{g NaOH}} \times$
$$\dfrac{1000\ \text{cm}^3}{1.0\ \text{dm}^3} = 0.20\ M$$

At 25°C, [H$^+$] × [OH$^-$] = $10^{-14}$
$$[H^+] \times 0.20 = 1.0 \times 10^{-14}$$
$$[H^+] = 5.0 \times 10^{-14}\ M$$

## Page 578

**6. a.** The pH of a solution is the negative logarithm to the base 10 of the hydrogen ion concentration.

•   **b.** The acidic pH values fall below 7.

**7. a.** A carbonated beverage is more acidic than orange juice.
   **b.** Rainwater is more acidic than sea water.
   **c.** Sodium bicarbonate is basic.

**8. a.** $[HNO_3] = [H^+] = 1.0 \times 10^{-14}$
$$pH = -\log(1.0 \times 10^{-4}) = 4.0$$
   **b.** $\dfrac{6.3\ \text{g HNO}_3}{1.00\ \text{dm}^3} \times \dfrac{1\ \text{mol HNO}_3}{63\ \text{g HNO}_3} = 0.10\ M\ HNO_3$
$$[HNO_3] = [H^+] = 0.10\ M = 1.0 \times 10^{-1}\ M$$
$$pH = -\log(1.0 \times 10^{-1}) = 1.0$$

**9.** $\dfrac{3.65\ \text{g HCl}}{1.00\ \text{dm}^3} \times \dfrac{1\ \text{mol HCl}}{36.5\ \text{g HCl}} = 0.100\ M$
$$[HCl] = [H^+] = 0.100\ M = 1.00 \times 10^{-1}\ M$$
$$pH = -\log(1.00 \times 10^{-1}) = 1.00$$

**10.** [H$^+$] = antilog($-$pH) = antilog($-10.00$) =
$$1.000 \times 10^{-10}\ M$$

## Page 580

**11. a.** pH = $-\log 1.39 \times 10^{-4}$ = 4 $-$ .143 = 3.86
   **b.** $10 - 0.391 = 9.61$
   **c.** $1 - 0.238 = 0.762$

**12. a.** [H$^+$] = antilog($-3.494$) = $3.206 \times 10^{-4}$
   **b.** [H$^+$] = antilog($-1.265$) = $5.433 \times 10^{-2}$
   **c.** [H$^+$] = antilog($-4.381$) = $4.159 \times 10^{-5}$

## Page 581

**13. a.** The function of buffers is to make a solution resistant to a change in its pH.
   **b.** The blood must maintain a pH between 7.3 and 7.5. Small changes above or below this range can be fatal.

**14. a.** When a buffer solution of sodium acetate and acetic acid has a small amount of 0.10 $M$ HCl

added to it, the acetate ions combine with the added hydrogen ions to form molecular acetic acid.
   **b.** When a small amount of 0.10 $M$ NaOH is added to this buffer, the hydrogen ions combine with the added hydroxide ions to form water.

**15. a.** The equilibrium occurring in a buffer solution of ammonia and ammonium chloride is
$$NH_3 + H_2O \rightleftarrows NH_4^+ + OH^-$$
   **b.** When a small amount of a strong acid is added to this buffer system, the hydrogen ions combine with hydroxide ions to form water, and the equilibrium is shifted to the right.
   **c.** When a small amount of a strong base is added to the system, the hydroxide ions from the strong base combine with the ammonium ions to form ammonia and water. The equilibrium shifts to the left.

## Page 583

**16. a.** The pH is about 10 or higher.
   **b.** A pH meter is more accurate for determining pH than pH paper is.

**17. a.** HIn $\rightleftarrows$ H$^+$ + In$^-$
   **b.** The molecules of the indicator have one color and its anions have another color.

**18.** Indicator colors:

|  | methyl orange | litmus | phenol-phthalein |
|---|---|---|---|
| **a. vinegar (pH = 3):** | red | red | colorless |
| **b. sea water (pH = 8):** | yellow | red-blue | colorless |

## Page 586

**19. a.** A neutralization reaction is one in which all of the H$^+$ ions of the acid combine with all of the OH$^-$ ions of the base.
   **b.** acid + base → salt + water

**20. a.** An acid-base titration is a procedure for determining the unknown concentration of one of the reactants in a neutralization reaction.
   **b.** A standard solution is a solution of known concentration that is used to determine the concentration of another solution.
   **c.** To determine the concentration of a basic solution, a carefully measured volume of the solution is placed in a beaker along with a few drops of an acid-base indicator. A standard solution of an acid is placed inside a buret. Acid is added until the indicator changes color. The unknown concentration can be determined from the reacting volumes of the solutions and the known concentration of the standard solution.

**21.** $V_a\,M_a = V_b\,M_b$
$$25.0\ \text{cm}^3 \times M_a = 10.0\ \text{cm}^3 \times 0.200\ M$$
$$M_a = 0.0800\ M$$

**22.** Note that 1 mol of $Ba(OH)_2$ neutralizes 2 mol of HCl.
$$V_a M_a = 2V_b M_b$$
$$15.0 \text{ cm}^3 \times 0.00300 \ M = 2(50 \text{ cm}^3 \times M_b)$$
$$M_b = 4.5 \times 10^{-4} \ M$$

**23.**
$$V_a M_a = V_b M_b$$
$$21.0 \text{ cm}^3 \times M_a = 25.0 \text{ cm}^3 \times 0.300 \ M$$
$$M_a = 0.357 \ M$$

**24.** Note that 1 mol of $H_2SO_4$ neutralizes 2 mol of KOH.
$$V_b M_b = 2V_a M_a$$
$$45.0 \text{ cm}^3 \times M_b = 2(15.0 \text{ cm}^3 \times 0.500 \ M)$$
$$M_b = 0.333 \ M$$

**Page 589**

**25. a.** The hydrolysis of a salt is the reaction of a salt with water, which may produce a weak acid, a weak base, or both.
  **b.** Salts of a weak base and a weak acid react with water to produce solutions that may be acidic, basic, or neutral, depending on how strongly the ions of the salt are hydrolyzed.
  **c.** The ions are hydrated but do not react with the water molecules.

**26.** When sodium acetate is dissolved in water,
  **a.** the acetate ions react with water molecules.
  **b.** The equation for this reaction is:
$$C_2H_3O_2^- + H_2O \rightleftarrows HC_2H_3O_2 + OH^-$$
  **c.** A sodium acetate solution is basic because acetate ions remove one of the hydrogen atoms from a number of the water molecules in the solution, which results in the formation of hydroxide ions.

**27. a.** The hydrolysis reaction of $NH_4Cl$ is
$$NH_4^+ + H_2O \rightleftarrows NH_3 + H_3O^+$$
  **b.** The solution is acidic because the $NH_4^+$ ion loses a proton to a water molecule, thus producing hydronium ions.

**28. a.** Ammonium carbonate produces a basic solution because the weak base, ammonia, is stronger as a base than the weak acid, carbonic acid, is as an acid.
  **b.** Ammonium acetate produces a neutral solution because ammonia, as a weak base, and acetic acid, as a weak acid, have about equal strength.
  **c.** Ammonium sulfite produces an acidic solution because the weak acid, sulfurous acid, has greater strength as an acid than the weak base, ammonia, has as a base.

**29. a.** phenolphthalein; **b.** methyl orange;
  **c.** any one of these three indicators.

**Page 593**

**30. a.** Sulfuric acid donates 2 protons to NaOH when it reacts to produce $Na_2SO_4$. Therefore, the gram equivalent mass of sulfuric acid in this reaction is:

$$\frac{\text{mass of 1 mol}}{2} = \frac{98 \text{ g}}{2} = 49 \text{ g}$$

  **b.** Because the formula of aluminum hydroxide is $Al(OH)_3$, 3 hydroxide groups are changed to water if all of them react:
$$\frac{\text{mass of 1 mol}}{3} = \frac{78 \text{ g}}{3} = 26 \text{ g}$$

**31.** In the reaction shown, both hydroxide groups of the $Ca(OH)_2$ react. The gram equivalent mass of $Ca(OH)_2$ is, therefore, 74.1 g $Ca(OH)_2$/2 = 37.0 g.
$$\frac{1.48 \text{ g } Ca(OH)_2}{500 \text{ cm}^3} \times \frac{1 \text{ g. eq. mass}}{37.0 \text{ g } Ca(OH)_2} \times \frac{1000 \text{ cm}^3}{1 \text{ dm}^3} = 0.0800 \ N$$

**32.**
$$N_a V_a = N_b V_b$$
$$0.300 \ N \times V_a = 0.225 \ N \times 36.0 \text{ cm}^3$$
$$V_a = 27.0 \text{ cm}^3$$

**Page 593, Electrolytic Titration**

**1.** Barium hydroxide is an electrolyte.
$$Ba(OH)_2 \rightarrow Ba^{2+} + 2OH^-$$

**2.** As the dilute sulfuric acid is added to the beaker, the barium ions are removed from solution as they combine with sulfate ions from the acid to produce the white precipitate of barium sulfate. The hydroxide ions also are removed as they combine with the hydrogen ions from the acid to form water. When enough dilute sulfuric acid is added to neutralize all the barium hydroxide, there are practically no free ions left in the beaker to conduct the current. Hence, the light goes out. However, when still more hydrogen and sulfate ions are added (when more dilute sulfuric acid is added), there are no more barium or hydroxide ions left in the solution with which they can react. The unreacted hydrogen and sulfate ions then conduct the current, causing the bulb to light again.

## Chapter Review 20

Page 594, Content Review

**1.** $HNO_3 = 1.0 + 14.0 + 3(16.0) = 63.0$ g/mol
$$M = \frac{25.2 \text{ g } HNO_3}{0.500 \text{ dm}^3} \times \frac{1 \text{ mol } HNO_3}{63.0 \text{ g}} \times \frac{1 \text{ mol } H^+}{1 \text{ mol } HNO_3} = 0.800 \ M$$

**2.** $NaOH = 23.0 + 16.0 + 1.0 = 40.0$ g/mol
$$[OH^-] = \frac{8.80 \text{ g } NaOH}{2.00 \text{ dm}^3} \times \frac{1 \text{ mol } NaOH}{40.0 \text{ g}} \times \frac{1 \text{ mol } OH^-}{1 \text{ mol } NaOH}$$
$$= 0.110 \ M = 1.10 \times 10^{-1} \ M$$

$$[H^+] = \frac{1.0 \times 10^{-14} \text{ mol}^2/1^2}{[OH^-]} = \frac{1.0 \times 10^{-14} \text{ mol}^2/1^2}{0.11 \ M} =$$
$$9.1 \times 10^{-14} \ M$$

**3. a.** By definition, pH = $-\log[H^+]$. Therefore,
pH = $-\log(1.0 \times 10^{-9} \ M) = -\log 1.0 - \log 10^{-9} =$
$$-0.00 - (-9) = 9.0$$

**b.** If $[OH^-] = 1.0 \times 10^{-9} \ M$,

then $[H^+] = \dfrac{1.0 \times 10^{-14}}{1.0 \times 10^{-9}} = 1.0 \times 10^{-5} \ M$

pH = $-\log(1.0 \times 10^{-5} \ M) = -\log 1.0 - \log 10^{-5}$
$$= -0.00 - (-5) = 5.0$$

**4.** By definition, pH = $-\log [H^+]$. Multiply this equation by $-1$. Then, take the antilog of both sides of the equation.
$$-pH = \log [H^+]$$
$$10^{-pH} = 10^{\log} [H^+] = [H^+]$$
$$[H^+] = 10^{-3.00} \ M = 1.00 \times 10^{-3} \ M$$
$$[OH^-] = \frac{1.0 \times 10^{-14}}{1.0 \times 10^{-3}} = 1.00 \times 10^{-11} \ M$$

**5.** From problem 4, $[H^+] = 10^{-pH}$.
$$[H^+] = 10^{-pH} = 10^{-7.50} \ M = 10^{-8 \ M + 0.50} \ M =$$
$$10^{-8} \times 10^{0.50} \ M = 3.16 \times 10^{-8} \ M$$

**6. a.** pH = $-\log(1.39 \times 10^{-4}) =$
$$- (\log 1.39 + \log 10^{-4}) =$$
$$-(0.1430 + -4) = -(-3.8570) = +3.86$$

**b.** pH = $-\log(5.43 \times 10^{-2}) =$
$$- (\log 5.43 + \log 10^{-2}) =$$
$$-(0.7348 + -2) = -(-1.2652) = +1.27$$

**c.** pH = $-\log(3.21 \times 10^{-4}) =$
$$-(\log 3.21 + \log 10^{-4}) =$$
$$-(0.5065 + -4) = -(-3.4935) = +3.49$$

**7.** $[H^+] = 10^{-pH}$
  **a.** $[H^+] = 10^{-9.609} = 10^{-10 + 0.391} = 2.460 \times 10^{-10} \ M$
  **b.** $[H^+] = 10^{-3.857} = 10^{-4 + 0.143} = 1.390 \times 10^{-4} \ M$
  **c.** $[H^+] = 10^{-0.762} = 10^{-1 + 0.238} = 1.73 \times 10^{-1} \ M$

**8.** A buffer solution is generally composed of a mixture of a weak acid and its conjugate base, or a mixture of a weak base and its conjugate acid. For example, acetate buffer is a mixture of acetic acid (a weak acid) and sodium acetate (its conjugate base). Ammonium buffer is ammonia (a weak base) and ammonium chloride (its conjugate acid).

**9. a.** The pH range in normal human blood is 7.3 to 7.5.
  **b.** If the pH dropped below 6.9 or rose above 7.7, a person could die. Therefore, the blood is buffered to keep the pH within the normal range.

**10.** $H^+ + CO_3^{2-} \rightleftharpoons HCO_3^-$
Excess acid would be neutralized by $CO_3^{2-}$, the conjugate base of this buffer pair.

**11.** $HIn \rightleftharpoons H^+ + In^-$
Adding acid shifts the equilibrium to the left,

producing HIn. The indicator solution is the color of the neutral HIn molecule. Adding base shifts the equilibrium to the right, so the indicator solution is the color of the anion, $In^-$.

**12. a.** The solution is yellow in methyl red, so its pH is above 6.0. It is also yellow in phenol red, so its pH is below 6.6. The fact that it is also yellow in alizarin yellow does not give any additional information.
  **b.** This solution is red in alizarin yellow, so its pH is 12.0 or higher. Its colors in methyl red and phenol red do not give any additional information.

**13.**

| | methyl red | phenol red | alizarin yellow |
|---|---|---|---|
| **a.** rainwater pH = 6.3 | yellow | yellow | yellow |
| **b.** ammonia water pH = 11.2 | yellow | red | yellow-red |

**14.** An acid and a base have neutralized each other when all of the $H_3O^+$ ions from the acid have combined with all of the $OH^-$ ions from the base.

**15. a.** $NaOH + HCl \rightarrow Na^+ + Cl^- + H_2O$
$$M_a = \frac{M_b V_b}{V_a} \times \frac{\text{mol acid}}{\text{mol base}} = \frac{(0.10 \ M)(25 \text{ cm}^3)}{(15 \text{ cm}^3)} \times \frac{1}{1} =$$
$$0.17 \ M$$

  **b.** 1 mol HCl = 36.5 g
$$\text{g HCl} = \frac{36.5 \text{ g}}{\text{mol}} \times \frac{0.17 \text{ mol}}{\text{dm}^3} \times 0.015 \text{ dm}^3 =$$
$$9.3 \times 10^{-2} \text{ g}$$

**16.** $NaOH + HCl \rightarrow Na^+ + Cl^- + H_2O$
$$M_b = \frac{M_a V_a}{V_b} \times \frac{\text{mol base}}{\text{mol acid}} = \frac{(2.76 \ M)(98.7 \text{ cm}^3)}{250 \text{ cm}^3} \times \frac{1}{1} =$$
$$1.09 \ M$$

**17.** When a strong acid and a strong base neutralize each other, they form a salt and water. This salt forms hydrated ions in aqueous solution, but it does not hydrolyze water. Therefore, the solution remains neutral, with a pH of 7.0.

**18. a.** Salts of a weak base and strong acid, a weak acid and strong base, and a weak acid and weak base are hydrolyzed by water.
  **b.** Salts of a weak base and weak acid can be hydrolyzed to produce acidic, basic, or neutral solutions, depending on the particular salt.

**19. a.** $CO_3^{2-} + H_2O \rightleftharpoons HCO_3^- + OH^-$
  **b.** The solution is basic because the reaction in **a** produces excess hydroxide ions.

**20. a.** Nitrous acid (a weak acid) and potassium hydroxide (a strong base) yield a basic solution, so use an indicator that changes color in the basic range, such as phenolphthalein.

  **b.** Sulfuric acid (a strong acid) and ammonia solution (a weak base) yield an acidic solution, so use an indicator that changes color in the acidic range, such as methyl orange.

  **c.** Sulfuric acid (a strong acid) and potassium hydroxide (a strong base) yield a neutral solution with the exact equivalence point at pH 7. However, the addition of only 1 drop of either the strong base or the strong acid will cause a change in pH of about 6 pH units. Therefore, practically any indicator can be used in such a titration.

**21. a.** $H_2SO_4 = 2(1) + 32 + 4(16.0) = 98$ g/mol

gram equivalent mass $= \dfrac{98g}{mol} \times \dfrac{mol}{1\ equivalent} =$

$98$ g/equivalent

  **b.** $H_3PO_4 = 3(1) + 31 + 4(16) = 98$ g/mol

gram equivalent mass $= \dfrac{98\ g}{mol} \times \dfrac{mol}{2\ equivalents} =$

$49$ g/equivalent

**22. a.** $N_a = \dfrac{10.0\ g\ H_2SO_4}{0.300\ dm^3} \times \dfrac{1\ mol}{98.1\ g} \times \dfrac{2\ equivalents}{mol} =$

$0.680\ N$

  **b.** $N_b = \dfrac{15.0\ g\ KOH}{0.200\ dm^3} \times \dfrac{1\ mol}{56.1\ g} \times \dfrac{1\ equivalent}{mol} =$

$1.34\ N$

**23.** $N_b = \dfrac{N_a V_a}{V_b} = \dfrac{(0.020\ N)\ (10.0\ cm^3)}{30.0\ cm^3} = 6.7 \times 10^{-3}\ N$

**Page 595, Content Mastery**

**24. a.** Some of the solutions may be acidic, some may be basic, and some may be neutral.

  **b.** The hydrolysis of this salt yields ammonia ($NH_3$) and hydrocyanic acid (HCN). The base is stronger than the acid. (The base has a higher ionization constant.)

  **c.** The ionization constant of the acid (HF) formed by hydrolysis is higher than that of the base ($NH_3$) that is formed. The solution, therefore, acquires an excess of hydrogen ions.

**25.** To determine the concentration of a solution of nitric acid, put a measured volume of the acid plus some indicator in a beaker. Add the standard KOH solution from a buret until the indicator changes color. The unknown concentration can be determined from the known concentration of the KOH solution and the volumes of reactants used to reach the end point.

**26. a.** $Bi(OH)_3 = 209 + 3(16) + 3(1) = 260$ g/mol

gram equivalent mass $= 260\ \dfrac{g}{mol} \times \dfrac{1\ mol}{equivalent} =$

$260$ g/equivalent

  **b.** $Pb(OH)_2 = 207 + 2(16) + 2(1) = 241$ g/mol

gram equivalent mass $= 241\ \dfrac{g}{mol} \times \dfrac{1\ mol}{equivalent} =$

$241$ g/equivalent

**27.** $H_2SO_4 + 2KOH \rightarrow K_2SO_4 + 2H_2O$

$M_b = \dfrac{M_a V_a}{V_b} \times \dfrac{moles\ base}{moles\ acid}$

$= \dfrac{15.0\ g\ H_2SO_4}{0.200\ dm^3} \times \dfrac{mol}{98.0\ g} \times \dfrac{15.0\ cm^3}{35.0\ cm^3} \times \dfrac{2\ mol\ base}{1\ mol\ acid}$

$= 0.656\ M$

**28.** $[H^+] = 0.080\ M\ HCl \times \dfrac{1\ mol\ H^+}{1\ mol\ HCl} \times \dfrac{1.00\ dm^3}{2.00\ dm^3} =$

$4.0 \times 10^{-2}\ M$

$[OH^-] = \dfrac{1.0 \times 10^{-14}\ mol^2/1^2}{4.0 \times 10^{-2}\ mol/1} = 2.5 \times 10^{-13}\ M$

**29.** $HA \rightleftarrows H^+ + A^-$

If $[HA] = [A^-]$, then they cancel out of the equation for $K_a$.

$K_a = \dfrac{[H^+]\cancel{[A^-]}}{\cancel{[HA]}} = [H^+]$

**30.** $pH = -\log[H^+] = -\log(1.0 \times 10^{-1}) =$

$-(0.0 + -1) = 1.0$

**31.** The pH of a carbonated drink is 3.0.

  **a.** Because this pH is less than 4.8, the solution will be red in methyl red.

  **b.** Because this pH is less than 8.2, the solution will be colorless in phenolphthalein.

**32.** $pH = -\log[H^+] = -\log(6.1 \times 10^{-4}\ M) =$

$-(\log 6.1 + \log 10^{-4}) = -(0.7853 + -4) = +3:21$

**33.** $H_3PO_4 = 3(1.01) + 31.0 + 4(16.0) = 98.03$ g/mol

$H_3PO_4 + 3NaOH \rightarrow Na_3PO_4 + 3H_2O$

gram equivalent mass $= 98.03\ \dfrac{g}{mol} \times \dfrac{1\ mol}{3\ equivalents} =$

$32.68$ g/equivalents

$M = \dfrac{44.4\ g}{0.250\ dm^3} \times \dfrac{mol}{98.0\ g} = 1.81\ M$

$N = \dfrac{44.4\ g}{0.250\ dm^3} \times \dfrac{1\ mol}{98.0\ g} \times \dfrac{3\ equivalents}{mol} = 5.43\ N$

**34.** $[H^+][OH^-] = 1.0 \times 10^{-14}\ mol^2/l^2$

$$[H^+] = \frac{1.0 \times 10^{-14}\ mol^2/l^2}{6.10 \times 10^{-4}\ mol/l} = 0.16 \times 10^{-10}\ M$$
$$= 1.6 \times 10^{-11}\ M$$
$$pH = -\log[H^+] = -\log(1.6 \times 10^{-11}\ M)$$
$$= -(\log 1.6 + \log 10^{-11})$$
$$= -(0.2041 + -11)$$
$$= +10.8$$

**35.** $2HCl + Ba(OH)_2 \rightarrow BaCl_2 + 2H_2O$

$$M_a = \frac{M_b\ V_b}{V_a} \times \frac{moles\ acid}{moles\ base}$$
$$= \frac{(1.38\ M)\ (98.7\ cm^3)}{250.0\ cm^3} \times \frac{2\ mol\ acid}{1\ mol\ base} = 1.09\ M$$

**36.** $[H^+] = 10^{-pH} = 10^{-0.61} = 10^{-1 + 0.39} =$
$$2.455 \times 10^{-1}\ M = 2.5 \times 10^{-1}\ M$$
$$[OH^-] = \frac{1.0 \times 10^{-14}}{[H^+]} = \frac{1.0 \times 10^{-14}}{2.455 \times 10^{-1}} =$$
$$4.1 \times 10^{-14}\ M$$

**37.** $Ba(OH)_2 = 137.3 + 2(16.0) + 2(1.0) =$
$$171.3\ g/mol$$
$$[OH^-] = \frac{8.55\ g}{1.0\ dm^3} \times \frac{mol\ Ba(OH)_2}{171.3\ g\ Ba(OH)_2} \times \frac{2\ mol\ OH^-}{1\ mol\ Ba(OH)_2}$$
$$= 0.10\ M$$

## Page 596, Concept Mastery

**38.** ***Concept:*** *The pH depends on the concentration of the hydrogen ion. Students sometimes think that the scale runs only from 1 to 14.*

***Solution:*** Yes, the pH can be less than 1 or greater than 14 and is limited only by the solubility of the solute. For example, if 80 grams or 2 moles of NaOH are dissolved in 1 $dm^3$ of solution, the pH would be slightly greater than 14.

For 2 $M$ $OH^-$, the $[H^+] = \dfrac{1.0 \times 10^{-14}\ M^2}{2\ M} =$
$$0.5 \times 10^{-14}\ M = 5.0 \times 10^{-15}\ M$$
$$pH = -\log[H^+] = -(\log 5.0 \times 10^{-15}) =$$
$$-(0.699 - 15) = +14.31$$

A 1 $M$ HCl solution has a pH equal to zero. A more concentrated acid that completely dissociates in water has a negative pH.
For 1 $M$ $H^+$, pH $= -\log(1) = -0 = 0$
For 2 $M$ $H^+$, pH $= -\log(2) = -0.301$

**39.** ***Concept:*** *Equivalent numbers of molecules of a strong acid and a strong base react to form water and a neutral salt.*

***Solution:*** See Figure 20-2.

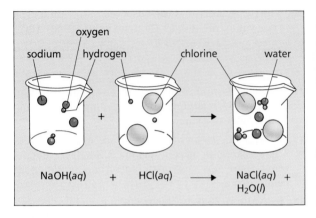

oxygen

sodium   hydrogen          chlorine        water

NaOH(aq)   +   HCl(aq)   $\longrightarrow$   NaCl(aq) + H$_2$O(l)

**Figure 20-2**

**40.** ***Concept:*** *Neutralizing a strong base with a weak acid yields a basic solution.*

***Solution:*** Mixing vinegar, which contains acetic acid, and sodium hydroxide yields water. Since acetic acid is a weak acid, the acetate ion reacts with water to form the molecular acetic acid. This reaction consumes some of the hydrogen ions present in the water, leaving an excess of hydroxide ions, resulting in a slightly basic solution.

**41.** ***Concept:*** *Water contains $H^+$ and $OH^-$ ions in small but significant quantities.*

***Solution:*** Even though water is a poor conductor of electricity, there are enough ions present to conduct electricity from the appliance through the person through the water to the ground.

**42.** ***Concept:*** *The pH scale is logarithmic.*

***Solution:*** Since pH uses a logarithmic scale (not a linear one), changing the pH by one unit is equivalent to changing the concentration of $H^+$ by $10^1$. The pH of rainwater is 2 units greater than the pH of tomato juice. Therefore, tomato juice has a hydrogen-ion concentration that is $10^2$ times greater than that of rainwater.

## Page 596, Cumulative Review

**43.** According to Arrhenius, a base is a substance whose water solution yields hydroxide ions as the only negative ion.

**44.** According to Brønsted-Lowry, an acid is a substance that can donate a proton to another substance.

**20**

**45.** The percent error is the observed value minus the true value, divided by the true value, times 100.

$$\% \text{ error} = \frac{271 \text{ K} - 273 \text{ K}}{273 \text{ K}} \times 100\% = \frac{-2}{273} \times 100$$
$$= -0.7\%$$

**46.** Chemical equilibrium exists when the forward and the reverse reactions are proceeding at the same rate under the same conditions.

**47.** A large $K_{eq}$ means that there are more products than reactants at equilibrium. A small $K_{eq}$ means that there are more reactants than products at equilibrium.

**48. b.** NaBr = 23.0 + 79.9 = 102.9 g/mol

$$\text{g Cl}_2 = 23.0 \text{ g NaBr} \times \frac{\text{mol NaBr}}{102.9 \text{ g}} \times \frac{2 \text{ Cl}}{2 \text{ NaBr}} \times \frac{35.5 \text{ g}}{\text{mol Cl}}$$
$$= 7.93 \text{ g}$$

**49. d.** The specific heat of water, the amount of heat required to raise the temperature of 1 g of water by 1 degree Celsius, is 4.18 joules.

$$4.18 \frac{\text{J}}{\text{g·°C}} \times 500 \text{ g} \times 21°\text{C} = 43890 \text{ J} = 4.4 \times 10^4 \text{ J}$$

**50.** The correct answer is **a.** Si has 14 electrons, whereas the others have 18 electrons.
  **a.** The atomic number of Si is 14, so a neutral atom has 14 electrons.
  **b.** The atomic number of S is 16, so a neutral atom has 16 electrons. $S^{2-}$ is a negative ion that has gained 2 electrons, for a total of 16 + 2 = 18.
  **c.** The atomic number of P is 15, so a neutral atom has 15 electrons. $P^{3-}$ is a negative ion that has gained 3 electrons, for a total of 15 + 3 = 18 electrons.
  **d.** The atomic number of Ne is 10, so the kernel has 10 electrons. The whole atom (which happens to be Ar) has 10 + 2 + 6 = 18 electrons.

**51.** The correct answer is **c.** isoelectronic, which is used to refer to 2 species (atoms, ions, or molecules) that have the same number of electrons.

**52. d.** $\dfrac{2 \text{ moles } X_2Y}{0.50 \text{ dm}^3} \times \dfrac{2X}{1X2Y} = 8.0 \text{ } M \text{ X ion}$

**Page 597, Critical Thinking**

**53.** Find the pH of each solution.
  **a.** NaOH is a strong base and dissociates completely.
  0.1 $M$ NaOH produces 0.1 $M$ OH$^-$.
  $$[H^+] = \frac{1.0 \times 10^{-14} \text{ mol}^2/1^2}{0.1 \text{ } M} = 1 \times 10^{-13} \text{ } M$$
  pH = 13
  **b.** HCl is a strong acid and dissociates completely.
  0.1 $M$ HCl produces 0.1 $M$ H$^+$.
  $[H^+] = 10^{-1} \text{ } M$, pH = 1

  **c.** From text Figure 20-6, the pH of lemon juice is 2.3.
  **d.** Acetic acid is a weak acid and does not ionize completely.
  HAc $\rightleftharpoons$ H$^+$ + Ac$^-$
  $$K_a = \frac{[H^+][Ac^-]}{[HAc]} = 1.8 \times 10^{-5} \text{ } M \text{ at } 25°\text{C}$$
  When acetic acid dissociates, the concentration of H$^+$ produced equals the concentration of Ac$^-$. Substitute into the equation and solve for [H$^+$].
  $$K_a = \frac{[H^+][H^+]}{0.1 \text{ } M} = 1.8 \times 10^{-5} \text{ } M$$
  $$[H^+]^2 = (1.8 \times 10^{-5} \text{ } M)(0.1 \text{ } M) = 1.8 \times 10^{-6} \text{ } M^2$$
  $$[H^+] = \sqrt{1.8 \times 10^{-6} \text{ } M^2} = 1.3 \times 10^{-3} \text{ } M$$
  $$\text{pH} = \log[H^+] = -\log(1.3 \times 10^{-3}) = -(0.1139 - 3) = 2.89$$
  **e.** The pH of tomato juice is 4.2.
  **f.** The pH of milk is 6.5. As the pH increases, the basicity increases. In the following chart, the most acidic substances are on the left, the most basic on the right.

| sub-stance | HCl | lemon juice | acetic acid | tomato juice | milk | NaOH |
|---|---|---|---|---|---|---|
| pH | 1 | 2.3 | 2.89 | 4.2 | 6.5 | 13 |
| letter | b | c | d | e | f | a |

**54.** Sometimes, an upset stomach is caused by acid indigestion, a condition in which too much acid is released into the stomach. Antacids contain basic substances that neutralize the excess stomach acid, thus relieving the indigestion.

**55.** Buffered solutions resist changes in pH, whereas unbuffered solutions do not. Adding a strong acid or base to an unbuffered solution causes a large change in the pH. In a buffered solution, the buffer reacts with the added acid or base and neutralizes it, so the pH remains relatively constant.

**56.** A solution that is blue in methyl violet and yellow in bromophenol blue has a pH above 1.6 and below 3.0. It will be red in methyl yellow.

**57.** See the following chart:

| Type | Titration of | Solution is | Suitable indicator |
|---|---|---|---|
| 1 | SA-SB | neutral | all |
| 2 | SA-WB | acidic | methyl yellow bromophenol blue |
| 3 | WA-SB | basic | alizarin yellow thymolphthalein |

**58.** The correct answer is **b** and **c**.
  **a.** This weak acid and its salt make a good buffer.
  **b.** While this is an acid and its salt, the acid is a strong acid rather than a weak acid, so the acid is completely ionized. There is no equilibrium.

There is plenty of $H^+$ to react with any base added to the solution, but using up the $H^+$ will raise the pH. There is no anion to react with any acid that is added to the solution.

c. This is not a weak base and its salt. $NH_3$ is a weak base, and NaOH is a strong base. They will both neutralize acids, but they cannot neutralize other bases that might be added to the solution.

### Page 597, Challenge Problems

**59. a.** $HS^- + H_2O \rightleftharpoons H_2S + OH^-$

$$K_h = \frac{[H_2S][OH^-]}{[HS^-]} = 9.1 \times 10^{-8}$$

**b.** $0.10$ $M$ NaHS dissociates completely to form $0.10$ $M$ $HS^-$. The concentration of $H_2S$ equals the concentration of $OH^-$ produced.

$[OH^-]^2 = K_h \times [HS^-] = 9.1 \times 10^{-8} \times 0.10 = 9.1 \times 10^{-9}$

$[OH^-] = \sqrt{91 \times 10^{-10}} = 9.5 \times 10^{-5}$ $M$

**c.** $[H^+] = \dfrac{K_w}{[OH^-]} = \dfrac{1.0 \times 10^{-14}}{9.5 \times 10^{-5}} = 1.1 \times 10^{-10}$ $M$

**d.** $pH = -\log[H^+] = -\log(1.1 \times 10^{-10})$

$= -(0.0414 + -10) = -(-9.9586) = +9.96$

**60. a.** $[H^+] = \dfrac{0.10 \text{ mol}}{1.00 \text{ dm}^3} = 1.0 \times 10^{-1}$ $M$

$pH = -\log[H^+] = -\log(1.0 \times 10^{-1}) = -(0 + -1)$
$= +1.0$

Therefore, the change in pH = $7.0 - 1.0 = 6.0$ pH units.

**b.** Write the equilibrium expression for the system before the acid is added and solve for the concentration of $H^+$. The problem gives [HA] and [A$^-$].

$HA \rightleftharpoons H^+ + A^-$

$$K_a = \frac{[H^+][A^-]}{[HA]} = \frac{[H^+](1.00)}{1.00} = 1.0 \times 10^{-7} = [H^+]$$

Because $K_a$ is small, the reaction favors the reactants. Most of the added acid will combine with $A^-$ to produce HA. Solve the problem by assuming that all of the added $H^+$ combines with $A^-$ to produce excess HA, and then a small amount of this HA, equal to $x$, dissociates. Now, write the equilibrium expression for this system.

$$K_a = \frac{[H^+][A^-]}{[HA]} = \frac{(10^{-7} + x)(1.00 - 0.10 + x)}{(1.00 + 0.10 - x)} =$$
$$1.0 \times 10^{-7}$$

Assume $x$ is negligible with respect to [HA] and [A$^-$] and solve for $x$.

$$K_a = \frac{(10^{-7} + x)(0.90)}{1.10)} = 1.0 \times 10^{-7}$$
$$x = \frac{1.10}{0.90} \times (1.0 \times 10^{-7}) - 1.0 \times 10^{-7} =$$
$$0.22 \times 10^{-7} \text{ } M$$

Notice that $x$ is, in fact, negligible with respect to [HA] and [A$^-$]. So, $[H^+] = 1.0 \times 10^{-7}$ $M + x = 1.0 \times 10^{-7}$ $M + 0.22 \times 10^{-7} = 1.22 \times 10^{-7}$ $M$.

$pH = -\log[H^+] = -\log(1.22 \times 10^{-7})$
$= -\log 1.22 - \log 10^{-7} = -0.086 - -7 = +6.91$

Therefore, the change in pH is $7.00 - 6.91 = 0.09$ pH units.

**c.** When 0.10 mol of acid is added to 1 dm$^3$ of solution, the change in the pH is almost 70 times greater for water than for the buffer!

$$\frac{6.00 \text{ units}}{0.09 \text{ unit}} = 67$$

**61.** Answers will vary depending on the samples each student chooses. Students probably will predict, for example, that cleaning solutions are basic and that carbonated beverages are acidic. They could verify their predictions by testing the samples with pH indicators.

20

# Oxidation and Reduction

**21**

## Chapter Planning Guide

| Text Section | Labs (Lab Manual) and Demonstrations (TE) | Supplementary Materials (Teacher's Resource Book) |
|---|---|---|
| **21-1** The Use of the Terms Oxidation and Reduction, pp. 599-600 **21-2** Oxidation Numbers, pp. 600-604 | | Transparency Master: Determining the Oxidation Number of Chromium in the Dichromate Ion, $Cr_2O_7^{2-}$, p. 21-1 Review Activity: Oxidation Numbers, p. 21-3 |
| **21-3** Identifying Oxidation-Reduction Reactions, pp. 604-610 **Application** Photography, p. 610 | | Review Activity: Oxidation and Reduction, p. 21-4 |
| **21-4** Balancing Redox Equations with Oxidation Numbers, pp. 611-613 **Career** Pharmacist, p. 612 | Demo 21-1: Decomposing Water with Your Bare Hands, p. TG-300 | Transparency Master: Balancing Redox Equations with Oxidation Numbers, p. 21-2 |
| **21-5** Balancing Redox Equations—The Half-Reaction Method, pp. 613-616 | Demo 21-2: Where's the Copper?, p. TG-301 Lab 41: Redox: Oxidation-Reduction Reactions | |
| | | Test—Form A, p. AT-80 Alternate Test—Form B, p. BT-80 |

☐ Core  ☐ Advanced  ☐ Optional

## Chapter Overview

In Chapter 21, we state and give examples of the original meanings of oxidation and reduction. The rules for assigning oxidation numbers to atoms in chemical formulas are given.

The extended meanings of oxidation and reduction are stated in terms of increases and decreases in oxidation number. Students use oxidation numbers to identify oxidation-reduction reactions (redox reactions) and the oxidizing and reducing agents in these reactions. The four categories of equations from Chapter 9 are classified as redox or non-redox reactions. Two methods of balancing redox equations are explained and applied. Students first learn to balance redox equations by using changes in oxidation numbers. Then we show them how to use the half-reaction method.

# Chapter Objectives

After students have completed this chapter, they will be able to:

1. Assign oxidation numbers to elements in various compounds and in the elemental state.
*21-1* and *21-2*

2. Identify oxidation-reduction reactions and the corresponding oxidizing and reducing agent.   *21-3*

3. Balance redox equations by the change-in-oxidation-number method.   *21-4*

4. Balance redox equations by the half-reaction method.   *21-5*

# Teaching Suggestions

## 21-1 The Use of the Terms Oxidation and Reduction, pp. 599-600, and

## 21-2 Oxidation Numbers, pp. 600-604

| Planning Guide | |
| --- | --- |
| Labs (Lab Manual) and Demonstrations (TE) | Supplementary Materials (Teacher's Resource Book) |
| | Transparency Master: Determining the Oxidation Number of Chromium in the Dichromate Ion, $Cr_2O_7^{2-}$, p. 21-1 Review Activity: Oxidation Numbers, p. 21-3 |

■ Discuss the original meaning of oxidation and give examples of oxidation reactions that are consistent with this definition.

■ Point out that the definition of oxidation has been broadened to encompass a larger number of reactions. Define oxidation number and oxidation state. Refer to text Figure 21-2 to emphasize the difference between ion charge and oxidation number. Discuss each of the rules for determining oxidation numbers in turn and work through examples of each rule. Ask the students to justify the zero oxidation number for the elements. Do the same for the monatomic ions for which the oxidation number is the same as the ionic charge. Emphasize the oxidation numbers of oxygen and hydrogen since they appear in so many compounds. Justify their usual values in terms of valence electrons and electronegativities. Then discuss the exceptions: the $-1$ value for hydrogen in hydrides, and the $-1$ value for the oxygen atom in peroxides. Use the Trans-

parency Master "Determining the Oxidation Number of Chromium in the Dichromate Ion, $Cr_2O_7^{2-}$" to illustrate how the oxidation numbers of atoms in polyatomic ions can be determined. Ask the students to use this method to verify the oxidation numbers of chromium in the compounds listed in text Figure 21-4. Point out to the students that in order to determine the oxidation numbers of elements with variable oxidation numbers (i.e., N, S, Cl, P, Cr, etc.), they should use the known values of other elements in the formula to solve for the unknown oxidation numbers.

■ **Application.** You may want to point out some familiar oxidation reactions to the students. For example, the tarnishing of silver is due to oxidation. In fact, the ease with which silver oxidizes makes this metal less desirable, and much less expensive, than gold and platinum. The oxidation of metals such as iron is commonly known as rusting. Discuss some of the common methods of preventing rusting such as varnishing, painting, and waxing.

## 21-3 Identifying Oxidation-Reduction Reactions, pp. 604-610

| Planning Guide | |
| --- | --- |
| Labs (Lab Manual) and Demonstrations (TE) | Supplementary Materials (Teacher's Resource Book) |
| | Review Activity: Oxidation and Reduction, p. 21-4 |

■ Re-define oxidation in terms of oxidation numbers and apparent loss of electrons. Define reduction in similar terms. Emphasize that a loss of electrons increases oxidation number, whereas a gain of electrons decreases oxidation number. Assign a number of redox equations and ask the students to identify the oxidized and reduced elements and the oxidizing and reducing agents. Their choices should be justified in terms of electron loss or gain and on the basis of an increase or decrease in oxidation state. Include some equations that are not redox to test the students' ability to differentiate between categories of reactions.

■ Remind the students of the classification scheme for chemical reactions introduced in Chapter 9. Point out that reactions that are classified as synthesis, analysis, and single replacement are redox reactions. None of the double replacement reactions is a redox reaction.

■ **Application.** You may want to point out that apple cider is one beverage that normally does not contain preservatives. Therefore, cider slowly undergoes fermentation and oxidation reactions in which the sugars ferment to ethyl alcohol and the alcohol is subsequently oxidized to acetic acid (vinegar).

21

■ **Concept Mastery.** The concepts covered so far in this chapter will be new to some students. Other students may be familiar with the common usage of the term oxidation and may have difficulty in relating to the more technical definition introduced in this section. Therefore, you may want to discuss Concept Mastery questions 30 through 33 (chapter-end questions). These questions can help you to determine the depth of your students' understanding of the term *oxidation*. Begin by writing several equations on the board. Some of these equations should contain oxygen and some should not, such as the equation discussed in question 30. Then show how the meaning of oxidation —an increase in oxidation number—is the broader definition.

## 21-4 Balancing Redox Equations with Oxidation Numbers, pp. 611-613

| Planning Guide | |
|---|---|
| Labs (Lab Manual) and Demonstrations (TE) | Supplementary Materials (Teacher's Resource Book) |
| Demo 21-1: Decomposing Water with Your Bare Hands, p. TG-300 | Transparency Master: Balancing Redox Equations with Oxidation Numbers, p. 21-2 |

■ If you choose to cover this Advanced Topic, begin by doing Demonstration 21-1, "Decomposing Water with Your Bare Hands." In this demonstration students observe a redox reaction, namely, the decomposition of water by electrolysis. Explain that, although the equation for this reaction can be balanced by the trial-and-error approach introduced in Chapter 9, other redox equations cannot be balanced by this approach. Point out that there are two different systematic methods for balancing redox equations: the change-in-oxidation-number method and the half-reaction method. Use the change-in-oxidation-number method to balance the equation for the electrolytic decomposition of water.

## 21-5 Balancing Redox Equations—The Half-Reaction Method, pp. 613-616

| Planning Guide | |
|---|---|
| Labs (Lab Manual) and Demonstrations (TE) | Supplementary Materials (Teacher's Resource Book) |
| Demo 21-2: Where's the Copper?, p. TG-301 Lab 41: Redox: Oxidation-Reduction Reactions | |

■ If you choose to cover this Advanced Topic, begin by doing Demonstration 21-2, "Where's the Copper?" In this demonstration the students observe the redox reaction between copper metal and a silver nitrate solution. They are asked to write the half-reactions and to balance the equation for this reaction. Use this demonstration as a motivating way to introduce the topic of half-reactions. Then discuss the step-by-step method for balancing redox equations using half-reactions. After you balance the equation for the reaction in Demonstration 21-2, work through Sample Problem 9 in the text. Assign Laboratory 41, "Redox: Oxidation-Reduction Reactions," in which the students observe numerous combinations of reactants and determine whether or not redox reactions occur. This lab also provides an opportunity to introduce the concept of standard electrode potentials.

# Demonstrations

## 21-1 Decomposing Water with Your Bare Hands

**Overview:** In this demonstration, you decompose water, using a hand generator. Your students are physically involved in supplying the energy for the chemical reaction that occurs.

**Materials:** d.c. hand generator (can generally be borrowed from the physics department); 500-mL beaker; 2 small test tubes with test-tube holder; insulated electrical wire; 2 electrodes; concentrated sulfuric acid ($H_2SO_4$); wooden splints; matches; safety goggles.

**Advance Preparation:** Set up the apparatus as shown in Figure 21-1. Add about 1 mL of concentrated sulfuric acid ($H_2SO_4$) to roughly 300 mL of water, to serve as an electrolyte. Fill the test tubes with the acidified water, pour roughly 250 mL of the water into a 500-mL beaker, and invert the filled test tubes into the water (keeping them stoppered during the inversion, so that no air enters them). Slip the tubes over the electrodes, as shown.

**Safety:** Be careful handling the sulfuric acid. Avoid allowing students to touch the electrodes or wires while the electricity is being generated. Be careful in carrying out the splint tests: hold the tubes at arm's length and wear goggles. Do not attempt to substitute large test tubes or other containers for the small ones. Carrying out the splint tests on larger quantities of hydrogen can produce a dangerous explosion and fire.

**Procedure:** 1. Have several students take turns rotating the handle of the generator to produce electric current. Have them continue to do so until one of the test tubes is filled with gas. Ask your students to observe the relative volumes and color of the two gases. 2. Keeping the test tube under water, remove the positive electrode from the test tube. Raise the tube to the level of the water surface so that all of the water is out of the tube but none of the gas can escape. Place a rubber stopper into the neck of the tube and remove it from the water. Hold the test tube with a test-tube holder. Light a wooden splint, and blow out the flame, leaving the tip of the splint glowing. Turn the test tube upright, remove the rubber stopper from it, and then, holding the tube at arm's length, insert the glowing splint, and ask your students to observe what happens. (Do not allow them to stand nearby.) 3. Repeat step 2 (observing the same cautions) for the tube that is over the negative electrode. This time, however, keep the tube inverted, and insert a still-burning splint into it. Ask students what they think the two gases are, and have them write a balanced equation for the decomposition reaction.

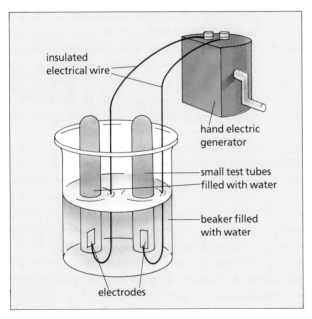

**Figure 21-1**

**Results:** Two gases will be collected, by water displacement, in the test tubes. The volume of gas over the negative electrode will be twice that over the positive electrode. Both gases will be colorless and nearly insoluble in water (since they were collected by water displacement). The gas collected at the negative electrode will be hydrogen, and the gas collected at the positive electrode will be oxygen, as indicated by the splint tests. The glowing splint thrust into the oxygen gas will glow brighter or burst into flame. The burning splint thrust into the hydrogen gas will burn with a pale-blue flame and/or produce a small explosion or "pop." The equation for the decomposition reaction

that will occur during the electrolysis is: $2H_2O(l) \rightarrow 2H_2(g) + O_2(g)$.

## 21-2 Where's the Copper?

**Overview:** In this demonstration, you cause copper and silver nitrate to undergo an oxidation–reduction reaction.

**Materials:** 30 cm of clean 16-gauge copper (Cu) wire; 250-mL beaker; 100 mL of 0.2 $M$ silver nitrate ($AgNO_3$); distilled water; watch glass.

**Advance Preparation: 0.2 $M$ $AgNO_3$:** mix 3.4 g of $AgNO_3$ in enough distilled water to make 100 mL of solution.

**Safety:** Be careful not to get any silver nitrate on your skin or clothing; it is poisonous and will also cause discoloration.

**Procedure:** 1. Add 100 mL of 0.2 $M$ $AgNO_3$ to a 250-mL beaker. Have students observe that the solution is colorless. Twist the copper wire into a coil shape (you can wrap it around a pencil or test tube, if you wish, and then slip it off). Have students observe the reddish color and the diameter of the copper wire. 3. Immerse the coiled copper wire in the silver nitrate solution, and bend the top end of the coil over the top of the beaker, to support the coil. Have students observe the copper wire and silver nitrate solution for a few minutes. Cover the beaker with a watch glass, and store it overnight. 4. The next day, have students again observe the beaker and its contents. Shake the copper wire to free it of its coating, and have students observe its diameter. Ask them to try to write half-reactions and a balanced oxidation–reduction equation for the reaction that has occurred.

**Results:** In step 3, immersion of the copper wire in the silver nitrate solution will rapidly cause the copper to appear to turn dark, suggesting that a chemical reaction is occurring. In step 4, a blue solution (characteristic of $Cu^{2+}$ ions) will be present in the beaker, and the copper wire that was immersed in the solution will be covered by small white-gray crystals of silver. The diameter of the copper wire will be reduced. The half-reactions and balanced overall equation are:

Reduction: $2Ag^+(aq) + 2e^- \rightarrow 2Ag(s)$

Oxidation: $$\frac{Cu(s) \rightarrow Cu^{2+}(aq) + 2e^-}{2Ag^+(aq) + Cu(s) \rightarrow 2Ag(s) + Cu^{2+}(aq)}$$

## Answers to Questions

**Page 603**

1. **a.** Oxidation number is the apparent charge assigned to an atom of a free or combined element.

21

**b.** The charge on a monatomic ion and its oxidation number are the same.

**c.** potassium ion: +1
calcium ion: +2
sulfide ion: −2

**2. a.** zero; **b.** +1

**3. a.** −2; **b.** −1

**4. a.** +1; **b.** −1

**5. a.** The sum of the oxidation numbers for all of the atoms in a neutral molecule or formula is zero.

**b.** $Al_2O_3$: 2 Al atoms $\times$ +3 = +6
$\phantom{Al_2O_3:}$ 3 O atoms $\times$ −2 = $\underline{-6}$
$\phantom{Al_2O_3: 3 O atoms \times -2 =}$ 0

**6. a.** The sum of the oxidation numbers for all of the atoms in the formula of a polyatomic ion is equal to the charge on the ion.

**b.** $SO_4^{2-}$: 1 S atom $\phantom{x}\times$ +6 = +6
$\phantom{SO_4^{2-}:}$ 4 O atoms $\times$ −2 = $\underline{-8}$
$\phantom{SO_4^{2-}: 4 O atoms \times -2 =}$ −2

**7. a.** 0; **b.** +2

**8.**
$$\overset{0}{\phantom{4}}\quad \overset{0}{\phantom{3}}\quad \overset{+3\,-2}{\phantom{2}}$$
**a.** $4Al + 3O_2 \rightarrow 2Al_2O_3$

$$\overset{0}{\phantom{F}}\quad \overset{+2\,-1}{\phantom{Sn}}\quad \overset{+2\,-1}{\phantom{Fe}}\quad \overset{0}{\phantom{S}}$$
**b.** $Fe + SnCl_2 \rightarrow FeCl_2 + Sn$

$$\overset{0}{\phantom{N}}\quad \overset{0}{\phantom{B}}\quad \overset{+1\,-1}{\phantom{Na}}$$
**c.** $2Na + Br_2 \rightarrow 2NaBr$

$$\overset{+1\,-1}{\phantom{HO}}\quad \overset{+1\,-2}{\phantom{HO}}\quad \overset{0}{\phantom{O}}$$
**d.** $2H_2O_2 \rightarrow 2H_2O + O_2$

**9. a.** +6; **b.** +5; **c.** +2

**10. a.** +5; **b.** −3; **c.** +7

**Page 609**

**11. a.** Oxidation is a chemical change in which the oxidation number of an element increases. Reduction is a chemical change in which the oxidation number of an element decreases.

**b.** Oxidation can also be defined as a change in which an element loses electrons, either partially or completely. Similarly, reduction is a change in which an element partially or completely gains electrons.

**12.** It is a redox reaction.

**13. a.** The oxidizing agent is the element whose oxidation number decreases; the reducing agent undergoes an increase in oxidation number.

**b.** The oxidizing agent gains electrons, partially or completely; the reducing agent loses electrons, partially or completely.

**14. a.** $4HCl + O_2 \rightarrow 2H_2O + 2Cl_2$

$\overset{0}{\phantom{xx}} \quad \overset{-2}{\phantom{xx}}$ (Oxygen reduced; is oxidizing agent.)

$-1 \;\text{———}\; 0$ (Chlorine oxidized; is reducing agent.)

**b.** $MnO_2 + 4HCl \rightarrow MnCl_2 + Cl_2 + 2H_2O$

$-1 \;\text{———}\; 0$ (Chlorine oxidized; is reducing agent.)

$+4 \;\text{———}\; +2$ (Manganese reduced; is oxidizing agent.)

**15. a.** Not a redox reaction (no change in oxidation numbers).

**b.** Phosphorus changes from 0 to +5. This increase in oxidation number identifies it as the reducing agent. Oxygen changes from 0 to −2. This decrease in oxidation number identifies it as the oxidizing agent.

**c.** Not a redox reaction (no change in oxidation numbers).

**d.** Tin changes from +2 to +4. This increase in oxidation number identifies it as the reducing agent. Iron changes from +3 to +2. This decrease in oxidation number identifies it as an oxidizing agent.

**Page 613**

**16.** Mn: from +7 to +2. Cl: from −1 to 0. The balanced equation is:
$2KMnO_4 + 16HCl \rightarrow$
$\phantom{xxxxxx} 2KCl + 2MnCl_2 + 8H_2O + 5Cl_2$

**17.** Cu: from 0 to +2. N: from +5 to +2 in the compound NO. The balanced equation is:
$3Cu + 8HNO_3 \rightarrow 3Cu(NO_3)_2 + 4H_2O + 2NO$

**18.** Cr: from +6 to +3. S: from 0 to +4. The balanced equation is:
$2K_2Cr_2O_7 + 2H_2O + 3S \rightarrow 3SO_2 + 4KOH + 2Cr_2O_3$

**Page 616**

**19.** N: from +5 to +2
Ag: from 0 to +1
$3e^- + 4H^+ + NO_3^- \rightarrow NO + 2H_2O$
$\phantom{xxxxx} 3(Ag \rightarrow Ag^+ + e^-)$
$\overline{3Ag + 4H^+ + NO_3^- \rightarrow 3Ag^+ + NO + 2H_2O}$

**20. a.** Mn: from +7 to +2,
C: from +3 to +4
The half-reactions are:
$2(MnO_4^- + 8H^+ + 5e^- \rightarrow Mn^{2+} + 4H_2O)$
$5(H_2C_2O_4 \rightarrow 2CO_2 + 2H^+ + 2e^-)$
$\overline{2MnO_4^- + 6H^+ + 5H_2C_2O_4 \rightarrow 2Mn^{2+} + 8H_2O + 10CO_2}$

**b.** $2KMnO_4 + 3H_2SO_4 + 5H_2C_2O_4 \rightarrow$
$\phantom{xxxxxx} 2MnSO_4 + 8H_2O + 10CO_2 + K_2SO_4$

# Chapter Review  21

**Page 617, Content Review**

**1. a.** Originally, oxidation was defined as a reaction between oxygen and another substance.
   **b.** Examples are iron rusting and paper burning.

**2.** Oxidation number is the apparent charge on an atom in a molecule or ion.

**3.** The oxidation number of an ion is its charge.
   **a.** oxide ion, $-2$
   **b.** barium ion, $+2$
   **c.** fluoride ion, $-1$
   **d.** sodium ion, $+1$

**4.** The sum of the oxidation numbers in a neutral molecule equals zero. Let $x$ be the unknown oxidation number.
   **a.** Since H is $+1$, 3 H are $+3$, so 1 N is $-3$.
   $x + 3(+1) = 0, x = -3$
   **b.** Since 1 O is $-2$, 2 O are $-4$, so 1 N is $+4$.
   $x + 2(-2) = 0, x = +4$
   **c.** Since 1 Ca is $+2$, 3 Ca are $+6$, so 2 N are $-6$, and 1 N is $-3$. $3(+1) + 2x = 0, x = -3$
   **d.** Since 1 I is $-1$, 3 I are $-3$, so 1 N is $+3$.
   $x + 3(-1) = 0, x = +3$

**5. a.** Since Ba is $+2$, 2 O are $-2$, so 1 O is $-1$.
   **b.** Since Ba is $+2$, 1 O is $-2$.
   **c.** Since K is $+1$, 2 K are $+2$, so 1 O is $-2$ (potassium oxide).
   **d.** Since K is $+1$, 2 K are $+2$, so 2 O are $-2$, and 1 O is $-1$ (potassium peroxide).

**6. a.** Na is $+1$, so H is $-1$ (sodium hydride).
   **b.** F is $-1$, so H is $+1$.
   **c.** H is $+1$ (rule 3).
   **d.** Be is $+2$, so 2 H are $-2$, so 1 H is $-1$ (beryllium hydride).

**7. a.**
$$\overset{+2\ \ -2}{\text{CuO}} = \overset{0}{\text{H}_2} \rightarrow \overset{0}{\text{Cu}} + \overset{+1\ -2}{\text{H}_2\text{O}}$$

   **b.**
$$\overset{-4\ +1}{\text{CH}_4} + \overset{0}{2\text{O}_2} \rightarrow \overset{+4\ -2}{\text{CO}_2} + \overset{+1\ \ -2}{2\text{H}_2\text{O}}$$

   **c.**
$$\overset{+4\ \ -1}{\text{SnCl}_4} + \overset{0}{\text{Fe}} \rightarrow \overset{+2\ \ -1}{\text{SnCl}_2} + \overset{+2\ \ -1}{\text{FeCl}_2}$$

   **d.**
$$\overset{+4\ \ -2+1}{\text{PbO}_2} + \overset{-1\ 0}{4\text{HI}} \rightarrow \overset{0}{\text{I}_2} + \overset{+2\ -1}{\text{PbI}_2} + \overset{+1\ \ -2}{2\text{H}_2\text{O}}$$

**8.** Find the answer by inspection or by solving for $x$, the unknown oxidation number.
   **a.** Mg is $+2$, 3 Mg are $+6$, 2 N are $-6$, so 1 N is $-3$.
   $3(+2) + 2x = 0, x = -3$
   **b.** 1 Na is $+1$, 3 Na are $+3$, 1 O is $-2$, 4 O are $-8$, so 1 As has to be $+5$.
   $3(+1) + x + 4(-2) = 0, x = +5$
   **c.** 1 H is $+1$, 2 H are $+2$, 1 O is $-2$, 3 O are $-6$, so 1 S has to be $+4$.
   $2(+1) + x + 3(-2) = 0, x = +4$
   **d.** 1 O is $-2$, 6 O are $-12$, so 4 P are $+12$, and 1 P is $+3$.
   $4x + 6(-2) = 0, x = +3$

**9.** Let $x$ equal the unknown oxidation number.
   **a.** $x + 4(-2) = -3, x = +5$
   **b.** $x + 4(-2) = -2, x = +6$
   **c.** $x + 3(-2) = -2, x = +4$
   **d.** $+1 + x + 3(-2) = -1, x = +4$

**10. a.** $+1 + x + 4(-2) = 0, x = +7$
   **b.** $+1 + x + 3(-2) = 0, x = +5$
   **c.** $+1 + x + -2 = 0, x = +1$
   **d.** $+1 + x = 0, x = -1$

**11. a.** $x + 2(-1) = 0, x = +2$
   **b.** $x + 2(-2) = 0, x = +4$
   **c.** $+1 + x + 3(-2) = 0, x = +5$
   **d.** $+1 + x + 4(-2) = 0, x = +7$

**12.** This reaction is an oxidation in terms of the older definition because something, namely zinc, reacts with oxygen. It is also an oxidation in terms of the modern definition, because the oxidation number of zinc increases, from 0 to $+2$, as it loses electrons.

**13. a.** This is a redox reaction because electrons are lost by one species and gained by another, as indicated by the change in oxidation numbers.
   **b.** Mg is oxidized from 0 to $+2$.
   **c.** Cl is reduced from 0 to $-1$.
   **d.** The oxidizing agent is the species that is reduced: $Cl_2$.
   **e.** The reducing agent is the species that is oxidized: Mg.

**14. a.**
$$\overset{+6\ -2}{\text{SO}_3} + \overset{+1\ \ -2}{\text{H}_2\text{O}} \rightarrow \overset{+1+6\ -2}{\text{H}_2\text{SO}_4}$$
There is no change in any oxidation number. This is not a redox reaction.

   **b.**
$$\overset{0}{2\text{Al}} + \overset{+1\ -1}{6\text{HCl}} \rightarrow \overset{+3\ \ -1}{2\text{AlCl}_3} + \overset{0}{3\text{H}_2}$$
This is a redox reaction. Aluminum is oxidized; hydrogen is reduced.

21

**c.**  0   +1 −2 +1  −1 +1 +1−2
        |    |  ∕ |  ∕   |  |  ∕
$Cl_2 + H_2O \rightarrow HCl + HClO$

This is a redox reaction. Some of the chlorine is oxidized, and some is reduced.

**d.**  +5−2  +1  −2 +1 +5 −2
        |∕    |   ∕   |  |  ∕
$P_4O_{10} + 6H_2O \rightarrow 4H_3PO_4$

This is not a redox reaction.

**e.**  +1 +5  −2 +1  −1  0
        |  |  ∕   |  ∕   |
$2KClO_3 \rightarrow 2KCl + 3O_2$

This is a redox reaction. Oxygen is oxidized, chlorine reduced.

**15.** The oxidation number of Cl in $Cl_2$ is 0. Of the six chlorine atoms undergoing reaction, one chlorine atom loses 5 electrons and is oxidized to +5 in $KClO_3$. The other five chlorine atoms each gain 1 electron and are thus reduced to −1 in KCl. The chlorine that loses electrons is oxidized; those that gain electrons are reduced.

**16.** Put up the oxidation numbers of the elements that are oxidized or reduced.

**a.**  0    +5    +2 +5   −3 +5
        |    |     |  ∕    |  |
$Zn + HNO_3 \rightarrow Zn(NO_3)_2 + NH_4NO_3 + H_2O$

Zinc loses 2 electrons and nitrogen gains 8, so there must be 4 Zn and 4 $Zn(NO_3)_2$.

$4Zn + HNO_3 \rightarrow 4Zn(NO_3)_2 + NH_4NO_3 + H_2O$

Balance the nitrogens, then the hydrogens, and check the oxygen.

$4Zn + 10HNO_3 \rightarrow 4Zn(NO_3)_2 + NH_4NO_3 + H_2O$

$4Zn + 10HNO_3 \rightarrow 4Zn(NO_3)_2 + NH_4NO_3 + 3H_2O$

**b.**  −1    +6    −2  0    +6
        |     |     |   |     |
$NaI = H_2SO_4 \rightarrow H_2S + I_2 + Na_2SO_4 + H_2O$

The iodine loses 1 electron, and sulfur gains 4.

$8NaI + H_2SO_4 \rightarrow H_2S + 4I_2 + Na_2SO_4 + H_2O$

Balance the sodium, the sulfates, and the hydrogens and check the oxygens.

$8NaI + H_2SO_4 \rightarrow H_2S + 4I_2 + 4Na_2SO_4 + H_2O$

$8NaI + 5H_2SO_4 \rightarrow H_2S + 4I_2 + 4Na_2SO_4 + H_2O$

$8NaI + 5H_2SO_4 \rightarrow H_2S + 4I_2 + 4Na_2SO_4 + 4H_2O$

**c.**  +3    −1    0    0
        |     |     |    |
$NF_3 + AlCl_3 \rightarrow N_2 + Cl_2 + AlF_3$

Nitrogen gains 3 electrons; chlorine loses 1. There are 3 chlorines per nitrogen.

$2NF_3 + 2AlCl_3 \rightarrow N_2 + 3Cl_2 + AlF_3$

Balance the aluminums, and check the fluorines.

$2NF_3 + 2AlCl_3 \rightarrow N_2 + 3Cl_2 + 2AlF_3$

**d.**  +3         +5        −1        +5
        |          |         |         |
$H_3AsO_3 + NaBrO_3 \rightarrow NaBr + H_3AsO_4$

As loses 2 electrons; Br gains 6. There are 3 As for every Br.

$3H_3AsO_3 + NaBrO_3 \rightarrow NaBr + 3H_3AsO_4$

Check that there are 9 H and 12 O on both sides.

**17.** $FeSO_4(aq) + KMnO_4(aq) + H_2SO_4(aq) \rightarrow$
        $MnSO_4(aq) + Fe_2(SO_4)_3(aq) + K_2SO_4 + H_2O$

Remove phase notations and spectator ions.

$Fe^{2+} + MnO_4^- \rightarrow Fe^{3+} + Mn^{2+}$

            +2        +3
            |         |
Oxidation: $Fe^{2+} \rightarrow Fe^{3+}$

            +7        +2
            |         |
Reduction: $MnO_4^- \rightarrow Mn^{2+}$

The half-reaction for the oxidation is balanced with respect to atoms, but not charge. Add 1 $e^-$ to the right side of the equation.

Oxidation: $Fe^{2+} \rightarrow Fe^{3+} + 1e^-$

For the reduction half-reaction, balance the atoms first, then the charge. Since the reaction takes place in acidic solution ($H_2SO_4$), add $H^+$ and $H_2O$ to balance the atoms.

$$MnO_4^- \rightarrow Mn^{2+} + 4H_2O$$
$$MnO_4^- + 8H^+ \rightarrow Mn^{2+} + 4H_2O$$

Add 5$e^-$ to the left side to balance the charge.

Reduction: $MnO_4^- + 8H^+ + 5e^- \rightarrow Mn^{2+} + 4H_2O$

Since the reduction reaction gains 5 electrons, multiply the oxidation half-reaction by 5 to make the number of electrons lost equal to the number of electrons gained.

Oxidation: $5Fe^{2+} \rightarrow 5Fe^{3+} + 5e^-$

Now, add the half-reactions together.

Oxidation: $5Fe^{2+} \rightarrow 5Fe^{3+} + 5e^-$
Reduction:

$MnO_4^- + 8H^+ + 5e^- \rightarrow Mn^{2+} + 4H_2O$
$\overline{5Fe^{2+} + MnO_4^- + 8H^+ + 5e^- \rightarrow}$
$\qquad\qquad 5Fe^{3+} + 5e^- + Mn^{2+} + 4H_2O$

Cancel out the 5$e^-$ on both sides of the equation.

$5Fe^{2+} + MnO_4^- + 8H^+ \rightarrow 5Fe^{3+} + Mn^{2+} + 4H_2O$

Check to make sure the oxygens balance. They do. To get the molecular equation, add the spectator ions, $K^+$ and $SO_4^{2-}$. Notice that the $H^+$ combine with $SO_4^{2-}$ to form $H_2SO_4$.

$5FeSO_4 + KMnO_4 + 4H_2SO_4 \rightarrow$
$$\frac{5}{2}Fe_2(SO_4)_3 + MnSO_4 + 4H_2O$$

Multiply the entire reaction by 2.

$10FeSO_4 + 2KMnO_4 + 8H_2SO_4 \rightarrow$
$$5Fe_2(SO_4)_3 + 2MnSO_4 + 8H_2O$$

Now, all of the atoms balance except for the $SO_4^{2-}$ and the $K^+$. There are $10 + 8 = 18 SO_4^{2-}$ on the left, but only $5(3) + 2 = 17$ on the right. There are $2K^+$ on the left, and none on the right. So, add 1 molecule of $K_2SO_4$ to the right side of the molecular equation.

$10FeSO_4 + 2KMnO_4 + 8H_2SO_4 \rightarrow$
$$2MnSO_4 + 5Fe_2(SO_4)_3 + K_2SO_4 + 8H_2O$$

### Page 618, Content Mastery

**18.** $Al(s) + H_2SO_4(aq) \rightarrow Al_2(SO_4)_3(aq) + H_2(g)$

Remove the spectator ions and phase notations.

$Al + 2H^+ \rightarrow Al^{+3} + H_2$

Oxidation: $Al \rightarrow Al^{+3} + 3e^-$

Reduction: $2H^+ + 2e^- \rightarrow H_2$

Multiply the oxidation reaction by 2 and the reduction reaction by 3 to get the number of electrons lost equal to the number of electrons gained. Then add the half-reactions together.

$$\frac{\begin{array}{l} 2Al \rightarrow 2Al^{+3} + 6e^- \\ 6H^+ + 6e^- \rightarrow 3H_2 \end{array}}{2Al + 6H^+ + 6e^- \rightarrow 2Al^{+3} + 6e^- + 3H_2}$$

Cancel the common terms and add the spectator ions to get the molecular equation.

$2Al + 6H^+ \rightarrow 2Al^{+3} + 3H_2$
$2Al + 3H_2SO_4 \rightarrow Al_2(SO_4)_3 + 3H_2$

Check to make sure the sulfates balance. They do.

**19.** The electron spends more of its time around the more electronegative atom in an ion or molecule, so the electron is assigned to the more electronegative atom when the bookkeeping is done to determine oxidation number, which is the apparent charge on the atom. The more electronegative atom has a lower oxidation number because it owns more electrons.

**20.** Both carbon and iron are oxidized when they combine with oxygen. For example, in the following reaction, carbon is oxidized; that is, its oxidation number increases from 0 to +4 when it reacts with oxygen to form carbon dioxide.

$$\begin{array}{ccc} 0 & 0 & +4 \ -2 \\ | & | & | \ / \\ C & + O_2 \rightarrow & CO_2 \end{array}$$

**21. a.** $\begin{array}{cc} +2 & -1 \\ | & / \\ \multicolumn{2}{c}{CaI_2} \end{array}$    **b.** $\begin{array}{c} 0 \\ | \\ O_2 \end{array}$

**c.** $\begin{array}{cc} -3 & +1 \\ | & / \\ \multicolumn{2}{c}{NH_3} \end{array}$    **d.** $\begin{array}{cc} +3 & -1 \\ | & / \\ \multicolumn{2}{c}{NF_3} \end{array}$

**22. a.** $\begin{array}{cc} +1 & -2 \\ | & / \\ \multicolumn{2}{c}{H_2O} \end{array}$

**b.** $\begin{array}{cc} +1 & -1 \\ | & / \\ \multicolumn{2}{c}{Na_2O_2 \text{ (sodium peroxide)}} \end{array}$

**c.** $\begin{array}{cc} +1 & -1 \\ | & / \\ \multicolumn{2}{c}{LiH \text{ (lithium hydride)}} \end{array}$

**d.** $\begin{array}{c} 0 \\ | \\ Ni \end{array}$

**e.** $\begin{array}{cc} +2 & -1 \\ | & / \\ \multicolumn{2}{c}{CuBr_2} \end{array}$

**23.** $Al(s) + HNO_3(aq) \rightarrow$
$$Al(NO_3)_3(aq) + NO_2(g) + H_2O(l)$$

Remove spectator ions and phase notations. Notice that some of the nitrate ions are reduced, and some are spectator ions.

$Al + NO_3^- \rightarrow Al^{3+} + NO_2$

Oxidation: $Al \rightarrow Al^{+3}$

Reduction: $NO_3^- \rightarrow NO_2$

Balance atoms first (by adding $H^+$ and $H_2O$ in acid solution), then the charge (by adding electrons).

Oxidation: $Al \rightarrow Al^{+3} + 3e^-$
Reduction: $NO_3^- \rightarrow NO_2 + H_2O$
$\qquad\qquad NO_3^- + 2H^+ \rightarrow NO_2 + H_2O$
$\qquad\qquad NO_3^- + 2H^+ + e^- \rightarrow NO_2 + H_2O$

Multiply the reduction reaction by 3 to get the number of electrons lost equal to the number of electrons gained.

$3NO_3^- + 6H^+ + 3e^- \rightarrow 3NO_2 + 3H_2O$

Add the two half-reactions together. Cancel common terms.

$$\frac{\begin{array}{l} Al \rightarrow Al^{+3} + 3e^- \\ 3NO_3^- + 6H^+ + 3e^- \rightarrow 3NO_2 + 3H_2O \end{array}}{\begin{array}{l} Al + 3NO_3^- + 6H^+ + 3e^- \rightarrow \\ \qquad Al^{+3} + 3e^- + 3NO_2 + 3H_2O \end{array}}$$

$Al + 3NO_3^- + 6H^+ \rightarrow Al^{+3} + 3NO_2 + 3H_2O$

Add the spectator ions to get the molecular equation. This involves adding 3 nitrates to the right to make $Al(NO_3)_3$. Then, add them to the left to balance the atoms. Notice that the $NO_3^-$ and $H^+$ ions combine to form $HNO_3$.

$Al + 3NO_3^- + 6H^+ \rightarrow Al(NO_3)_3 + 3NO_2 + 3H_2O$
$Al + 6NO_3^- + 6H^+ \rightarrow Al(NO_3)_3 + 3NO_2 + 3H_2O$
$Al + 6HNO_3 \rightarrow Al(NO_3)_3 + 3NO_2 + 3H_2O$

**24. a.** $x + 4(-2) = -3, x = +5$
   **b.** $2(+1) + 1 + x + 4(-2) = 0, x = +5$

**25. a.** $+1 + 1 + x + 4(-2) = 0, x = +6$
   **b.** $+1 + 1 + x + 3(-2) = 0, x = +4$

**26. a.** nitrite ion $= NO_2^-, x + 2(-2) = -1, x = +3$

21

**b.** nitrate ion = $NO_3^-$, $x + 3(-2) = -1$, $x = +5$

**27. a.** solid carbon = C, $x = 0$

   **b.** $x + 4(+1) = 0$, $x = -4$

   **c.** $x + -2 = 0$, $x = +2$

   **d.** $x + 3(-2) = -2$, $x = +4$

**28.** $CrO_4^{2-}(aq) + H^+(aq) + Cl^-(aq) \rightarrow$
$$Cr^{3+}(aq) + Cl_2(g) + H_2O(l)$$

Remove spectator ions and phase notations.

$CrO_4^{2-} + Cl^- \rightarrow Cr^{3+} + Cl_2$

Oxidation: $Cl^- \rightarrow Cl_2$
$$2Cl^- \rightarrow Cl_2$$
$$2Cl^- \rightarrow Cl_2 + 2e^-$$

Reduction: $CrO_4^{2-} \rightarrow Cr^{3+}$
$$CrO_4^{2-} \rightarrow Cr^{3+} + 4H_2O$$
$$CrO_4^{2-} + 8H^+ \rightarrow Cr^{3+} + 4H_2O$$
$$CrO_4^{2-} + 8H^+ + 3e^- \rightarrow Cr^{3+} + 4H_2O$$

Multiply the oxidation reaction by 3 and the reduction reaction by 2 to get the number of electrons lost equal to the number of electrons gained.

$6Cl^- \rightarrow 3Cl_2 + 6e^-$
$2CrO_4^{2-} + 16H^+ + 6e^- \rightarrow 2Cr^{3+} + 8H_2O$
Add the two half-reactions together.
$6Cl^- \rightarrow 3Cl_2 + 6e^-$
$\underline{2CrO_4^{2-} + 16H^+ + 6e^- \rightarrow 2Cr^{3+} + 8H_2O}$
$6Cl^- + 2CrO_4^{2-} + 16H^+ + 6e^- \rightarrow$
$$3Cl_2 + 6e^- + 2Cr^{3+} + 8H_2O$$

Cancel common terms.

$6Cl^- + 2CrO_4^{2-} + 16H^+ \rightarrow 3Cl_2 + 2Cr^{3+} + 8H_2O$

Add the spectator ions. Add 6 $Cl^-$ to the right to make $CrCl_3$. Add 6 $Cl^-$ to the left to keep the atoms balanced. Then combine $H^+$ and $Cl^-$ to form HCl, and $H^+$ and $CrO_4^{2-}$ to form $H_2CrO_4$.

$6Cl^- + 2CrO_4^{2-} + 16H^+ \rightarrow 3Cl_2 + 2CrCl_3 + 8H_2O$
$12Cl^- + 2CrO_4^{2-} + 16H^+ \rightarrow 3Cl_2 + 2CrCl_3 + 8H_2O$
$12HCl + 2H_2CrO_4 \rightarrow 3Cl_2 + 2CrCl_3 + 8H_2O$

**29.** $MnO_4^-(aq) + H_2S(g) + H^+(aq) \rightarrow$
$$Mn^{2+}(aq) + S(s) + H_2O(l)$$
Remove the spectator ions and phase notations.

$MnO_4^- + H_2S \rightarrow Mn^{2+} + S$

Oxidation: $H_2S \rightarrow S$
$$H_2S \rightarrow S + 2H^+$$
$$H_2S \rightarrow S + 2H^+ + 2e^-$$

Reduction: $MnO_4^- \rightarrow Mn^{2+}$
$$MnO_4^- \rightarrow Mn^{2+} + 4H_2O$$
$$MnO_4^- + 8H^+ \rightarrow Mn^{2+} + 4H_2O$$
$$MnO_4^- + 8H^+ + 5e^- \rightarrow Mn^{2+} + 4H_2O$$

Multiply the oxidation by 5 and the reduction by 2 to get the number of electrons lost equal to the number of electrons gained.

$5H_2S \rightarrow 5S + 10H^+ + 10e^-$
$\underline{2MnO_4^- + 16H^+ + 10e^- \rightarrow 2Mn^{2+} + 8H_2O}$
$5H_2S + 2MnO_4^- + 16H^+ + 10e^- \rightarrow$
$$5S + 10H^+ + 10e^- + 2Mn^{2+} + 8H_2O$$
Cancel common terms.
$2MnO_4^- + 5H_2S + 6H^+ \rightarrow 2Mn^{2+} + 5S + 8H_2O$

## Page 618, Concept Mastery

**30. Concept:** *Oxidation is an increase in oxidation number due to a loss of electrons. It does not depend on the presence of oxygen.*

  **Solution:** No, chlorine is reduced, not oxidized, because its oxidation number decreases from 0 in the uncombined state to $-1$ in NaCl. The chlorine gains an electron from the sodium, so it is reduced, not oxidized. The sodium is oxidized even though it does not combine with oxygen. The sodium is still oxidized because it loses an electron to chlorine, thus increasing its oxidation number.

**31. Concept:** *Oxidation is the loss of electrons.*

  **Solution:** All reactions in which molecular oxygen combines with another element are redox reactions. Oxygen is reduced from 0 in the uncombined state to $-1$ or $-2$ in a peroxide or other compound. Many reactions involving oxygen are, in fact, oxidations, because oxygen is electronegative and often accepts electrons from another atom. However, the presence of oxygen among the reactants does not make the reaction a redox reaction. Oxygen can be an element in a species in a double displacement reaction, for example, in which there is no redox reaction.

$CaBr_2 + Pb(NO_3)_2 \rightarrow PbBr_2 + Ca(NO_3)_2$

**32. Concept:** *Oxidation is the loss of electrons, which have a negative charge.*

  **Solution:** When a metal atom is oxidized to a cation, it loses electrons. The charge on the metal increases because it has lost the negative charge associated with the electron. Losing a negative charge results in increasing the positive charge.

**33. Concept:** *The oxidation number of hydrogen can be either +1 or −1.*

  **Solution:** Hydrogen often reacts by losing 1 electron, just like the elements in Group 1. In these reactions, the oxidation number of hydrogen is +1. Hydrogen is also a diatomic gas, like $F_2$ and $Cl_2$. Like these gases in Group 17, hydrogen can gain 1 electron and have an oxidation number of $-1$. The electronegativity of the element with which hydrogen reacts determines whether hydrogen gains or loses 1 electron, and the gain or loss determines hydrogen's oxidation number.

## Page 619, Cumulative Review

**34.** The electronic configuration given is $2 + 2 + 6 + 2 = 12$ electrons. The correct answer is **c.**
  **a.** $Cl^{-1}$ has $17 + 1 = 18$ electrons.
  **b.** $S^{-2}$ has $16 + 2 = 18$ electrons.
  **c.** $P^{+3}$ has $15 - 3 = 12$ electrons.
  **d.** Ne has 10 electrons.

**35. a.** Electronegativity increases from left to right and from bottom to top in the periodic table. Fluorine is the most electronegative element.

**36. b.** The SI unit for mass is the gram, not the atomic mass unit. Hydrogen has a mass of 1.0 gram/mole or 1.0 amu/atom.

**37.** In pure water at 25°C, $[H^+] = [OH^-] = 1.0 \times 10^{-7} M$.

**38.** $2H_2O \rightleftarrows H_3O^+ + OH^-$

**39.** The apparent charge on oxygen in most compounds is $2-$.

**40.** Types of electromagnetic radiation are gamma rays, X rays, ultraviolet radiation, visible light, infrared radiation, radar, microwaves, and radio waves.

**41.** The atomic mass is an average mass for the naturally occurring mixture of isotopes.

**42.** Forms of energy are potential, kinetic, heat, sound, chemical, mechanical, electrical, magnetic, and electromagnetic.

**43.** Nonmetals, on the right side of the periodic table, form anions by gaining electrons. Therefore, the ionic radius is larger than the atomic radius.

## Page 619, Critical Thinking

**44.** In $H_2$, both atoms have the same electronegativity, so the electrons are shared equally. The hydrogen neither loses nor gains an electron, so its oxidation number is zero. In $H_2O$, the oxygen is more electronegative, so hydrogen loses its electron to oxygen and, therefore, has a positive oxidation number.

**45.** All three metals react with oxygen to form an oxide. The iron oxide is called rust; the silver oxide, tarnish; the copper oxide, patina.

**46.** Bromine is more electronegative than phosphorus, so it gains electrons from phosphorus in $PBr_3$. Thus, bromine has a negative oxidation number.

**47.** Each can be classified as:
  element (E)
  polyatomic ion (P)
  ionic compound (I)
  molecular compound (M)
  **a.** I; $Fe^{+3}$, $Cl^{-1}$
  **b.** M; $H^{+1}$, $O^{-1}$
  **c.** E; $Br^0$
  **d.** M; $C^{+4}$, $O^{-2}$
  **e.** I; $Ca^{+2}$, $H^{-1}$
  **f.** I; $K^{+1}$, $S^{+6}$, $O^{-2}$
  **g.** P; $N^{+5}$, $O^{-2}$
  **h.** P; $Cl^{+5}$, $O^{-2}$
  **i.** I; $Na^{+1}$, $O^{-1}$
  **j.** M; $N^{-3}$, $H^{+1}$
  **k.** E; $Pb^0$
  **l.** P; $P^{+5}$, $O^{-2}$

**48.** In peroxides, the oxygens are bound to each other and share the electrons equally. Their oxidation number is $-1$ because they only gain 1 electron from another atom. In most compounds, oxygen gains 2 electrons from the other atoms and has an oxidation number of $-2$. The number of electrons lost determines the total increase in oxidation number. Similarly, the number of electrons gained determines the total decrease in oxidation number. Because the number of electrons lost must equal the number of electrons that are gained in any redox reaction, the total increase in oxidation number must equal the total decrease in oxidation number.

## Page 619, Challenge Problems

**49.** Air contains oxygen. When air is mixed with the exhaust gases, the pollutants are oxidized to less harmful substances. Carbon monoxide is oxidized to carbon dioxide. Unburned gasoline consists mainly of hydrocarbons, $C_xH_y$. These substances can be oxidized to carbon dioxide and water.

**50.** Students' answers will vary considerably. Some common oxidizing agents are free nonmetals such as $O_2$, $Cl_2$, and $Br_2$, and cations such as $Ag^+$, $H^+$, $Cu^{2+}$, $Fe^{3+}$, and $Cr_2O_7^{2-}$. Common reducing agents are metals such as Zn and Na, and nonmetals such as C, $SO_3^{2-}$, and NO.

Many progressive deteriorations in the presence of oxygen, such as rotting or discoloring or rusting, are oxidations. The reverse, such as cleaning and polishing reactions, are reductions.

**51.** $C_6H_{12}O_6 + O_2 \rightarrow CO_2 + H_2O$

$C_6H_{12}O_6 + 6O_2 \rightarrow 6CO_2 + 6H_2O$

$CO_2 = 12.0 + 2(16.0) = 44.0$ g/mol

$$\frac{0.350 \text{ g } CO_2}{\text{minute}} \times \frac{\text{mol}}{44.0 \text{ g}} \times \frac{1 \text{ mol } O_2}{1 \text{ mol } CO_2} \times \frac{60 \text{ min.}}{\text{hour}} \times$$

$$\frac{24 \text{ hours}}{\text{day}} = 11.5 \text{ mol } O_2/\text{day}$$

$$\frac{11.5 \text{ mol } O_2}{\text{day}} \times \frac{1 \text{ mol } C_6H_{12}O_6}{6 \text{ mol } O_2} = 1.92 \text{ mol } C_6H_{12}O_6/\text{day}$$

21

# Electrochemistry

## Chapter Planning Guide

| Text Section | Labs (Lab Manual) and Demonstrations (TE) | Supplementary Materials (Teacher's Resource Book) |
|---|---|---|
| **22-1** Two Branches of Electrochemistry, p. 621 | | |
| **22-2** Half-reactions and Half-reaction Equations, pp. 622-625 | | |
| **22-3** The Electric Current, pp. 625-626 | Lab 42: Electrolysis | |
| **Break-through** Superconductors, p. 626 | | |
| **22-4** Current Through an Electrolyte—Electrolysis, pp. 627-630 | | |
| **22-5** Electrolysis of Molten Sodium Chloride, pp. 630-631 | | |
| **22-6** Electrolysis of Water, pp. 631-634 | | Transparency Master: The Electrolysis of Water, p. 22-1 |
| **22-7** Electrolysis of Concentrated Sodium Chloride Solution (Brine), pp. 634-635 | | Review Activity: Electrolytic Cells, p. 22-5<br>Review Activity: Labeling an Electrolytic Cell, p. 22-6 |
| **22-8** Electroplating, pp. 635-637 | | Transparency Master: Electroplating a Fork, p. 22-2 |
| **22-9** The Electrochemical Cell, pp. 637-641 | | |
| **22-10** The Porous Cup and Salt Bridge, pp. 641-643 | | Transparency Master: The Daniell Cell, p. 22-3 |
| **22-11** The Voltage of an Electrochemical Cell, pp. 643-645 | | |
| **22-12** The Standard Hydrogen Half-cell, pp. 645-647 | | |

| Text Section | Labs (Lab Manual) and Demonstrations (TE) | Supplementary Materials (Teacher's Resource Book) |
|---|---|---|
| **22-13** Standard Electrode Potentials, pp. 649-653 | | Transparency Master: Table of Standard Reduction Potentials, p. 22-4<br>Review Activity: Galvanic Cells, p. 22-7<br>Review Activity: Labeling a Galvanic Cell, p. 22-8<br>Review Activity: Standard Electrode Potentials, p. 22-9 |
| **22-14** Voltages of Galvanic Cells Not Containing the Standard Hydrogen Half-cell, pp. 653-655 | Lab 43: Electrochemical Cells | |
| **Biography** Guadalupe Fortuño, p. 654 | | |
| **22-15** The Chemical Activities of Metals, pp. 655-656<br>**22-16** Some Practical Applications of Electrochemical Cells, pp. 656-658<br>**22-17** The Corrosion of Metals—An Electrochemical Process, pp. 658-660 | Demo 22-1: Charging and Discharging a Lead Storage Battery with Your Bare Hands, p. TG-313<br>Demo 22-2: Plumbers' Chemistry, p. TG-314<br>Lab 44: Corrosion of Iron | Critical and Creative Thinking: Ranking Things and Ideas, p. CCT-63 |
| **Can You Explain This?** Light from Chemical Energy, p. 660 | | |
| | | Test—Form A, p. AT-84<br>Alternate Test—Form B, p. BT-84 |

☐ Core   ☐ Advanced   ☐ Optional

## Chapter Overview

In Chapter 22 we describe the nature of electrochemical processes. This is accomplished by first presenting an overview of electrolysis and electrochemical reactions. For those students who may not have covered Section 21-5 (an Advanced Topic), we discuss the basic facts regarding oxidation and reduction half-reactions and their equations. A brief review of electric current is presented and includes such topics as sources of current, metallic conduction, and ionic conduction.

The electrolytic cell and the electrochemical cell, along with some of their applications, are described in detail. We present a detailed discussion of the electrolysis of water, molten sodium chloride, and brine (a concentrated water solution of sodium chloride). We then discuss the process of electroplating.

The chapter ends with a thorough introduction to standard electrode potentials. We first explain the significance of the standard hydrogen electrode and show how the standard hydrogen half-cell is used to derive standard electrode potentials for other half-cells. We then explain how to use this information to predict, from given pairs of half-cells, which half-reaction will be oxidized and which half-reaction will be reduced in a spontaneous reaction. We conclude with several applications of electrochemical cells.

22

# Chapter Objectives

After students have completed this chapter, they will be able to:

1. Describe the operation of an electrolytic cell. *22-1*
2. Write equations showing the reactions that occur when several compounds are electrolyzed.
                              *22-2 to 22-7*
3. Explain the operation of a setup for electroplating with metals.                           *22-8*
4. Describe the operation of a galvanic cell.
                              *22-9 and 22-10*
5. Determine the net voltage obtained when standard half-cells are paired to form a galvanic cell.
                              *22-11 to 22-13*
6. Predict reaction products by using standard reduction potentials and an activity series.
                              *22-14 to 22-17*

# Teaching Suggestions

## 22-1 Two Branches of Electrochemistry, p. 621, and

## 22-2 Half-reactions and Half-reaction Equations, pp. 622-625

■ Remind the students that a partial or complete transfer of electrons occurs during a redox reaction. Electrochemistry deals with those reactions in which there is a complete transfer of electrons. Define the two main electrochemical processes: electrolysis and electrochemical reactions.

■ It is very important for students to understand the nature of oxidation and reduction half-reactions and their equations. This topic is included in Section 21-5, which may have been omitted in some classes. For this reason, the basic facts regarding this topic are repeated in this chapter. Discuss the definitions of oxidation and reduction in terms of a loss and gain of electrons. The students should be able to write the half-reaction equations for redox reactions.

## 22-3 The Electric Current, pp. 625-626, and

## 22-4 Current Through an Electrolyte—Electrolysis, pp. 627-630

| Planning Guide | |
|---|---|
| Labs (Lab Manual) and Demonstrations (TE) | Supplementary Materials (Teacher's Resource Book) |
| Lab 42: Electrolysis | |

■ Review the basic facts about electricity, including the nature of an ordinary electric current, sources of current, metallic conduction, and ionic conduction. Distinguish between direct and alternating current.

■ Point out that reactions in electrolytic cells are not spontaneous. They can only occur when an external source of electrical energy is supplied. Refer to text Figures 22-7 through 22-10 to aid in teaching the definitions of electrolysis, anode, cathode, electrolyte, internal circuit, and external circuit. Assign Laboratory 42, "Electrolysis," in which the students set up a typical electrolysis apparatus and use it to electrolyze an aqueous solution of potassium iodide.

■ **Application.** You may want to discuss the important commercial application of electrolysis to the production of aluminum, which is covered in more detail in Chapter 23. The overall process has three major steps. In the first step, some impurities are removed from $Al_2O_3(s)$ ore by dissolving the ore in concentrated NaOH solution:

$$Al_2O_3 + 6OH^- + 3H_2O \rightleftharpoons 2Al(OH)_6^{3-}$$

In the second step, the solution is filtered to remove any undissolved impurities and acidified with $CO_2$ to precipitate the purified $Al_2O_3(s)$:

$$6CO_2 + 2Al(OH)_6^{3-} \rightleftharpoons Al_2O_3(s) + 6HCO_3^- + 3H_2O$$

In the final step, $Al_2O_3$ is electrolyzed in the presence of cryolite:

Anode Reaction: $2Al^{3+} + 6e^- \rightleftharpoons 2Al(s)$

Cathode Reaction: $\dfrac{3O^{2-} \rightleftharpoons \frac{3}{2}O_2(g) + 6e^-}{2Al^{3+} + 3O^{2-} \rightleftharpoons 2Al(s) + \frac{3}{2}O_2(g)}$

## 22-5 Electrolysis of Molten Sodium Chloride, pp. 630-631

■ Discuss the electrolysis of molten sodium chloride and use it to test the students' understanding of the terminology related to electrolysis. Ask the students to describe the flow of electric current in the internal and external circuits and to write the half-reaction equations taking place at the anode and the cathode.

## 22-6 Electrolysis of Water, pp. 631-634

| Planning Guide | |
|---|---|
| Labs (Lab Manual) and Demonstrations (TE) | Supplementary Materials (Teacher's Resource Book) |
| | Transparency Master: The Electrolysis of Water, p. 22-1 |

■ Discuss the reactions involved in the electrolysis of water in a dilute solution of sodium sulfate. Point out that both sodium ions and water are present at the negative electrode. It may be helpful, at this time, to point out that some ionic and molecular species are reduced or oxidized more easily than others. Ask the students to predict which of these two substances, the sodium ions or the water molecules at the negative electrode, is more easily reduced. Then ask students to write the half-reaction equations and the complete redox equation for the electrolysis of water.

■ **Concept Mastery.** If your students need to review the concepts of gas volumes, the particle nature of matter, and Avogadro's hypothesis as they apply to electrolysis reactions, assign Concept Mastery question 38 (chapter-end question). If possible, demonstrate the electrolysis of water. The equipment for this is relatively inexpensive. Observing an actual electrolysis of water helps students to realize why an ionic substance such as sodium sulfate must be added to the water, how the presence of this substance does not change the ratio of hydrogen to oxygen but does affect the rate of the reaction, and why disconnecting one wire lead stops the entire reaction.

## 22-7 Electrolysis of Concentrated Sodium Chloride Solution (Brine), pp. 634-635

| Planning Guide | |
| --- | --- |
| Labs (Lab Manual) and Demonstrations (TE) | Supplementary Materials (Teacher's Resource Book) |
| | Review Activity: Electrolytic Cells, p. 22-5<br>Review Activity: Labeling an Electrolytic Cell, p. 22-6 |

■ Remind the students that the previous two sections dealt with the electrolysis of water and the electrolysis of molten sodium chloride. Ask them to predict what will happen when a mixture of these two substances is electrolyzed. Discuss the competing reactions at each electrode. Ask the students to explain the source of the sodium hydroxide solution. Then ask the students to write equations for each half-reaction.

■ **Application.** You may want to discuss a very unusual electrolytic cell used for the electrolysis of a concentrated sodium chloride solution and constructed by Dow Chemical Company. This Chlor-Alkali Electrolytic Cell is built on a large salt bed. To dissolve the salt, water is pumped into the natural salt bed at approximately 2000 m below the surface. A saturated solution of the dissolved salt is pumped back to the surface. A continuous electrolysis of this solution is then carried out according to the following net equation:

$$2H_2O(l) + 2Cl^-(aq) \rightarrow H_2(g) + Cl_2(g) + 2OH^-(aq)$$

Although the water is a stronger reducing agent than the chloride ion, the oxidation of water is a relatively slow reaction. If a large enough voltage is applied, the chloride ion is oxidized at a much faster rate. All of the products of this reaction are used commercially. The hydrogen gas and the chlorine gas react to produce muriatic (hydrochloric) acid. The chlorine gas is dried, cooled, and compressed into a liquid, for commercial use. The sodium hydroxide solution is concentrated by evaporation and sold as aqueous caustic soda.

■ **Concept Mastery.** You may want to discuss Concept Mastery question 39 (chapter-end question) as a summary of Section 22-7. The reaction discussed in the question is identical to that of sodium chloride, except for the name of the halide involved. Try to dispel the idea of magic in chemical reactions. There is a difference between surprise about the outcome of a reaction and magic. In magic there is no natural explanation for the occurrence.

## 22-8 Electroplating, pp. 635-637

| Planning Guide | |
| --- | --- |
| Labs (Lab Manual) and Demonstrations (TE) | Supplementary Materials (Teacher's Resource Book) |
| | Transparency Master: Electroplating a Fork, p. 22-2 |

■ Explain that a useful application of electrolysis is electroplating. Emphasize the importance of the composition of the electrodes in the electroplating apparatus.

## 22-9 The Electrochemical Cell, pp. 637-641

■ Remind the students that many chemical reactions liberate energy in the form of heat or light. Point out that under suitable conditions energy from a chemical reaction can take the form of an electric current. Explain that an electrochemical cell is a device that can separate the oxidation and reduction half-reactions in order to make electrons travel through an external circuit, thus producing an electric current in that circuit. Emphasize that the redox reaction in an electrochemical cell is spontaneous.

■ Discuss text Figures 22-17 through 22-20. Define electromotive force. Compare the galvanic cell to the electrolytic cell.

## 22-10 The Porous Cup and Salt Bridge, pp. 641-643

| Planning Guide | |
| --- | --- |
| Labs (Lab Manual) and Demonstrations (TE) | Supplementary Materials (Teacher's Resource Book) |
| | Transparency Master: The Daniell Cell, p. 22-3 |

22

■ Discuss the construction and operation of a typical electrochemical cell. Explain the reactions that are taking place at each electrode. Ask the students what happens to the electric current when the salt bridge is removed. Define half-cell and discuss the notation used to represent half-cells.

## 22-11 The Voltage of an Electrochemical Cell, pp. 643-645, and

## 22-12 The Standard Hydrogen Half-cell, pp. 645-647

■ Point out that the electromotive force of the current produced in an electrochemical cell is measured in volts. The voltage is a measure of the force that causes the electrons to flow from the substance that is oxidized to the substance that is reduced. The greater the tendency of the cell reactions to occur is, the higher the electromotive force of the cell is.

■ Explain that in order to quantitatively measure the tendency of any half-reaction to occur as an oxidation or a reduction, it is necessary to establish a standard half-cell that is assigned a specific potential value. Then, other half-cells of unknown potential can be paired with the standard cell. Explain the construction and operation of a standard hydrogen half-cell. Point out the conditions under which it is assigned a zero potential. Explain how it can be used to determine the relative potentials of other half-cells such as $Zn/Zn^{2+}$ and $Ag/Ag^+$ cells.

## 22-13 Standard Electrode Potentials, pp. 649-653

| Planning Guide | |
|---|---|
| **Labs (Lab Manual) and Demonstrations (TE)** | **Supplementary Materials (Teacher's Resource Book)** |
| | Transparency Master: Table of Standard Reduction Potentials, p. 22-4 |
| | Review Activity: Galvanic Cells, p. 22-7 |
| | Review Activity: Labeling a Galvanic Cell, p. 22-8 |
| | Review Activity: Standard Electrode Potentials, p. 22-9 |

■ Refer to the Transparency Master "Table of Standard Reduction Potentials." Explain how the electrode potentials in this table are derived, using the following three half-cells paired with the standard hydrogen half-cell as illustrations: $Ag/Ag^+$, $Cu/Cu^{2+}$, and $Zn/Zn^{2+}$. Demonstrate how the information in this table can be used to ascertain the voltage developed be-

tween a half-cell and the standard hydrogen electrode. Work through Sample Problem 2 in the text, which illustrates how the table of standard reduction potentials can be used to determine the product of a given set of reactants in an electrochemical cell.

## 22-14 Voltages of Galvanic Cells Not Containing the Standard Hydrogen Half-cell, pp. 653-655

| Planning Guide | |
|---|---|
| **Labs (Lab Manual) and Demonstrations (TE)** | **Supplementary Materials (Teacher's Resource Book)** |
| Lab 43: Electrochemical Cells | |

■ Explain how the table of standard reduction potentials can be used to obtain the net voltage for a cell that results from the pairing of two half-cells. Point out that the potentials for the oxidation reactions are the same as those for the reduction reactions except for the sign of the voltage. Ask the students to calculate net voltages that result when the silver and copper half-cells are paired. Have them do the same for the zinc-silver and the zinc-copper cells. Emphasize that the net reactions are spontaneous only when the sums of the half-reaction potentials are positive. Ask which half-reaction should be the oxidation and which should be the reduction to yield a spontaneous reaction.

■ Assign Laboratory 43, "Electrochemical Cells." In this lab the students set up and measure the voltage of several different electrochemical cells. Then they compare the experimental voltages with the theoretical voltages derived from the table of standard electrode potentials.

## 22-15 The Chemical Activities of Metals, pp. 655-656,

## 22-16 Some Practical Applications of Electrochemical Cells, pp. 656-658, and

## 22-17 The Corrosion of Metals—An Electrochemical Process, pp. 658-660

| Planning Guide | |
|---|---|
| **Labs (Lab Manual) and Demonstrations (TE)** | **Supplementary Materials (Teacher's Resource Book)** |
| Demo 22-1: Charging and Discharging a Lead Storage Battery with Your Bare Hands, p. TG-313 | Critical and Creative Thinking: Ranking Things and Ideas, p. CCT-63 |
| Demo 22-2: Plumbers' Chemistry, p. TG-314 | |
| Lab 44: Corrosion of Iron | |

■ Explain that the table of standard electrode potentials can be used to rank metals in the order of their activities. Because a metal's activity is directly related to its ability to lose electrons, the more active metals have lower reduction potentials. Ask the students to relate the activities of metals to their reduction potentials and to list the more common metals in the order of their activities. They can compare their list to the one in text Figure 22-36. Then ask the students to list common nonmetals in the order of their activities or their ability to be reduced.

■ Begin the discussion of applications of electrochemical cells by discussing the construction and operation of a dry cell, both alkaline and acid forms. Then do Demonstration 22-1, "Charging and Discharging a Lead Storage Battery with Your Bare Hands." In this demonstration, you construct a simple lead storage battery. Compare this lead storage battery to the one in text Figure 22-40. Discuss the operation and use of this type of battery. Then compare the lead storage battery to a nickel-cadmium rechargeable battery. Point out that although the nickel-cadmium battery is more expensive than the lead storage battery, it has certain advantages. For example, the freezing point of the KOH electrolyte is very low ($-30°C$), the capacity does not drop as sharply with a drop in temperature, and the battery can be charged and discharged without a loss of efficiency. The major disadvantage is that the KOH in the nickel-cadmium battery reacts with the $CO_2$ in the air and must be replaced periodically. The nickel-cadmium battery is used in some European autos, electric razors, calculators, and power tools.

■ An interesting way to introduce the topic of corrosion is to do Demonstration 22-2, "Plumbers' Chemistry." In this demonstration students observe the acceleration of the rate of corrosion of an iron pipe because of its contact with a copper pipe. Point out that the corrosion of metals is an electrochemical process. Assign Laboratory 44, "Corrosion of Iron," in which the students investigate the factors that affect the rate of corrosion of an iron nail.

■ **Application.** You may want to point out to the students that acid rain is harmful to things other than plants and animals. It has also increased the rate of corrosion in metals. Ask the class to describe the galvanic cell that is formed when a sample of impure iron is in contact with acid rain. Ask the students to indicate the anode, cathode, and electrolyte. Students should also be able to explain why zinc or magnesium prevents the corrosion of iron when they are in contact with the iron.

■ **Concept Mastery.** You may want to discuss Concept Mastery question 42 to address some students' misconception regarding corrosion of metals. Students often think that when something corrodes, it automatically wears away and therefore decreases in mass.

Actually, when metals corrode, they increase in mass because of the additional mass of the metal oxide that is formed. Only when the corrosion is removed does the original metal sample decrease in mass.

■ **Critical Thinking.** In the Critical and Creative Thinking worksheet "Ranking Things and Ideas" students rank several metals according to their suitability for the cathodic protection of underground pipelines. The students use the table of standard reduction potentials (text Figure 22-30) and other factors such as cost in their evaluations.

## Demonstrations

### 22-1 Charging and Discharging a Lead Storage Battery with Your Bare Hands

**Overview:** In this demonstration, you charge a small lead storage battery, using a d.c. hand generator. Evidence that the battery has been charged is demonstrated by the lighting of a bulb.

**Materials:** d.c. hand generator (can generally be borrowed from the physics department); 2 thin lead sheets, 3 cm × 5 cm × 1 mm; sandpaper; 2 pieces of gauze or coated screening, 2 cm × 5 cm; 2% solution, by mass, of anhydrous sodium sulfate ($Na_2SO_4$); concentrated sulfuric acid ($H_2SO_4$); medicine dropper; 50-mL beaker; 4 alligator clips; coated copper electrical wire; 1 miniature lamp with leads, 1.5 volts, 0.025 amp; 2 rubber bands; safety goggles.

**Advance Preparation:** 1. Cut the two pieces of lead into the shape shown in Figure 22-1(a). Using a sharp, hard object, scratch a plus sign ($+$) on the small protruding square of one lead sheet, and a minus sign ($-$) on the square of the other sheet. Each protruding square will serve as a terminal contact. 2. **2% $Na_2SO_4$:** Mix 2 g of $Na_2SO_4$ in 98 mL of water. Acidify the solution by adding $1-2$ mL of concentrated sulfuric acid ($H_2SO_4$). 3. Because d.c. hand generators may differ considerably, you should carry out a trial run of the demonstration before class, in order to determine the number of minutes needed to charge the lead storage battery so that it will light a miniature lamp.

**Safety:** Be careful in handling the sulfuric acid, the lead battery, and the generator. Wear goggles throughout. Warn students who assist you not to touch the electrodes or wire leads, and have the students wear goggles.

**Procedure:** 1. Place one piece of gauze or coated screening onto a desk or table. Place the "$-$" lead electrode on top of the gauze or screening, followed by the second piece of gauze or screening. Finally, lay the "$+$" lead electrode on top. (See Figure 22-1(b).) 2. Roll

22

the pile of lead sheets and gauze or screening into a roll. (See Figure 22-1(c).) Do not allow the lead plates to come into direct contact with one another. Hold the lead cell together by using rubber bands. Place the lead cell into a 50-mL beaker, and cover all but the terminals of the cell with 2% sodium sulfate ($Na_2SO_4$) solution. 3. Connect the electrodes of the generator to the miniature lamp (see Figure 22-1(d)) and show what happens when the handle of the generator is turned. 4. Disconnect the electrodes of the generator, and connect them to the terminal contacts of the lead storage battery, using alligator clips and wire. Have student volunteers turn the handle of the generator (in the same direction always), and have the class observe what happens. Have the volunteers continue to generate electricity for the length of time that was previously required to charge the lead storage battery (see "Advance Preparation"). Ask students how such charging occurs in the battery of an automobile. 5. After the lead storage battery is charged, disconnect the wire leads from the generator, and connect the miniature lamp to the lead battery. Have students observe what happens. Ask them to discuss the energy conversions that have taken place throughout the demonstration.

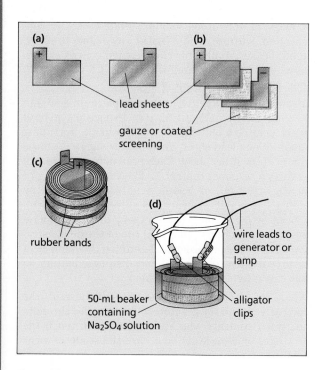

**Figure 22-1**

**Results:** When the handle of the generator is turned, in step 3, the miniature lamp will light up. The mechanical energy expended in turning the armature of the generator in its magnetic field will be converted into electrical energy. Electrons will pass through the wire into the filament of the miniature lamp and some of their energy will be changed to light and heat. Total energy will be conserved throughout. When the d.c. generator is connected to the battery, in step 4, mechanical energy will again be changed to electrical energy. An electric current will be produced, and electrons will flow into the lead storage plates in the battery. The electrical energy will be stored as potential energy in the chemical bonds in the lead storage battery. Some $H_2$ gas will form at the positive plate, and $PbO_2$ will form at the negative plate.

Reduction $PbSO_4(s) + 2e^- \rightarrow Pb(s) + SO_4^{2-}(aq)$

Oxidation $PbSO_4(s) + 2H_2O(l) \rightarrow$
$$2e^- + SO_4^{2-}(aq) + 4H^+(aq) + PbO_2(s)$$

Overall $\overline{2PbSO_4 + 2H_2O(l) \rightarrow}$
$$Pb(s) + PbO_2(s) + 4H^+(aq) + 2SO_4^{2-}(aq)$$

Lead storage batteries do not become charged spontaneously. Energy must be expended to charge them. The alternator and rectifier in an automobile convert the electrical energy produced by the car's generator into direct current. This current, like that from the hand generator in this demonstration, stores energy in the automobile's battery. Once a lead storage battery is charged, a spontaneous reaction can occur and the potential energy stored in the chemical bonds can be converted back to electrical energy. This will be demonstrated in step 5, when you connect the miniature lamp to the lead storage battery and the lamp lights. The production of an electric current by the lead storage battery is accomplished by the oxidation of lead in the anode to $Pb^{2+}$ ions. These lead ions react with the $SO_4^{2-}$ ions in the electrolyte and precipitate as lead sulfate ($PbSO_4$) on the lead plates. Lead dioxide ($PbO_2$) that was produced during the charging is also converted to $PbSO_4$ that is precipitated at the cathode. The half-reactions and overall reaction that occur are:

$Pb(s) + SO_4^{2-}(aq) \rightarrow 2e^- + PbSO_4(s)$

$PbO_2(s) + 4H^+(aq) + SO_4^{2-} + 2e^- \rightarrow$
$$PbSO_4(s) + 2H_2O(l)$$

$\overline{Pb(s) + 2SO_4^{2-}(aq) + 4H^+(aq) + PbO_2(s) \rightarrow}$
$$2PbSO_4(s) + 2H_2O(l)$$

## 22-2 Plumbers' Chemistry

**Overview:** In this demonstration, you set up a system in which an electrochemical reaction involving two different metals occurs.

**Materials:** short length (roughly 15 cm) of new copper pipe; short length of new iron pipe; piece of corroded iron pipe; 500-mL beaker; tap water; concentrated sulfuric acid ($H_2SO_4$); galvanometer; two lengths of wire with alligator clips; sandpaper.

**Advance Preparation:** 1. Obtain the new pipes from a

hardware store. You may be able to obtain the piece of corroded iron pipe from a local plumber. 2. Place 300 mL of tap water into the 500-mL beaker, and add to it 1–2 mL of concentrated sulfuric acid, so as to allow the water to conduct electricity.

**Safety:** Be careful in handling the sulfuric acid.

**Procedure:** 1. Show the students the lengths of new pipe, and tell them that similar piping is used in many homes, schools, and offices to carry fresh water and waste water. Remove any traces of grease or oxide from the surface of the pipes by rubbing them lightly with sandpaper. 2. Set up the apparatus as shown in Figure 22-2. When attaching the alligator clips to the pipes, be sure that they make good contact with the metal. Before connecting the galvanometer, ask students why you are using it rather than a light bulb to detect current. Connect the galvanometer and have students observe it. (If you do not obtain a reading, adjust the alligator clips.) Have the students observe the direction of the current, as well as its magnitude, and ask them to explain what is happening. 3. Show the students an example of a corroded iron pipe to illustrate the effects of such processes. Point out that copper and iron plumbing pipes are kept apart in order to help prevent such corrosion from occurring.

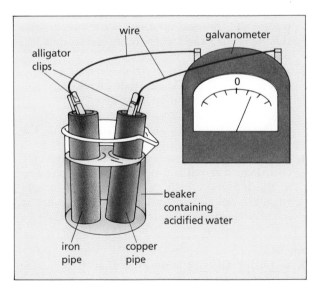

**Figure 22-2**

**Results:** The filament of a light bulb may offer too much resistance for the cell's low current to overcome; therefore, a galvanometer, which is more sensitive in detecting low currents, is used instead. A low current will be detectable. The electrons will flow from the iron pipe to the copper pipe. (You can further confirm the direction of this electron flow by referring to a chart of standard reduction potentials for half-

reactions.) $Fe^{2+}$ ions will form at the surface of the iron pipe and will drift away from the pipe, exposing more iron to oxidation. Hydrogen gas will slowly (and invisibly) form at the copper pipe and leave the system, allowing the electrochemical reaction to continue.

## Answers to Questions

**Page 624**
1. **a.** During an electrolysis, electrical energy is converted to chemical energy.
   **b.** During the operation of an electrochemical cell, chemical energy is changed to electrical energy.
2. The redox reaction in which electrons are completely gained or lost plays an important role in electrochemistry.
3. A half-reaction is either the oxidation or the reduction part of the redox reaction.
4. **a.** $Ca \rightarrow Ca^{2+} + 2e^-$ (the oxidation)
   **b.** $Cl_2 + 2e^- \rightarrow 2Cl^-$ (the reduction)

**Page 630**
5. **a.** An electric current is any flow of electrical charge.
   **b.** Metallic conduction is the movement of loosely held valence electrons in the atoms of the metals.
   **c.** Ionic conduction results from the movement of positive and negative ions along some path.
6. A direct current is a form of electric current in which the electrons travel in one direction only.
7. **a.** In text Figure 22-7, electrons are accepted by molecules or ions in the solution.
   **b.** These electrons come from ions or molecules in the solution.
8. **a.** The battery, the two wires, and the metal strips make up the external circuit.
   **b.** The electrolyte is the internal circuit.
9. Electrolysis is the process by which an electric current causes a redox reaction to take place.
10. A source of direct current supplies the energy needed to cause the reaction to occur. The cathode is the electrode where reduction occurs. It has a negative charge, having acquired electrons from the power source. The anode is the electrode where oxidation occurs. It has a positive charge and attracts anions in the electrolyte. The electrolyte is a liquid that permits the flow of ions between the electrodes.
11. **a.** Oxidation occurs at the anode.
    **b.** Reduction occurs at the cathode.
    **c.** The anode is positively charged.
    **d.** The cathode is negatively charged.

**Page 631**

12. **a.** During the electrolysis of molten NaCl, sodium ions are attracted to the negative electrode, gain electrons, and become neutral sodium atoms.
   **b.** $Na^+ + e^- \rightarrow Na$
   **c.** The chloride ions are attracted to the positive electrode where they lose electrons and become neutral chlorine atoms. Two chlorine atoms combine to form a chlorine molecule.
   **d.** $2Cl^- \rightarrow Cl_2 + 2e^-$ (at the "+" electrode)
   **e.** $2NaCl \rightarrow 2Na + Cl_2$ (overall reaction)

**Page 634**

13. **a.** $2H_2O \rightarrow O_2 + 4H^+ + 4e^-$ (at the anode)
   **b.** $4H_2O + 4e^- \rightarrow 2H_2 + 4OH^-$ (at the cathode)
   **c.** $6H_2O \rightarrow 2H_2 + O_2 + 4H^+ + 4OH^-$ (sum a + b)
   **d.** $2H_2O \rightarrow 2H_2 + O_2$ (final equation)
14. **a.** Water contains very few ions, and the electrolysis would be extremely slow. The added electrolyte supplies ions that cause the rate of the reaction to increase.
   **b.** These electrolytes are catalysts because they speed up the reaction without being permanently altered.

**Page 635**

15. **a.** $2Cl^- \rightarrow Cl_2 + 2e^-$
   **b.** $2H_2O + 2e^- \rightarrow H_2 + 2OH^-$
   **c.** $2H_2O + 2Cl^- \rightarrow H_2 + Cl_2 + 2OH^-$
16. **a.** Sodium hydroxide, chlorine gas, and hydrogen gas are produced during the electrolysis of brine.
   **b.** Sodium hydroxide is produced by evaporating the final solution.
   **c.** $2H_2O + 2NaCl \rightarrow H_2 + Cl_2 + 2NaOH$

**Page 637**

17. **a.** The object to be plated is the cathode, the negative electrode.
   **b.** The other electrode is composed of the plating metal.
   **c.** A nonconductor can be coated with a conducting material such as graphite.
   **d.** The ions of the metal that is to form the plate must be present in the electroplating solution.
18. **a.** The anode is silver, the cathode is the spoon, and the electrolyte is a soluble silver compound such as silver nitrate.
   **b.** $Ag^+ + e^- \rightarrow Ag$ (cathode reaction)
   **c.** $Ag \rightarrow Ag^+ + e^-$ (anode reaction)
   **d.** One silver atom goes into solution for each silver atom that plates out.

**Page 641**

19. Galvanic cell and voltaic cell are synonyms for electrochemical cell.

20. $Cu^{2+}$ ions, $SO_4^{2-}$ ions, and water molecules are present in an aqueous solution of $CuSO_4$.
21. See Figure 22-3.

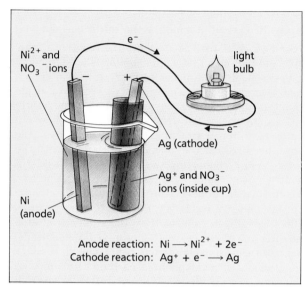

Anode reaction:  $Ni \longrightarrow Ni^{2+} + 2e^-$
Cathode reaction:  $Ag^+ + e^- \longrightarrow Ag$

**Figure 22-3**

22. The temperature, the composition of the electrodes, and the concentrations of the ions in solution determine the voltage of an electrochemical cell.
23. **a.** The mass of the Zn electrode decreases.
   **b.** The mass of the Cu electrode increases.
   **c.** Zinc ion concentration increases.
   **d.** Copper ion concentration decreases.
   **e.** The spectator ion concentration remains the same.
24. In both an electrolysis and electrochemical cell, there is an internal and external circuit. Ions flow in the internal circuit, a redox reaction occurs when the cell is in operation, oxidation occurs at the anode, and reduction occurs at the cathode.

**Page 643**

25. **a.** During the operation of a Daniell cell, zinc atoms from the electrode pass into solution as zinc ions.
   **b.** Copper ions from the solution are deposited on the cathode.
   **c.** Sulfate ions from the cathode compartment pass through the walls of the porous cup into the anode compartment.
26. A half-cell consists of the electrode (anode or cathode) and the chemicals that react in that portion of the cell.
27. $Ag/Ag^+$

**Page 647**

**28.** The voltage or electromotive force is a measure of the difference in electrical potential between the electrodes.

**29. a.** The hydrogen electrode is a platinum strip coated with finely divided platinum.

    **b.** $H_2 \rightarrow 2H^+ + 2e^-$; $2H^+ + 2e^- \rightarrow H_2$

    **c.** reduction

    **d.** oxidation

**30.** The concentration of hydrogen ions is 1 $M$, the temperature is 25°C, and the hydrogen gas pressure is 101.3 kPa in a standard hydrogen half-cell.

**31.** Exactly 0 volts has been assigned to the standard hydrogen half-cell.

**32. a.** When the $H^+$ ion is the stronger oxidizing agent, oxidation occurs in the other half-cell.

    **b.** When the $H_2$ gas is the stronger reducing agent, reduction occurs in the other half-cell. The oxidizing agent in the other half-cell is a stronger one than the $H^+$ ions.

**33.** Use a salt bridge to connect the zinc half-cell with a standard hydrogen half-cell. Connect a voltmeter to this arrangement as shown in text Figure 22-28. The needle swings to the right, showing that zinc metal is a stronger reducing agent than hydrogen gas.

**Page 653**

**34.** Standard conditions for standard electrode potentials: The temperature is 25°C, ion concentrations are 1 $M$, and the pressure of gases is 101.3 kPa.

**35. a.** Reducing agents are on the right.

    **b.** Oxidizing agents are on the left.

**36. a.** In text Figure 22-30, $F_2$ is the strongest oxidizing agent.

    **b.** Li is the strongest reducing agent.

    **c.** $2Li + F_2 \rightarrow 2LiF$

**37.** It means that this half-reaction will proceed only in a solution that is acidic.

**38. a.** $3K + Al^{3+} \rightarrow 3K^+ + Al$

    **b.** $Br_2 + Cl^- \rightarrow N.R.$

    **c.** $Ca + ZnCl_2 \rightarrow CaCl_2 + Zn$

**Page 655**

**39. a.** −0.14 volt

    **b.** −0.76 volt

    **c.** The $Sn^{2+}$ is the stronger oxidizing agent. It is higher in the table of standard reduction potentials and therefore is more easily reduced.

    **d.** $Zn + Sn^{2+} \rightarrow Zn^{2+} + Sn$

    **e.** See Figure 22-4.

**40. a.** Temperature, 25°C; $Cu^{2+}$ ion concentration, 1 $M$.

    **b.** Anode reaction: $Al \rightarrow Al^{3+} + 3e^-$
        Cathode reaction: $Cu^{2+} + 2e^- \rightarrow Cu$

    **c.** $2Al + 3Cu^{2+} \rightarrow 2Al^{3+} + 3Cu$

    **d.** (+1.66 volts) + (+0.34 volt) = 2.00 volts

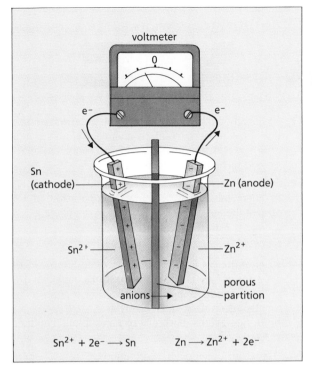

**Figure 22-4**

**Page 660**

**41. a.** Iron and zinc would be practical metals for the lab preparation of $H_2$ with HCl.

    **b.** Lithium and sodium would create very vigorous, and possibly explosive, reactions. Copper will not react with HCl solution.

**42.** It consists of six 1½-volt cells connected in series.

**43.** During the discharge of a lead storage battery, the acid reacts with the electrodes to form $PbSO_4$ and $H_2O$. Therefore, the acid concentration decreases.

**44.** Pb, $PbO_2$, and $H_2SO_4$ are reactants during the discharge of a lead storage battery.

**45.** Four ways to prevent metallic corrosion: 1) Coating the metal with paint, lacquer, etc.; 2) Plating with another metal; 3) Alloying with another metal or metals; 4) Making it the cathode in a cell where the anode is a more expendable metal.

**Page 660, Light from Chemical Energy**

  **1.** The bubbles are hydrogen gas.

  **2.** $Mg + 2H^+ \rightarrow Mg^{2+} + H_2$

In this setup, magnesium atoms reduce the hydrogen ions in solution to produce hydrogen gas. The copper is an inert electrode. As $Mg^{2+}$ ions are formed, electrons are left behind on the magnesium electrode. These electrons flow through the wire (and the light bulb) to the copper electrode, where they reduce the hydrogen ions. This current lights the bulb.

22

# Chapter Review 22

## Page 662, Content Review

1. Electrochemistry deals with the relation of the flow of electric current to chemical changes and with the conversion of chemical to electrical energy and electrical to chemical energy.

2. During electrolysis, electrical energy is converted to chemical energy. During the operation of an electrochemical cell, the reverse takes place.

3. **a.** $2K \rightarrow 2K^+ + 2e^-$
   **b.** $Cl_2 + 2e^- \rightarrow 2Cl^-$

4. **a.** Metallic conduction consists of a flow of electrons, as in an electric current in a copper wire. Ionic conduction consists of a flow of ions, as in a solution used in electrolysis.
   **b.** In neon signs, both electrons and ions conduct the current.

5. Oxidation takes place at an anode.

6. Electrolysis is the process by which an electric current produces a redox reaction in a conducting liquid or fluid.

7. **a.** At the negative electrode, electrons are accepted by a molecule or ion.
   **b.** A molecule or ion gives up electrons to the positive electrode.
   **c.** Negative ions move toward the positive electrode, and positive ions move toward the negative electrode.

8. A half-reaction is the oxidation or reduction part of a redox reaction. During the electrolysis of molten NaCl, $Na^+$ is reduced and $Cl^-$ is oxidized. The half-reactions for reduction and oxidation, respectively, are
   $$Na^+ + e^- \rightarrow Na$$
   $$2Cl^- \rightarrow Cl_2 + 2e^-$$

9. During the electrolysis of water, oxidation of water occurs at the anode, producing acidic (low pH) conditions and generating oxygen gas.

10. $4H_2O + 4e^- \rightarrow 2H_2 + 4OH^-$

11. $2H_2O + 2NaCl(aq) \xrightarrow{\text{electrolysis}} H_2(g) + Cl_2(g) + 2NaOH(aq)$

12. **a.** Water molecules are more easily reduced, requiring a lower voltage than that needed for the sodium ions.
   **b.** At the anode, chloride ions are more easily oxidized than water molecules.

13. **a.** The iron bar is made the cathode (negative electrode). The anode is made of zinc. The electrolyte is a solution of a soluble zinc salt, containing zinc ions.
   **b.** Anode reaction: $Zn \rightarrow Zn^{2+} + 2e^-$
   Cathode reaction: $Zn^{2+} + 2e^- \rightarrow Zn$

14. An electrochemical cell is a device that uses a redox reaction as a means of producing an electric current.

15. $Zn + Cu^{2+} \rightarrow Zn^{2+} + Cu$

16. **a.** Some zinc atoms go into solution as zinc ions and, briefly, electrons flow in the external circuit.
   **b.** Because copper has less tendency to form ions than zinc does, the net result is that some copper ions gain electrons released by the zinc and form neutral copper atoms. This leaves an excess of sulfate ions in solution.
   **c.** The excess positive charge in solution at the zinc electrode and the excess negative charge in the solution at the copper electrode prevent the further formation and flow of electrons.

17. **a.** Zinc ions in the solution flow toward the excess sulfate ions; sulfate ions flow toward the zinc ions. Therefore, the solution is kept electrically neutral, allowing electrons to be formed and to flow in the external circuit.
   **b.** A salt bridge can be used.

18. Voltage is the measure of the difference in electrical potential between two points in an electrical circuit.

19. Standard electrode potentials are measured relative to the reduction of $H^+$ to $H_2$ gas being assigned 0.0 volts and under the conditions of concentration of 1.0 $M$, 25°C, and 101.3 kPa (1.00 atm).

20. **a.** It adsorbs hydrogen gas, holding the atoms in an activated form in which they enter an equilibrium reaction with the hydrogen ions in solution.
   **b.** 0.00 volts.

21. **a.** $H_2 \rightarrow 2H^+ + 2e^-$
   **b.** $Fe^{3+} + e^- \rightarrow Fe^{2+}$
   **c.** $H_2 + 2Fe^{3+} \rightarrow 2H^+ + 2Fe^{2+}$

22. The reaction will not occur spontaneously because the voltage is negative. That is, $E°$ for the oxidation of Fe (+0.44 volt) plus $E°$ for the reduction of $Zn^{2+}$ (−0.83 volt) is negative (−0.39 volt).

23. **a.** 0.14 volt + 0.80 volt = 0.94 volt
   **b.** $Sn \rightarrow Sn^{2+} + 2e^-$
   **c.** The tin is oxidized.
   **d.** The tin is the reducing agent.

24. **a.** 0.45 volt + $x$ = 0.60 volt; $x$ = 0.15 volt
   **b.** $Sn^{4+} + 2e^- \rightarrow Sn^{2+}$

25. **a.** 2.37 volts − 0.76 volt = 1.61 volts
    **b.** 1.66 volts + 1.36 volts = 3.02 volts
    **c.** −0.77 volt + 1.09 volts = 0.32 volt

26. Lithium is the most reactive metal.

27. $MnO_2$ and $NH_4Cl$ are reduced, and zinc is oxidized.
    $E_{reduction} + E°_{oxidation\ of\ Zn} = 1.50$ volts
    Using text Figure 22-30, the $E°$ for the oxidation of Zn is −(−0.76 volt).
    $E_{reduction} + 0.76$ volt = 1.50 volts
    $E_{reduction} = 0.74$ volt

28. Zinc is more reactive than iron. Thus, the blocks of Zn will oxidize before Fe oxidizes (rusts). This arrangement protects the iron ship.

## Page 663, Content Mastery

29. There is no difference among electrochemical, galvanic, and voltaic cells. These are different names for the same electrochemical setup.

30. **a.** 2 moles of $OH^-$ for every 1 mole of $Cl_2$.
    **b.** 1 mole of $OH^-$ for every 1 mole of $Cl^-$.

31. **a.** $2H_2O + 2e^- \rightarrow H_2 + 2OH^-$
    $2H_2O \rightarrow O_2 + 4H^+ + 4e^-$
    **b.** $2H_2O \rightarrow 2H_2 + O_2$

32. **a.** The anode is copper; it is immersed in a solution of copper(II) nitrate. The cathode is silver; it is immersed in a solution of silver nitrate.
    **b.** At the anode: $Cu \rightarrow Cu^{2+} + 2e^-$
    At the cathode: $Ag^+ + e^- \rightarrow Ag$
    **c.** Electrons flow from the copper anode to the silver cathode.
    **d.** Copper ions at the anode flow toward the nitrate ions at the cathode; nitrate ions flow toward the copper ions.

33. **a.** It will have an Sn electrode in a solution of an $Sn^{2+}$ salt in one compartment and an Fe electrode in a solution of an $Fe^{2+}$ salt in the other. A salt bridge or porous partition is used.
    **b.** $Sn^{2+} + 2e^- \rightarrow Sn$; $Fe \rightarrow Fe^{2+} + 2e^-$
    **c.** The tin electrode is the cathode; the iron electrode is the anode.
    **d.** The cathode is positive; the anode is negative.
    **e.** $Fe + Sn^{2+} \rightarrow Fe^{2+} + Sn$

34. **a.** Yes. **b.** No. **c.** No. **d.** Yes.

35. From text Figure 22-30, we see that the strongest oxidizing agent is $F_2$ and the strongest reducing agent is Li. Combining these two species theoretically would produce the largest voltage. Therefore, we would create a battery that has the reduction of $F_2(g)$ for the cathode and the oxidation of Li(s) for the anode. The equation is as follows:
    $F_2(g) + 2Li(s) \rightarrow 2Li^+(aq) + 2F^-(aq)$.

The voltage $= E°_{ox} + E°_{red} = -(-3.04$ volts$) + 2.87$ volts $= 5.91$ volts.

36. **a.** The negative terminal has an excess of electrons, or negative charge. The positive terminal is deficient in its number of electrons and has an excess positive charge.
    **b.** At the negative terminal, the electrons are moving out of the terminal into one end of the light-bulb filament. At the positive terminal, electrons are being drawn out of the filament into the terminal.

37. **a.** The net potential is 2.37 volts + (−1.66 volts) = 0.71 volt. This is positive, and the reaction proceeds spontaneously.
    **b.** The net potential is 0.14 volt + (−0.45 volt) = −0.31 volt. The reaction is not spontaneous.
    **c.** The net potential is 1.09 volts + (−0.54 volt) = 0.55 volt. The reaction is spontaneous.
    **d.** The net potential is −1.36 volts + 1.23 volts = −0.13 volt. The reaction is not spontaneous.

## Page 664, Concept Mastery

38. ***Concept:*** *Electrolysis of water produces gases in which the molecules are widely separated.*
    *Solution:* The volume of hydrogen to oxygen is 2:1 because the spaces between the molecules are vast as related to the volume of an individual molecule. Avogadro's hypothesis indicates that equal volumes of an ideal gas will contain the same number of molecules.

39. ***Concept:*** *Electrolytic reactions take place readily if the conditions are right.*
    *Solution:* An electrolytic reaction is occurring in which the iodide ion is being oxidized to free iodine and the water is producing the hydroxide ion and hydrogen gas. The ink that appears is $I_2$.

40. ***Concept:*** *Voltage can be positive or negative.*
    *Solution:* Voltage is not a physical entity. This does not make it something unreal. It is the tendency for electrons to flow. The number itself is somewhat arbitrary, like the numbers given for the boiling point and freezing point of water on the Celsius scale. A temperature of −20°C is real. The scale is based on a comparison of the ability of metal ions to be reduced with that of the hydrogen ion.

41. ***Concept:*** *Batteries are dead when chemical activity is at an equilibrium.*

22

*Solution:* Batteries are not really dead. Either the reaction has ceased because one of the products has been allowed to escape and therefore the reaction is irreversible, or the reactants are at equilibrium. In the case of batteries that can be revived by recharging, the products of the reactions are solids that do not escape. The reaction is forced in the opposite direction by applying an external voltage. When this is removed, the reaction then proceeds as it had originally.

**42. *Concept:*** *Corrosion is a redox reaction in which the metal wears away.*

*Solution:* In a redox reaction it is true that the metal wears away because of its reaction with oxygen to form the oxide. As the oxide forms, the mass of the metal that is corroding will increase unless the corrosion is removed. Because the corrosion contains the metal ions, less metal remains than was originally present.

### Page 664, Cumulative Review

**43. d.** Double replacement reactions are not redox.

**44. c.** $2H_2S + 3O_2 \rightarrow 2H_2O + 2SO_2$

$$\frac{3 \text{ mol } O_2 \times 5.0 \text{ dm}^3 \text{ H}_2S}{2 \text{ mol } H_2S} = 7.5 \text{ dm}^3 \text{ O}_2$$

**45. c.** $Ca(OH_2) + H_2SO_4 \rightarrow 2H_2O + CaSO_4$

Molar concentration of $Ca(OH)_2$ solution =
$$\frac{15.0 \text{ cm}^3 \text{ H}_2SO_4 \times 0.100 \text{ } M \text{ H}_2SO_4}{35.0 \text{ cm}^3 \text{ Ca(OH)}_2} = 0.0429 \text{ } M;$$

$$\frac{0.0429 \text{ mol/dm}^3 \times 35.0 \text{ cm}^3}{1000 \text{ cm}^3/\text{dm}^3} = 0.00150 \text{ mol};$$

$0.00150 \text{ mol} \times 74.0 \text{ g/mol} = 0.111 \text{ g Ca(OH)}_2$

**46. a.** Mg has the largest atomic radius.

**47.** Oxidation first referred to the combination of a substance with oxygen. Today the term oxidation includes any chemical change in which the oxidation number of an element increases.

**48.** When a substance melts, its particles acquire enough kinetic energy to leave their fixed locations (in the solid phase).

**49. a.** In an ionic solid, the ions (e.g., Na$^+$ and Cl$^-$) exist in a regular pattern called a crystal lattice, in which there are no separate, covalently bonded units that correspond to the formula (e.g., NaCl) of the compound.

**b.** The ions in a crystal lattice are strongly held in fixed positions by electrical attractions of ions around them. A large amount of energy is needed to break up the structure, so that ionic crystals have high melting points.

**c.** In the solid state, the ions are immobile, but melting or dissolving frees the ions to move about and thus to conduct a current.

**50. a.** $1s^2 2s^2 2p^6 3s^2 3p^4$

**b.** $p_x$, 2; $p_y$, 1; $p_z$, 1

**c.** 6

**51.** A scientific theory provides a general explanation for the observations related to the problem, while a scientific law states a relationship among observed facts.

**52.**
$$\frac{72.0 \text{ g HCl} \times 1 \text{ mol } H_2 \times 2.0 \text{ g/mol } H_2}{2 \text{ mol HCl} \times 36.5 \text{ g/mol HCl}} = 1.97 \text{ g}$$

### Page 664, Critical Thinking

**53.** Silver and other precious metals provide a coating that resists corrosion. They also increase the value of objects such as jewelry because of their attractive shine.

**54.** Activity in a metal is the readiness to give up valence electrons, to undergo oxidation. Metals that are easily oxidized are difficult to reduce, so they have low reduction potentials.

**55.** In both cases, Cl$^-$ gets oxidized at the anode. In the electrolysis of molten NaCl, Na$^+$ gets reduced at the cathode. In the electrolysis of brine, however, it is easier to reduce the H$_2$O that is present than it is to reduce Na$^+$.

**56.** Zinc would be more useful. Anodic protection is meant to protect a metal by having a more active metal be oxidized instead. Zinc is more active than iron and will work. Copper is less active than iron and, thus, will not work.

**57. a.** No, a reducing agent is needed.

**b.** and **c.** Yes.

**d.** No, a reducing agent is needed.

**e.** Yes.

**58.** K > Ba > Na > Zn > Pb > Hg > Au

**59.** The electrode potential for reducing Ag$^+$ is +0.80 volt, so the electrode potential for the reverse reaction in which Ag is oxidized is −0.80 volt. Since the reaction is written in the other direction, the sign of the electrode potential must be changed. Since the reaction is now an oxidation, the electrode potential is an oxidation potential, not a reduction potential.

**60. a.** See Figure 22-5.

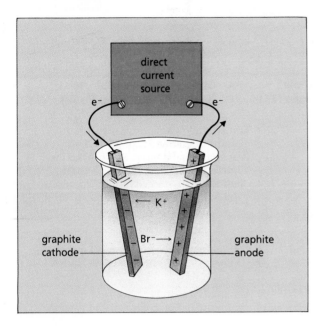

**Figure 22-5**

**b.** $K^+ + e^- \rightarrow K$ (cathode reaction)
$2Br^- \rightarrow Br_2 + 2e^-$ (anode reaction)
$2K^+ + 2Br^- \rightarrow 2K + Br_2$

**61. a.** It turns blue because of the hydroxide ions produced in the cathode reaction.
  **b.** It turns red because of the hydrogen ions produced in the anode reaction.
  **c.** They combine to form water.

**62. a.** Its polarity keeps changing. When the electrode is positive, silver goes into solution as ions; when the electrode is negative, ions plate out on the electrode.
  **b.** Its polarity also changes. When the electrode is negative, the spoon is plated with silver; when the electrode is positive, the silver goes back into solution as ions.
  **c.** For practical purposes, neither electrode undergoes a net change.

**63.** A prospector can make money by placing "worthless" used tin cans in a stream containing the more valuable copper, because, as text Figure 22-30 indicates, tin is more reactive than copper. As Figure 22-30 also shows, the following reaction proceeds spontaneously:
$Sn(s) + Cu^{2+}(aq) \rightarrow Sn^{2+}(aq) + Cu(s)$
$E° = +0.48$ volt

22

# Chemistry of Selected Elements

23

## Chapter Planning Guide

| Text Section | | Labs (Lab Manual) and Demonstrations (TE) | Supplementary Materials (Teacher's Resource Book) |
|---|---|---|---|
| 23-1 | Descriptive Chemistry, p. 667 | | Transparency Master: Some Alkali Metal Compounds, p. 23-1 |
| 23-2 | The Alkali Metals, pp. 667-669 | | Transparency Master: Some Alkaline Earth Metal Compounds, p. 23-2 |
| 23-3 | The Alkaline Earth Metals, pp. 669-670 | | Open-Ended Demonstration: The Behavior of Plaster of Paris, p. 23-6 |
| 23-4 | The Transition Metals, pp. 670-672 | Demo 23-1: Iron in Cereal, p. TG-326<br>Demo 23-2: Pennies That Float, p. TG-327 | Transparency Master: Some Transition Elements and Their Uses, p. 23-3 |
| Biography | Ignacio Tinoco, Jr., p. 672 | | |
| 23-5 | Aluminum, pp. 672-673 | | |
| 23-6 | Iron and Steel, pp. 673-676 | | Transparency Master: Properties and Uses of Several Steels, p. 23-4 |
| 23-7 | The Recovery of Copper, pp. 676-678 | | |
| 23-8 | Oxygen, pp. 678-679 | Lab 46: Oxygen: Its Properties<br>Lab 47: Hydrogen: Preparation and Properties | |
| Career | Dietitian, p. 679 | | |
| 23-9 | Hydrogen, pp. 679-680 | | |
| 23-10 | Sulfur, pp. 680-682 | Lab 45: Allotropes of Sulfur<br>Demo 23-3: Making Acid from Burning Sulfur, p. TG-327 | Open-Ended Demonstration: The Dehydration of Sucrose, p. 23-7 |
| 23-11 | Nitrogen, pp. 682-684 | | |
| 23-12 | The Halogens, pp. 684-686 | | Transparency Master: Some Halogen Compounds, p. 23-5<br>Societal Issues: Chlorofluorocarbons and the Ozone Layer, p. SI-41 |

| Text Section | Labs (Lab Manual) and Demonstrations (TE) | Supplementary Materials (Teacher's Resource Book) |
|---|---|---|
| **23-13**  The Noble Gases, pp. 686-687 | | Review Activity: Selected–Elements Vocabulary, p. 23-8 |
| | | Test—Form A, p. AT-88 Alternate Test—Form B, p. BT-88 |

■ Core   ■ Advanced   ■ Optional

## Chapter Overview

In Chapter 23 we describe the occurrence, preparation, reactions, and compounds of the alkali metals and the alkaline earth metals. We then describe individual metals from other groups—silver, copper, iron, and aluminum. Next, the Hall-Heroult process for extracting aluminum and the commercial production of steel and copper are discussed. We present highlights of the descriptive chemistry of the nonmetals oxygen, hydrogen, nitrogen, sulfur, and the halogens. The chapter concludes with a survey of the noble gases.

## Chapter Objectives

After students have completed this chapter, they will be able to:

1. Compare the preparations, properties, and uses of the alkali metals and the alkaline earth metals.
   *23-1 to 23-3*

2. Identify some compounds of metals in Group 1 and Group 2 and state their uses.   *23-2 and 23-3*

3. Describe some representative transition metals.
   *23-4*

4. Explain how aluminum, iron, and copper are extracted from their ores.   *23-5 to 23-7*

5. Describe the sources, properties, and uses of oxygen, hydrogen, sulfur, and nitrogen. *23-8 to 23-11*

6. Define allotropes, using oxygen and sulfur as examples.   *23-8 and 23-10*

7. Describe the preparation, reactions, and uses of the halogens and noble gases.   *23-12 and 23-13*

## Teaching Suggestions

**23-1 Descriptive Chemistry, p. 667,**

**23-2 The Alkali Metals, pp. 667-669, and**

**23-3 The Alkaline Earth Metals, pp. 669-670**

| Planning Guide | |
|---|---|
| Labs (Lab Manual) and Demonstrations (TE) | Supplementary Materials (Teacher's Resource Book) |
| | Transparency Master: Some Alkali Metal Compounds, p. 23-1 Transparency Master: Some Alkaline Earth Metal Compounds, p. 23-2 Open-Ended Demonstration: The Behavior of Plaster of Paris, p. 23-6 |

■ To begin the chapter, you may want to point out to students that although descriptive chemistry is the main focus of Chapter 23, many other chapters in the text also have descriptive content that is tied in closely with theoretical material. Examples may be found especially in Chapters 1, 2, 4, 11, 16, 19, 24, and 25.
■ Relate the properties of the alkali metals to their electron structure. Discuss with students how the ease with which these elements lose electrons accounts for their high conductivity and chemical reactivity. The high mobility of the electrons also results in metallic bonds that give metals their high boiling points and good malleability and ductility. Because each of the alkali metals has the largest atomic radius of any element in its period, there is a wide separation of the electrons form the nucleus. This accounts for the softness of the alkali metals. When discussing this point, have students refer to text Figure 14-20, show-

23

ing spheres as models for easy visual comparison of atomic radii. Use the periodic table to explain the increasing activity, with increasing atomic number, of the elements in Group 1.

You may want to compare the chemical reactivities of the Group 2 metals with those of the Group 1 metals. Referring students again to Figure 14-20, discuss how differences in the atomic sizes and nuclear charges of the elements in these two groups account for the difference in their activity.

■ Using the Transparency Masters "Some Alkali Metal Compounds" and "Some Alkaline Earth Metal Compounds," ask students to name alkali and alkaline earth metal compounds that they have used at home.

■ For average or above-average students, you may wish to do the Open-Ended Demonstration "The Behavior of Plaster of Paris." In this demonstration, you mix gypsum with water and students observe the changes that occur as the mixture sets under water, in a paper cup, and in a rubber mold. Students then explain their observations and tell how they would test the correctness of their explanations.

## 23-4 The Transition Metals, pp. 670-672, and

## 23-5 Aluminum, pp. 672-673

| Planning Guide | |
|---|---|
| Labs (Lab Manual) and Demonstrations (TE) | Supplementary Materials (Teacher's Resource Book) |
| Demo 23-1: Iron in Cereal, p. TG-326<br>Demo 23-2: Pennies That Float, p. TG-327 | Transparency Master: Some Transition Elements and Their Uses, p. 23-3 |

■ For a motivating opener to the discussion of transition metals, you may do Demonstration 23-1, "Iron in Cereal," and/or Demonstration 23-2, "Pennies That Float." Students may be surprised to learn from these demonstrations that iron is added to cereal in metallic form and that post-1982 pennies contain only 2.4% copper.

■ Have students locate Groups 3 to 11 in the periodic table. Remind them that these elements are metals because their outermost shells contain so few electrons. Discuss with students how the sizes of atoms of transition metals help to explain why these metals are harder, are more brittle, and have higher melting points than the metals of Groups 1 and 2. Again, have students use Figure 14-20 for easy comparison of atomic sizes.

■ You may want to tell your students the story about Charles Hall. When he was a young graduate student at Oberlin College in Ohio, his chemistry professor said

that fame and fortune awaited the person who could find an inexpensive way of extracting aluminum from its ores. It was in response to this challenge that Hall set up a crude electrolysis cell in his backyard laboratory and produced aluminum from bauxite dissolved in melted cryolite. Hall was 23 years old at the time (1886).

Working independently, Paul Heroult, also at the age of 23, made the same discovery in France a few months later. Coincidentally, Hall and Heroult not only were born in the same year (1863) but also died in the same year (1914).

■ The Transparency Master "Some Transition Elements and Their Uses" can give students a broad perspective on the diverse uses of these metals. Ask students to generalize the properties of the transition elements from this table.

■ **Application.** You may wish to have students compare the observable properties of several common alloys used in household articles and jewelry with the properties of the metals from which they are formed. In addition to stainless steel, which is described in text Figure 23-14 along with other kinds of steel, some of these alloys are: sterling silver, 92% silver and 8% copper; brass, variable amounts of copper and zinc; and yellow gold, 90% gold, 10% copper.

■ **Application.** You might want to inform your students that aluminum — unlike wood, for example — is a non-renewable resource. For aluminum to be available to future generations, the earth's supply must be recycled. You may suggest to students that they keep track of the amount of aluminum (foil and cans) that they discard in a week.

## 23-6 Iron and Steel, pp. 673-676

| Planning Guide | |
|---|---|
| Labs (Lab Manual) and Demonstrations (TE) | Supplementary Materials (Teacher's Resource Book) |
| | Transparency Master: Properties and Uses of Several Steels, p. 23-4 |

■ To help students understand the chemistry of the blast furnace, walk them through the diagram in text Figure 23-11, relating the equations in the text to the relevant parts of the furnace. You may explain that all of the reactions that occur are not known with great accuracy, but that the equations given are probably correct enough summaries of highly complex processes. Next, have students use Figure 23-13 to relate the parts of the basic-oxygen-process furnace to the reactions as described in the text.

■ Use the Transparency Master "Properties and Uses of Several Steels" to help students see how steels of different compositions have different sets of properties and diverse uses that are often highly specialized.

## 23-7 The Recovery of Copper, pp. 676-678

■ Students will recall that the uses of copper were discussed in Section 23-4. Here, the emphasis is on the chemistry used to produce copper that will have the high degree of purity needed in electrical conductors.

Have students relate the electrolytic refining of copper to their study of electrolysis in Chapter 22. Ask them to note, for example, that oxidation occurs at the anode and reduction at the cathode.

You may want to discuss with students the fact that the electrolytic refining of copper would be quite expensive because of the cost of the electricity, but that this cost is offset by the value of the gold and silver that are recovered from the anode mud.

## 23-8 Oxygen, pp. 678-679, and

## 23-9 Hydrogen, pp. 679-680

| Planning Guide | |
| --- | --- |
| Labs (Lab Manual) and Demonstrations (TE) | Supplementary Materials (Teacher's Resource Book) |
| Lab 46: Oxygen: Its Properties<br>Lab 47: Hydrogen: Preparation and Properties | |

■ The scientists whose names are tied in closely with the discovery and properties of oxygen and hydrogen made their contributions during the same decade: Scheele (1771) and Priestley (1774), both of whom are credited with the preparation of oxygen; Lavoisier (1774) who explained the role of oxygen in burning; and Cavendish (1776) who discovered hydrogen. Cavendish also discovered that hydrogen forms water when it burns.

■ Have students do Laboratory 46, "Oxygen: Its Properties," in which students investigate the relative insolubility of oxygen in water and its ability to support combustion. Then have students do Laboratory 47, "Hydrogen: Preparation and Properties." In this lab, students prepare hydrogen by the reaction of zinc with dilute sulfuric acid and show that hydrogen is relatively insoluble in water, is less dense than air, and produces water when it burns.

■ **Concept Mastery.** It is a common belief (of unknown origin) among students that hydrogen is a major component of the atmosphere. In case any of your students have this idea, you may use Concept Mastery question 40 (chapter-end question) to correct this misconception and to remind them that air is made up chiefly of nitrogen and oxygen.

## 23-10 Sulfur, pp. 680-682

| Planning Guide | |
| --- | --- |
| Labs (Lab Manual) and Demonstrations (TE) | Supplementary Materials (Teacher's Resource Book) |
| Lab 45: Allotropes of Sulfur<br>Demo 23-3: Making Acid from Burning Sulfur, p. TG-327 | Open-Ended Demonstration: The Dehydration of Sucrose, p. 23-7 |

■ You may want to introduce sulfur by doing Laboratory 45, "Allotropes of Sulfur." Students observe the preparation of rhombic, monoclinic, and amorphous sulfur, and they investigate the structure and properties of each of these forms.

■ Use text Figure 23-19 as the basis for your discussion of the Frasch process. Help students to understand the mining of sulfur by having them relate the physical properties of sulfur to the stages shown in the illustration.

■ Next, do Demonstration 23-3, "Making Acid from Burning Sulfur." In this demonstration, students see how sulfur burns to form sulfur dioxide, which is then combined with water to produce sulfurous acid, a component of acid rain. You may want to compare and contrast the formation of sulfurous acid with the commercial production of sulfuric acid by the contact process.

■ Be sure to discuss the reputation of sulfuric acid for being the most important of all manufactured compounds. You may wish to tell students that the tonnage of sulfuric acid produced by a nation has been called a direct measure of that country's degree of development, so widespread is the commercial use of the acid.

■ You can do the optional Open-Ended Demonstration "The Dehydration of Sucrose," a dramatic example of the action of concentrated sulfuric acid as a dehydrating agent. In this activity, you may have students suggest explanations and ways to test their correctness. You may also use the demonstration to show students one reason why concentrated sulfuric acid is especially destructive to all organic matter, including natural clothing fibers and skin.

■ Point out that the great affinity of concentrated sulfuric acid for water is one reason for being careful to dilute the acid only by pouring it (slowly, and with stirring) into the water, not vice versa. If water is poured into the acid, the heat given off in the vigorous exothermic reaction does not dissipate fast enough, causing the water to boil and the water-acid mixture to splatter.

■ **Concept Mastery.** Students sometimes fail to distinguish between allotropes and isotopes. You may

23

wish to use Concept Mastery question 43 (chapter-end question) to review both definitions and the difference between them.

## 23-11 Nitrogen, pp. 682-684

▪ In connection with your class discussion of the preparation of pure nitrogen by fractional distillation, you may point out that recent experiments with superconductivity have been carried out at the temperature of liquid nitrogen.

▪ Be sure to stress the practical importance of the relative inactivity of elementary nitrogen. Students will recall from the account of the Haber process in Chapter 18 that the fixation of nitrogen was a major achievement of historic significance. You may explain that nitrogen is a constituent of protein, but that most living things cannot use atmospheric nitrogen to make proteins or other compounds from which proteins might be made. Have students who have studied biology recall the crucial role of bacteria in the fixation of nitrogen in biological systems.

## 23-12 The Halogens, pp. 684-686

| Planning Guide | |
| --- | --- |
| Labs (Lab Manual) and Demonstrations (TE) | Supplementary Materials (Teacher's Resource Book) |
| | Transparency Master: Some Halogen Compounds, p. 23-5 Societal Issues: Chlorofluorocarbons and the Ozone Layer, p. SI-41 |

▪ You may want to discuss the discovery of fluorine by Moissan (1886), of chlorine by Scheele (1774), of bromine by Balard (1826), and of iodine by Courtois (1811). The cyclotron at Berkeley, California, was used to prepare astatine in 1940. Its most stable isotope has a half-life of only 8 hours.

▪ You can ask a number of stimulating questions in the class discussion of the halogens. Why, at ordinary temperatures, do the physical phases of the halogens progress from gaseous to liquid to solid? (Discuss van der Waals forces.) Should all salt be iodized? How is radioactive iodine used medically?

▪ The Transparency Master "Some Halogen Compounds" might be used to initiate a discussion of the varied ways in which we use halogen compounds.

▪ The Societal Issues worksheet "Chlorofluorocarbons and the Ozone Layer" gives students more information about ozone (introduced in Section 23-8) and halogen compounds in the context of a current scientific con-

cern. The critical thinking questions that accompany the article help the students to evaluate this complex issue.

## 23-13 The Noble Gases, pp. 686-687

| Planning Guide | |
| --- | --- |
| Labs (Lab Manual) and Demonstrations (TE) | Supplementary Materials (Teacher's Resource Book) |
| | Review Activity: Selected–Elements Vocabulary, p. 23-8 |

▪ In June of 1962 the first report of a noble gas forming a stable compound was made by Canadian chemist Neil Bartlett. He had reacted xenon with platinum hexafluoride to form a yellow powder, probably $XePtF_6$. Later that year, investigators at the Argonne National Laboratory near Chicago reported the formation of $XeF_4$ by reacting xenon and fluorine gas for one hour at 400°C and then cooling the reaction to −78°C. The colorless solid, stable at room temperature, was the first compound known to contain an inert gas combined with only one other element. Other compounds of xenon and radon with fluorine have also been made.

In discussing the chemistry of noble gases, you may ask students why efforts to produce compounds of helium, neon, and argon, similar to the efforts to produce compounds of xenon and radon, have been unsuccessful.

▪ The Review Activity "Selected Elements Vocabulary" is appropriate for reviewing Chapter 23.

# Demonstrations

## 23-1 Iron in Cereal

**Overview:** In this demonstration, you use a magnet to remove iron particles from a bowl of iron-fortified cereal.

**Materials:** cereal with high iron content; white magnetic stirring bar; magnetic stirrer; 1000-mL beaker.

**Procedure:** 1. Pour about half of a box of an iron-fortified cereal into a 1000-mL beaker. Add water and stir until the cereal becomes soggy. 2. Place a magnetic stirring bar into the beaker, and stir for about 20–30 minutes, using the magnetic stirrer. 3. Carefully remove the magnetic stirring bar, and have students examine it. Ask the students why the particles they see were added to the cereal.

**Results:** The stirring bar will have particles of elemental iron adhering to it. The elemental iron dissolves in the hydrochloric acid in the stomach and forms $Fe^{2+}$, which is more useful to the body than the more common $Fe^{3+}$. The reason most manufacturers add elemental iron to the package instead of $Fe^{2+}$ is that $Fe^{2+}$ would tend to oxidize in the box, to form $Fe^{3+}$.

## 23-2 Pennies That Float

**Overview:** In this demonstration, you place post-1982 pennies into hydrochloric acid. After a few hours, the pennies float to the surface.

**Materials:** post-1982 penny; 6 *M* hydrochloric acid (HCl); 100-mL beaker; triangular file; crucible tongs.

**Advance Preparation: 6 *M* HCl:** mix concentrated HCl and water in a 1:1 ratio by volume.

Safety: Be careful in handling the hydrochloric acid.

**Procedure:** 1. Using a triangular file, make a few small notches on the edges of a post-1982 penny. 2. Place the penny into the HCl solution. Allow the system to stand overnight. 3. Have students observe the penny the next day. Ask them to account for its position in the beaker. 4. Using tongs, remove the penny, rinse it in water, wipe it dry, and have students observe it. Ask the students to attempt to write a balanced equation representing what has occurred.

**Results:** The zinc in the post-1982 penny, which contains 2.4% Cu and 97.6% Zn (pre-1982 pennies contain 94% Cu and 6% Zn) will react with the hydrochloric acid, according to the equation: $Zn(s) + 2HCl(aq) \rightarrow H_2(aq) + ZnCl_2(aq)$. Hydrogen gas trapped inside the penny will cause it to float.

## 23-3 Making Acid from Burning Sulfur

**Overview:** In this demonstration, you burn sulfur in air to form sulfur dioxide, which then reacts with water to form sulfurous acid. Acid rain, which can result from similar reactions of nonmetallic oxides with water in rain, is then discussed.

**Materials:** powdered sulfur; deflagrating spoon or bent spatula; gas-collecting bottle; glass plate to cover the mouth of the bottle; red and blue litmus paper; Bunsen burner.

Safety: Work at the fume hood, as sulfur dioxide fumes are toxic and irritating to the respiratory tract. Be careful in handling the hot sulfur.

**Procedure:** 1. Place a volume of sulfur, about the size of a pea, into the deflagrating spoon or onto the bent spatula. Hold the spoon over the flame of a burner until the sulfur begins to burn with a blue flame. Immediately insert the spoon into a gas-collecting bottle, and cover the bottle as closely as possible with a glass plate, trapping as much gas as possible. Allow the sulfur to burn as completely as possible. Ask students to write a balanced equation to represent this reaction. 2. Remove the spoon and add about 100 mL of water to the bottle. Shake carefully to dissolve the

gas. Add pieces of red and blue litmus paper to the bottle, and have students observe the resulting color of the paper. Ask the students to write a balanced equation for the reaction of the sulfur dioxide with water. Ask them how gases such as sulfur dioxide (formed during the burning of high-sulfur coal) can contribute to the formation of acid rain.

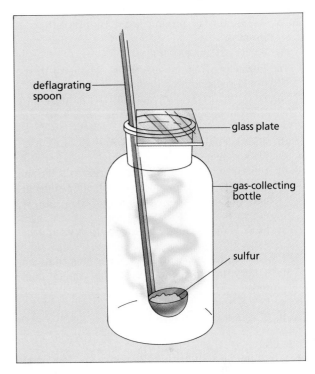

**Figure 23-1**

**Results:** The sulfur will burn in air to form sulfur dioxide, according to the equation: $S(s) + O_2(g) \rightarrow SO_2(g)$. The $SO_2$ will combine with water to form sulfurous acid, according to the equation: $SO_2(g) + H_2O(l) \rightarrow H_2SO_3(aq)$. The litmus paper will turn pink, indicating the presence of an acid. Sulfur dioxide gas can combine with atmospheric water to produce sulfurous acid, which contributes to acid rain.

## Answers to Questions

**Page 672**
1. These elements are quite active.
2. **a.** Sodium is used in sodium vapor lamps and as a coolant in nuclear reactors. **b.** Coolant: low melting point and high heat conductivity. Lamp: produces yellow light that penetrates fog.
3. $MgCl_2 \xrightarrow{\text{elec.}} Mg + Cl_2$

4. The transition metals are harder, are more brittle, have higher melting points, show variable oxidation states, and have colored ions.

5. When exposed to air, Mg and Cu form films of compounds that protect them from corrosion, whereas Ca and Fe lack these films and continue to oxidize until completely corroded.

## Page 678

6. **a.** Aluminum is produced by the Hall-Heroult process.

   **b.** $2Al_2O_3 \xrightarrow{\text{elec.}} 4Al + 3O_2$

   **c.** Because $Al^{3+}$ gains electrons, the metal in the ore is reduced.

7. **a.** $Fe_2O_3$ (ore), C (coke), and $CaCO_3$ (limestone) are the components of the charge in a blast furnace.

   **b.** $3CO + Fe_2O_3 \rightarrow 2Fe + 3CO_2$; $C + O_2 \rightarrow CO_2$; $CaO + SiO_2 \rightarrow CaSiO_3$

8. **a.** Cast iron contains impurities such as S, P, and Si, whereas steel contains controlled percentages of C plus other elements (Cr, Ni, V, Mn, W, etc.).

   **b.** Steel is made chiefly by the basic oxygen process.

9. Froth flotation concentrates copper ores that contain very low percentages of the copper compounds.

10. **a.** $2Cu_2S + 3O_2 \rightarrow 2Cu_2O + 2SO_2$

    **b.** $2Cu_2O + Cu_2S \rightarrow 6Cu + SO_2$

## Page 682

11. Air is liquefied under high pressure and low temperature. The nitrogen and argon, which boil at lower temperatures than oxygen, are boiled away, and nearly pure oxygen remains. This process is called fractional distillation.

12. **a.** Ozone is a bluish gas with a sharp odor. It is a much stronger oxidizing agent than oxygen. In the upper atmosphere, it absorbs ultraviolet radiation from the sun. **b.** Ozone, $O_3$, is an allotropic form of oxygen, $O_2$.

13. **a.** Priestley discovered oxygen.

    **b.** Cavendish discovered hydrogen.

    **c.** Frasch invented the Frasch process for mining sulfur.

14. **a.** Oxygen is used industrially in the manufacture of steel, in the treatment of respiratory ailments, and in rockets. **b.** Hydrogen is used industrially in the production of ammonia, in the hydrogenation of oils, in welding torches, and as a rocket fuel.

15. **a.** $S + O_2 \rightarrow SO_2$;

    $2SO_2 + O_2 \xrightarrow{V_2O_5} 2SO_3$;

    $SO_3 + H_2SO_4 \rightarrow H_2SO_4 \cdot SO_3$;

    $H_2SO_4 \cdot SO_3 + H_2O \rightarrow 2H_2SO_4$

**b.** Sulfuric acid is the most important industrial compound.

## Page 687

16. The strong triple bond in $N_2$.

17. Nitric acid. It is used to make fertilizers and to make explosives.

18. $2NaI + Cl_2 \rightarrow 2NaCl + I_2$

    $2NaI + 2H_2SO_4 + MnO_2 \rightarrow$
    $\qquad\qquad I_2 + MnSO_4 + Na_2SO_4 + 2H_2O$

19. The reaction between antimony and bromine would be less vigorous, because chlorine is more active than bromine.

20. $2Sb + 3Cl_2 \rightarrow 2SbCl_3$

    $2Sb + 3Br_2 \rightarrow 2SbBr_3$

21. **a.** A solution of chlorine has a strong oxidizing effect.

    **b.** Freon is used as refrigerant. Silver bromine is used in photographic film. Sodium iodide is used to prevent goiter.

22. **a.** The noble gases are not inert: compounds of xenon, krypton, and radon have been made.

    **b.** The noble gases are not all rare because argon and helium are relatively abundant.

## Chapter Review  23

### Page 688, Content Review

1. Descriptive chemistry is the aspect of chemistry that describes the sources, properties, and uses of specific elements and their compounds.

2. The alkali metals are malleable, ductile, very soft, and lustrous, and are good conductors of electricity and heat. They have low melting points and are the most reactive family of metals.

3. Alkali metals have lower melting points than most other metals.

4. Alkali metals are softer than most other metals.

5. Sodium can be prepared by the electrolysis of sodium chloride.

   $2NaCl(l) \xrightarrow{\text{elect.}} 2Na(s) + Cl_2(g)$

6. Alkaline earth metals have 2 valence electrons and form ions with a charge of 2+.

7. Magnesium's strength and light weight make it useful for building aircraft.

8. Calcium can be prepared by reducing calcium oxide.

   $3CaO(s) + 2Al(s) \rightarrow 2Al_2O_3(s) + 3Ca(g)$

9. The transition metals are harder, are more brittle, and have higher melting points than the metals of

Groups 1 and 2. They also show variable oxidation states and have colored ions.

10. Iron is the most abundant transition metal in the earth's crust.

11. Aluminum is the most abundant metal in the earth's crust.

12. Aluminum and its alloys are used as structural materials in truck bodies, airplanes, and railroad cars. They are also used in cooking utensils and aluminum foil.

13. A flux is a substance that causes mineral impurities in an ore to melt more readily. Slag is a light, easily-melted, glass-like material formed in smelting.

14. Silver and gold are recovered from the electrolysis of impure copper.

15. $2MnO_2(s) + 2H_2SO_4(l) \rightarrow$
$$2MnSO_4(aq) + 2H_2O(l) + O_2(g)$$
(Scheele's method)

$2HgO(s) \rightarrow 2Hg(l) + O_2(g)$ (Priestley's method)

16. $2KClO_3(s) \xrightarrow{MnO_2} 2KCl(s) + 3O_2(g)$

17. $Zn(s) + 2HCl(aq) \rightarrow ZnCl_2(aq) + H_2(g)$

18. Sulfur is used in the manufacture of sulfuric acid, fungicides, insecticides, matches, fireworks, dyes, drugs, asphalt, and vulcanized rubber.

19. Nitrogen gas is used to surround foods, to prevent their oxidation.

20. Pure nitrogen is produced by the fractional distillation of liquid air.

21. The most reactive nonmetal is fluorine.

22. The least reactive halogen is astatine.

23. The halogens are fluorine, chlorine, bromine, iodine, and astatine.

24. The noble gases are inactive because of their stable electron configurations.

25. The noble gases are helium, neon, argon, krypton, xenon, and radon.

### Page 689, Content Mastery

26. The least reactive family of nonmetals is Group 18 (the noble gases).

27. Oxygen is the most abundant element in the earth's crust.

28. Calcium carbonate occurs naturally as deposits of limestone, marble, and chalk. These deposits were formed in past geological ages from compressed layers of the shells of marine animals.

29. Alkalis are more reactive than most other metals.

30. The Frasch process uses three concentric pipes. Hot water is forced down the outermost pipe to melt the sulfur. Hot, compressed air pumped through the innermost pipe mixes with the molten sulfur and forces it up the middle pipe.

31. Transition metals are usually harder, more brittle, less reactive, and have higher melting points.

32. Yes. X, Kr, and Rn form compounds with $F_2$.

33. The reactivity of the halogens decreases as their atomic numbers increase.

34. Silver is the best conductor of heat and electricity.

35. Alkali metals have 1 valence electron and form ions with a charge of 1+.

36. The most reactive family of nonmetals is Group 17.

37. Allotropes are different molecular structures of the same element, which can exist in the same phase. Examples are oxygen ($O_2$) and ozone ($O_3$), rhombic $S_8$ and monoclinic $S_8$.

38. The oxidation of Na can be prevented by keeping Na under an inert liquid, such as kerosene.

39. The Hall-Heroult process uses an electrolytic cell in which aluminum oxide in solution is reduced to aluminum. The oxygen produced at the carbon anodes reacts with them, forming carbon dioxide. Eventually, the anodes must be replaced.

### Page 689, Concept Mastery

40. **Concept:** *$H_2$ is not a major component of air.*
    *Solution:* $H_2$ is very light and floats to the upper atmosphere. It is also reactive and oxidizes in $O_2$ to water. Air is primarily $N_2$ (78%) and $O_2$ (21%) — not $H_2$.

41. **Concept:** *Metals are not always shiny solids.*
    *Solution:* The black substance is finely divided pieces of copper metal that have been reduced by the zinc and precipitated out of solution. If this copper were melted and cooled, it would look like a solid piece of commercial copper, shiny and orange.

42. **Concept:** *The arrangement of atoms differs for solutions (alloys), heterogeneous mixtures, and compounds.*
    *Solution:* See Figure 23-2.

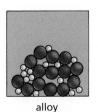
alloy

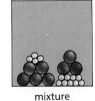
mixture

compound

**Figure 23-2**

43. ***Concept:*** *Isotopes have different atomic struc-tures: allotropes have different molec-ular structures.*

    *Solution:* The four isotopes of sulfur have 16 protons and 16 electrons. They differ in their number of neutrons. Allotropes of sulfur are molecules in which the sulfur atoms are arranged differently.

44. ***Concept:*** *Aluminum forms a protective covering of aluminum oxide.*

    *Solution:* Scouring a blackened aluminum pot removes the surface layer of aluminum oxide. The pot looks better and cooks better because aluminum conducts heat better than aluminum oxide. Each scouring removes some aluminum.

## Page 690, Cumulative Review

45. **c.** The bond in $N_2$ is a triple bond.

46. **a.** Sublimation: phase change from solid to gas.

47. **c.** Adding a catalyst does not affect a system at chemical equilibrium.

48. **b.** Vapor pressure of $H_2$
    = total pressure − vapor pressure of water
    = 101.3 kPa − 2.8 kPa = 98.5 kPa

49. **c.** $V = \dfrac{320 \text{ K} \times 30.0 \text{ dm}^3}{310 \text{ K}} = 31.0 \text{ dm}^3$

50. Electrolysis is the process by which an electric current causes a redox reaction in the water solution of an electrolyte or in a pure electrolyte in the liquid phase.

51. Oxidation occurs at the anode, reduction at the cathode.

52. **a.** Proceeding from left to right in the third period, the type of element changes from metal to semi-metal to nonmetal. **b.** Atomic radius decreases.

53. **a.** Elements in the same group of the periodic table have similar electron structures. **b.** Noble gases are found at the end of each period.

## Page 690, Critical Thinking

54. Silver is much less reactive than iron, oxidizing (tarnishing) slowly over time.

55. Since sodium has such a high oxidation potential, it is hard to find something with a still higher oxidation potential capable of reducing sodium.

56. Aluminum has strength, light weight, and forms a self-protective oxide.

57. Elements at the left side of the table are reactive, forming compounds by donating electrons. On the other hand, elements at the right are also reactive, forming compounds by accepting electrons.

58. Rusting is the major disadvantage of using iron in outdoor furniture.

59. Al is so abundant it is considered less valuable.

60. They must have different boiling points. In fractional distillation, the temperature of a mixture is raised slowly. The component with the lowest boiling point boils first. Its vapor is collected and condensed. As the temperature of the mixture increases, other components boil off at their boiling points and are also collected. If two components have the same boiling point, they cannot be separated by this method.

61. Airships are filled with helium rather than hydrogen because helium does not burn or explode.

## Page 691, Challenge Problems

62. $SO_2$ can be reacted with water and an oxidizing agent (such as oxygen) to produce sulfuric acid. The commercial value of the sulfuric acid should make recovery of $SO_2$ economically viable.

63. **a.** $NaAlSi_3O_8$
    formula weight = 1(23.0) + 1(27.0) + 3(28.1) + 8(16.0) = 262.3
    $$\frac{\text{weight of Al}}{\text{weight of ore}} \times 100\% = \frac{27.0}{262.3} \times 100\% = 10.3\%$$
    **b.** $KAlSi_2O_6$
    formula weight = 1(39.1) + 1(27.0) + 2(28.1) + 6(16.0) = 218.3
    $$\frac{\text{weight of Al}}{\text{weight of ore}} \times 100\% = \frac{27.0}{218.3} \times 100\% = 12.4\%$$
    **c.** $CaAl_2Si_2O_8$
    formula weight = 1(40.1) + 2(27.0) + 2(28.1) + 8(16.0) = 278.3
    $$\frac{\text{weight of Al}}{\text{weight of ore}} \times 100\% = \frac{2(27.0)}{278.3} \times 100\% = 19.4\%$$

64. $Fe_2O_3$ is $\dfrac{111.6}{159.6} \times 100\% = 69.9\%$ by weight iron.
    $$100 \text{ kg ore} \times \frac{27 \text{ kg Fe}_2\text{O}_3}{100 \text{ kg ore}} \times \frac{69.9 \text{ kg Fe}}{100 \text{ kg Fe}_2\text{O}_3} =$$
    $$18.9 \text{ kg Fe}$$

65. The luster of metals comes from the free electrons at the surface of the crystal. When these electrons absorb light, they vibrate. Energy is radiated in all directions, giving metals their shiny appearance.

66. The lenses are coated with a clear silver halide, which decomposes in sunlight.
    $$AgX \xrightleftharpoons{\text{light}} Ag + X, \text{ where } X = \text{halogen}$$
    The silver halide is usually AgCl or AgBr. In brighter light, more silver halide decomposes, so the lenses get darker.

# Organic Chemistry

24

## Chapter Planning Guide

| Text Section | Labs (Lab Manual) and Demonstrations (TE) | Supplementary Materials (Teacher's Resource Book) |
|---|---|---|
| **24-1** The Nature of Organic Compounds, p. 693 | Lab 48: Melting Point Determination of an Organic Compound | |
| **24-2** General Properties of Organic Compounds, pp. 694-695 | | |
| **24-3** Bonding in Organic Compounds, pp. 695-696 | | |
| **24-4** Structural Formulas and Isomers, pp. 696-697 | Demo 24-1: Mobilizing Molecules, p. TG-339 | Transparency Master: Aliphatic Hydrocarbons, p. 24-1 |
| **24-5** Hydrocarbons, pp. 698-700 | | |
| **24-6** Saturated Hydrocarbons—The Alkanes, pp. 700-702 | | Transparency Master: The Isomers of Pentane, p. 24-2 |
| **24-7** The IUPAC Naming System, pp. 702-705 | | |
| **24-8** Unsaturated Hydrocarbons —Alkenes, Alkynes, and Alkadienes, pp. 706-708 | | |
| **24-9** Aromatic Hydrocarbons—The Benzene Series, pp. 708-710 | | Review Activity: IUPAC Nomenclature, p. 24-8 |
| **24-10** Reactions of the Hydrocarbons, pp. 710-714 | | Transparency Master: Reactions of the Hydrocarbons, p. 24-3 Open-Ended Demonstration: Chromatography, p. 24-6 Review Activity: Chemistry of Carbon, p. 24-10 Review Activity: Classifying Hydrocarbons, p. 24-11 Review Activity: Writing Structural Formulas for Organic Compounds, p. 24-13 |

24

| Text Section | | Labs (Lab Manual) and Demonstrations (TE) | Supplementary Materials (Teacher's Resource Book) |
|---|---|---|---|
| Biography | Dorothy Crowfoot Hodgkin, p. 712 | | |
| 24-11 | Petroleum, pp. 714-715 | | |
| 24-12 | Alcohols, pp. 716-720 | | Transparency Master: Common Functional Groups in Organic Chemistry, p. 24-4 |
| 24-13 | Aldehydes, pp. 721-722 | | Transparency Master: The Effect of a Hydroxyl Group on the Solubility in Water of an Organic Compound, p. 24-5 |
| 24-14 | Ketones, pp. 722-723 | | |
| 24-15 | Ethers, pp. 723-724 | | |
| 24-16 | Carboxylic Acids, pp. 724-725 | Lab 49: Esters | Review Activity: Classifying Organic Compounds by Functional Group, p. 24-15 |
| 24-17 | Esters and Esterification, p. 726 | | Review Activity: Naming Organic Compounds That Contain Functional Groups, p. 24-17 |
| | | | Review Activity: Writing Structural Formulas for Organic Compounds That Contain Functional Groups, p. 24-19 |
| | | | Review Activity: Classes of Organic Compounds, p. 24-21 |
| | | | Critical and Creative Thinking: Ethical Judgments, p. CCT-67 |
| 24-18 | Soaps and Detergents, pp. 727-729 | | Critical and Creative Thinking: Categorical Arguments, p. CCT-51 |
| | | | Societal Issues: Hazardous Wastes, p. SI-44 |
| Can You Explain This? | Spinning a Thread, p. 729 | | |
| | | | Test—Form A, p. AT-92 |
| | | | Alternate Test—Form B, p. BT-92 |

☐ Core    ■ Advanced    ☐ Optional

## Chapter Overview

Chapter 24 begins with discussion of some general characteristics of organic compounds, which are compared to inorganic compounds in terms of properties such as conductivity, reactivity, and rate of reaction. We review the bonding between the atoms making up molecules of organic compounds and the effect of that bonding on the properties of those compounds. We discuss the use of structural formulas to represent organic molecules, especially to show the relationship between isomers.

We give a general description of hydrocarbons, compare saturated and unsaturated compounds, and differentiate five homologous series of hydrocarbons:

alkanes, alkenes, alkynes, alkadienes, and aromatics. Students write structural formulas for hydrocarbons, apply the IUPAC rules for naming hydrocarbons, and write equations for four categories of reactions of hydrocarbons.

We describe several groups of hydrocarbon derivatives characterized by functional groups: alcohols, aldehydes, ketones, ethers, and carboxylic acids. Esters and esterification reactions and, finally, soaps and saponification reactions are explained.

## Chapter Objectives

After students have completed this chapter, they will be able to:

1. State some general properties and describe some reactions of organic compounds.   *24-1* and *24-2*

2. Describe the bonding between atoms in the molecules of many organic compounds.   *24-3* and *24-4*

3. Compare the general formulas of several hydrocarbon series and apply the IUPAC system in naming their members.   *24-5* to *24-7*

4. Compare saturated and unsaturated compounds with respect to structure and properties.
   *24-6* to *24-11*

5. State the names, structural formulas, and uses for members of several types of hydrocarbon derivatives.   *24-12* to *24-18*

## Teaching Suggestions

### 24-1 The Nature of Organic Compounds, p. 693,

### 24-2 General Properties of Organic Compounds, pp. 694-695, and

### 24-3 Bonding in Organic Compounds, pp. 695-696

| Planning Guide | |
|---|---|
| **Labs (Lab Manual) and Demonstrations (TE)** | **Supplementary Materials (Teacher's Resource Book)** |
| Lab 48: Melting Point Determination of an Organic Compound | |

■ To begin the chapter, you may want to discuss with students the history of the use of the term "organic chemistry." Its meaning, as used today, originated when Wöhler prepared urea, $NH_2CONH_2$, in a reaction using ammonium chloride, $NH_4Cl$, and silver cyanate,

AgOCN. Neither of these compounds had been made by a living thing. You may want to describe how, about 50 years earlier, Karl Scheele prepared oxalic acid, $H_2C_2O_4$, an organic compound, by reacting sugar with nitric acid. This showed that an organic compound could be made in the laboratory. However, it was argued that the "vital force" needed for the creation of this organic compound came from the sugar, which had once been part of a living sugar-cane plant. Thus, the vitalistic theory remained unchallenged until Wöhler's work, which was supported by that of other chemists.

■ Use text Figure 24-2 to emphasize the general properties of organic compounds and to show the differences between organic and inorganic compounds.

■ You may want to build models of the solid phase of simple organic compounds, consisting of aggregates of molecules (such models are not usually available commercially) and compare these with models of ionic compounds such as sodium chloride and/or calcium carbonate.

■ Have students do Laboratory 48, "Melting Point Determination of an Organic Compound," in which they determine the melting points of maleic acid, salicylic acid, tannic acid, and urea. Relate the discussion of the experiment to the concepts of covalent bonding and ionic bonding. Explain how the nature of the forces of attraction between molecules and between ions determines the major characteristics of both organic and inorganic compounds. Thus, for most organic compounds phase changes such as melting and boiling involve the separating of molecules, while similar phase changes for ionic compounds require the separation of oppositely charged ions, which takes a stronger force.

■ **Concept Mastery.** Students will have heard the term "organic" used in a variety of ways. To relate its chemical meaning to students' experience, you may wish to use Concept Mastery questions 49 and 50 (chapter-end questions) to begin the chapter. You may review the chemical meaning of "decompose," pointing out that it is not synonymous with "decay," although in everyday language the two terms are sometimes used interchangeably.

■ **Application.** You may want to use the comparison of the molecular masses and boiling points of two organic compounds to give students an opportunity to relate structure, bonding, and properties. Have them recall that ethylene glycol (molecular mass = 62, boiling point = 198°C) is used as an antifreeze in automobiles. Butane (molecular mass = 58, boiling point = 0°C) is used in butane lighters, where it remains as a liquid under pressure until it is slowly released when the lighter is in use.

24

## 24-4 Structural Formulas and Isomers, pp. 696-697, and

## 24-5 Hydrocarbons, pp. 698-700

| Planning Guide | |
|---|---|
| **Labs (Lab Manual) and Demonstrations (TE)** | **Supplementary Materials (Teacher's Resource Book)** |
| Demo 24-1: Mobilizing Molecules, p. TG-339 | Transparency Master: Aliphatic Hydrocarbons, p. 24-1 |

■ Use text Figure 24-6 to show the two isomers of $C_4H_{10}$. Provide molecular model kits so that students can make models of the structures being discussed as you point out their characteristics. The frequent use of models throughout the chapter will help students to understand the concept of isomers. Use both ball-and-stick and space-filling models, if they are available, so that students will appreciate the strengths and weaknesses of each type. It will be helpful to apply the principles of recognition and naming of isomers to examples from Sections 24-6, 24-8, and 24-12. (See also Section 24-6 for suggestions on teaching isomers that you may want to use here.)

■ You may use Section 24-5 to begin to organize your work on hydrocarbons. Almost any systematic arrangement of the information will help your students. One approach is to fill out a table similar to that in the Transparency Master "Hydrocarbons" found in the *Teacher's Resource Book*. See accompanying Figure 24-1 for a mostly blank table that lacks the informa-

tion contained under the column headings in the transparency master for several types of hydrocarbons. This table can be used to organize the information in Sections 24-5 and the following four sections. You and your students can complete each column of the table as you come to the section of the text that discusses the class of compounds for that column. Students can use the completed table as a summary of Sections 24-5 to 24-9. The completed table will show relationships between classes of compounds and will help your students to avoid the temptation of trying to memorize isolated, unconnected bits of information.

## 24-6 Saturated Hydrocarbons—The Alkanes, pp. 700-702, and

## 24-7 The IUPAC Naming System, pp. 702-705

| Planning Guide | |
|---|---|
| **Labs (Lab Manual) and Demonstrations (TE)** | **Supplementary Materials (Teacher's Resource Book)** |
| | Transparency Master: The Isomers of Pentane, p. 24-1 |

■ Use models to show molecules of the saturated hydrocarbons, including isomers of some of these compounds. Use the Transparency Master "The Isomers of Pentane" together with three-dimensional models to help students see the geometrical relationships between these models. Then, on paper, represent several other isomers of compounds as two-dimensional structural formulas. One of the biggest

**Hydrocarbons**

| | Aliphatic | | | | Aromatic |
|---|---|---|---|---|---|
| | **Alkane** | **Alkene** | **Alkyne** | **Alkadiene** | **Benzene** |
| General formula | $C_nH_{2n+2}$ | | | | |
| Typical structural formula | 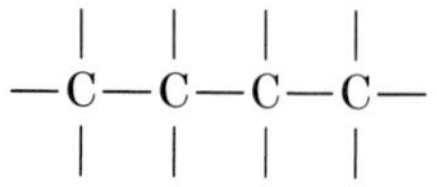 $-C-C-C-C-$ butane | | | | |
| Carbon-carbon bond type | all single bonds | | | | |
| Naming suffix | -ane | | | | |

Figure 24-1

hurdles is to convince students that, for example,

is not an isomer of

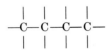

but is, in fact, the same molecule. Although most ball-and-stick models show this principle quite clearly, it still bothers some students.

■ The exotic names of chemicals are interesting to many students. Ask them to bring in labels from food, health, or other products showing names of organic compounds. Point out that they will learn to understand the meanings of many of these names.

■ Once students catch the spirit of the seven rules for naming organic compounds, they can become quite skillful at giving structural formulas and the corresponding names for many alkanes. Be sure to provide plenty of practice in applying the rules.

## 24-8 Unsaturated Hydrocarbons—Alkenes, Alkynes, and Alkadienes, pp. 706-708

■ Fill in the columns titled "Alkene," "Alkyne," and "Alkadiene" in Figure 24-1 (found with the Teaching Suggestions for Sections 24-4 and 24-5). Discuss what the differences in the arrangement of atoms into molecules are and how these differences in structure affect the properties of compounds.

## 24-9 Aromatic Hydrocarbons—The Benzene Series, pp. 708-710

| Planning Guide | |
| --- | --- |
| Labs (Lab Manual) and Demonstrations (TE) | Supplementary Materials (Teacher's Resource Book) |
| | Review Activity: IUPAC Nomenclature, p. 24-8 |

■ Emphasize the connection between the term aromatic and the benzene ring structure with its characteristic resonance bonds between adjacent carbon atoms. If you use ball-and-stick (coil spring) models for benzene, be sure to point out the inadequacy of the alternating-single-and-double-bond version that is usually associated with these models.

You and your students should fill out the last column (titled "Benzene") in Figure 24-1 (found with the Teachings Suggestions for Sections 24-4 and 24-5).

Use the completed table to point out the similarities and differences in the arrangements of atoms into molecules among the various classes of compounds. Discuss how these similarities and differences in structure affect the properties of compounds.

## 24-10 Reactions of the Hydrocarbons, pp. 710-714

| Planning Guide | |
| --- | --- |
| Labs (Lab Manual) and Demonstrations (TE) | Supplementary Materials (Teacher's Resource Book) |
| | Transparency Master: Reactions of the Hydrocarbons, p. 24-3 Open-Ended Demonstration: Chromatography, p. 24-6 Review Activity: Chemistry of Carbon, p. 24-10 Review Activity: Classifying Hydrocarbons, p. 24-11 Review Activity: Writing Structural Formulas for Organic Compounds, p. 24-13 |

■ As suggested in Sections 24-5 to 24-9, a systematic organization of reactions of hydrocarbons is recommended to help students get the "big picture" rather than a collection of unconnected facts. For this purpose, you may want to use the summary provided in the Transparency Master "Reactions of Hydrocarbons."

## 24-11 Petroleum, pp. 714-715

■ Discuss the chemistry of petroleum, especially the processes of refining. Have students recall the concept of fractional distillation as a method of preparing nitrogen, oxygen, and other components of air (Chapter 23). Point out the similarities and differences of the two processes.

## 24-12 Alcohols, pp. 716-720

| Planning Guide | |
| --- | --- |
| Labs (Lab Manual) and Demonstrations (TE) | Supplementary Materials (Teacher's Resource Book) |
| | Transparency Master: Common Functional Groups in Organic Chemistry, p. 24-4 |

24

| Alcohols | | | |
| --- | --- | --- | --- |
| **Category** | **General formula** | **Example, IUPAC name** | **Additional information** |
| Alcohol | $R$—OH | | good solvents; many soluble in water |
| Monohydroxy | | | isomeric forms; different chemical and physical properties |
| Primary | $R$—C—OH (with vertical bonds) | —C—C—C—C—OH <br> 1-butanol | |
| Secondary | 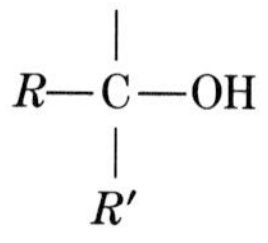 $R$—C—OH <br> $R'$ | 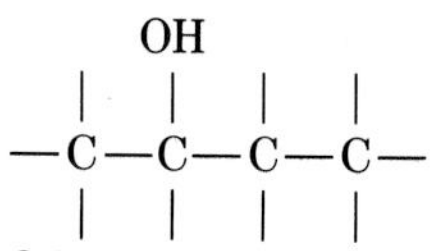 OH <br> —C—C—C—C— <br> 2-butanol | |
| Tertiary | 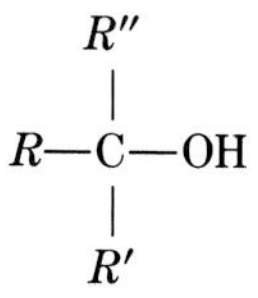 $R''$ <br> $R$—C—OH <br> $R'$ | 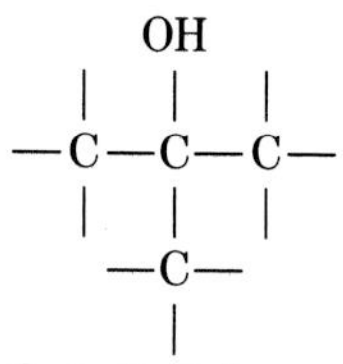 OH <br> —C—C—C— <br> —C— <br> 2-methyl-2-propanol | |
| Dihydroxy | | 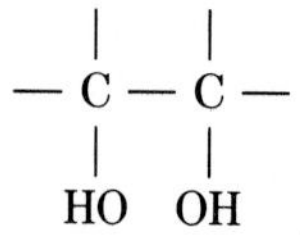 —C—C— <br> HO  OH <br> 1,2-ethanediol | ethylene glycol used as antifreeze |
| Trihydroxy | | 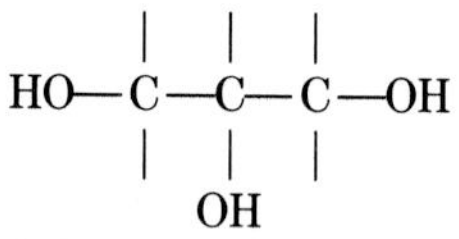 HO—C—C—C—OH <br> OH <br> 1,2,3-propanetriol | glycerine used in cosmetics as lubricant |

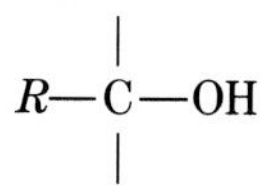

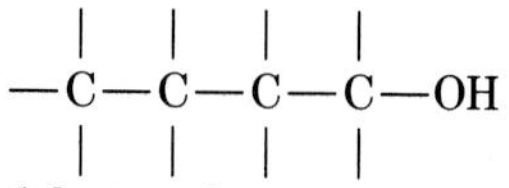

**Figure 24-2**

■ To organize information about the categories of hydrocarbon derivatives that are described in Sections 24-12 to 24-17, you may develop a series of tables to supplement the one in the Transparency Master "Common Functional Groups in Organic Chemistry." Figure 24-2 is the first of the supplementary tables. It shows the different types of alcohols.

■ You may wish to compare and contrast destructive distillation, referring to text Figure 24-31, with the process of fractional distillation (Section 24-11).

■ **Concept Mastery.** Students may have the idea that a chemical made synthetically is different from one that occurs naturally. You may wish to use Concept Mastery question 53 (chapter-end question) to raise the issue. Explain that although the final product may be slightly different because it is not 100% pure, the compounds are identical. You may also want to ask students about the quality of other synthetic products such as food extracts, vitamins, and generic brand drugs.

## 24-13 Aldehydes, pp. 721-722

## 24-14 Ketones, pp. 722-723, and

## 24-15 Ethers, pp. 723-724

| Planning Guide | |
| --- | --- |
| Labs (Lab Manual) and Demonstrations (TE) | Supplementary Materials (Teacher's Resource Book) |
| | Transparency Master: The Effect of a Hydroxyl Group on the Solubility in Water of an Organic Compound, p. 24-5 |

■ You may develop the table shown in Figure 24-3 to organize information about aldehydes, ketones, and ethers. Point out to students that each of the three kinds of compounds has an oxygen atom bonded to a hydrocarbon chain. In the case of aldehydes and ketones, there is a double bond between one carbon atom and the oxygen atom. If the oxygen atom is bonded to a terminal carbon atom, the compound is an aldehyde. If the oxygen atom is bonded to two carbon atoms, one from each of two alkyl groups, the compound is an ether.

■ Use the Transparency Master "The Effect of a Hydroxyl Group on the Solubility in Water of an Organic

Compound" as an example of how a difference in structure is related to a difference in properties.

## 24-16 Carboxylic Acids, pp. 724-725, and

## 24-17 Esters and Esterification, p. 726

| Planning Guide | |
| --- | --- |
| Labs (Lab Manual) and Demonstrations (TE) | Supplementary Materials (Teacher's Resource Book) |
| | Review Activity: Classifying Organic Compounds by Functional Group, p. 24-15<br>Review Activity: Naming Organic Compounds That Contain Functional Groups, p. 24-17<br>Review Activity: Writing Structural Formulas for Organic Compounds That Contain Functional Groups, p. 24-19<br>Review Activity: Classes of Organic Compounds, p. 24-21<br>Critical and Creative Thinking: Ethical Judgments, p. CCT-67 |

| Aldehydes, Ketones, and Ethers | | | |
| --- | --- | --- | --- |
| Category | Formula | Example, IUPAC name | Additional information |
| Aldehyde | 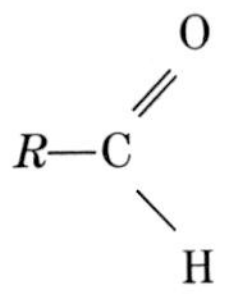 $R-C\!\!\begin{array}{c}\nearrow O \\ \searrow H\end{array}$ | 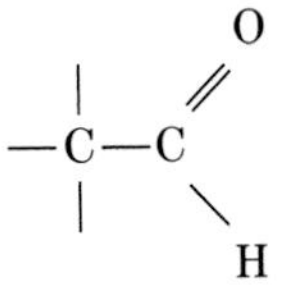 $-C-C\!\!\begin{array}{c}\nearrow O \\ \searrow H\end{array}$ ethanal | ethanal used in the preparation of acetic acid |
| Ketone | 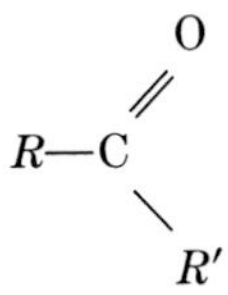 $R-C\!\!\begin{array}{c}\nearrow O \\ \searrow R'\end{array}$ | 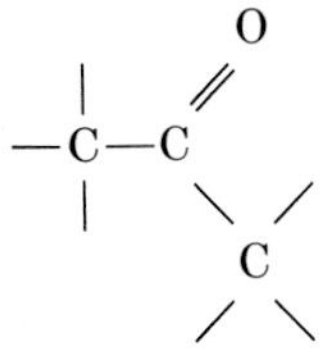 propanone | propanone used as a solvent |
| Ether | $R-O-R'$ | 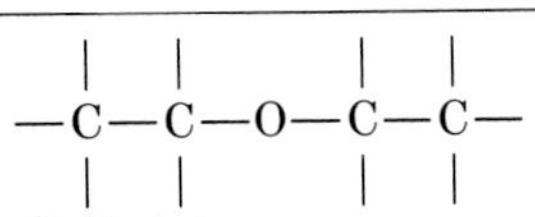 $-C-C-O-C-C-$ diethyl ether | diethyl ether used as a solvent |

Figure 24-3

| Carboxylic Acids | | | |
| --- | --- | --- | --- |
| Category | Formula | Example, IUPAC name | Additional information |
| Carboxylic acid | 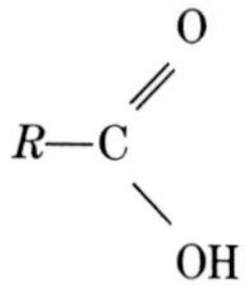 R—C double bond O, single bond OH | 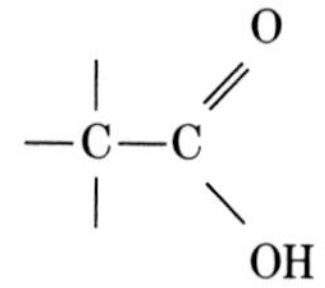 —C—C double bond O, OH; ethanoic acid | reacts with alcohols to form esters; see Section 24-17 |

Figure 24-4

- Emphasize the structural formulas and corresponding names for several carboxylic acids. You may develop the table shown in Figure 24-4. Have students recall, from Chapters 19 and 20, their study of weak acids, a prime example of which they know by the name of acetic acid (IUPAC name: methanoic acid). Have students note the ways in which organic acids resemble and differ from inorganic acids.

- Students are generally interested in esters. To motivate interest in these compounds, do Laboratory 49, "Esters," in which students observe the preparations of ethyl acetate, amyl acetate, and methyl salicylate and identify the products by their pleasant odors—apple, banana, and wintergreen, respectively.

- You may use models to show an esterification reaction. Have students note, in Equation 13, that the H atom leaves the alcohol and the —OH group leaves the acid. Point out the role of $H_2SO_4$ as a dehydrating agent in the formation of water during the reaction. This is also an opportunity to recall Le Chatelier's principle and show how it applies to the removal of water in an esterification reaction.

- You may want to prepare another table to organize the information in Figure 24-5 or use the information to extend a table prepared for Sections 24-13 to 24-16.

- **Application.** Students may be interested in knowing that two compounds, with similar shapes and similar-looking functional groups, elicit dramatic responses from worker honeybees. One of the compounds is the ketone 2-heptanone, which helps to organize the bees in anticipation of an attack on their beehive by robber bees or other offenders. The other compound is the ester isopentyl acetate, which is released during stinging. This ester brings out very aggressive behavior and seems to direct other bees to sting in the same location. If someone inadvertently kills a bee while doing garden work, the ester may be released and cause other bees to swarm to the site. The formulas for these compounds are

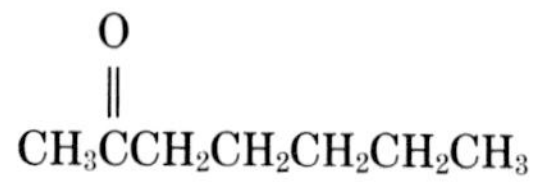

$$CH_3CCH_2CH_2CH_2CH_2CH_3 \quad \text{2-heptanone}$$

(with O double bonded above the second carbon)

$$CH_3C\,OCH_2CH_2CH\,{<}^{CH_3}_{CH_3} \quad \text{isopentyl acetate}$$

(with O double bonded above the first C)

| Esters | | | |
| --- | --- | --- | --- |
| Category | Formula | Example, IUPAC name | Additional information |
| Ester | 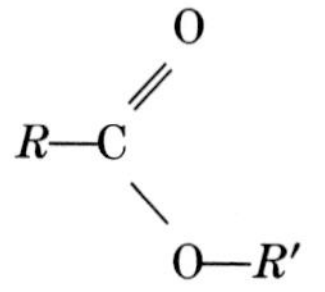 R—C double bond O, single bond O—R' | 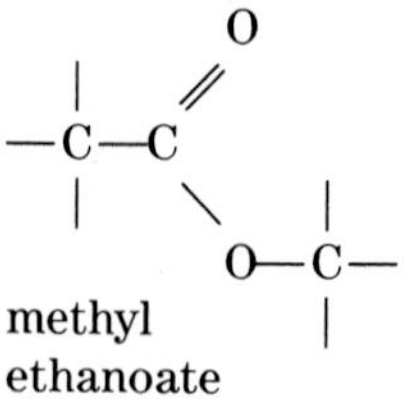 —C—C double bond O, O—C—; methyl ethanoate | formed from alcohol and carboxylic acid |

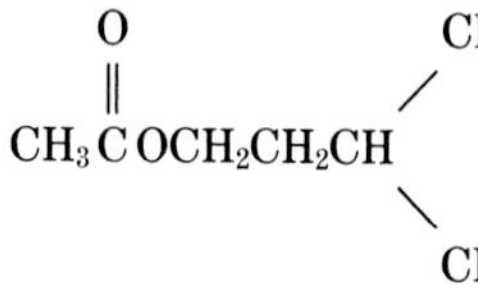

Figure 24-5

■ **Critical Thinking.** In the Critical and Creative Thinking worksheet "Ethical Judgments" students make a difficult decision between alternative methods of destroying obsolete chemical weapons. This is an important skill, which students can apply to the many issues that affect their lives.

## 24-18 Soaps and Detergents, pp. 727-729

| Planning Guide | |
| --- | --- |
| Labs (Lab Manual) and Demonstrations (TE) | Supplementary Materials (Teacher's Resource Book) |
| | Critical and Creative Thinking: Categorical Arguments, p. CCT-51 Societal Issues: Hazardous Wastes, p. SI-44 |

■ Emphasize the chemical reaction that produces soap. Include the effects of the minerals in hard water when it is used with ordinary soaps. Show how soap behaves differently in hard water and in pure (distilled) water. Point out that detergents work like soap but are chemically very different from soap.

■ You may wish to look ahead to the discussion of fats in Chapter 25 and perform Laboratory 50, "Saponification," at this time. See the teaching suggestions for Section 25-3.

■ **Critical Thinking.** Too often students attempt to memorize all of the material in this chapter, with frustrating results. The Critical and Creative Thinking worksheet "Categorical Arguments" helps students to classify organic compounds using the rules of classification and simple logic.

## Demonstration

### 24-1 Mobilizing Molecules

**Overview:** In this demonstration, you construct a mobile of organic molecules that illustrates molecular symmetry.

**Materials:** 3–4 ball-and-stick molecular-model sets (as attractive as possible); spool of transparent thread; scissors; thick wire; wire cutters.

**Advance Preparation:** none

**Procedure:** 1. Construct a number of models of organic compounds, both of your choosing and of your students'. Have the students examine each so that they can better visualize the spatial arrangements of the atoms. Also, have them attempt to find axes or planes of symmetry in the molecules. (See (a) in Figure 24-6, as an example.) Have them distinguish symmetrical molecules from asymmetrical ones. Be sure to include

at least a dozen of the former type. Examples can include ethane ($C_2H_6$), benzene ($C_6H_6$), carbon tetrachloride ($CCl_4$), and 1,2-dichloroethane ($CH_2ClCH_2Cl$). 2. Tie a length of clear plastic thread to each of the symmetrical molecules in such a way that when the model is supported by the string, its weight is equally distributed on both sides and the model hangs in a balanced position. Ask students where the point of contact is located relative to the axis or plane of symmetry in each case. 3. Cut one or more pieces of wire to serve as a support system for the mobile. Tie the midpoints of the wires together with string. (See (b) in Figure 24-6 for a simple example; the actual number of possibilities is very high, so you should feel free to design your own mobile, with student input.) 4. Vary the lengths of the clear plastic threads attached to the models, and tie the free end of each to different points along various wires, preserving overall balance. (If you wish, you can place chemically related molecules on the same wire.) 5. Hang the mobile from the ceiling, preferably in a place in which drafts of air will cause its parts to rotate.

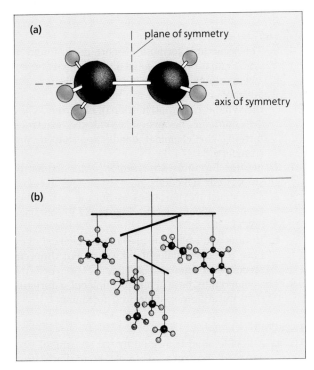

**Figure 24-6**

**Results:** Axes and planes of symmetry will depend upon the specific molecules chosen. The support string (or the geometrical extension of it) will, in each case, be attached at a point on the axis or plane or at a point of intersection of an axis with a plane.

# Answers to Questions

**Page 695**

1. **a.** Originally, the term "organic" came from the belief that certain compounds could be produced only by organisms.
   **b.** The compounds of carbon are studied in organic chemistry.
2. In many organic compounds, the only forces of attraction between molecules are the relatively weak van der Waals forces. Therefore, organic liquids tend to have high vapor pressure. For similar reasons, organic solids tend to have low solubility in polar solvents.
3. Organic liquids made up of nonpolar molecules can dissolve nonpolar solutes and are nearly insoluble in polar solvents.
4. The rates of organic reactions are slow because organic molecules contain covalent bonds.
5. **a.** When many organic compounds are heated to a high temperature in air, combustion is likely to occur.
   **b.** When heated in the absence of air, those compounds tend to decompose.

**Page 697**

6. **a.** The structural formula of methane is found in text Figure 24-3 (on page 695).
   **b.** The methane molecule is tetrahedral.
   **c.** Molecules of methane are nonpolar because of the symmetrical distribution of electrons. They are nonionic because the valence electrons forming the chemical bonds are shared, not transferred.
7. Structural formulas are used in order to distinguish between isomers.
8. **a.** The structural formulas of butane and isobutane are given in text Figure 24-6 (on page 697).
   **b.** Butane and isobutane are isomers because they have the same molecular formula but different structural formulas.
9. The compounds have the same molecular formula ($C_2H_6O$) but different structural formulas.

**Page 700**

10. **a.** A double bond is formed by the sharing of two pairs of electrons. A triple bond has three shared pairs of electrons.
    **b.** A saturated compound contains no double or triple bonds between carbon atoms.
    **c.** In a saturated hydrocarbon, all of the bonds between carbon atoms are single bonds.
    **d.** An unsaturated hydrocarbon has at least one double or triple C − C bond per molecule.

11. **a.** All of the members of a homologous series of compounds have the same general formula.
    **b.** The increment in a series of hydrocarbons is given by the difference between the molecular formulas of any two consecutive members of a homologous series.
    **c.** The increment in the alkane series is $CH_2$.
12. **a.** Hydrocarbons are organic compounds that contain only carbon and hydrogen.
    **b.** Hydrocarbons are found in petroleum and natural gas.
    **c.** Straight open-chain, branched open-chain, and cyclic (closed-chain) structures are found in hydrocarbons.
    **d.** In an open-chain molecule, the carbon atoms are arranged in a chain that is not a ring. Thus, each molecule has at least two end carbon atoms, more if the chain is a branched-chain.
13. **a.** Hydrocarbons made of small molecules tend to be gases at ordinary conditions. Midsize molecules tend to be liquids, while large molecules are usually solids.
    **b.** As molecular size increases, van der Waals attractions increase and melting points and boiling points increase.
    **c.** Hydrocarbons are used chiefly as fuels.
14. The alkane that contains three carbon atoms is propane. Its structural formula is shown in text Figure 24-10 on page 699.
15. **a.** An alkadiene has two double bonds between two different and separate pairs of carbon atoms.
    **b.** An aromatic hydrocarbon is a ring compound with one or more six-carbon rings. The bonds between the six carbons exhibit resonance such that each bond is equivalent to approximately one and a half bonds between carbon atoms.

**Page 702**

16. **a.** The general formula for an alkane is $C_nH_{2n+2}$.
    **b.** The alkanes are slow to react with many reagents because the carbon-carbon bonding in alkanes is saturated; that is, all carbon atoms are bonded with single bonds.
    **c.** The forces of attraction between molecules of alkanes are van der Waals forces.
    **d.** The boiling and melting points of the hydrocarbons are relatively low because the van der Waals forces are relatively weak.
17. The prefixes used in the names of the alkanes correspond to the number of carbon atoms:
    **a.** 1, *meth-*; **b.** 2, *eth-*; **c.** 3; *prop-*; **d.** 4, *but-*; **e.** 5, *pent-*
18. **a.** An alkyl group is an alkane molecule from which a hydrogen atom has been removed at one end.

**b.** Alkyl groups containing one to four carbon atoms:

$CH_3-$ methyl; $C_2H_5-$ ethyl; $C_3H_7-$ propyl; $C_4H_9-$ butyl

**19.** Octane has more isomers than pentane or heptane because octane has more carbon atoms.

**Page 705**

**20. a.** The parent chain in a branched alkane is the longest unbranched string of carbon atoms in a molecule. **b.** The direction of numbering the carbon atoms in a parent chain is chosen in order to give the lowest possible locator numbers to substituted groups. **c.** The locator numbers are used to specify the carbon atom to which a substituted group is attached.

**21.** Molecular formulas, structural formulas, and names for some hydrocarbons are:

**a.** $CH_3CH_2CH_3CHCH_2CH_3$
3-methylpentane

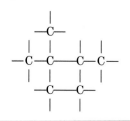

**b.** $CH_3CH_3CHCH_2CH_2CH_3$
2-methylpentane

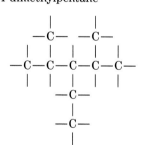

**c.** $CH_3CH_3CH_3CCH_3$
2,2-dimethylpropane

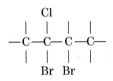

**d.** $CH_3CH_3CHCHCH_3CH_3$
2,3-dimethylbutane

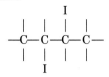

**22.** Some halogen derivatives of hydrocarbons are:

**a.** $CH_3CHICHICH_3$
2,3-diiodobutane

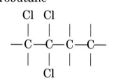

**b.** $CH_3CBr_2CH_2CH_3$
2,2-dibromobutane

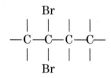

**c.** $CH_3CBrClCHBrCH_3$
2,3-dibromo-2-chlorobutane

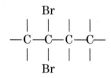

**d.** $CH_3CH_2CCl_2CClH_2$
1,2,2-trichlorobutane

**23.** The IUPAC names of the compounds are

**a.** 2,2,3-trimethylpentane

**b.** 4-ethyl-2-methylhexane

**c.** 3-methylhexane

**24. a.** 3-ethyl-2,4-dimethylpentane

**b.** 2,2,3-trimethylbutane

**c.** 4-ethyl-2,3-dimetylhexane

$$
\begin{array}{c}
\mid\\
-\text{C}-\\
\mid \quad \mid \quad \mid \quad \mid \quad \mid \quad \mid\\
-\text{C}-\text{C}-\text{C}-\text{C}-\text{C}-\text{C}-\\
\mid \quad \mid \quad \mid \quad \mid \quad \mid \quad \mid\\
-\text{C}- \quad -\text{C}-\\
\mid \qquad \mid\\
-\text{C}-\\
\mid
\end{array}
$$

**Page 708**

**25. a.** $C_nH_{2n}$.

**b.** An alkene has one carbon-carbon double bond.

**c.** The first five alkenes are: $C_2H_4$, ethene; $C_3H_6$, propene; $C_4H_8$, butene; $C_5H_{10}$, pentene; and $C_6H_{12}$, hexene.

**26. a.** A characteristic of the alkynes is the presence of one triple carbon-carbon bond.

**b.** $C_nH_{2n-2}$.

**c.** The first four alkynes are: $C_2H_2$, ethyne; $C_3H_4$, propyne; $C_4H_6$, butyne; and $C_5H_8$, pentyne.

**27. a.** In an alkadiene, there are two carbon-carbon double bonds. They are not placed consecutively in the molecule.

**b.** $C_nH_{2n-2}$.

**c.** The IUPAC name for isoprene is 2-methyl-1,3-butadiene.

**28. a.** polyethylene;

**b.** polypropylene;

**c.** synthetic rubber;

**d.** synthetic rubber.

**29. a.** 1-pentyne

$$
\begin{array}{c}
\mid \quad \mid \quad \mid\\
-\text{C}\equiv\text{C}-\text{C}-\text{C}-\text{C}-\\
\mid \quad \mid \quad \mid
\end{array}
$$

**b.** 3-methyl-1-pentyne

$$
\begin{array}{c}
\mid\\
-\text{C}-\\
\mid \quad \mid \quad \mid\\
-\text{C}\equiv\text{C}-\text{C}-\text{C}-\text{C}-\\
\mid \quad \mid \quad \mid
\end{array}
$$

**c.** 1,3-pentadiene

$$
\begin{array}{c}
\mid \quad \mid \quad \mid \quad \mid\\
-\text{C}=\text{C}-\text{C}=\text{C}-\text{C}-\\
\mid
\end{array}
$$

**d.** 2,3-dimethyl-1,3-pentadiene

$$
\begin{array}{c}
\mid \quad\ \ \mid\\
-\text{C}- \ -\text{C}-\\
\mid \quad\ \ \mid \qquad \mid\\
-\text{C}=\text{C}\!-\!-\!-\!-\text{C}=\text{C}-\text{C}-\\
\mid \qquad\quad \mid \quad \mid
\end{array}
$$

**Page 710**

**30.** An aromatic hydrocarbon has at least one ring of six carbon atoms with resonance hybrid bonds between the carbon atoms. Such rings with resonance bonds are not found in aliphatic compounds.

**31. a.** $C_nH_{2n-6}$

**b.** The structural formula for benzene is shown in text Figures 24-21 and 24-22 on pages 708 and 709.

**32. a.** Coal tar is the richest natural source of aromatic hydrocarbons.

**b.** Dyes, explosives, aspirin, and sulfa drugs are made from aromatic hydrocarbons.

**33. a.** The carbon-carbon bonds in benzene are resonance hybrid bonds. They are equivalent to the sharing of three electrons (rather than the usual two, four, or six). This creates a sort of bond-and-a-half.

**b.** Benzene behaves sometimes like a saturated compound and sometimes like an unsaturated compound.

**34.** See accompanying Figure 24-7.

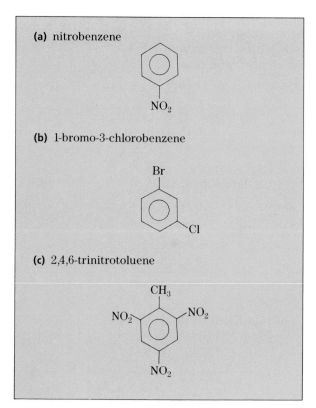

**(a)** nitrobenzene

**(b)** 1-bromo-3-chlorobenzene

**(c)** 2,4,6-trinitrotoluene

Figure 24-7

**Page 714**

**35. a.** The alkanes are less reactive than the alkenes.

Alkanes react by substitution only, whereas alkenes are more likely to react by addition.

**b.** The complete combustion of methane in oxygen is:
$$CH_4 + 2O_2 \rightarrow CO_2 + 2H_2O$$

**c.** Carbon monoxide, CO, and carbon are often found as products of incomplete combustion.

**36. a.** In a substitution reaction, a different atom, usually a halogen, is substituted for a hydrogen atom on a hydrocarbon chain.

**b.** Some chlorine substitution products of methane are:

$CCl_4$, tetrachloromethane (carbon tetrachloride)
$CHCl_3$, trichloromethane (chloroform)
$CH_2Cl_2$, dichloromethane (methylene chloride)
$CH_3Cl$, chloromethane (methyl chloride)

**c.** The formula for Freon is $CF_2Cl_2$. Its IUPAC name is dichlorodifluoromethane.

**37. a.** A polymer is a giant molecule formed by joining simple molecules into long chains.

**b.** A monomer is any one of the many simple units that make up polymers.

**c.** Polyethylene is an example of an addition polymer.

**d.** Butyl rubber is an example of a copolymer.

**e.** Isobutylene and isoprene are the monomers found in the copolymer butyl rubber.

**38. a.** The alkenes can undergo addition reactions because each molecule has one double bond between carbon atoms. Alkanes, having single bonds only, cannot react by addition.

**b.**
$$\begin{array}{ccc} | & | & \\ C=C & + & Cl-Cl \rightarrow \end{array} \begin{array}{cc} | & | \\ -C-C- \\ | & | \\ Cl & Cl \end{array}$$

**c.** Product name: 1,2-dichloroethane

**39. a.** 1,2-dibromoethane

**b.** iodoethane

$$\begin{array}{cc} | & | \\ -C=C-I \\ | & | \end{array}$$

**c.** 1,2-dibromoethane

$$\begin{array}{cc} -C=C- \\ | & | \\ Br & Br \end{array}$$

**d.** 1,1,2,2-tetrabromoethane

**Page 715**

**40. a.** Petroleum is typically a mixture of aliphatic and aromatic hydrocarbons.

**b.** This mixture can be separated into its components by successive distillations with fractions being drawn off based upon differences in boiling points.

**c.** Among the products of fractional distillation are gasoline, kerosene, furnace oil, naphtha, and lubrication products.

**41. a.** In the process of cracking, a mixture of hydrocarbons is heated under pressure.

**b.** The chief purpose of cracking is to break larger molecules into smaller molecules and thus to increase the supply of gasoline.

**c.** During thermal cracking, heat is applied while keeping the system under high pressure.

**d.** In catalytic cracking, a catalyst is used in addition to heat and pressure.

**e.** Gasoline from catalytic cracking is superior to that from thermal cracking because it contains more alkenes and more branched-chain and ring compounds, which increase octane ratings.

**Page 720**

**42.** A functional group is a group of atoms that gives characteristic properties to organic compounds.

**43.** The hydroxide ion is an ion with a negative charge. The hydroxyl group is found in alcohols and other compounds covalently bonded to a carbon atom. It possesses no charge.

**44. a.** In an alcohol, one hydroxyl group or more is bonded to an alkyl group.

**b.** R–OH

**c.** ethanol, $C_2H_5OH$

**45. a.** A primary alcohol is one in which the carbon atom attached to the —OH group is bonded to one and only one other carbon atom. Ethyl alcohol is an example: $CH_3-CH_2-OH$.

**b.** In a secondary alcohol, the carbon atom attached to the —OH group is bonded to two other carbon atoms. An example is 2-propanol:

$$CH_3-\underset{\underset{OH}{|}}{CH}-CH_3$$

**c.** In a tertiary alcohol, the carbon atom bonded to the —OH group is bonded to three other carbon atoms. An example is 2-methyl-2-propanol:

46. **a.** methanol; **b.** ethanol; **c.** wood alcohol, methyl alcohol; **d.** grain alcohol, ethyl alcohol.
47. **a.** Methanol (methyl alcohol) tastes like ethanol, attacks the nervous system, and is miscible with water; it is used as a solvent and fuel, and to produce formaldehyde.
    **b.** Ethanol (ethyl alcohol) is volatile, colorless, and flammable; it is used in beverages and as a solvent and fuel.
    **c.** Methyl alcohol is sometimes called wood alcohol because it was originally obtained by the destructive distillation of wood.
    **d.** Denatured alcohol is ethanol that has been made unfit to drink, often by the addition of methanol.
48. **a.** 1,2-dihydroxyethane, ethylene glycol
    **b.** 1,2,3-trihydroxypropane, glycerine
    **c.** Ethylene glycol is used as an antifreeze in automobile engines.
    **d.** Glycerine is used to manufacture plastics and cosmetics.
49. **a.** Alcohols possess properties of both polar and nonpolar molecules because the hydroxyl group, —OH, is polar whereas the alkyl group to which it is bonded is generally nonpolar.
    **b.** Butyl alcohol is less soluble in water than is ethyl alcohol because the nonpolar alkyl group is a larger part of the butyl alcohol molecule.
    **c.** Glycerine is more polar than is ethylene glycol because glycerine has three —OH groups per molecule whereas ethylene glycol has only two.

**Page 725**

50.

| | **a.** one-carbon aldehyde | **b.** two-carbon aldehyde |
|---|---|---|
| Structural formula: |  |  |
| IUPAC name: | methanal | ethanal |
| Common name: | formaldehyde | acetaldehyde |
| Two uses: | germicide; disinfectant | preparation of aniline dyes and synthetic rubber |

51. **a.** and **b.** These structural formulas appear as marginal annotations on text page 725.
    **c.** The IUPAC name for acetone is propanone.
    **d.** Acetone is used primarily for a solvent.
52. **a.** The general formula for an ether is $R$—$O$—$R'$.
    **b.** This structural formula appears as a marginal annotation on text page 725.
    **c.** The use of ether as an anesthetic has been largely discontinued because ether is irritating, nauseating, and extremely flammable.
    **d.** The major industrial use of ether is as a solvent.
53. These structural formulas and names appear as marginal annotations on text page 725.
54. **a.** The general formula of a fatty acid is $C_nH_{2n+1}COOH$.
    **b.** Fatty acids are so named because they are found in natural fats.
55. **a.** Like inorganic acids, carboxylic acids ionize to form hydronium ions when they are dissolved in water. Both kinds of acids can be neutralized by inorganic bases such as NaOH.
    **b.** The part of the carboxylic acid that gives it polarity is the —COOH group.
    **c.** The solubility of carboxylic acids decreases as the number of carbon atoms increases because the nonpolar group becomes an increasingly greater part of the molecule.

**Page 728**

56. **a.** The reaction between a carboxylic acid and an alcohol is called esterification.
    **b.** The formation of ethyl ethanoate is:

    $$CH_3COOH + C_2H_5OH \rightarrow CH_3COOC_2H_5 + HOH$$

    Ethyl ethanoate is also known as ethyl acetate.
    **c.** To increase the rate of reaction, the system is warmed and $H_2SO_4$ is added as a dehydrating catalyst.
57. **a.** A soap is a metallic salt of a higher carboxylic acid.
    **b.** Four common soaps include sodium stearate, potassium stearate, sodium palmitate, and potassium palmitate.
    **c.** Potassium soaps are softer and lather more readily than sodium soaps.
    **d.** The molecular formula for sodium stearate, the most common soap, is $C_{17}H_{35}COONa$.
58. **a.** Three ions that are often present in hard water are $Ca^{2+}$, $Mg^{2+}$, and $Fe^{2+}$.
    **b.** When a soluble soap is added to hard water, a precipitate of calcium, magnesium, or iron(II) stearate forms.
    **c.** The stearate precipitate is undesirable because it forms a greasy, scummy coating on the tub, shower, or laundry.

**59. a.** and **b.** These structural formulas appear as marginal annotations on text page 729.

**60.** The equation for the formation of ethyl methanoate from ethanol and methanoic acid appears as a marginal annotation on text page 729.

**Page 729, Spinning a Thread**

1. It might be used to make synthetic fibers. The thread is, in fact, nylon.

2. Some tests could be done to determine whether the reaction could be done on a large scale in a practical manner. Other tests would depend on the proposed use for the fibers. For example, if the fiber was to be used in fabric, tests should be carried out to determine the fiber's solubility in water, its flammability, how easily it can be dyed, its insulating properties, its feel against the skin, its strength, etc.

# Chapter Review 24

**Page 731, Content Review**

1. **a.** The word "organic," applied to chemical compounds, originally meant "produced by a living organism."
   **b.** Wöhler made urea from inorganic compounds.

2. Van der Waals forces, dipole-dipole attractions, and hydrogen bonds exist in organic compounds.

3. Organic liquids exist as molecules, not as ions.

4. The ability of carbon atoms to bond to other carbon atoms accounts for the large number of organic molecules.

5. The structural formula shows the arrangement of the atoms.

6. These two compounds have the same molecular formula but different structural formulas.

7. **a.** In a saturated organic compound, all four valence bonds of each carbon atom are utilized to the fullest extent in holding other atoms.
   **b.** In an unsaturated compound, the carbon atoms that are involved in double or triple bonds can add additional atoms through reaction.

8. Unsaturated hydrocarbons are more reactive than the saturated hydrocarbons because they have more electrons available to form new bonds.

9. The aliphatic series are the alkanes, alkenes, alkynes, and alkadienes.

10. **a.** $C_7H_{16}$, $C_8H_{18}$, $C_9H_{20}$
    **b.** Van der Waals forces become stronger with increasing molecular mass because the number of electrons increases.

11. The butane molecule becomes a butyl group upon the removal of a hydrogen atom from a terminal carbon atom.

12. The straight-chain isomer of $C_8H_{18}$ is called normal octane.

13. **a.** n-butane

$$CH_3 - CH_2 - CH_2 - CH_3$$

**b.** 2-methylbutane

$$CH_3 - CH - CH_2 - CH_3$$
$$|$$
$$CH_3$$

**c.** 2,5-dimethylhexane

$$CH_3 - CH - CH_2 - CH_2 - CH - CH_3$$
$$|\qquad\qquad\qquad\quad|$$
$$CH_3\qquad\qquad\qquad CH_3$$

14. **a.** 1,3-dibromopentane

$$\begin{array}{ccc} Br & & Br \\ | & & | \\ H - C - CH_2 - CH - CH_2CH_3 \\ | \\ H \end{array}$$

**b.** 2,2,3-trichloropentane

$$\begin{array}{cc} Cl & Cl \\ | & | \\ CH_3 - C - CH - CH_2 - CH_3 \\ | \\ Cl \end{array}$$

**c.** 2-bromo-3-methylpentane

$$\begin{array}{c} CH_3 - CH_2 - CH - CH - CH_3 \\ |\quad\ | \\ CH_3\ \ Br \end{array}$$

15. **a.** $CH_2{=}CH - CH_2 - CH_2 - CH_2 - CH_3$
    $CH_3 - CH{=}CH - CH_2CH_2CH_3$
    $CH_3 - CH_2 - CH{=}CH - CH_2 - CH_3$

**b.** 1-hexene, 2-hexene, 3-hexene

16. **a.**

$$\begin{array}{ccc} & CH_3 & CH_3 \\ & | & | \\ CH_3 - C{=}CH - C - CH_3 \\ & & | \\ & & CH_3 \end{array}$$

24

**b.**

$$CH \equiv C - \underset{\underset{CH_3}{|}}{\overset{\overset{Br}{|}}{CH}} - CH - CH_3$$

**c.**

$$CH_2{=}C - \underset{\underset{CH_3}{|}}{C}{=}CH_2$$
$$\qquad \overset{|}{CH_3}$$

**d.** $CH_3{-}CH{=}CH{-}CH{=}CH{-}CH_3$

**17.**    ortho          meta          para

**18. a.** $2C_4H_{10} + 13O_2 \rightarrow 8CO_2 + 10H_2O$

**b.** $2C_8H_{18} + 25O_2 \rightarrow 16CO_2 + 18H_2O$

**19. a.**

$$H - \underset{\underset{H}{|}}{\overset{\overset{H}{|}}{C}} - H + 2Cl_2 \rightarrow H - \underset{\underset{H}{|}}{\overset{\overset{Cl}{|}}{C}} - Cl + 2HCl$$

**b.**

$$H - \underset{\underset{H}{|}}{\overset{\overset{H}{|}}{C}} - \underset{\underset{H}{|}}{\overset{\overset{H}{|}}{C}} - H + Br_2 \rightarrow H - \underset{\underset{H}{|}}{\overset{\overset{H}{|}}{C}} - \underset{\underset{H}{|}}{\overset{\overset{H}{|}}{C}} - Br + HBr$$

**c.**

$$H - \underset{\underset{H}{|}}{\overset{\overset{H}{|}}{C}} - \underset{\underset{H}{|}}{\overset{\overset{H}{|}}{C}} - H + 2Cl_2 \rightarrow H - \underset{\underset{Cl}{|}}{\overset{\overset{Cl}{|}}{C}} - \underset{\underset{H}{|}}{\overset{\overset{H}{|}}{C}} - H + 2HCl$$

**20.** 1,2-dichloroethane

$$H - \underset{\underset{H}{|}}{\overset{\overset{Cl}{|}}{C}} - \underset{\underset{H}{|}}{\overset{\overset{Cl}{|}}{C}} - H$$

**21.** Petroleum is the principal source of aliphatic hydrocarbons.

**22.** The hydroxyl group, —OH, is characteristic of the alcohols.

**23. a.** Ethanol is denatured to make it unfit to drink.
**b.** Ethanol is denatured by adding methanol to it.

**24.** Ethylene glycol has a low freezing point and a high boiling point. It is also soluble in water.

**25.** Methanal is known as formaldehyde.

**26.** The structural formula for butanal is

$$H - \underset{\underset{H}{|}}{\overset{\overset{H}{|}}{C}} - \underset{\underset{H}{|}}{\overset{\overset{H}{|}}{C}} - \underset{\underset{H}{|}}{\overset{\overset{H}{|}}{C}} - \overset{\overset{O}{\parallel}}{C}{\diagdown} H$$

**27.** A ketone is a compound with a carbonyl group.

**28.** The structural formula for 5-methyl-3-hexanone is

$$CH_3 - CH_2 - \overset{\overset{O}{\parallel}}{C} - CH_2 - \underset{\underset{CH_3}{|}}{CH} - CH_3$$

**29. a.** Diethyl ether is a very volatile, flammable liquid.
**b.** The general formula for ethers is $R{-}O{-}R'$.

**30.** The "fatty acid series" is a homologous series of saturated carboxylic acids, so named because many of these acids are found in natural fats.

**31. a.** Ethyl propanoate would be made from the reaction between ethanol and propanoic acid.

**b.**

$$CH_3 - CH_2 - \overset{\overset{O}{\diagup\!\!\parallel}}{\underset{\diagdown}{C}}{\phantom{i}} + C_2H_5 - OH \rightarrow$$
$$\qquad\qquad OH$$

$$CH_3 - CH_2 - \overset{\overset{O}{\parallel}}{C} - O - C_2H_5 + H_2O$$

**32.** A bathtub "ring" forms as a product of the reaction between the metallic ions in water (such as $Ca^{2+}$ ions) and the stearate ion from the soap. The product is a scum-like deposit, such as calcium stearate.

**33.** Lye reacts with grease to make the soluble products of soap and glycerine. This is the soap-making reaction known as saponification.

## Page 732, Content Mastery

**34. a.** Gasoline is insoluble in water.
**b.** Covalent bonds are strong and, therefore, are difficult to break. This property results in slow reactions.

**35. a.** $C_2H_6$, $C_3H_8$; **b.** $C_3H_6$, $C_4H_8$

**36.** Carbon is the "backbone" of all organic compounds and life itself.

**37. a.** 2,2-dimethylbutane
**b.** 2-methylbutane
**c.** 4-ethyl-3-methylheptane

**38. a.**

$$CH_3-\underset{\underset{Cl}{|}}{\overset{\overset{Cl}{|}}{C}}-\underset{\underset{}{|}}{\overset{\overset{CH_3}{|}}{CH}}-CH_3$$

**b.**

$$CH_3-CH-\underset{\underset{CH_3}{|}}{\overset{\overset{CH_3}{|}}{C}}-CH_2-CH_3 \quad \underset{CH_3}{}$$

**c.**

$$CH_3-CH_2-\underset{\underset{CH_2}{|}}{\overset{\overset{CH_3}{|}}{C}}-CH_2-CH_2-CH_3$$
$$\underset{CH_3}{|}$$

**39. a.**

$$H-\underset{\underset{Cl}{|}}{\overset{\overset{Cl}{|}}{C}}-\underset{\underset{H}{|}}{\overset{\overset{Cl}{|}}{C}}-H$$

**b.**

$$F-\underset{\underset{F}{|}}{\overset{\overset{F}{|}}{C}}-\underset{\underset{H}{|}}{\overset{\overset{Br}{|}}{C}}-Cl$$

**c.**

$$H-\underset{\underset{Br}{|}}{\overset{\overset{H}{|}}{C}}-CH_2-\underset{\underset{CH_2}{|}}{CH}-CH-CH_2-CH_3$$
$$\underset{CH_3}{|}$$

**40. a.** 5-chloro-2-pentene
**b.** 3,3-dibromo-1-pentyne
**c.** 2,3,4-trichloro-4-methyl-2-hexene

**41.** The structural formula for ethane, which does not have any isomers because it has only two carbon atoms, is as follows:

$$H-\underset{\underset{H}{|}}{\overset{\overset{H}{|}}{C}}-\underset{\underset{H}{|}}{\overset{\overset{H}{|}}{C}}-H$$

**42.** There are four structural formulas for $C_4H_8$. They are listed in Figure 24-8.

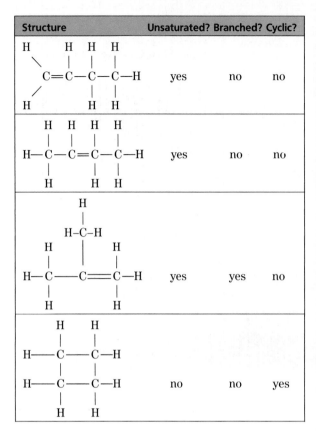

| Structure | Unsaturated? | Branched? | Cyclic? |
|---|---|---|---|
| $C=C-C-C-H$ | yes | no | no |
| $H-C-C=C-C-H$ | yes | no | no |
| $H-C-C=C-H$ | yes | yes | no |
| $H-C-C-H$ / $H-C-C-H$ | no | no | yes |

**Figure 24-8**

**43.** With all of benzene's excellent properties, it is seldom used by chemistry students because it is a known cancer-causing compound, i.e., a carcinogen.

**44.** Decane has a higher boiling point because it has a higher molecular mass, creating greater intermolecular forces.

**45.** To make soap, pioneers had to add NaOH (lye) to animal fat. They often used potash ($K_2CO_3$ and sometimes $K_2O$) from the ashes of wood for their base.

**46. a.** Catalytic hydrogenation is one type of addition reaction in which hydrogen is added to alkenes and/or alkynes in the presence of suitable catalysts, such as platinum, palladium, or nickel.
**b.** If a sample of propyne were subjected to this process, it would be converted to propene, which in turn would be converted to propane.

**47.** The number 2 refers to a specific carbon atom; the prefix *di* refers to two atoms or groups of atoms attached to a carbon atom.

**48.** See Figure 24-9, page TG-348.

24

## Page 733, Concept Mastery

**49. Concept:** *Organic compounds do not necessarily produce odors when they decompose.*

**Solution:** Some organic materials will decompose into products that have unpleasant odors. This is especially true if hydrogen sulfide is present. Strictly speaking, decomposition of a substance into simpler substances does not include additional chemical reactions in which elements react to form new products. Most of the products would be odorless —this is especially true when they are reduced to elemental form.

**50 Concept:** *Organic chemistry is the chemistry of carbon compounds.*

**Solution:** Organic farming refers to the use of natural waste products of animals as fertilizers. These fertilizers are carbon compounds. In nonorganic farming, inorganic fertilizers are also used.

**51. Concept:** *Isomers are chemical compounds with the same molecular formula but different structural formulas.*

**Solution:** Isomers have to do with compounds while allotropes and isotopes have to do with elements. Isomers and allotropes are similar in that each has to do with the same elements. Isomers have the same number and kind of elements but different structural formulas. Allotropes have the same kind of element but vary in the number of atoms in the molecule. Isotopes are atoms of the same element with different numbers of neutrons.

**52. Concept:** *Saturated hydrocarbons have the maximum number of hydrogen atoms that they can hold.*

**Solution:** Both have all that they can contain. Saturated solutions have the maximum solute that will dissolve in the solvent at a given temperature. Saturated hydrocarbons have the maximum number of hydrogen atoms that can be bonded to the carbon atoms.

**53. Concept:** *The structural formula identifies the organic compound.*

**Solution:** There should be no price difference in terms of the quality. Both should be identical if they are pure substances. There could be a difference if they are impure as they could contain different kinds or amounts of impurities.

### Types of Organic Compounds

| Structure | IUPAC name | Functional group |
|---|---|---|
| 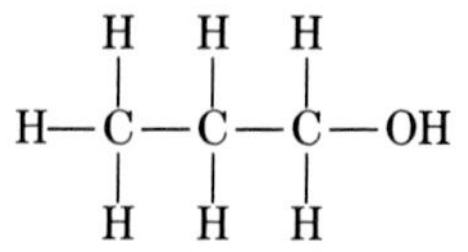 | 1-propanol | alcohol |
| 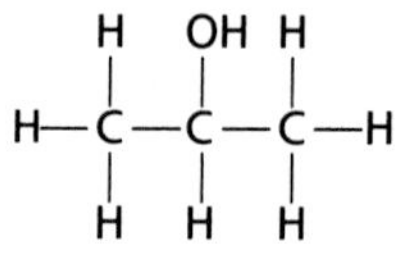 | 2-propanol | alcohol |
| 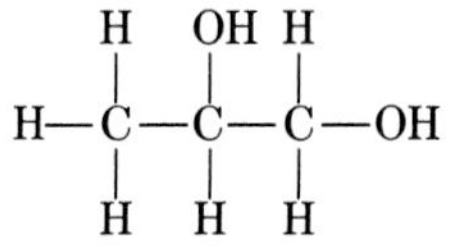 | 1,2-propanediol | dihydroxy alcohol |
| 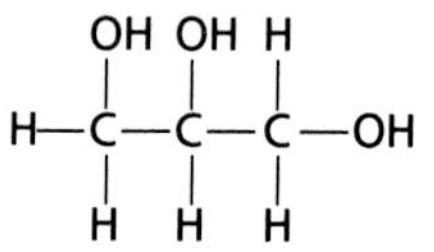 | 1,2,3-propanetriol (glycerine) | trihydroxy alcohol |
| 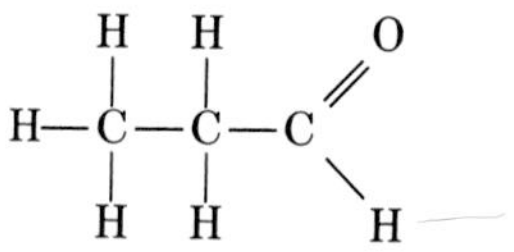 | propanal | aldehyde |
| 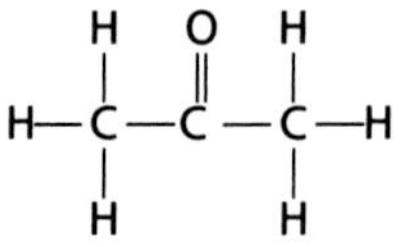 | propanone | ketone |
| 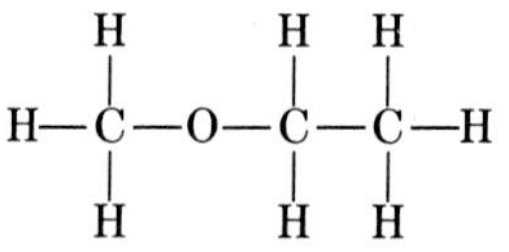 | ethyl methyl ether | ether |
| 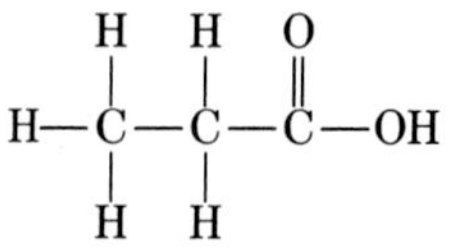 | propanoic acid | carboxylic acid |
| 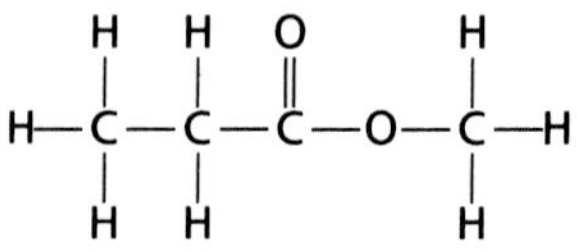 | methyl propanoate | ester |

**Figure 24-9**

## Page 734, Cumulative Review

**54. a.** Aluminum is the most common metal in the earth's crust.

**55. d.** Aluminum is not a transition metal.

**56. b.** Oxygen is the most abundant element in the earth's crust.

**57. b.** Hybridization of orbitals occurs in covalent bonding.

**58. d.** $\dfrac{33.5\ \text{g}}{134\ \text{g/mol}} \times \dfrac{1000\ \text{cm}^3/\text{dm}^3}{100\ \text{cm}^3} = 2.50\ M$

**59.** $\dfrac{273\ \text{K} \times 202.6\ \text{kPa}}{300\ \text{K}} = 184.4\ \text{kPa}$

**60. a.** nitrogen monoxide; nitrogen(II) oxide;
  **b.** carbon dioxide; carbon(IV) oxide;
  **c.** diphosphorous trioxide; phosphorous(III) oxide

**61. a.** 100 g has 40.0 g C, 6.67 g H, 53.3 g O.
  40.0 g C/12.0 g/mol C = 3.33 mol C atoms
  6.67 g H/1.01 g/mol C = 6.60 mol H atoms
  53.3 g O/16.0 g/mol O = 3.33 mol O atoms
  The whole-number ratio is 1 C atom to 2 H atoms to 1 O atom, so the empirical formula is $CH_2O$.
  **b.** Molecular mass of $CH_2O$ would be 30.0 u. Molecular mass of fructose is 180 u.
  180/30.0 = 6; 6($CH_2O$) = $C_6H_{12}O_6$

**62.** 200 cm³ $H_2$ × $\dfrac{1\ \text{dm}^3}{1000\ \text{cm}^3}$ × $\dfrac{1\ \text{mol}}{22.4\ \text{dm}^3}$
  = 0.00893 mol $H_2$ produced
  $\dfrac{2\ \text{mol Al}}{3\ \text{mol }H_2}$ × 0.00893 mol $H_2$ × $\dfrac{27\ \text{g Al}}{\text{mol}}$ = 0.161 g Al

**63. a.** 100 g has 85.7 g C and 14.3 g H.
  85.7 g C/12.0 g/mol C = 7.14 mol C atoms
  14.3 g H/1.01 g/mol H = 14.2 mol H atoms
  The whole-number ratio is 2 H atoms to 1 C atom, so the empirical formula is $CH_2$.
  **b.** Molecular mass of $CH_2$ would be 14.0 u.
  Molecular mass of hydrocarbon = 56.1 u.
  56.1/14.0 = 4; 4($CH_2$) = $C_4H_8$

## Page 734, Critical Thinking

**64. a, b,** and **i** are alkanes; **c, g,** and **h** are alkynes *or* alkadienes; **d, e, f,** and **j** are alkenes.

**65.** An alkyl group is part of an alkane. If the alkane loses one hydrogen, it becomes an alkyl group, reactive and ready for bonding to something else.

**66.** Alkynes are the most reactive because the electrons in the triple bond are less tightly held and, therefore, are more reactive than electrons in the double or single bonds of alkenes and alkanes. The order is alkynes > alkenes > alkanes.

**67.** Petroleum is a complex mixture of hydrocarbons and their derivatives. These compounds can be separated by fractional distillation because of the difference in their boiling points. The molecules with the longer hydrocarbon chains usually boil at higher temperatures.

**68.** Because organic molecules have such varied and complex structures, and because there are so many organic molecules, chemists needed a systematic approach to naming them. It would be difficult to keep the compounds straight if they were referred to by their common or trivial names. Because science depends on accurate communication between scientists, a clear and unambiguous system that is not redundant was needed. The system has to be detailed enough to give every distinct compound a unique name.

## Page 735, Challenge Problems

**69.** The structure of polyethylene is as follows:

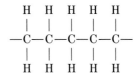

Replacing the appropriate hydrogens with methyl groups yields this structure, polypropylene:

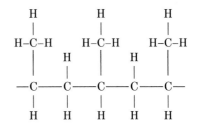

**70.** 3-chloro-6-butyl-4,4-dimethyldecane

**71. a.** $CH_3$—$CH_2$—OH vs. $CH_3$—O—$CH_3$
  ethanol and dimethyl ether

  **b.** $CH_3$—$CH_2$—C=O vs. $CH_3$—C=O
  (with H below first) (with $CH_3$ below second)
  propanal and propanone

  **c.** $CH_3$—$CH_2$—C=O vs. $CH_3$—C=O
  (with OH below first) (with O—$CH_3$ below second)
  propanoic acid and methyl ethanoate

24

# Biochemistry

**25**

## Chapter Planning Guide

| Text Section | Labs (Lab Manual) and Demonstrations (TE) | Supplementary Materials (Teacher's Resource Book) |
|---|---|---|
| **25-1** The Compounds of Life, pp. 737-738 <br><br> **25-2** Carbohydrates, pp. 738-740 | | Transparency Master: Classes of Biologically Important Substances, p. 25-1 <br> Transparency Master: Glucose, p. 25-3 <br> Transparency Master: Three Simple Sugar Isomers, p. 25-2 <br> Societal Issues: Artificial Sweeteners, p. SI-47 |
| **25-3** Lipids, pp. 740-742 | Lab 50: Saponification | Transparency Master: Formation of a Fat, p. 25-4 |
| **25-4** Proteins, pp. 742-744 <br><br> **25-5** Biochemical Reactions and Enzymes, pp. 744-745 | Demo 25-1: Protein Anyone?, p. TG-353 | Transparency Master: Formation of a Peptide Bond, p. 25-5 |
| **Break-through** The Robot Chemist, p. 745 | | |
| **25-6** Nucleic Acids, pp. 746-749 | | |
| **25-7** The Role of Energy in Biochemistry, pp. 749-750 | | Review Activity: Biochemistry, p. 25-6 <br> Critical and Creative Thinking: Secondhand Sources, p. CCT-7 |
| | | Test—Form A, p. AT-99 <br> Alternate Test—Form B, p. BT-99 |

■ Core    ■ Advanced    ■ Optional

## Chapter Overview

In Chapter 25 we present a survey of four classes of biochemical compounds and some of their properties and reactions. These classes are: (1) carbohydrates, which function as sources of energy and as structural material; (2) lipids, which have structural and regulatory functions; (3) proteins, which have structural, regulatory, protective, and other functions; and (4) nucleic acids, which control development. We show how many biochemical reactions can be classified as condensation polymerizations (i.e., the synthesis of polymers from monomers) or as hydrolyses (i.e., the breakdown of polymers into monomers). We give special attention to enzymes, a category of proteins that catalyze biochemical reactions. The chapter ends with a discussion of energy as it relates to biochemical reactions.

# Chapter Objectives

After students have completed this chapter, they will be able to:

1. Give molecular structures and uses of some examples of each of the four classes of biochemical compounds.                          *23-1 to 25-6*
2. Describe the role of polymerization in reactions for the synthesis of those classes of biochemical compounds.                          *25-2 to 25-6*
3. Describe the hydrolysis reactions by which the polymers of biochemical compounds are broken down into monomers.                          *25-2 to 25-6*
4. Explain the role of enzymes in biochemical reactions.                          *25-5*
5. Describe the role of energy changes in some biochemical reactions.                          *25-7*

# Teaching Suggestions

## 25-1 The Compounds of Life, pp. 737-738, and 25-2 Carbohydrates, pp. 738-740

| Planning Guide | |
| --- | --- |
| Labs (Lab Manual) and Demonstrations (TE) | Supplementary Materials (Teacher's Resource Book) |
| | Transparency Master: Classes of Biologically Important Substances, p. 25-1 |
| | Transparency Master: Three Simple Sugar Isomers, p. 25-2 |
| | Transparency Master: Glucose, p. 25-3 |
| | Societal Issues: Artificial Sweeteners, p. SI-47 |

■ To introduce the chapter, have students refer to Figure 25-2, or use the Transparency Master "Classes of Biologically Important Substances." Point out the relationship of biochemistry to organic chemistry.

■ To help students understand optical isomers, first use differently colored spheres like those in text Figure 25-4. Next, use the Transparency Master "Three Simple Sugar Isomers." Then have students examine the structures of glucose, galactose, and fructose, as shown in the transparency and in text Figure 25-3. You may also use models of these compounds.

■ One way to help your students understand the complex vocabulary of biochemistry is to use illustrations and models liberally. You may wish to start your

discussion of carbohydrates with the Transparency Master "Glucose." Then you might show students a model of the glucose molecule, emphasizing the 2–to–1 ratio of H to O atoms. Next, show models of an "aldehyde" sugar and a "ketone" sugar, pointing out different locations of the $\overset{\backslash}{\underset{/}{C}} = O$ group.

■ Call attention to text Figure 25-6 to help explain the polymerization of carbohydrates, and have students compare the structure of a monosaccharide, such as glucose, and a disaccharide, such as sucrose. In your discussion of polysaccharides, have students point out the similarity and difference between starch and cellulose as shown in text Figure 25-7. You may also use models to show the processes of polymerization and of hydrolysis of carbohydrates.

■ The Societal Issues worksheet "Artificial Sweeteners" examines the health issues of sugar and sugar substitutes. The critical thinking questions at the end of the article are designed to lead the students through a critical evaluation and decision process concerning usage of these substances.

## 25-3 Lipids, pp. 740-742

| Planning Guide | |
| --- | --- |
| Labs (Lab Manual) and Demonstrations (TE) | Supplementary Materials (Teacher's Resource Book) |
| Lab 50: Saponification | Transparency Master: Formation of a Fat, p. 25-4 |

■ To set the stage for the study of lipids, have students recall their study of esters and soaps from Sections 24-17 and 24-18, or discuss these classes of compounds for the first time if they were not studied earlier. Review the definition of fats as glyceryl esters of carboxylic acids of relatively high molecular masses (i.e., those that contain long carbon chains) and the definition of soaps as metallic salts of such fatty acids. To show the relationship between fats and soaps, do Laboratory 50, "Saponification," in which students observe the preparation of a soap from a liquid fat and a strong base.

Refer students to text Figures 25-9 and 25-10 to show the relationship between fatty acids and fats. Discuss dehydration synthesis using the Transparency Master "Formation of a Fat." Then you may want to have students compare Figure 25-10 with text Figure 25-12 and note the striking difference between a fat and cholesterol. The biochemical processes in which fats contribute to the buildup of cholesterol in the body are obviously complex and beyond the scope of our brief survey of the subject.

■ **Application.** Students may be interested in knowing

some facts about coconut oil, a lipid found in many commonly used products. Explain that coconut oil is a triglyceride that contains an unusual array of fatty acids. Unlike many other vegetable oils that are largely unsaturated, coconut oil is the most saturated fat known. The lack of double bonds in its carbon chains makes this oil less reactive than unsaturated oils. Discuss with students how this property increases the chemical stability of the fat, and hence the shelf life of products made with it. Ask why consumers may be misled by advertising that states that the food contains "pure vegetable oil." (It has been claimed that the comsumption of some vegetable oils that contain large amounts of *un*saturated fats keeps one's blood cholesterol at an acceptable level.)

Coconut oil is also used for making bath soaps. Its fatty acids have relatively short chains of 12 or 14 carbons. Fatty acids with short carbon chains make coconut oil soaps more hydrophilic and thus more soluble, which makes it easy to develop a lather. The other major lipid used to make soap is beef tallow, which has fatty acid chains that are mostly 18 carbons long. As a result, tallow soaps do not lather well in water at temperatures normally used for bathing. Most soaps are made from a blend of the more expensive coconut oil and the cheaper tallow in order to give both economy and lathering properties. You could have students read the labels on soap bars and look for terms that suggest the use of tallow and coconut oil.

■ **Concept Mastery.** You may wish to use Concept Mastery questions 30 and 33 (chapter-end questions) to make students more aware of the relationship of chemistry to health. A discussion of these questions should help students to understand that even though some fatty foods, like margarine, contain no cholesterol, they can contribute to the manufacture of cholesterol by the body.

### 25-4 Proteins, pp. 742-744, and

### 25-5 Biochemical Reactions and Enzymes, pp. 744-745

| Planning Guide | |
|---|---|
| **Labs (Lab Manual) and Demonstrations (TE)** | **Supplementary Materials (Teacher's Resource Book)** |
| Demo 25-1: Protein Anyone?, p. TG-353 | Transparency Master: Formation of a Peptide Bond, p. 25-5 |

■ You may wish to introduce proteins by doing Demonstration 25-1, "Protein Anyone?" Students observe chemical testing for the presence of protein in food samples.

■ Emphasize the nature of amino acids and their role in the formation of protein molecules by walking students through text Figures 25-13 and 25-14. You may also use the Transparency Master "Formation of a Peptide Bond" and molecular models to illustrate peptide formation. To help students appreciate the size and complexity of protein macromolecules, call attention to the model in text Figure 25-16.

■ Have students recall concepts from Chapter 17 related to the driving forces associated with chemical reactions. Show how enzymes can lower $E_{ACT}$ for many reactions that invole biochemical molecules.

■ **Application.** The chemistry involved in curling hair may be of interest to some students. You may explain that strands of hair protein take particular shapes because of disulfide bonds between different protein chains, thus restricting the motion of the protein molecules. Disulfide bonds can be cleaved by reduction with "thio" ($HSCH_2COOH$) to convert the disulfide bonds in proteins to free —SH groups. As a result, the protein chains have more freedom to move about and to assume new shapes when hair is wound around a curler. The new shapes are then fixed by treating the hair with a mild oxidizing agent such as potassium bromate, $KBrO_3$, which causes new disulfide bonds to form between the protein chains.

■ **Concept Mastery.** Students frequently fail to relate chemistry to their own bodies. You may wish to use Concept Mastery questions 28, 31, and 32 (chapter-end questions) to remind students that their bodies are made of chemicals that are taking part in chemical reactions. In discussing question 32, point out that principles learned in previous chapters, such as limiting reactants, also hold for reactions within their bodies.

### 25-6 Nucleic Acids, pp. 746-749, and

### 25-7 The Role of Energy in Biochemistry, pp. 749-750

| Planning Guide | |
|---|---|
| **Labs (Lab Manual) and Demonstrations (TE)** | **Supplementary Materials (Teacher's Resource Book)** |
| | Review Activity: Biochemistry, p. 25-6 Critical and Creative Thinking: Secondhand Sources, p. CCT-7 |

■ To help students understand the similarities and differences in the structures of RNA and DNA, call attention to text Figures 25-20 and 25-21. Discuss how the letters T, C, A, and G represent the four nitrogen bases shown in text Figure 25-22. Be sure students can identify the lines that represent hydrogen bonds between pairs of these bases in adjacent strands of the double helix.

■ The Review Activity "Biochemistry" is appropriate, at this time, to review the material in Chapter 25.

■ **Critical Thinking.** In the Critical and Creative Thinking worksheet "Secondhand Sources" students assess information given by two advertisements regarding sources of calcium in the diet. The students evaluate the reliability of these secondhand sources, based on the bias of the advertisers. In a follow-up activity this skill is applied to questioning the reliability of a standard reference source, the periodic table.

■ Point out how the laws of thermodynamics apply to biochemical systems. You may want to trace through the logic of the changes in $\Delta G$, $\Delta S$, and $\Delta H$ as described in this section. Explain that despite their superficial resemblence to structural formulas, the diagrams in text Figure 25-24 are simplified models of the compounds represented. Point out that the process shown can harvest energy from one reaction and store that energy as chemical energy in a nearby system. Describe the interplay between exergonic and endergonic reactions, and show how this can result in the net storage of energy for future use.

## Demonstration

### 25-1 Protein Anyone?

**Overview:** In this demonstration, you test several foods for the presence of protein.

**Materials:** concentrated nitric acid ($HNO_3$); concentrated ammonia water; 0.05 $M$ copper sulfate ($CuSO_4$) solution; 6 $M$ potassium hydroxide (KOH) solution; 12 test tubes; test-tube holder; Bunsen burner; various food samples.

**Advance Preparation:** 1. **0.05 $M$ $CuSO_4$**: mix 25.0 g of $CuSO_4 \cdot 5H_2O$ in sufficient water to make 100 mL of solution. 2. **6 $M$ KOH:** mix 5.6 g of KOH in sufficient water to make 100 mL of solution. 3. Select as samples several food items such as nuts, cheese, hard-boiled egg whites, and sugar candy.

**Safety:** Be careful in handling the various chemical substances—in particular, the $HNO_3$ and KOH. Work at a fume hood.

**Procedure:** 1. Place into separate test tubes a small amount of each food to be tested. Cover the samples with concentrated nitric acid, and gently and carefully heat each at a fume hood. Carefully pour off the nitric acid, and rinse the food samples with water. Have students observe the color of the samples. Add a small amount of concentrated ammonia water to each sample. Have students observe the resulting color of the food samples. Tell students that this test for protein is known as the xanthoproteic test. 2. Place fresh samples of foods into separate test tubes. Add one drop of 0.05 $M$ $CuSO_4$ solution and five drops of 6 $M$ KOH solution. Have students observe the resulting color of the samples. Tell the students that this test for protein is known as the Biuret test.

**Results:** The food samples (such as nuts, cheese, and egg white) that contain protein will turn yellow after submersing and heating in nitric acid, and will turn orange after addition of ammonia. The protein-containing samples will also produce a purplish color after addition of copper sulfate and potassium hydroxide solutions.

## Answers to Questions

**Page 740**

1. Biochemistry is the study of the compounds that make up living things and the chemical reactions that are associated with their life processes.

2. **a.** Structural isomers have the same molecular formulas but different structures. Stereoisomers have the same molecular structures but different arrangements of the atoms in space.
   **b.** Glucose and galactose are stereoisomers.

3. When glucose dissolves in water, the carbonyl group does not remain intact. See text Figure 25-5.

4. **a.** Monosaccharides are converted to polysaccharides by polymerization.
   **b.** Polysaccharides are converted to monosaccharides by hydrolysis.
   **c.** In polymerization, a water molecule is lost. In hydrolysis, a water molecule is added.

5. *Glucose:* source of energy.
   *Starch:* storage of energy.
   *Cellulose:* rigid plant structures (wood, cotton).

**Page 742**

6. **a.** The groups of compounds classified as lipids are fats, waxes, phospholipids, and steroids.
   **b.** These compounds are classified together because they all have low solubility in water.

7. **a.** The molecular structures of all fatty acids are alike in that each molecule contains the carboxyl group, −COOH, and a hydrocarbon chain.
   **b.** In the hydrocarbon chain of a saturated fat, there are no double bonds between carbon atoms. In an unsaturated fat, there is one or more double or triple bonds between carbon atoms.

8. **a.** Fats serve as a source of energy.
   **b.** Waxes form waterproof coatings.
   **c.** Phospholipids regulate movement of substances into and out of cells.
   **d.** Steroids are used to build cell membranes.

25

**Page 745**

9. The general formula for an amino acid appears as a marginal annotation on text page 745.

10. **a.** A peptide bond is formed between the nitrogen atom of an amino acid and the carboxylic carbon of other amino acid. See text Figure 25-14.
   **b.** A peptide molecule is formed by bonding two or more amino acids.
   **c.** A protein is a polypeptide made up of 100 or more amino acids.

11. **a.** A protein polymer is produced by the formation of many peptide bonds.
   **b.** A protein polymer is broken down by hydrolysis. As water is added, the polypeptide breaks down into protein monomers.
   **c.** Water is removed during polymerization. Water is added during hydrolysis.

12. Several types of proteins and their functions are given in text Figure 25-17.

13. Enzymes act as catalysts for many biochemical reactions. These enzymes control the rate of reaction of substrate molecules.

14. A substrate molecule "just fits" onto the proper enzyme molecule. The enzyme weakens the bonds of the substrate, thereby allowing the substrate to be converted to the intended product.

**Page 748**

15. **a.** Nucleic acids are macromolecules that control the development of organisms and production of substances essential to life.
   **b.** A nucleotide is made up of a 5-carbon sugar, a phosphate, and a ring-shaped nitrogen-containing base. See text Figure 25-20.
   **c.** In DNA, the sugar is deoxyribose and in RNA the sugar is ribose.

16. Condensation polymerization reactions occur when nucleotides form nucleic acids.

17. **a.** In a single strand of DNA, the sugar of one nucleotide molecule is bonded to the phosphate of another nucleotide molecule.
   **b.** Hydrogen bonding between pairs of nitrogen-containing bases holds together the two strands in the DNA double helix.

**Page 750**

18. **a.** $\Delta H$ is defined as change in enthalpy.
   **b.** $\Delta S$ is defined as change in entropy.
   **c.** $\Delta G$ is defined as change in free energy.

19. **a.** An endergonic reaction is not spontaneous. Its value for $\Delta G$ is positive.
   **b.** An exergonic reaction is spontaneous. Its value for $\Delta G$ is negative.

20. The free energy available from an exergonic reaction drives a nearby endergonic reaction.

## Chapter Review    25

**Page 751, Content Review**

1. The four classes of biochemical compounds are carbohydrates, lipids, proteins, and nucleic acids.

2. The general formula of carbohydrates is $(CH_2O)_n$.

3. The carbonyl group is located at an end position in the molecule in aldehyde sugars and at an interior position in a ketone sugar.

4. Simple sugars (monosaccharides) are formed during the hydrolysis of a polysaccharide.

5. The reaction is called dehydration synthesis because during the synthesis of the disaccharide, one molecule of water is produced from the two simple sugars.

6. Body fat stores energy and serves as a shock absorber and as insulation.

7. Fats are digested by hydrolysis, which causes the polymers to break down into monomers.

8. Lipids dissolve in nonpolar organic solvents, such as ether and benzene.

9. Protein is digested by hydrolysis. With the addition of water, the protein breaks down into amino acids.

10. There are 20 different amino acids.

11. Polypeptide chains may link together by various means including hydrogen bonds, ionic bonds, and bonds between sulfur atoms.

12. An enzyme is a protein that acts as a catalyst for a biochemical reaction.

13. Only small amounts of enzyme are needed to catalyze large amounts of substrate because the enzyme is not changed or used up during the biochemical reaction.

14. High activation energies protect organic molecules from uncontrolled and undesirable reactions.

15. The three parts making up a nucleotide are a 5-carbon sugar, a phosphate group, and a ring-shaped base containing nitrogen.

16. **a.** Adenine, cytosine, guanine, and thymine are the nitrogen bases found in DNA nucleotides.
   **b.** Adenine, cytosine, guanine, and uracil are the bases found in RNA.

17. In the DNA double helix, adenine and thymine bind together and cytosine and guanine bind together.

18. The energy stored in ATP's phosphate bonds can be used to drive certain endergonic reactions.

### Page 752, Content Mastery

19. Starch and cellulose are examples of polysaccharides.

20. Two molecules having the same structure but in a different arrangement in space are called optical isomers, or steroisomers.

21. A peptide bond is formed when proteins are synthesized via polymerization of amino acid monomers.

22. A biological catalyst is called an enzyme and is a protein.

23. The general formula for carbohydrates is $(CH_2O)_n$. From this formula we can see that there are twice as many hydrogen atoms as carbon atoms. Therefore, the number of hydrogen atoms is $2 \times 36$, or 72.

24. The principal source of energy for living things is carbohydrates.

25. The body efficiently "couples" an endergonic reaction with an exergonic reaction. The exergonic reaction provides energy to drive the endergonic reaction.

26. Polypeptides contain ten or more amino acid monomers; proteins contain 100 or more amino acid monomers. Thus, all proteins are polypeptides, but not all polypeptides are proteins.

27. Number of nucleotides per DNA molecule equals
$$\frac{1 \times 10^7 \text{ g/mol DNA}}{3 \times 10^2 \text{ g/mol nucleotides}} =$$
$$3 \times 10^4 \text{ nucleotides per DNA molecule}$$
Number of nucleotides per RNA molecule equals
$$\frac{3 \times 10^4 \text{ g/mol RNA}}{3 \times 10^2 \text{ g/mol nucleotides}} =$$
$$1 \times 10^2 \text{ nucleotides per RNA molecule}$$

### Page 752, Concept Mastery

28. *Concept:* *The human body is composed of biochemicals.*
    *Solution:* If it were not a chemical, it would have to be a form of energy, as matter and energy make up the physical world.

29. *Concept:* *Complex sugars have the same chemical properties as simple sugars once they hydrolyze.*
    *Solution:* The sucrose changes to fructose when it comes in contact with water. Therefore, the chemical reactions would be the same.

30. *Concept:* *Animal fats contain cholesterol.*
    *Solution:* Lard and butter are both animal fats that contain cholesterol. Margarine is made from vegetable oils. Although it does not contain cholesterol, it contains saturated fats which are known to cause the body to manufacture cholesterol.

31. *Concept:* *Chemical reactions occur in the body.*
    *Solution:* When the chemical reactions occur in your body, they produce heat. The excess heat from uncontrolled reactions that occur when you are ill cause an increase in body temperature.

32. *Concept:* *Enzymes are catalysts.*
    *Solution:* Small additions of the enzyme will increase the reaction rate. Excessive amounts will not increase the reaction rate because the carbohydrate is the limiting reactant. If the enzyme is not eliminated from the saliva, since it is a catalyst, it should be regenerated.

32. *Concept:* *Margarine is a fat that contains saturated fats.*
    *Solution:* Because margarine contains saturated fats, and saturated fats cause the body to produce cholesterol, margarine intake should be limited.

### Page 752, Cumulative Review

34. **d.** The alkali metal family is most reactive.

35. **a.** Sulfur is mined by the Frasch process.

36. **c.** A carbon atom has four valence electrons.

37. During boiling, heat energy causes the molecules to overcome the forces of attraction in the liquid. The molecules now become freely moving particles in the gaseous phase.

38. The crystal lattice of ice is an open structure which, when the ice melts, collapses. As a result, liquid water is denser than ice.

39. Silver: $150 \text{ g}/10.5 \text{ g/cm}^3 = 14.3 \text{ cm}^3$
    Gold: $100 \text{ g}/19.3 \text{ g/cm}^3 = 5.18 \text{ cm}^3$
    The silver occupies $14.3 \text{ cm} - 5.18 \text{ cm}^3$
    $= 9.1 \text{ cm}^3$ more volume.

40. This energy is used to remove valence electrons from sodium atoms and to break the bonds between chlorine atoms in diatomic molecules of chlorine.

41. The $CO_2$ molecule is a three-atom, linear molecule with the carbon atom in the middle. In this symmetrical structure, the polarities of the carbon-to-oxygen bonds counterbalance each other. The $H_2O$ molecule is nonsymmetrical with the two hydrogen-to-oxygen bonds forming an approximate right angle that leaves a partial positive

25

charge at the hydrogen end of the molecule and a partial negative charge at the other end.

42. 1 mol of $NO_2$ has: 1 mol = 14.0 g N and 2 mol × 16.0 g/mol = 32 g O, total 46 g. 14 g/46 g = 30% N; 32 g/46 g = 70% O

43. 50.0 cm$^3$ × 1.50 g/cm$^3$ = 75.0 g of solution 60% × 75.0 g = 45 g $H_2SO_4$

## Page 753, Critical Thinking

44. Glucose and fructose are two simple sugars that form sucrose when they are bonded together in a particular way. Glucose and fructose are monosaccharides, or monomers; sucrose is a disaccharide.

45. Simple sugars have many polar OH groups, so they readily dissolve in a polar solvent, such as water.

46. Yes, female hormones (estrogens) are steroids because they have the same four-ring structure as testosterone (which is a steroid).

47. Protein from animals is more likely than protein from plants to have the balance of amino acids the body requires because animal protein is much more like that found in the human body.

48. The "wasted" energy could be used to provide heat to maintain the proper body temperature, which is approximately 37°C.

49. The general formula for carbohydrates is $(CH_2O)_n$. This formula is a carbon atom and a water molecule and appears to be a hydrated carbon atom. Thus, the name carbohydrates is derived from carbon and hydrate.

50. In the DNA double helix, adenine and thymine bind together and guanine and cytosine bind together.

## Page 753, Challenge Problems

51. An inhibitor is a molecule that is structurally similar to a substrate but not identical; that is, it looks like the right key. Its structure is close enough that it binds to the active site on the enzyme; that is, the key goes into the lock. When the key is turned, however, a real substrate is catalyzed by the enzyme and released, leaving the enzyme free to bind other substrates. An inhibitor gets stuck in the lock, thus preventing the enzyme from binding to other substrates and catalyzing any more reactions.

52. **a.** Saturated. There are no C-C double bonds.
    **b.** Unsaturated. There are two $CHCHCH_2$ groups, each of which has 2 C-C double bonds.
    **c.** Saturated. There are no C-C double bonds.
    **d.** Unsaturated. There is one C-C double bond: $CH_3(CH_2)_5CH=CH(CH_2)_7COOH$

53. In Section 24-10, it is mentioned that addition reactions are much more characteristic of unsaturated hydrocarbons than of saturated hydrocarbons. Bromine is one of the more active halogens that will take part in addition reactions. A simple test to determine whether a fat was saturated would be to put a sample of the fat in a test tube with some bromine. Shake. If a reaction takes place, the fat is unsaturated. If not, the fat is saturated.

# Nuclear Chemistry

**26**

## Chapter Planning Guide

| Text Section | Labs (Lab Manual) and Demonstrations (TE) | Supplementary Materials (Teacher's Resource Book) |
|---|---|---|
| **26-1** Changes in the Nucleus, pp. 755-756<br><br>**26-2** Types of Radiation, pp. 756-757 | Demo 26-1: Detection of Radioactivity, p. TG-361<br>Lab 51: Radioactivity<br>Demo 26-2: Distance, Shielding, and Radiation, p. TG-362 | Transparency Master: Separation of Alpha, Beta, and Gamma Radiation by Charged Plates, p. 26-2<br>Review Activity: Radiation, p. 26-5<br>Critical and Creative Thinking: Identifying Reasons, p. CCT-27 |
| **26-3** Half-Life, pp. 757-759<br><br>**26-4** Natural Radioactivity, pp. 559-760<br><br>**26-5** The Uranium-238 Decay Series, pp. 760-763<br><br>**Biography** Chien-Shiung Wu, p. 759 | Demo 26-3: Simulation of Half-Life, p. TG-362<br>Lab 52: Determining Half-Life | Practice Problems, p. 26-8<br>Concept Mastery: Half-Life, p. CM-35<br>Transparency Master: The Uranium-238 Decay Series, p. 26-3 |
| **26-6** Artificial Radioactivity (Induced Radioactivity), pp. 763-765<br><br>**26-7** Biological Effects of Radiation, pp. 765-766<br><br>**26-8** Beneficial Uses of Radiation, pp. 766-767 | | |
| **26-9** Radioactive Dating, p. 768 | | |
| **26-10** Particle Accelerators, pp. 768-769 | | |
| **26-11** Nuclear Energy: The Mass-Energy Relation, pp. 770-771<br><br>**26-12** Nuclear Fission, pp. 772-773<br><br>**26-13** Fission Reactors, pp. 773-775<br><br>**26-14** Fusion Reactions, pp. 775-776 | Demo 26-4: A Chain Reaction, p. TG-363 | Transparency Master: The Reaction of a Proton with Lithium-7, p. 26-4<br>Review Activity: Nuclear Reactions, p. 26-6<br>Societal Issues: Nuclear Energy, p. SI-50 |

26

| Text Section | Labs (Lab Manual) and Demonstrations (TE) | Supplementary Materials (Teacher's Resource Book) |
|---|---|---|
| | | Test—Form A, p. AT-99<br>Alternate Test—Form B, p. BT-99 |

☐ Core    ■ Advanced    ☐ Optional

## Chapter Overview

We begin Chapter 26 with an account of the discovery of radioactivity, noting the contributions of Becquerel, the Curies, and Rutherford. We distinguish alpha, beta, and gamma radiation and then explain the concept of half-life. Students acquire the skill of writing equations for nuclear reactions, including some that occur naturally in the U-238 decay series and some that are brought about artificially.

The balance of the chapter focuses primarily on practical applications of nuclear chemistry. We describe the adverse biological effects of radiation as well as its uses in medicine, industry, and research, including radioactive dating. Particle accelerators, radioactive dating, and Einstein's mass-energy relation are explained. We describe nuclear fission reactions and the uses of fission reactors for nuclear power. The chapter concludes with a discussion of nuclear fusion reactions and the experimental fusion reactor.

## Chapter Objectives

After students have completed this chapter, they will be able to:
1. Compare natural and induced radioactivity.
   *26-1 to 26-6*
2. Write nuclear equations for the decay of alpha and beta emitters in the U-238 series, the first artificial transmutation, and the synthesis of Pu-239.
   *26-4 to 26-14*
3. Describe the use of U-238 and C-14 in dating.
   *26-9*
4. Compare three types of particle accelerators.
   *26-10*
5. Solve problems based on the Einstein formula $E = mc^2$.
   *26-11*
6. Distinguish between nuclear fission and fusion and describe reactions of both types.   *26-12 to 26-14*
7. Describe and discuss some benefits and problems of nuclear energy.   *26-7 and 26-8*

## Teaching Suggestions

### 26-1 Changes in the Nucleus, pp. 755-756, and

### 26-2 Types of Radiation, pp. 756-757

| Planning Guide | |
|---|---|
| Labs (Lab Manual) and Demonstrations (TE) | Supplementary Materials (Teacher's Resource Book) |
| Demo 26-1: Detection of Radioactivity, p. TG-361<br>Lab 51: Radioactivity<br>Demo 26-2: Distance, Shielding, and Radiation, p. TG-362 | Transparency Master: Separation of Alpha, Beta, and Gamma Radiation by Charged Plates, p. 26-2<br>Review Activity: Radiation, p. 26-5<br>Critical and Creative Thinking: Identifying Reasons, p. CCT-27 |

■ To open the chapter, discuss with students the nature of background radiation. Explain that we are continually being bombarded by cosmic rays, ultraviolet rays, and other radiation from the sun and stars. We are also hit by radiation from radioactive materials in the earth beneath us and in building materials. Save the details of the nuclear reactions that result in such radiation for your discussion of Sections 26-4 and 26-5.

Take advantage of the fascination most students have with the Geiger counter by using it to demonstrate the presence of background radiation. You may wish to do steps 1 to 3 of Demonstration 26-1, "Detection of Radioactivity," in which you first test a classroom-safe radioactive source and then test for background radiation. Alternatively, you may do Part A of Lab 51, "Radioactivity," in which you first test for background radiation and then compare the results with those obtained from radioactive sources.

■ Although X rays are caused by electron displacement and not by nuclear change, they are related historically to the discovery of radioactivity. You may want to point out not only some differences between the two types but also some similiarities of the two types of radiation, such as the use of both in treating cancer.

■ Use the Transparency Master "Separation of Alpha,

Beta, and Gamma Radiation by Charged Plates" to help students differentiate between the three types of radiation given off by radioactive substances.

■ Next, you may wish to proceed with steps 4 and 5 of Demonstration 26-1, "Detection of Radioactivity," showing students how an electroscope and a cloud chamber can also be used to detect radioactivity.

■ To demonstrate some properties of radiation, complete Parts B and C (after doing Part A if it was not done before) of Lab 51, "Radioactivity," in which students observe the shielding effects of different materials and the relationship between distance and radiation. Alternatively, you can use Demonstration 26-2, "Distance, Shielding, and Radiation," to show some properties of the different kinds of radiation.

■ The Review Activity "Radiation" is appropriate for use after Section 26-2.

■ **Critical Thinking.** Becquerel's experiment is the subject of the Critical and Creative Thinking worksheet "Identifying Reasons," which is appropriate for use with Section 26-2.

## 26-3 Half-Life, pp. 757-759,

## 26-4 Natural Radioactivity, pp. 759-760, and

## 26-5 The Uranium-238 Decay Series, pp. 760-763

| Planning Guide | |
|---|---|
| **Labs (Lab Manual) and Demonstrations (TE)** | **Supplementary Materials (Teacher's Resource Book)** |
| Demo 26-3: Simulation of Half-Life, p. TG-362 Lab 52: Determining Half-Life | Practice Problems, p. 26-8 Concept Mastery: Half-Life, p. CM-35 Transparency Master: The Uranium-238 Decay Series, p. 26-3 |

■ You may begin your discussion of half-life with Demonstration 26-3, "Simulation of Half-Life." Pennies are used to simulate decay of a radioactive substance and to determine a quantity analogous to half-life. Then have students study text Figure 26-4 to help clarify the concept.

■ Use Laboratory 52, "Determining Half-Life," to demonstrate how the Geiger counter can be used to determine the half-lives of two radioisotopes, iodine-131 and phosphorus-32. Students record data observed over a period of weeks and construct graphs of the data.

■ The Practice Problems worksheet (TRB) can be used to give students further practice with half-life calculations.

■ Although radioactive dating is described in detail in Section 26-9, you may want to point out now that such dating is an important application of half-life, and give some examples of how it works.

■ Use the Transparency Master "The Uranium-238 Decay Series" to help students understand the sequence of changes in nuclei from U-238 to Pb-206.

■ **Concept Mastery.** When discussing Concept Mastery question 31 (chapter-end question), be aware that some students may be confused about the change in the charge on the nucleus when a beta particle is emitted. The students' intuition leads them to the erroneous conclusion that if a particle is emitted from the nucleus, the atomic number of the atom decreases, rather than increases. That is, some students expect that beta emission will produce a nucleus with a less positive charge rather than one with a more positive charge. You may wish to ask students to cite similarities and differences between the loss of an electron in a chemical reaction and the loss of an electron (beta particle) in a nuclear reaction.

Students often make errors with half-life calculations because they confuse the reactant remaining with the product formed when using the half-life equation. The Concept Mastery worksheet "Half-Life" (TRB) can help students to overcome this by visualizing the decay process.

## 26-6 Artificial Radioactivity (Induced Radioactivity), pp. 763-765,

## 26-7 Biological Effects of Radiation, pp. 765-766, and

## 26-8 Beneficial Uses of Radiation, pp. 766-767

■ In your discussion of artificial (induced) radioactivity, emphasize the contributions of Rutherford, who produced the first artificial transmutation that resulted in a stable isotope, and of the Joliot-Curies, who carried out the first artificial transmutation that resulted in a radioisotope. You may challenge students to suggest how some elements might be changed to radioisotopes without undergoing transmutation and then show them how the Joliot-Curies achieved this with NaCl.

■ Have students recall from their study of biology the distinction between *somatic* and *genetic*. An example of a somatic effect of excessive radiation is the uncontrolled production of white blood cells (leukemia). Genetic effects include birth defects.

■ When discussing how radiation may be beneficial, you may want to give students the following additional examples. Radioimmunoassay (RIA) uses radiotracers to detect early stages of disease. By monitoring the rate of glucose metabolism in the brain, positron emission transaxial tomography (PET) can detect early stages of serious ailments.

■ **Application.** You may want to discuss with students

26

a clever approach to using radiation for killing cancer cells known as boron-10 neutron-capture therapy. When boron is bombarded with neutrons, alpha particles are released according to the following equation:

$$^{10}_{5}B + ^{1}_{0}n \rightarrow ^{7}_{3}Li + ^{4}_{2}He$$

Because neutrons are uncharged, they readily pass through body tissue and interact specifically with boron atoms. Neither boron nor lithium is radioactive; therefore, neither presents a radiation hazard. The alpha particles that form, however, are the most massive of the common forms of radiation and therefore, are, the most destructive to tumor cells. The strategy is to bind the boron to some chemical compound, deliver the compound to a tumor site, and then radiate from outside the body with a source of neutrons. Even a small dose of boron can result in exposure to alpha particles exactly where the radiation is needed and with relatively little damage to healthy tissues.

■ **Concept Mastery.** Students have heard much about radioactivity from the media and may have many ideas about it that conflict with reality. Two of these are illustrated in Concept Mastery questions 33 to 35 (chapter-end questions). You may need to point out that the emission or absorption of a neutron does not necessarily produce a new element. It may simply produce a different isotope of the same element that may be unstable and decompose or emit radiation (question 33). Explain that if everything that has been exposed to radiation became radioactive, then everything on earth would be radioactive because the earth is continually being bombarded by cosmic rays (question 34).

The human species has always been exposed to some form of radiation and has adapted to it. You may use Concept Mastery question 32 (chapter-end question) to make this point. You can ask students to make other calculations about their exposure to radiation over their lifetime.

## 26-9 Radioactive Dating, p. 768

■ In your discussion of radioactive dating, emphasize why different naturally occurring radioisotopes are ued for dating objects of different origins and ages. For dating mineral objects with ages over 40 000 years, the measurement of uranium-238 and its decay product lead-206 is suitable because of the relatively long half-life of uranium-238. For dating objects of organic origin up to the age of 40 000 years, the measurement of carbon-14 and carbon-12 (as detailed in Section 26-9) is suitable not only because of the relatively short half-life of carbon-14 but also because carbon-14 is assimilated by organisms only as long as they remain alive.

■ **Application.** You might want to make students aware of the Rb-87/Sr-87 method of radioactive dating, known as the rubidium-strontium clock. It is suitable for dating mineral objects older than about 40 000 years. The Rb-87/Sr-87 approach is based on the following reaction:

$$^{87}_{37}Rb \rightarrow ^{87}_{38}Sr + ^{0}_{-1}e$$

Rubidium-87 has a half-life of $4.7 \times 10^{16}$ years, and strontium-87 is not radioactive. Thus, while the amount of Rb-87 steadily decreases with age, the amount of Sr-87 increases. By comparing the amounts of the two isotopes in a rock sample, its age can be determined. This technique has been used to find the age of the earth (4.5 billion years) and to date some samples of rock ($3.3 \times 10^{10}$ years) brought back from the moon during the Apollo 15 mission.

## 26-10 Particle Accelerators, pp. 768-769

■ In discussing particle accelerators, you may want to describe the gradual increase in speeds achieved since their introduction. The first cyclotron accelerated protons to energies equivalent to 80 000 electron-volts. Improved cyclotrons and synchrotrons produce energies of about 400 million electron-volts and the cosmotron produces hundreds of billions of electron-volts.

Use text Figure 26-13 to discuss with students each part of the cyclotron. Have students note that the electrical and/or magnetic fields in accelerators speed up only charged particles, so that neutrons cannot be used as "bullets."

## 26-11 Nuclear Energy: The Mass-Energy Relation, pp. 770-771,

## 26-12 Nuclear Fission, pp. 772-773,

## 26-13 Fission Reactors, pp. 773-775, and

## 26-14 Fusion Reactions, pp. 775-776

| Planning Guide | |
|---|---|
| **Labs (Lab Manual) and Demonstrations (TE)** | **Supplementary Materials (Teacher's Resource Book)** |
| Demo 26-4: A Chain Reaction, p. TG-363 | Transparency Master: The Reaction of a Proton with Lithium-7, p. 26-4 Review Activity: Nuclear Reactions, p. 26-6 Societal Issues: Nuclear Energy, p. SI-50 |

■ To help students appreciate how much energy, theoretically, is available from a small amount of mass by the Einstein equation, you may use the following example. One gram of matter converted to energy would produce $9 \times 10^{13}$ J, equal to burning 3000 tons of coal, or enough energy to allow a 30-watt bulb to burn continuously for 1000 years.

■ Use the Transparency Master "The Reaction of a Proton with Lithium-7" to help students see how the amount of energy emitted is equivalent to the loss of mass when measured experimentally or when using the Einstein equation.

■ Discuss text Figures 26-15 and 26-16 in detail to help students understand the concepts of nuclear fission and chain reactions. Then have students examine text Figure 26-17, showing how a chain reaction is controlled in a fission reactor. Students should be able to relate the diagram in Figure 26-16 to that in Figure 26-17. You may wish to do Demonstration 26-4, "A Chain Reaction," to simulate the role of the control rods in a fission reactor.

■ Compare and contrast nuclear fission and nuclear fusion reactions. Have students note that both produce energy, one by breaking down nuclei and the other by building up nuclei. Discuss the advantages of the fusion reactors, which may be used as a practical energy source in the future, over the fission reactors that are not in use. You may want to discuss the problems of making the fusion reactor workable. These include the possibility of thermal pollution of the atmosphere and nearby bodies of water and the application of the technology of fusion reactors to thermonuclear weapons. Use the Societal Issues worksheet "Nuclear Energy" to present both sides of the nuclear power controversy.

■ The Review Activity "Nuclear Reactions" is suitable for use at the end of Section 26-14.

# Demonstrations

## 26-1 Detection of Radioactivity

**Overview:** In this demonstration, you use a Geiger counter, electroscope, and cloud chamber to detect radiation from various radioactive sources, including a smoke detector, luminous watch dial, and classroom-safe radioactive sources procured from suppliers. You also demonstrate the existence of background radiation.

**Materials:** Geiger counter; electroscope; alpha source; beta and/or gamma source; smoke detector; old watch with luminous dial; rubber rod; piece of fur; cloud chamber (commercially available); ethanol; dry ice; tongs; gloves; flashlight with powerful beam.

**Safety:** Use only radioactive sources that are classroom-safe and designed for the purpose, and follow the directions that accompany them. Do not directly touch any radioactive substances. Also, be careful in using the dry ice. Wear gloves and use tongs during handling. Caution students not to look directly into the flashlight beam.

**Procedure:** 1. Bring a classroom-safe radioactive source (obtained from a supplier) close to the tube of the Geiger counter, and have students note the results. First use an alpha emitter and then a beta and/or gamma emitter. 2. Remove all radioactive sources from the area of the Geiger counter, turn on the counter for a set period of 2 minutes, and have students note and attempt to explain what occurs. Repeat this process two or three times. 3. Use the Geiger counter to test a smoke detector and an old watch with a luminous dial. 4. Use fur to rub a rubber rod. Touch the knob of an electroscope with the charged rod to produce a negative charge on the electroscope. Bring a classroom-safe radioactive source near the knob of the charged electroscope and have students note the result. 5. Pour some ethanol into the cloud chamber, and allow the absorbent material around the sides of the chamber to become saturated with the alcohol. Insert a classroom-safe radioactive alpha source into the chamber, and place the chamber onto several large pieces of dry ice. Allow 5 minutes for the chamber to become cold. Turn off the classroom lights, darken the room as much as possible, and shine a powerful beam of light at an angle through the top on the sides of the chamber. Ask students to describe what they observe. Replace the alpha source with a beta source, and repeat the process.

**Results:** In step 1, the number of counts per minute (cpm) for the beta and/or gamma source is likely to be greater than that for the alpha source. In step 2, the Geiger counter should detect background radiation whose cpm will be much lower than that for the radioactive sources. This background count is due to all types of radiation in the environment and to cosmic rays from space. The background count will not be exactly the same for the various 2-minute intervals. In step 3, the smoke detector and watch should produce cpm higher than the background source, but probably not as high as those produced by the sources from suppliers. In step 4, when the charged rod touches the knob of the electroscope, the knob and leaves will become negatively charged and the leaves will repel each other and move apart. When a radioactive source is brought near the knob, the air around the knob will become ionized by the radiation. The positive charges around the knob will cause electrons to move up from the leaves, and the leaves will no longer repel each other and, consequently, will come together. In step 5, vapor trails should be visible in the cloud chamber. Alpha particles will leave shorter, thicker tracks than will the faster-moving beta particles.

## 26-2 Distance, Shielding, and Radiation

**Overview:** In this demonstration, you record the counts per minute (cpm) for a radioactive source at various distances from a Geiger-counter tube to show a mathematical relationship between cpm detected and distance. You also determine what type of shielding is needed to stop alpha radiation and beta and/or gamma radiation.

**Materials:** Geiger counter; classroom-safe sources of radioactivity (alpha, and beta and/or gamma emitters); ruler; thin sheets of paper, of cardboard, of aluminum, and of lead, cut into small squares roughly 6 cm × 6 cm.

**Advance Preparation:** Cut the paper, cardboard, and metal sheets into the 6 cm × 6 cm squares.

**Safety:** Use only radioactive sources that are classroom-safe and designed for the purpose, and follow the directions that accompany them.

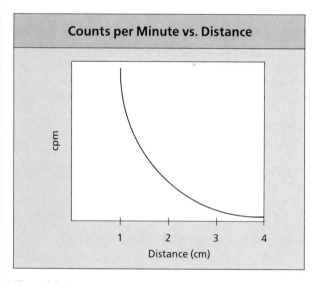

**Figure 26-1**

**Procedure:** 1. Find the background count over a 2-minute interval. Record and repeat this process two or three more times, and record the average cpm. 2. Place an alpha emitter about 4 cm from the Geiger counter tube for 2 min, and have students record the resulting cpm, after first subtracting the average background count. Have students plot cpm ($y$-axis) versus distance of source from the Geiger-counter tube ($x$-axis). Ask them to describe the resulting curve. 4. Place an alpha emitter 2 cm from the tube, place 1 sheet of paper between the source and the tube, and find the average background corrected cpm. Repeat, keeping the distance constant and using more sheets of paper until the cpm is reduced essentially to the background

count. Repeat the same procedure, using sheets of cardboard, then sheets of aluminum, and, finally, sheets of lead. Have students compare the materials' abilities to act as shields against alpha particles. 6. Repeat step 4, using a beta and/or gamma emitter.

**Results:** The curve produced in step 4 should illustrate an inverse square relationship of the general shape shown in accompanying Figure 26-1. (Vertical-axis units will depend upon the particular source used.) In step 4, alpha radiation essentially will be stopped by a few sheets of cardboard, relatively few sheets of paper, 1 sheet of lead, and 1–2 sheets of aluminum. Beta and/or gamma radiation will not be affected significantly by the paper; a relatively large number of sheets of aluminum or several sheets of lead will be required to essentially stop the radiation.

## 26-3 Simulation of Half-Life

**Overview:** Pennies are used to simulate radioactive decay and to determine a quantity analogous to half-life.

**Materials:** 80 pennies; shoe box or cigar box with lid.

**Advance Preparation:** Place all 80 pennies, with the head side up, inside the box.

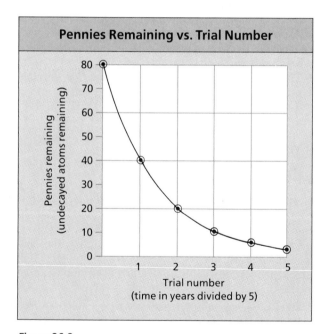

**Figure 26-2**

**Procedure:** 1. Show the class that the box contains 80 pennies, all with the head side up. 2. Shake the box thoroughly and set it down. Have a student volunteer remove all of the pennies with the tail side facing upward. Record the number of pennies that are left. 3. Repeat step 2 four times (to give a total of 5 trials).

4. Have students graph the number of pennies remaining ($y$-axis) versus the trial number ($x$-axis). Tell students that trial number, or shake number, is analogous to time in decay situations, and that the number of heads-up pennies is analogous to the number of undecayed atoms remaining. Then ask students: If each trial is assumed to represent 5 years, what is the "half-life" revealed by analyzing the graph?

**Results:** After each trial shake, about half of the pennies remaining at the end of the preceding trial will have the head side facing upward. The graph of pennies left versus trial number should be an inverse relationship (see accompanying Figure 26-2). The "half-life" is the "time" (number of trials × 5) required for the number of "undecayed atoms" (heads-up pennies) to be cut in half. The "time" required in this case is 5 years (1 trial).

### 26-4 A Chain Reaction

**Overview:** In this demonstration, you set up dominoes to simulate a chain reaction and to simulate the role of the control rods in a fission reactor.

**Materials:** box of dominoes

**Advance Preparation:** none

**Procedure:** 1. Discuss the fission of uranium-235 by a neutron. Write the nuclear equation for this reaction on the board:

$$^{235}_{92}U + ^{1}_{0}n \rightarrow ^{92}_{36}Kr + ^{141}_{56}Ba + 3^{1}_{0}n + energy$$

Tell students that each of the 3 neutrons released can start another fission reaction and that this overall process, called a chain reaction, can proceed very rapidly. 2. Illustrate this concept, using a domino setup: Set up 21 dominoes in a triangular (bowling-pin-type) arrangement, with one domino in the front row, two in the second row, etc. (the sixth row should have six dominoes in it). The space between each pair of rows should be slightly more than half of the length of a domino. Tip over the first domino, so that it causes the second row to tip over, and so on. Have students get a sense of the number of dominoes that fall. 3. Set up the dominoes as before. Ask students to suggest some ways to slow down or stop this domino effect. Remove some dominoes from the setup and tip over the first domino again. Repeat, restoring the removed dominoes and removing a different set of them. Try this repeatedly, having students observe the various results. Ask students what controls the fission rate in nuclear fission reactors.

**Results:** In step 2, all of the dominoes should fall. Removal of dominoes will cause the total number of fallen dominoes to decrease significantly in ways that depend upon the number and specific positions of the dominoes removed. (If the second row of dominoes is removed, for example, the entire process will be stopped.) Cadmium or boron control rods whose number and position depend upon the desired rate of fission absorb neutrons in a fission reactor.

## Answers to Questions

**Page 758**
1. X rays are electromagnetic waves with short $\lambda$.
2. It ionizes air, causes phosphorescent materials to glow, kills bacteria, and raises the temperature of surrounding air.
3. Transmutation involves the change of an element into an entirely different one.
4. **a.** Alpha rays are deflected toward the negative plate. Beta rays are deflected toward the positive plate. Gamma rays are not deflected by an electric field. **b.** The penetrating power of gamma rays is greater than that of beta rays, which is greater than that of alpha rays. **c.** The ionizing ability of gamma rays is greater than that of alpha rays, which is greater than that of beta rays.
5. **a.** The half-life of an isotope is the time it takes for one-half of the atoms of the sample to decay. **b.** After four half-lives, 1/16 of the original mass of the isotope remains.
6. In 48 days, there are 6 cycles of the 8-day half-life period. Therefore, 4.00 g × $(1/2)^6$ = 0.062 g of the mass remaining after 48 days.
7. While the mass decreases from 8.00 g to 0.25 g, five half-life periods pass. Therefore, the half-life is 30 days/5 = 6.0 days.
8. **a.** See accompanying Figure 26-3.

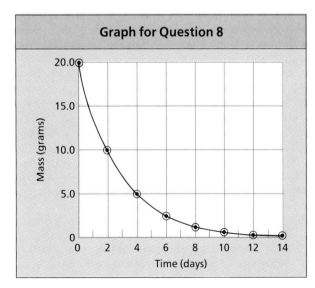

**Figure 26-3**

**b.** 14 days/2 days per half-life = 7 half-lives.
20.0 g × $(1/2)^7$ = 0.156 g remaining.

$$\frac{0.156 \text{ g}}{20.0 \text{ g}} \times 100\% = 0.78\% \text{ of the original mass}$$

remaining after 14 days.

## Page 763

**9. a.** A nuclear reaction is one that involves changes in the nuclei of atoms. **b.** Alpha emission causes the mass number to decrease by 4 and the nuclear charge to decrease by 2.

**10.** Both types of equations (chemical and nuclear) must be balanced with respect to charge and mass. However, in a nuclear reaction, new elements are produced whereas in a chemical reaction new combinations of elements are produced.

**11. a.** The change of a neutron to a proton is responsible for the emission of an electron. **b.** The mass number remains the same and the nuclear charge (atomic number) increases by 1 unit when an electron is emitted from a nucleus.

**12. a.** A beta particle (electron). **b.** An alpha particle.

**13. a.** A radioactive series is a chain of transmutations starting with a radioactive isotope and ending with a nonradioactive element. **b.** Three radioactive series are the U-238 series, the Th-232 series, and the U-235 series. **c.** A stable isotope of lead is the final element produced by these series.

**14. a.** $^{214}_{84}\text{PO} \rightarrow {}^{210}_{82}\text{Pb} + {}^{4}_{2}\text{He}$
  **b.** $^{214}_{83}\text{Bi} \rightarrow {}^{214}_{84}\text{Po} + {}^{0}_{-1}\text{e}$
  **c.** $^{210}_{84}\text{Po} \rightarrow {}^{206}_{82}\text{Pb} + {}^{4}_{2}\text{He}$

## Page 767

**15. a.** In the first case of artificial transmutation, nitrogen was changed to an isotope of oxygen.
  **b.** Ernest Rutherford. **c.** Rutherford bombarded nitrogen gas with alpha particles.

**16. a.** Irene and Frederic Joliot-Curie bombarded aluminum with alpha particles. **b.** Phosphorus-30 was produced. **c.** Phosphorus-30 is radioactive whereas oxygen-17 is stable.

**17. a.** $^{27}_{13}\text{Al} + {}^{4}_{2}\text{He} \rightarrow {}^{30}_{15}\text{P} + {}^{1}_{0}\text{n}$
  **b.** $^{30}_{15}\text{P} \rightarrow {}^{30}_{14}\text{Si} + {}^{0}_{1}\text{e}$

**18. a.** The positron has the same mass as the electron but its charge is 1+. **b.** Antimatter is a collection of antiparticles, which are particles of the same mass but of opposite charge.

**19. a.** neutrons;
  **b.** $^{23}_{11}\text{Na} + {}^{1}_{0}\text{n} \rightarrow {}^{24}_{11}\text{Na}$; **c.** $^{37}_{17}\text{Cl} + {}^{1}_{0}\text{n} \rightarrow {}^{38}_{17}\text{Cl}$

**20.** A rem is the unit used to measure exposure of living things to radiation.

**21. a.** A tracer is a radioactive isotope that can be followed in its movements with a radiation counter. **b.** Radioactive phosphorus can be fed to plant roots. Its position in the plant will tell how much and how fast the phosphorus is absorbed by the plant.

**22.** 67 + (50 to 100) + 2 + 20 mrems = 139 to 189 mrems ≈ 140 to 190 mrems per year

## Page 769

**23. a.** Radioactive dating is the determination of the age of rocks, relics, and past events by use of radioactive isotopes. **b.** After one half-life, a 1-gram sample of U-238 will produce 0.43 g of Pb-206 and 0.07 g of He. One-half of the original gram of U-238 will remain. The age of the mineral can be determined by comparing the actual amount of U-238 in the sample to the amount of Pb-206 or He present.

**24.** The ratio of C-14 to C-12 in a living organism is the same as in the atmosphere. When the organism dies, the C-14 starts to decay to nitrogen. By measuring the ratio of C-14 to C-12 in the remains and comparing it to the atmospheric ratio, we can calculate how long ago organisms died.

**25.** It accelerates, or speeds up, charged particles that are then used to bombard elements.

**26.** $^{14}_{6}\text{C} \rightarrow {}^{14}_{7}\text{N} + {}^{0}_{-1}\text{e}$

## Page 771

**27.** The energies produced in such reactions are enormous. They can be measured and related to the loss of mass involved.

**28. a.** $E = mc^2$
  $= 1.00 \text{ kg} \times (3.00 \times 10^8 \text{ m/sec})^2$
  $= 9.00 \times 10^{16} \text{ kg-m}^2/\text{sec}^2 = 9.00 \times 10^{16} \text{ J}$
  **b.** $9.00 \times 10^{16} \text{ J} \times \dfrac{1.00 \text{ kg coal}}{3.00 \times 10^7 \text{ J}} =$
  $3.00 \times 10^9 \text{ kg coal}$
  $3.00 \times 10^9 \text{ kg coal} \times \dfrac{2.2 \text{ pounds}}{1.00 \text{ kg}} =$
  $6.6 \times 10^9 \text{ pounds coal}$
  $6.6 \times 10^9 \text{ pounds coal} \times \dfrac{1 \text{ ton}}{2000 \text{ pounds}} =$
  $3.3 \times 10^6 \text{ tons coal}$

**29.**   $E = mc^2$
  $90 \text{ J} = m \times (3.00 \times 10^8 \text{ m/sec})^2$
  $m = \dfrac{90 \text{ J}}{9.00 \times 10^{16} \text{ m}^2/\text{sec}^2} = 1.0 \times 10^{-15} \text{ kg}$

## Page 773

**30. a.** Atomic fission is the splitting of the atomic nucleus.
  **b.** The purpose of a fission reactor is to carry out nuclear splitting at a controlled rate so that the released energy can be harnessed.

**31. a.** The neutrons must be captured by other U-235 nuclei to produce additional fissions. **b.** Critical mass is the minimum mass of fissionable material that will support a self-sustained chain reaction.

**32.** $^{235}_{92}U + ^1_0n \rightarrow ^{141}_{56}Ba + ^{92}_{36}Kr + 3^1_0n$

**Page 775**

**33. a.** Graphite slows down neutrons so that they can be captured more easily by the nuclei of the fuel.

**b.** The control rods absorb neutrons in order to keep the number of neutrons available for fission equal to the number used up by fission. In this manner, the chain reaction is controlled.

**34. a.** The fuel used in many fission reactors is U-238 enriched with U-235.

**b.** The U-238 is changed to Pu-239.

**35. a.** When U-238 captures a neutron, it becomes U-239 with a mass number of 239 and an atomic number of 92.

**b.** Neptunium and plutonium.

**36. a.** The chief use of plutonium is as a nuclear fuel supplying atomic energy.

**b.** Transuranium elements are elements with atomic numbers greater than those of uranium (92).

**37. a.** Three products of fission reactors are new synthetic elements, valuable radioisotopes, and heat, which is converted into electricity.

**b.** Radioactive wastes must be disposed of safely. The heated water can cause thermal pollution of streams and thus endanger marine life.

**Page 776**

**38. a.** In a fusion reaction, two or more nuclei combine to form a single nucleus of slightly less total mass.

**b.** Two examples of fusion reactions are the combination of 4 hydrogen nuclei to form 1 helium nucleus
$4(^1_1H) \rightarrow ^4_2He + 2(^0_1e)$
and the combination of a deuteron and a triton to form helium
$^2_1H + ^3_1H \rightarrow ^4_2He + ^1_0n$

**c.** In a fusion reaction, high energies are needed to overcome the forces of repulsion between the nuclei and to allow them to collide with sufficient force to cause fusion.

**39. a.** The source of the sun's energy may be the conversion of hydrogen to helium.

**b.** $4(^1_1H) \rightarrow ^4_2He + 2(^0_1e) + Q$

**40. a.** A thermonuclear device is an explosive device based on a fusion reaction.

**b.** Fusion reactors produce very little radioactive waste. Also, the fuel source for these reactors is easily obtainable and inexpensive water.

## Chapter Review

**Page 778, Content Review**

**1.** When a nuclear reaction occurs and a nuclide changes from one element to another, the reaction is called transmutation. For example, $^{14}_6C \rightarrow ^{14}_7N + ^0_{-1}e$.

**2.** The three types of nuclear radiation found in nature are alpha, beta, and gamma radiation.

**3.** After one half-life, one-half of the original mass will remain; after two half-lives, one-half of that amount, or one-quarter, will remain. After three half-lives, one-half of one-quarter, or one-eighth (⅛) will remain.

**4.** After 30 days, the radioactive isotope would have gone through two half-lives. Thus, one-quarter of its original mass would remain. One-quarter of 10.0 g is 2.50 g.

**5.** $^{235}_{92}U \rightarrow ^{231}_{90}Th + ^4_2He$

**6.** Bi-209

**7.** sodium-24

**8.** Radiation dose in a brick house equals $(50 + 100)/2 = 75$ mrem/year.
Radiation dose in a wooden house equals $(30 + 50)/2 = 40$ mrem/year.
The difference between these values is 26 mrem/year; the wooden house results in a lower total dosage.

**9. a.** $^4_2He$; **b.** $^0_{-1}e$; **c.** $^1_0n$; **d.** $^1_1H$; **e.** $^2_1H$

**10.** Somatic injuries are biological changes within body tissues caused by the breaking of chemical bonds or the ionization of atoms in molecules causing cells to die or to be modified. Genetic injuries affect the reproductive cells in a similar manner, which may result in heredity changes.

**11.** The radiation from cobalt-60 is directed toward the tumor at various angles, resulting in a high concentration of gamma rays at the tumor site. The DNA molecules of the faster growing cancer cells are more susceptible to disruption by the gamma radiation than are the normal cells.

**12.** The ratio of the isotopes after one half-life period is half as great as that in the atmosphere. For the ratio to become ¹⁄₁₆ as great, it would take four half-life periods. 5700 years × 4 = 22 800 years

**13.** If there is an equal number of atoms of the two isotopes, then half of the original mass of U-238

has decayed. Thus, the mineral has gone through one half-life and must be about 4.5 billion years old, the half-life of U-238.

14. **a.** Both accelerators use electric and magnetic fields. The cyclotron differs because it focuses a beam of accelerated particles by means of a series of electromagnets.
    **b.** Linear accelerators do not use magnetic fields; they use synchronized fields of electric force.

15. 8.023 g reactants − 8.016 g products = 0.007 g mass lost during the reaction.
    $E = mc^2$
    $$= 0.007 \text{ g} \times \frac{1 \text{ kg}}{10^3 \text{ g}} \times (3.0 \times 10^8 \text{ m/s})^2 =$$
    $$6 \times 10^{11} \text{ J}$$

16. Atomic fission is started by one neutron hitting a U-235 atom. More than one neutron is emitted; the neutrons produce fission in nearby atoms.

17. The critical mass is the quantity that allows the capture of released neutrons to be sufficient to support a self-sustaining chain reaction. If too little mass is used, too many released neutrons will escape without striking any nuclei. If too much mass is used, a rapid buildup in the rate of fission will occur, resulting in an explosion.

18. $^{235}_{92}\text{U} + ^1_0\text{n} \rightarrow ^{144}_{58}\text{Ce} + ^{90}_{38}\text{Sr} + 4(^0_{-1}\text{e}) + 2(^1_0\text{n})$

19. **a.** U-235 is present in extremely small amounts in its ores. Its separation from the mineral is slow and expensive. A mixture of U-235 and U-238 that will sustain a chain reaction can be made.
    **b.** The U-238 in the mixture undergoes fusion to produce another atomic fuel, plutonium-239.

20. $^{238}_{92}\text{U} + ^1_0\text{n} \rightarrow ^{239}_{92}\text{U}$
    $^{239}_{92}\text{U} \rightarrow ^{239}_{93}\text{Np} + ^0_{-1}\text{e}$
    $^{239}_{93}\text{Np} \rightarrow ^{239}_{94}\text{Pu} + ^0_{-1}\text{e}$

21. **a.** $^{12}_6\text{C}$, $^{16}_8\text{O}$, $^{32}_{16}\text{S}$
    **b.** $3(^4_2\text{He}) \rightarrow ^{12}_6\text{C}$
    $4(^4_2\text{He}) \rightarrow ^{16}_8\text{O}$
    $8(^4_2\text{He}) \rightarrow ^{32}_{16}\text{S}$

## Page 779, Content Mastery

22. **a.** $^{218}_{85}\text{At}$; **b.** $^{17}_8\text{O}$; **c.** $^{10}_5\text{B}$; **d.** $^{52}_{25}\text{Mn}$

23. **a.** $^{14}_7\text{N} + ^4_2\text{He} \rightarrow ^{17}_8\text{O} + ^1_1\text{H}$
    **b.** $^{27}_{13}\text{Al} + ^4_2\text{He} \rightarrow ^{30}_{15}\text{P} + ^1_0\text{n}$
    **c.** O-17 is stable; P-30 is radioactive.
    **d.** Si-30
    **e.** Induced (artificial) radioactivity is shown.

24. A radiation detector, such as the Geiger counter or scan, is brought near the patient's throat in the vicinity of the thyroid gland.

25. Seven general applications of radioisotopes include: (1) diagnostic or environmental tracer stud-

ies, (2) sterilization of material, (3) diagnostic viewing of organs (X rays, for example), (4) therapeutic treatments against tumors, (5) measurement of thicknesses of industrial materials, (6) dating objects, and (7) production of energy.

26. With the assumption that the half-life of C-14 is 5730 years, the age of a wooden spoon having a C-14 radioactivity of 12.5% of a contemporary spoon is determined as follows:
    1.00 half-life implies 50.0%
    2.00 half-lives imply 25.0%
    3.00 half-lives imply 12.5%
    Therefore, age = (3.00 half-lives) × (5730 years/half-life) = 17 200 years

27. Using Einstein's equation,
    $E = mc^2$
    $m = E/c^2 = (6.3 \times 10^9 \text{ J}) / (3.0 \times 10^8 \text{ m/s})^2$
    $= 7.0 \times 10^{-5} \text{ g}$

28. **a.** Three uses of fission reactors are (1) to synthesize new elements or make radioisotopes, (2) to make steam for the production of electricity, and (3) to power submarines and surface vessels. **b.** Nuclear power is not used in aircraft because the reactors require heavy and costly shielding. **c.** Mix the radioactive wastes with molten glass, convert the glass into cylinders, and package and bury the cylinders.

29. The two methods of producing nuclear energy are fission and fusion. Fission produces the most energy, whereas fusion produces the least pollution.

30. Radon-222 undergoes 4 alpha emissions, 4 beta emissions, and 3 gamma emissions. The gamma radiation does not change the mass number or atomic number of the nuclide, so each gamma radiation can be ignored. For each alpha emission, the mass number decreases by 4 and the atomic number decreases by 2. For each beta emission, the atomic number increases by 1. The mass number of the stable element equals 222 − 4(4), or 206. The element's atomic number equals 86 − 4(2) + 4(1), or 82. The stable element is $^{206}_{82}\text{Pb}$.

## Page 779, Concept Mastery

31. ***Concept:*** *When a negative particle is lost, the remaining particle increases in positive charge.*
    *Solution:* When the beta particle is emitted from the nucleus of an atom, a neutron changes into a proton. This results in an additional proton.

32. ***Concept:*** *Excessive radiation is harmful.*
    *Solution:* Humans have always been exposed to a certain level of radiation from outer space and have adapted quite well to it. When radiation becomes excessive, it

proves to be harmful, such as in the Chernobyl accident. Scientists are not yet certain about what constitutes harmful levels. It appears that short intensive doses are more harmful than longer low-level doses.

33. ***Concept:*** *Radioactive decay causes nuclear changes.*

    *Solution:* Not every change in the nucleus of an atom makes a new atom. The addition of a neutron produces another isotope of the same element.

34. ***Concept:*** *Radioactive decay causes nuclear changes.*

    *Solution:* Sometimes a substance bombarded by another particle will become radioactive and sometimes it does not. A harmless isotope, or even a familiar element, could be produced.

35. ***Concept:*** *Antimatter is matter.*

    *Solution:* Since antimatter has mass and volume, it is truly matter. It is called antimatter because when one particle is combined with a particle of identical mass but opposite charge, the two particles are annihilated.

## Page 779, Cumulative Review

36. **d.** $15 \text{ dm}^3 \times \dfrac{1.0 \text{ atm}}{2.0 \text{ atm}} \times \dfrac{300 \text{ K}}{273 \text{ K}} = 8.2 \text{ dm}^2$

37. **b.** J.J. Thomson is credited with the discovery of the electron.

38. **d.** Atoms and ions of the same element never differ in the number of protons.

39. **c.** Dmitri Mendeleev was the first to publish a classification of the elements that became the basis for the modern periodic table.

40. Heat is a form of energy; temperature is a measure of the average kinetic energy of a body of matter.

41. $400 \text{ g} \times 2.26 \times 10^3 \text{ J/g} = 9.04 \times 10^5 \text{ J}$

42. $4HNO_3(l) \rightarrow 4NO_2(g) + O_2(g) + 2H_2O(l)$

43. In the Bohr model, the electron can travel around the nucleus only in circular orbits with definite radii. When the electron is in the ground state, it moves in the orbit of smallest radius. In the wave-mechanical model, only the probability of finding an electron in a certain region is indicated. For hydrogen, this region is a spherical shell centered on the nucleus.

44. **a.** Li· ·C̈l̈:

    **b.** Li· + ·C̈l̈: → Li$^+$[:C̈l̈:]$^-$

45. $2Al + 3H_2SO_4 \rightarrow Al_2(SO_4)_3 + 3H_2$
    $2Al + 6H_3O^+ \rightarrow 2Al^{3+} + 6H_2O + 3H_2$

## Page 780, Critical Thinking

46. Both fission and fusion are nuclear reactions that produce energy. In fission, one nucleus splits into approximately equal fragments. In fusion, two or more nuclei combine to form a single, heavier nucleus.

47. No. Transmutations involve changing one element into another. The atomic number identifies the element, so the atomic number must change in a transmutation. If sodium-23 is bombarded with neutrons, some of the sodium will be converted to sodium-24. This reaction produces a different isotope, to be sure, but it is still sodium. No transmutation has occurred.

48. The half-life of carbon-24 is 5730 years. Therefore, the amount of carbon-14 will not change very much in just a few hundred years. This technique is best applied to samples thought to be between 1000 and 75000 years old.

49. Students' answers to this question will vary, depending on how they interpret "serious." There is no right answer. Somatic effects that can cause disease or death are more important for the individual. Genetic effects have greater consequences for the progress and survival of the species.

50. Answers will vary, depending on each student's stance on the political issue. Without a doubt, nuclear reactors can produce energy. The problems are the possibility of an accident or terrorism at a nuclear reactor, the storage of radioactive wastes, and the attitudes of members of society.

51. Low-energy neutrons are more effective than high-energy neutrons in producing nuclear reactions, because they not only have a greater chance of being captured by the nuclei of the atoms of fuel, but also give up energy in the form of heat when their velocity is reduced.

## Page 780, Challenge Problems

52. $^{238}_{92}U + ^{12}_{6}C \rightarrow ^{246}_{98}Cf + 4^{1}_{0}n$

53. 20% of 68 kg is 13.6 kg or 13600 g.
    $(13600 \text{ g}) / 12 \text{ g/mol} = 1133 \text{ mol C}$
    $(1133 \text{ mol C}) \times (6.02 \times 10^{23} \text{ atoms/mol}) =$
    $6.8 \times 10^{26} \text{ carbon atoms}$
    $(6.8 \times 10^{26} \text{ C atoms}) \times (1 \text{ C-14 atom}/10^{12} \text{ C atoms}) =$
    $6.8 \times 10^{14} \text{ C-14 atoms}$

54. $E = mc^2$
    $m = E/c^2$
    $= (10^{17} \text{ J/s}) / (3 \times 10^8 \text{ m/s})^2 = 1 \text{ kg/s}$
    $(1 \text{ kg/s}) \times (60 \text{ s/min}) \times (60 \text{ min/hr}) \times (24 \text{ hr}) =$
    $9 \times 10^4 \text{ kg}$

26